Lecture Notes in Computer Science   6998

Commenced Publication in 1973
Founding and Former Series Editors:
Gerhard Goos, Juris Hartmanis,

Manfred A. Jeusfeld   Lois Delcambre
Tok Wang Ling (Eds.)

Conceptual Modeling – ER 2011

30th International Conference, ER 2011
Brussels, Belgium, October 31 - November 3, 2011
Proceedings

 Springer

Volume Editors

Manfred A. Jeusfeld
Tilburg University
Warandelaan 2
5037 AB Tilburg, The Netherlands
E-mail: manfred.jeusfeld@acm.org

Lois Delcambre
Portland State University
Maseeh College of Engineering and Computer Science
P.O. Box 751
Portland, OR 97207-0751, USA
E-mail: lmd@cs.pdx.edu

Tok Wang Ling
National University of Singapore
Department of Computer Science
13 Computing Drive
Singapore 117417
E-mail: lingtw@comp.nus.edu.sg

ISSN 0302-9743   e-ISSN 1611-3349
ISBN 978-3-642-24605-0   e-ISBN 978-3-642-24606-7
DOI 10.1007/978-3-642-24606-7
Springer Heidelberg Dordrecht London New York

Library of Congress Control Number:

CR Subject Classification (1998): D.2, F.3, D.3, I.2, F.4.1, D.2.2-4

LNCS Sublibrary: SL 3 – Information Systems and Application, incl. Internet/Web
and HCI

Typesetting: Camera-ready by author, data conversion by Scientific Publishing Services, Chennai, India

Printed on acid-free paper

Springer is part of Springer Science+Business Media (www.springer.com)

Foreword

We are proud to present the proceedings of the International Conference of Conceptual Modeling (ER 2011) lasted in Belgium. We devoted all our energy to make it a scientific, social, and artistic success.

Belgium has a long tradition, rooted in the early 1970s, in database research and particularly in database modeling. This 30th ER conference was organized by the CoDE Research department of the Université libre de Bruxelles and the PReCISE Research Center of the Université de Namur, both very active in the database community.

Belgium is also the country of beer, character cheese, French fries, comic strips, Art Nouveau, and surrealism, but above all of institutional intricacy. This was thus the ideal venue for an anniversary conference of a series devoted to reducing and mastering information system complexity.

Nothing would have been possible without the unfailing and experienced contribution of the ER Steering Committee as well as the Program, Publicity, Workshop, Tutorial, Panel, Industrial Track (a new one), Demos and Posters, and Doctoral Consortium Chairs and Committees. Organizing such a wide-scope international conference and making it a success require countless competences, ranging from financial manager to webmaster. They all did an excellent job. Special thanks also to all our sponsors and sister scientific societies for their support: FNRS, Microsoft Research, NSF, Euranova, IBM, FWO, Intergraph, Springer, la Ville de Bruxelles, OM Partners, CETIC, Océ, ReveR, ACM SIGMIS, ACM SIGMOD, as well as the Université libre de Bruxelles and the Université de Namur.

Finally, there is no scientific conference without high-quality contributors, attendees, and readers: thanks to all of you.

On behalf of all the persons and partners that contributed to making this conference a success, we hope you find the proceedings interesting and valuable for your research.

July 2011

Esteban Zimányi
Jean-Luc Hainaut

Preface

The ER conference is the leading international forum for presenting research results and discussing future trends in conceptual modeling. ER 2011 was the 30th such meeting and took place in Brussels, the vibrant "capital" of Europe.

While keeping a strong focus on conceptual modeling, the ER conference has always been open to new trends, such as goal modeling and process modeling. In 2011, the extension of conceptual modeling to requirements engineering, human and social factors in modeling, ontologies, model development and evolution, and data model theory were major trends among the papers accepted for the main conference.

The Program Committee (PC) received 157 submissions to the main program. Each paper was reviewed by at least three members of the Program Committee. Additionally, six senior reviewers moderated the discussion on disputed papers and wrote meta-reviews when necessary. The PC ultimately decided to accept 39 papers of excellent academic quality for the main program, of which 25 regular-length papers and 14 short papers. The overall acceptance rate was thus 24.8%. The acceptance rate of regular-length papers is 15.9%. The reason for the distinction between regular-length and short papers was the observation that a number of submissions had a very good technical quality, but were perhaps a bit less fully developed. So, the PC wanted these papers in the main program but to have them in some sense distinguished from the regular-length papers.

The scientific program included three keynote talks by Alon Halevy, Stefano Spaccapietra, and Carson Woo, spanning a breadth of topics in conceptual modeling. The proceedings also include a summary of the panel discussion and of the tutorial program. We graciously thank the authors for submitting their work, the PC members for writing reviews and participating in lively discussions, and the six senior reviewers for processing all the reviews and providing recommendations.

July 2011

Manfred Jeusfeld
Lois Delcambre
Tok Wang Ling

Organization

General Conference Chairs

Esteban Zimányi — Université Libre de Bruxelles, Belgium
Jean-Luc Hainaut — Université de Namur, Belgium

Program Committee Co-chairs

Manfred A. Jeusfeld — Tilburg University, The Netherlands
Lois Delcambre — Portland State University, USA
Tok Wang Ling — National University of Singapore, Singapore

Industrial Co-chairs

Alkis Simitsis — HP Labs, USA
Hans Van Mingroot — IBM, Belgium

Workshops Co-chairs

Olga De Troyer — Vrije Universiteit Brussel, Belgium
Claudia Bauzer Medeiros — University of Campinas, Brazil

PhD Colloquium Co-chairs

Christophe Claramunt — Naval Academy Research Institute, France
Markus Schneider — University of Florida, USA

Poster and Demonstration Chair

Roland Billen — Université de Liège, Belgium

Tutorials Co-chairs

Alejandro Vaisman — University of Buenos Aires, Argentina
Jef Wijsen — Université de Mons, Belgium

Panel Chair

Torben Bach Pedersen — Aalborg University, Denmark

Publicity Chair

Anthony Cleve   Université de Namur and Université Libre
                                  de Bruxelles, Belgium

Travel Award Chair

Min Song   New Jersey Institute of Technology, USA

Financial Chair

Frédéric Servais   Université Libre de Bruxelles, Belgium

Steering Committee Liaison

Sudha Ram   University of Arizona, USA

Local Organization Committee

Stijn Vansummeren (Chair)   Université Libre de Bruxelles, Belgium
Vinciane de Wilde   Université Libre de Bruxelles, Belgium
Serge Boucher   Université Libre de Bruxelles, Belgium
François Picalusa   Université Libre de Bruxelles, Belgium

Webmaster

Boris Verhaegen   Université Libre de Bruxelles, Belgium

Program Committee

Jacky Akoka   CNAM, France
Paolo Atzeni   Università Roma Tre, Italy
Carlo Batini   University of Milano-Bicocca, Italy
Boualem Benatallah   University of New South Wales, Australia
Sonia Bergamaschi   Università di Modena e Reggio Emilia, Italy
Arne Berre   SINTEF, Norway
Sourav Saha Bhowmick   Nanyang Technological University, Singapore
Alexander Borgida   Rutgers University, USA
Mokrane Bouzeghoub   Université de Versailles, France
Shawn Bowers   Gonzaga University, USA
Stephane Bressan   National University of Singapore, Singapore
Marco A. Casanova   Pontificia Universidade Catolica do Rio
                                  de Janeiro, Brazil

Silvana Castano	Università degli Studi di Milano
Dickson Chiu	Dickson Computer Systems, China
Isabel Cruz	University of Illinois at Chicago, USA
Karen Davis	University of Cincinnati, USA
Umeshwar Dayal	HP Labs, USA
Olga De Troyer	Vrije Universiteit Brussel, Belgium
Gillian Dobbie	University of Auckland, New Zealand
Johann Eder	University of Klagenfurt, Austria
Jérôme Euzenat	INRIA & LIG, France
Joerg Evermann	Memorial University of Newfoundland, Canada
Xavier Franch	Universitat Politècnica de Catalunya, Spain
Helena Galhardas	Technical University of Lisbon, Portugal
Jaap Gordijn	Vrije Universiteit Amsterdam, The Netherlands
Giancarlo Guizzardi	Universidade Federal do Espirito Santo, Brazil
Peter Haase	Fluid Operations, Germany
Sven Hartmann	Clausthal University of Technology, Germany
Brian Henderson-Sellers	University of Technology Sydney, Australia
Howard Ho	IBM Almaden Research Center, USA
Arantza Illarramendi	Basque Country University, Spain
Matthias Jarke	RWTH Aachen, Germany
Paul Johannesson	Stockholm University, Sweden
Kamalakar Karlapalem	IIIT Hyderabad, India
Larry Kerschberg	George Mason University, USA
Vijay Khatri	Indiana University, USA
Michael Kifer	State University of New York at Stony Brook, USA
Hiroyuki Kitagawa	University of Tsukuba, Japan
Alberto Laender	Universidade Federal de Minas Gerais, Brazil
Wolfgang Lehner	Technical University of Dresden, Germany
Julio Cesar Leite	Pontifícia Universidade Catolica do Rio de Janeiro, Brazil
Qing Li	City University of Hong Kong, China
Mong Li Lee	National University of Singapore, Singapore
Stephen Liddle	Brigham Young University, USA
Mengchi Liu	Carleton University, Canada
Peri Loucopoulos	Loughborough University, UK
Jiaheng Lu	Renmin University of China, China
Kally Lyytinen	Case Western Reserve University, USA
Jan Mendling	Humboldt University Berlin, Germany
Xiaofeng Meng	Renmin University of China, China
Michele Missikoff	IASI-CNR, Italy
Wilfred Ng	Hong Kong University of Science and Technology, China
Antoni Olivé	Universitat Politècnica de Catalunya, Spain

Jose Palazzo M. de Oliveira	Universidade Federal do Rio Grande do Sul, Brazil
Andreas Opdahl	University of Bergen, Norway
Sylvia Osborn	University of Western Ontario, Canada
Jeffrey Parsons	Memorial University of Newfoundland, Canada
Oscar Pastor	Technical University of Valencia, Spain
Barbara Pernici	Politecnico di Milano, Italy
Alain Pirotte	Université Catholique de Louvain, Belgium
Dimitris Plexousakis	University of Crete, Greece
Rachel Pottinger	University of British Columbia, Canada
Erik Proper	Public Research Center Henri Tudor, Luxemburg
Sandeep Purao	Penn State University, USA
Christoph Quix	RWTH Aachen, Germany
Jolita Ralyté	University of Geneva, Switzerland
Colette Rolland	University Paris 1 Pantheon-Sorbonne, France
Michael Rosemann	Queensland University of Technology, Australia
Gustavo Rossi	Universidad de la Plata, Argentina
Motoshi Saeki	Tokyo Institute of Technology, Japan
Klaus-Dieter Schewe	Software Competence Center Hagenberg, Austria
Mário Silva	IST, Portugal
Richard Snodgrass	University of Arizona, USA
Il-Yeol Song	Drexel University, USA
Veda C. Storey	Georgia State, USA
Ernest Teniente	Universitat Politècnica de Catalunya, Spain
James Terwilliger	Microsoft Corporation, USA
Riccardo Torlone	Università Roma Tre, Italy
Juan Trujillo	University of Alicante, Spain
Susan Urban	Texas Tech University, USA
Inge Van De Weerd	Utrecht University, The Netherlands
Axel Van Lamsweerde	Université Catholique de Louvain, Belgium
Panos Vassiliadis	University of Ioannina, Greece
Vania Vidal	Universidade Federal do Ceara, Brazil
Gerd Wagner	Brandenburg University of Technology, Germany
Masatoshi Yoshikawa	Kyoto University, Japan
Eric Yu	University of Toronto, Canada
Ge Yu	Northeastern University, China
Yanchun Zhang	Victoria University, Australia
Xiaofang Zhou	University of Queensland, Australia
Shuigeng Zhou	Fudan University, China

Senior Reviewers

David W. Embley	Brigham Young University, USA
Avigdor Gal	Technion - Israel Institute of Technology, Israel
John Mylopoulos	Università di Trento, Italy
Moira Norrie	ETH Zurich, Switzerland
Sudha Ram	University of Arizona, USA
Bernhard Thalheim	University of Kiel, Germany

External Reviewers

Mohammad Allah-Bakhsh	Behzad Hezarkhani	Dumitru Roman
	Guangyan Huang	Marcus Roy
Yubin Bao	Felipe Hummel	Altigran S. Da Silva
Moshe Chai Barukh	Zheng Huo	Emanuel Santos
George Baryannis	Sergio Ilarri	Yingjie Shi
Seyed M.R. Beheshti	Ritu Khare	Gonçalo Simões
Domenico Beneventano	Yicong Liang	Fabrizio Smith
Maria Bergholtz	Hui Ma	Serena Sorrentino
Yi Cai	Jiangang Ma	Young-Kyoon Suh
Cinzia Cappiello	Youzhong Ma	Francesco Taglino
Cyril Carrez	José Macedo	Ornsiri Thonggoom
Marco Comerio	Fabiana Marinho	Wee Hyong Tok
Evangelia Daskalaki	Bruno Martins	Gaia Varese
Julian Eberius	Andrea Maurino	Kevin Vlaanderen
Alfio Ferrara	Eduardo Mena	Haiyong Wang
Giorgos Flouris	Stefano Montanelli	Jing Wang
Bernhard Freudenthaler	Mirella M. Moro	Ingo Weber
Lizhen Fu	Christine Natschläger	Haoran Xie
Rigel Gjomemo	Oana Nicolae	Chrysostomos Zeginis
Roy Grønmo	Marius Octavian Olaru	Rui Zhang
Francesco Guerra	Matteo Palmonari	Xiaojian Zhang
Dirk Habich	Laura Po	Ming Zhong
Stephen Hegner	Raúl Mazo	

Organized by

Université Libre de Bruxelles, Belgium
Université de Namur, Belgium

In Cooperation with

ACM SIGMIS
ACM SIGMOD

Gold Sponsors

Silver Sponsors

Bronze Sponsors

Table of Contents

Data Model Theory

Model Development and Maintainability

User Interfaces and Software Classification

Evolution, Propagation and Refinement

UML and Requirements Modeling

Views, Queries and Search

Requirements and Business Intelligence

MDA and Ontology-Based Modeling

Process Modeling

The Role of Conceptual Modeling in Managing and Changing the Business

Carson Woo

Sauder School of Business,
The University of British Columbia
carson.woo@ubc.ca

Abstract. Conceptual modeling has been used mainly for supporting information systems (IS) development. In order to better capture requirements for developing IS, we have been extending conceptual models to include more business context (e.g., mission of the organization). This seems to interest organizational workers in using those conceptual models to solve problems. We propose dual roles for conceptual modeling: developing IS, and managing the changes occurring in the business. To fulfill the second role, conceptual modeling must provide constructs that are not biased toward IS background and thinking, but assist organizational workers to better understand the business and its operations. Research and literature on management will be useful to accomplish this objective. Our research in this direction suggests much potential in expanding conceptual modeling to support organizational workers.

Keywords: information systems analysis, business perspective, business context, management concepts, organizational actors, organizational goals, thought process.

1 Introduction

Traditionally, conceptual modeling has been used mainly by information systems developers. We see a lot of potential in expanding conceptual modeling to support organizational workers in their problem solving. The objective of this paper is to explain this potential, provide examples, and suggest research directions.

Mylopoulos [14] defines conceptual modeling as "the activity of formally describing some aspects of the physical and social world around us for purposes of understanding and communication." The outcome of conceptual modeling is usually some kind of a diagram or conceptual model. However, conceptual modeling has been used mainly as a means for systems analysts to gather requirements from organizational workers so that information systems can be developed. As stated by Olive [15], "the main purpose of conceptual modeling is to elicit the conceptual schema of the corresponding information system".

Unfortunately, every business evolves and changes over time, due to growth, downsizing, product changes, and new generations of consumers. The changes can be so complex that even organizational workers involved in the change may have only their own narrow perspective of the business. This can result in problems such as

M. Jeusfeld, L. Delcambre, and T.W. Ling (Eds.): ER 2011, LNCS 6998, pp. 1–12, 2011.

duplication of work and conflicting messages to customers. For a systems analyst in such an organization, it can be very challenging to gather requirements for conceptual modeling.

An approach to addressing this challenge is to incorporate more business context when gathering requirements. We have been extending conceptual models to capture more contextual information such as the vision and mission of the company. When communicating these conceptual models to users, we found that users discovered previously unknown information, and utilized the conceptual models to support their problem solving. For example, the conceptual models we developed for a unit in a business school helped some middle managers to revise their interpretations of the school's need, and aligned them with the strategic intent [18].

Including business context in conceptual models can therefore lead users to discover new information, and this is an opportunity for conceptual modeling. Systems analysts are trained to map abstract knowledge into explicit knowledge in the conceptual models needed to develop information systems. If systems analysts could go one step further and utilize their conceptual models to assist organizational workers in problem solving, then conceptual modeling will have a dual role: developing IT, and facilitating the changes occurring in the business.

In Section 2, we explain the limitations of existing work in capturing business context and what can be done to overcome them. Section 3 discusses how conceptual modeling can provide values for organizational workers, and examples from our research in accomplishing this objective. Finally, Section 4 concludes this paper and calls for more work in this direction.

2 Limitations of Existing Work and Possible Extensions

This section is not meant to be a complete literature review. Rather, we hope that a few examples will show the limitations of existing work and the potential for extending the role of conceptual modeling.

The idea of using conceptual models to support organizational workers in their problem solving is not new. Business process diagrams have been used by managers to reengineer their organization [7] for over a decade now. Managers would discover the inefficiency and ineffectiveness of their existing business processes and utilize the diagrams to design more effective and efficient ones. The same business process diagrams were later used to develop information systems. This is the only conceptual modeling framework we are aware of that has been used to support organizational workers in their problem solving (i.e., designing business processes). However, not every aspect of the business can be represented using business process diagrams, and the potential for extending conceptual modeling lies in discovering whether other types of conceptual models can be used to represent the business. We will provide some examples later in the paper.

The idea of providing more business context in requirements gathering for conceptual modeling is also not new. For examples, the work system approach [1] includes both the information technology (IT) and non-IT parts of organizational work and describes both of them from a business viewpoint; Penker and Han-Erik [17] extend UML for modeling business (business vision, structure, processes, and behavior); the i* diagram represents the underlying motivations behind organizational work and can aid early phase requirements gathering [23]; the enterprise architecture frameworks such as the Zackman Framework [24], TOGAF [20], and DoDAF [3] capture both the business and information systems perspectives for describing the organization. However, the major outcome of these frameworks is to provide business capabilities to help management understand, manage, prioritize, and/or invest in information systems development. We could not find much use of conceptual models beyond supporting information systems development. To elaborate this point, we will use the i* strategic dependency model and the "goal" concept.

2.1 The Strategic Dependency Model in the i* Framework

The strategic dependency model in the i* framework represents the dependency of the depender who needs something from the dependee [23]. The idea of resource dependency was proposed for studying how organizations adapt to changes in the environment [16; 21]. The proposal is that organizations lacking certain resources will seek to establish relationships with others in order to acquire the needed resources. A resource can be anything valued by the organization, including information, materials, capital, and access to markets. In order to ensure continuing access to the needed resources, a depender will seek to formalize *agreements* with the dependee that govern the exchange of resources. The i* strategic dependency model represents the relationship for acquiring resources but does not include the agreements that govern the exchange of resources. This is because the relationships are needed to develop information systems, but the agreements governing exchanges are outside the scope of developing information systems.

Tillquist et al. [19] developed a Dependency Network Diagram (DND) to capture both the relationships for acquisition and the agreements governing exchange. In their case study, they found the addition of governance control (i.e., agreements governing exchange) in the DND, enables senior management to better understand organizational relationships, to design control and coordination of organizational work explicitly, and to diagnose the impact of IT implementation. The conceptual model, in this case, plays the dual role of providing requirements for information systems development and helping senior management to solve problems outside of information systems development. Although the i* strategic dependency model can also help senior management to solve some of their problems, adding governance control extends the contribution of conceptual modeling to organizational work.

Figure 1 provides a pictorial view of the potential extension of conceptual modeling. The figure has two circles, representing the problem solving needs in business and the requirement-gathering (or IT) needs in information systems development. Most of the current work that provides business context focuses on the business needs that intersect with IT needs. The potential for conceptual modeling lies in extending it beyond IT needs, and into the business context.

2.2 The Different Facets of Goals in Business and IT

The concept of goals in goal-based requirements engineering [9] is another example of the intersection of business and IT needs, and it can potentially be extended into the full business needs area in Figure 1.

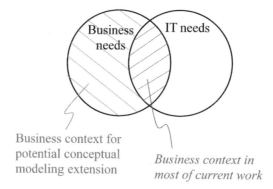

Fig. 1. Potential area of expansion for conceptual modeling

A goal is, in general, considered an objective to achieve [10; 23]. It can be decomposed into sub-goals comprising finer and more structured tasks that can be designed or performed. Decomposition, in general, can be done using AND or OR [2], where AND means all the sub-goals must be achieved in order to accomplish the goal, while OR means alternative ways of accomplishing the same goal. The contribution analysis shows how achieving a particular goal can help to reach a higher level goal. This works well for information systems development because this goal structure helps in designing the modules of the information systems and provides a rationale for management to make decisions on the IT project. However, this view is too general for business use.

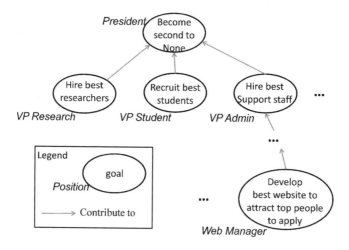

Fig. 2. A Contribution Analysis Diagram

We will use the contribution analysis diagram in Figure 2 to explain why the current view of goals is too general for business use. Let's say a University's President sets a mission for the university, like "become second to none." To accomplish this objective, she relies on her Vice Presidents to do something in their respective roles. Let's say the Vice President of Administration sees "hiring the best support staff" as a goal that can contribute to the top strategic goal of "becoming second to none." This hiring goal is then interpreted by the Web Manager as "developing the best web site" as a goal that will eventually contribute to the "becoming second to none" goal, because the site will attract the best people to apply. When we look at the Web Manager's goal, we start to ask questions such as, can an attractive web site really contribute to the "becoming second to none" goal? If yes, by how much? Is it possible that, because a Web Manager always thinks about web development, it is not surprising that he sees "developing an attractive web site" as contributing to all higher level goals? Should the President invest in this web development project and how much money should she invest? Obviously, more information is needed in order to answer these questions.

Goal-setting at different levels of the organization has different meanings, considers different factors, and is dependent on the organizational workers at each level. For example, at the top organizational level, the President and Vice Presidents consider external factors and may set higher than possible to achieve goals that lack operational considerations. At the operation level, organizational workers consider factors such as resources available to them, the importance of their role (so that they will not be laid off), and maximizing budgets for their projects, but may be less interested in enterprise wide achievements. This is why simply showing how a goal contributes to another goal in a contribution analysis diagram will not provide sufficient information for top management to make a decision.

An example of research that tries to address the different characteristics or attributes associated with goals at different levels of organizations, and the relationships between those goals, is that of Singh and Woo [18]. This approach will be further discussed in Section 3.1.

3 Providing Values for Organizational Workers

There is evidence that organizational workers are already using conceptual models for their problem solving. For example, Fettke [5] reported in his survey that practitioners are using conceptual model diagrams for non-IT related work such as human resource management. He also reported that a critical success factor for conceptual modeling is that nontechnical people should easily understand the models. This means that organizational workers will use conceptual models more often if we use familiar terminology, and show them the value that can result. To illustrate how conceptual models can assist organizational workers in problem solving, we present examples from our research.

We focused on developing approaches to conceptual modeling that are derived from research on management. Examples include strategic management literature, human resource management literature, and personnel psychology literature. We looked for management concepts (rather than IT concepts) to use in conceptual models that could potentially support the organizational worker. We also sought to avoid any biases in our IT background and thinking.

To reach this objective, we viewed business as consisting of organizational actors, who each represent a role in organizational work having a goal and a thought process. The idea of looking into organizational worker is not new. Jacobson et al. [8] used the concept of *actors,* and identify cases as a starting point for understanding requirements in their use-case analysis; Yu [23] used *agent* as the focus to understand dependencies and rationales. Checkland [4] stated that "... at a higher level, every situation in which we undertook action research was a human situation in which people were attempting to take purposeful action which was meaningful for them" (p.S14). This is consistent with our view of considering business as a context where organizational workers play roles, and have goals and thought processes.

When an organizational worker performs his/her work, other organizational workers might be interested in knowing how the work affects or contributes to their work (inter-actor view) and why the work was performed in a specific way (intra-actor view). We can capture these inter-actor and intra-actor views in conceptual models. A specific type of inter-actor view occurs in the business-IT alignment, where an organizational worker's accomplishments might contribute to his/her supervisor's goal. Regarding the intra-actor view, the different backgrounds, beliefs, and abilities of organizational workers affects their thought processes or what Checkland [4] called "(what is) meaningful for them." Representing their thought processes in conceptual models might help organizational workers to better understand each other and react accordingly, when cooperating or collaborating.

3.1 Conceptual Models for Business-IT Alignment

Singh and Woo [18] did an extensive search in management literature and came up with these types of goals that need to be distinguished in organizations. They are:

(1) **Strategic goals:** These are the goals of the organizational vision. They are set by and for top management.
(2) **Assigned goals:** These are operational goals that will contribute to the achievement of the strategic goals. They are set by top management for middle managers.
(3) **Interpreted goals:** These are interpretations by individual organizational workers of the assigned goals.

Distinguishing these goals is necessary because of the goal-setting issues mentioned at the end of Section 2.2. Interpreted goals are needed because organizational workers can interpret goals differently due to factors such as experience, ability, past success, task complexity, and performance constraints. Interpretations that are not aligned with strategic goals can, therefore, affect organizational performance or outcomes.

The attributes associated with (or concepts used in) each of these goals, and the relationships between the goals, are discussed in greater detail in [18]. For the purpose of this paper, we will provide examples of the attributes associated with the strategic goal. Strategic choice (or vision) and strategic process (a set of related procedures to implement the strategic choice) are concepts used to formulate strategic goals. Factors such as internal competencies and the environment guide the selection of strategic choice and strategic process.

We conducted two case studies using this framework of goals. In the first study, we found that the three types of goals are insufficient to provide a contribution analysis diagram that would be meaningful for organizational workers. Both assigned and interpreted goals can occur at different levels of organizations and it is important to further distinguish the goals according to different levels of organizations.

In the second case study, we retained the strategic goals but added tactical level goals and operation level goals. Tactical goals are set by and for middle level managers while operation goals are set by and for the lowest level managers. This distinction is important because middle managers play a critical role in operationalizing strategic goals. Figure 3 shows an example of a contribution analysis diagram that we presented to organizational workers to assist their problem solving.

In these two case studies, we discovered that these conceptual models help organizational workers to

- Understand the coherence of and congruency among operational, tactical, and strategic goals.
- Identify critical goals at the operational level that directly contribute to multiple strategic goals. This is an important discovery because organizations often lay off employees when they eliminate the need to accomplish certain goals, but this elimination and lay off indirectly hurts other strategic goals. Having such a diagram helps senior management to understand the impact of their intended changes.
- Better understand their interpretation of strategic goals. For example, the diagram forced a human resources manager to think through the goals in depth, and revised her interpretation of the assigned goal so that it aligned with the strategic intent.

We also discovered that the distinction between assigned goals and organizational workers' interpretation of the assigned goals (i.e., interpreted goals) is more pronounced among middle management than at the higher and lower levels of the organization. This illustrates the need to incorporate tactical level goals in the contribution analysis diagram. It will be useful to study how conceptual models can aid middle managers in better aligning their goals with strategic goals.

In addition, it was interesting to discover that decomposing goals using ORs (alternative ways of accomplishing the same goal) was not needed by upper and middle managers, because of the nature of the tactical goals and the process used to determine them. The process seemed to include an agreement among managers to accomplish organizational intent in a coherent and consistent way. Having alternatives would make it more difficult for them to ensure the intended organizational outcomes.

3.2 Conceptual Models for Thought Process

We mentioned earlier in Section 3 that representing thought processes might help organizational workers to better understand each other, and react accordingly when cooperating or collaborating. In this section we report our research experience and findings in this line of work.

8   C. Woo

We use the following concepts to represent the internal behavior of organizational workers: *perception/input, belief, learning, goal, intention, reasoning, capability, output*, and *action* [13]. We called this the *organizational actor* framework. *Perception/input* represents the attributes of things in the world that the organizational worker is aware of. *Beliefs* are assumptions about the world that are based on the organizational worker's observations of the world. The mechanism by which the observations turn into *beliefs* is represented by *learning*. The *goal* is the main

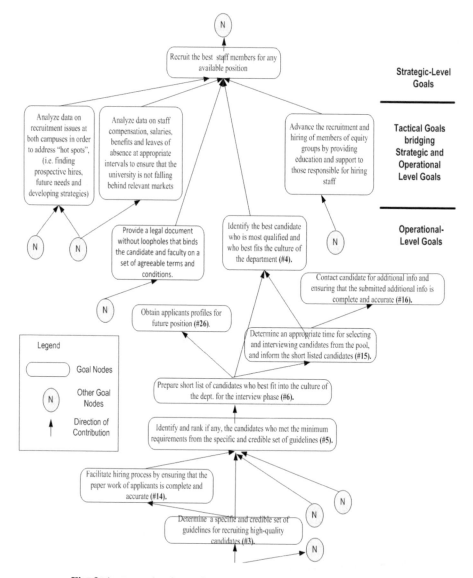

Fig. 3. An example of mapping operational goals to strategic goals [18]

objective of the organizational worker, and how the organizational worker wants to act to achieve a goal is called an *intention*. The process by which an actor decides what to do is represented by *reasoning*. The actual changes s/he creates in the environment are represented by *actions* that create some output (or specific attribute of the environment).

None of the above concepts in the organizational actor framework are new and they have been used in the field of intelligent agents and multi-agent systems for many years. However, we are unaware of work that uses these concepts to help organizational workers in their problem-solving. Monu and Woo [13] provided evidence that organizational workers unintentionally use those concepts in their problem solving. In an exploratory study with 10 subjects, we found that subjects prefer to use the organizational actor model, over i* models, in explaining a domain application to other people. From the rationale provided by the subjects, we found the *learning* and *reasoning* concepts of organizational workers (which are not available in the i* models) are useful for understanding and communication. *Learning* and *reasoning* are concepts that represent the thought process of organizational workers.

An example of an organizational actor diagram is shown in Figure 4. We used the description and i* diagrams provided in [6] to derive this organizational actor diagram. It will provide a useful comparison to the corresponding i* diagrams in [6].

To further understand the usefulness of the organizational actor framework, we applied it to two domains: marketing and disaster management. For the marketing case study [11], we represented a scenario involving a price war between two companies so that we could use the organizational actor diagram to create a simulation of agents in this situation. The marketing expert used the diagram and discovered that the objectives of the respective retailer actor was not solely what drove pricing behavior but the actors' reasoning and learning.

In the disaster management case study [12], where we represented the conceptual model of actors in a disaster management scenario, senior disaster professionals found that a major resource for them was not technical manuals but everyday sources (e.g., student newspapers and community meetings) that provided information about the "pulse" of the community. In addition, disaster recovery personnel were able to discover assumptions in the disaster plan. For example, they discovered that their major assumption had been that key personnel in the disaster recovery would always be able to interact during the disaster. Assumptions are represented in the organizational actor diagram as beliefs, and beliefs can be changed by learning. This is therefore another example of the usefulness of representing the thought process of organizational workers in a conceptual model.

4 Conclusion

Conceptual modeling started in the area of database design, and expanded into gathering requirements for information systems development. In this paper, we provide a further extension, because we realize we can move away from using it purely for IT; we can help organizational workers to better understand the organization and support them in their problem solving. To do this, we needed to represent aspects that we had not modeled previously, and we needed to base the development of those aspects in management literature. In this paper, we provided a few examples of how to accomplish this: (a) agreements that govern the exchange of resources in Section 2.1, (b) attributes associated with goals at different levels of organizations in Section 3.1, and (c) the thought process of reasoning and learning in Section 3.2.

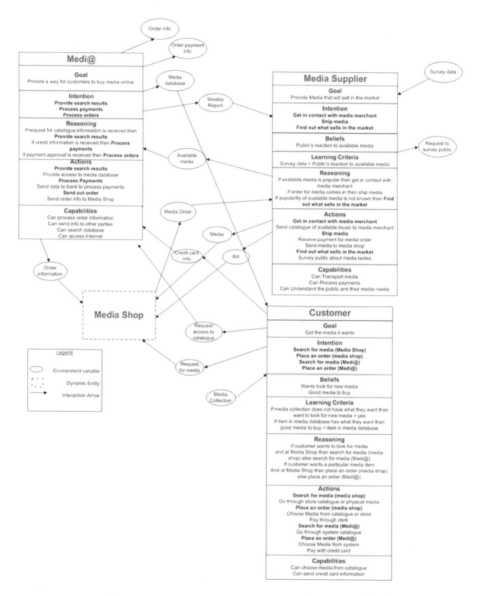

Fig. 4. An Example Organizational Actor Diagram [13]

We are extending our object-oriented modeling approach to include business context [22]. When applying the approach in real world situations, we discovered that most of our diagrams are too complex for use by organizational workers. One way to resolve this challenge is to provide summary information useful for their problem solving (e.g., a bar chart showing hours spent in different activities) or allow them to query the database containing the conceptual model (e.g., what are the sub-goals that contribute to a higher level goal). However, in order to produce this kind of aggregated information for organizational workers, we need to ensure consistency in capturing requirements and in the meanings used by different people in this open-ended world.

We see a lot of potential in expanding conceptual modeling to support organizational workers. Although these conceptual models might need some intermediate mapping before they can be used for IT development, the conceptual models developed for organizational workers should help to refine the requirements needed to develop information systems, and this can open up many avenues for future research.

Acknowledgement. This research was funded in part by a grant from the Natural Sciences and Engineering Research Council of Canada (NSERC). The author is indebted to the comments and feedback of this work from Izak Benbasat, Andrew Burton-Jones, Kafui Monu, and Yair Wand.

References

[1] Alter, S.: The Work System Method: Conncecting People, Process, and IT for Business Results. Work System Press, Larkspur (2006)

[2] Bresciani, P., Giorgini, P., Giunchiglia, F., Mylopoulos, J., Perini, A.: TROPOS: An Agent-Oriented Software Development Methodology. Autonomous Agents and Multi-Agent Systems 8, 203–236 (2004)

[3] The Department of Defense Architecture Framework (DoDAF), http://cio-nii.defense.gov/sites/dodaf20/ (access June 29, 2011)

[4] Checkland, P.: Soft Systems Methodology: A Thirty Year Retrospective. In: Systems Research and Behavioral Science, Syst. Res., vol. 17, pp. S11–S58. John Wiley & Sons, Ltd., Chichester (2000)

[5] Fettke, P.: How Conceptual Modeling Is Used. Communications of the Association for Information Systems 25(1), 571–592 (2009)

[6] Giunchiglia, F., Mylopoulos, J., Perini, A.: The Tropos Software Development Method: Processes, Models and Diagrams. In: Proceedings of the First International Joint Conference on Autonomous Agents and Mutiagent Systems: Part 1 Bologna, Italy (July 2002)

[7] Hammer, M., Champy, J.: Reengineering the Corporation. HarperCollins Publishers, Inc., New York (2001)

[8] Jacobson, I., Christerson, M., Jonsson, P., Overgaard, G.: Object-Oriented Sofware Engineering: A Use Case Driven Approach. ACM Press, New York (1992)

[9] Kavakli, E., Loucopoulos, P.: Goal Driven Requirements Engineering: Evaluation of Current Methods. In: Proceedings of the 8th CAiSE/IFIP8.1 International Workshop on Evaluation of Modeling Methods in Systems Analysis and Design (EMMSAD), Velden, Austria, June 16-17 (2003)

[10] van Lamsweerde, A.: Goal-Oriented Requirements Engineering: A Guided Tour. In: Proceedings of the 5th IEEE International Symposium on Requirements Engineering, August 27-31 (2001)

[11] Monu, K., Wand, Y., Woo, C.: Intelligent Agents as a Modelling Paradigm. In: Proceedings of the International Conference on Information Systems (ICIS 2005), Las Vegas, December 12-14, pp. 167–179 (2005)

[12] Monu, K., Woo, C.: Conceptual modeling in disaster planning using agent constructs. In: Laender, A.H.F., Castano, S., Dayal, U., Casati, F., de Oliveira, J.P.M. (eds.) ER 2009. LNCS, vol. 5829, pp. 374–386. Springer, Heidelberg (2009)

[13] Monu, K., Woo, C.: Determining the Usefulness of Representing Organizational Actor Thought-Processes Using Conceptual Modeling. In: Proceedings of the tenth AIS SIGSAND Symposium, Bloomington, Indiana, USA, June 3-4 (2011)

[14] Mylopoulos, J.: Conceptual modeling and Telos. In: Loucopoulos, P., Zicari, R. (eds.) Conceptual Modeling, Databases, and case: an Integrated view of Information Systems Development, pp. 50–68. John Wiley & Sons, Inc., Chichester (1992)

[15] Olivé, A.: Conceptual Modeling of Information Systems. Springer, Heidelberg (2007)

[16] Pfeffer, J., Salancik, G.: The External Control of Organizations: A Resource Dependence Perspective. Harper and Row, New York (1978)

[17] Penker, M., Han-Erik, E.: Business Modeling with UML: Business Patterns at Work. Wiley, New York (2000)

[18] Singh, S.N., Woo, C.: Investigating Business-IT Alignment Through Multi-Disciplinary Goal Concepts. In: Requirements Engineering, vol. 14, pp. 177–207. Springer, Heidelberg (2009)

[19] Tillquist, J., King, J.L., Woo, C.: A Representational Scheme for Analyzing Information Technology and Organizational Dependency. Management Information Systems Quarterly (MISQ) 26(2), 91–118 (2002)

[20] The Open Group Architecture Framework (TOGAF), http://pubs.opengroup.org/architecture/togaf9-doc/arch/ (access June 29, 2011)

[21] Ulrich, D., Barney, J.: Perspectives on Organizations: Resource Dependence, Efficiency and Population. Academy of Management Review 9(3), 471–481 (1984)

[22] Wand, Y., Woo, C., Wand, O.: Role and Request Based Conceptual Modeling – A Methodology and a CASE Tool. In: Li, Q., Spaccapietra, S., Yu, E., Olivé, A. (eds.) ER 2008. LNCS, vol. 5231, pp. 540–541. Springer, Heidelberg (2008)

[23] Yu, E.: Modelling Organizations for Information Systems Requirements Engineering. In: Proceedings of the First IEEE Symposium on Requirements Engineering, San Diego, U.S.A, pp. 34–41 (January 1993)

[24] Zackman, J.A.: Zackman Framework, http://www.zachman.com/ (access June 28, 2011)

Adding Meaning to Your Steps
(Keynote Paper)

Stefano Spaccapietra[1] and Christine Parent[2]

[1] Swiss Federal Institute of Technology (EPFL), IC, Station 14, 1015 Lausanne, Switzerland
[2] University of Lausanne, HEC-ISI, 1015 Dorigny, Switzerland
stefano.spaccapietra@epfl.ch, christine.parent@unil.ch

Abstract. Mobility data is becoming an important player in many application domains. Many techniques have been elaborated to extract statistical knowledge from the data sets gathering raw data tracks about the moving objects of interest to an application. These data tracks obey the physical-level specifications of the devices used for data acquisition (GPS, GSM, RFID, smart phones, and other sensors). Nowadays, interest has shifted from raw data tracks analysis to more application-oriented ways of analyzing more meaningful movement records suitable for the specific purposes of the application at hand. This trend has promoted the concept of semantically rich trajectories, rather than raw movement, as the core object of interest in mobility studies.

This keynote paper intends to provide the foundations of a semantic approach to data about movement. It focuses on the definitions of the most important concepts about mobility data, concepts that are frequently used but rarely rigorously defined.

Keywords: Mobility data, moving objects, movement tracks, trajectory, semantic trajectory, trajectory behavior.

1 Introduction

Mobility is one of the major keywords that characterize the current development of our society. People, goods, and ideas are moving faster and more frequently than ever. This entails a considerable boom in all logistics geared to make moving easier. From the computer science perspective such logistics targets on the one hand the provision of contextualized information (via location-based systems), and on the other hand the capture, management and exploitation of movement data (generated via the use of GPS, sensors, RFIDs, cellphones, smartphones, and alike). Tracking moving objects can produce huge amounts of movement data. Unfortunately these data, basically GPS records containing sequences of spatio-temporal positions, do not readily convey information about their meaning from an application viewpoint. Hence their use remains quite limited.

To enable richer use of movement data, recent research has been investigating ways to enrich movement tracks to make them better correspond to application requirements and scenarios. These enriched movement tracks are nowadays referred to as semantic trajectories.

M. Jeusfeld, L. Delcambre, and T.W. Ling (Eds.): ER 2011, LNCS 6998, pp. 13–31, 2011.

As a new type of objects, semantic trajectories call for new definitions in terms of modeling and manipulation, including the ability to define multiple interpretations on the basis of application criteria. This paper provides a set of basic definitions that form a consistent framework to talk about how GPS records of movement tracks can be turned into meaningful information, the semantic trajectories. Definitions follow the inspirational work on semantic trajectories first done within the GeoPKDD project [8] (in particular [4], [15], [22]), and currently continued within the MODAP EU Coordination Action [20]. Other important prior background work includes work on spatio-temporal databases [13] and the work by Güting et al. on moving objects [11].

The next section discusses the step leading from raw movement to raw trajectories. Section 3 moves us from raw trajectories to semantic trajectories. In section 4 we analyze how the concept of behavior inherently applies to trajectory analyses. Section 5 concludes this short contribution.

2 Raw Movement Tracks

Movement in this paper refers to time-stamped changes in the spatial position of an object, called the *moving object*. It is therefore, by the virtue of this definition, movement in geographical space, as opposed, for instance, to metaphorical movements such as the career path expressing the progression of a person in a work-related abstract space. Intuitively, movement can be defined as the result of an action performed to 1) go from one place to another, if the moving object controls its movement (e.g. a person, an animal, a car), or 2) move an object from one place to another, if the moving object is passive and is moved (e.g., a parcel). We do not include in this study other kinds of movements that are not intended for changing the spatial position: E.g., eye or finger movements, body movements as in gymnastic exercises, or movement intended to change the spatial distribution of a set of objects, as e.g. in military games.

We also do not address issues related to shape and shape deformations that may accompany movement. For example, a pollution cloud is likely to change shape over time while it moves. To avoid dealing with the complexity of tracking the shape of the object, we ignore the object's shape and consider that the moving object is spatially represented as a single moving point. The chosen point may be the centroid of the object's shape or any other point deemed to suitably represent the current position of the object.

The object's movement is usually captured using GPS devices, as is the case for GPS embedded in cars, cell phones, and various transmitters attached to animals. It may also be sensed via tags (e.g., RFID tags), attached to the moving object, a technique frequently used with passive objects, e.g., parcels and products. The accumulation of captured data forms the *movement track* of the moving object, defined as the sequence of spatio-temporal positions, i.e. (instant, point) pairs, that contains the evolving position of the object. In Figure 1 the dotted line shows part of a movement track in space and time where X and Y are the spatial coordinates and time is the vertical axis. The continuous line in the X, Y plan shows the spatial trace of the moving object. Notice that the three vertical segments of the spatio-temporal trace, (t1, P1)–(t2, P1), (t3, P2)–(t4, P2), and (t5, P3)–(t6, P3), show that the object did not move during the three time intervals: [t1,t2], [t3,t4] and [t5,t6].

Figure 2 uses a 2D visualization on the background geographical map to show the spatial trace of a pedestrian visiting the EPFL campus.

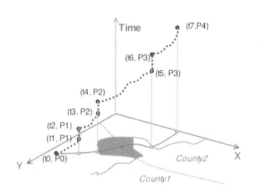

Fig. 1. A movement track in a 3D   **Fig. 2.** The spatial trace of a movement
(2D space + time) representation   on a background map

To differentiate the captured track from other kinds of tracks that will be introduced in the sequel, we call *raw data* the captured data. Notice that while simple devices only transmit (id, t, x, y [, z]) spatio-temporal positions (where id denotes the device identifier and x, y, z are the spatial coordinates in either 2D or 3D space), more sophisticated devices can transmit more data, such as the instant speed or stillness, instant direction, instant rotation, instant acceleration.

The movement track of an object can be captured all along the lifespan of the object. However, many applications are not interested in keeping and analyzing exhaustive movement records. For example, ecologists tracking the movement of birds may be interested in analyzing birds' movement only during their annual migration periods, in spring and autumn. During the other seasons the signals transmitted by the devices equipping the birds are simply ignored (not stored). We call *trajectories* the segments of the object's movement that are of interest for a given application (see Figure 3). Each trajectory is identified by its performing object and two specific spatio-temporal positions, called *Begin* and *End*, which are the first and the last positions of the object for this trajectory [22].

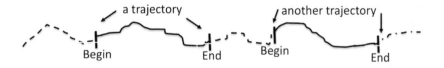

Fig. 3. Trajectories extracted from a movement track visualized as a line

We call *raw trajectory* a trajectory containing only raw data. A raw trajectory is formally defined as:

(trajectoryID, movingObjectID, track: LISTOF position(instant, point))

Notice that the movement track contains only positions recorded at some sampling instants. Therefore it is an approximation of the real movement. Interpolation functions are frequently used to compute the likely position of the moving object for any instant between two consecutive sampled positions. The computed positions complement the captured positions, thus reconstructing continuity.

It is, however, often the case that a movement track shows an abnormal (greater than the sampling rate) temporal gap between two consecutive positions. This means that over some periods of time the information on the movement of the object is missing. If this is accidental (e.g., because of device malfunction) we say there is a *hole* in the track. If this is deliberate (e.g., an employee deactivating her GPS when going for lunch) we say there is a *semantic gap*. Semantic gaps have to be explicitly recorded in order to differentiate them from the holes. Holes may sometimes be "filled", using e.g. linear interpolation algorithms that compute the missing positions. Semantics gaps, instead, are not to be filled, as the positions are intentionally missing.

3   From Raw Trajectories to Semantic Trajectories

Even when complemented with the definition of semantic gaps, raw trajectories are not sufficient for many applications that need more semantics. Raw trajectories are well fitted for applications that aim only at locating some moving objects (e.g. where was parcel #371 at 8am PST on October 30, 2011?) or computing statistics on the spatio-temporal characteristics of the trajectory (e.g. which percentage of trajectories show speed over 50km/h?). On the other hand, most applications analyses require trajectories that are linked to the application context. For example, understanding characteristics of persons' trajectories in a city usually requires knowledge of the underlying city map. Thanks to city information, spatio-temporal coordinates can be replaced with streets and crossings names, or with names of places of interest, such as buildings, housings, shops, restaurants, cafes, schools, enterprises, and sports centers. Traffic monitoring applications, for example, also need information about ongoing events, e.g. football games, fairs, and concerts, to be able to differentiate what happens under normal traffic conditions from what happens under exceptional traffic conditions. Such information is recovered from external data sources, in particular sources containing geo- and time-referenced objects. Let us generically call *application data repository* these external sources, be they application's databases or other sources such as GIS or web pages.

All these information, as well as others, may be attached to the trajectory track or to specific parts of it. For example, an application may need to record the goal of each trajectory trip, e.g. was it for visiting a customer or a provider? An application dealing with apes may need to record at each instant the activity pursued by the animals, e.g. resting, feeding, moving, and escaping. An application monitoring persons in a city may need to record the transportation means used at each instant by each moving person. Following today's practice we call *annotation* any additional data that enriches the knowledge about a trajectory (or about any part of the trajectory) and that is stored with the trajectory data. Annotations may be captured by observers (e.g., the activity of apes) or by sensors (e.g. instant speed), or may be inferred by reasoning (e.g., the transportation means of the persons in a city may be inferred from the velocity and acceleration of the person, and from knowledge about the transport and road networks) [10]. An annotation value is an attribute value (e.g. in the apes' trajectories, the string "feeding" is a value for the activity annotation) or a link to an object of the application data repository (e.g. in a relational database about persons' trajectories in a city, the key of the tuple "bus_line_13" of the Transportation table may be a value for the transportation means annotation). It may also be a complex value composed of attribute values and links to objects. For instance in the apes application, a complex annotation value for a trajectory of the ape 26 could be ("picking lice off", ape_33) where ape_33 is a reference to the object representing another ape of the studied group.

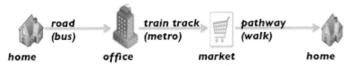

Fig. 4. Different annotations on a trajectory: kind_of_place (home, office, market), kind_of_path (road, train_track, pathway), means_of_transportation (bus, metro, walk)

Another way of enhancing the knowledge on trajectories is to identify, within them, specific segments that are semantically meaningful for the application in view of specific trajectory data analyses. An *episode* [17] is a maximal sub-sequence of a trajectory such that all its spatio-temporal positions comply with a given predicate that bears on the spatio-temporal positions and/or their annotations. Usually a trajectory is segmented into a list of episodes of several types according to a set of predicates, each predicate defining a type of episodes. For instance, a vehicle trajectory may be segmented into episodes of two types, "stop" and "move", according to the two predicates: 1) for stops: speed<3km/h, 2) for moves: speed≥3km/h.

Fig. 5. Segmentation into episodes by mode of transportation

A given trajectory may be structured into episodes in many different ways, i.e. using different sets of predicates. For example, a trajectory of a person within a city may be segmented into episodes based on 1) the value of the annotation "means_of_transportation" (e.g., on_foot, by_bus, by_car) [28], 2) the time period corresponding to the instant of the spatio-temporal position (e.g. morning, noon, afternoon, evening, night), and 3) the category of the area of the city corresponding to the location of the spatio-temporal position (e.g. residential, mixed residential-commercial, commercial, industrial, special). We call each list of episodes an *interpretation* of the trajectory. We call **semantic trajectory** a trajectory enhanced with annotations and/or one or several alternative interpretations.

Episodes themselves can be annotated. For instance, in the case of persons' trajectories in a city, the episodes of type stop may be annotated with the reference to the application object of type "Point of Interest" that is the nearest one and most likely to have been visited by the moving person during this stop.

At this point we can formally define a trajectory of an object as:

Trajectory = (trajectoryID, objectID, trajAnnotations,
        track: LISTOF position(t, p, posAnnotations),
        semanticGaps: LISTOF gap(t_1,t_2),
        interpretations : SETOF interpretation(interpretationID,
                episodes: LISTOF episode(t'_1, t'_2, type, episodeAnnotations)))

where:

trajectoryID is the identifier of the trajectory;

objectID is the identifier of the moving object;

trajAnnotations is the (possibly empty) set of annotations associated to the trajectory as a whole (e.g. its goal or cause, its duration, its length)

track is the list of spatio-temporal positions of the moving object. The list is temporally ordered, according to ascending t

t, t_i specify a temporal element. Usually they are instants. All t_i are disjoint.

p specifies a spatial element. Without loss of generality we assume it is a point, i.e. 2D coordinates (x, y) or 3D coordinates (x, y, z)

posAnnotations denotes a (possibly empty) set of annotations (e.g. activity, transportation means) associated with the spatio-temporal position.

The first spatio-temporal position is called Begin: Begin=(t_{Begin}, p_{Begin}, annotations$_{Begin}$)

The last spatio-temporal position is called End: End=(t_{End}, p_{End}, annotations$_{End}$);

semanticGaps is a (possibly empty) list of semantic gaps in the trajectory. Each gap is defined by two instants t_1 and t_2 where t_1 and t_2 are instants (t) in positions, such that t_2 immediately follows t_1 in positions: t_1=position$_i$.t and t_2=position$_{i+1}$.t

interpretations is the (possibly empty) set of interpretations of the trajectory

interpretationID is the identifier of the interpretation, e.g. "StopMoveEpisodes" or "activityEpisodes";

episodes is the list of episodes for this interpretation

t'_1 and t'_2 are instants (t) recorded in two positions, such that:
        $t'_1 < t'_2$ and episode$_{i+1}$.$t'_1 \geq$ episode$_i$.$t'_2 + 1$

type is the type of the episode, e.g. "stop" or "move" for the interpretation "stop/moveEpisodes", "playing", "eating", or "resting" for the interpretation "activityEpisodes";

episodeAnnotations is the (possibly empty) set of annotations associated to the episode.

Let us use the example of trajectories of cars in a city with a unique interpretation, StopMoveEpisodes, and only one annotation: an annotation of episodes of type stop containing the reference to a place of interest. Then the above definition reduces to:

(trajectoryID, objectID, positions: LISTOF position(t, p),
    episodes: LISTOF episode (t'_1, t'_2, type, episodeAnnotations))

where: type = "stop" or "move"
episodeAnnotations =
    for stops: a link to a PlaceOfInterest object of the application data repository
    for moves: /

A raw trajectory is formally defined as:
(trajectoryID, ObjectID, positions: LISTOF position(t, p))

Knowing what is in a trajectory, we can now look at how to analyze trajectories to infer further characterization of the information they convey.

4   Basic Concepts for Describing Trajectory Behaviors

The goal of this section is to introduce, identify, and define a set of basic concepts for understanding past and future works on analyses of trajectory behaviors. Behavioral analysis is not a new discipline. The last 20+ years have seen numerous contributions from computer science as well as from many application domains (e.g. transports, ecology). However, on the one hand the analysis techniques and tools (e.g. data mining and knowledge extraction) have significantly evolved, and on the other hand the growth of mobility data has recently lead to new facilities, new problems and new solutions. Thus, an introduction on trajectory behaviors and their identification and use seems appropriate.

The number of behaviors that can be defined is unbounded, as any application domain has its own typical requirements and any application adds its specific requirements. We purposely abstain from trying to define a behavior taxonomy. We instead discuss ways to classify behaviors based on their important and identifiable features. Of particular importance in clarifying the broad vision of behaviors is the separation between individual and collective behaviors, which we discuss in subsections 4.2 and 4.3. Other categorizations of interest are discussed in subsections 4.4 to 4.6. Compliance to behaviors is introduced in subsection 4.7. Finally, subsection 4.8 suggests a categorization of research concerns about trajectory behaviors.

4.1   Introducing Trajectory Behaviors and Their Identification

There are many ways to use trajectory data. The simplest one is by querying the data to find mobility facts about some moving object. For example, the tracking database of an express delivery company allows customers to find out where their shipment is at any point in time. Similarly, relatives of airline passengers can ask when a given flight departed and when it arrived. More frequently applications focus on analytical querying, to extract higher-level information from the trajectory database. For example, a city traffic management application may statistically analyze trajectories to identify the most traveled routes depending on time periods within a day or depending on days within a week. This kind of knowledge is not about a specific trajectory or about a specific moving object. It is related to the fact that a sufficient number of trajectories share something in common. For example, if many car trajectories traverse a given square in the city within the same one-hour period one can infer that during this hour the square qualifies as a traffic congestion area. By "congestion area" we refer to both the location and the time period. Actually, the higher-level information targeted by our traffic application will rather be to find all congestion areas within the city. Once this factual result achieved, the application may wish to further analyze trajectories to check if alternative traffic regulations (e.g. using a different network of one-way streets) could possibly lead to the removal of some congested areas. One way to address this goal can be to analyze, for each congestion area, the set of trajectories participating in the congestion and look for groups of trajectories that follow similar routes before and after they traverse the congestion area. Then the remaining task is to find alternate routes for the largest groups.

This complex analysis process uses two kinds of trajectory characterization:

1) Identifying which trajectories cross the congestion area. The filtering of the trajectories is done by applying the predicate "Does the trajectory cross the congestion area during the congestion period?" to each one of the trajectories in the trajectory database.

2) Among the set of trajectories selected for a given congestion area, select the groups of trajectories that use similar routes before and after the congestion area. The predicate for this selection is: "Do all trajectories in the group follow similar routes at least from 1km before up to 1km after the congestion?" Unlikely to the previous case, this condition has to be checked not for each trajectory, but for each potential maximal group of trajectories crossing the congestion.

In the literature on mobility, the predicate used to characterize trajectories is said to define a **trajectory behavior** (or trajectory pattern or behavioral pattern). The trajectories selected by the predicate are said to show the corresponding behavior. Both terms behavior and pattern denote some characteristic that is typically distinguishable in the trajectories provided some appropriate technique (from simple selections to complex knowledge extraction processes) is used to analyze the set of trajectories. In this paper we consider the terms behavior and pattern as synonyms and choose to use behavior as this term has a more definite flavor of spatio-temporality that goes well with trajectories.

The predicate defining a behavior can just be anything. It totally depends on the application at hand. It may rely on the spatio-temporal characteristics of the trajectories, like speed (e.g. the *Speeding* behavior that characterizes vehicles speeding above the limit), or the starting or ending points (e.g. the *Meet* behavior [7] that characterizes a group of trajectories ending at the same place at the same time). These spatio-temporal predicates usually use spatial, temporal and spatio-temporal relationships, like crossing a specific area or line during a specific time interval. The behavior predicate may also rely on the semantic information conveyed via the annotations of the trajectory, in particular on any object of the application repository (and therefore of the environment) that is referenced by an annotation (see Section 3 for more about annotations and the links between the trajectory and the environment).

For instance, the predicate of the behavior *HomeToWork* relies on the types of the starting and ending places of the trajectory (respectively HomePlace and WorkPlace types). These semantic information may be stored directly in the annotations of the Begin and End positions of the trajectory (e.g. the annotation "PlaceType" whose values are: 'work', 'home', 'shop', 'restaurant'...), or they may be characteristics of the objects referenced by the annotation (e.g. the annotation "PlaceOfInterest" whose value is a reference to an object in the environment database and one characteristics of this object is its type which says if the object is a work place, a home place or another kind of place).

It is essential for a mobility application to define the trajectory behaviors that are relevant to its goals. Being able to choose or get inspiration from an existing taxonomy certainly helps application designers. For this reason research has been devoted to build such taxonomy. For example, Dodge et al. [7] undertook a study of the literature on data mining and visual analysis dealing with movement data and extracted definitions of various movement behaviors, most of which refer to behaviors of groups of moving objects. The extracted types of behaviors have been organized in an informal taxonomy. Their classification is based on the spatial and temporal characteristics of the trajectories with no semantic annotation. It provides intuitive rather than formal definitions and classification. The authors have also set up a web site where interested researchers can contribute to the further development of the taxonomy (http:// movementpatterns. pbworks.com/w/page/21692527/Patterns-of-Movement).

Similar efforts towards a list of behaviors include Thériault et al. [23], whose main focus is on spatio-temporal behaviors, Laube et al. [14] whose peculiarity is studying movement of individuals within a group, Andrienko and Andrienko [3] who addresses single and collective behavior taking also into consideration terrain features (e.g. obstacles) as well as some semantic annotations (e.g. means of transportation), and Wood and Galton [26] who develop a deeper investigation into concepts for collective behaviors. The latter is particularly interesting as it discusses in detail the works we just quoted, including [7]. Their conclusion is that no work is sufficiently mature and comprehensive to establish a general taxonomy.

4.2 Individual Trajectory Behavior versus Collective Behavior

Back to our example on using car trajectories to determine congestion areas, we have seen that for the purpose of finding how to prevent congestions we need two kinds of characterizations of trajectories:

1) Characterizing each trajectory individually, by associating to it the congestion areas it traverses, if any. Other examples include qualifying each human trajectory in a city as: a *Shopping* trajectory (a trajectory that stops in several shops or shopping centers), a *Tourist* trajectory (a trajectory that stops in hotels, museums, and monuments), a *HomeToWork* trajectory (a trajectory that goes form the home place of the object to her/his work place), and son on. Similarly, we can seek to qualify each animal trajectory as e.g. a *Leadership* trajectory (a trajectory that moves in front of the trajectories of the other animals of its group);

2) Characterizing groups of trajectories, e.g. in the traffic application the groups of vehicle trajectories traversing the same congestion area with similar routes.

Characterization of groups of trajectories is very frequent in animal monitoring applications as animals of many species use to move in groups. Popular examples include *V-Shape* trajectories for migrating birds and *Meet* trajectories for humans (a group of people that reach the same place roughly at the same time).

The conclusion from the examples is that two kinds of trajectory behavior exist: individual trajectory behaviors, and collective behaviors.

Figure 6 illustrates that for individual behaviors each trajectory is checked against the behavior predicate. This determines if the trajectory shows this behavior or not. Collective behaviors cannot be checked by considering a single trajectory. They need multiple, usually simultaneous trajectories by different objects. Two trajectories may be checked against e.g. a *Meet* behavior, while more trajectories are needed to check for a *Flock* behavior [5].

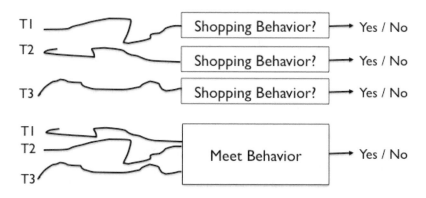

Fig. 4. Individual (Shopping) versus Collective (Meet) Behaviors

Definition: Let T be a trajectory. A ***trajectory individual behavior*** is a Boolean predicate p(T). The predicate can bear on any characteristics of the trajectory.

Trajectories satisfying the predicate are said to show the corresponding behavior.

Behaviors can be formally defined. We use for this purpose a generic logic formalism. A quite different formalism, tailored for collective behaviors, has been proposed by Laube et al. [14]. For example, let us define a *TrajectoryByBus* behavior for trajectories that have an interpretation called TransportModeInterpretation with episodes of type: bus, foot, car, train, subway and bike. We define *TrajectoryByBus* as the fact of having at least one episode by bus and possibly some episodes by foot, but no other type of episode (no car, train, subway or bike episode). The formal definition of the TrajectoryByBus behavior then is:

Let T be a trajectory with a formal definition as defined in Section 2.

TrajectoryByBus(T):
∃i∈T.interpretations (i.interpretationID="TransportModeInterpretation" ∧
    ∃e∈ i.episodes (e.type=bus) ∧
¬∃e∈i.episodes (e.type=train ∧ e.type=subway ∧ e.type=bike ∧ e.type=car)
)

In this example the defining predicate requires that the trajectory data include a specific interpretation (TransportModeInterpretation), because the behavior predicate bears on the associated episodes. A much simpler example is the *CrossTheChamps-Elysées* behavior that bears only on the spatial data (the trajectory route) used to evaluate the involved topological Cross relationship with the line representing the Champs-Elysées.

Definition. Let ST be a set of trajectories such that $|ST|>1$. A ***trajectory collective behavior*** is a Boolean predicate p(ST). The predicate can bear on any characteristics of the trajectories.

A collective behavior can be defined for:

- known pre-existing groups. E.g. a herd of sheep shepherded by a dog shows the Flock behavior, and the same applies to a platoon of soldiers.
- groups that are defined on the spot by the evaluation of the behavior predicate. E.g. the groups of similar trajectories that follow the same route before and after crossing a congestion area.

Consider, for example, a crowd making a protest march. We can decide that the whole set of people in the crowd makes up a single group, and analyze the behavior of the group, e.g. in terms of initial gathering, peaceful marching, stopping, listening to a speaker, and disbanding. We could also identify a group of individuals in the crowd that do not show the expected behavior, for example frequently moving from one position within the crowd to a different position, frequently getting in and out of the crowd, tending to reach the border between the crowd and security staff. Such atypical behavior can be defined as the behavior of a group of potential rioters. We have coexistence of behaviors for a known group (the crowd) and behaviors for a group (the rioters) that can only be identified a posteriori.

Following Dodge et al., we use group to denote a priori known groups, and cohort to denote groups identified by applying the behavior predicate.

As an example of formal definition for a collective behavior, let us give the definition of the Convergence behavior:

Let ST be a set of trajectories, SPACE the set of points of the application space, and Δs the desired spatial approximation threshold (a distance),

$$convergence(ST, \Delta s): \exists p_c \in SPACE (\forall T \in ST (distance(T.p_{End}, p_c) \le \Delta s) \land$$
$$\forall T \notin ST (distance(T.p_{End}, p_c) > \Delta s))$$

This convergence behavior can be turned into a Meet (spatio-temporal) behavior by adding a temporal condition requiring that convergence of ST happens within a certain timeframe:

Let ST be a set of trajectories, SPACE the set of points of the application space, TIME the set of instants of the application time, Δs a spatial threshold (a distance), and Δt a temporal threshold (a duration):

$$meet(ST, \Delta s, \Delta t): \exists p_m \in SPACE \ \exists t_m \in TIME ($$
$$\forall T \in ST (distance(T.p_{End}, p_m) \le \Delta s \land |T.t_{End} - t_m| \le \Delta t) \land$$
$$\forall T \notin ST (distance(T.p_{End}, p_m) > \Delta s \lor |T.t_{End} - t_m| > \Delta t))$$

4.3 More on Collective Behaviors

Groups are essential for collective behaviors. But what exactly is a group and what are its relevant properties? Wood and Galton have produced several papers on an ontological analysis of the group concept (called collective in their approach) [25] and the group motion concept [26, 27]. Identified properties of a group include:

- Membership: Does the group have always the same set of members?
- Location: Does the group have a location? Is it fixed or variable? How is it related to the location of its members?
  - Causal versus purpose: Does the group exist because of a cause or purpose?
  - Roles: Do all the members have the same role, or are there various roles?
  - Depth: Are some members themselves groups?

Given these properties, an application can move from the analysis of collective trajectory behaviors to the analysis of the corresponding groups of moving objects. Considering movement of groups raises further questions on the interplay between the movement of the group and the movement of each member of the group (e.g., are movements coordinated or not?), as well as interplays between movements of different members in the group (e.g. the typical leadership/follower behaviors inside groups of animals).

The analysis of trajectory behavior remains a very open research domain and significant new results can be expected by ongoing and future work. In the next three subsections we turn our attention to providing some more categorizations to help organizing the research domain. These three categorizations are orthogonal to each other, i.e. all combinations are possible.

4.4 Spatial / Temporal / Spatio-Temporal / Semantic Behaviors

Different views on the characteristics of trajectories lead to different categorizations of their behaviors. Following the definition of trajectory in Section 3, trajectory characteristics include spatio-temporal positions, annotations (at various levels) and interpretations consisting of episodes. The latter is clearly semantic, application-driven information. The former, positions, is by definition spatio-temporal information, offering the possibility of considering space and time separately or together, as needed. Annotations may be: 1) of spatio-temporal nature, e.g. instant speed at each position, 2) semantic information, e.g. the activity of observed apes or the transportation means of moving persons, and 3) a combination of spatio-temporal and semantic information, e.g. the average speed during an episode.

Based on the trajectory characteristics, the following behavior categories for both individual and collective behaviors can be found e.g. in [7] taxonomy:

- **Spatial behaviors**, whose defining predicate only bears on the spatial information, i.e. the points of the spatio-temporal positions. These predicates usually use spatial relationships like those defined in [11]. Examples of individual spatial behaviors include: the CrossAreaA behavior that selects the trajectories that cross the spatial extent of the area identified as A, and all "shape" behaviors that select the trajectories whose path shows the corresponding shape, e.g., Straight pattern, Loop pattern, Star pattern. Examples of spatial collective behaviors include Co-location and Concentration [7].

- **Temporal behaviors**, whose defining predicate uses only the temporal information, i.e. the instants of the spatio-temporal positions. These predicates usually use temporal relationships like those defined in [1, 11, 19]. Examples of individual temporal behaviors include: Trajectories that start before 7am in the morning, trajectories whose total stop duration exceeds the total move duration, and trajectories during a given time interval. An example of temporal collective behavior is Synchronization [7].

- **Spatio-temporal behaviors**, whose defining predicate uses both spatial and temporal information. These predicates usually use spatial, temporal and spatio-temporal relationships like those defined in [11, 19]. Simple individual behaviors include: the TemporalCross behavior that adds a temporal constraint to the CrossAreaA behavior, e.g., cross the area A within a given time interval, the StartAt behavior selecting trajectories that start at some given point at some given time, and the Speeding behavior that selects car trajectories where speed reaches higher than a given threshold. A popular behavior in this category is the Sequence behavior: It is a complex behavior that selects the trajectories that satisfy a list of spatial (or spatio-temporal) simple predicates in a given temporal order, e.g. start at a given point P1, later cross the area A1, and later stop during a while inside the area A2. Examples of spatio-temporal collective behaviors include Convergence/Divergence, Expansion/Contraction, Progression/Regression, and Deformation [23], Flock [7].

More recently trajectories have been enhanced with semantic features, thus enabling an additional category:

- **Semantic behaviors**, whose defining predicate uses the semantic information, i.e. the semantic annotations and episodes. A popular example is behaviors related to episodes of type stop [22], trying to characterize for which purpose the moving object stopped, e.g., persons' trajectories that stop at a restaurant, car trajectories that stop at a petrol station belonging to a competitor petrol company. Already quoted examples are Shopping behavior, denoting any trajectory such that at least 70% of its stop duration is made in places of interest of kind Shop, and HomeToWork behavior, denoting any trajectory such that its Begin is in a place of kind HomePlace and its End is in a place of kind WorkPlace.

- **Mixed behaviors**, whose defining predicate uses some semantic characteristics together with spatial, temporal and/or spatio-temporal characteristics. They are the most frequent behaviors. Most of the spatio-temporal behaviors have their mixed counterpart. The CrossTheChampsElysées we already mentioned illustrates this mix. It characterizes the trajectories that cross the spatial extent of a given geo-object of the application. Examples of collective mixed behavior are FlockEscapingFromPredator and TouristGroup. The TouristGroup behavior denotes a Flock behavior with most of its stops in places of kind Museum, Monument, SouvenirShop, and Restaurant.

4.5 Global versus Local Behaviors

This classification, orthogonal to the two previous one, is rooted on the scope of the defining predicate which may be either the whole trajectory or a segment of it. This defines two classes of behavior:

- **Global behaviors**, defined by predicates that constrain the whole trajectory, like selecting trajectories that spend more time during the stops than during the moves, or trajectories whose global shape is a star.

- **Local behaviors**, defined by predicates that constrain only a sub-segment of the trajectory, i.e., the predicate selects the trajectories that contain at least a sub-segment that satisfies the predicate. Trajectories that start before 7am, trajectories that pass nearby a given geo-object during their first episode are two examples of local behaviors.

Some predicates may be used to define both global and local behaviors. For instance, the predicate that selects trajectories that contain at least a move that draws a star shape is a local star behavior, while the predicate that selects trajectories whose whole sequence of positions draws a star shape is a global star behavior.

4.6 Simple versus Complex Behaviors

As trajectories are temporally ordered lists of positions, many individual behaviors do not specify a predicate on a unique position of the trajectory, they specify a sequence of predicates that have to be satisfied in the order of the sequence: The trajectory has to satisfy each predicate in turn as the moving object makes its trajectory. These sequences of predicates are usually called sequence patterns or **sequence behaviors**. An example of sequence behavior is: Trajectories that begin in place P1, then cross area A2, and later stop in place P3 for at least 10 minutes. Sequence behaviors have been thoroughly investigated.

As sequence behaviors may be quite complex, a language has to be defined for expressing the various sequence operators. The most usual operators are:

- THEN_NEXT: the next spatio-temporal position, the next instant, or the next episode must comply with the predicate
- THEN_LATER: there must be, later within the trajectory, a spatio-temporal position, instant, or episode that complies with the predicate
- repetitions: for exactly (or at least, at most) N consecutive spatio-temporal positions, instants, or episodes the predicate must be fulfilled
- optionality: for 0 or 1 consecutive spatio-temporal position, instant, or episode the predicate must be fulfilled.

The languages that are most frequently used for defining sequence behaviors are ad hoc languages based on lists of predicates coupled to temporal constraints ("time ordered sequence of query atoms"), and languages based on regular grammar or expressions. An example of the first kind are the "sequence queries" defined in [12]. A sequence query is a list of spatial predicates coupled to temporal constraints that are either absolute (e.g. "on November 1st, 2011") or relative (e.g. "10 days later" or simply "later"). Another example is the query language defined in [16]. This language is based on constraints languages.

Regular grammars and expressions work on sequences of characters, so their principles can be easily adapted to trajectories that are sequences of positions or episodes. For instance in [18] a trajectory is the recording of the list of zones that the moving object crossed with associated time durations. In [9] a trajectory is made up of episodes of kind stop and move. Each stop is annotated with a place of interest. In both cases, a language based on regular grammars allows defining predicates on these sequences of zones or places of interest.

Laube et al. followed a similar approach. They defined a language for describing individual and collective behaviors (respectively called sequence and incident patterns) based on the spatio-temporal characteristics of the trajectories, like speed or direction [14]. Their language is also based on regular expressions. The novelty is that the language may define individual and collective behaviors, thanks to a model that represents the trajectories and the set of moving objects. The repetition and optional operators can be applied to the sequence of instants of a trajectory or to the set of moving objects, thus supporting the description of collective behaviors that involve sets of objects.

In [21] Sakr and Güting follow another approach. Based on their long experience on databases for moving objects, they designed a powerful language that relies on "lifted predicates". A lifted predicate is any regular predicate (like "Is the car over-speeding?" or the spatial predicate "Is the car inside area A?") that is applied to time-varying objects, and in particular to moving objects (instead of being applied to a snapshot view). The result of a lifted predicate is a time-varying Boolean, i.e. a function from Time to Boolean. For instance, the predicate "Is the car over-speeding?" may generate the following result for the day November 1st, 2011: (False [8h05, 8h45]), (True [8h46, 9h12]), (False [9h12, 10h08])... These lifted predicates allow Sakr and Güting to express any kind of complex sequence behavior. In particular, they allow expressing sequence operators of kind THEN_NEXT, THEN_LATER, DURING, BEFORE...

Our last classification of behaviors defines **simple and complex behaviors**. We call simple those behaviors whose defining predicate consists in a set of conditions connected by the regular Boolean operators AND, OR, and NOT. We call complex those behaviors whose defining predicate consists in a set of conditions connected by the Boolean operators and by at least one sequence operator. According to this last classification, sequence patterns are complex behaviors

4.7   Checking If Trajectories Comply with a Behavior

Behavioral analysis includes checking if given trajectories comply with given behavior predicates, or finding which trajectories from a trajectory database comply with given behavior predicates.

For individual behaviors, the predicate that defines the behavior may refer only to the trajectory itself (e.g. HomeToWork, CrossLine, Star), or refer to the trajectory and some other one(s) (e.g. the PeacockCourtshipDance behavior of a peacock in front of a few peahens), or refer to the "semantic" group to which the trajectory belongs (e.g. the Leadership behavior that characterizes the alpha wolf of a pack of wolves).

Checking collective behaviors on pre-existing groups runs as a check for individual behaviors, except that compliance is evaluated at the group level instead of at the individual level.

On the other hand, checking collective behaviors on cohorts (groups that are defined by the collective behavior) runs as an iterative process. Assume we have a set of n trajectories {T1, T2, ..., Tn}, and we are looking for subsets of converging trajectories (same end point). We can use the following algorithm (Convergence behavior):

Initialize a first cohort, C1 := {T1}
FOR each trajectory T in {T2, T3,..., Tn}, DO:
    Check with the existing cohorts {C1, C2,..., Ck} IF T converges with one of
        these cohorts (say Cj)
        THEN add T to Cj
        ELSE create a new cohort, Ck+1 := {T}
END of FOR

As an example of why finding cohorts may be very useful, let us consider an application willing to determine places of interest within a city or a region. Running the compliance evaluation for the behavior SharedStop (the trajectories share at least a common stop location) will determine how many moving objects stop at the same place. The higher the number of involved objects, the higher the appropriateness of qualifying this point as a place of interest.

In most cases the matching between a behavior and trajectories does not need to be an exact match (in Section 4.2 our definition of Meet includes both a spatial and a temporal approximation) thus replacing a point with a region around it. An alternative approach is to introduce a compliance measure to replace the compliant/not compliant result by a rating such as e.g., 80% compliant.

Local behaviors (Section 4.5) introduce an additional complexity in compliance checks. Given a local individual behavior LB, a trajectory T can be searched to find if it complies with the LB trajectory behavior. Although conceptually very simple, matching T against LB requires the LB predicate to be checked for all possible sub-sequences of spatio-temporal positions of T (LB defines a kind of sliding window continuous query). Similar reasoning applies to local collective behaviors.

4.8 Looking for Behaviors a Posteriori versus Using Predefined Behaviors

Two types of trajectory behavior research exist. On the one hand we have researches that, given a set of trajectories, aim at identifying which behaviors can be found in the set. No a priori behavior or application-defined behavior is assumed. Techniques for this kind of research typically include data mining, machine learning, and knowledge extraction in general. It is worth noting that in some application domains, e.g. video-surveillance, trajectories are indeed analyzed to find characteristic behaviors but the found behaviors are not of interest per se, they are only used to detect unusual behaviors, i.e. trajectories that do not comply with any of the characteristic behaviors. Tung et al. [24] survey a number of proposed techniques to find unusual behaviors, mainly based on neural networks once the characteristic behaviors have been identified in a training phase.

On the other hand we have researches that for a given problem domain use a set of behaviors that have been predefined by the experts in the domain. For example, Carey et al. [6] analyze behavior of flies in a cage by looking for six predefined behaviors: walking, moving, flying, feeding, drinking, and resting. Issues in these approaches basically relate to detection, quantification-evaluation, and visualization of the considered behaviors.

Relevant work is analyzing trajectories frequent behaviors in order to infer semantic information about the environment, like finding the places of interest in a city, the places favored by migrating birds for feeding and resting or the places that are the most dangerous for them.

Finally, there are research efforts aiming at defining behaviors in a given domain in a more abstract way, e.g. not for the purpose of a specific application. The already quoted taxonomic work of [7] belongs to this category, as do the works in [4] and [2], where for example the Flock, Leadership and SingleFile behaviors are proposed. These behaviors stem from an observation of possible spatio-temporal configurations of moving objects and are assumed to be relevant to a variety of applications.

4.9 Conclusion

In this paper we have first defined the basic concepts that underline trajectory management, emphasizing aspects related to a semantic view of trajectories. Secondly we have shown how trajectory behaviors can be described by predicates involving movement attributes and/or relations to the context and/or semantic annotations. Complex behaviors can be decomposed into simpler behaviors linked by various temporal relations. We have introduced the concepts of individual and collective behaviors and considered the distinction between local and global behaviors. We have also considered on a general level three kinds of behavior analysis: (1) checking for compliance with a particular behavior; (2) searching for occurrences of particular behaviors; and (3) observing and describing existing behaviors.

We do expect the corpus of concepts and techniques related to semantic trajectories to significantly increase in the short term. We hope this paper provides a stable basis for evolution. We expect an even more important development of new applications and new domains where semantic trajectories will significantly help new results.

Acknowledgments. This paper results from preparatory work we did to contribute to a survey on semantic trajectories [20]. The work was done within Working Group 3 of the MODAP EU project (www.modap.org). We are definitely indebted to the colleagues with whom we shared the surveying task: Chiara Renso, Natalya and Gennady Andrienko, Vania Bogorny, Maria Luisa Damiani, Aris Gkoulalas-Divanis, Jose Macedo, Nikos Pelekis, Yannis Theodoridis, and Zhixian Yan.

References

1. Allen, J.F.: Maintaining knowledge about temporal intervals. Communications of the ACM 26(11) (November 1983)
2. Andersson, M., Gudmundsson, J., Laube, P., Wolle, T.: Reporting leadership pattern among trajectories. In: 22nd Annual ACM Symposium on Applied Computing, Seoul, Korea, pp. 3–7 (2007)
3. Andrienko, N., Andrienko, G.: Designing visual analytics methods for massive collections of movement data. Cartographica 42(2), 117–138 (2007)
4. Andrienko, N., Andrienko, G., Pelekis, N., Spaccapietra, S.: Basic concepts of movement data. In: Giannotti, F., Pedreschi, D. (eds.) Mobility, Data Mining and Privacy, pp. 15–38. Springer, Heidelberg (2008)

5. Benkert, M., Gudmundsson, J., Hübner, F., Wolle, T.: Reporting flock patterns. Ecological Modelling 113(1-3), 141–156 (1998)
6. Carey, J.R., et al.: A high-resolution system for recording the daily and lifetime behavioral and movement patterns of individual tephritid fruit flies. In: Proceedings of Measuring Behavior 2010, Eindhoven, The Netherlands, August 24-27 (2010)
7. Dodge, S., Weibel, R., Lautenschütz, A.K.: Taking a systematic look at movement: Developing a taxonomy of movement patterns. In: The AGILE Workshop on GeoVisualization of Dynamics, Movement and Change, Girona, Spain (May 5, 2008)
8. Giannotti, F., Pedreschi, D. (eds.): Mobility, Data Mining and Privacy. Springer, Heidelberg (2008)
9. Gomez, L., Kuijpers, B., Vaisman, A.: Aggregation languages for moving object and place of interest. In: Proceedings SAC 2008, Fortaleza, Ceara, Brazil, March 16-20 (2008)
10. Guc, B., May, M., Saygin, Y., Korner, C.: Semantic annotation of GPS trajectories. In: 11th AGILE International Conference on Geographic Information Science, Gerona, Spain (2008)
11. Güting, R.H., Böhlen, M.H., Erwing, M., Jensen, C.S., Lorentzos, N.A., Schneider, M., Vazirgiannis, M.: A foundation for representing and querying moving objects. ACM Transactions on Database Systems 25(1), 1–42 (2000)
12. Hadjileftheriou, M., Kollios, G., Balakov, P., Tsotras, V.: Complex spatio-temporal pattern queries. In: Proc. of VLDB 2005, Trondheim, Norway, August 30 - September 2 (2005)
13. Koubarakis, M., et al. (eds.): Spatio-Temporal Databases: The CHOROCHRONOS Approach. LNCS, vol. 2520. Springer, Heidelberg (2003)
14. Laube, P., Van Kreveld, M., Imfeld, S.: Finding REMO - Detecting relative motion patterns in geospatial lifelines. In: Developments in Spatial Data Handling, Part 5, pp. 201–215. Springer, Heidelberg (2005)
15. Macedo, J., et al.: Trajectory data models. In: Giannotti, F., Pedreschi, D. (eds.) Mobility, Data Mining and Privacy, pp. 123–150. Springer, Heidelberg (2008)
16. Mokhtar, H.M.O., Su, J.: A query language for moving object trajectories. In: Proc. of the 17th Int. Conf. on Scientific and Statistical Database Management, Santa Barbara, CA (2005)
17. Mountain, D., Raper, J.F.: Modelling human spatio-temporal behaviour: a challenge for location-based services. In: Proceedings of the 6th International Conference on GeoComputation, Brisbane, Australia, September 24–26 (2001)
18. Du Mouza, C., Rigaux, P.: Mobility patterns. Geoinformatica 9(4), 297–319 (2005)
19. Parent, C., Spaccapietra, S., Zimanyi, E.: Conceptual Modeling for Traditional and Spatio-Temporal Applications: The MADS Approach. Springer, Heidelberg (2006)
20. Parent, C., et al.: Survey on Semantic Trajectories Modeling and Analysis, submitted for publication (2011)
21. Sakr, M.A., Güting, R.H.: Spatiotemporal pattern queries, Geoinformatica, August 12 (2010), doi:10.1007/s10707-010-0114-3
22. Spaccapietra, S., Parent, C., Damiani, M.L., Macedo, J.A., Porto, F., Vangenot, C.: A conceptual view on trajectories. Data & Knowledge Engineering 65, 126–146 (2008)
23. Thériault, M., Claramunt, C., Villeneuve, P.Y.: A spatio-temporal taxonomy for the representation of spatial set behaviours. In: Böhlen, M.H., Jensen, C.S., Scholl, M.O. (eds.) STDBM 1999. LNCS, vol. 1678, pp. 1–18. Springer, Heidelberg (1999)
24. Tung, F., Zelek, J.S., Clausi, D.A.: Goal-Based trajectory analysis for unusual behavior detection in intelligent surveillance. Image and Vision Computing (29), 230–240 (2011)

25. Wood, Z., Galton, A.: A taxonomy of collective phenomena. Applied Ontology 4, 267–292 (2009)
26. Wood, Z., Galton, A.: Classifying Collective Motion. In: Gottfried, B., Aghajan, H. (eds.) Behavior Monitoring and Interpretation – BMI, pp. 129–155. IOS Press, Amsterdam (2009)
27. Wood, Z., Galton, A.: Zooming in on collective motion. In: Bhatt, M.H., Guesgen, H., Hazarika, S. (eds.) Spatio-temporal dynamics, Proceedings of Workshop 21, 19th European Conference on Artificial Intelligence, ECAI 2010, Lisbon, Portugal, August 16-20, pp. 25–30 (2010)
28. Zheng, Y., Chen, Y., Xie, X., Ma, W.-Y.: Understanding transportation modes based on GPS data for Web applications. ACM Transaction on the Web 4(1) (January 2010)

Best-Effort Modeling of Structured Data on the Web

Alon Halevy

Google Research,
1600 Amphitheatre Parkway,
Mountain View, California, USA

The World-Wide Web provides access to millions of data tables with high-quality content, formatted either in HTML tables, HTML lists, or other structured formats, or stored in on-line data management services. These tables contain data about virtually every domain of interest to mankind. Several reasearch projects aim at enabling search over these data sets and ultimately the ability to answer queries and to combine data from multiple sources.

In addition to the challenges involved in extracting the high-quality data sets from the Web, there is a fundamental challenge concerning how and whether to create a conceptual model of the data that can be used by the higher-level services. Creating a conceptual model, in the traditional sense, for such a collection of data is impractical because of (1) the breadth of the data, (2) the fact that domains overlap in complex ways, and (3) that modeling assumptions differ depending on the level of detail and cultural context.

Several projects at Google have the goal of leveraging this collection of data and to make it easier to create and share new data sets. In each case, interesting challenges arise from the lack of a conceptual model. In the WebTables Project [1,3] we collected over 100 million high-quality HTML tables, developed search over this collection. We used information from text on the Web to recover some of the semantics of these tables. In Google Fusion Tables [2], we make it easy for data owners to upload and manipulate their data, create visualizations and discover other data sets that may be relevant to them, all this without requiring them to a priori create a model of their data. The experiences from these projects suggest that we may require a fundamentally different approach to data modeling in the context of the Web.

References

1. Cafarella, M.J., Halevy, A.Y., Wang, D.Z., Wu, E., Zhang, Y.: WebTables: Exploring the Power of Tables on the Web. PVLDB 1(1), 538–549 (2008)
2. Gonzalez, H., Halevy, A., Jensen, C., Langen, A., Madhavan, J., Shapley, R., Shen, W., Goldberg-Kidon, J.: Google Fusion Tables: Web-Centered Data Management and Collaboration. In: SIGMOD (2010)
3. Venetis, P., Halevy, A., Madhavan, J., Pasca, M., Shen, W., Wu, F., Miao, G., Wu, C.: Recovering semantics of tables on the web. In: PVLDB (2011)

M. Jeusfeld, L. Delcambre, and T.W. Ling (Eds.): ER 2011, LNCS 6998, p. 32, 2011.
© Springer-Verlag Berlin Heidelberg 2011

CSRML: A Goal-Oriented Approach to Model Requirements for Collaborative Systems

Miguel A. Teruel, Elena Navarro, Víctor López-Jaquero, Francisco Montero,
and Pascual González

LoUISE Research Group,
Computing Systems Department,
University of Castilla - La Mancha
{MiguelAngel.Teruel,Elena.Navarro,VictorManuel.Lopez,
Francisco.MSimarro,Pascual.Gonzalez}@uclm.es

Abstract. A collaborative system is software which allows several users to work together and carry out collaboration, communication and coordination tasks. To perform these tasks, the users have to be aware of other user's actions, usually by means of a set of awareness techniques. In previous works, we found by means of empirical studies that the most suitable Requirements Engineering approach to specify the requirements of this kind of systems is the Goal-Oriented one, and more precisely *i** approach. In this paper, CSRML (Collaborative Systems Requirements Modelling Language) is presented, an extension of *i** to deal with the specification of the requirements of these systems in which the collaboration and the awareness of other users presence / actions are crucial. In order to validate this proposal, a case study has been carried out by modelling a jigsaw activity: a cooperative-learning technique in which students individually do some research in a proposed problem and then they teach each other what they have learned by sharing each individual view of the problem.

Keywords: Collaborative systems, Awareness, Requirements Engineering, Goal-Oriented, *i**, CSRML.

1 Introduction

Requirements elicitation is one of the first stages in the Software Development Process [1,2]. If this phase fails to properly capture the requirements of the application, it is very likely that the rest of the process will fail as well, hence entailing important time and monetary costs. Therefore, the generation of an accurate requirements model is a highly important issue for any kind of system.

Collaborative Systems (a.k.a. Computer Supported Cooperative Work system, CSCW system) are not exempt from this need. They are a special kind of software whose users can perform collaboration, communication and coordination tasks. Unlike conventional single-user systems, CSCW systems have to be specified by using a special set of requirements, usually of a non-functional nature, which usually result from the users' need of being aware of the presence and activity of other remote

M. Jeusfeld, L. Delcambre, and T.W. Ling (Eds.): ER 2011, LNCS 6998, pp. 33–46, 2011.

or local users with who to perform the above mentioned collaborative tasks, that is, the *Workspace Awareness*.

Gutwin et al. [3] define *Workspace Awareness* (WA) as "the up-to-the-moment understanding of another person's interaction within a shared workspace". WA involves knowledge about *where* others are working, *what* they are doing *now*, and *what* they are going to do *next*. They presented a conceptual framework to establish what information makes up workspace awareness. This information is obtained by answering the questions "who, what and, where". That is, when several users work jointly in a physical shared space, they know who they are working with, what they are doing, where they are working, when various events happen, and how these events happen.

In this context, a proper specification of the system, identifying clearly the requirements of the system-to-be, specially the awareness requirements, is one of the first steps to overcome this problem. Awareness requirements can be considered as non-functional requirements (NFR) or extra-functional requirements (EFR), because they are usually constraints regarding quality (e.g. functionality, usability) [4]. However, the specification of this kind of requirements is not a trivial issue, because of the high number and diversity of requirements they are related to, and their high impact in terms of the final architecture of the system. Therefore, the proper selection of the requirements specification technique becomes a challenging and important decision.

We can define our research methodology as follows: in a previous work [5], it was analyzed, by using the DESMET guidelines [6], which is the is more appropriate technique, Goal-Oriented (GO) [7], Use Cases [8,9] or Viewpoints [10], to specify the requirements of collaborative systems. It was found that GO provides more facilities to model the requirements of this kind of systems. Once we determined GO as the most suitable technique, we analyzed which GO approach deals with CSCW systems in a better way [11]. The analyzed approaches for the specification of collaborative systems were NFR Framework [12], *i** Framework [13] and KAOS Methodology [7], paying special attention to awareness requirements. In order to carry out this study, the awareness requirements of a real system (Google Docs) [14] were specified. After modelling the system, an empirical analysis was conducted in order to compare these different GO techniques. As a result of this experiment we concluded that the analyzed GO approaches are not fully appropriate to model collaborative systems characteristics because of its lack of representation for the collaboration mechanisms between users and the awareness requirements, as well as the inappropriate actors and roles management for CSCW systems.

These conclusions, together with the results of [5] support our initial hypothesis: a RE technique to address the problems detected during this study is required. This technique should adopt some features from the analyzed GO approaches and should cover the lack of expressiveness in certain aspects that current GO techniques present. This constitutes the main aim of this work: to adapt/extend a GO notation for this kind of systems. Concretely, and according to the conclusions of our previous study [11], the most appropriate approach to deal with this kind of systems is *i**. Therefore, in this paper CSRML (Collaborative Systems Requirements Modelling Language) notation is described, as an extension of *i** notation aiming at providing the necessary expressiveness to model the special characteristics of CSCW systems requirements. In addition, a set of heuristics and restrictions are applied to the original *i** approach aimed at improving the ease of use of the proposed graphical language and the understandability of the models created by using CSRML.

This paper is structured as follows. After this introduction, in Section 2, we offer an analytical background about Goal-Oriented techniques and, specially, about the *i** approach. In Section 3, we present CSRML, our proposal for dealing with Requirements Engineering in CSCW systems. In Section 4, we present our case study: a collaborative learning jigsaw activity that will be modelled in Section 5 by using CSRML. Finally, in Section 6, conclusions and future work are presented.

2   Goal-Oriented Techniques and the *i** Approach

This section provides an analytical background about GO techniques, focusing on *i** approach, which constitutes the main foundation of our proposal.

2.1   Goal-Oriented Requirements Engineering

In the context of RE, GO approach [7] has been found useful for eliciting and defining requirements. Other techniques, such as Use Cases [8], only focus on establishing the features (i.e. activities and entities) that the system-to-be should support. Nevertheless, GO proposals focus on why systems are being constructed, by providing the motivation and rationale to justify the software requirements specification. Furthermore, they are not only useful for analyzing goals, but also for elaborating and refining them.

A GO model can be specified in a variety of formats, by using a more or less formally defined notation. It is built as a directed graph by means of a refinement of the systems goals. This refinement is performed until goals have enough granularity and detail so as to be assigned to an agent (software or environment). Thus, they are verifiable within the system-to-be. This refinement process is performed by using AND/OR/XOR refinement relationships. There is a wide number of proposals ranging from elicitation to validation activities in the RE process (see [15] for an exhaustive survey). However, some concepts are common to all of them:

- *Goal* describes why a system is being developed, or has been developed, from the point of view of the business, organization or the system itself. In order to specify it, both *functional goals*, i.e., expected services of the system, and *softgoals*, related to quality of service, constraints on the design, etc., should be determined.
- *Agent* is any active component, either from the system itself or from the environment, whose cooperation is needed to define the operationalization of a goal, that is, how the goal is going to be provided by the system-to-be. This operationalization of the goals is exploited to maintain the traceability throughout the Software Development Process.
- *Refinement Relationships*: AND/OR/XOR relationships enable the construction of the goal model as a directed graph. These relationships are applied by means of a refinement process (from generic goals towards sub-goals) until they have enough granularity to be assigned to a specific operationalization.

It must be pointed out that one of the main advantages exhibited by this approach is that it introduces mechanisms for reasoning about the specification. Thus, it facilitates the process of evaluating designs or alternative specifications of the system-to-be [16].

2.2 *i** Framework

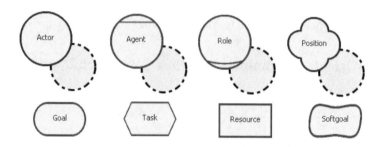

Fig. 1. Objects of *i** Framework

The *i** Framework [2,13] distinguishes between two kinds of elements: objects (Fig. 1) and relationships (Fig. 2). The objects considered in *i** are:

- An *actor* is a person or a system that has a relationship with the system to be developed. *i** identifies three kinds of actors:
    - *Agent* is an actor who has a concrete physical representation, e.g. a person or a system.
    - *Role* defines the behaviour of an actor within a specific context. An actor can have several roles, and a role can be assigned to multiple actors.
    - *Position* is a set of roles that can be typically played by one agent. An agent can play several positions.
- *Goal*: A goal answers "why?" questions. It describes a certain state in the world that an actor would like to achieve. However, a goal does no prescribe how it should be achieved.
- *Task*: A task specifies a particular way of doing something. Typically a task consists of a number of steps (or sub-tasks) that an actor must perform to execute it.
- *Resource*: A resource is a (physical or informational) entity that the actor needs to achieve a goal or perform a task. The main concern about a resource is whether it is available and from whom.
- *Softgoal*: A softgoal is a condition in the world that the actor would like to achieve, but unlike the concept of (hard) goal, the condition to achieve it is not sharply defined. A softgoal is typically a quality attribute that constrains other element, such as a goal, a task or a resource. A softgoal is considered to be fulfilled if there is sufficient positive evidence for its fulfilment and little evidence against it.

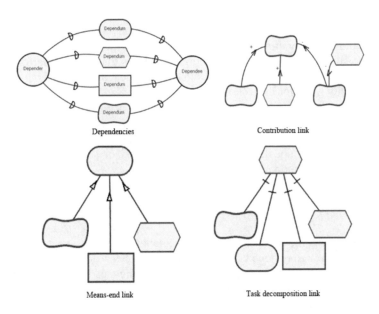

Fig. 2. Relationships of the *i** Framework

The previous objects are related between them through this set of relationships:

- *Dependency*: A dependency in *i** documents a relationship between a depender and a dependee for a dependum. The depender and the dependee are actors. The depender depends on the dependee for achieving a goal, performing a task, or using a resource. The dependum is the object which the dependee must deliver and which the depender depends on. It can be a goal, a task, a resource, or a softgoal. If the dependee fails to deliver the required dependum, the depender's ability to achieve its own goals is affected. In other words, it becomes difficult or impossible for the depender to achieve a goal, perform a task, or use a resource. Based on the type if dependum, *i** distinguishes four types of dependencies: (i) *Goal dependency* determines that the depender assumes that the dependee achieves the goal, but does not prescribe how it should achieve the goal; (ii) *Task dependency* defines that the dependee must perform the assigned task to achieve a goal; (iii) *Resource dependency*: expresses that the depender depends on the availability of a physical or informational resource that is provided by the dependee; (iv) *Softgoal dependency* expresses that the depender depends on the dependee to perform a task that leads to the achievement of a *soft*goal. The criteria to determine how to achieve the softgoal are not clearly defined. Typically, the dependee offers several alternatives for achieving the softgoal, and the judgement of whether the softgoal is achieved or not is up to the depender.
- *Means-end link*: A means-end link documents which softgoals, tasks, and/or resources contribute to achieving a goal. A means-end link also facilitates the documentation and evaluation of alternative ways to satisfy a goal, i.e., different decompositions of goal into subgoals, tasks, and resources.

- *Task decomposition link*: A task decomposition link documents the essential elements of a task. A task decomposition link relates the task to its components, which can be any combination of sub-goals, sub-tasks, resources, or softgoals. The decomposition of a task can thus comprise sub-tasks that must be performed, sub-goals that must be achieved, resources that are needed, and softgoals that typically define quality goals for the task.
- *Contribution link*: A contribution link documents a positive (+) or negative (-) influence on softgoals from tasks or other softgoals. A contribution link describes whether a task or a softgoal contributes to satisfy a softgoal positively or negatively. It does not define precisely which kind of support is offered or the extent of the given support.

3   CSRML: A Requirement Language for Collaborative Systems

In order to deal with the special kind of requirements of CSCW systems, and based on the two studies aforementioned [5,11], CSRML has been developed (Collaborative Systems Requirements Modelling Language). This language consists in an extension of *i** including some elements to model the special collaboration features of CSCW systems that can be applied to several domains that implies collaboration between users. CSRML elements (Fig. 3), excluding those whose meaning is the same as in *i**, are:

- *Role*: A role is a designator for a set of related tasks to be carried out. The difference between *i** and CSRML is that an actor playing a role can participate in individual or collaborative tasks (through participation links) and can be the responsible for the accomplishment of a goal (through responsibility links). In addition, the graphical notation is also different from the *i** role (the concept of role/actor boundary is not used in CSRML).*Actor*: An actor is a user, program, or entity with certain acquired capabilities (skills, category, and so forth) that can play a role in executing (using devices) or being responsible for actions [17]. An actor has to play a role (specified by means of a playing link, see Fig. 3) in order to participate in the system.
- *Task:* The concept of task in CSRML is the same as in *i**. They only differ in the introduced notation to define the importance of a task: one, two or three exclamation marks, depending on the importance of the task. Two kinds of CSRML tasks has been identified:
  - Abstract task: This kind of task consists in an abstraction of a set of concrete tasks and, possibly, other elements. We are not able to assign participation links directly to this kind of tasks. It helps in task decomposition.
  - Concrete task: These are the tasks the participants are involved in. The abstract tasks are refined in these ones. Participants will be assigned to the task through participation links. There are four types of these tasks:
    - o *Individual task* is a task that an actor can perform without any kind of interaction with other actors.

    o *Collaboration / Communication / Coordination task* two or more actors are involved in order to perform any kind of collaboration / communication / coordination among them.

- *Awareness softgoal*: CSRML refines the *i** concept of softgoal into a new specialization: awareness softgoal, that represents a special need of perception of other user's presence / actions, without which the task the user wants to perform would be affected negatively or even could not be done.
- *Awareness resource*: This special kind of resource corresponds to an implementation or a design solution to accomplish an awareness softgoal.
- *Playing link*: A playing link is used to represent when an actor assumes a role. This link has a guard condition that represent when a role can be played by an actor.
- *Participation link*: A participation link denotes who are involved in a task. This link has an attribute to specify its cardinality, i.e., the number of users that can be involved in a task.
- *Responsibility link*: A responsibility link assigns a role (played by an actor) to a (soft)goal or task. This link represents who is the stakeholder responsible for a goal/task accomplishment. It is not necessary that this stakeholder is involved in the goal sub-tasks. Nevertheless, if the role is responsible for a goal or task, this role is also responsible for the elements it is divided into, unless a responsibility link reaches one of the elements it is divided into.

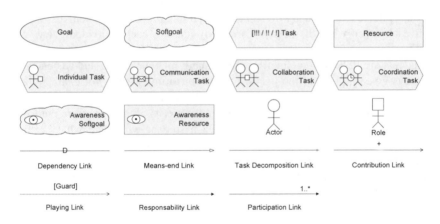

Fig. 3. CSRML elements

    The reason to introduce these new elements was despite *i** already had enough elements, these elements suffered an important expressivity overload, especially when dealing with CSCW systems. Due to this, we refined some elements and relationships into new ones. For example, based on *i** softgoals, we defined our awareness softgoals to model those requirements related to the users need of be aware of others users with whom to perform collaboration tasks.

    It is worth noting an additional difference between CSRML and *i**: CSRML is practically hierarchical (see Fig. 4 to Fig. 10). Thus, it fosters the scalability of the model created by using this notation. In a first level, we have the *Responsibility diagram*, in which the system's main goal is decomposed into main tasks and quality softgoals. Also, in this diagram, the goals and tasks responsibilities are defined.

In a second level appear *Task refinement diagrams*, in which the system's main tasks are decomposed into new goals, softgoals, tasks and resources, and roles are assigned to tasks. This constitutes another difference between CSRML and *i**. Because CSRML has been thought for collaborative systems, *i** boundaries for actors/roles were discarded, since they would not allow for assigning a task to more than one role. In addition, the *Quality factors diagram* completes the system specification showing the quality softgoals and the elements that contribute to their accomplishment.

Some guidelines to model a collaborative system can be seen in Section 5, in which we model the case study defined in Section 4. Nevertheless, we consider as a further work to define more formal guidelines to model CSCW systems with CSRML.

4 Case Study: Jigsaw Activity

Classroom Assessment Techniques (CATs) can help students in developing problem solving and group work skills. There are many types of collaborative activities that students can carry out. One simple activity that can be put into practice in a wide range of contexts is the *jigsaw activity* [18]. This is a cooperative-learning technique in which students individually do some research in a proposed problem and then they teach each other what they have learned by sharing each individual view of the problem.

Students are divided into small groups, usually of four or six students each. Each student is given a piece of the jigsaw to learn or to investigate. For example, a long reading assignment can be broken into six smaller pieces. Each student takes a piece and becomes an expert on that content. When the pieces of the jigsaw are put together or when the group comes back together, each student will share what he/she has learnt. There are a lot of jigsaw activity variants. In our study case, we are going to use the following one, based on an interactive and real-time e-learning approach. When this activity is carried out by means of a Computer Assisted Learning system, it entails five steps:

1. *Create teams*: All the students should enter into the system. Then, the teacher creates the student's groups and assigns the students. The number of groups depends on the number of students who participate into the activity. To do this, the teacher has to be aware of connected student's status. When all the students become part of a team, we can proceed to the next step.
2. *Individual work*: First, the group members have to designate a coordinator for the team. Then, each group member must select a jigsaw piece. In this step each member has to do research individually to explain what he/she has learnt to the rest of the group later. Each student has to make an individual work report describing what he/she has found out.
3. *Experts meeting*: In this step, students with the same jigsaw piece have an "experts meeting". First, each experts group designates a coordinator. Then, each member

explains his/her individual work to the rest of the group in order to improve each member's work. Each expert group have to make an experts report in a collaborative manner.

4. *Team meeting*: After the experts meeting, the work teams meet again to teach each other what they have learnt and improved thanks to the other expert's knowledge. Similarly to the previous step, they have to elaborate a collaborative team report.

5. *Evaluate activity*: The last step consists of the evaluation of the student's individual and collaborative work. To do this, the teacher evaluates the individual, experts and team report. Finally, the teacher provides feedback to the students through an evaluation document.

In addition, in order to ensure certain success level, the activity must pursue these educational quality factors:

- *Heterogeneous grouping*: It is necessary that the students work together in heterogeneous groups in terms of gender, ethnicity, academic performance level, etc. Also, the group size must be between two and six students.
- *Positive interdependence*: The student must be aware that he/she only will be successful if his/her partners are successful too.
- *Individual responsibility*: passive students who take advantage of his/her partners' work to obtain his/her goals must be avoided.
- *Equal opportunities for success*: All the students, regardless of his/her level, have to be able of making contributions to the improvement of the group results.
- *Promoter interaction*: Students have to promote and facilitate the progress of his/her partners through mutual aid, support and encouragement of efforts to learn from all group members.
- *Cognitive information processing*: The primary goal is to improve the academic performance of all students, promoting the construction of higher quality learning. The cognitive processing of information involves to balancing different points of view, explanations, interpretations, clarify doubts, formulating examples, etc.
- *Using cooperative skills*: The teacher should pay the same attention and rigor to the treatment of interpersonal skills and group work practice, that to the content of the school syllabus.
- *Group evaluation*: The effectiveness of cooperative learning depends largely on the establishment of group evaluation dynamics within the teams, which serve to regulate their own performance.

5   The Jigsaw Activity with CSRML

In this section, the previous case study is modelled by using the CSRML notation in order to illustrate its expressiveness capacity for CSCW systems. First, in Fig. 4, we can see the *system goals diagram*, in which the system main goals are defined. As can be seen, we are going to achieve the system goals by means of the realization of the system's main task: the Jigsaw activity

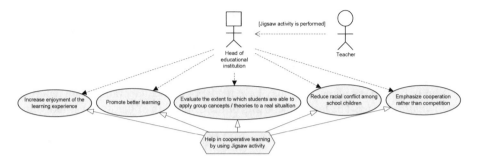

Fig. 4. System goals diagram

Fig. 5 shows the *responsibility diagram* with the main system's task and its decomposition in quality softgoals and tasks. In this figure, it can be observed that the use of *responsibility links* shows who is responsible for goals and tasks. Note that if a role is responsible for a goal or task, this role is also responsible for the elements it is divided into, unless a responsibility link is specified to one of the elements it is divided into. Also, the *playing links* are used to represent the condition that must be met for an actor to play a role. For the sake of model readability, task decomposition will be shown in subsequent figures.

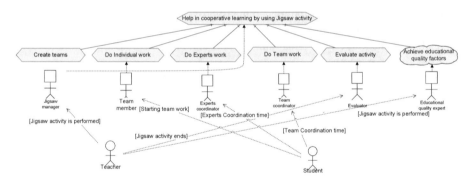

Fig. 5. Responsibility diagram

Fig. 6 depicts *Create teams* task refinement diagram. In this figure, tasks are refined into more specific ones and into new goals until individual or collaborative (collaboration, coordination or communication) tasks are specified. It can be observed that for collaborative tasks, more than an actor (playing a role) is involved through *participation links*. Also, an *awareness softgoal*, namely *Be aware of unassigned students*, has been specified related to the *Create student teams* task. The rationale for include this awareness softgoal is that to perform *Create student teams* task, a teacher must be aware of what students are waiting to be assigned to a team. To achieve this, an *awareness resource*, namely *Participant list with assignment status*, has been introduced, that is, a likely implementation of the *Be aware of unassigned students* softgoal.

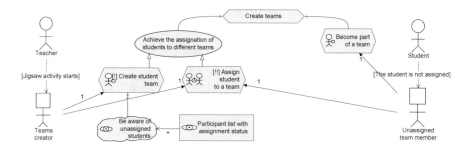

Fig. 6. *Create teams* task refinement diagram

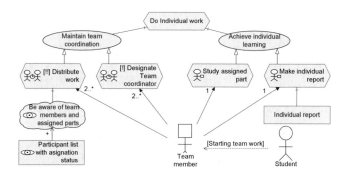

Fig. 7. *Individual work* task refinement diagram

Next, Fig. 7 presents the decomposition of the *Individual work* task. In this figure different cardinalities for *participation links* are used. For example, to *Distribute work*, two or more (at most the team maximum number of components) must participate. This cardinality has been specified with 2..* in Fig. 7.

Fig. 8 illustrates the four degrees of priority that can be assigned to tasks: normal, high ([!]), very high ([!!]) and highest ([!!!]). Additionally, this figure includes two awareness softgoals. One of them is similar to the one above mentioned, but the other awareness softgoal corresponds to the use of remote cursors (an implementation of Gutwin's telepointers [19]).

Fig. 9 shows another system tasks refinements. *Do team work* task refinement diagram is similar to that on Fig. 8.

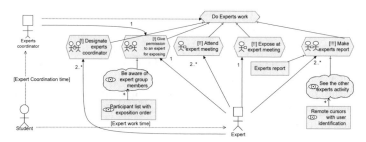

Fig. 8. *Do experts work* task refinement diagram

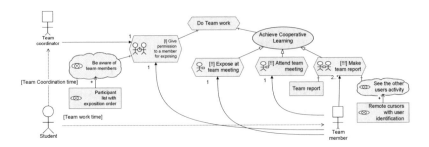

Fig. 9. *Do team work* task refinement diagram

Finally, Fig. 10 corresponds to the *Quality factors diagram*. In this model, the quality factors that contribute to achieve the jigsaw activity with a high quality level are shown. These factors are represented as softgoals and they are related to the main quality softgoal by means of contribution links with positive contributions. The achievement of all these quality softgoals is obtained in different ways. For instance, the *Heterogeneous grouping* softgoal is achieved by means of an awareness softgoal and its corresponding awareness resource consists of a students' video embodiment, and the *Group evaluation* softgoal is accomplished through the *Evaluate team members* of the *Evaluate activity* task refinement diagram.

With this last diagram, we have defined the entire system, verifying the applicability of CSRML to the CSCW systems specification, trying to cover the deficiencies found in *i** for this kind of systems.

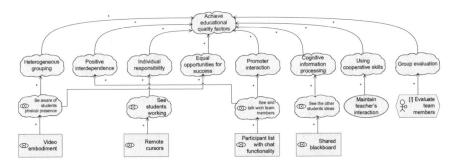

Fig. 10. Quality factors diagram

6   Conclusions and Further Works

In our previous works [5,11], we found out that GO techniques (and especially *i**) can be used to deal with collaborative systems requirements modelling. Nevertheless, we also found out that this ilk of specifications suffer from an important lack of expressiveness for some characteristics related to user collaboration, awareness representation or quality factors. To address these shortcomings, we propose CSRML, an extension of *i** Goal-Oriented specification to model CSCW systems requirements.

To illustrate the use of this language, we have modelled a collaborative system. For the sake of clarity, in this paper an excerpt of this system, consisting in a cooperative e-learning jigsaw activity, has been presented. This case study was modelled because it has a set of characteristics that were hard or impossible to be represented with the original *i** notation. These characteristics were properly described by introducing a set of new elements and links into *i** notation. The quality and awareness representation has been made possible by means of new awareness elements and the inclusion of a new set of diagrams in order to provide some structure to the specification.

To sum up, CSRML helps in improving understandability and maintainability of requirements models for CSCW systems by adding new elements and relationships to *i**. These new elements facilitate the specification of awareness requirements, which are paramount in the Software Development Process of any CSCW systems.

One of our ongoing works is closely related to the development of e-learning systems. Since LoUISE research group [20] has been working during the last years in this kind of systems, several patterns have been described up to date. One of the main problems they have is that they have been specified in an informal way that cannot be easily reused for the specification of different systems. Therefore, we are studying how CSRML can be used to improve their specification.

In addition we are currently working in the definition of formal guidelines to use our proposal. Finally, we are assessing the *understandability* of CSRML models by means of a family of empirical experiments. Its results are currently being analysed.

Acknowledgements. This work has been partially supported by the grant (PEII09-0054-9581) from the Junta de Comunidades de Castilla-La Mancha and by the grant (DESACO, TIN2008-06596-C02-01) from the Spanish Government.

References

[1] Pressman, R.S.: Software engineering: a practitioners approach. McGraw-Hill Science/Engineering/Math (2009)

[2] Pohl, K.: Requirements Engineering: Fundamentals, Principles, and Techniques. Springer, Heidelberg (2010)

[3] Gutwin, C., Greenberg, S.: A Descriptive Framework of Workspace Awareness for Real-Time Groupware. Computer Supported Cooperative Work 11, 411–446 (2002)

[4] Hochmuller, H.: Towards the Proper Integration of Extra-Functional Requirements. Australasian Journal of Information Systems 6, 98–117 (1999)

[5] Teruel, M.A., Navarro, E., López-Jaquero, V., Montero, F., González, P.: An Empirical Evaluation of Requirement Engineering Techniques for Collaborative Systems. In: 15th International Conference on Evaluation and Assessment in Software Engineering, Durham, UK (2011)

[6] Kitchenham, B.: A methodology for evaluating software engineering methods and tools. In: Rombach, H., Basili, V., Selby, R. (eds.) Experimental Software Engineering Issues: Critical Assessment and Future Directions. LNCS, vol. 706, pp. 121–124. Springer, Heidelberg (1993)

[7] van Lamsweerde, A.: Goal-Oriented Requirements Engineering: A Guided Tour. In: Proceedings of the Fifth IEEE International Symposium on Requirements Engineering, pp. 249–263. IEEE Computer Society, Los Alamitos (2001)

[8] Cockburn, A.: Writting Effective Use Cases. Addison-Wesley, Reading (2000)

[9] Booch, G., Rumbaugh, J., Jacobson, I.: The Unified Modeling Language User Guide. Addison-Wesley, Reading (2005)

[10] Finkelsetin, A., Kramer, J., Nuseibeh, B., Finkelstein, L., Goedicke, M.: Viewpoints: A Framework for Integrating Multiple Perspectives in System Development. International Journal of Software Engineering and Knowledge Engineering 2, 31–57 (1992)

[11] Teruel, M.A., Navarro, E., López-Jaquero, V., Montero, F., González, P.: A Comparative of Goal-Oriented Approaches to Modelling Requirements for Collaborative Systems. In: 6th International Conference on Evaluation of Novel Software Approaches to Software Engineering, Beijing, China (2011)

[12] Cysneiros, L.M., Yu, E.: Non-Functional Requirements Elicitation (Perspectives on Software Requirements). Springer, Heidelberg (2003)

[13] Castro, J., Kolp, M., Mylopoulos, J.: A requirements-driven development methodology. In: Dittrich, K.R., Geppert, A., Norrie, M.C. (eds.) CAiSE 2001. LNCS, vol. 2068, pp. 108–123. Springer, Heidelberg (2001)

[14] Google, Google Docs (2001)

[15] Kavakli, E., Loucopoulos, P.: Goal Modeling in Requirements Engineering: Analysis and Critique of Current Methods. In: Information Modeling Methods and Methodologies, pp. 102–124 (2004)

[16] Chung, L., Nixon, B., Yu, E., Mylopoulos, J.: No Non-Functional Requirements in Software EngineeringTitle. Kluwer Academic Publishers, Dordrecht (1999)

[17] Noguera, M., González, M., Garrido, J.L., Hurtado, V., Rodríguez, M.: System Modeling for Systematic Development of Groupware Applications. In: International Conference on Software Engineering Research and Practice, pp. 750–756 (2006)

[18] Pozzi, F.: Using Jigsaw and Case Study for supporting online collaborative learning. Computers & Education 55, 67–75 (2010)

[19] Gutwin, C., Greenberg, S., Roseman, M.: Workspace Awareness in Real-Time Distributed Groupware: Framework, Widgets, and Evaluation. In: Proceedings of HCI on People and Computers XI, pp. 281–298. Springer, Heidelberg (1996)

[20] Fardoun, H., Montero, F., López-Jaquero, V.: eLearniXML: Towards a model-based approach for the development of e-Learning systems considering quality. Advances in Engineering Software 40, 1297–1305 (2009)

Establishing Regulatory Compliance for Software Requirements

Silvia Ingolfo, Alberto Siena, and John Mylopoulos

University of Trento,
Trento, Italy
silvia.ingolfo@studenti.unitn.it, a.siena@disi.unitn.it,
jm@cs.toronto.edu

Abstract. A software system complies with a regulation if its operation is consistent with the regulation under all circumstances. The importance of regulatory compliance for software systems has been growing, as regulations are increasingly impacting both the functional and nonfunctional requirements of legacy and new systems. HIPAA and SOX are recent examples of laws with broad impact on software systems, as attested by the billions of dollars spent in the US alone on compliance. In this paper we propose a framework for establishing regulatory compliance for a given set of software requirements. The framework assumes as inputs models of the requirements (expressed in i*) and the regulations (expressed in Nòmos). In addition, we adopt and integrate with i* and Nòmos a modeling technique for capturing arguments and establishing their acceptability. Given these, the framework proposes a systematic process for revising the requirements, and arguing through a discussion among stakeholders that the revisions make the requirements compliant. Our proposed framework is illustrated through a case study involving fragments of the HIPAA regulation.

Keywords: Regulatory compliance, requirement engineering, argumentation.

1   Introduction

The problem of legal compliance of information systems is gaining relevance in recent years. Government regulations that impact software systems are becoming ever-more prevalent in current legislative scenarios around the world. Organizations that don't comply with regulations are vulnerable to fines and prosecution that could damage both their financial and marketing prospects both in the short and long term. The impact of this situation has been immense on Software Engineering as much as on business practices. It has been estimated that in the Healthcare domain, organizations have spent $17.6 billion over a number of years to align their systems and procedures with a single law, the Health Insurance Portability and Accountability Act (HIPAA), introduced in 1996[1]. In the

---

[1] Medical privacy – national standards to protect the privacy of personal health information. Office for Civil Rights, US Department of Health and Human Services, 2000.

M. Jeusfeld, L. Delcambre, and T.W. Ling (Eds.): ER 2011, LNCS 6998, pp. 47–61, 2011.

Business domain, it was estimated that organizations spent \$5.8 billion in one year alone (2005) to ensure compliance of their reporting and risk management procedures with the Sarbanes-Oxley Act (SOX)[2]. In short, compliance is a costly proposition and dealing with it is not an option.

A key issue for the requirements compliance problem concerns the form of evidence provided that indeed a requirements model complies with a given law (fragment). There is an abundance of formal method techniques developed in AI and Software Engineering (SE) for dealing with this issue [1,2,3]. Unfortunately, such techniques are generally heavy-weight in the notations they use for modeling laws and requirements, as well as in the reasoning tools they employ to establish compliance.

In our work, we lower the bar. Instead of capturing the essence of laws and requirements by using heavy-handed techniques for establishing compliance through formal reasoning, we adopt a conceptual modeling approach whereby laws and requirements are captured through conceptual models. Moreover, compliance is not established through automated proof, but rather through argumentation among the stakeholders who state positions, e.g., "this requirement does not comply with this part of the law" and argue for or against them until (hopefully) consensus is reached.

The objective of this paper is to propose a systematic process for establishing compliance of system requirements to a given law using argumentation as a means. The process takes as input a requirements model R and a law model L. Designers iteratively revise R = R(0) into revised requirements models R(1), ..., R(i), ... and discuss each with stakeholders until the stakeholders agree that a revised model R(N)indeed complies with L.

The contribution of the paper includes an extension of the Nòmos framework [4] for dealing with compliance. With this extension we are able to both detect compliance and pinpoint which requirements does not comply and need to be revised. To do this, we integrate into Nòmos the structural and algorithmic richness of an argumentation framework. Through a systematic process, compliance of software requirements to a given law is established. The process ends with a revised version of the input model that is compliant with the law.

The rest of the paper is structured as follows. Section 2 presents an overview of the modeling concepts and the validation method we have adopted. Section 3 presents our framework for supporting a compliance discussion. Section 4 describes the process we propose for establishing compliance through argumentation. Section 5 presents a case study involving fragments of the HIPAA regulation that shows how our proposed method works. Section 6 summarizes related work. Finally, section 7 concludes the paper.

2   Research Baseline

Requirements Models. Requirements engineering frameworks are generally based on the study and analysis of stakeholder needs. i* [5] is an agent-oriented

---

[2] Online news published in dmreview.com, November 15, 2004.

modeling framework for requirements centering on the intentions of stakeholders and their inter-dependencies. The two main components of an i* model are a Strategic Dependency (SD) model and a Strategic Rationale (SR) model. The former is used to describe the dependencies that actors have to accomplish their goals. The latter models the goals within an actor, and the tasks by which these can be fulfilled.

i* doesn't natively support the representation of legal concepts, but it can be extended for this purpose. Nòmos [4] is an extension of i*, specifically tailored to express legal concepts. Nòmos is goal-oriented, law-driven intended to generate requirements through which the system-to-be can comply to a given law (these are referred to as compliance requirements). It relies on a metamodel, based on the concept of right [6]. A right is held by a legal subject towards another subject. Rights are declared in normative propositions (NP) [1], which are the most atomic piece of law able to carry a normative meaning. Normative propositions also contain a legal modality (whether it is a duty, privilege or else) and the actual object of the right. Legal rights are put in (compliance) relation with intentional elements to derive compliance requirements. When an actor of the domain is recognized to be a subject of law (e.g., when "John" is recognized to be of such class of actors referred to as "Doctor" in a certain law), the actor is put in `embodiment` relation with the legal subject. To represent an actor actually complying with a given normative proposition, the `realization` relation is introduced, which links an actor's goal with the normative proposition it is intended to comply with. Finally, in order to cope with the rich expressivity of the language used in law, the Nòmos framework introduces a `dominance` relation to establish the priority of a right over another: $NP_1 > NP_2$ characterizes the fact that as long as NP_1 holds, NP_2 doesn't.

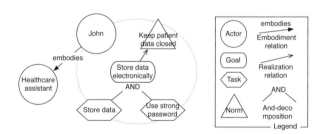

Fig. 1. A Nòmos model representing a compliance solution

The i*/Nòmos model is shown in figure 1. In the figure John, who *embodies* the figure of Healthcare operator, has by law the duty of keeping old patient records. A possible solution to this, is that of assigning to John the responsibility for storing patient data only electronically; this, in turn, can operationally be done by storing the data and using a strong password to protect it.

However, a major drawback of this model-based approach is that the semantics of the compliance relations is extremely rich and doesn't depend only on the strategic decisions of the analyst. For example, the relation between John and

Healthcare operator depends on the definition of Healthcare operator, which has to be differently interpreted. Similarly, the thesis that the "Store data electronically" goal is all that is necessary to comply with the given prescription can be debated and refuted. Moreover, regulations are often subject to changes over time, so the parameters that shape and define compliance change accordingly. It is often the case that interpretations by the court or revisions of a regulation lead to revised policies and procedures that need to be reflected accordingly in operational systems

This example shows how challenging is dealing with compliance of software requirements. A truth-theoretic proof of compliance is beyond the state of the art, so we need alternative ways to support compliance evidence of a requirement.

Argumentation. The fundamental objective of Requirement Engineering (RE) concerns how to effectively capture the needs of stakeholders. While the analysis of the system-to-be proceeds, there is the need to verify and validate the requirements against the stakeholders. [7] proposes the ACceptability Evaluation framework (ACE) a propositional reasoning framework that allows the representation of a discussion and provides algorithms to automatically verify the acceptability of the proposed RE artifacts.

When discussing the validity of a solution, stakeholders iteratively provide arguments for/against its validity. Eventually the discussion reaches an end and a decision about the topic is taken. The core element of a discussion is therefore this set of statements, for or against the validity of a given solution.

All information gathered during the discussion is represented in ACE as a directed labeled graph G, with a set of vertices and lines. A proposition is represented as a vertex $v \in V(G)$ and can have four labels $\{i, I, C, P\}$. The label i is for information vertex (i.e. statements made by participants), while the other vertices identify an Implication, Conflict or Preference vertex. The resulting graph connecting information, the propositions and some labeling functions form the syntax of the language.

Together with a syntax, two important algorithms are defined in [7]. The `FindDiscussion` algorithm returns a specific discussion by performing a breadth-first search to retrieve all vertices in favor or against a given vertex. The `EvaluateDiscussion` algorithm traverses the discussion while evaluating the acceptability of the proposed solution (root vertex). Based on some labeling deduction rules and to some procedures handling cycles and transitive relations, all vertices of the graph are labelled. Depending on the label of the vertex representing the proposed solution, its acceptability is either accepted, rejected or inconclusive.

3   Proposed Framework

The key idea proposed here is that the evidence of requirements compliance with respect to a given law results from a *discussion* about the requirements and how they relate to the law. If acceptance is established, then the discussion is said to support the claim of compliance. Otherwise, new information is added

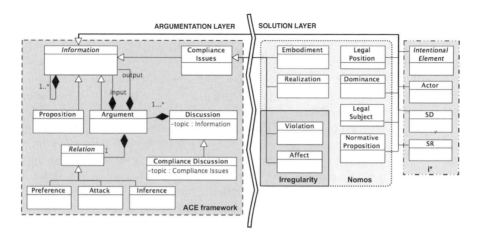

Fig. 2. Metamodel of the argumentation framework for a compliance discussion

to the discussion. If no more information can be added, and no acceptance is established, then the discussion is said to reject the claim. The discussion is represented by means of the ACE language, and its algorithms are used to evaluate its acceptability.

The cost to maintain this argumentation-based treatment of compliance though, is the introduction of additional elements in the models, which may result in comprehension bottlenecks. We address this problem by splitting the model in 2 layers: in the first layer (*argumentation layer*) the discussions takes place; in the second layer (*solution layer*) the compliance solution is modeled. The *argumentation layer* records the structure and other information regarding every discussion behind any change in the solution layer. If a change is not accepted by a discussion at the argumentation level, it is not recorded in the solution layer. The *solution layer* represents the goal-oriented soon-to-be-compliant version of the model and consequently it is expressed within the Nòmos framework. This way, the argumentation layer provides a justification for the solution layer. Modifications accepted in the argumentation layer are represented in this layer. Rejected changes and their discussions are still recorded at argumentation layer and are maintained for both traceability and possible future reuse.

As the ACE framework handles two types of information (Propositions and Arguments), we need to expand and integrate its model to allow us to evaluate and discuss the validity of Nòmos relations. We have therefore expanded this argumentative framework and integrated with Nòmos within the context of a discussion (figure 2). As we can see in the metamodel of figure 2, we have combined the Nòmos modeling language with the metamodel of the ACE framework. A discussion handles regular statements made by participants (Propositions), i* entities represent strategic requirements, and Nòmos concepts represent the law fragments addressing requirements. Some Nòmos elements need to be discussed so they capture a different type of information ("compliance issues"). The structure of the discussion allows us to relate *Information* with the three relations offered by the ACE framework. Their combination, called an *Argument*, is the core concept of a discussion. When arguments are put forward, a discussion is generated and it eventually evaluates the acceptability of the subject. For more details on the metamodel of the framework see [8]. The justification framework of ACE, combined with the expressivity of Nòmos, allows to discuss the acceptability the latest version of the requirements model with respect to compliance. These discussions (*compliance discussions*) can manage not only information provided by participants, but also all existing components of the Nòmos model.

So how do we *define compliance in terms of argumentation*? Anytime a regulation applies, we can loosely say that its compliance is determined by two facts: the new legal requirements are met by the system [compliance], and no part of the system is in conflict with the regulation [conformity] [9]. The compliance with new regulations can be identified and represented with the *realize* relation in Nòmos, a concept expressing the suitability of an element to fulfill a NP. To argue non-conformity, we need to be able to identify which part of the system does not comply and needs to be amended. We have therefore introduced the concept of *irregularity* in Nòmos (see figure 2). We define as *irregular* a situation where either an element of the model directly *violates* a norm, or where an element is *addressed* by a regulation and therefore needs to be checked for compliance. For example, a task such as "Post original CD tracks in a webpage for public download" is in violation with copyright regulations as its aim is directly against regulation. A goal like "Share music" identifies the more general situation not in direct violation, but that it is surely *affected* by copyright regulations and that therefore needs to be investigated. Eventually, two compliance conditions (compliance and conformity) can be related to the existence or absence in the model of these specific key relations (realize, affect/violate). The proof of compliance of our system is therefore based on the discussions and the argumentations regarding these relations. To prove compliance, argumentation regulates the introduction of *realize* relation in the model. To prove conformity, the absence of irregularity relations in the model (*affect/violate*) has to be achieved.

4   Compliance Process

The definition of compliance we have provided before, clearly outlines that reaching compliance is a gradual process to achieve some compliance properties. We therefore need a systematic process to modify and revise the initial requirements model to guarantee that these two properties are met by the final model. The procedure we propose is structured along three logical phases:

1. The *analysis phase* [step 1 and 2] takes as input the model of requirements, expressed as a set of goals to be achieved and tasks to be performed by stakeholders, and a set of NPs with possible irregularities highlighted.
2. The model is then followed by a *compliance check* [step 3] where the criteria for compliance are evaluated. If the model is compliant, the process returns the model, else we move to the next phase.

3. The *modeling phase* [steps 4 and 5] aims at amending a requirements model that is not compliant. The model is expanded and revised by requirement engineers to satisfy the two compliance constraints. A discussion evaluates the acceptability and validity of the solution proposed.

Since this last step modifies the initial model, the process is iterated to ensure that no irregularities have been introduced during modeling. When a cycle is completed without introducing modifications in the solution layer – i.e., in the models – the process ends and compliance is said to be achieved.

The key part of the approach is to be able to guarantee that the revisions actually make the system compliant: all the corrections made to the system — as well as the assumptions behind the corrections — are based on the fundamental concept of providing validation through argumentation. In the next sections we will see in detail the five steps of the compliance process.

4.1 Step 1. Embodiment

The main goal of this step is to ensure a correct and exhaustive binding between the legal subjects addressed in the NPs and the actor of the system. All the actors addressed by the law have to comply with the respective set of NPs that concern them. Once the correspondence is given, all NPs related to the legal entity are added to the actor boundary.

In this step we therefore evaluate the possible embodiments between actors and legal subjects (algorithm 1). When the validity of an embodiment is accepted by a discussion, the *embody* link is added in the solution layer between the actor and the legal subject. Also, the NPs associated to that legal subject are added to the actor boundary.

Forall *legal subject* ls_i and **forall** *stakeholder* s_j **do:**
   evaluate "$s_j \xrightarrow{\text{embody}} ls_i$"
   if discussion accepts $s_j \xrightarrow{\text{embody}} ls_i$ **then**
      add "$s_j \xrightarrow{\text{embody}} ls_i$" in the solution layer;
      add NPs in the actor boundary
   else skip
$\rightarrow$ [step 2]

Algorithm 1. Embodiment step (step 1)

4.2 Step 2. Find Irregularities

The main goal of this step is to identify the irregularities that the model has with respect to the newly added NPs. The model is therefore analyzed with the purpose of finding *all* the elements of the model that contribute to the noncompliance of the system.

Forall *normative* np_i and forall *element* ie_j **do:**

    evaluate "$ie_j \xrightarrow{\text{violate}} np_i$"

      if discussion accepts $ie_j \xrightarrow{\text{violate}} np_i$ **then**

        add "$ie_j \xrightarrow{\text{violate}} np_i$" in the solution layer;

      else evaluate "$np_i \xrightarrow{\text{affect}} ie_j$"

          if discussion accepts $np_i \xrightarrow{\text{affect}} ie_j$ **then**

            add "$np_i \xrightarrow{\text{affect}} ie_j$" in the solution layer;

          else skip

$\rightarrow$ [step 3]

Algorithm 2. Identification of irregularities in a requirements model (step 2)

With the same argumentation process used in the previous step, the validity of each *affect/violate* relation introduced at solution-level has to be supported by a discussion at argumentation level that accepts it. All elements of the model are analyzed by a discussion that assess the situation between every one of them and the NP. A discussion evaluates a possible *violate* relation between the two. When it doesn't subsist, then the *affect* relation is considered. Upon the acceptance of either relation, the link is added to the solution layer, otherwise the next pair [element,NP] can be analyzed. With this systematic approach, all IEs are evaluated by a discussion as possible irregularity in the system.

4.3 Step 3. Compliance Check

The important goal of this step is to evaluate whether the given model satisfies the compliance properties.

---

if forall $np_i \in NP$

$\left[\{\exists\ ie : ie \xrightarrow{\text{realize}} np_i\} \text{ or } \{\exists np_j \in NP : np_j < np_i \text{ and } \exists ie : ie \xrightarrow{\text{realize}} np_j\} \right.$

  and

$\left. \{\nexists\ ie : np \xrightarrow{\text{affect}} ie\} \right]$

then system is compliant $\rightarrow$ exit

else system is not compliant $\rightarrow$ [step 4]

Algorithm 3. Pseudocode for the compliance check procedure (step 3)

As we have seen, the definition of compliance is expressed by two conditions that the system has to meet (algorithm 3): 1) each NP in the system must: have (at least) one goal that realizes it or have a correct dominance relation with a realized one; 2) no element in the system is irregular with respect to any NP. When these two conditions are met, the system is compliant and the process terminates, otherwise it proceeds in the modeling phase.

4.4   Step 4. Solve Irregularities

The main goal of this step is to solve all irregularities that are present in the model. The model has to be revised by requirement engineers that propose new elements, new operalizations and changes. A discussion will then evaluate whether the changes made are sufficient for the irregularity to be considered solved (algorithm 4). The model is revised until the discussion rejects the validity of the irregularity (e.g. $topic_1 = ie \xrightarrow{\text{affect}} np$ is rejected) and the relation is deleted from the solution layer. At the end of this step each irregularity has been considered and solved by revising the model.

Forall ie_i such that ($np_j \xrightarrow{\text{affect}} ie_i$ or $ie_i \xrightarrow{\text{violate}} np_j$)
    repeat: revise model;
           start discussion evaluating the irregularity
    until: ("$np_j \xrightarrow{\text{affect}} ie_i$" is rejected) or ("$ie_i \xrightarrow{\text{violate}} np_j$" is rejected)
$\rightarrow$ [step 5]

Algorithm 4. Addressing irregularities in the requirements model (step 4)

4.5   Step 5. Find Realizations

The main goal of this step is to identify all elements of the model that contribute and prove its compliance. In fact it is necessary that all legal requirements expressed as NPs are met by the system.

In this step we search the model for elements that directly realize each NP. A discussion will evaluate whether each element can be considered as realization for the considered NP. Then we consider all NPs for which a realize relation was not found, and go through the same revision process used to solve irregularities. Requirement engineers will revise the model and a discussion will evaluate the acceptability of the realization of a suggested element.

  Forall np_i and forall ie_j **do:**
        start discussions evaluating $ie_j \xrightarrow{\text{realize}} np_i$
  Forall $np_i \not\exists ie_j : ie_j \xrightarrow{\text{realize}} np_i$
    repeat: revise model;
          start discussion evaluating the realization

Algorithm 5. Pseudocode for finding a realization for all NPs (step 5)

At the end of this fifth step — also the end of the modeling phase — the identified irregularities have been solved and all NP are realized in the model. With respect to the model that has been analyzed in the analysis phase, the output of this phase is inevitably different in some parts. Before entering the compliance check again it is necessary to analyze this new model to check whether possible irregularities have been introduced. Also, in case new actors have been added during the modeling revision, there is also the need to reevaluate possible embodiments. Consequently the output model is passed on to the analysis phase for a back up check.

5   Preliminary Evaluation: A Case Study

In this section we exemplify the described process by means of a case study regarding the HIPAA regulation.[3] We consider a scenario where a hospital wants to collect PHI (Personal Health Information) to evaluate the quality of its services. The input to our model is an i* requirements model and the NPs extracted from §164.502 and related to the non-disclosure of PHI (see [4]).

1. Embodiment. In the following example we consider the legal subject "Covered Entity" (CE) defined in the HIPAA regulation (§160.103) and how the actors of a hospital system are affected by the regulation. As we have seen, the main goal of this step is to correctly bind all actors with the legal subjects. As we can see from figure 3, our process evaluates the possible embodiment between all actors and the legal entity we are considering. A discussion is then started to evaluate the acceptability of the relation.

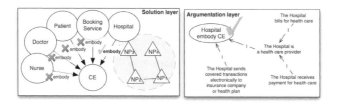

Fig. 3. The solution and argumentation layer evaluating the embodiments for the legal subject "Covered Entity"

For example, when evaluating whether a "Patient" is a CE, statements are made to reject the validity of this embodiment: p_1 = "*The patient receives health care services*", p_2 = "*The patient doesn't transmit any information*", and so on. The embodiment relation is eventually rejected and the next embodiment is then evaluated. When evaluating the relation "Hospital $\xrightarrow{embody}$ CE", a user immediately points out that p_3 = "*The Hospital bills for health care*" and p_4 = "*The Hospital receives payment for health care*". As a consequence p_5 = "*The Hospital is a health care provider*" ($p_3, p_4 \xrightarrow{imply} p_5$). After another user says that p_6 = "*The Hospital sends health care information electronically*", the discussion is concluded and accepts the validity of the relation. The *embody* relation is therefore added to the solution layer and all the NPs associated with the legal entity are added to the actor boundary.

---

[3] http://www.hipaa.org/, http://www.hhs.gov/ocr/privacy/index.html

2. Find Irregularities. In the following example we consider the Hospital actor and the NP regarding the non disclosure of PHI (np_1). We assume that the initial goal-model of the hospital is the one depicted in the left side of figure 4 All the element of the model are analyzed by a discussion to evaluate possible irregularity. For example, when g_2 is analyzed as a possible *violation* of the NP ($t_1 = g_2 \xrightarrow{violate} np_1$), immediately a user points out that $p_7 =$ "*The aim of the collection is research*" ($p_7 \xrightarrow{attack} t_1$) and $p_8 =$ "*The collection of PHI is allowed for research purposes*" ($p_8 \xrightarrow{imply} p_7$). As the discussion terminates, it is evaluated and the topic rejected. When the *affect* relation is evaluated ($t_2 = np_1 \xrightarrow{affect} g_2$), the users agree that $p_9 =$ "*The user must be informed if the purpose of disclosure*" ($p_9 \xrightarrow{imply} t_2$) and $p_{10} =$ "*PHI should be collected with the patient's consent*" ($p_{10} \xrightarrow{imply} t_2$). As the discussion terminates, the acceptability of the topic is evaluated and since it is accepted, the *affect* relation is added to the model.

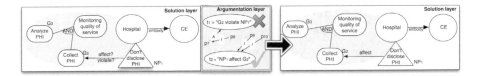

Fig. 4. The solution and argumentation layer evaluating the irregularity relation between np_1 and g_2

3. Compliance Check. Considering the example of the Hospital goal-model from figure 4, we can see that the (lone) normative proposition is not realized by any element of the model, so the step terminates and we move to the modeling phase. In fact, if either constraint fails, we have established non-compliance.

4. Solve Irregularities. Considering the example of figure 4, we are asked to revise the model in order to solve the irregularity $np_1 \xrightarrow{affect} g_2$. After the revision, a discussion evaluates the acceptability of the new model. Despite the assessment that previously identified problems (expressed by the propositions $p_{16}, p_{17}, p_{22}, p_{23}$ and p_{24}) have been addressed in the present model ($G_4, \ldots, G_8$ support their validity), some other issues are still open and the irregularity is still valid. In fact the participants point out that G_2 is still affected by NP_1 because $p_{25} =$ "*The collected PHI might be accessed by unauthorized person-nel*" ($p_{25} \xrightarrow{imply} t_2$). Also, other users argue that $p_{26} =$ "*After PHI are collected, the forms could be accessed by unauthorized personnel*" and also $p_{27} =$ "*The electronic access to PHI has to be protected*". As the acceptability of the *affect* relation is still accepted (left side of figure 5), the model has to be revised again. The following revision (right side of figure 5) is evaluated by a discussion that assesses that the irregularity doesn't hold anymore, and it is therefore deleted from the model.

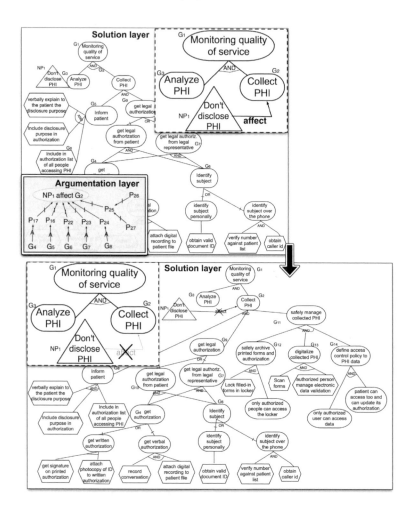

Fig. 5. Requirement engineers revise the model on the left into the right one, as a discussion assesses that the irregularity is still present in the model

5. Find Resolutions. In this last step an irregularity-free version of the model is passed as input and it is searched for elements that realize the NP (right side of figure 6). Discussions evaluate the validity of each element of the model as a possible realization for the NP. For example, when G_{11} is considered (discussion with topic $t_3 = G_{11} \xrightarrow{realize} NP_1$) a participant states that $p_{33} =$ "*PHI disclosure depends on the way information with PHI is handled after collection*" and that in the present model $p_{34} =$ "*Collected PHI is not disclosed without authorization*". As evidence of this last statement, goals g_{12}, g_{13} and g_{14} are in fact presented ($\{g_{12}, g_{13}, g_{14}\} \xrightarrow{imply} p_{34}$). As this discussion ends, the algorithm EvaluateDiscussion accepts the realization, and the relation is added to the model (see figure 6).

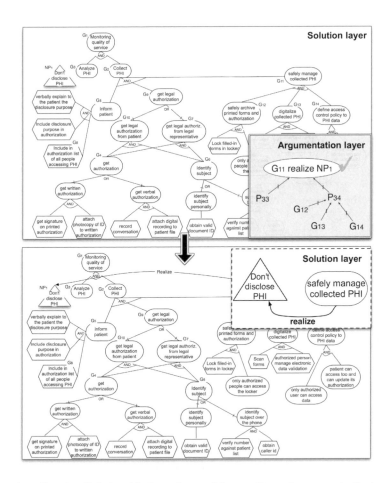

Fig. 6. A realization link is added to the model as a discussion accepts that goal g_{11} realizes the normative proposition np_1

6 Related Work

Analysis of regulatory compliance of a system has been also examined in [10] where the authors suggest using a production rule model to check for compliance. Differently from our work, their work was aimed at providing support for a compliance check, while our work extends this concept with both a framework and a systematic process for obtaining compliance through the traceability and soundness provided by argumentation.

A more targeted approach dealing specifically with privacy law, was investigated by Ghanavanti et al. [2]. They use the Goal-oriented Requirements Language (GRL) to model goals and actions prescribed by laws and they introduce a framework that models the business processes of a hospital and binds it with the legislation on privacy of health information. Our work instead relies on argumentation to establish compliance. Similarly Rifaut et al.[11] developed a framework based on the i* goal model to capture legal requirements and analyze business process compliance with respect to related published regulations.

Also, Antón and Young [3] extract software requirements by analyzing the commitments, privileges, and rights conveyed within online policy documents. Differently from our goal-oriented approach, their work involved a systematic analysis of policy documents to obtain software requirements.

Robinson developed the REQMON framework to monitor at runtime software requirements to ensure compliance with regulations [12]. While his approach focused on runtime compliance with system requirements, we aim establishing design-time compliance to an initial model thanks to a framework that directly integrates the means to obtain compliance (argumentation) within the modeling capabilities of Nòmos.

I. Habli et al. [13] have shown how argumentation is used to assure the decomposition and traceability of requirements. C.B. Haley et al. [14] have shown how argumentation can be successfully employed to clarify how a system can satisfy its security requirements. Moreover, T. Ghetiu et al. [15] pioneer the concept Argument-Driven Validation (ADV), structured arguments used as validity building blocks. Our work improves these approaches as we provide an actual extension to the argumentation framework that directly integrates the legal concepts needed to manage the compliance of requirements.

7   Conclusions

The present work proposes goal-oriented, norm-driven requirements modeling framework for modeling law, requirements and compliance solutions of requirements with respect to law. However, a number of issues remain open, because the semantics of constructs, such as "realization" or "embodiment" is hardly formalizable, often subjective and therefore debatable in concrete situations. Laws are also soften subject to changes over time, so a flexible approach is needed to manage these situations. The key idea proposed in this paper is that argumentation can be adopted to establish compliance. Through a systematic process, irregularities are identified in the models and solutions, once found, are associated to an argumentation tree, which justifies them. Given a discussion, compliance amounts to evaluating the acceptability of the argumentations. This process has been successfully applied to a case study, revising an input requirements model with respect to a law fragment and returning its compliance-acceptable version. However, research is currently ongoing to make more systematic the whole framework.

A number of issues still remain open. Firstly, our systematic process for establishing compliance needs to be refined to offer better guidelines for interpreting concepts such as "realization" and "embodiment". Secondly, laws are subject to amendments and revisions. Accordingly, we need to enrich our framework to accommodate the co-evolution of laws and requirements for a given software system.

References

1. Sartor, G.: Fundamental legal concepts: A formal and teleological characterisation. Artificial Intelligence and Law 14, 101–142 (2006)
2. Ghanavati, S., Amyot, D., Peyton, L.: Towards a framework for tracking legal compliance in healthcare. In: Krogstie, J., Opdahl, A.L., Sindre, G. (eds.) CAiSE 2007 and WES 2007. LNCS, vol. 4495, pp. 218–232. Springer, Heidelberg (2007)
3. Young, J.D., Anton, A.I.: A method for identifying software requirements based on policy commitments. In: IEEE Int. Conf. Req. Eng., pp. 47–56 (2010)
4. Siena, A.: Engineering law-compliant requirements. The Nòmos framework. PhD thesis, University of Trento, Italy (2010)
5. Yu, E.: Modelling Strategic Relationships for Process Reengineering. PhD thesis, University of Toronto, Canada (1995)
6. Hohfeld, W.N.: Fundamental Legal Conceptions as Applied in Judicial Reasoning. Yale Law Journal 23(1) (1913)
7. Jureta, I., Mylopoulos, J., Faulkner, S.: Analysis of multi-party agreement in requirements validation. In: IEEE Int. Conf. Req. Eng., pp. 57–66 (2009)
8. Ingolfo, S.: Establishing compliance of software requirements through argumentation, Master's thesis, University of Trento, Italy (2010)
9. Guzman, A.T.: A compliance-based theory of international law. California Law Review 90(6), 1823–1887 (2002)
10. Maxwell, J., Anton, A.: Checking existing requirements for compliance with law using a production rule model. In: Second International Workshop on Requirements Engineering and Law (RELAW), pp. 1–6 (2009)
11. Rifaut, A., Dubois, E.: Using goal-oriented requirements engineering for improving the quality of iso/iec 15504 based compliance assessment frameworks, pp. 33–42. IEEE Computer Society, Los Alamitos (2008)
12. Robinson, W.N.: Implementing rule-based monitors within a framework for continuous requirements monitoring. In: Hawaii International Conference on System Sciences, vol. 7, p. 188a (2005)
13. Habli, I., Wu, W., Attwood, K., Kelly, T.: Extending argumentation to goal-oriented requirements engineering. In: Hainaut, J.-L., Rundensteiner, E.A., Kirchberg, M., Bertolotto, M., Brochhausen, M., Chen, Y.-P.P., Cherfi, S.S.-S., Doerr, M., Han, H., Hartmann, S., Parsons, J., Poels, G., Rolland, C., Trujillo, J., Yu, E., Zimányie, E. (eds.) ER Workshops 2007. LNCS, vol. 4802, pp. 306–316. Springer, Heidelberg (2007)
14. Haley, C.B., Moffett, J.D., Laney, R., Nuseibeh, B.: Arguing security: validating security requirements using structured argumentation. In: SREIS 2005 (2005)
15. Ghetiu, T., Polac, F., Bown, J.: Argument-driven validation of computer simulations - a necessity, rather than an option. In: Advances in System Testing and Validation Lifecycle (VALID), pp. 1–4 (August 2010)

Making Explicit Some Implicit *i** Language Decisions

Lidia López, Xavier Franch, and Jordi Marco

Universitat Politècnica de Catalunya (UPC)
c/Jordi Girona, 1-3, E-08034 Barcelona, Spain
{llopez,jmarco}@lsi.upc.edu, franch@essi.upc.edu

Abstract. The *i** (i-star) framework is one of the most widely adopted modelling approaches by several communities (business modelling, requirements engineering, ...). Probably due to its highly strategic nature, the definition of the modelling language offered by the framework does not make explicit the full behaviour of some basic constructs, leaving them thus open to several interpretations. This looseness may not be important in some contexts, even it may be beneficial since it leaves room for researchers to customize the framework to their needs. However, it becomes an obstacle in other situations, e.g., model interoperability and model-driven development. In this paper we identify ambiguities and silences in the *i** language definition in a systematic manner, and then we propose an interpretation to deal with them. In some cases, the proposal may include the addition of some annotation into some language construct. The result is a formal definition taking the form of a UML conceptual data diagram (a metamodel) with several important integrity constraints.

Keywords: *i** framework, i-star, iStar, ambiguity, silence.

1 Introduction

The *i** (pronounced *eye-star*) framework [1] is currently one of the most widespread goal- and agent-oriented modelling and reasoning frameworks. It has been applied for modelling organizations, business processes and system requirements, among others.

Throughout the years, different research groups have proposed variations to the modelling language proposed in the *i** framework (for the sake of brevity, we will name it "the *i** language"). Some variations come from paradigm shifts (e.g., using *i** for modelling services [2], see [3] for a compilation), others propose some particular type of new construct (e.g., for dealing with security aspects [4]), but others just issue slight modifications related to the core of the *i** language (from now on, "the *i** language core"). This third type of variations mainly appear because the definition of the *i** language core is loose at some parts, and researchers may have interpreted the same constructs in different ways. The absence of a universally agreed metamodel has accentuated this effect [5].

Looseness is partly due to the high strategic nature of the *i** framework: the emphasis is more on high-level concepts like actors, goals and dependencies, than on low-level details. Thus, it may be argued that the mentioned ambiguities and silences may not be important in some contexts (e.g., interactive creativity meetings with

M. Jeusfeld, L. Delcambre, and T.W. Ling (Eds.): ER 2011, LNCS 6998, pp. 62–77, 2011.

stakeholders). Being this true, it also happens that there are other contexts in which ambiguities and silences become an obstacle:

- Model interoperability. Accepting a community scenario in which different variants for *i** exist, supporting the interchange of models and the interconnection of tools seems to be a reasonable goal. In a previous work [6], we have reported how different interpretations of the *i** language core may hamper and eventually prevent automatic model interchange among tools.
- Model-driven development (MDD). Several works are addressing the use of *i** diagrams as starting point in MDD processes [7]. Due to their very nature, MDD processes require models with a clear and non-ambiguous meaning.
- Precise definition of some *i** constructs. In the available definitions of the *i** language core, some constructs were not defined up to the last level of detail. For instance, in [8] we have explored the *i** subtyping construct at the level of Strategic Rationale (SR) diagrams. In this work, we have identified some looseness that forced us to make some decisions about the *i** language.

Our position is that each and every modeling language definition should be complete and consistent regardless of its intended use. This is the ultimate motivation of our work. Those contexts that require a more informal or agile use should lead to lighter versions of the language but still these should be complete and consistent, as well as compatible with the full version.

The work presented here addresses these problems and specifically tries to answer the following research questions:

- RQ1. Which ambiguities and silences exist in the current definition of the *i** language core?
  o RQ1.1. What constructs can be considered to form the *i** language core?
- RQ2. What decisions can be made to solve these ambiguities and silences?
  o RQ2.1. Is it necessary to include additional features in the *i** language core to implement these decisions?
  o RQ2.2. Are there particular issues that deserve further research before an informed decision can be made?
- RQ3. What is the final form that an ambiguity- and silence-free *i** language core definition should take?

The rest of the paper is structured as follows. Section 2 enumerates and analyses the sources consulted. Section 3 shows the methodology used to drive our work. Sections 4 to 7 are the core of the work, complemented with section 8 where we formulate our final proposal for the *i** language core. Section 9 provides the conclusions and future work. Basic knowledge of *i** is assumed, see [1] and the *i** wiki [9] for details.

2   Background: Analysis of the *i** Framework

There is a great deal of research made by the *i** community that is relevant to our objectives. This section tries to summarize the most important observations after analysing eight types of sources. It is clear that we cannot aim at giving details in the paper for every individual type of source, so we have decided just to enumerate the most significant sources considered in each type and provide in the second subsection a global consolidation of observations.

2.1 Sources of Our Work

The types of inputs considered have been the following:

Main dialects. Arguably, we may consider that there exist three main streams of *i** variants: 1) the seminal proposal of the *i** framework [1], updated in [9]; 2) the Goal-oriented Requirement Language (GRL) which is part of the User Requirements Notation (URN) [10]; 3) Tropos, an agent-oriented software methodology that adopts *i** as its modelling language [11].

Metamodels. Several contributions exist that propose metamodels for *i** with different purposes: 1) metamodels for particular *i** variants like GRL's [12] and Tropos' [13]; 2) metamodels for supporting model interoperability [14]; 3) metamodels for providing a reference framework [15][16]; 4) metamodels as the basis for tool construction [17].

Literature. In [14] we performed a literature review as a baseline for model interoperability analysis. Since we focused on the analysis of *i** constructs, the results of the review are applicable also in this paper. The review was conducted over the following conferences and journals for the period 2006-2010: ER, CAiSE, REJ, DKE, IS Journal, RE, RiGiM, WER, *i** workshop, and it included also the recent book on *i** [3]. After some filtering, we selected 63 contributions proposing addition, removal or modification of basic *i** constructs as described in Table 1.

Tools. We experimented with the some of the most (if not the most) used *i** modeling tools: Open OME [18], jUCMNav [19], REDEPEND [20] and TAOM4E [21]. Being modelling tools, they necessarily provide (intentionally or not) answers to some of these ambiguities and silences.

Techniques. Similarly to tools, what makes interesting the definition of techniques is that they provide an interpretation to all *i** constructs. Two main types of techniques exist, evaluation procedures [22][23] and qualitative reasoning techniques [24].

Evaluation reports. Some works exist that similarly to our aim, have provided an analysis of different aspects of *i**: 1) Analysis of current uses, best practices and misunderstandings [25][26]; 2) direct comparison of several major proposals [15][16]; 3) reflections about *i** subordinated to the analysis of its visual notation [27]; 4) definition of a model interchange format [28].

Real experiences. The experiences of *i** in real projects provides insights about how the framework has been used in industrial projects, cf. [29][30][31] among others.

Personal feedback. Last but not least, interaction with researchers in the community, discussions, attendance to talks, etc., had provided us useful insights on the use of *i**.

Table 1. Variations proposed by the *i** community in the last 5 years (selected venues only). Each paper increments each column at most in 1

	Actors	Actor links	Dependencies	Intentional elements (IE)	IE links
New	4	24	10	21	21
Removed	8	5	2	1	0
Changed	3	1	1	36	43

2.2 Observations

We have built our work from the analysis of the sources above. The first output is the decision of which elements form the *i** language core. The rationale adopted is: an element is included in the *i** language core if it is adopted or accepted (sometimes implicitly) by all the sources mentioned above. To start with, we consolidate this core into a preliminary UML conceptual data schema that includes classes for the core concepts and associations among them (see Fig. 1). In the next sections we will add the required information into this conceptual schema until we reach a non-ambiguous and complete definition of the core.

The data schema shows the three key concepts of *i**: Actor, Dependency and IntentionalElement. Actors have a boundary that includes their InternalElements, a subtype of intentional element. Both actors and internal elements may be related through Links. Concerning dependencies, they connect DependencyParticipant (either actors or internal elements) acting as dependers or dependees through some Dependum (another type of intentional element). We remark that in this initial model we are not including any type of constraint (even we do not include cardinality), since for all the concepts we may find several interpretations that could violate these constraints, regardless how general we try to be.

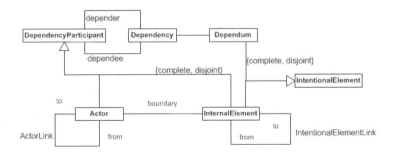

Fig. 1. The *i** language core: preliminary representation as a UML conceptual data schema

3 Systematic Management of Ambiguities and Silences

To proceed further in the formulation of the core of the *i** language, we wanted to apply some systematic process to ensure the completeness of the analysis. We opted for designing a set of questions to apply to each element in the core. Since elements are represented in a data schema, we derived these questions from the analysis of the

UML superstructure [32] regarding to the metaelements that we will use in the core definition: classes, associations, specializations and attributes.

Table 2 summarizes the most important questions. In the analysis, we left out from the very beginning information that appears in the UML metamodel but that it is not of interest in our context, e.g. questions related to visibility. We have not shown in the table either some questions that were applied but that have provided a consistent result in all cases (e.g., we first had two questions to find out if some association or attribute were derived, or also to check for overlapping specializations, but since the answer was always negative, we do not show them). Concerning the rest of questions:

Table 2. Summary of questions for ambiguity and silence systematic detection

Concept	Id	Question
Class	C1	Is the class specialized according to some criteria (type, ...)?
	C2	For each criterion in C1, is the specialization complete or incomplete?
	C3	Does the class have any attribute?
Associations	A1	Which are the characteristics of the different roles (cardinality, ordering, ...)?
	A2	Is the association of a specific type (composition, aggregation)?
	A3	Is it an association class? (if so, Class' questions also apply)
Attributes	P1	Which type is it?
	P2	Which is the cardinality (univalued, multivalued, optional, ...)?
All types	T1	Is there any other constraint involving one or more elements of the model?

- r classes, most questions are related to their possible participation in specialization hierarchies: possible classification criteria and their completeness. The last question refers to the existence of attributes.
- Concerning associations, the questions are designed to find out: characteristics of roles; nature of the association (e.g., aggregation, composition...); and if it is an association class (and then class questions also apply).
- For attributes, fundamental questions are about their type and cardinality.
- Last, a general question was applicable to all type of elements, searching for properties that relate different elements of the model or express characteristics of one particular type of element (e.g., reflexivity, transitivity, ...).

The next sections discuss the application of these questions to the different parts of the data schema shown in Fig. 1, although we will not show continuously the questions and how they were applied. References to elements of the final metamodel presented in Section 8 are written in Courier style.

4   Actors and Actor Links

Question C1 applied over Actor could be matter of discussion, since not all the proposals found in the literature propose distinguishing types of actors. However, those that do, adhere to the classical distinction: Role, Position, Agent. The most remarkable exception is GRL/URN in all its sources (language report, metamodel and jUCMNav tool) but even here we may find some ambiguity, since at some documents it is said that the type of actor can be stated using metadata, therefore we conclude that introducing `ActorTypes` does not cause a severe conflict with GRL/URN.

Question C2 over actors reveals one typical situation of silence in most sources. However, we find some examples in which non-classified actors coexist with actors of a particular type. Another argument that could be given is that if we consider the model development process, even if we want to end up with a model with all actors belonging to a given type, intermediate states could still keep actors whose type is still not determined. Therefore, we allow `General` actors to coexist with specialized ones.

When it comes to `ActorLink`, first of all we find several `ActorLinkTypes` in the literature. Those sources that distinguish actor types, also provide the classical links `plays`, `occupies` and `covers`, applied to the correct types (`IC5-7`). In addition, specialization (`is-a`) and aggregation (`is-part-of`) are often mentioned and for those sources that don't, it seems more that simply it was not an objective of the work than an intended decision. Therefore, we also propose them. The main problem at this moment is the instance (`INS`) relationship among agents. This concept appears in the seminal Yu's proposal but it is not formally defined, it is just used in the examples. A fundamental question arises here: is it really a construct that must appear at the model itself, or does it belong to a different modelling level? In some sense, referring to the MOF specification [33], it could be argued that agents' instances belong to M0 whilst the rest of an *i** model is at M1. Therefore, we do not include the instance relationship in our current core proposal, instead we formulate our open issue (OI):

OI1: Does the `instance` relationship belong to the *i** core?

When we explore the `ActorLink` association (A1 and A2, and also T1), we find the typical scenario that we feel justifies the need of this paper. There are very permissive scenarios that do not include any constraint (e.g., the OpenOME tool) and others that state some concrete rules (e.g., the Tropos metamodel). Several issues get different responses in different sources, or they are not mentioned at all:

- Cardinalities: e.g., may an actor be specialization of more than one actor (see Fig. 2, left)? May different actor links have different cardinalities?
- Constraints among types of connected actors: e.g., may an actor of a given type be a subtype or part of an actor of another type (see Fig. 2, center)?
- Simultaneous application of actor links: e.g., may an actor be at the same part a subtype and a part of two other actors, or even of the same actor (see Fig. 2, right)?

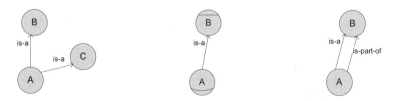

Fig. 2. Some forbidden situations in the *i** language core for actor links

As a result of this analysis, we make the following decisions:

– We do not allow an actor being a subtype of more than one actor (IC8). Reason is simplicity: multiple inheritance is known as a source of confusion for modellers. Specially because, as we will see in Section 5, there are a lot of questions about the meaning of these links when intentional elements are considered.
– We do not allow neither is-a nor is-part-of to involve actors of different type (IC3) or to be applied to the same pair of actors (IC4). Not just simplicity is behind this decision, also conceptual clarity (from an ontological point of view) and compliance to community behaviour: some proposals state this constraint explicitly (remarkably the Wiki does) and those that don't, seem more not having paid attention to the issue that having made a conscious decision.
– We do not allow cycles, not just for the same type of link, but for all (IC2). We have not found any meaningful situation where cycles should be allowed.
– There is no special property for the ActorLink association. We just paid attention to the possibility of plays being an association derived from covers and occupies, but clearly this is not the case, since an agent may play a role without an intermediate position. Also we discarded is-part-of to be an aggregation.

5   Internal Elements and Internal Element Links

Internal elements configure the rationale of actors. A review of the sources shows a clear consensus in four types (albeit some minor terminological differences): goal, softgoal, task and resource. The existence of a fifth type, belief, is not so clear. The main dialects use it inconsistently: whilst Yu's thesis named them, in fact it does not make use of them, but then the wiki clearly defines them. URN/GRL includes beliefs from the very beginning, whilst Tropos just do it sometimes. Similar dissimilarities may be found in the rest of sources. In our core proposal, we are including beliefs in the IEType intentional elements' type because we think that they are really modelling something that cannot be modelled otherwise ("a condition about the world that the actor holds to be true" [9]). Following GRL metamodel, they cannot be part of a dependency (IC9,14). Since this could be a controversial point we identify an OI:

OI2: Does the belief relationship belong to the *i** core?

When it comes to internal element links (IELinks), we find fundamental questions that are typically answered differently by different sources:

Types of Links. There is agreement on task decompositions (TD), means-end links (ME) and contributions to softgoals (CSG). Other variants are rare and it does not seem advisable to include them. Still some problems arise (see Fig. 3):

– For TD, the elements that decompose are considered in AND relationship. Therefore, it is not possible to decompose any other type of internal element other than task with an AND decomposition.
– For ME, there is no consensus about which relationships are valid between sources and targets of the links, e.g., may a resource be an end? Also, it is not clear whether the means are exclusive (XOR) or not (OR).

– For CSG, there is agreement that contributions must be typed, but there is no consensus about the admitted types. One of the most used values' domain includes also AND and OR types, and then it is not clear whether this prevents the use of softgoals as root for TD and ME.

Joint Use. In general, it is not stated whether an internal element may be decomposed using more than one type of link. E.g., if it is a task, may it be both decomposed with TD and ME?

Cycles. Although in general cycles are not allowed, we have the specific case of CSG: if softgoal A contributes negatively to softgoal B and the other way round, is it possible to state both relationships together in the model?

Roots. Usually it is not stated if more than one root is possible inside an actor's boundary, although by observation of examples this seems to be the usual case. Constraints on the type of the root(s) are usually not given either.

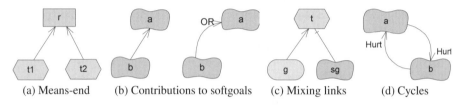

| (a) Means-end | (b) Contributions to softgoals | (c) Mixing links | (d) Cycles |

Fig. 3. Some extreme situations in *i** decomposition links

Below we show the decisions made at this respect. We have tried to combine the following criteria: conceptual clarity, keeping the language as understandable as it could be; soundness, avoiding situations that could drive to meaningless models; flexibility, avoiding unnecessary restrictions; expressive power, trying to exploit full capabilities of goal models; alignment with community, to foster acceptance.

Types of Links

– For TD, we allow the possibility of having other types than `task` in the root, therefore the name should change to just `decomposition`. This could be a highly controversial point, but in fact note that currently: 1) decomposition of goals into subgoals is currently proposed in some documents as: first, provide a `task` means to the `goal` end, and then decompose the `task` into `goals`, which we believe just introduces some noise in the model with the same objective; 2) AND-`decomposition` of softgoals is supported by `contribution` as defined e.g. in Wiki.
– For ME, we take the most permissive option and interpret OR instead of XOR.
– In both cases, aligning with URN/GRL position, we tend to remove as many constraints as possible concerning valid types of internal elements. In other words, we want the core to be as inclusive as possible since the sources' analysis has demonstrated great diversity. Therefore, we just control the use of beliefs: a belief can be decomposed just into beliefs; a belief can contribute to softgoals (`IC10`).

 – For `contribution`, we adhere to the proposal in the Wiki and URN/GRL (excluding AND/OR contributions, that we consider as decomposition, see above), a `ContType` formed by values `make`, `help`, `some+`, `unknown`, `some-`, `hurt`, `break`.

Joint Use. An internal element cannot be decomposed using more than one decomposition type (`IC13`). A decomposed softgoal may be the target of contribution links.

Cycles. Only cycles among softgoals are allowed (`IC12`).

Roots. More than one root of any type is allowed.
The connexion between internal elements and actors is implemented through the `boundary` association (see Fig. 1). It is declared as composition since an internal element belongs to exactly one actor and its life is dependant of its actor's life.

A last point that needs attention is the effect of actor links on internal elements. In other words, if there is a link from actor A to actor B, what effect has this on the internal elements in A? This question arose when we used intensively the `is-a` relationship in our models and motivated a line of research that is still ongoing [8]. A lot of open issues had been to be tackled, e.g., which modifications are allowed inside A of the elements inherited from B? We foresee that the same questions may arise when considering the other types of actor links. The answer to these questions motivates an OI that in fact is many-fold (one for each type of actor link):

OI3: Which are the consequences on internal elements of actors that are related to other actors via actor links?

6   Dependencies

`Dependums` are at the heart of dependencies and their nature is one of the most agreed concepts in *i**: they have the same type `IEType` than internal elements but not including beliefs (`IC9`), so we adhere to this position.

When it comes to `dependencies`, we find several issues that deserve discussion:

Source and Target Elements. We may find all possible situations of connection among internal elements and actors depending on the internal knowledge about involved actors. Therefore, we allow any possible situation. The initial metamodel at Fig. 1 supports this decision with the `IntentionalElement` class. However, a twilight zone appears when considering what happens e.g. with a dependency among two actors when a third actor inherits from one of the former [8]. We identify an OI:

OI4: Which are the relationships between dependencies and actor links?

Strength. Basically the discussion is whether strengths should be part of the core or not. A lot of researchers in the community simply do not use strengths. However, we still believe that they have a potential and their use could be of interest in several contexts (since they provide both information about criticality and effort).

Multiplicity. A situation that is not completely specified in *i** proposals is whether a dependency can have multiple dependees or dependers and in this case, what is the meaning. We find two different style repetitions: the dependum is repeated in different dependencies; or the dependum has several links stemming or going to. After examining the existing proposals, the decision made is (see Fig. 4):

– We allow both: 1) one dependency with multiple dependers and dependees (see Fig. 4, left); 2) several dependencies with the same dependum, provided that the same pair (depender, dependee) does not appear in more than one of them (IC14).
– If a dependency has several dependees, then the satisfaction of the dependum depends on all of them altogether. This is the most usual intent in the models in which we have found this situation. As drawback, this decision prevents to express that a single dependee could make a dependum satisfied.
– If a dependency has several dependers, then all the dependers depend on that dependum the same way. If needed for clarity of the drawing, we admit to split the dependency into several since no ambiguity is possible (see Fig. 4, right, bottom).
– If there are two dependencies with the same dependum *d* (see Fig. 4, right, top), it means that *d* is describing some kind of entity that appears in 2 different contexts.

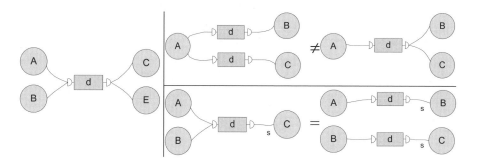

Fig. 4. General framework for dependencies in the *i** language core

We remark that we explicitly avoid in our core some scarce uses that may be found in some proposals (more in examples than in formal definitions themselves), e.g.: dependencies involving intentional elements inside an actor, or dependency links that include some contribution value.

7   Some Addition of Information into *i** Models

In the previous analysis we have strictly adhered to consensus and intentionally avoid any proposal that could be considered out of the current trends in *i** (with the only exception of task-decomposition converted into decomposition). However, we still find some situations whose resolution cannot be implemented without adding some information in *i** models. We are identifying next these situations and providing a way of modelling them (shown in Fig. 5). Remarkably, we will provide default actions that makes the classical *i** models compliant to our definition. We also try to provide a uniform graphical view in terms of notation, as the figure shows.

Generalization Sets. In some models we have needed to specialize an actor according to different criteria. For instance, in a Travel Agency case, we needed to specialize the

TravelAgency actor with respect to the target type of customer (Individual, Organization) and the type of agency (Internet, Traditional). We faced two problems: first, *i** does not support the grouping of subactors by criterion, so that the model didn't catch the intended meaning; second, we were not able to distinguish the disjoint nature of the first criterion from the overlapping criterion of the second one. We propose to make *i** more expressive at this respect, adding: 1) the ability to group subactors; 2) the ability to classify the specialization according to completeness and disjointness. We propose to use the UML metamodel concept of `GeneralizationSet` to specify these issues. As default case, we choose one single `complete` and `disjoint` specialization criterion without explicit `name`.

Decomposition Links. As commented in Section 4, we are proposing an AND-decomposition link beyond task decomposition, and we also have the means-end links that are a kind of OR-decomposition. Putting both things together, we propose to follow Tropos' proposal in which we have just the `Decomposition` link that can be qualified as AND or OR, and in fact we propose also XOR as a third type of qualification to support expressiveness to obtain then an attribute of type `LogicalType`. By default, AND-decomposition links are interpreted as `decomposition`, and OR- and XOR-decomposition links as `means-ends`.

Dependency Links. We find a similar situation than above for dependency links in the dependee's side. We propose the same solution: to qualify the type of combination of dependees with AND, OR, XOR (attribute in `Dependency` of type `LogicalType`).

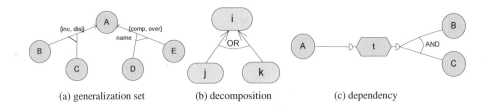

(a) generalization set   (b) decomposition   (c) dependency

Fig. 5. Proposals for the *i** language core

To conclude with, we identify a final OI:

OI5: How much acceptable those proposals could be in the *i** community.

8   The *i** Language Core: Final Representation

In this section we show the result of the analysis undertaken in the four previous sections. The metamodel is shown in Fig. 6 and the integrity constraints in Table 3.

It is important to remark that we have a degree of freedom when one class has some specialization criterion with respect to the representation in UML of each value of this criterion. Given a class C in which a classification criterion may take values $k_1, ..., k_n$, we may create k subclasses of C, one for each k_i, or we may create an

Table 3. Integrity constraints over the *i** core language

Id.	Concept	Integrity Constraint
IC1	name attribute	There cannot be two model elements with the same `name` except for:
IC1.1	InternalElement	`internal elements`: name restriction applies inside `actors'` boundary
IC2	ActorLink	Cycles are not allowed regardless of the type of `ActorLink`
IC3		The links `is-a` and `is-part-of` must connect actors of the same type
IC4		The `is-a` and `is-part-of` links cannot be applied to the same pair of `Actors`
IC5		The link `occupies` must connect an `Agent` with a `Position`
IC6		The link `covers` must connect an `Position` with a `Role`
IC7		The link `plays` must connect an `Agent` with a `Role`
IC8		An `Actor` cannot be a subtype of more than one `Actor`
IC9	Dependum	`Dependums` cannot have `Belief` as type
IC10	InternalElement Link	`Beliefs` can be `decomposed` only into `beliefs`
IC11		`Contributions` can only have `softgoals` as `to`
IC12		The only cycles allowed are those that involve only `contribution` links
IC13		An internal element can be `decomposed` using one type of decomposition
IC14	Dependency	A `dependum` cannot appear twice among the same pair of `Actors`
IC15		Depender and dependee actors must be different
IC16		`Beliefs` cannot be neither `depender` nor `dependee`

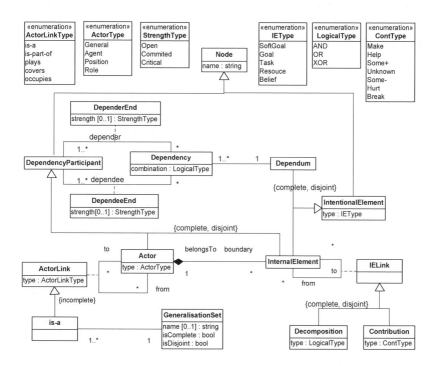

Fig. 6. The *i** language core: final representation as a UML conceptual data schema

Enumeration type with values k_1, ..., k_n and then an attribute of this type in C. We have decided to avoid creation of specialization relationships to keep the model simple, and thus the only situation in which sub-classes are created is when some attribute has to be defined in at least one of the k_i. This is a change with respect to some former metamodels we have proposed (e.g., [16]), but after some experience with them we think that it is worth keeping the class diagram simple. The rest of the metamodel just reflects the decisions made in the paper.

9   Conclusions

In this paper we have formulated a precise definition of the core constructs of the $i*$ language. We have organized the research into several research questions (see Section 1) which we hope have been satisfactorily answered:

- We have undertaken a comprehensive analysis of the existing body of knowledge for the $i*$ framework with focus on the language. The analysis has relied upon several types of sources. As a result, we have identified the $i*$ language constructs whose formal definition is not completely defined (research question RQ1) and determined which part of the language can be considered to be the core (RQ1.1).
- We have proposed how to deal with the identified ambiguities and silences. For most of them, we have provided in this paper our interpretation of the problem and then we have made a particular decision to solve it (RQ2). In some cases, we have added and formally defined some minor notational elements to the $i*$ language to fulfil this goal (RQ2.1). These new elements are always optional in nature. Last, we have identified some open issues that cannot be decided in the paper but require a more detailed analysis (RQ2.2). We remark the intended decision of keeping separated RQ2 from RQ1: whilst RQ1 is answered through analysis, RQ2 is requiring decisions to be made, which can always be a matter of discussion.
- We have articulated our proposal around a UML data schema with integrity constraints to fully define the meaning of the $i*$ language constructs (RQ3).

As a summary, we may say that we have provided a first consolidated step towards having a community agreement of the formal meaning of $i*$ constructs up to a level of detail that is not currently available. As mentioned in the introduction, we think that the results of this work can be useful in several contexts that really require this level of detail, like model-driven development, model interchange and tool interoperability. We also remark that although the paper has focused on the $i*$ language, we believe that the method and criteria used could eventually be applied in other domains facing a similar scenario.

In this paper, we have assumed that "a" (i.e., exactly one) $i*$ language core exists. An open question that requires further investigation is whether different contexts could require different language cores. For instance, does the $i*$ language needed for conducting creativity meetings share the same core with model-driven development-oriented $i*$?

At a first sight, this work may seem to contradict somehow some of our previous work on the construction of an $i*$ metamodel [15][5][16][14]. In these works, we advocate for an $i*$ metamodel general enough to host most of the proposed variants of *i*. But in fact we argue that the two approaches are complementary. In these cited works, we design a general metamodel but the *i** language core is embedded into it. What we are proposing here is to make more accurate the expression of the core. Thus putting both lines of research together, we could include the decisions made in this paper into the metamodel proposed in these sources. Thus, any new *i** variant could configure the metamodel to its own needs (e.g., by adding some new type of intentional element, or restricting the allowed types of links decomposition) but at the same time, relying on a stable *i** core with a clearly defined semantics, eventually shared by all variants.

As future work, we first mention the consideration of the open issues identified in the paper. In addition, we have identified two lines of research:

1) building an ontological foundation for the *i** core language, using a foundational ontology like UFO [34];

2) adapting existing techniques to the proposed *i** language core, which requires reflecting about the concept of satisfactibility of intentional elements.

Acknowledgments. This work has been supported by the Spanish project TIN2010-19130-c02-01. The authors want to thank Carlos Cares for his suggestions in early versions of the work; Renata and Giancarlo Guizzardi for our fruitful discussions on the topic; and the anonymous reviewers for their valuable feedback.

References

1. Yu, E.: Modelling Strategic Relationships for Process Reengineering. PhD.Computer Science University of Toronto, Toronto (1995)
2. Estrada, H., Martínez, A., Pastor, O., Mylopoulos, J., Giorgini, P.: Extending organizational modeling with business services concepts: An overview of the proposed architecture. In: Parsons, J., Saeki, M., Shoval, P., Woo, C., Wand, Y. (eds.) ER 2010. LNCS, vol. 6412, pp. 483–488. Springer, Heidelberg (2010)
3. Yu, E., Giorgini, P., Maiden, N., Mylopoulos, J. (eds.): Social Modeling for Requirements Engineering. The MIT Press, Cambridge (2011)
4. Mouratidis, H., Giorgini, P., Manson, G.: Integrating Security and Systems Engineering: Towards the Modelling of Secure Information Systems. In: Eder, J., Missikoff, M. (eds.) CAiSE 2003. LNCS, vol. 2681, Springer, Heidelberg (2003)
5. Franch, X.: Fostering the Adoption of *i** by Practitioners: Some Challenges and Research Directions. In: International Perspectives on Information Systems Engineering. Springer, Heidelberg (2010)
6. Colomer, D., López, L., Franch, X., Cares, C.: Model Interchange and Tool Interoperability in the *i** Framework: An Experiment. In: WER 2011 (2011)
7. Alencar, F., Marín, B., Giachetti, G., Pastor, O., Castro, J., Pimentel, J.H.: From i* requirements models to conceptual models of a model driven development process. In: Persson, A., Stirna, J. (eds.) PoEM 2009. LNBIP, vol. 39, pp. 99–114. Springer, Heidelberg (2009)
8. López, L., Franch, X., Marco, J.: Defining Inheritance in *i** at the Level of SR Intentional Elements. In: iStar 2008 (2008)
9. The *i** Wiki, http://istar.rwth-aachen.de (last accessed July 2011)
10. ITU-T Recommendation Z.151 (11/08), User Requirements Notation (URN) - Language Definition (2008), http://www.itu.int/rec/T-REC-Z.151/en

11. Bresciani, P., Giorgini, P., Giunchiglia, F., Mylopoulos, J., Perini, A.: Tropos: An Agent-Oriented Software Development Methodology. Autonomous Agents and Multi-Agent Systems 8(3) (2004)
12. Amyot, D., Horkoff, J., Gross, D., Mussbacher, G.: A lightweight GRL profile for i* modeling. In: Heuser, C.A., Pernul, G. (eds.) ER 2009. LNCS, vol. 5833, pp. 254–264. Springer, Heidelberg (2009)
13. Susi, A., Perini, A., Mylopoulos, J.: The Tropos Metamodel and its Use. Informatica (2005)
14. Cares, C., Franch, X.: A metamodelling approach for i* model translations. In: Mouratidis, H., Rolland, C. (eds.) CAiSE 2011. LNCS, vol. 6741, pp. 337–351. Springer, Heidelberg (2011)
15. Ayala, C., Cares, C., Carvallo, J.P., Grau, G., Haya, M., Salazar, G., Franch, X., Mayol, E., Quer, C.: A Comparative Analysis of i*-Based Agent-Oriented Modeling Languages. In: SEKE 2005 (2005)
16. Cares, C., Franch, X., Mayol, E., Quer, C.: A Reference Model for i*. Book chapter in [3] (2011)
17. Lucena, M., Santos, E., Silva, C., Alencar, F., Silva, M.J., Castro, J.: Towards a unified Metamodel for i*. In: RCIS 2008 (2008)
18. OpenOME Tool, http://www.cs.toronto.edu/km/openome/ (last accessed, March 2011)
19. jUCMNav Tool, http://jucmnav.softwareengineering.ca (last accessed, March 2011)
20. Lockerbie, J., Maiden, N.: REDEPEND: Extending i* Modelling into Requirements Processes. In: RE 2008 (2008)
21. TAOM4E Tool, http://selab.fbk.eu/taom/ (last accessed, March 2011)
22. Horkoff, J., Yu, E.: Finding solutions in goal models: An interactive backward reasoning approach. In: Parsons, J., Saeki, M., Shoval, P., Woo, C., Wand, Y. (eds.) ER 2010. LNCS, vol. 6412, pp. 59–75. Springer, Heidelberg (2010)
23. Amyot, D., Ghanavati, S., Horkoff, J., Mussbacher, G., Peyton, L., Yu, E.: Evaluating Goal Models within the Goal-oriented Requirement Language. International Journal of Intelligent Systems 25(8) (2010)
24. Giorgini, P., Mylopoulos, J., Nicchiarelli, E., Sebastiani, R.: Reasoning with goal models. In: Spaccapietra, S., March, S.T., Kambayashi, Y. (eds.) ER 2002. LNCS, vol. 2503, p. 167. Springer, Heidelberg (2002)
25. Horkoff, J., Elahi, G., Abdulhadi, S., Yu, E.: Reflective analysis of the syntax and semantics of the i* framework. In: Song, I.-Y., Piattini, M., Chen, Y.-P.P., Hartmann, S., Grandi, F., Trujillo, J., Opdahl, A.L., Ferri, F., Grifoni, P., Caschera, M.C., Rolland, C., Woo, C., Salinesi, C., Zimányi, E., Claramunt, C., Frasincar, F., Houben, G.-J., Thiran, P. (eds.) ER Workshops 2008. LNCS, vol. 5232, pp. 249–260. Springer, Heidelberg (2008)
26. Webster, I., Amaral, J., Cysneiros, L.M.: A Survey of Good Practices and Misuses for Modelling with i* Framework. In: WER 2005 (2005)
27. Moody, D., Heymans, P., Matulevicius, R.: Visual Syntax does matter: Improving the Cognitive Effectiveness of the i* Visual Notation. Req. Engineering Journal 15(2) (2010)
28. Cares, C., Franch, X., Perini, A., Susi, A.: Towards Interoperability of i* Models using iStarML. Computer Standards & Interfaces 33(1) (2011)
29. Carvallo, J.P., Franch, X.: On the use of i* for architecting hybrid systems: A method and an evaluation report. In: Persson, A., Stirna, J. (eds.) PoEM 2009. LNBIP, vol. 39, pp. 38–53. Springer, Heidelberg (2009)

30. Annosi, A., Pascale, A., Gross, D., Yu, E.: Analyzing Software Process Alignment with Organizational Business Strategies using an Agent- and Goal-oriented Analysis Technique. In: iStar (2008)
31. Maiden, N., Jones, S., Ncube, C., Lockerbie, J.: Using i* in Requirements Projects: Some Experiences and Lessons Learned. Book chapter in [3] (2011)
32. OMG 2.2 Unified Modelling Language Superstructure (2009)
33. MOF 2.0 Core Final Adopted Specification (2006)
34. Guizzardi, G., Wagner, G.: Using UFO as a Foundation for General Conceptual Modeling Languages. In: Theory and Application of Ontologies. Springer, Heidelberg (2010)

The Impact of Perceived Cognitive Effectiveness on Perceived Usefulness of Visual Conceptual Modeling Languages

Kathrin Figl[1] and Michael Derntl[2]

[1] Institute for Information Systems and New Media, Vienna University of
Economics and Business, Austria
kathrin.figl@wu.ac.at
[2] Information Systems and Databases, RWTH Aachen University, Germany
derntl@dbis.rwth-aachen.de

Abstract. Users' perceptions and beliefs are relevant for the adoption
of conceptual modeling languages in practice. This paper examines the
relationship between user perception of the quality of a conceptual modeling language from a cognitive point of view and its perceived usefulness.
The article builds on Moody's framework of quality characteristics of visual modeling languages. By means of an empirical study with 198 user
ratings of diagrams drawn with different modeling languages used in the
e-learning domain, we provide evidence that users' perception of criteria
such as perceptual discriminability, graphic economy, a balanced combination of text and symbols, and semiotic clarity influence perceived
usefulness of visual conceptual modeling languages. These findings and
their implications for practice and research are discussed.

1 Introduction

Conceptual models are known to support the analysis, design, development, and
documentation of software and data intensive systems. In particular, they are
used for defining stakeholder requirements and for conceptualizing diffuse knowledge in a domain. Models document the stakeholders' understanding of a domain
and the functionality of an information system. One main goal of requirements
engineering is "conveying and promoting the understanding of the application
domain" [1]. Consequently, models can improve the requirements engineering
process and facilitate common understanding of domains and processes between
users and system engineers [2]. Because of the positive effects, a large number
of different modeling approaches targeting different levels or viewpoints within
information systems—also addressing different domains—have been proposed.
Yet, there is a discrepancy between (a) the attention paid to creating and developing modeling languages in research and (b) their actual usage by practitioners
in real-world applications. For instance, in the e-learning domain, instructional
designers find it difficult in practice to use visual modeling languages to describe
their design artifacts due to their unfamiliarity and the intrinsic complexity of
the languages used [3].

M. Jeusfeld, L. Delcambre, and T.W. Ling (Eds.): ER 2011, LNCS 6998, pp. 78–91, 2011.
© Springer-Verlag Berlin Heidelberg 2011

The broad spectrum of available modeling languages makes beliefs and choices of users an important issue. Choice of modeling language is particularly relevant because "the world (reality) is never given to us in and of itself, but only through interpretation in some language" [4, p.148]. The perception of the (cognitive) effectiveness of a modeling language is likely to influence whether or not users perceive a language as useful and become interested in using the language. This is highly relevant in fields where there is no de-facto standard modeling language. Prior research showed that perceived ontological deficiencies in a modeling language negatively influence perceived usefulness and ease of use [5]. Other characteristics may have similar effects and influence the users' intentions to use a modeling language. For instance, research in several domains has shown that design aesthetics positively influence usage perceptions [6]. This paper follows up on this line of research. It goes beyond identifying and discussing cognitive effectiveness criteria of conceptual modeling languages, by connecting them to practitioners' usage beliefs. This approach differs from prior studies in that we investigate not only one, but a variety of criteria for cognitive effectiveness that users would be able to judge from a first impression of a language. Based on this we analyze which criteria are relevant for users' perception of the usefulness of the languages.

We use a theoretical framework on desirable cognitive characteristics of visual modeling languages [7] to assess the users' perceptions. Although there are already a number of frameworks available for evaluating modeling approaches, empirical research is still rare [1]. In previous research these frameworks were primarily used to conduct analytical expert evaluations of different modeling languages and analyze these in detail (e.g. [8,9,10,11]). We complement this thread of work by turning to the users' point of view and examine specifically how users' perception of quality characteristics relate to usage beliefs of conceptual modeling languages. In an empirical study 198 domain experts' ratings of different diagrams were collected. The ratings reflect the experts' judgment of three different visual modeling languages with regard to perceived cognitive characteristics and perceived usefulness. The data analysis demonstrates that these two dimensions are positively associated, which offers relevant input to understanding of the interaction between people and the conceptual modeling languages they use.

The rest of this paper is structured as follows. We begin with an overview of quality aspects in conceptual modeling. Then, we describe the research questions and the method employed in our empirical study. The next section presents our data analysis and an examination of the results. Finally, we present the implications of our research and discuss the limitations of our work.

2   Theoretical Background

2.1   Visual Modeling Languages

From a practical point of view, a conceptual modeling language is fundamental in order to allow a community to share their practices [12]. Using a visual modeling language—that is, a conceptual modeling language with a visual notation system—is the first step in narrating practices, and therefore to engage in reflective thinking as presented, for example, in Schön's *reflection on action* [13]. In the context of this paper we are interested in modeling languages that come with a visual notation. Such languages include "a set of graphical symbols, a set of compositional rules for how to form valid visual sentences, and definitions of their meanings" [7, p.756]. On the one hand, there are general-purpose visual modeling languages like the UML (Unified Modeling Language) [14] which can be used for modeling various perspectives on almost any kind of (information) system. On the other hand there are domain specific languages which are tailored for use by persons in a particular domain. A domain specific modeling language "directly represents the problem space by mapping modeling concepts to domain concepts" [15, p.19]. It matches vocabularies and mental representations of the domain experts and can therefore be a powerful and easy-to-use tool in a particular domain.

Visual models can support practitioners and their community to conceptualize problem spaces by providing a 'workbench' and toolkit for problem solving in exploring, creating, refining and redesigning design solutions. A shared, common language means that a community has a means to name and describe its environment and its inner dynamics, to identify problems, analyze them, and describe design solutions. As such, a shared language is the medium for the creation of a common ground [16], i.e. a shared understanding of a problem and of its possible solutions, and eventually of a shared culture in terms of the collection and construction of solutions and principles over time. Therefore, the language may improve communication, e.g. in design team meetings with fewer misunderstandings between experts and stakeholders due to the existence of a consistent terminology. It further enables designers and developers to generate and share design patterns by capturing the essential bits and pieces of a design solution to be adapted and reused for similar problems [17,18,19]. Last, but not least, by specifying requirements in specific settings, visual models may help to bridge the gap between design and implementation of a system. The provision of a detailed and unambiguous model can then be transformed into a working application.

2.2   Quality of Conceptual Models and Modeling Languages

Lindland et al. [20] proposed one of the first frameworks on the quality of conceptual models. It distinguishes three types of quality, namely syntactic quality, pragmatic quality and semantic quality. The framework is based on linguistics and considers four main elements: language, the modeling domain, the actual model, and the respective user. In this framework the *syntactic quality* refers to the consistency between the language and a model that was created by using the language. This consistency can be controlled via a comparison with the corresponding language grammar—that is, the modeling language's meta-model—and is therefore simple to assess. *Pragmatic quality*, however, describes a model's ability to help users in understanding the domain. In doing so, pragmatic quality connects the dimensions 'model' and 'user interpretation' of the model. Up to now, empirical studies often included the assessment of the user's perception (i.e. how easy/difficult it was to understand) and the usability (i.e. the perceived value, perceived ease of use, user satisfaction, and ease of use) [21]. *Semantic quality* captures the relationship between the domain and a model and determines how well a model conveys the intended meaning. Krogstie et al. [22] extended Lindland's framework with a fourth dimension: the *perceived semantic quality*. This dimension refers to the correspondence between the user interpretation (what a user thinks a model depicts) and the domain knowledge (what a user thinks a model should include). Semantic quality is difficult to measure, because it is hard to define what part of 'reality' is actually visualized in a specific model. There is a variety of studies comparing models against meta-models, or studies conducting ontological analyses to find out whether a grammar includes ontological deficiencies that may lead to scripts with low semantic quality [21].

Maes and Poels [21] additionally stress that a discussion of the quality of conceptual models from the users' point of view is relevant. By adapting measures stemming from popular information system success models to the area of conceptual modeling, they demonstrate that beliefs such as perceived ease of understanding and perceived semantic quality influence various attitudes such as perceived usefulness and, eventually, user satisfaction. Perceived usefulness is an important concept for measuring the users' overall quality evaluation of a modeling language. Since the actual objective of using a concepual model or a modeling language can have a variety of external influence factors, perceived usefulness is generally a robust success measure [21]. In the realm of conceptual modeling, we define perceived usefulness by replacing the term 'system' with 'conceptual model' in the original definition by Davis [23, p. 320]: "the degree to which a person believes that using a particular [conceptual model] would enhance his or her job performance".

There are several factors contributing to the quality of a modeling language. *Effectiveness* means how well a modeling language assists in accomplishing modeling goals, and *efficiency* refers to the resources needed to use a modeling language [1]. The users' interaction with modeling languages includes two main aspects, namely (*a*) the creation (authoring) of models, and (*b*) the understanding (assimilation) of models [1]. Not all modeling languages require the same effort (e.g. time, subjective ease-of-use) to learn to read and use the language. That is, models created with different modeling languages are likely to differ according to the effort required to interpret them and to develop an understanding. The form of visual information representation can have a significant impact on the efficiency of information search, the explicitness of information, and problem solving [24]. Moody [7] proposed 9 principles for high-quality design of visual languages from a cognitive viewpoint. These are semiotic clarity, graphic economy, perceptual discriminability, visual expressiveness, dual coding, semantic transparency, cognitive fit, complexity management and cognitive integration. Since one main interest in our study is to investigate users' perception of modeling languages, we will detail quality characteristics which users can perceive and judge also based on a first impression, i.e. without training on reading and using the language. Criteria like cognitive fit, complexity management, and cognitive integration are not further considered here, since users will only be able to judge these criteria after they develop interest in the language and become familiar with it to a certain degree. From Moody's criteria we therefore adopt the following for our study:

Perceptual Discriminability: Perceptual discriminability is defined as the "ease and accuracy with which graphical symbols can be differentiated from each other" [7].

Graphic Economy: A reasonable balance between the expressiveness of a language and the number of the symbols is demanded by the principle of graphic economy.

Dual Coding: A wise combination of text and graphical representation is referred to as dual coding, representing a further dimension for cognitively effective visual languages [7].

Visual Expressiveness: Visual languages which fully exploit the range of visual variables (e.g. spatial dimensions, shape, size, color, brightness, orientation, and texture) for their symbols offer a higher degree of visual expressiveness. If symbols differ according to several visual variables (e.g. color and size), they can be easily distinguished, and if a symbol has a unique value in the form of a visual variable, it is easily recognized.

Semantic Transparency: Semantic transparency describes whether symbols and their corresponding concepts are easily associated [7]. Similarly, McDougall [25, p. 489] refers to *semantic distance* to describe the continuum of "the closeness of the relationship between the symbol and what it is intended to represent". Icons, for example, are easily associated with their referent real-world concepts, because there is a direct relationship between them and their meaning.

Semiotic Clarity: Semiotic clarity refers to the importance of a one-to-one correspondence between selected concepts and their visual representation by a symbol. Anomalies such as symbol redundancy (more than one symbol representing the same concept), overload (one symbol representing more than one concept), symbol excess and deficit (when there are graphical symbols without a correspondence to a semantic construct, or vice versa) should be avoided, since they lead to ambiguity and additional unnecessary cognitive load for the user [7]. Research on the creation of domain-specific modeling languages reveals typical problems, e.g. that too many generic concepts for the domain or too many semantically overlapping concepts are chosen for a language; or that the language developer puts too much emphasis on specific concepts while neglecting other equally important concepts [26].

3   Research Questions

Having laid out the relevant theoretical background to examine cognitive effectiveness criteria related to the quality of visual modeling languages, we will now

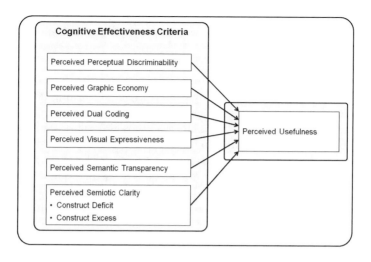

Fig. 1. Research model

explore how perceived usefulness varies depending on the perception of these quality characteristics. Hence, the main research question is: "How are users' perceptions of cognitive effectiveness criteria associated with their beliefs about the usefulness of the modeling language?"

The research model shown in Fig. 1 proposes that perceived usefulness is influenced by perceivable cognitive effectiveness criteria. The main proposition is that secondary quality criteria of a modeling language influence the formation of beliefs towards the language. This is backed up by previous research in conceptual modeling (e.g. [5]) and research on product perceptions (e.g. [6]). Prior research has found that there is a positive relationship between perceived usefulness and quality characteristics such as semiotic clarity of a language [5], perceived semantic quality and perceived ease of understanding [21]. Therefore, we expect a positive influence on perceived usefulness in case that users perceive symbols as highly discriminable, visually expressive and semantically transparent, graphic-economically chosen, and with appropriate use of the dual coding principle. Additionally, we hypothesize that perceived existence of construct deficit and excess would negatively affect perceived usefulness, since construct deficit is expected to limit expressiveness and modeling options.

4 Method

4.1 Design

To answer the research question and test the hypotheses we used a correlational study design. In a web-based questionnaire nine examples of diagram types from three different modeling languages were presented to users in random order. The users were asked to rate each diagram according to its cognitive effectiveness and its usefulness. They were instructed to rate the visual characteristics of the diagrams without paying specific attention to the actual content in the examples.

4.2   Materials

For the study, three modeling languages used in the e-learning domain for instructional design of learning processes and environments were selected as the object of evaluation. This specific domain was chosen because we had access to a large number of experts in that domain. Visual instructional design languages are important tools for e-learning design practitioners for several reasons related to the complexity of the domain [27]: for instance, instructional designers typically work in teams and therefore need a means of communication; for ensuring consistency between idea and implementation while retaining compliance with needs, goals and constraints; also, constraints and affordances of the available technologies need to be considered, which is becoming increasingly complex given the rate of technological innovation.

A visual instructional design language is defined as a set of concepts that support the structuring of the instructional design (i.e. specification) and/or the development (i.e. production) to support conceiving innovative solutions [28]. It is a conceptual tool for achieving more standardized and, at the same time, more creative design solutions, as well as enhancing communication and transparency in the design process. The main goal of a visual instructional design language is therefore the description of the "content and process within a 'unit of learning' from a pedagogical perspective in order to support reuse and interoperability" [29, p.10].

For this study we selected 9 diagram types defined in 3 different instructional design languages. As depicted in Fig. 2 we used diagram types from the following languages:

- *Educational Environment Modeling Language* (E^{2}ML) [30]: Goal Diagram, Dependencies Diagram, and Activity Flow Diagram;
- *Perspective-oriented Educational Modeling Language* (PoEML) [31]: Functional Goals Perspective Diagram, Participants' Perspective Diagram, and Order Perspective Diagram;
- *Cooperative UML* (coUML) [32]: Course Activity Diagram, Document Diagram, and Role Diagram.

4.3   Instrument

For most cognitive quality characteristics of modeling languages, there were no existing scales available. We therefore constructed two-item scales for each criterion in a way that they could be answered based on a single given diagram. The item construction was theoretically grounded on Moody's framework of desirable properties of visual languages [7]. The only exception was semiotic/ontological clarity, for which we could build on items previously developed by [5]. As mentioned in Section 2.2, knowledge of more diagram types and their relationships

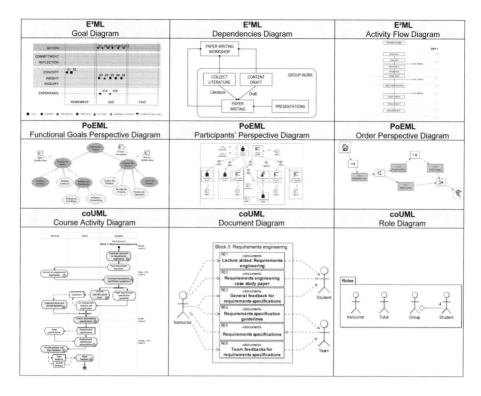

Fig. 2. Diagrams used in the user evaluation

would be necessary to evaluate the criteria of cognitive fit, complexity management and cognitive integration. Therefore, these criteria were not included in the questionnaire. To measure perceived usefulness of diagram types we adapted a scale proposed by [21] for the specific domain of the languages.

We ran a pre-test with 3 participants for ensuring content validity and for ensuring the understandable formulation of items before administering the questionnaire. Reliability analysis revealed adequate internal consistency for all scales (Cronbach's $\alpha > .8$), with the exception of visual expressiveness ($\alpha = .6$) and semiotic clarity ($\alpha = .2$). Cronbach's α should be greater than or equal to .7 to consider items to be uni-dimensional, therefore we analyzed single item scores instead of scale means for semiotic clarity. All items as well as detailed results of the reliability analysis can be found in the Appendix.

4.4   Sample

The final sample consisted of 198 user ratings of diagrams. Each of the 22 domain experts (12 males, 10 females), aged 34 years on average, had evaluated all 9 diagrams. Most participants were higher education teachers (13); the others were e-learning support staff at different universities (3) or researchers in the context of instructional design (6). Concerning experience with the domain, on

Table 1. Influence factors for perceived usefulness

Parameter	Estimate	Std. Error	df	t	Sig.
Intercept	-.33	.60	73	-.54	.588
Perceptual Discriminability	.18	.10	89	1.76	.082 +
Graphic Economy	.20	.11	67	1.87	.066 +
Dual Coding	.28	.10	85	2.93	.004 *
Visual Expressiveness	-.10	.12	92	-.84	.404
Semantic Transparency	.15	.11	90	1.34	.182
Semiotic Clarity: Absence of Construct Deficit	.21	.07	82	2.90	.005 *
Semiotic Clarity: Absence of Construct Excess	.06	.08	88	.74	.464

$^{+}\ldots p < .1$ $^{*}\ldots p < .05$

average each participant had already been involved in the creation of 5 different instructional designs (e.g. courses or trainings).

5   Results

Hypotheses were tested using the linear mixed-effects models (MIXED) procedure in SPSS 19.0 with cognitive effectiveness criteria as independent variables and perceived usefulness as the dependent variable. The MIXED procedure can handle fixed and random effects. We included the variables 'domain expert' and 'diagram' as random factors in the model and assumed that each expert as well as each diagram would have a different intercept. The different experts had different intercepts ($Wald\,Z = 2.21, p = .027$), while the different diagrams did not have different intercepts ($Wald\,Z = 1.52, p = .128$).

Table 1 provides details of the analysis showing the parameter estimates of the fixed effects and significance levels. As expected, dual coding ($p = .004$) and absence of construct deficit ($p = .005$) had a significant positive effect. Additionally there was a trend that perceptual discriminability ($p = .082$) and graphic economy ($p = .066$) had a positive effect on perceived usefulness. The subjects' perceptions of semantic transparency, visual expressiveness and absence of construct excess did not have a statistically significant effect on perceived usefulness.

6   Discussion

The empirical study set out to investigate associations between users' perceptions of cognitive effectiveness of a modeling language and their beliefs about its usefulness. Results reveal that users' perception of criteria as perceptual discriminability, graphic economy, a balanced combination of text and symbols and absence of construct deficit are relevant influence factors for perceived usefulness of a visual modeling language. In line with our hypotheses, these results demonstrate that if users have the overall impression that a language is not well constructed, they will also tend to disregard its usefulness.

6.1   Limitations

Although the effects found in this study are evident and in line with previous research, there are some noteworthy limitations.

First, we acknowledge that the relationships between the variables could be examined in greater detail with artificially constructed test materials in which the criteria systematically vary. This could also shed more light on why criteria such as semantic transparency, visual expressiveness and construct excess were not relevant for perceived usefulness. One could argue that these are simply not as important. However, there may be other possible interpretations. Although we selected 9 different diagrams for the evaluation it could be that the diagrams did not vary enough for these criteria to be measured. Another explanation could be that these criteria were harder to judge for study participants.

Second, we recognize that further factors in the experimental materials (e.g. semantic quality of the diagrams) could have a deterring influence on the relationships that were investigated. However, in order to control for this possible threat to validity we had included nine different diagrams from different languages. In doing so, influences of external factors should be negligible. Nevertheless, future research could include even more diagrams and their evaluations to provide additional evidence.

Third, another limitation is that this study used a specific domain (instructional design) as a research object. Future research will have to take other domains into account to test the effects found in this study. Practitioners and modeling languages from other domains that have more (or less) tradition and affinity with visual modeling could be included.

Fourth, the selection of variables in the research model could further be extended and the influence or perception of quality characteristics on actual or intended use should be investigated in greater detail. Future research could examine additional variables—e.g. the perceived ease of use or actual use—to extend the research model we used.

6.2   Implications

The work presented in this paper carries implications for both research and practice.

For research streams investigating user attitudes and beliefs of conceptual modeling languages, our study adds to the current body of knowledge by investigating cognitive effectiveness criteria of modeling languages and their effect on perceived usefulness. Our results provide further indication into the importance of cognitive quality criteria of modeling languages as proposed by [7]. The results add to the growing body of analytical expert evaluations of modeling languages using this framework. Additionally, our work provides a first contribution on how to measure these quality criteria empirically through questionnaires.

From a practical viewpoint, the results reported here offer valuable suggestions for the design and construction of visual modeling languages. If adoption in practice is an objective (which it should be), efforts should not only be spent on the underlying basic concepts and constructs of the modeling language, but also on quality characteristics such as visual appearance and choice of symbols.

7 Conclusion

The study reported in this paper investigated the association of users' perception of quality criteria in visual modeling languages with their perceived usefulness. Based on Moody's criteria of cognitive effectiveness [7] we built a research model that enabled testing the effect of selected criteria on the perceived usefulness of visual modeling languages. The selection of criteria enables judgment of specific diagrams without requiring previous knowledge or expertise with the modeling language.

A set of 9 diagrams from 3 different visual instructional design languages was presented to study participants to judge. The results showed that four of the criteria included in the research model have a statistically significant positive influence on perceived usefulness. These are:

- Easy discrimination between different visual symbols (*perceptual discriminability*);
- Balance between high expressiveness and limited number of symbols (*graphic economy*);
- Balanced combination of textual and symbolic representations (*dual coding*);
- Absence of construct deficit, i.e. all relevant concepts are or can be represented in the modeling language (*semiotic clarity*).

These findings enable developers of visual modeling languages to propel the adoption by practitioners by considering the relevant criteria and thus improving the perceived usefulness of a language. This paper is intended as a contribution to raise awareness about and demonstrate the importance of cognitively effective design of visual conceptual modeling languages.

References

1. Gemino, A., Wand, Y.: A framework for empirical evaluation of conceptual modeling techniques. Requirements Engineering 9(4), 248–260 (2004)
2. Moody, D.L.: Theoretical and practical issues in evaluating the quality of conceptual models: Current state and future directions. Data and Knowledge Engineering 15(3), 243–276 (2005)
3. Boot, E.W., Nelson, J., van Merriënboer, J., Gibbons, A.S.: Stratification, elaboration, and formalization of design documents: Effects on the production of instructional materials. British Journal of Educational Technology 38(5), 917–933 (2007)
4. Hirschheim, R., Klein, H.K., Lyytinen, K.: Information Systems Development and Data Modeling: Conceptual and Philosophical Foundations. Cambridge University Press, Cambridge (1995)

5. Recker, J., Rosemann, M., Green, P., Indulska, M.: Do ontological deficiencies in modeling grammars matter. Management Information Systems Quarterly 35(1) (2011)
6. Sonderegger, A., Sauer, J.: The influence of design aesthetics in usability testing: Effects on user performance and perceived usability. Applied Ergonomics 41(3), 403–410 (2010)
7. Moody, D.L.: The physics of notations: Towards a scientific basis for constructing visual notations in software engineering. IEEE Transactions on Software Engineering 35(5), 756–779 (2009)
8. Moody, D.L., Heymans, P., Matulevicius, R.: Improving the effectiveness of visual representations in requirements engineering: An evaluation of i* visual syntax. In: Proceedings of the 17th IEEE International Requirements Engineering Conference, RE 2009, pp. 171–180. IEEE Computer Society, Washington, DC, USA (2009)
9. Moody, D., Hillegersberg, J.: Software Language Engineering, pp. 16–34. Springer, Heidelberg (2009)
10. Genon, N., Heymans, P., Amyot, D.: Analysing the cognitive effectiveness of the BPMN 2.0 visual notation. In: Malloy, B., Staab, S., van den Brand, M. (eds.) SLE 2010. LNCS, vol. 6563, pp. 377–396. Springer, Heidelberg (2011)
11. Figl, K., Mendling, J., Strembeck, M., Recker, J.: On the cognitive effectiveness of routing symbols in process modeling languages. In: Aalst, W., Mylopoulos, J., Rosemann, M., Shaw, M.J., Szyperski, C., Abramowicz, W., Tolksdorf, R. (eds.) BIS 2010. Lecture Notes in Business Information Processing, vol. 47, pp. 230–241. Springer, Heidelberg (2010)
12. Lave, J., Wenger, E.: Situated Learning: Legitimate Peripheral Participation. Cambridge University Press, Cambridge (1991)
13. Schön, D.: The Reflective Practitioner. How professionals think in action. Temple Smith, London, UK (1983)
14. Object Management Group: Unified Modeling Language (UML) 2.3 (2010), http://www.omg.org/spec/UML/2.3/
15. Cao, L., Ramesh, B., Rossi, M.: Are domain-specific models easier to maintain than uml models? IEEE Software 26(4), 19–21 (2009)
16. Clark, H.H., Brennan, S.E.: Grounding in communication. In: Resnick, L.B., Levine, J.M., Teasley, S.D. (eds.) Perspectives on Socially Shared Cognition, pp. 127–149. American Psychological Association, Hyattsville (1991)
17. Alexander, C., Ishikawa, S., Silverstein, M., Jacobson, M., Fiksdahl-King, I., Angel, S.: A Pattern Language - Towns, Buildings, Construction. Oxford University Press, New York (1977)
18. Gamma, E., Helm, R., Johnson, R.E., Vlissides, J.: Design patterns: Abstraction and reuse of object-oriented design. In: European Conference on Object-Oriented Programming (ECOOP), Kaiserslautern, Germany, pp. 406–431 (1993)
19. Derntl, M., Botturi, L.: Essential use cases for pedagogical patterns. Computer Science Education 16(2), 137–156 (2006)
20. Lindland, O.I., Sindre, G., Sølvberg, A.: Understanding quality in conceptual modeling. IEEE Softw. 11, 42–49 (1994)
21. Maes, A., Poels, G.: Evaluating quality of conceptual modelling scripts based on user perceptions. Data & Knowledge Engineering 63(3), 701–724 (2007)
22. Krogstie, J., Sindre, G., Jorgensen, H.D.: Process models representing knowledge for action: a revised quality framework. European Journal of Information Systems 15(1), 91–102 (2006)

23. Davis, F.D.: Perceived usefulness, perceived ease of use, and user acceptance of information technology. MIS Quarterly 13(3), 319–340 (1989)
24. Larkin, J.H., Simon, H.A.: Why a diagram is (sometimes) worth ten thousand words. Cognitive Science 11(1), 65–100 (1987)
25. McDougall, S.J.P., Curry, M.B., Bruijn, O.D.: Measuring symbol and icon characteristics: Norms for concreteness, complexity, meaningfulness, familiarity, and semantic distance for 239 symbols. Behavior Research Methods, Instruments, & Computers 31(3), 487–519 (1999)
26. Kelly, S., Pohjonen, R.: Worst practices for domain-specific modeling. IEEE Software 26(4), 22–29 (2009)
27. Derntl, M., Parrish, P., Botturi, L.: Beauty and precision: Weaving complex educational technology projects with visual instructional design languages. International Journal on E-Learning 9(2), 185–202 (2010)
28. Gibbons, A.S., Brewer, E.: Elementary principles of design languages and design notation systems for instructional design. In: Spector, M., Wiley, D. (eds.) Innovations to Instructional Technology: Essays in Honor, Lawrence Erlbaum, New Jersey (2004)
29. Rawlings, A., van Rosmalen, P., Koper, R., , M., Rodrguez Artacho, M., Lefrere, P.: Cen/isss ws/lt learning technologies workshop - survey of educational modelling languages (emls) (2002), http://www.eifel.org/publications/standards/elearning-standard/cenissslt/emlsurvey
30. Botturi, L.: E^2ML: A visual language for the design of instruction. Educational Technology Research and Development 54(3), 265–293 (2006)
31. Caeiro-Rodríguez, M.: PoEML: A separation-of-concerns proposal to Instructional Design. In: Botturi, L., Stubbs, T. (eds.) Handbook of Visual Languages in Instructional Design: Theories and Practices, pp. 185–209. Information Science Reference, Hershey (2008)
32. Derntl, M., Motschnig-Pitrik, R.: coUML – A Visual Language for Modeling Cooperative Environments. In: Botturi, L., Stubbs, T. (eds.) Handbook of Visual Languages for Instructional Design: Theories and Practices, pp. 155–184. Information Science Reference, Hershey (2008)

Appendix: Questionnaire

- What is your age? (__ years)
- What is your gender? (Male/Female)
- What is your main role in the context of instructional design? (Instructor/E-learning support team of a university/Instructional design support of a university/Researcher in the context of instructional design)
- In the creation of how many different instructional designs (e.g. courses) have you already been involved? (__ instructional designs)

Instruction: "Please take a look at the following instructional design models and answer the questions based on these models! Details of the model content are less important as the models are only examples!"

The 9 different diagrams were shown as depicted in Fig. 2 followed by these questions:

- Dimension: **Perceptual Discriminability** (Cronbach's $\alpha = .956$)
  - There are symbols that are difficult to differentiate.
  - There are symbols that can easily be confused with each other.
- Dimension: **Graphic Economy** (Cronbach's $\alpha = .904$)
  - The diagram is difficult to understand due to the large number of symbols.
  - I think the amount of different symbols should be reduced.
- Dimension: **Dual Coding** (Cronbach's $\alpha = .846$)
  - The combination of text and symbols makes the diagram type easier to understand.
  - Textual annotations improve understanding of the diagram type.
- Dimension: **Visual Expressiveness** (Cronbach's $\alpha = .597$)
  - The visual expressiveness of the symbols should be increased by variation of color, size, form or brightness.
  - I perceive the symbols as visually expressive.
- Dimension: **Semantic Transparency** (Cronbach's $\alpha = .924$)
  - The symbols are intuitively understandable.
  - Even without explanation it is clear what the symbols represent.
- Dimension: **Semiotic Clarity** (adapted from [5]) (Cronbach's $\alpha = .223$)
  - Construct deficit - The diagram type could be made more complete by adding new symbols to represent relevant real-world phenomena of instructional design.
  - Construct excess - There are symbols that do not represent any relevant real-world phenomena of instructional design.
- Dimension: **Perceived Usefulness** (adapted from [21]) (Cronbach's $\alpha = .930$)
  - Overall, I think the diagram improves my performance when understanding the instructional design.
  - Overall, I found the diagram useful for understanding the instructional design.
  - Overall, I think the diagram would be an improvement to a textual description of the instructional design.

Effects of External Conceptual Models and Verbal Explanations on Shared Understanding in Small Groups

Wolfgang Maass[1,3], Veda C. Storey[2], and Tobias Kowatsch[3]

[1] Saarland University, 66123 Saarbrücken, Germany
[2] University Plaza, Georgia State University, Atlanta 30399 United States
[3] Institute of Technology Management (ITEM), University of St. Gallen, Switzerland
`wolfgang.maass@iss.uni-saarland.de, vstorey@gsu.edu,`
`tobias.kowatsch@unisg.ch`

Abstract. Effective conceptual modeling requires a shared understanding of the concepts that are found in an application domain. Achieving such understanding, especially for large design problems, is a challenging, and long-standing problem. Conceptual models tend to be either subjective representations of individuals that require mutual knowledge sharing between members of a modeling team or externalized normative representations that require knowledge transfer from model preceptors to model receptors. Model preceptors have either created a conceptual model or conceived it by another preceptor. In prior studies, normative conceptual models were used to investigate knowledge transfer between preceptors and receptors. This research, in contrast, investigates knowledge transfer of conceptual models between model owners and receptors. A 2x2 study design with modeling novices was used that varied the type of conceptual modeling language and the type of information system. Further testing investigated whether knowledge transfers were affected by additional verbal explanations given by the preceptor. Each modeler was provided access to two conceptual modeling languages that naturally support structure or process representations. The study investigated whether the use of particular conceptual modeling languages differ in their effects on shared understanding between two persons and whether additional verbal explanations might increase shared understanding. The results of this exploratory empirical study provide useful insights into the use of Conceptual Modeling Language pairs for shared understanding in conceptual modeling in small groups.

1 Introduction

The conceptual modeling phase of systems development involves the process of abstracting the real world to represent it by a model that focuses on key entities and relationships of an application domain [1]. Conceptual models that accurately represent an application domain provide a critical means for shared understanding in an information system development team [2, 3]. A long-standing challenge in information systems research is that many information systems projects fail either completely or partially [2, 4]. Prior studies have concluded that mis-understanding between team members is one of the key issues for such failures [5, 6]. People from

M. Jeusfeld, L. Delcambre, and T.W. Ling (Eds.): ER 2011, LNCS 6998, pp. 92–103, 2011.

different departments use incompatible languages for expressing their ideas and understandings of the envisioned information system [7]. Software engineers, for example, use UML tools, database modelers use ER diagrams; graphical designers are accustomed to scribbles and storyboards; and people from marketing use textual descriptions on customer relationship measurements.

There have been few empirical studies on understanding these communication problems in terms of the social processes associated with conceptual modeling [2]. Little empirical research has been conducted that examines how different conceptual modeling languages (CML) support shared understandings within modeling teams. Instead, researchers have focused on how normative conceptual models represented by a particular CML support individual understanding of a conceptual model (CM) [3]. In such studies, CMs were created and evaluated by modeling experts. In practice, however, CMs are rarely created by modeling experts; rather, they are created quite loosely for transferring individual understandings of a subjective CM to another team member. It is an open research question as to how non-experts use various CML for creating CMs and then use these CMs for creating a shared understanding with other non-experts.

The objective of our exploratory research is to examine the subjective side of understanding the conceptual modeling process with emphasis on supporting shared understanding amongst information systems non-expert modelers. To do so, an empirical analysis is carried out on small groups participating in a design task. The contribution of the research is to understand whether (and how) different types of CML with additional verbal explanations can assist small groups of non-experts in a shared understanding of domain concepts in order to create effective conceptual models.

2 Theoretical Background

2.1 Conceptual Models

A conceptual model expresses the meaning of terms and concepts used by domain experts to discuss a design problem, and to identify the relationships among different concepts [8]. The conceptual modeling phase of information systems development is intended to clarify the meaning of various terms, and to ensure that problems with different interpretations do not occur. The conceptual model is mapped into the physical design for implementation. It is, thus, important that conceptual models are well defined and represent the essence of an application domain. A conceptual model can be described using various notations, such as UML or OMT for object modeling, or IE or IDEF1X for entity-relationship models [9].

Regardless of the notation, it is crucial that the essence of the domain be accurately captured. The process involved in conceptual modeling involves collaboration between requirements engineering (RE) participants (e.g., user-representatives and systems analysts) where knowledge regarding the system requirements is shared, absorbed, and constructed. The main challenge of the collaborative interaction is for the participants to arrive at a shared frame of reference and conceptualization regarding system requirements. This requires understanding the process of "collaborative sense-making and knowledge transfer that results in the convergence of diverse mental models" [2]. Conceptual models are complex knowledge structures that can be normative versus subjective; semi-formal versus formal, external (documented) versus internal (mental) representations; and individual understanding and mental models versus cross understanding and shared understanding.

Several CML have been proposed that focus on (1) business process modeling (e.g., [10]), (2) general software engineering (e.g., [11]), (3) semantic data models (e.g., [12]), and meta-data models and computational ontologies [13]. Grammars provided by CMLs require ontologies for defining the fundamental entities and structures that should be focused by CMs [14].

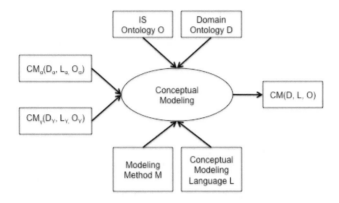

Fig. 1. Generic model of conceptual modeling

Figure 1 provides a generic model for conceptual modeling. In an idealized form, conceptual modeling transforms existing external or internal CMs into an integrated CM(D, L, O), by means of a modeling method M and a conceptual language L based on a domain ontology D and a fundamental information systems ontology O.

Initially a CM is a subjective conceptualization of a domain created by an individual, also called a mental model [15]. By explication processes and a CM language (CML), an individual translates his/her subjective CM into an external CM. CML support informal, semi-formal, or formal representations. External conceptual models are either used in knowledge transfers or knowledge sharing activities. Knowledge transfer situations are governed by principal-agent settings between preceptors and receptors and thus use external CM in a normative manner. Normative CMs are either explained to receptors by the creator of this external CM or by trained preceptors. In the latter case, the external CM supports indirect knowledge transfers. If knowledge transfers are based on a normative CM alone, it will support individual understanding of an objective conceptualization whereas a receptor's understanding of the creator's model must be derived by additional reasoning. Indirect knowledge transfers of normative conceptual models without additional explanations by preceptors has been the core focus of empirical studies (e.g., [16]).

It could be argued that additional explanations given by a preceptor might provide additional cues that allow receptors to directly gain an understanding of the creator's subjective CM. Davidson argues that the theoretic assumption of knowledge transfers based on normative CMs contradict the reality of requirements elicitation, often described as "chaotic and non-linear" [17] and non-deterministic [2]. This means that external CM are not isolated but embedded into a communication discourse between various members of a group. Because conceptual models based on current CML are static descriptions, it is reasonable to expect that, at least for some domains and organizational settings, knowledge transfers can be improved by additional verbal explanations and discussions.

2.2 Design and Mental Models

Based on a representational theory of the mind [18], the concept of an individual mental model has been introduced that represents models of real-world or idealistic situations. Mental models are representations that are formed by individuals as internal descriptions of perceived and imagined situations [19]. For representations of perceived situations, mental models are conceived as model representations of external realities that can be used for mental processing such as mental rotations [20, 21]. During the design phases of an Information System, an internal CM is a mental model that cannot be derived by direct perception but from auxiliary descriptions such as narratives and diagrams. For framing the general problem during early design stages, narratives are more helpful representations for qualitative and ambiguous descriptions than graphics [22]. However, diagrammatic representations are very helpful during later design phases. Therefore, we assume that external CMs in the form of narratives are used early for conceiving a basic internal CM that can be enhanced by subsequently given diagrammatic CM.

2.3 Shared Understanding

Shared understanding should help to produce a better CM, by helping the people involved in the design realize a shared mental model, i.e. similar individual mental models [23]. This is especially important in designs that require a group effort in the requirements analysis and conceptual modeling phases. Group performance, in general, depends on interactions between group members for choosing goals and objectives, selecting solutions to achieve the group's goals, resolving conflicts, and performing activities that help to achieve group tasks [24]. These interactions require communication between group members that are intended to promote group behavior [25]. In the requirements elicitation phase, textual and diagrammatic CML have been created that facilitate communication and subsequent shared understanding by building shared mental models between members of a design team [2, 3].

Effective group performance requires that groups hold common or overlapping mental representations (referred to as shared mental models or team mental models), of goals, task requirements, procedures, role responsibilities, and situations [23]. Shared experience and information is the basis for further information sharing and, thus, strengthens understanding and collaboration within a team [26]. With respect to requirements engineering, shared mental models are mental representations of a conceptual model that are assumed by group members to be mutually agreed upon and used as a basis for group behavior, such as consensus building, problem solving, decision making, and inferencing [27, 28].

3 Research Model and Hypotheses

In the following, we describe an exploratory study that investigates the effects of different conceptual modeling languages (CMLs) on individual and shared understanding in small information systems (IS) design groups. By adopting a non-normative stance, we also investigate the role of CML for knowledge transfer between team members.

The key questions addressed are:

− How do different CML affect individual understanding and shared understanding?
− How do textual explanations of external CM affect individual and shared understanding?
− Is shared understanding on CM affected by different types of information systems?

Our study is framed by the following constraints:

− How do external conceptual models support a shared understanding in non-normative situations with low heterogeneity of prior modeling knowledge between members of small teams?
− How do additional verbal explanations affect this shared understanding (same moderating factors).

4 Research Method

This research tests 'surface understanding' [16] in the sense of shared understanding. If shared understanding is missing, problem-solving is not possible. An external conceptual model is not tested because the study is intended to test how CM and explanations affect knowledge transfers in a small team from an originating modeler to a model user. Otherwise, we would need to test how a normative, objective CM would be explained by one person to another.

4.1 Study Design

A laboratory experiment with two-person teams was carried out to investigate our research questions. Each subject was given one of the following two situations representing different types of IS, i.e. one Online IS and one Ubiquitous IS:

− Online IS: Michael is overweight and suffers from hazelnut allergy. Today he wants to order at his preferred online restaurant FirstMeal that supports him during his diet program. Due to his profile a series of salads and several vegetarian dishes, including such vegetarian pizza and potato dishes, are proposed. He opts for a vegetarian pizza and chooses an additional tofu topping from a list. Because he has met his last week's training program, he is awarded to choose a complimentary dessert from a menu. He opts for a smoothie with mango-coconut flavor from the category of lactose-free desserts.

– Ubiquitous IS: Anna gets site-specific weather information when she is brushing her teeth in the bathroom. Based on weather information and her calendar, free-time event suggestions are given, e.g. "Today, 8 p.m. - Miss Marple Night at CinemaOne. Do you want to order tickets?"

With ubiquitous computing technologies [29], information services can be integrated in any kind of physical environment and provide information to users when they enter these environments. These technologies provide the basis for the class of information systems, called ubiquitous information systems [30], that support individual users and groups by providing information and communication services adapted to dynamically changing situations and user needs. Ubiquitous information systems are appropriate to include because of the increase in ubiquitous computing, emphasis on inter-organizational applications, and demands for shorter project life-cycles which have introduced new techniques and changed the risk profile of requirements development project [31].

To develop an external model of these situations, two conceptual modeling languages (CML) were introduced to the subjects. The first CML combines ontologies and UML activity diagrams, both of which are denoted as CML1. On one hand, ontology describes subsumptions and other relationships between concepts, i.e. it reflects explicitly formal specifications of the terms in the domain of question and relationships among them [32]. Sharing common understanding of the structure of information among people or software agents is one of the more common goals in developing ontologies [32, 33]. On the other hand, UML activity diagrams describe interactions between instances of concepts over time that are also called workflows (cf. OMG 2011, http://www.uml.org).

The second CML combines the notations of UML use case diagrams and sequence diagrams. This combination is denoted as CML2. UML use cases show a set of use cases and actors with an association between each interacting pair of actor and use case [34]. In contrast, a UML sequence diagram shows how messages within an IS are exchanged by considering the order of interactions (cf. OMG 2011, http://www.uml.org). Both CMLs have been selected as they provide a tool to model: (1) general structures and static relations of an IS (Ontology and UML use case diagram notations); and (2) workflows within an IS (UML activity diagrams and UML sequence diagrams).

The study was carried out in three steps. First, both subjects were asked to model one IS from one of the two situations with a given CML separately. To account for the bias that would appear from a static IS-CML combination, subjects in a team were assigned to crosswise different IS-CML combinations. Each subject was given a short introduction to the corresponding CML and exemplary diagrams were presented. By this procedure, each subject was able to become accustomed to the assigned CML. Then, each subject was allowed 30 minutes to develop an external model of the assigned situation with pen and paper. In the second step of the survey, each subject had to evaluate the teammate's model without any further explanations with regard to unambiguity, consistency and understandability of the model. These constructs were derived from [35] and corresponding questionnaire items have been created (cf. Table 2).

In the third and final step of the survey, each subject had to explain his or her own model in no more than five minutes to his or her teammate. Then, again, each subject had to evaluate the teammate's model with regard to the items given in Table 2. In addition to demographical data, two constructs were also measured during this step: first, the extrinsic power of a CML for an individual understanding of the future IS regarding the given situation and second, the extrinsic power of a CML for a shared (team) understanding. In summary, the experimental design is shown in Table 1 and the questionnaire items are given in Table 2. All questionnaire items were rated on 7-point Likert scales ranging from strongly disagree (1) to strongly agree (7).

Table 1. Study design. Note: 34 subjects were randomly assigned to the four groups

		Type of Information System	
		Online IS	**Ubiquitous IS**
Type of Conceptual Modeling Language (CML)	**CML1:** Ontology & UML activity diagram	Group 1 (n=9)	Group 2 (n=9)
	CML2: UML use case diagram & sequence diagram	Group 3 (n=8)	Group 4 (n=8)

4.2 Results and Discussion

Ten female and 24 male students from a media informatics department participated in the lab experiment. Their age ranged between 19 and 24 (n=25) and between 25 and 29 (n=6). Three subjects were over 30. The subjects understood the semantics and practical application of the CMLs (Mean: 5.76; SD: .89) and judged themselves to be competent in evaluating the corresponding external conceptual models (Mean: 5.32; SD: 1.06). Overall, the instructions of the study have been understood (Mean: 5.53; SD: .89) and the length of the study was perceived acceptable (Mean: 4.26; SD: 1.56). The descriptive statistics of all constructs are presented in Table 2.

Paired-sample t-tests were used to identify any significant differences of evaluations before and after an explanation was provided regarding one particular external CM. The results indicate that explanations significantly increased comprehensibility of the external CMs for both types of information systems (cf. COM5-9 in Table 2).

Furthermore, high mean values on unambiguity and comprehensibility indicate that the subjects perceived the provided CM as a sufficient basis for deriving an internal CM of high quality. With respect to consistency, no significant change was found when test persons received additional explanations. For consistency, in general, it can be argued that structural and process elements are well captured by Use cases / sequence diagrams and ontologies / activity diagrams alike. Only for Ubiquitous IS and CML2 (UML use case diagrams & sequence diagram) was the consistency of the external CMs judged higher after the explanation (cf. CON4/6/8 in Table 2). This could be explained by deficiencies of use case diagrams / sequence diagrams with respect to modeling domains for UIS.

Table 2. Instrument and descriptive statistics. Note: SD = standard deviation, MO = Model Only, M+E = Model + Explanation, Situation 1 = Online IS, Situation 2 = Ubiquitous IS; */** = .05/.01 significance levels for paired-sample t-test (MO versus M+E).

Construct	Mean (SD) MO	Mean (SD) M+E
Unambiguity: I think this model of type [CML1/2] accurately represents Situation [1/2].		
UNA1: CML1 + Online IS (n=9)	6.11 (0.60)	5.78 (1.20)
UNA2: CML1 + Ubiquitous IS (n=9)	6.00 (1.00)	6.22 (0.44)
UNA3: CML2 + Online IS (n=8)	5.75 (0.89)	5.87 (0.64)
UNA4: CML2 + Ubiquitous IS (n=8)	5.63 (1.06)	6.00 (0.00)
UNA5: Total CML1 (n=18)	6.06 (0.80)	6.00 (0.91)
UNA6: Total CML2 (n=16)	5.69 (0.95)	5.94 (0.44)
UNA7: Total Online IS (n=17)	5.94 (0.75)	5.82 (0.95)
UNA8: Total Ubiquitous IS (n=17)	5.82 (1.02)	6.12 (0.33)
UNA9: Total (n=34)	**5.88 (0.88)**	**5.97 (0.72)**
Consistency: I think that this model of type [CML1/2] is consistent as such with regard to Situation [1/2].		
CON1: CML1 + Online IS (n=9)	5.78 (0.67)	5.67 (1.00)
CON2: CML1 + Ubiquitous IS (n=9)	5.78 (1.20)	6.22 (0.83)
CON3: CML2 + Online IS (n=8)	5.38 (1.41)	5.50 (1.93)
CON4: CML2 + Ubiquitous IS (n=8)	5.13 (0.84)	5.75 (1.04)*
CON5: Total CML1 (n=18)	5.78 (0.94)	5.94 (0.94)
CON6: Total CML2 (n=16)	5.25 (1.13)	5.62 (1.50)*
CON7: Total Online IS (n=17)	5.59 (1.06)	5.59 (1.46)
CON8: Total Ubiquitous IS (n=17)	5.47 (1.07)	6.00 (0.94)*
CON9: Total (n=34)	**5.53 (1.05)**	**5.79 (1.23)**
Comprehensibility: I think this model of type [CML1/2] is easy to understand with regard to Situation [1/2].		
COM1: CML1 + Online IS (n=9)	6.11 (0.78)	6.44 (0.73)
COM2: CML1 + Ubiquitous IS (n=9)	6.11 (1.67)	6.67 (0.50)
COM3: CML2 + Online IS (n=8)	6.25 (0.71)	6.63 (0.74)
COM4: CML2 + Ubiquitous IS (n=8)	5.75 (1.39)	6.63 (0.52)
COM5: Total CML1 (n=18)	6.11 (0.96)	6.56 (0.62)*
COM6: Total CML2 (n=16)	6.00 (1.01)	6.63 (0.62)*
COM7: Total Online IS (n=17)	6.18 (0.73)	6.53 (0.72)*
COM8: Total Ubiquitous IS (n=17)	5.94 (1.25)	6.65 (0.49)*
COM9: Total (n=34)	**6.06 (1.01)**	**6.59 (0.61)****
Extrinsic power of CML for individual understanding (EPIU): I think that this model of type [CML1/2] made it easy for me to create an individual understanding of the conceptual model regarding Situation [1/2].		
EPIU1: CML1 + Online IS (n=9)		5.78 (0.67)
EPIU2: CML1 + Ubiquitous IS (n=9)		5.56 (1.88)
EPIU3: CML2 + Online IS (n=8)		5.87 (0.64)
EPIU4: CML2 + Ubiquitous IS (n=8)		4.88 (2.03)

Table 2. (*Continued*)

EPIU5: Total CML1 (n=18)	5.67 (1.37)
EPIU6: Total CML2 (n=16)	5.38 (1.54)
EPIU7: Total Online IS (n=17)	5.82 (0.64)
EPIU8: Total Ubiquitous IS (n=17)	5.24 (1.92)
EPIU9: Total (n=34)	**5.53 (1.44)**

Extrinsic power of CML for a shared (team) understanding (EPSU): I think that, in general, the external conceptual model of type [CML1/2] supports a shared understanding in our team with respect to Situation [1/2].

EPSU1: CML1 + Online IS (n=9)	5.78 (0.97)
EPSU2: CML1 + Ubiquitous IS (n=9)	6.44 (0.53)
EPSU3: CML2 + Online IS (n=8)	5.63 (1.41)
EPSU4: CML2 + Ubiquitous IS (n=8)	6.25 (1.17)
EPSU5: Total CML1 (n=18)	6.11 (0.83)
EPSU6: Total CML2 (n=16)	5.94 (1.29)
EPSU7: Total Online IS (n=17)	5.71 (1.16)
EPSU8: Total Ubiquitous IS (n=17)	6.35 (0.86)
EPSU9: Total (n=34)	**6.03 (1.06)**

No effects can be found for unambiguity. However the subjects were confident that all CMs for all CMLs represent target situations on a high level. Further research is required to assess whether this confidence is stable or whether it is related to a lack of modeling experience. Nonetheless reassurance after receiving an explanation might indicate stable confidence. The mean value (5.53) for the extrinsic power of CML for individual understanding (EPIU) shows that all models are perceived important for creating internal conceptual models. Only use case diagrams / sequence diagrams provide less support. However, it might indicate that internal CM extracts structural information on concepts and relationships from an originating external CM but loses direct links to the external CM itself. This complex relationship requires further research.

By conducting an analysis of variance, we could not find any significant differences with regard to the extrinsic power of a CML for individual or shared (team) understanding by varying the factors CML and the type of IS. Thus, type of IS and CML as used in the current study have not influenced the extrinsic power of a CML for individual understanding or for a shared (team) understanding. However, mean values show differences for individual and shared understanding (EPIU9 and EPSU9) that are significant at the .06 level by applying a paired-sample t-test. This could be explained by different metrics that are used for the internal CM and shared understanding between team members. For individual CM a test person seems to have higher requirements than for shared understandings.

The overall high mean values for all variables are surprising because all test persons were modeling novices. No significant differences were found for the CML with ontologies / activity diagrams compared to the CML with use cases / sequence diagrams. This is unexpected because ontologies can be considered rather new tools for conceptual modeling. In contrast, CM based on use cases diagrams / sequence diagrams were significantly improved by explanations with respect to consistency and comprehensibility. CM represented by ontologies / activity diagrams did not gain from explanations for consistency but for comprehensibility only. Furthermore, comprehensibility of both types of CM for both IS types are significantly improved by verbal explanations. In summary, it can be argued that advantages exist of some CML types for particular types of IS (e.g., CML1 - UIS). Differences between extrinsic power of CML combinations for individual and shared understanding indicate that CML play different roles on individual and group levels. A tentative conclusion is that it is not important which grammar is used as long as it provides basic diagrammatic elements. This complex relationship between models and conceptual models needs further in-depth studies.

5 Summary

This research has investigated how conceptual modeling languages enhanced with verbal explanations can affect shared understanding of conceptual models between members of non-expert design teams. An empirical study was carried out in which two types of information systems (online and ubiquitous) were tested to assess whether narratives and diagrammatic conceptual modeling languages could provide rich information so that individuals would perceive them as being unambiguous, consistent, and comprehensible.

This research is one response to the need for empirical research on topics related to conceptual modeling [3]. However, further research involving field studies are required to demonstrate the application of the results to real world requirements engineering work. This study also raises further research questions; for example, would similar effects be found for expert groups. Further research is also required to expand the study to include formal ontology representation tools.

References

1. Stachowiak, H.: Allgemeine Modelltheorie. Springer, Heidelberg (1973)
2. Chakraborty, S., Sarker, S., Sarker, S.: An Exploration into the Process of Requirements Elicitation: A Grounded Approach. J. Assoc. Inf. Syst. 11, 212–249 (2010)
3. Burton-Jones, A., Meso, P.: The Effects of Decomposition Quality and Multiple Forms of Information on Novices' Understanding of a Domain from a Conceptual Model. J. Assoc. Inf. Syst. 9, 748–802 (2008)
4. CIO Update, http://www.cioupdate.com/insights/article.php/3813646/Why-Software-Development-Projects-Fail-Part-IV-Release.htm
5. Vlaar, P., van Fenema, P., Tiwari, V.: Cocreating Understanding and Value in Distributed Work: How Members of Onsite and Offshore Vendor Teams Give, Make, Demand, and Break Sense. Mis Quart. 32, 227–255 (2008)
6. Lin, L., Geng, X., Whinston, A.: A Sender-Receiver Framework for Knowledge Transfer. Mis Quart. 29, 197–219 (2005)

7. Urquhart, C.: Exploring Analyst-Client Communication: Using Grounded Theory Techniques to Investigate Interaction in Informal Requirements Gathering. In: Lee, A., Liebenau, J., DeGross, J. (eds.) Information Systems and Qualitative Research, pp. 149–181. Chapman & Hall, London (1997)

8. Wand, Y., Storey, V.C., Weber, R.: Analyzing the Meaning of a Relationship. ACM Trans. Database Systems 24, 494–528 (1999)

9. Fowler, M.: Analysis Patterns, Reusable Object Models. Addison-Wesley, Longman, Amsterdam (1997)

10. Scheer, A.-W.: ARIS. Modellierungsmethoden, Metamodelle, Anwendungen. Springer, Berlin (1998)

11. Booch, G., Rambaugh, J., et al.: The Unified Modeling Language User Guide. Addision-Wesley, Redwood City (1999)

12. Chen, P.: The Entity-Relationship Model–Toward a Unified View of Data. ACM Transactions on Database Systems 1, 9–36 (1976)

13. Bera, P., Krasnoperova, A., Wand, Y.: Using Ontology Languages for Conceptual Modeling. Journal of Database Management 21, 1–28 (2010)

14. Wand, Y., Monarchi, D., Parsons, J., Woo, C.: Theoretical foundations for conceptual modelling in information systems development. Decis Support Syst. 15, 285–304 (1995)

15. Storey, V.C., Fracchia, F., Müller, H.: Cognitive design elements to support the construction of a mental model during software exploration. Journal of Systems and Software 44, 171–185 (1999)

16. Burton-Jones, A., Meso, P.: Conceptualizing Systems for Understanding: An Empirical Test of Decomposition Principles in Object-Oriented Analysis. Inform. Syst. Res. 17, 38–60 (2006)

17. Davidson, E.J.: Technology Frames and Framing: A Socio-Cognitive Investigation of Requirements Determination. Mis Quart. 26, 329–358 (2002)

18. Fodor, J.A., Pylyshyn, Z.W.: Connectionism and Cognitive Architecture: A Critical Analysis. In: Pinker, S., Mehler, J. (eds.) Connections and Symbols, pp. 3–71. MIT Press, Cambridge (1988)

19. Gentner, D., Stevens, A.L.: Mental Models. Lawrence Erlbaum Associates, Hillsdale (1983)

20. Kosslyn, S.M.: Image and Mind. Harvard University Press, Cambridge (1980)

21. Shepard, R.N., Metzler, J.: Mental rotation of three-dimensional objects. Science 171, 701–703 (1971)

22. Kuechler, W., Vaishnavi, V.: On theory development in design science research: anatomy of a research project. Eur. J. Inform. Syst. 17, 489–504 (2008)

23. Cannon-Bowers, J.A., Salas, E., Converse, S.: Shared mental models in expert team decision making. In: Castellan, N.J. (ed.) Individual and Group Decision Making, pp. 221–246. Lawrence Erlbaum Associates, Hillsdale (1993)

24. McGrath, J.E.: Groups: Interaction and Performance. Prentice-Hall, Englewood Cliffs (1984)

25. Habermas, J.: The Theory of Communicative Action, Reason and the Rationalization of Society, vol. 1. Heinemann, London (1984)

26. Wittenbaum, G.M.: Putting communication into the study of group memory. Human Communication Research 29, 612–623 (2003)

27. Rasker, P., Post, W., Schraagen, J.: Effects of two types of intra-team feedback on developing a shared mental model in Command & Control teams. Ergonomics 43, 1167–1189 (2000)

28. Stout, R.J., Cannon-Bowers, J.A., Salas, E., Milanovich, D.: Planning, shared mental models, and coordinated performance: An empirical link is established. Human Factors 41, 61–71 (1999)
29. Lyytinen, K., Yoo, Y.: Issues and Challenges in Ubiquitous Computing. Communication of the ACM 45, 62–65 (2002)
30. Maass, W., Janzen, S.: Pattern-based approach for designing with diagrammatic and propositional conceptual models. In: Jain, H., Sinha, A.P., Vitharana, P. (eds.) DESRIST 2011. LNCS, vol. 6629, pp. 192–206. Springer, Heidelberg (2011)
31. Mathiassen, L., Tuunanen, T., Saarinen, T., Rossi, M.: A Contingency Model for Requirements Development. Journal of the Assoication for Information Systems 8, 569–597 (2007)
32. Gruber, T.R.: A translation approach to portable ontologies. Knowledge Acquisition 5, 199–220 (1993)
33. Noy, N.F., McGuinness, D.L.: Ontology Development 101: A Guide to Creating Your First Ontology. Technical Report and Stanford Medical Informatics Technical Report SMI-2001-0880, Stanford Knowledge Systems Laboratory (2001)
34. Cockburn, A.: Writing effective use cases. Addison-Wesley, Upper Saddle River (2001)
35. Fettke, P.: How Conceptual Modeling Is Used. Communications of the Association for Information Systems 25, 571–592 (2009)

Sociotechnical Trust: An Architectural Approach

Amit K. Chopra, Elda Paja, and Paolo Giorgini

Department of Information Engineering and Computer Science,
University of Trento, Italy
{chopra,paja,paolo.giorgini}@disi.unitn.it

Abstract. Current approaches in sociotechnical systems consider trust to be either *cognitive*—referring to actors' mental models of each other—or *technical*—referring to an actor's trust of a technical artifact. In this paper, we take a more expansive view of trust: in addition to the cognitive, we also consider trust in the *architectural* sense. Broadly, architectural trust applies at the level of roles. Our principal claim is that sociotechnical systems are essentially specified in terms of architectural trust. Whereas previous work has considered dependencies between actors as a fundamental social relation, we claim that no dependency can exist without the corresponding architectural trust.

1 Introduction

Sociotechnical Systems (STS) are complex: they consist of humans, organizations, and their information systems. While STS have been around for a while, sociotechnical approaches to building such systems are still in their infancy. Traditional approaches to building information systems focus solely on operational aspects; sociotechnical approaches would require taking into account even the social relationships among the actors involved. One of the key challenges in software engineering is coming up with the right abstractions for modeling sociotechnical systems. Various high-level models for STS have been proposed—for example, intentional [3], goal-oriented [19], based on responsibility [18], and so on.

In this paper, we propose *sociotechnical trust* as the fundamental social relationship among actors of an STS. When we say *sociotechnical trust*, we refer to the trustworthiness of an STS. Our key intuition is that STS are organized along trust relationships. Any STS exists in the first place because actors are not omnipotent; they necessarily depend on each other to get things done. It is trust that makes dependence on others reasonable. When an actor trusts another for something, it expects the latter to do that thing. Lacking such a trust relationship, an actor can hardly depend on another for anything. We want to make explicit these trust relationships in order to provide prospective participants with information regarding the dependencies they would have upon the STS in case they decide to interact with it. For example, let's consider a healthcare STS. Alice would not make a payment to ModernLabs if she did not trust that ModernLabs would deliver test results if she paid. We use the notation T(Alice, ModernLabs, paid, delivered) to mean that Alice trusts ModernLabs to deliver the results if she has paid for the tests.

This paper is about the engineering of *sociotechnical trust*: how should we design an STS so that it *ensures* trust relationships such as the above between Alice and

M. Jeusfeld, L. Delcambre, and T.W. Ling (Eds.): ER 2011, LNCS 6998, pp. 104–117, 2011.

ModernLabs in the healthcare STS? Ensuring means that we want this relationship to hold not only between Alice and ModernLabs, but between every patient-laboratory pair relationship participating in the healthcare STS. In other words, the trust relationship has to be somehow encoded into the architecture of the STS irrespective of individual actors. Hence, we refer to such trust relationships as *architectural*.

Further, we want to be able to compare two STS in a particular domain, and be able to objectively say which STS fares better from the trust perspective. For example, all other things being equal, one could objectively say that the healthcare system which encodes the above trust relationship between patients and laboratories is better for (all) patients than the system without. Objectively means that anyone, even someone who has no intention or need of participating in the STS being compared, would come to the same conclusion.

We make such comparisons all the time in our day to day lives. For example, we intuitively know that from a customer's point of view, an online marketplace that mandates that merchants refund customers for returned products within a month of purchase is better than one that does not allow such returns; the customers trust the merchants more in the former. It is the same reason why we deem credit card holders to be better off in the credit card system resulting from the passage of the Credit Card Act of 2009 [1]—in the new system, credit card holders now trust that banks will not arbitrarily raise interest rates, and so on. This paper explores the computational basis behind such intuitions.

Contributions. Singh proposed the notion of architectural trust [17]; our contributions are in applying this notion to the engineering of STS, for which we coin the term *sociotechnical trust.*

- We characterize the notion of what it means for an STS to ensure more trust than another. We do this via the notion of one trust relationship *supporting* another trust relationship. We give a computational grounding for sociotechnical trust in terms of communication (commitments). Our conceptual model enables one to claim if one system is more trustworthy than another from a particular role's perspective.
- We show the notion of sociotechnical trust to be different from cognitive or technical trust, two kinds of trust relationships commonly modeled in STS software engineering.
- We evaluate our approach through a case study on European food safety law (understood as an STS for ensuring food safety)

Organization. The rest of the paper is organized as follows. Section 2 introduces a conceptual model of sociotechnical trust, discussing the computational grounding of trust connectors in terms of commitments. It also discusses what it means to objectively compare STS from a trust perspective, presenting as well a notation for representing the system. Section 3 discusses how sociotechnical trust is different from the prevalent notions of trust and places them all in a single framework. Section 4 evaluates our approach against a case study from the European food safety law. Section 5 concludes the paper with a survey of the literature and future directions.

2   A Conceptual Model of Sociotechnical Trust

Our conceptual model emphasizes the social entities abstracted away as roles and the trust relationships among them. In contrast to other approaches in the literature, our conceptual model is notable in that it does not rely upon intentional—varying from actor to actor—concepts such as goals, capabilities, risk, and so on.

Following [6], we conceptualize an STS system as a specification of trust relationships with reference to roles, not particular actors. Individual actors, perhaps completely unknown at the time of the design of STS, would adopt roles in an STS depending on their business requirements and constraints.

Our idea of a *sociotechnical system* is that of a set of roles and the trust relationships that hold between them. Formally, let ϕ be a set of symbols. Let $\mathcal{P}$ be the set of all propositions over ϕ (including $\top$, the constant for truth) using the connective of propositional logic. Let $p, q, \ldots$ range over $\mathcal{P}$. Let $\mathcal{R}$ be a set of roles; let $x, y, \ldots$ be variables over roles. A system $\mathcal{S}$ is a set such that $S \subseteq \mathcal{R} \times \mathcal{R} \times \mathcal{P} \times \mathcal{P}$. We say $\mathsf{T}(x, y, p, q)$ if and only if $(x, y, p, q) \in \mathcal{S}$.

For instance, taking again into consideration the healthcare domain, one system, let's call it HealthcareSystem1, could be the one composed of the roles Hospital and Patient. In this system, the Patient trusts the Hospital will provide accurate test results (1).

Another system, HealthcareSystem2, includes the roles Hospital, Patient, and Lab. In this setting, the Patient trusts the Hospital will provide accurate test results (2). On the other hand, the Hospital depends on the Lab to analyze test outcomes and produce accurate results (3). Labs are more specialized entities, hence the reason for Hospitals to outsource the tests. Also, the Hospital commits to the Patient that personal data will be confidential and not disclosed to other third parties (4).

$$\mathsf{T}(\mathsf{Patient, Hospital, takeTest, receiveAccurateResults}) \qquad (1)$$

$$\mathsf{T}(\mathsf{Patient, Hospital, takeTest, receiveAccurateResults}) \qquad (2)$$

$$\mathsf{T}(\mathsf{Hospital, Lab}, \top, \mathsf{provideAccurateResults}) \qquad (3)$$

$$\mathsf{T}(\mathsf{Patient, Hospital, providePersonalData, ensureConfidentiality}) \qquad (4)$$

2.1   Computational Grounding

Architecturally, sociotechnical trust is what connects two given participants of the STS. We propose a commitment-based approach to engineering sociotechnical trust (in the rest of the paper, when we say *trust* we mean *sociotechnical trust*, unless otherwise specified). Recent advances have proposed commitment-based architectural styles for SOA [15]. The notion of sociotechnical trust exploits the connection between commitments and architecture. Commitments are a simple yet powerful abstraction to model interactions between two agents in terms of a contractual relation [16]. A commitment is a quaternary relation C(debtor, creditor, antecedent, consequent) that stands for a promise made by the debtor to the creditor that if the antecedent is brought about, the consequent will be brought about. Engineering STS for trust means reasoning from a role-based perspective and establish enough commitments into the system so that an agent adopting a role would trust others adopting other roles. Alice trusts ModernLabs for delivery upon payment, that is, $T(\text{Alice}, \text{ModernLabs}, \text{paid}, \text{delivered})$ if ModernLabs has committed to Alice for doing so, in other words $C(\text{ModernLabs}, \text{Alice}, \text{paid}, \text{delivered})$. In the case of trust relationships, we refer to x and y as the *truster* and *trustee*, respectively, whereas in the case of commitments, we refer to x and y as the *creditor* and *debtor*, respectively. Commitments have been extensively studied in multiagent systems [16], and have been recently applied to understanding the notion of dependencies in systems involving multiple actors [7]. Commitments are rooted in communication: they are created and they evolve when agents exchange messages. Commitments can be *created*, *discharged*, *canceled*, and *released*. $T(x, y, r, u)$ is created when $C(x, y, r, u)$ is created. Similarly, the trust is discharged and violated when the corresponding commitment is discharged and violated; analogously for canceled and released.

Within a given domain there is a variety of STS operating on the basis of trust relationships among their actors, as explained by the aforementioned example. They offer different levels of trust with respect to a particular role's perspective. An actor can either *Join* or *Leave* an STS. Joining means binding to a role and therefore instantiating (partially perhaps) the trust relationships in which the role appears. Ideally, an actor should not leave the system without fulfilling the expectations that others have of him by way of instantiated trust relationships. Referring to the two healthcare systems, HealthcareSystem1 and HealthcareSystem2, we could, intuitively and objectively speaking, say that the second system is better or more trustworthy than the first one from the point of view of the Patients, as it includes additional trust relationships that contribute positively to the fulfillment of the basic requirement of receiving accurate test results, thereby enhancing Patients' trust in this system. However, this might not be the case when it come to Hospitals. From their point of view the first healthcare system is better, as it produces only one commitment from their part, that is, provide accurate results to the Patients, whereas the second healthcare system imposes on them more restrictions. They have to ensure accuracy of results and depend on Labs for this activity. Furthermore, to ensure confidentiality of Patients' personal data, they might have to undertake measures to satisfy this requisite.

Essentially, through the conceptual model we want to make clearer the role perspective in order to provide each prospective participant of any of the systems within a given domain with a clear view while choosing the system he wants to play a role at.

However, establishing enough commitments into the system may be not enough; we also need mechanisms that can support them. Having mechanisms for *monitoring* or *enforcing* commitments supports the establishment of trust relations.

2.2 Trust Supporting Mechanisms

Some of the trust relationships present in the system influence positively on other trust relationships. We say that these relationships *support* the satisfaction of other relationships, with respect to a given role's perspective, enhancing the trust this role has about the system. We represent this type of relation as in (5). This means that the trust relation $T(x,y,p,q)$ *supports* (positively) the trust relation $T(x,z,r,s)$ from x's perspective.

$$T(x, y, p, q) \succ T(x, z, r, s) \tag{5}$$

If we denote T(x,y,p,q) with T_1 and T(x,z,r,s) with T_2, to express that T_1 *supports* T_2 from x's perspective, we use $T_1 \succ_x T_2$ (more generally $T_1 \succ_{\mathcal{R}} T_2$, for any $x \in \mathcal{R}$).

But, what is the meaning of *supports* and why it actually increases trust from a role's perspective? Our intuition is that $T_1 \succ_{\mathcal{R}} T_2$ only if T_1 handles exceptions that arise from T_2. Following this intuition, we specify the *supports* relation through a series of mechanisms (Table 1), which are used to enhance trust of a role about the system. The purpose of these mechanisms is to handle exceptions that might arise from the existing trust relations. By doing so, the resulting system is more robust, and thus more trustworthy for the given role. Table 1 gives a list of basic trust supporting mechanisms induced from the set of patterns presented in [15]. It is basic because they refer to the basic operations concerning commitments such as create, delegate, cancel, etc.

Table 1. Some trust enhancing mechanisms

Name	Trust Encoding
$delegation(x, y, z, p, q)$	$\mathsf{T}(x, y, \mathsf{threatened}(x, y, p, q), \mathsf{T}(x, z, p, q))$
$compensate(x, y, p, q, r, s)$	$\mathsf{T}(x, y, \mathsf{violated}(x, y, p, q), \mathsf{T}(x, y, r, s))$
$undo(x, y, p, q, r)$	$\mathsf{T}(x, y, \mathsf{undo}(q), \mathsf{T}(x, y, r, \mathsf{undo}(p)))$
$renegotiate(x, y, p, q, r, s)$	$\mathsf{T}(x, y, \mathsf{unreasonable}(p, q), \mathsf{T}(x, y, \mathsf{renegotiated}(r, s), \mathsf{T}(y, x, r, s)))$

The propositions violated, threatened, undo, unreasonable, renegotiated, and so on are domain-specific. Referring to our running example, in case ModernLabs cannot deliver the test results to Alice, the Hospital can take care of that, offering yet another way to satisfy Alice's needs. Delegating the responsibility of delivering the results to the Hospital, makes the relationship between Alice and ModernLabs more robust (as long as Alice gets the results, she does not care how they got to her).

Redundancy is another mechanism, but we consider it as a special case of delegation. The system that offers redundancy is better not only for Alice, but for any patient that would decide whether to pay and take a test at ModernLabs or any other laboratory that offers the same services. Generally speaking, for any patient p interacting with some laboratory l, if T_a and T_b stand for $\mathsf{T}(\mathsf{p}, \mathsf{l}, \mathsf{paid}, \mathsf{delivered})$ and $\mathsf{T}(\mathsf{p}, \mathsf{l}, \mathsf{threatened}(p, l, paid, \mathsf{delivered}), \mathsf{T}(\mathsf{p}, \mathsf{h}, \mathsf{paid}, \mathsf{delivered}))$ respectively, (h stands for hospital), then $T_b \succ_p T_a$.

Compensate and undo can be used to capture return-refund scenarios. For example, let T_g and T_v be $\mathsf{T}(\mathsf{p}, \mathsf{l}, \mathsf{paid}, \mathsf{delivered})$ and $\mathsf{T}(\mathsf{p}, \mathsf{l}, \mathsf{violated}(\mathsf{p}, \mathsf{l}, \mathsf{paid}, \mathsf{delivered}),$ refund $\wedge$ discountCoupon)) respectively. $T_v \succ T_g$, since the trust relationship for delivering the test results upon payment is violated by the laboratory, then a trust relationship that ensures refunds along with a discount coupon for future tests makes the relationship more robust from the patient's point of view. Basically, the laboratory is compensating for the violation by offering a discount coupon and undoing the payment done by the patient. As a result, the patient considers the latter system to be a better choice for him (more trustworthy).

Renegotiate on the other hand offers more alternatives for the role to choose. For example, in case of T_x: $\mathsf{T}(\mathsf{p}, \mathsf{l}, \mathsf{paid}, \mathsf{delivered})$ the laboratory might deliver the results of the test in a moment of time that is considered late for the patient. The patient may renegotiate for the time of the delivery by getting a commitment from the laboratory that will deliver the results on time, T_y: $\mathsf{T}(\mathsf{p}, \mathsf{l}, \mathsf{paid}, \mathsf{deliverOnTime})$. Again $T_y \succ_p T_x$.

The *supports* relationship shows how trust within a system is improved, from a roles perspective, and it helps possible participants while choosing a system from a range of systems in the domain. By looking at these relationships prospective participants can determine when an entire system (a set of trust relationships) is better than the rest of the systems, within the same domain, from their perspective. Taking this into account we could for instance establish that, if $T_1 \succ_R T_2$, a system $\{T_1, T_2\}$ is better from R's perspective than a system having only $\{T_2\}$.

We provide a graphical representation of the notions composing the system (Fig. 1). Roles are graphically represented as ovals, while trust relationships are shown using double stroke arrows pointing to the trustee, labeled with the actual trust relationship among two given roles (1a). Fig. 1b depicts the usage of the delegation as a trust *supporting* mechanism. The *supports* relation is labeled with the subscript "Alice" to show how Alice's trust is enhanced.

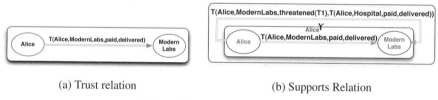

(a) Trust relation   (b) Supports Relation

Fig. 1. Graphical representation of the system

Apart from the mechanisms shown in Table 1 there could be others that influence the trustworthiness of a system. These mechanisms are domain specific and emerge from the study and analysis of the given domain. We will use a case study to discover new mechanisms to support trust (section 4). Our approach for sociotechnical trust is based on commitments, thus to enhance trust in the system enough commitments are built to make it more trustworthy. The *supports* relation reflects this intuition as well. For instance, let us consider two healthcare systems from our running example, say system $S_1 = \{T_i\}$ and system $S_2 = \{T_i, T_j, T_k\}$.

S_1 represents a system in which only one trust relationship holds (6). Hospitals commit on ensuring confidentiality of Alice's personal data (to comply with HIPAA[1]), hence the trust relationship between Alice and the Hospital that if Alice provides her personal data to adhere to Hospital's services, the Hospital will ensure confidentiality of those data. Information included in the medical records of the patients should also be protected and not shared with other parties, unless the patient gives a written permit for that.

S_2 ((7),(8), and (9)) represents a system in which the Hospital commits to ensure confidentiality of patient's personal data, it also commits to share patient's personal data only upon their written permission, and the doctor attending the patient commits to protect and ensure privacy of patient information and medical records. The trust

---

[1] https://www.cms.gov/hipaageninfo/

relationships present in S_2 emerge from these commitments. S_2 involves the trust relationships T_j and T_k, each of which supports the trust relation T_i (that is, $T_j \succ_{Alice} T_i$ and $T_k \succ_{Alice} T_i$). Having two more trust relationships (hence more *commitments*) that support the basic trust relationship, will influence the overall trust of the system.

We could say that S_2 is more trustworthy from the patient's (Alice) point of view than S_1 because it provides more commitments to ensure confidentiality.

$$T_i = \mathsf{T}(\mathsf{Alice}, \mathsf{Hospital}, \mathsf{personalData}, \mathsf{ensureConfidentiality}) \tag{6}$$

$$T_i = \mathsf{T}(\mathsf{Alice}, \mathsf{Hospital}, \mathsf{personalData}, \mathsf{ensureConfidentiality}) \tag{7}$$

$$T_j = \mathsf{T}(\mathsf{Alice}, \mathsf{Doctor}, T, \mathsf{privacyOfMedicalRecords}) \tag{8}$$

$$T_k = \mathsf{T}(\mathsf{Alice}, \mathsf{Hospital}, \mathsf{permit}, \mathsf{sharePersonalData}) \tag{9}$$

Definition 1. *Let S_1 and S_2 be two systems. We say that S_2 is more trustworthy than S_1 from x's perspective ($S_2 \gg_x S_1$) if and only if:*

1. $(x, y, p, q) \in S_1$ implies $(x, y, p, q) \in S_2$, and
2. $\exists (x, z, r, s) \in S_2$ such that $\mathsf{T}(x, z, r, s) \succ \mathsf{T}(x, y, p, q)$

The definition captures the intuition behind the fact that a participant (x) will trust more the system that will provide more commitments to him (i.e more trust relationships) that *support* the initial interaction he wants to start with that system. This initial interaction is a relation that is provided by both systems to x (1); x considers S_2 more trustworthy because it provides other relations that *support* the basic interaction (2).

In the aforementioned example, there are two trust relationships in S_2, namely T_j and T_k, that support the trust relation in S_1, T_i. Therefore, the system S_2 is said to be more trustworthy from Alice's point of view.

3   Kinds of Trust in Sociotechnical Systems

We highlight the difference between sociotechnical trust and two other notions of trust that have been applied to modeling and reasoning about sociotechnical systems. We show with the help of examples that the three are orthogonal notions, and that each plays a role in the smooth functioning of a live STS.

3.1   Technical Trust

By actors, we refer only to *social* entities. In practice, this means only humans and organizations (or their software surrogates). For example, consider a healthcare system. Hospitals, patients, doctors, laboratories, insurance companies, and so on are all actors in the system. A hospital may provide the service of appointment scheduling via a Web application; clearly, the application itself is not an actor in the same sense that a hospital is. Similarly, a laboratory may use several devices in providing testing services to patients, for example, a CT scanner; clearly, the CT scanner too is not an actor. Thus, in this paper, we do not talk about *technical trust*—whether the hospital trusts the scheduling Web application (to work well) or whether the laboratory trusts the CT scanner. We broadly identify technical trust with assurance [13], also sometimes referred to as dependability [8].

The contrast with technical trust is an important one. Technical trust necessarily treats the system under consideration as a monolithic entity that can be deployed and evaluated for desirable properties. However, sociotechnical systems are not monolithic. Each actor is necessarily *autonomous* and will implement the functionality it desires independently from other actors. For example, a hospital will implement its information systems independently from a laboratory. Therefore, it is impractical to dwell upon whether a hospital considers a laboratory's information systems and devices dependable; however, it is critically important that the hospital trusts the laboratory for providing accurate test results. In general, technical trust applies at a lower level than social trust. Figure 2 illustrates in an architectural sense the difference between social and technical trust. Incidentally, the traditional model of sociotechnical systems from RE is similar to Figure 2(B).

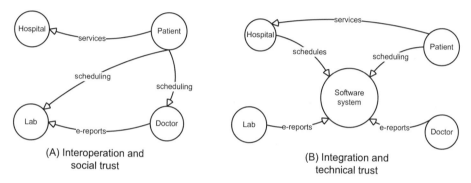

(A) Interoperation and social trust

(B) Integration and technical trust

Fig. 2. Social versus technical trust

Let T_T denote the technical trust relation. For example, T_T(ModernLabs, CTScanner, operatedProperly, deliveredAccurateResults) means that ModernLabs trusts the CTScanner to deliver accurate results if operated properly.

Technical trust is not relevant for us. It is not the scope of our work. Instead, we concentrate on the roles interacting in the system, not the information systems or devices being used. We are interested in the actual actors operating the technical systems, so the technical trust is encapsulated within the social trust. Alice trusts ModernLabs to deliver accurate results, but she does not care how ModernLabs achieves that. It is ModernLabs' responsibility assuring the correctness of the results. As long as the results are delivered being accurate, Alice trusts ModernLabs. It is this kind of relationship that we want to exploit.

3.2   Cognitive Trust

Most of the predominant computational approaches to trust have a cognitive bias. In such approaches, each agent has a mental, and therefore necessarily private, model of other agents, based on which it chooses whom to interact with. Some approaches to trust are based on reputation. Although reputation itself is a social concept in that an agent's reputation is public, it also is mostly applied in a cognitive way—as an input to the agents' mental models.

Let T_C denote the cognitive trust relation. For example, T_C(Alice, ModernLabs, paid, delivery) means that Alice cognitively trusts ModernLabs. Sociotechnical trust wants to influence in some way the enhancement of cognitive trust, however we cannot enforce the latter. If a system inspires more trust than other systems in the same domain, it might be the case that prospective participants become more willing to participate in that system.

3.3   Orthogonality

Our conceptual model helps determine whether a system is trustworthy, architecturally speaking. However we do not address issues dealing with cognitive trust, such as *"within a system, who to interact with?"*, nor issues concerning technical trust. Each of them has a different consequence on the actors' decisions (or influences differently actors' decisions). Let's consider a situation where hospital SantaChiara is known to be better than hospital SanCamillo, and in which Alice trusts more (cognitively) Dr.Giusti rather than Dr.Falconi. Based on sociotechnical trust considerations, we could say objectively that Alice would rather be visited by Dr.Giusti (Dr.G) in hospital SantaChiara (S.Ch) than by Dr.Falconi (Dr.F) in hospital SanCamillo (S.Cam) (10). However, we could not say anything about Alice's trust (where would she get a visit) in case doctor Dr.Giusti were to work at hospital SanCamillo and Dr.Falconi were to work at hospital SantaChiara (11).

$$T(\text{Alice}, \text{Dr.G}, \text{S.Ch}, \text{goodVisit}) \gg_{Alice} T(\text{Alice}, \text{Dr.F}, \text{S.Cam}, \text{goodVisit}) \quad (10)$$

$$T(\text{Alice}, \text{Dr.G}, \text{S.Cam}, \text{goodVisit}) \not\gg_{Alice} T(\text{Alice}, \text{Dr.F}, \text{S.Ch}, \text{goodVisit}) \quad (11)$$

Similarly, if Alice trusts cognitively ModernLabs to deliver the results once she has paid for the tests, this does not mean that she technically trusts ModernLabs, and vice versa.

4   The Food Law Case Study

The European Parliament and the Council adopted Regulation (EC)178/2002[2] on January 2002, to harmonize all Member States food legislation in a general Food Law regulation, whose primary objective is consumer protection throughout Europe. Food Law lays down all requirements on food safety. It imposes requirements on any substance that is intended or expected to be incorporated into a food/feed during its manufacture, preparation or treatment [5]. These requirements should be applied by all food operators in order to comply with the regulation.

Identifying Roles and Trust Relationships. Food law exposes the following participants (roles): Member States (MS), Food Safety Authority(FSA), Food Business Operator (FBO), European Consumer (EC). Stakeholders in the food/feed chain are a lot, among which food/feed manufacturers, importers, brokers, farmers, distributors, etc., but we classify all as FBO. To be in compliance with (EC)178/2002 requirements and specifications, the trust relations in Table 2 should hold.

---

[2] http://ec.europa.eu/food/food/foodlaw/index_en.htm

Table 2. Trust relations based on roles perspective

Trust relation	Description
European Consumers' Perspective	
$T(C, FBO, onMarket(x), safe(x))$	Consumers trust food operators that every product they placed in the market is safe
$T(C, FBO, onMarket(x), labelAdequately(x))$	Consumers trust food operators that every product they placed in the market is labeled adequately
$T(C, FSA, \neg safe(x), prohibitPlacingOnMarket(x))$	Consumers trust the authorities that if food is found to be unsafe, it will be prohibited to be placed on the market
$T(C, FBO,$ $violated(C, FBO, onMarket(x), safe(x)),$ $T(C, FBO, informOn(x), withdraw(x)))$	Consumers trust food operators that if food is found to be unsafe when it had already been placed on the market, they will be informed and food will be withdrawn from the market
$T(C, FBO, hazardsIdentifiedOn(x),$ $assessRisksRelatedTo(x))$	Food operators should perform risk assessment and analysis for any identified possible hazard related to a given food product
$T(C, FBO, product(x, FBO) \wedge ingredients(x, y_0) \wedge$ $\ldots \wedge ingredients(x, y_n), record(y_0, supplier) \wedge \ldots \wedge$ $record(y_n, supplier) \wedge record(x, customer))$	Food operators should keep record of all the suppliers of ingredients of the products they sell and of all the immediate customers
Food Business Operator Responsibility	
$\forall suppliers T(FSA, FBO, monitor(suppliers),$ $risksEarlyDetected)$	Problems with food will be detected early if food operators monitor their suppliers
$T(FSA, FBO, onRisk, notify)$	Food safety authority expects to receive notification on risk
$T(MS, FSA, notify, inform)$	Food safety authority should inform member states when notified for some risk

Enhancing Consumers' Trust. We provide a semi-formal graphical representation in a multilayer perspective (Figure 3) starting from the basic situation (container denoted with R). The core requirement is that consumers are provided with safe food, that is, every food that is placed on the market is safe and adequately labeled. Food operators are responsible for ensuring this, therefore we show the trust relation that should hold between consumers and food operators. The Food Safety Law specifies mechanisms that will help improve this situation, thereby enhancing the chances of achieving the primary goal of having safe food on the market. These mechanisms are actually the *supports* relations specific to this domain. The structuring of the trust relationships performed in Figure 3 serves the purpose of applying the *supports* relations to improve the sociotechnical trust at each layer, introducing them at the appropriate layer. Thus, in the second

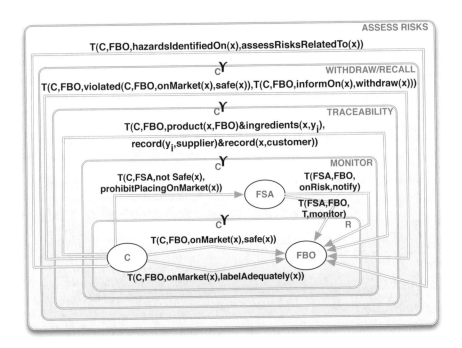

Fig. 3. Food Law System Enhancing Consumers' Trust

layer (*Monitoring*) monitoring mechanisms are enabled, such as the ones for monitoring suppliers and food. Monitoring will increase the level of trust consumers will have on the products placed on the market. However, monitoring alone is not enough. That is why *Traceability* mechanisms are applied on top of monitoring (third layer), so that any time a given risk is identified, it is possible to find the node in the food chain in which the breach occurred. Whenever a hazard is encountered, traceability is used to identify the source of such risk, afterward food operators can perform risk assessment to verify the status of the given product. If it is found to violate food safety requirements, customers should be notified and the product needs to be withdrawn or recalled (forth layer: *Withdraw/Recall*). Risk assessment procedures will influence the decision to withdraw or recall a product from the market (fifth layer: *Assess Risks*).

We use the *supports* relationship notation labeled with C, at the border between the subsequent layers, to represent the fact that trust relationships in the above layer *support* trust relationships in the layer below, enhancing at each subsequent layer Consumers' trust about the system.

Conclusion. We presented a graphical representation of an STS from the Food Law case study showing trust relations that hold between the different roles (mainly consumers and food operators) along the food chain. We used the case study to identify domain specific *supports* relationships that aim to increase a consumer's trust in this STS. Based on the identified *supports* relationships, we built a structured graphical representation of the trust relations that hold in the system to help possible participants decide which system they want to play a role at. This representation makes the role perspective clearer by showing the relations they may be involved. Furthermore, this structuring allows to see how trust is increased after each layer by representing the trust supporting mechanisms. All mechanisms represented in terms of *supports* trust relationships serve the purpose of ensuring consumers' safety and inspiring their trust in the system.

Is the Approach Scalable for Larger Case Studies? Our approach depends on the clarity of the information regarding the considered domain, as the process of discovering *supports* relationships is domain specific.

5 Discussion

In this paper, we captured the intuition behind sociotechnical trust, as referring to the trustworthiness of an STS. We consider an STS to be organized along trust relationships. We want to make make explicit these trust relationships in order to provide prospective participants with information regarding the dependencies they would have upon the STS in case they decide to play a role in. Based on this information, one is able to decide whether, on his perspective, an STS is more trustworthy than another. This requires that we capture *sociotechnical* trust in an architectural sense as a relationship among roles in the system. When specific actors adopt the roles, those relationships are instantiated. We showed the notion of sociotechnical trust to be different from cognitive and technical trust, two prominent concepts in sociotechnical systems research. We analyzed the European food safety regulation on the basis of our approach. The case study reveals that a STS is not a list of trust relationships, but there is structure in the sense that some trust relationships enhance some others. Understanding the structure of a system will prove valuable for those who want to decide their participation in a system. A key feature of our conceptual model is that we take the role perspective in saying whether one system is more trustworthy than another. Thus whereas a healthcare STS may be more trustworthy from the patient point of view; it may be less trustworthy from a laboratory's point of view. Such a perspective follows naturally from the fact that trust is a directed relationship.

The *trustworthiness* of a software is traditionally seen as a measure of assurance that the software is free from vulnerabilities [13]. Notably, such a notion of trustworthiness treats software as a monolithic entity; it is technical trust. Examples of such software include operating systems and browsers. Many trustworthy computing initiatives, including Microsoft's [12], to mitigate security concerns fall under this category. Castelfranchi [4] lists different kinds of trust that often come into play: trust in the environment and infrastructure (technical trust), trust in one's own agent (technical trust because it amounts to trust in the software that an actor uses), and trust in authorities and partners (both cognitive). These are all important kinds of trust; however none of these is sociotechnical. Asnar *et al.* [2] model trust relationships among actors in order to analyze risk; however in their approach, trust is an agent's subjective belief about another, in other words, cognitive. Similar to our approach, Giorgini *et al.* [9] model social trust at the role level. They present examples where any agent adopting some role must trust another adopting some role for something, however, cognitively it may not. Giorgini *et al.* deem this as a conflict. In our approach, such a situation is not a conflict—social and cognitive trust are orthogonal concepts. Our idea of assuming domain-specific trust enhancing (the *supports*) relationships is not unfounded. Jones *et al.* [11] present a list of trust requirements for e-business. Haley *et al.* [10] introduce the notion of trust assumptions to help discharge concerns about system security. Siena *et al.* [14] care about compliance of actors with regulations, we care about understanding the structure of the regulations themselves, and how the regulation may have potentially come about in the first place.

Future Directions. In order to build architecturally better systems in terms of trust, we want to explore a formal semantics for the *supports* relationship. However, given the diversity of domains and trust relationships, this is an especially challenging task. Our initial approach for defining supports was via formulating trust enhancing mechanisms. We will further exploit commitments to identify more such mechanisms.

Acknowledgments. This work has been partially supported by the EU-FP7-IST-IP-ANIKETOS and EU-FP7-IST-NOE-NESSOS project. Amit K. Chopra was supported by a Marie Curie Trentino cofund award.

References

1. Credit card accountability responsibility and disclosure act of (2009),
   http://www.govtrack.us/congress/bill.xpd?bill=h111-627
2. Asnar, Y., Giorgini, P., Massacci, F., Zannone, N.: From trust to dependability through risk analysis. In: Proceedings of the Second International Conference on Availability, Reliability and Security, pp. 19–26 (2007)
3. Bresciani, P., Perini, A., Giorgini, P., Giunchiglia, F., Mylopoulos, J.: Tropos: An agent-oriented software development methodology. Autonomous Agents and Multi-Agent Systems 8(3), 203–236 (2004)
4. Castelfranchi, C., Tan, Y.-H.: The role of trust and deception in virtual societies. International Journal of Electronic Commerce 6(3), 55–70 (2002)
5. Standing Committee on The Food Chain and Animal Health. Food law implementation guidelines. World Wide Web electronic publication, January 2010, Lastchecked (December 2010)
6. Chopra, A.K., Dalpiaz, F., Giorgini, P., Mylopoulos, J.: Modeling and reasoning about service-oriented applications via goals and commitments. In: Pernici, B. (ed.) CAiSE 2010. LNCS, vol. 6051, pp. 113–128. Springer, Heidelberg (2010)
7. Chopra, A.K., Dalpiaz, F., Giorgini, P., Mylopoulos, J.: Modeling and Reasoning about Service-Oriented Applications via Goals and Commitments. In: Pernici, B. (ed.) CAiSE 2010. LNCS, vol. 6051, pp. 113–128. Springer, Heidelberg (2010)
8. Dewsbury, G., Sommerville, I., Clarke, K., Rouncefield, M.: A Dependability Model for Domestic Systems. In: Anderson, S., Felici, M., Littlewood, B. (eds.) SAFECOMP 2003. LNCS, vol. 2788, pp. 103–115. Springer, Heidelberg (2003)
9. Giorgini, P., Massacci, F., Mylopoulos, J., Zannone, N.: Requirements engineering for trust management: Model, methodology, and reasoning. International Journal of Information Security 5, 257–274 (2006)
10. Haley, C., Laney, R., Moffett, J., Nuseibeh, B.: Using trust assumptions with security requirements. Requirements Engineering 11, 138–151 (2006)

11. Jones, S., Wilikens, M., Morris, P., Masera, M.: Trust requirements in e-business. Communications of the ACM 43(12), 81–87 (2000)
12. Lipner, S.: The trustworthy computing security development lifecycle. In: Proceedings of the 20th Annual Computer Security Applications Conference, pp. 2–13 (December 2004)
13. Mead, N.R., Jarzombek, J.: Advancing software assurance with public-private collaboration. IEEE Computer 43(9), 21–30 (2010)
14. Siena, A., Armellin, G., Mameli, G., Mylopoulos, J., Perini, A., Susi, A.: Establishing regulatory compliance for information system requirements: An experience report from the health care domain. In: Parsons, J., Saeki, M., Shoval, P., Woo, C., Wand, Y. (eds.) ER 2010. LNCS, vol. 6412, pp. 90–103. Springer, Heidelberg (2010)
15. Singh, M.P., Chopra, A.K., Desai, N.: Commitment-based service-oriented architecture. Computer 42(11), 72–79 (2009)
16. Singh, M.P.: An ontology for commitments in multiagent systems: Toward a unification of normative concepts. Artificial Intelligence and Law 7, 97–113 (1999)
17. Singh, M.P.: Trust as a basis for social computing (2010), http://www.csc.ncsu.edu/faculty/mpsingh/papers/positions/Trust-formal-architecture-talk.pdf
18. Strens, R., Dobson, J.: How responsibility modelling leads to security requirements. In: Proceedings of the New Security Paradigms Workshop, pp. 143–149 (1993)
19. van Lamsweerde, A.: From system goals to software architecture. In: Bernardo, M., Inverardi, P. (eds.) SFM 2003. LNCS, vol. 2804, pp. 25–43. Springer, Heidelberg (2003)

Generating SPARQL Executable Mappings to Integrate Ontologies[*][**]

Carlos R. Rivero, Inma Hernández, David Ruiz, and Rafael Corchuelo

University of Sevilla, Spain
{carlosrivero,inmahernandez,druiz,corchu}@us.es

Abstract. Data translation is an integration task that aims at populating a target model with data of a source model by means of mappings. Generating them automatically is appealing insofar it may reduce integration costs. Matching techniques automatically generate uninterpreted mappings, a.k.a. correspondences, that must be interpreted to perform the data translation task. Other techniques automatically generate executable mappings, which encode an interpretation of these correspondences in a given query language. Unfortunately, current techniques to automatically generate executable mappings are based on instance examples of the target model, which usually contains no data, or based on nested relational models, which cannot be straightforwardly applied to semantic-web ontologies. In this paper, we present a technique to automatically generate SPARQL executable mappings between OWL ontologies. The original contributions of our technique are as follows: 1) it is not based on instance examples but on restrictions and correspondences, 2) we have devised an algorithm to make restrictions and correspondences explicit over a number of language-independent executable mappings, and 3) we have devised an algorithm to transform language-independent into SPARQL executable mappings. Finally, we evaluate our technique over ten scenarios and check that the interpretation of correspondences that it assumes is coherent with the expected results.

Keywords: Information Integration, Data Translation, Semantic-web Ontologies, SPARQL Executable Mappings.

1 Introduction

Data in current databases are usually modelled using relational or nested relational models, which include relational and semi-structured schemata [4]. However, there is an increasing shift towards representing these data by means of ontological models due to the popularity and maturity of the Semantic Web [35].

---

[*] Supported by the European Commission (FEDER), the Spanish and the Andalusian R&D&I programmes (grants TIN2007-64119, P07-TIC-2602, P08-TIC-4100, TIN2008-04718-E, TIN2010-21744, TIN2010-09809-E, TIN2010-10811-E, and TIN2010-09988-E).

[**] See [31] for a demo regarding this paper.

M. Jeusfeld, L. Delcambre, and T.W. Ling (Eds.): ER 2011, LNCS 6998, pp. 118–131, 2011.
© Springer-Verlag Berlin Heidelberg 2011

In this paper, we focus on semantic-web ontologies that are represented using RDF, RDF Schema and OWL ontology languages to model structure and data, and their data are queried by means of the SPARQL query language [3,10,25].

Existing databases comprise a variety of models, created by different organisations for different purposes, and there is a need to integrate them [4,19,22]. Mediators provide a well-known solution to the problem of integrating models since they can help bridge the semantic gap amongst them [11,33]. A mediator relates a source model, which contains the data of interest, to a target model, which usually contains no data. Mediators can perform two tasks: data integration and data translation [19,22]. The former deals with answering queries posed over the target model, which is virtual, using the source model only [15,19,37]. The latter, which is the focus of this paper, aims at populating a target model with data of a source model [8,12,24,28,29].

Mappings, which are the cornerstone components of mediators, relate source and target models in different ways [8,9,11,18,19]. Building and maintaining mappings automatically is appealing insofar this relieves users from the burden of writing them, checking whether they work as expected or not, making changes if necessary, and restarting this cycle [4,27]. Mappings can be of various types but, in this paper, we focus on two: correspondences and executable mappings.

On the one hand, correspondences may be handcrafted with the help of a visual tool [1], or generated automatically using matching techniques [9,11,30]. They are hints that specify which elements from the source and target models are related in some unspecified way [5]. Therefore, they must be interpreted to perform the data translation task. However, this interpretation is far from trivial since it is not unique, i.e., different approaches interpret correspondences in different ways [2,5,28]. Consequently, it is mandatory to check whether the resulting target data are coherent with the expected results.

On the other hand, executable mappings, a.k.a. operational mappings, encode an interpretation of correspondences in a given query language [14,28,29]. These mappings are executed by means of a query engine to perform the data translation task. The main benefit of using these mappings is that the data translation task is simplified, making it more efficient and flexible: thanks to executable mappings, instead of relying on ad-hoc programs that are difficult to create and maintain, the query engine is used as the transformation engine [14]. Furthermore, these engines incorporate a vast knowledge on query manipulation, from which it is derived that the executable mappings are automatically optimised for better performance of the data translation task.

In the bibliography, there are a number of techniques to automatically generate executable mappings. Unfortunately, none of them can be straightforwardly applied to semantic-web ontologies in the context of the data translation task due to the following reasons, namely (for further details, see Section 2):

- Some of them are based on instance examples of the target model [29], which are suitable in scenarios in which the target model is already populated. However, we focus on scenarios in which the target model has no instances at all, which seems to be quite usual in practice [2,4,28].

– Others focus on nested relational models, which represent trees [13,20,28,36]; however, they cannot be straightforwardly applied to ontologies, which represent graphs, due to a number of differences between them [17,21,23,32].

In this paper, we present a technique to automatically generate SPARQL executable mappings to perform the data translation task between OWL ontologies. To illustrate it, we use an example that is contextualised in the domain of films and reviews, using DBpedia and Revyu as data sources. The original contributions of our technique are that it is based on restrictions and correspondences, instead of instance examples, which makes it appealing in many practical cases. Furthermore, we have devised an algorithm to generate language-independent executable mappings that makes restrictions and correspondences explicit. Finally, we have devised an algorithm to transform language-independent into SPARQL executable mappings by creating triple patterns and linking variables of these patterns.

This paper is organised as follows: Section 2 presents the related work; in Section 3, we present the algorithms to automatically generate SPARQL executable mappings; Section 4 presents the evaluation of our technique; and, finally, Section 5 recaps on our conclusions.

2   Related Work

In this section, we study the techniques to automatically generate executable mappings in both the semantic-web and database research fields.

In the semantic-web research field, Qin et al. [29] devised a technique to generate executable mappings between ontologies in a semi-automatic way. Their technique is divided into five modules. The first module deals with the automatic discovering of correspondences. The second module determines whether two instances in different ontologies represent the same real-world entity. The third module deals with the clustering of correspondences that are related. The fourth module takes a set of source and target instances as input and generates a set of frequent queries of interest between them. Note that target instances have to be provided by the user when the target is not populated. Finally, the fifth module generates executable mappings based on frequent queries and correspondences. This technique generates a set of executable mappings that can be specified in Web-PDDL (an ontology language devised by the authors), Datalog or SWRL.

Regarding the database research field, Popa et al. [28] proposed a technique to automatically generate executable mappings for performing the data translation task between nested relational models. A nested relational model defines a tree that comprises nested nodes with attributes. The first step of their technique consists of computing primary paths, each of which is the unique path from the tree root to a node. Furthermore, this step comprises the identification of referential constraints that relate two primary paths by an equality expression between two attributes. The second step consists of applying an extension of the relational chase algorithm to compute logical relations, each of which is an enumeration of the logical joins specified by referential constraints. Therefore, a logical relation comprises a number of primary paths that are related by referential constraints. This step is applied in both source and target models. The third step computes the executable mappings by performing the Cartesian product between source and target logical relations. For each pair, the technique analyses the correspondences that relate source and target elements in this pair. Note that this technique takes only one type of correspondence into account: source attribute to target attribute. Finally, the fourth step deals with the transformation of the previous executable mappings, which are represented in an intermediate nested-relational query language, into XQuery or XSLT queries.

The technique devised by Popa et al. [28] was the starting point to a number of subsequent approaches: Fuxman et al. [13] proposed the use of nested mappings that are generated by correlating Popa et al's mappings, which are called basic mappings. Basic and nested mappings can produce redundant target instances, which motivated the research on the generation of laconic/core mappings that produce target instances with no redundancy [20,36]. Mappings systems like Clio or Clip are also based on this technique [1,14].

Finally, ontology and schema matching approaches focus on the automatic generation of correspondences. Choi et al. [9], Euzenat and Shvaiko [11], and Rahm and Bernstein [30] are good surveys on the state of the art of schema and ontology matching techniques. However, it is important to notice that, in this paper, we assume that correspondences already exist, so we make no contribution to the schema or ontology matching research fields.

As a conclusion, Qin et al. [29] is suitable to generate executable mappings in scenarios in which the target model is already populated. In the rest of scenarios, the user must provide an adequate set of instance examples to ensure that the technique works properly, not only with the aforementioned examples, but also with new instances. If the set of instance examples does not capture variability well-enough, the technique may fail to cover some cases. Furthermore, the technique may suffer from overfitting, i.e., an overfitted technique works well with training examples, but may not be able to generalise to adapt to new instances from the real world.

Regarding the techniques based on nested relational models [13,20,28,36], they cannot be straightforwardly applied to ontologies due to the following differences:

- Structure: a nested relational model comprises a number of nodes, which may be nested and have a number of attributes. This model represents a tree in which there is a unique path from the root to any node or attribute. Contrarily, an ontology comprises three types of nodes: classes, data properties and object properties. This ontology represents a graph in which there may be zero, one or more paths connecting two arbitrary nodes. Note that these graphs do not have a unique root and may contain cycles.
- Instances: an instance in a nested relational model has a unique type that corresponds to an existing node. Contrarily, an instance in an ontology may have multiple types that correspond to a number of existing classes, which need not be related by specialisation. Furthermore, in a nested relational model, an instance of a nested node exists as long as there exists an instance

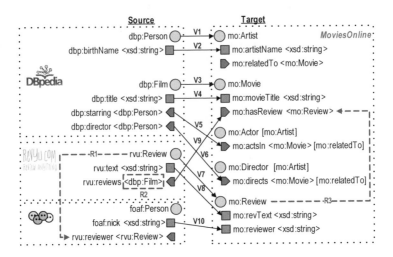

Fig. 1. Data translation scenario of our running example

of the corresponding parent node. Contrarily, in an ontology, classes, data properties and object properties can be instantiated independently from each other by default.

– Queries: in the context of nested relational models, queries to perform the data translation task are encoded using XQuery or XSLT, which depend on the structure of the XML documents on which they are executed. Contrarily, in an ontology, these queries must be encoded in a language that is independent of the structure of XML documents, since the same ontology can be represented by different XML documents.

3   Mapping Generation

In this section, we present our technique to automatically generate SPARQL executable mappings based on restrictions and correspondences, which is divided into two steps: Kernel Generation and SPARQL Transformation.

To illustrate it, we use a running example in the domain of movies and reviews. Our running example builds on a fictitious video-on-demand service called Movies Online. It provides information about the movies it broadcasts and reviews of these movies. Movies Online have a number of knowledge engineers in their staff, and they devised the target ontology of Figure 1, which models movies and reviews. Instead of performing a handcrafted population of the ontology, Movies Online decided to translate information of movies and reviews from DBpedia [7] and Revyu [16], which are the source ontologies. Note that the Revyu ontology references the Friend of a Friend ontology, following the principles of Linked Data [6]. Note also that, throughout this paper, 'dbp', 'rvu', 'foaf' and 'mo' are the prefixes of DBpedia, Revyu, FOAF and Movies Online, respectively.

To represent ontologies, we use a tree-based notation in which classes are represented as circles, data properties as squares and object properties as pentagons. Furthermore, the domain of a data or object property is represented by nesting the property into the domain class, e.g., *dbp:birthName* is a data property whose domain is *dbp:Person*. The range of a data or object property is represented by '<' and '>', e.g., *dbp:starring* is an object property whose range is *dbp:Person*. Finally, class and property specialisations are represented by '[' and ']', e.g., *mo:Actor* is subclass of *mo:Artist*, and *mo:actsIn* is subproperty of *mo:relatedTo*.

In the following subsections, we present the restrictions and correspondences that our technique is able to process, and the algorithms to automatically generate SPARQL executable mappings.

3.1   Restrictions and Correspondences

In this section, we present the restrictions and correspondences of our technique. Regarding restrictions, we assume that source and target ontologies pre-exist, so they contain a number of inherent restrictions, e.g., *"foaf:Person* is the domain of *foaf:nick"*. Furthermore, it is possible to specify user-defined restrictions to adapt existing source and target ontologies to the requirements of a specific scenario, e.g., *R1* restricts reviews to have, at least, one reviewer.

Our technique is able to process six types of restrictions, namely:

- Domain(x, y): data or object property x is domain of class y. For instance, in Figure 1, Domain(*foaf:nick, foaf:Person*).
- Range(x, y): object property x is range of class y, e.g., *R2* corresponds to Range(*rvu:reviews, dbp:Film*).
- StrongDomain(x, y): class x is domain of data or object property y, whose minimal cardinality is one, e.g., StrongDomain(*foaf:Person, foaf:nick*). Note that this restriction is equivalent to a minimal cardinality of one over the domain class.
- StrongRange(x, y): class x is the range of object property y, whose minimal cardinality is one, e.g., *R1* corresponds to StrongRange(*rvu:Review, rvu:reviewer*). Note that this restriction is equivalent to a minimal cardinality of one over the range class.
- Subclass(x, y): class x is subclass of class y, e.g., Subclass(*mo:Director, mo:Artist*).
- Subproperty(x, y): data or object property x is subproperty of data or object property y, e.g., Subproperty(*mo:actsIn, mo:relatedTo*).

We deal with three types of correspondences, namely:

- ClassCorrespondence(x, y): instances of the y target class are copied from instances of the x source class, e.g., *V1* that corresponds to ClassCorrespondence(*dbp:Person, mo:Artist*).
- DataPropertyCorrespondence(x, y): instances of the y target data property are copied from instances of the x source data property, e.g., *V2* that corresponds to DataPropertyCorrespondence(*dbp:birthName, mo:artistName*).

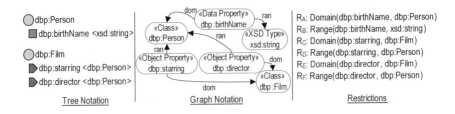

Fig. 2. An example of the restrictions of an ontology

– ObjectPropertyCorrespondence(x, y): instances of the y target object property are copied from instances of the x source object property, e.g., V5 that corresponds to ObjectPropertyCorrespondence(*dbp:starring*, *mo:actsIn*).

Therefore, for a particular scenario, we have a number of source and target restrictions, and a number of correspondences. Figure 2 presents a part of the source ontology in our running example that is represented in our tree-based notation, in a graph-based notation, and the restrictions that are associated to this part of the ontology, respectively. Note that each of these restrictions models a directed edge in the ontology graph that has a left and a right entities, e.g., the left entity of R_A in Figure 2 is *dbp:birthName*, and the right part is *dbp:Person*.

Finally, it is important to notice that correspondences in isolation are usually not suitable enough to perform the data translation task. For instance, assume that we use V5 in isolation to translate instances of *dbp:starring* into *mo:actsIn*. In this context, we translate the domain and range of *dbp:starring* into the domain and range of *mo:actsIn*, respectively. Unfortunately, by doing this, we are translating *dbp:Film* into *mo:Actor*, and *dbp:Person* into *mo:Movie*, which is obviously incorrect. This is the reason why we must take both restrictions and correspondences into account to generate executable mappings.

3.2   Kernel Generation

In this section, we present the algorithm to automatically generate kernels. Intuitively, a kernel of a correspondence is a language-independent executable mapping that comprises those source restrictions, target restrictions and correspondences that we must take into account to produce coherent target data. The algorithm is shown in Figure 3(a) and it takes a set of correspondences C, and a set of source and target restrictions as input, R_S and R_T, respectively. For each correspondence, it creates a new kernel that is added to the output set K. A kernel is a three-element tuple (R'_S, R'_T, C') that comprises a set of source restrictions R'_S, a set of target restrictions R'_T, and a set of correspondences C'.

To create each kernel, it first calls the *Expand* algorithm (cf. Figure 3(b)), which is responsible for finding all restrictions that have to be explicit regarding an entity. Recall that an entity may be a class, a data property or an object property. This algorithm takes an entity and a set of restrictions as input, and it finds all restrictions that are related to this input entity. First, this input entity

Generate Kernels
Input
  C: Set of Correspondence
  R_S, R_T: Set of Restriction
Output:
  K: Set of Kernel
Variables:
  e_S, e_T: Entity
  R'_S, R'_T: Set of Restriction
  C': Set of Correspondence

$K = \emptyset$
For each (e_S, e_T) in C
  R'_S = Expand (e_S, R_S)
  R'_T = Expand (e_T, R_T)

  C' = FindCorrespondences (C, R'_S, R'_T)

  $K = K \cup \{ (R'_S, R'_T, C') \}$
End for

Expand
Input
  e: Entity
  R: Set of Restriction
Output:
  O: Set of Restriction
Variables:
  E: Set of Entity
  e_L, e_R: Entity

$(O, E) = (\emptyset, e)$

Do until no new entity is added to E
  For each (e_L, e_R) in R
    If $e_L \in E \wedge (e_L, e_R) \notin O$
      $O = O \cup \{ (e_L, e_R) \}$
      $E = E \cup \{ e_L, e_R \}$
    End if
  End for
End do

Find Correspondences
Input
  C: Set of Correspondence
  R_S, R_T: Set of Restriction
Output:
  O: Set of Correspondence
Variables:
  E_S, E_T: Set of Entity
  e_S, e_T: Entity

$O = \emptyset$
$(E_S, E_T) = (\text{Entities}(R_S), \text{Entities}(R_T))$

For each (e_S, e_T) in C
  If $e_S \in E_S \wedge e_R \in E_R$
    $O = O \cup \{ (e_S, e_T) \}$
  End if
End for

(a) Generate Kernels   (b) Expand   (c) Find Correspondences

Fig. 3. Algorithms to compute kernels

is added to the set of entities E. Then, for each restriction, it is added to the output if it is not already present and the left entity of the restriction belongs to E. Therefore, the *Expand* algorithm computes the maximal connected subsets of restrictions out of all of the source or target restrictions. Note that it is called two times to compute source and target restrictions, respectively.

Finally, the *Find Correspondences* algorithm finds all correspondences C' that relate the entities of source and target restrictions that were found by means of algorithm *Expand* (cf. Figure 3(c)). This algorithm takes a set of correspondences, and a set of source and target restrictions as input. First, it computes all the entities contained in source and target restrictions by means of *Entities* algorithm, which is not described because it is straightforward. Then, for each correspondence, it is added to the output if the entities that are related by this correspondence belong to source and target entities.

The *Generate Kernels* algorithm terminates in $O(c(s^2 + t^2 + c))$ time in the worst case, where c is the total number of input correspondences, and s and t are the total number of input source and target restrictions, respectively. Furthermore, this algorithm generates a total number of c kernels. Note that the proof of this analysis has been omitted due to space restrictions.

Figure 4 illustrates how this algorithm works. It takes correspondence *V9* as input (cf. Figure 4(a)), which is an object property correspondence that relates *rvu:reviews* with *mo:hasReview*.

The first step (cf. Figure 4(b)) is to expand *rvu:reviews* using source restrictions. In this case, the domain of *rvu:reviews* is *rvu:Review* and the range is *dbp:Film*, both restrictions are added. Then, *rvu:Review* has a minimal cardinality restriction with *rvu:reviewer*, so this restriction is added as well. Our technique continues with the expansion until no new source restriction is added.

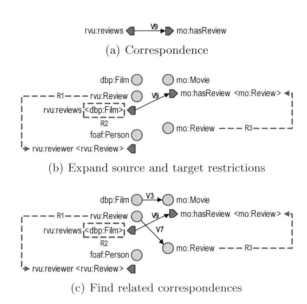

(a) Correspondence

(b) Expand source and target restrictions

(c) Find related correspondences

Fig. 4. Example of the Generate Kernels algorithm

The second step (cf. Figure 4(b)) is to expand *mo:hasReview* using target restrictions, the domain of *mo:hasReview* is *mo:Movie*, and its range is *mo:Review*, both restrictions are added. Furthermore, *mo:Review* has a minimal cardinality restriction with *mo:hasReview*, this restriction is added too and, in this case, the expansion is finished since no new target restriction is added.

Finally, our technique finds correspondences that relate the entities of both source and target restrictions (cf. Figure 4(c)). In this case, correspondences *V3* and *V7* that relate *dbp:Film* with *mo:Movie* and *rvu:Review* with *mo:Review*, respectively. Therefore, the final kernel of correspondence *V9* is shown in Figure 4(c). Note that the kernel for correspondence *V9* groups correspondences *V3* and *V7*. However, the kernel for correspondence *V3* does not group any other correspondences, i.e., the correspondence itself is a kernel. Therefore, this is the reason why our technique must process all input correspondences.

3.3   SPARQL Transformation

In this section, we present the algorithm to transform kernels into SPARQL executable mappings. A key concept of the SPARQL language is the triple pattern, which is a three-element tuple that comprises a subject, a predicate and an object. A SPARQL executable mapping is a two-element tuple (T_C, T_W) that comprises a set of triple patterns of the source and target ontologies, T_C (the CONSTRUCT clause) and T_W (the WHERE clause), respectively.

The transformation algorithm is shown in Figure 5(a). Note that *Initialise*, *Compute Graph* and *Compute Variables* algorithms are not described in detail due to space limitations. However, we use an example to illustrate them. The

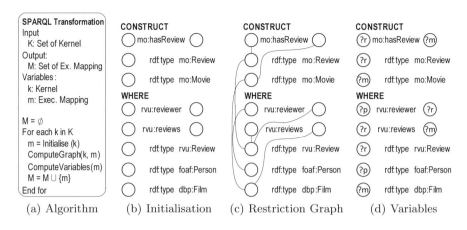

(a) Algorithm   (b) Initialisation   (c) Restriction Graph   (d) Variables

Fig. 5. Algorithm and example of SPARQL Transformation

transformation algorithm takes a set of kernels K as input and it transforms each kernel into a SPARQL executable mapping, which is added to the output set M. To compute each SPARQL executable mapping, in the first step, the algorithm initialises the source triple patterns and the target triple patterns by means of *Initialise* algorithm. In this initialisation, for each class, it generates a triple pattern with an empty node, e.g., *mo:Review* in Figure 5(b); and for each data property or object property, it generates a triple pattern with two empty nodes, e.g., *mo:hasReview* in Figure 5(b). These empty nodes are assigned with variables in the following steps.

The second step computes the restriction graph that consists of relating the empty nodes previously generated by means of source and target restrictions and correspondences. This restriction graph is computed by the *Compute Graph* algorithm. Note that m is an input/output parameter of this algorithm, i.e., m is modified and returned by the *Compute Graph* algorithm. Finally, the third step computes the variables of the *CONSTRUCT* and *WHERE* clauses by using the same variable for nodes that are connected by an edge. These variables are computed by the *Compute Variables* algorithm, which also has m as an input/output parameter.

An example of the SPARQL Transformation algorithm is shown in Figures 5(b), 5(c), and 5(d). In this case, it transforms the kernel of Figure 4 into a SPARQL executable mapping. The first step (cf. Figure 5(b)) is to create a triple pattern for each entity that appears in the kernel, e.g., for *foaf:Person*, it creates a triple pattern in the *WHERE* clause that specifies a subject node of this type, but it does not assign a variable yet. Furthermore, for *rvu:reviews*, it creates a triple pattern in which subject and object nodes have blank variables. The final result of this step is a template of a SPARQL executable mapping that comprises a set of empty nodes, which are assigned with variables in the following steps.

The second step (cf. Figure 5(c)) consists of computing the restriction graph for the triple patterns of the previous template. This step is achieved by

Table 1. Results of our evaluation

	MO	O2M	C	LP	SP	ERC	ESB	ESP	SRC	SS
Classes	9	72	728	728	728	365	365	365	365	365
Data Properties	8	41	100	100	100	100	100	100	100	100
Object Properties	8	90	726	0	0	363	0	0	363	0
Correspondences	10	11	777	414	414	414	51	51	51	51
Source restrictions	17	695	776	413	413	50	50	50	1502	413
Target restrictions	20	118	776	413	413	1502	170	463	50	50
Executable mappings	10	10	777	414	414	51	51	51	51	51
Time (seconds)	0.08	0.67	0.23	0.19	0.17	18.29	0.22	0.21	27.46	0.25

specifying an edge between two nodes of the triple patterns if there exists a restriction or correspondence that relates those nodes. For example, since *rvu:Review* is the domain of *rvu:reviews*, there exists an edge between the subject of the triple pattern of *rvu:Review* and the subject of the triple pattern of *rvu:reviews*. Furthermore, since *V3* relates *dbp:Film* with *mo:Movie*, there is an edge between the subjects of their triple patterns. Finally, the third step (cf. Figure 5(d)) assigns the same variable for nodes that are connected by edges, e.g., *?m* is the variable used for the subject of *dbp:Film* and the object of *rvu:reviews* triple patterns. The final SPARQL executable mapping for correspondence *V9* is shown in Figure 5(d).

This algorithm terminates in $O(k((e+2)(s+t+c)+e^2))$ time in the worst case, where k is the total number of input kernels, e is the total number of entities in the source and target ontologies, c is the total number of correspondences, and s and t are the total number of source and target restrictions, respectively. Furthermore, this algorithm generates a total number of k executable mappings. Note that the proof of this analysis has been omitted due to space restrictions.

4   Implementation and Evaluation

In this section, we describe the implementation and evaluation of our technique. We have implemented the algorithms described in Section 3 using Java 1.6 and the Jena framework 2.6.3. In this evaluation, we compute the time taken by our technique to automatically generate SPARQL executable mappings. Note that, to compute these times, we ran the experiments on a PC with a single 2.66 GHz Core 2 Duo CPU and 4 GB RAM, running on Windows XP (SP3) and JRE 1.6.0. Furthermore, to make these times more precise, we repeated each experiment 25 times and computed the maximum value.

We have tested our technique with ten different scenarios and the results are shown in Table 1. Note that we measure the number of classes, data properties and object properties of both source and target ontologies, the number of correspondences and source and target restrictions, the total number of generated executable mappings, and the maximum time taken to generate them.

An important issue is whether the interpretation of the correspondences is coherent with respect to the expected interpretation by experts. Regarding the example presented in Section 3 (MO in Table 1), the resulting target instances after performing the data translation task are as expected by experts. Furthermore, another scenario deals with the integration of semantic-web services with successful results. Semantic-web services try to reduce the number of limitations of (non-semantic) web services by enriching them with semantic annotations to improve their discovery and composition. Therefore, each of these services is related to one or more ontologies that describe it. In this context, we integrate OWL-S as the source ontology and the Minimal Service Model (MSM) as the target ontology [26] (O2M in Table 1). Thanks to our technique, we are able to automatically populate iServe, which comprises a number of semantic-web services represented using MSM, based on a number of semantic-web services represented using OWL-S [26].

Finally, we have tested our technique with a benchmark that provides eight data translation patterns, which are inspired by real-world data translation problems [34]. In this benchmark, the data translation task is performed by a set of queries that are automatically instantiated from a number of query templates that have been devised by experts. These patterns are the following:

- Copy (C): each class, data property and object property source instance is copied into a class, data property or object property target instance.
- Lift Properties (LP): the data properties of a set of subclasses in the source are moved to a common superclass in the target.
- Sink Properties (SP): the data properties of a superclass in the source are moved to a number of subclasses in the target.
- Extract Related Classes (ERC): the data properties of a class in the source are grouped into a number of new classes in the target, which are related to the original one by a number of object properties.
- Extract Subclasses (ESB): a class in the source is split into several subclasses in the target and data properties are distributed amongst them.
- Extract Superclasses (ESP): a class in the source is split into several superclasses in the target, and data properties are distributed amongst them.
- Simplify Related Classes (SRC): source classes, which are related by a set of object properties, are transformed into a target class that aggregates them.
- Simplify Specialisation (SS): a set of specialised classes in the source are flattened into a single target class.

In all of these patterns, our technique generates the same target instances as the benchmark. Therefore, we conclude that the interpretation of the correspondences is coherent with the expected results by experts in these patterns.

5   Conclusions

In this paper, we present a technique to automatically generate SPARQL executable mappings. Our technique has been devised for semantic-web ontologies that are represented using the OWL ontology language. It is based on correspondences and source and target restrictions, and it generates SPARQL executable mappings in two steps: kernel generation and SPARQL transformation.

As a conclusion, we have devised a technique that, building on our experiments, seems promising enough for real-world scenarios: we evaluate it over ten scenarios and, in our evaluation results, executable mappings are generated in less than thirty seconds in the worst case. Furthermore, we also test the interpretation of correspondences that our algorithm assumes, and the result is that it is coherent with the results expected by experts.

The original contributions of our technique are as follows: 1) Instead of relying on instance examples of the target ontology, we automatically generate executable mappings based on restrictions and correspondences, which makes it appealing in many practical cases. 2) We have devised an algorithm to generate kernels, which are language-independent executable mappings that makes restrictions and correspondences explicit. 3) We have devised an algorithm to transform kernels into SPARQL executable mappings by linking the variables of triple patterns in these mappings.

References

1. Alexe, B., Chiticariu, L., Miller, R.J., Pepper, D., Tan, W.C.: Muse: a system for understanding and designing mappings. In: SIGMOD, pp. 1281–1284 (2008)
2. Alexe, B., Tan, W.C., Velegrakis, Y.: STBenchmark: towards a benchmark for mapping systems. PVLDB 1(1), 230–244 (2008)
3. Antoniou, G., van Harmelen, F.: A Semantic Web Primer, 2nd edn. The MIT Press, Cambridge (2008)
4. Bernstein, P.A., Haas, L.M.: Information integration in the enterprise. Commun. ACM 51(9), 72–79 (2008)
5. Bernstein, P.A., Melnik, S.: Model management 2.0: manipulating richer mappings. In: SIGMOD, pp. 1–12 (2007)
6. Bizer, C.: The emerging web of linked data. IEEE Int. Sys. (2009)
7. Bizer, C., Lehmann, J., Kobilarov, G., Auer, S., Becker, C., Cyganiak, R., Hellmann, S.: DBpedia - a crystallization point for the web of data. J. Web Sem. (2009)
8. Bizer, C., Schultz, A.: The R2R framework: Publishing and discovering mappings on the web. In: COLD (2010)
9. Choi, N., Song, I.-Y., Han, H.: A survey on ontology mapping. SIGMOD Record 35(3), 34–41 (2006)
10. Euzenat, J., Polleres, A., Scharffe, F.: Processing ontology alignments with SPARQL. In: CISIS, pp. 913–917 (2008)
11. Euzenat, J., Shvaiko, P.: Ontology Matching. Springer, Heidelberg (2007)
12. Fagin, R., Kolaitis, P.G., Miller, R.J., Popa, L.: Data exchange: semantics and query answering. Theor. Comput. Sci. 336(1), 89–124 (2005)
13. Fuxman, A., Hernández, M.A., Ho, C.T.H., Miller, R.J., Papotti, P., Popa, L.: Nested mappings: Schema mapping reloaded. In: VLDB, pp. 67–78 (2006)
14. Haas, L.M., Hernández, M.A., Ho, H., Popa, L., Roth, M.: Clio grows up: from research prototype to industrial tool. In: SIGMOD, pp. 805–810 (2005)
15. Halevy, A.Y.: Answering queries using views: A survey. VLDB J. 10(4), 270–294 (2001)
16. Heath, T., Motta, E.: Revyu: Linking reviews and ratings into the web of data. J. Web Sem. 6(4), 266–273 (2008)

17. Karvounarakis, G., Magkanaraki, A., Alexaki, S., Christophides, V., Plexousakis, D., Scholl, M., Tolle, K.: Querying the semantic web with RQL. Computer Networks 42(5), 617–640 (2003)
18. Kensche, D., Quix, C., Li, Y., Jarke, M.: Generic schema mappings. In: Parent, C., Schewe, K.-D., Storey, V.C., Thalheim, B. (eds.) ER 2007. LNCS, vol. 4801, pp. 132–148. Springer, Heidelberg (2007)
19. Lenzerini, M.: Data integration: A theoretical perspective. In: PODS, pp. 233–246 (2002)
20. Mecca, G., Papotti, P., Raunich, S.: Core schema mappings. In: SIGMOD, pp. 655–668 (2009)
21. Motik, B., Horrocks, I., Sattler, U.: Bridging the gap between OWL and relational databases. J. Web Sem. 7(2), 74–89 (2009)
22. Noy, N.F.: Semantic integration: A survey of ontology-based approaches. SIGMOD Record 33(4), 65–70 (2004)
23. Noy, N.F., Klein, M.C.A.: Ontology evolution: Not the same as schema evolution. Knowl. Inf. Syst. 6(4), 428–440 (2004)
24. Papotti, P., Torlone, R.: Schema exchange: A template-based approach to data and metadata translation. In: Parent, C., Schewe, K.-D., Storey, V.C., Thalheim, B. (eds.) ER 2007. LNCS, vol. 4801, pp. 323–337. Springer, Heidelberg (2007)
25. Parreiras, F.S., Staab, S., Schenk, S., Winter, A.: Model driven specification of ontology translations. In: Li, Q., Spaccapietra, S., Yu, E., Olivé, A. (eds.) ER 2008. LNCS, vol. 5231, pp. 484–497. Springer, Heidelberg (2008)
26. Pedrinaci, C., Liu, D., Maleshkova, M., Lambert, D., Kopecký, J., Domingue, J.: iServe: a linked services publishing platform. In: ORES (2010)
27. Petropoulos, M., Deutsch, A., Papakonstantinou, Y., Katsis, Y.: Exporting and interactively querying web service-accessed sources: The CLIDE system. ACM Trans. Database Syst. 32(4) (2007)
28. Popa, L., Velegrakis, Y., Miller, R.J., Hernández, M.A., Fagin, R.: Translating web data. In: VLDB, pp. 598–609 (2002)
29. Qin, H., Dou, D., LePendu, P.: Discovering executable semantic mappings between ontologies. In: Chung, S. (ed.) OTM 2007, Part I. LNCS, vol. 4803, pp. 832–849. Springer, Heidelberg (2007)
30. Rahm, E., Bernstein, P.A.: A survey of approaches to automatic schema matching. VLDB J. 10(4), 334–350 (2001)
31. Rivero, C.R., Hernández, I., Ruiz, D., Corchuelo, R.: Mosto: Generating sparql executable mappings between ontologies. In: Jeusfeld, M., Delcambre, L., Ling, T.W. (eds.) ER 2011. LNCS, vol. 6998, pp. 118–131. Springer, Heidelberg (2011)
32. Rivero, C.R., Hernández, I., Ruiz, D., Corchuelo, R.: On using database techniques for generating ontology mappings. In: SWWS (2011)
33. Rivero, C.R., Hernández, I., Ruiz, D., Corchuelo, R.: A reference architecture for building semantic-web mediators. In: IWSSA (2011)
34. Rivero, C.R., Ruiz, D., Corchuelo, R.: On benchmarking data translation systems for semantic-web ontologies (Tech. Report), http://tdg-seville.info/Download.ashx?id=205
35. Shadbolt, N., Berners-Lee, T., Hall, W.: The semantic web revisited. IEEE Int. Sys. 21(3), 96–101 (2006)
36. ten Cate, B., Chiticariu, L., Kolaitis, P.G., Tan, W.C.: Laconic schema mappings: Computing the core with SQL queries. PVLDB 2(1), 1006–1017 (2009)
37. Yu, C., Popa, L.: Constraint-based XML query rewriting for data integration. In: SIGMOD, pp. 371–382 (2004)

Enterprise Monitoring Ontology

Patrício de Alencar Silva and Hans Weigand

Department of Information Management
Tilburg University, P.O. Box 90153
5000LE Tilburg, The Netherlands
{p.silva,h.weigand}@uvt.nl

Abstract. A value constellation is an economic system of actors exchanging objects of value to satisfy a consumer's need. Its operation is driven by strategic goals, such as shared profit generation and strengthening of long-term business relationships. Its stability, though, depends on how efficiently its actors perform their operations and, consequently, on how value is produced. How to enforce actual value delivery gives rise to several conceptual and practical issues on service monitoring, being the former the subject of this paper. We hereby propose a framework comprising an ontology and method for deriving monitoring requirements *from* and *to* value constellations. The framework is evaluated via case study in electricity markets, where a smart metering constellation provides monitoring services to another constellation from the electricity imbalance market. The feasibility analysis shows how to use the ontology to derive multiple alternatives to monitor a value constellation, and how to choose the (potentially) most value-adding one.

Keywords: Enterprise Ontology, Electricity Markets, Requirements Engineering, Service Monitoring, Value Constellations.

1 Introduction

A value constellation is an economic system of actors collaborating via exchange of objects of value, so as to fulfill a consumer's need [1]. In such a system, actors share common interests, such as to increase profit generation and preserve long-term collaborations. The stability of a value constellation, though, is a product of individual operational performances on value production and delivery, whereby collective value generation emerges. Indispensably for medium and small-scale participant enterprises, it is essential not only to engage but also remain on one or many constellations, for the sake of individual business survival and resilience.

Enforcement of operational performance somewhat depends on the design and application of monitoring mechanisms. The main research question here is *how a value constellation can be monitored*. This question can be decomposed into many conceptual and practical ones, which the former comprehends the subject of research reported in this paper. Hence, taking the representation of a value constellation as a starting point (i.e. the specification of its constituent actors, operations and exchanged objects), the conceptual sub-questions of interest here are: (1) *what the monitoring*

M. Jeusfeld, L. Delcambre, and T.W. Ling (Eds.): ER 2011, LNCS 6998, pp. 132–146, 2011.

requirements of a value constellation are and (2) *how these requirements can be derived and represented.* To our best knowledge, there is no systematic approach available to derive monitoring requirements for value constellations on the business strategy level. There are sufficient motivations to treat such research questions, though. Among them, we emphasize the possibility of furnishing business analysts with a reasoning tool for designing monitoring requirements for an enterprise operating in the context of a value constellation.

To cope with the before mentioned research questions, we propose a framework to derive monitoring requirements *from* and *to* value constellations. The framework comprises an ontology, named Enterprise Monitoring Ontology (EMO) and a (business strategy) reasoning method. EMO can be used to re-produce a value monitoring viewpoint from an individual actor/enterprise which has a monitoring need that can be fulfilled by a (monitoring) value constellation. Taking this actor's perspective as predominant over the other ones', EMO builds a value monitoring sub-system, with a proper set of monitoring roles, operations and objects. That is, EMO is a representation of a micro-level (individual) behavioral specification of *operational stereotypes* for monitoring to be embodied within a value constellation. EMO comprises three sub-ontologies, representing different but complementary views relative to a value level monitoring viewpoint: (1) *monitoring goal ontology*, (2) *monitoring policy ontology*, and (3) *monitoring metric ontology*. The reasoning method can be used on the derivation of the views, which are further reified into alternative value constellations that supply other constellations with monitoring objects. Not only are monitoring constellations expected to be economically self-sustainable, but also value-adding sub-systems. Ultimately, the reasoning method assists on selecting the (potentially) best pay-off monitoring constellation.

The paper is organized as follows. Section 2 provides some of the main premises of the theories adopted as references to describe the operation of value constellations, and how they can be extended and used as meta-modeling constructs for building value constellations. In Section 3, EMO is introduced, along with a detailed description of its constituent sub-ontologies. In Section 4, the use of the reasoning method is demonstrated on the feasibility analysis of monitoring constellations for a business case in electricity markets. Discussion and future outlook are provided in Section 5.

2 Theoretical Background

A handful of theories have been proposed to explain how value constellations (a.k.a. enterprise collaborations, value systems, service networks, etc.) form and operate, and other ones continue to appear. Each of these theories focuses on a different business aspect or phenomena. Some aspects conflict, some overlap. We cite here three of these theories, along with their corresponding modeled aspects. The first one is the e^3value, a framework with ontology and method, proposed by Gordijn [1]. E^3value models a value constellation as a system of actors exchanging objects of economic value. It focuses primarily on the *profitability analysis* and assessment of a value constellation as an economically sustainable system. The second one is the Resource Event Agent Ontology (REA), proposed by McCarthy [2]. REA models a value constellation as a system of agents performing economic events that change the state of resources.   REA focuses on describing the enterprise *accounting phenomena*, by typifying business events and relating them to their corresponding actors, via commitment relationships. The third one is the Business Modeling Ontology (BMO), proposed by Osterwalder [3]. BMO can be used to build a model of a firm for an individual enterprise, making use of four different views that much resembles to the four perspectives of the Balance Scorecard, proposed by Kaplan and Norton [4]. BMO focuses on the aspect of the relationship between the enterprise and the *environment* characterized by customer's demands.

A few contributions have been done on merging these and other satellite theories in order to find a common denominator that could explain why and how modern enterprises operate in business collaboration contexts. Andersson et al. [5] have merged the before mentioned theories into a (Business) Reference Ontology. Among many motivations of this work, the authors highlight the importance of identifying intersections among the merged ontologies as a mean for individual ontology evolution. The proposed ontology comprises approximately 17 basic concepts and 40 core relationships (incl. generalizations and aggregations). As alternative business ontologies continue to be proposed, other reconciliations can succeed towards a core understanding of the phenomena of business collaboration.

One of the most comprehensive theories on enterprise modeling proposed thus far is the Enterprise Ontology, by Dietz [6]. Grounding on a Language Action Perspective (LAP), the author defines and articulates three basic concepts and two relationships to describe how modern enterprises operate. A brief description of the theory follows. An enterprise system is composed by three power sets: *actors, production operations* and *coordination operations*. An actor reifies the notion of *authority* to be able to perform both types of operations. A production operation relates an actor to the object to be produced. A coordination operation relates two actors by the object they communicate. Actors are assigned to production operations via *competence* relationships, and to coordination via *responsibility* relationships. Operations are still classified by its state: before being performed, operations are *acts*, whereas after successful execution, they produce *facts*. These basic concepts and relationships define the first of four axioms of the theory: the *operational axiom*. The other ones comprise the *transactional axiom* (describing how operations follow a transactional pattern), the *composition axiom* (describing how transactions can be composed) and the *distinction axiom* (describing how human actors within an enterprise perform ontological, infological and datalogical acts). The ontology defines a closure *organizational theorem*, which assigns the realization of ontological, infological and datalogical acts to distinct subsystems within the enterprise.

In order to answer the question of *how a value constellation can be monitored*, we reconcile concepts from the Enterprise Ontology of Dietz, the Reference Ontology of Andersson et al., and the e^3value ontology of Gordijn. The output of this reconciliation is the so-called Enterprise Monitoring Ontology (EMO). According to Dietz, the elements of the Enterprise Ontology can be extended by stereotypes to model different interfaces an enterprise operation can expose to the outside world. More precise enterprise actor's stereotypes can be described via assignments to these operations. We therefore use the Enterprise Ontology as a reference meta-theory and extend it with stereotypes for characterizing monitoring operations. Some of the stereotypes are reified by concepts from the Reference Ontology of Andersson et al. and further realized by e^3value elements. Finally, the monitoring stereotypes are instantiated with some parameters from a business case. EMO is described in details in the next section.

3 Enterprise Monitoring Ontology (EMO)

EMO defines the static abstract space of a value monitoring system. It comprises three distinct but aligned sub-ontologies, each describing a different view on the system: (1) the *monitoring goal ontology*, (2) the *monitoring policy ontology*, and (3) the *monitoring metric ontology*. This section is dedicated to explain the formulation and integration of these views into the value monitoring viewpoint.

3.1 Monitoring Goal Ontology

The *monitoring goal ontology* is the starting and ending point for deriving a value monitoring viewpoint. Actually, it comprises a process ontology, whereby one can navigate across the other sub-ontologies. It is described as follows and is depicted in **Fig. 1**. The ontology grounds on three foundational concepts: *actor*, *operation* and *object*, all stereotyped as «metaclass». The concept of *object* is equivalent to the concept of *resource* from the Reference Ontology, which defines resources as "valuable objects to the actors". An *actor* aims to achieve a *goal*. Here, at least two types of goals can be distinguished: a *core business goal*, to be accomplished via core business operations, and a *monitoring goal*, derived from the core goal and providing means to achieve it. A *metric* parameterizes a goal. As a mean to accomplish a goal, an actor may engage on performing operations, which are classified into *production* and *coordination* [6].

A *coordination operation* relates two actors via «commitment» of *responsibility*. Dietz identifies a basic set of coordination operations, such as *request*, *promise*, *state* and *accept*.

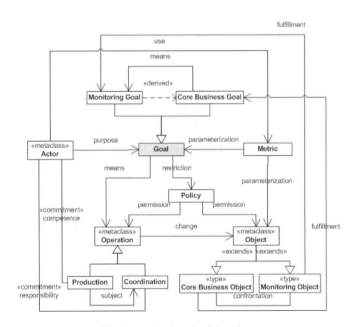

Fig. 1. Monitoring Goal Ontology

Coordination operations always have production ones as a subject (i.e. as a propositional content). Actors get committed to production acts by *competence*. Anderson et al. have identified two stereotypes of production acts: *conversion* and *transfer*. Examples of conversion are to *use*, *consume* or *produce* an object, whereas examples of transfer are to *give* or to *take* (the right on) some object. In the end, all of these operations somewhat change some feature of the object in discourse.

At this point, at least two types of object must be identified: *core business objects* and *monitoring objects*. A core business object represents a promise of value production, from one actor to another, whereas a monitoring object regards the evidence of real value delivery. Actors use metrics to parameterize both goals and objects. A core business object fulfils a core business goal, whereas a monitoring business object fulfils a monitoring goal. The parameterization provided by a metric allows for confrontation of a value promise (i.e. the core object) with the real value delivery (i.e. the monitoring object). The internal feedback loop closes when the actor tracks whether his monitoring goal was achieved or not, and in turn, how it supported the achievement of a core business goal.

The instantiation of these relationships provides a characterization of a value monitoring goal. The next step comprises the definition of monitoring policies restrictions on the type of operations to be performed by each actor in a value monitoring system.

3.2 Monitoring Policy Ontology

The *monitoring policy ontology* describes a view that *quantitatively* restricts how monitoring goals can be achieved. It grounds on the core elements of the Role Based Access Control (RBAC) model [7]. RBAC provides a core set of policy concepts, whose precise semantics definition depends on the system under design. The semantics of a value monitoring policy is depicted in Fig. 2 and is described as follows. A policy is defined by two assignment relationships: one for relating roles to performing actors, and one for relating actors to permissions. A policy, therefore, defines who can do what and how. The stereotypes for monitoring actors were identified from the literature in Contract Law [8], specifically on what concerns contract enforcement parties. For a given monitoring policy, an actor can play one of the four roles: (1) a *monitor*, an active actor that wants to monitor a *monitoree*; (2) a *monitoree*, a passive actor committed to a monitor via promise to deliver a core business object; (3) a *third-party*, a neutral party acting on behalf of the monitor to execute monitoring operations; and (4) a *regulator* (e.g. certification authorities, regulation bodies, etc.), who is in the exercise and possession of a monitoring system norm.

According to Coyne and Davis [9], good RBAC engineering practices include firstly characterizing policy permissions and, further, assigning them to build stereotyped roles to be played by actors. *Permissions* are logical containers relating operation types to object types. They can provide access to operations and disclosure of objects. As mentioned before, operations (coordination or production) are typified by the changes they cause on features of objects. To provide a characterization of the *production* operations, we describe the relationships between operations and objects, by using the *conversion events* from Andersson et al. [5], stereotyped as «conversion». Two types of operations are identified: *monitored* and *monitoring operations*. A *monitoring operation* produces «conversion» a *monitored object* (i.e. the primary evidence). A *monitoring operation* in turn uses «conversion» *monitoring* and *regulatory objects* to produce «conversion» a *monitoring object*. Here, regulatory objects stand for all kinds of objects that unlock or disclosure private

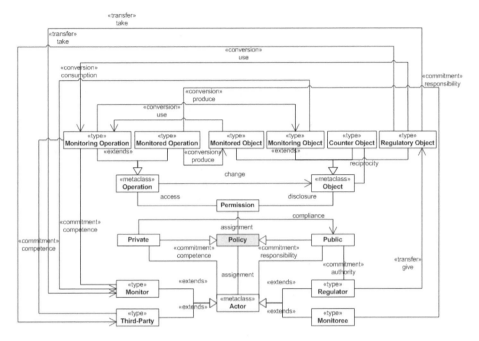

Fig. 2. Monitoring Policy Ontology

verifiable information. Examples are: accreditations, certifications, public keys, property rights, etc.). Another type of object comprises the *counter objects*. They are also part of a policy, being provided in reciprocity to all other objects. The crucial importance of these objects will become clear on the monitoring metric ontology. Yet from a production perspective, it is important to define the monitoring operations performed by each role. Firstly, regulators have authority to define public policies. Public policies are templates subsuming the allowed alternatives whereby all the actors can perform operations. In theory, all the private policies must be compliant (i.e. subsumed by) the public ones. All actors have responsibility «commitment» on defining their own private monitoring policies. A *monitoree* has the responsibility «commitment» on performing monitored operations, whereas *monitors* and *third-parties* may have the competence «commitment» on performing monitoring ones.

From a coordination perspective, it is worth to define what objects are communicated from and to whom. We use the *transfer events* from Andersson et al. [5], stereotyped as «transfer». Thus, a *monitoree* gives «transfer» monitoring objects to other monitors and/or third-parties (indirectly, from monitored operations). A *regulator* gives «transfer» regulatory objects to *monitors* and/or *third-parties*. Yet, *monitors* and *third-parties* can take «transfer» regulator objects from *regulators*. To close the monitoring policy loop with the main production operation, *monitors* can consume «conversion» monitoring objects (indirectly, via third-party monitoring operations, or directly, via his own monitoring operations).

The subtlest conceptual distinction of this sub-ontology is the *stereotyping of monitoring operations*. By means of that, any domain-specific monitoring operation (e.g. collecting, filtering, processing, publishing, etc) could expose a monitoring or monitored behavior. The difference relies on how an actor uses or exposes his operations via monitoring interfaces (described in terms of monitoring objects converted or transferred).

3.3 Monitoring Metric Ontology

Complementary to the monitoring policy ontology, the monitoring metric ontology aims to restrict qualitatively how monitoring goals can be fulfilled by monitoring objects. Another important aspect is that it takes the perspective of the *monitor* role on typifying and evaluating monitoring objects according to the (potential) value they return. The ontology is depicted in Fig. 3 and is described as follows. An actor playing the role of a monitor uses metrics to parameterize his goals and objects. In order to be consistently traceable via objects, the semantics of goals and metrics must be equivalent. That is, as the fulfillment of goals depends on the monitoring objects, the monitorability of a goal becomes dependent on the monitorability these objects.

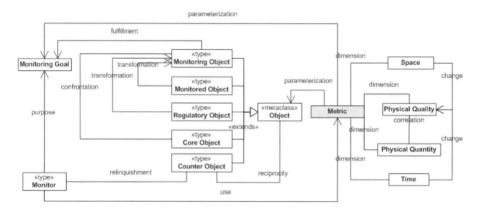

Fig. 3. Monitoring Metric Ontology

A metric is defined as a quaternary relationship with four dimensions, each of them constituting a proper universe of discourse: *physical quantity, physical quality, time* and *space*. According to Gruber and Olsen [10], *physical quantities* represent a whole universe of ontological discourse. The authors propose a comprehensive ontology for classifying physical quantities according to their mathematical dependencies. The ontology is aimed to support diverse applications on mathematics, engineering and physics, where there is a need for consensus on comparability and order. Examples of quantity classes are tensor quantities, units of measure and magnitudes. Regarding *physical qualities*, these are properties that distinguish a certain object in reality as unique. The value attributed to these properties may depend on relative human interpretation, in opposition to the exact nature of quantities. Specifically on the context of value modeling, Weigand et al. [11] have defined qualities of value objects as *second-order values*. In practice, such properties depend on the existence of the object they qualify. In the ontological discourse, they are independent entities. Examples of second-order values are aesthetics, experience and convenience. It is worth noting that such properties are much more comprehensive than non-functional properties of services [12]. In the business context, McCannon discusses on empirical evidences of trade-offs and correlations between quantity and quality of provisioned economic objects [13]. For instance, considering the time of manufacturing an economic object as constant, increasing demand for quantity may cause decreases on quality. Finally, *time* and *space* dimensions close the description of a monitoring metric. These dimensions can somehow change quality properties of a physical object. For instance, the economic value of an apartment may vary according to the location and the season of the year. When parameterizing an object of value, a metric can be used on the design of (business) Key Performance Indicators, as referred by Parmenter [14]. Ram and Liu [15] employ some of the mentioned metric dimensions to provide semantics for data provenance in terms of characterization of events (and not objects, as here). Besides, time and space can be used as consistency parameters for traceability of monitoring goals by means of monitoring objects.

The ultimate purpose of the monitoring metric is the parameterization of all the objects of value being exchanged in a value monitoring system. A monitoring object fulfills a monitoring goal of the monitor role, as it attests on the delivery of the value promised in terms of a core business object. The confrontation of these two objects is one of the most important monitoring relationships to be traced. It is worth to highlight the importance of the counter objects in this context. Among the Ten Principles of Economics discussed by Mankiw [16], the second one states that *the value of something is what you give up to get it*. Cost here is much more comprehensive than monetary value, and is equivalent to value. Thus, as counter objects are offered in economic reciprocity in return of all the other types of objects, they can be used to assess directly the value of the monitoring within a value monitoring sub-system. As the regulatory and the monitored objects are also used and transformed into a monitoring object, they can be used to assess indirectly the value of monitoring in this case. The loop closes when a monitoring object fulfills a monitoring goal, which is the purpose of the monitor role. Instances of value monitoring constellations can be assessed and adapted via cyclic interactions from the goal, through the policy, to the metric ontologies.

4   Case Study Evaluation

In this section we demonstrate how to derive a value monitoring viewpoint using EMO in conjunction with a strategic reasoning method. The case is provided by the Energy Research Center of the Netherlands (ECN) and is concerned with the need for monitoring electricity production in the market of renewable energy sources.

4.1   Business Case Description

The case comes from the electricity markets, where the commodity is traded. A full description of the roles played in this system is provided by the Directive 2004/54/EC [17]. The case is briefly described as follows. All the electricity suppliers accredited as Balance Responsible Parties (BRP) have the obligation to provide estimates on the amount of electricity to be produced to the Transmission System Operator (TSO). Such estimates, called *energy programs,* must be provided each 15 minutes, so as the TSO can have a big picture on the energy flow in the whole system. Yet, environmental drivers have pushed the inclusion of renewable energy sources (e.g. biomass, solar and wind energy) in the electricity market, which can also be accredited as BRPs. However, intermittent resources such as solar panels and wind turbines often fail on delivering the expected amount of electricity, causing extra imbalances to the system. When a wind turbine fails, it has to pay balancing costs to the TSO. There are two ways the BRP can cope with the implied penalties: (1) to pay the imbalance costs directly to the TSO, which can be high as the TSO offers transparent balancing by using its own reserves; or (2) to use its own portfolio of small-scale Distributed Energy Resources (DER) to cope (potentially) with the imbalance. The second option pushes the BRP to freelance on the electricity wholesale market so as to discover a bundle of DERs to cope with the imbalance. This last option has a high business value to the BRP, as it may not only cope with the caused imbalance, but also generate profit.

A value constellation for this case is depicted in Fig. 4, using the e^3value graphical representation. A BRP has a need to balance its electricity production, which can be fulfilled by exchanging electricity «core object» for money «counter object» in three ways: (1) directly with DERs; (2) indirectly, via Aggregators; and (3) both. Aggregators bundle electricity produced by small-scale DERs, and sell it to the BRPs. Aggregators have been implemented in reality in the agriculture sector in the Netherlands (bundling large scale DERs). Implementing aggregators for scalable management of small-scale DERs is still subject of research. Any of the actors can fail on delivering the amount of electricity promised, causing a chain of imbalances in the system. At this point, our research question can be applied to this case: *how a value constellation from the electricity imbalance reduction market can be monitored?*

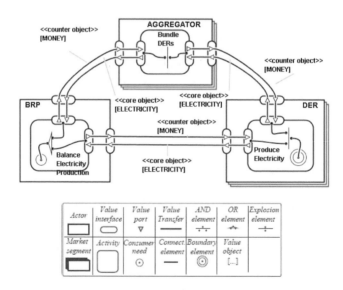

Fig. 4. Electricity Imbalance Reduction Value Constellation

4.2   Reasoning on EMO: Strategic Value Monitoring Method

To provide alternative answers to the previous question, we develop on the use of EMO and its reasoning method so as to produce a value monitoring viewpoint of an individual actor willing to monitor value delivery from his business partners. The method comprises five steps, which are explained as follows.

Step 1 – *Monitoring Scenario and Private Goal Setting:* a monitoring scenario identifies who wants to monitor whom, i.e. *monitor* and *monitoree*. The *monitor* has a monitoring goal, which is derived from his core business goals and can be fulfilled by monitoring objects, as specified in the goal monitoring ontology (vide Fig. 1). This approach leads to monitoring a value constellation by interactions involving pairs of actors. In this case, the monitoring of the whole constellation is not centralized, but emerges from its constituent monitoring interactions. This approach much conforms to the shareholder's perspective of the enterprise, discussed by Smith [18]. An actor operating within a constellation as a shareholder has selfish interests on profitability as a priority over social responsibility. The opposite approach represents the stakeholder's perspective. Squazzoni [19] also analyses this kind of phenomena on understanding global behavior of social systems, starting from the analysis of individual behavior.

We select the monitoring scenario involving the *aggregators* (as monitors) and the *DERs* (as monitorees). The monitor has core business and monitoring goals which can be parameterized via metric ontology. For example, an aggregator may have a core business goal represented by the tuple: <Unit of measure|Quality|CommodityTime|Location>. An instance of this goal is <2.775 kW|Predictability 0.85|Electricity|15 min.|Noord-Brabant>, where: kW are used as unit of measure for electricity; 0.85 is the predictability factor (i.e. a second order value) that the amount of electricity will be produced; 15 minutes is the energy program time window; and Noord-Brabant, a geographic region in the Netherlands. From this core business goal, multiple *monitoring goals* can be derived and parameterized. As each instance of a metric tuple produces a different goal characterization, individual metric dimensions can be taken as consistency variables for metric derivation. For instance, if the *physical* quantity is the consistency variable, the amount of electricity of individual DERs can be monitored and confronted with the total amount to be produced. If the *time* dimension is the consistency variable, it makes sense to check the production into time slots shorter than 15 minutes. Complexity on metric decomposition increases as multiple dimensions are chosen as consistency variables. An example of monitoring goal would be represented by the tuple <XkW|0.85|Electricity|15min.|Tilburg>, which reads as *"to verify whether an X amount of electricity, with a predictability factor of 85% is produced by a DER from Tilburg, each 15 minutes"*. As Tilburg is a sub-region of the Noord-Brabant Dutch province, the monitoring goal decomposition would be derived taking the spatial dimension as a consistency variable. Having derived the monitoring goal from a core business one, the next step comprises how to get the monitoring objects that will fulfill this goal.

Step 2 – *Public Monitoring Policy Design*: after setting his monitoring goal, a monitor must reason on the possible ways to fulfill it. In this case, monitoring becomes a "value need", and the problem is how to configure a value constellation to fulfill this need with monitoring objects. According to the monitoring policy ontology, a monitoring policy consists on what monitoring objects can be provided and communicated, from whom to whom and via what kind of operation. A public monitoring policy (theoretically) includes all the allowed alternatives to get monitoring objects. *Regulators* are responsible for defining public policies governing the operation of business collaboration domains.

An example of a monitoring policy for our business case is depicted in Fig. 5. This policy is a value representation of the original policy stated by the NMa/DTe Electricity

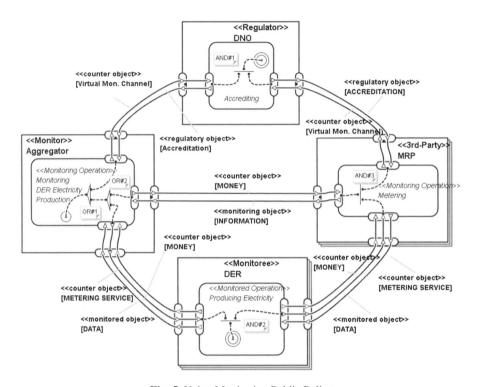

Fig. 5. Value Monitoring Public Policy

Metering Code, in the Netherlands [20]. Its description follows. An aggregator, assigned with a *monitor* role, wants to monitor the production of electricity of the DERs, which operate as *monitorees*. DERs are responsible for the production operation of "producing electricity", which in this case is stereotyped as a monitored operation, as it provides monitored objects in exchange of counter objects (vide Fig. 2). All types of objects are communicated via coordination operations which, in *e³value*, are instantiated by value exchanges. Boundary elements graphically define where the monitored objects are produced, whereas a consumer's need element indicates where the monitoring objects are consumed. An aggregator can get the monitoring objects (information) of interest via three alternatives: (1) directly from the DERs; (2) indirectly, via Metering Responsible Parties (MRPs), which are the third-parties that can perform metering operations; and (3) from both ways, which would allow for evidence confrontation.

In the first alternative, the monitoring is self-enforced, as the monitor has to transform the monitored object into a monitoring one, using his own internal production operations. In this business market, aggregators can only become competent to perform metering operations if accredited by the Distribution Network Operator (DNO), which has the authority to provide the accreditation «regulatory object» for the exercise of the Metering Responsibility. In this case, an accreditation does not require a monetary object in reciprocity, but a special object, called *virtual monitoring channel* «counter object», whose relative value to the DNO comprises the controllability over the monitoring objects produced by the system. Thus, accreditations work as public keys to unlock the access to the monitored objects and to transform them into monitoring ones.

In the second alternative, the monitoring is third-party enforced. The MRPs, acting on behalf of the aggregators, get the data from the DERs and transform it into monitoring objects (information), via metering operation (stereotyped as «monitoring operation»). In the third alternative, double enforcement happens. This situation is more appropriate for cases when the risk of fraud on value delivery is high. In short, a value monitoring policy specifies monitoring stereotypes of objects, operations and actors. It works as a template to define possible instances of value constellations allowed to fulfill a monitoring goal. Here, all the stereotypes defined in the monitoring policy apply.

Step 3 – *Private Monitoring Policy Discovery*: still reasoning on the monitoring policy sub-ontology, a monitor is responsible for elaborating his own private monitoring policies. These in turn must be compliant with (i.e. subsumed by) public ones. Private monitoring policies can also be discovered from public ones. From the policy depicted in Fig. 5, it is easy to discover the only three alternatives which could constitute private monitoring policies followed by the monitor. However, as the number of policy alternatives increases (specified in terms of traces, via AND/OR connectors), it may become necessary to discover alternative ways to satisfy a monitoring goal. Each alternative comprises a different value monitoring constellation, with different object flows. That is, taking a simple pair of actors from a given core business collaboration as a basic monitoring scenario (with a *monitor* and a *monitoree* as respective starting and ending points), multiple value monitoring constellations can be derived to support that collaboration with monitoring services.

Step 4 – *Private Monitoring Policy Selection*: as many monitoring constellations may be derived to achieve the same monitoring goal, a monitor actor is probably interested on selecting the constellation whereby he could get the monitoring objects with the best payoff. It is critical for a monitoring constellation to be self-sustainable. It is desirable, though, that it adds value to a core business constellation, i.e. generate profit. One way to select the best payoff monitoring constellation is to parameterize all the stereotyped objects using the monitoring metric sub-ontology.

Considering the practical definition of value stated by Mankiw [16], that *the value of something is what you give up to get it*, one stereotyped object deserves special consideration: the **counter objects**. According to the policy and metric sub-ontologies, these objects are offered in reciprocity of all the other stereotyped objects. Considering yet that regulatory and monitored objects are used to produce monitoring objects and that core business objects do not belong to the monitoring subsystem, but to the core business one, the definition of the value of monitoring can be simplified to the difference between the value of counter objects provided and received by the monitor actor. Indeed, counter-objects represent what the monitor relinquishes so as to ultimately get the monitoring objects. If the difference is positive, the monitoring constellation is self-sustainable and value-adding for the monitor. If the difference is null, the monitoring constellation is effective on mitigating risks of value creation in the core business the monitor participates. If the difference is negative, the monitoring payoff actually decreases the monitor's value production on the core business. Nevertheless, if monetary value cannot be assigned to counter objects, the assessment of the value of monitoring becomes more difficult to be performed. In this case, would be more relative than absolute, more qualitative than quantitative.

Step 5 – *Private Monitoring Goal Tracing*: the traceability of a monitoring goal depends primarily on how the monitoring objects are parameterized, and how they are confronted with core business objects. As the monitoring objects constitute evidence of real value delivery, they must be confronted with their corresponding value promises, stated in terms of core business objects, which flow in the core business constellation. As explained before, quantities, time and space can be used for metric consistency and for goal decomposition and tracing. Finally, goals are also related to each other. A monitoring goal has to be accomplished as a mean to achieve higher-level business goals of the actor playing the role of a monitor.

These five steps constitute a strategic method to be used with EMO to derive and reason upon monitoring requirements of a value constellation. Its application on the mentioned business case aims to show feasibility (rather than completeness) of the proposed approach.

5 Discussion

This paper has addressed some of the conceptual issues on how value constellations can be monitored. Its main contribution comprised an ontology and method that can be used to derive monitoring requirements of a value constellation. One of the most distinguishable aspects of this approach is that it considers monitoring as a *behavioral phenomena* occurring across the operations performed by an enterprise. A possible implication from adopting such a point-of-view on engineering monitoring requirements whatsoever is that a monitoring system does not necessarily need to be constructed from entirely new operations to fulfill a certain monitoring demand. Instead, it can be built through *stereotypes* defining behavioral specifications (contracts) to be fulfilled by actors, operations and objects that typically compose a monitoring system. Within the enterprise modeling domain, it means that the effort paid on designing new operations can be substantially reduced, as long as existing operations expose monitoring interfaces to the outside world.

Concerning related approaches, the one that most closely relates to this research is the *e3control* framework, proposed by Kartseva [21]. *E3control* aims to design enterprise level controls against organizations behaving opportunistically within a value constellation. Our approach differs from *e3control* in three main aspects. The first one is that monitoring comprises one among many instruments of organizational control. Thus, we provide a treatment for (value level) monitoring in a much deeper level of detail of what *e3control* does (with the specification of only two patterns for monitoring). The second aspect is that, *e3control* relies on *patterns* to describe recurrent controlling scenarios, whereas we use the concept of *operational stereotyping*, which is more flexible on encompassing multiple monitoring scenarios without confusing the designer with too many intermediate models. Besides, patterns rarely fit smoothly on covering complex scenarios, often demanding adjustment by the use of "glue patterns". The third and most important differing aspect is that, in *e3control*, controlling objects often interleave core business networks, being exchanged for core business objects. Such an approach makes difficult to assess the economic sustainability of controlling strategies, as they become dependent on the business they control. In our approach, there is a clear separation of the type of objects flowing in a core business constellation and the objects flowing within the monitoring constellation. The distinction goes even further, via stereotyping of monitoring operations and roles.

Regarding the case study evaluation, the contribution is dual. This case has furnished our framework with problems on the interleaving of imbalance reduction value constellations with the smart metering ones. One of the main barriers on the adoption of smart metering programs in many European countries is that the benefits of this technology may accrue to other parties than the ones that bear the costs. Without a clear definition of operational flows, value creation may outflow from one constellation to another, leaving no room for traceability. In this sense, the Enterprise Monitoring Ontology also represents a contribution for this business case, on assisting to separate supporting constellations without disconnecting them, specifically for modeling constellations that provide monitoring services to other ones.

As a future research direction, the next step comprises how to go from a value viewpoint to a process viewpoint on service monitoring. In this case, value creation becomes dependent on the execution of business activities. We are currently investigating how the Language Action Perspective (LAP) can be primarily used to formalize monitoring commitments on the process viewpoint.

References

1. Gordijn, J., Akkermans, H.: Value based Requirements Engineering: Exploring Innovative e-commerce Idea. Requirements Eng. Journal 8(2), 114–134 (2003)
2. McCarthy, W.E.: The REA Accounting Model: A Generalized Framework for Accounting Systems in a Shared Data Environment. Accounting Review 57, 554–578 (1982)
3. Osterwalder, A.: The Business Model Ontology: A Proposition in a Design Science Approach. PhD Thesis. University of Lausanne (2004)
4. Kaplan, R.S., Norton, D.P.: The Balanced Scorecard: Translating Strategy into Action. Harvard Business Press, Cambridge (1996)
5. Andersson, B., Bergholtz, M., Edirisuriya, A., Ilayperuma, T., Johannesson, P., Gordijn, J., Grégoire, B., Schmitt, M., Martinez, F.H., Abels, S., Hahn, A., Wangler, B., Weigand, H.: Towards a Reference Ontology for Business Models. In: Embley, D.W., Olivé, A., Ram, S. (eds.) ER 2006. LNCS, vol. 4215, pp. 482–496. Springer, Heidelberg (2006)
6. Dietz, J.: Enterprise Ontology: Theory and Methodology. Springer, Heidelberg (2006)
7. Sandhu, R., Ferraiolo, D.F., Kuhn, D.R.: The NIST Model for Role-Based Access Control: Toward a Unified Standard. In: Proc. of the 5th ACM Workshop on Role-Based Access Control, pp. 47–63 (2000)
8. Smith, S.A.: Contract Theory. Clarendon Law Series. Oxford University Press, USA (2004)
9. Coyne, E.J., Davis, J.M.: Role Engineering for Enterprise Security Management. Artech House, Inc., Norwood (2007)
10. Gruber, T.R., Olsen, G.R.: An Ontology for Engineering Mathematics. In: Doyle, J., Torasso, P., Sandewall, E. (eds.) 4th Int. Conf. on Principles of Knowledge Representation and Reasoning, Gustav Stresemann Institut, Bonn, Germany. Morgan Kaufmann, San Francisco (1994)
11. Weigand, H., Johannesson, P., Andersson, B., Bergholtz, M., Edirisuriya, A., Ilayperuma, T.: Strategic Analysis Using Value Modeling–The c3-Value Approach. In: Proc. of the 40th HICSS, p. 175c. IEEE Computer Society, Washington, DC, USA (2007)
12. O'Sullivan, J., Edmond, D., ter Hofstede, H. M.: Formal Description of Non-Functional Service Properties. Technical FIT-TR-2005-01, Queensland University of Technology, Brisbane (2005), http://www.wsmo.org/papers/OSullivanTR2005.pdf
13. McCannon, B.C.: The Quality-Quantity Trade-off. Eastern Economic Journal 34(1) (2008)
14. Parmenter, D.: Key Performance Indicators: Developing, Implementing, and Using Winning KPIs. Wiley, Chichester (2007)

15. Ram, S., Liu, J.: Understanding the semantics of data provenance to support active conceptual modeling. In: Chen, P.P., Wong, L.Y. (eds.) ACM-L 2006. LNCS, vol. 4512, pp. 17–29. Springer, Heidelberg (2007)
16. Mankiw, N.G.: Principles of Economics, 4th edn. South-Western College Pub.(2006)
17. European Parliament and Council. Common Rules for the Internal Market in Electricity. EU Directive 2004/54/EC. Official Journal of the European Union (July 15, 2003)
18. Smith, H. J.: The Shareholders vs. Stakeholders Debate. MIT Sloan Management Review, 85–90 (2003)
19. Squazzoni, F.: The Micro-Macro Link in Social Simulation. Sociologica (January 2008), http://www.sociologica.mulino.it/doi/10.2383/26578
20. NMa/DTe.: Electricity Metering Code: Conditions within the meaning of Section 31, sub-section 1b of the Electricity Act 1998, Informal Translation. Office of Energy Regulation (part of the Netherlands Competition Authority) (September 4, 2007)
21. Kartseva, V., Gordijn, J., Tan, Y.-H.: Designing Value-Based Inter-organizational Controls Using Patterns. In: Lyytinen, K., Loucopoulos, P., Mylopoulos, J., Robinson, B. (eds.) Design Requirements Engineering. LNBIP, vol. 14, pp. 276–301. Springer, Heidelberg (2009)

Multilingual Ontologies for Cross-Language Information Extraction and Semantic Search

David W. Embley[1], Stephen W. Liddle[2], Deryle W. Lonsdale[3],
and Yuri Tijerino[4]

[1] Department of Computer Science
[2] Information Systems Department
[3] Department of Linguistics and English Language,
Brigham Young University, Provo, Utah 84602, U.S.A.
[4] Department of Applied Informatics,
Kwansei Gakuin University, Kobe-Sanda, Japan

Abstract. Valuable local information is often available on the web, but encoded in a foreign language that non-local users do not understand. Can we create a system to allow a user to query in language L_1 for facts in a web page written in language L_2? We propose a suite of multilingual extraction ontologies as a solution to this problem. We ground extraction ontologies in each language of interest, and we map both the data and the metadata among the language-specific extraction ontologies. The mappings are through a central, language-agnostic ontology that allows new languages to be added by only having to provide one mapping rather than one for each language pair. Results from an implemented early prototype demonstrate the feasibility of cross-language information extraction and semantic search. Further, results from an experimental evaluation of ontology-based query translation and extraction accuracy are remarkably good given the complexity of the problem and the complications of its implementation.

1 Introduction

Many users, especially those traveling abroad or doing business in multiple countries and cultures, would like to be able to query foreign-language sites on the web in their own language. An ideal app would allow users to pose queries in their own language, run these queries against foreign-language sites, and return results in their own language. A user U, for example, who speaks only English, may wish to enquire about nearby restaurants while visiting Osaka, Japan. Using an iPhone, U may wish to pose a query to find a "BBQ restaurant near the Umeda station, with typical prices less than \$40." The app should rewrite U's inquiry in Japanese, access Japanese web pages to find restaurants that satisfy the criteria, respond with answers in English, and allow U to tap on answers to obtain more detail in English. Figure 1 gives actual answers retrieved from the web for this sample query. Figure 2 shows an interface with the query in a type-in text field, the English version of the answers retrieved, and a list of additional

M. Jeusfeld, L. Delcambre, and T.W. Ling (Eds.): ER 2011, LNCS 6998, pp. 147–160, 2011.
© Springer-Verlag Berlin Heidelberg 2011

店名	住所	ジャンル	予算
新焼肉屋	梅田1-10-19	焼肉	2000
肉屋	梅田1-11-29	焼肉	3000
美味焼肉	梅田2-30-22	焼肉	1500
焼肉屋	梅田3-19-28	焼肉	3000
焼き焼き	梅田2-18-26	焼肉	1000

Fig. 1. Results Extracted from Japanese Web Pages

BBQ restaurant near the Umeda station, with typical prices less than $40.

	Name	Address	Cuisine Type	Price Range
☑	Shin-YakinikuYa	1-10-19 Umeda	BBQ	$15-30
☐	NikuYa	1-11-29 Umeda	BBQ	$30-50
☐	OishiiYakiniku	2-30-22 Umeda	BBQ	$15-30
☐	YakinikuYa	3-19-28 Umeda	BBQ	$30-50
☐	Yakiyaki	2-18-26 Umeda	BBQ	$5-15

More details: Hours of Operation, Payment Method, Rating, Serving Style, Tipping Protocol

Fig. 2. English Query over Japanese Data with Results Translated to English

available information about the restaurants. If U then checks the check-box for one or more of these restaurants (e.g., the checked box for Shin-YakinikuYa) and clicks on PaymentMethod, the additional information in Figure 3 appears.

More Details (Shin-YakinikuYa, 1-10-19 Umeda, BBQ, $15-30)

Payment Method: Cash, MasterCard, Visa

Back to Results

Fig. 3. Payment Method Information

Although within-language information extraction and semantic search is a common research topic (e.g., [1,2]), much less effort has been devoted to cross-language information extraction and query processing, where the user's query and the information sources are not in the same language (e.g., [3]). The U.S. government[1], the European Union[2], and Japan[3] all have initiatives to help

---

[1] See http://trec.nist.gov

[2] See http://www.clef-campaign.org

[3] See http://research/nii.ac.jp/ntcir

further the development and evaluation of multilingual and crosslinguistic information retrieval and information extraction systems. Of course, companies interested in web content and market share are also working on ways to provide multilingual access to the Internet. Many of the existing crosslinguistic efforts involve a scenario that includes a hybrid of variously configured extraction and machine-translation technologies [4]. Such approaches are complicated by the status of efficient, accurate machine-translation engines, as yet another ongoing research effort. One group mitigates this problem by directly annotating web pages with conceptual vectors in an interlingua representation [5] to assure direct extraction against queries in any language. The use of an interlingua [6] also represents the central paradigm for translating between languages in several machine-translation systems [7]. The use of conceptual ontologies in this type of work is fairly common (see, for example, [8]).

To address the multitude of problems in cross-language information extraction and semantic search, we propose here ML-OntoES (MultiLingual Ontology Extraction System). ML-OntoES is a conceptual-modeling approach to crosslinguistic information processing based on extraction ontologies. An extraction ontology is a linguistically grounded conceptual model capable of populating its schema with facts automatically extracted from web pages [9,10]. Extraction ontologies also automatically extract information from free-form user queries, match the information with ontological conceptualizations, and generate formal queries over populated schemas [11]. The key idea that makes ML-OntoES work is the mapping of each language-specific extraction ontology to and from a central, language-agnostic ontological conceptualization of a narrow domain of interest. The basic premise draws on machine translation through interlinguas, but our application of this notion to extraction ontologies is new.

To illustrate our approach consider the user query in Figure 2. ML-OntoES "translates," "extracts," and "translates again" as follows: we (1) apply an English restaurant extraction ontology to match the query to a conceptual model, (2) use pre-determined mappings through a central language-agnostic conceptual model to a Japanese restaurant extraction ontology, (3) extract both requested facts and ontologically related facts from Japanese web sites with the Japanese restaurant extraction ontology, (4) map returned results (e.g., Figure 1) and related results through the central language-agnostic conceptualization back to the English restaurant extraction ontology, and (5) display results and links to additional information (e.g., Figures 2 and 3).

The contributions of this work include: (1) development of an architecture with a central language-agnostic ontological conceptualization for cross-language information extraction and semantic search (Sections 2.1–2.2) (2) specification of mapping types to and from the central conceptualization along with scalable, pay-as-you-go ways to establish both mappings and new language-specific extraction ontologies (Section 2.3), and (3) implementation of prototypes demonstrating proof-of-concept feasibility and providing encouraging results for cross-language query translation and extraction accuracy (Sections 3.1–3.2).

2   Architecture

In this section we propose an architecture for ML-OntoES and emphasize how this proposal provides the feature set and scalability required to support rich multilingual interactions. We begin by describing extraction ontologies (Section 2.1) and multilingual ontologies (Section 2.2). Then we discuss the multilingual mappings that connect different languages and locales in a meaningful way, thus making a multilingual ontology useful for a variety of information processing tasks, supporting users in their native locales (Section 2.3).

2.1   Extraction Ontologies

In general, *ontology* is the study of reality. More specifically, **an** *ontology* is an expression of a particular model of reality, including a specification of concepts, relationships among concepts, and constraints that exist in the model. An *extraction ontology* is an ontology that has enough information in the model to be able to drive the process of extracting concepts and relationships from some source document such as an HTML page or a PDF document.

Figure 4 gives the conceptual-model component of an extraction ontology that describes aspects of the *Restaurant* concept that an international traveler might be interested in exploring, such as price range of meals, menu items available, hours of operation, payment methods accepted, and tipping protocols.

The notation of Figure 4 conforms to OSM (Object-oriented Systems Modeling) [12]. Names written in rectangles constitute concepts (*object sets*) of the ontology. Solid borders denote nonlexical concepts (e.g., *Restaurant* and *Rating* in Figure 4), while dashed borders indicate lexical concepts (e.g., *Address* and *Geo Location*). Lines between concepts denote relationship sets, and arrow heads mark functional associations. For example, in Figure 4 a *Rating* has at most one *Agency*, one *Value*, and one *Scale*, but an *Agency* may give many *Rating*s to multiple *Restaurant*s. A triangle represents a generalization/specialization (ISA) relationship between object sets. For example, *Beverage* is a generalization that has two specializations: *Alcoholic Beverage* and *Non-Alcoholic Beverage*. The half solid dot on *Alcoholic Beverage* is an *object-set object* that represents the *Alcoholic Beverage* object set itself, so that by connecting *Regulations* to the object-set object we mean that regulations apply to the whole set of *Alcoholic Beverages* as a collection, not individually to each member of the collection.

The conceptual model in Figure 4 is only one part of the restaurant extraction ontology, namely the conceptual structure. The other part of the extraction ontology is a collection of *data frames* that describe the individuals, contextual clues, and keywords associated with—or signaling the presence of—concepts in the ontology. We use a variety of techniques to encode data frames. For relatively narrow domains, lexicons can simply list the corresponding terms (e.g., *Payment Method*'s data frame could be a lexicon containing the names of credit card companies and other terms such as "personal check" or "cash"). For richer concepts we use regular expressions (e.g., *Price* would be difficult to enumerate, but a simple regular expression such as \d+\.\d\d can represent a large set

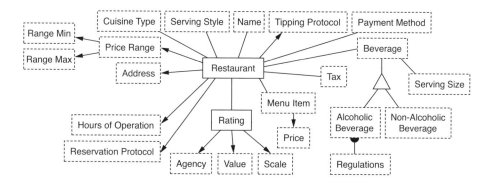

Fig. 4. Conceptual-Model Component of a Restaurant Extraction Ontology

of prices in a compact way). Contextual clues are also important for the data extraction process, and we again use lexicons and regular expressions to specify contextual details. For example, "$" is a strong signal that a *Price* concept follows, especially if it matches one of the regular expressions of *Price*.

It is common to use OWL, the Web Ontology Language, to describe the details of an ontology. Numerous tools leverage the OWL standard for ontology creation and use. We use OSM because we have built a data extraction system, OntoES, around the OSM structure and the data-frame extensions that support data extraction. OntoES automatically extracts data from ontologically narrow application domains with relatively high precision and recall, using ontology specifications that are robust with respect to different web sites or changes in document structure within the target domains. In order to interoperate with other tools and systems, OntoES is able to generate an OWL/RDF version of a populated OSM conceptual-model instance queriable with SPARQL.

2.2 Multilingual Ontologies

In ML-OntoES, a *multilingual ontology* localized to n contexts $\{\mathcal{C}_1, ..., \mathcal{C}_n\}$ is an $n+1$-tuple $\mathcal{O} = (\mathcal{A}, \mathcal{L}_1, ..., \mathcal{L}_n)$, where $\mathcal{A}$ is a language-agnostic ontology representing concepts and facts in the ontology from a language-agnostic perspective, and each $\mathcal{L}_i$, $1 \leq i \leq n$, is a localization[4] of $\mathcal{A}$ to one of the n contexts. $\mathcal{A}$ is an extraction ontology that consists of a set of structural concepts (e.g., object sets, relationship sets, data frames) and facts (e.g., objects, relationships) that describe a domain of interest in a language-agnostic way. Each localization is a 4-tuple $\mathcal{L}_i = (\mathcal{C}_i, \mathcal{O}_i, \mathcal{M}_{\mathcal{A} \mapsto \mathcal{L}_i}, \mathcal{M}_{\mathcal{L}_i \mapsto \mathcal{A}})$, where $\mathcal{C}_i$ is a local context label, $\mathcal{O}_i$ is an extraction ontology, $\mathcal{M}_{\mathcal{A} \mapsto \mathcal{L}_i}$ is a set of mappings from $\mathcal{A}$ to $\mathcal{L}_i$, and $\mathcal{M}_{\mathcal{L}_i \mapsto \mathcal{A}}$

---

[4] We use "localization" rather than "language" because even within the same language there may be local variants we wish to capture (e.g., Australia uses both a different measurement system and a different currency than the U.S. even though both languages are English).

is a set of mappings from $\mathcal{L}_i$ to $\mathcal{A}$. Each concept in $\mathcal{O}_i$ must map to a single concept in $\mathcal{A}$, but concepts in $\mathcal{A}$ may map only partially to concepts in $\mathcal{O}_i$ (i.e., $\mathcal{M}_{\mathcal{A} \mapsto \mathcal{L}_i}$ is surjective, while $\mathcal{M}_{\mathcal{L}_i \mapsto \mathcal{A}}$ is injective).

The key idea of the ML-OntoES architecture is that each localized ontology maps to a central language-agnostic representation and vice versa. This "star architecture" avoids the n^2 complexity of mapping each localized ontology to all other localizations, and instead provides a nearly linear scaling. Adding another localization involves constructing the localized extraction ontology ($\mathcal{O}_i$) along with mappings ($\mathcal{M}_{\mathcal{L}_i \mapsto \mathcal{A}}$ and $\mathcal{M}_{\mathcal{A} \mapsto \mathcal{L}_i}$) to and from $\mathcal{A}$. In the process, it may be necessary to adjust $\mathcal{A}$ so that all concepts in $\mathcal{O}_i$ are represented directly in $\mathcal{A}$, and this may in turn require adjusting some of the mappings for other localizations. But since most mappings are trivial, the expected case is a linear effort required to add an additional localization to $\mathcal{O}$—indeed, sublinear since many language resources exist to aid in constructing the mappings.

It is customary to identify language and culture contexts by spoken language and country name such as German/Switzerland (de-CH) or Spanish/Guatemala (es-GT). But in general there could be many contexts associated with a given language/country pair, such as Swiss German/Switzerland in contrast to High German/Germany, or even tourist Spanish/Mexico versus business Spanish/Mexico. The concepts chosen for a particular localization may vary for many reasons. Ultimately, the precise meaning of "context" is defined by the author of the localization who expresses a selected set of ideas in a particular language. In our definition, we only need to note that a context has a chosen label, $\mathcal{C}_i$ (though conventional locale labels such as "en-US" or "de-CH" could easily be used where appropriate). As a convention, we may replace i with $\mathcal{C}_i$ when referring to elements of $\mathcal{O}$. For example, the English/U.S. localization $\mathcal{L}_i$ could be designated $\mathcal{L}_{en-US} = (\text{"en-US"}, \mathcal{O}_{en-US}, \mathcal{M}_{\mathcal{A} \mapsto \mathcal{L}_{en-US}}, \mathcal{M}_{\mathcal{L}_{en-US} \mapsto \mathcal{A}})$.

For our running example, Figure 4 shows the English/U.S. (en-US) localization and Figure 5 shows the Japanese/Japan (ja-JP) localization. The language-agnostic component $\mathcal{A}$ (not shown) is similar to these two. $\mathcal{A}$ includes *Geo Location* (地理座標) from Figure 5 and *Range Min/Range Max* from Figure 4. Concept labels in $\mathcal{A}$ can be written in any language or symbol system the ontology developer finds most useful. For example, the concept for *Geo Location* could be written 地理座標, *Geo Location*, $\mathcal{C}_1$, or anything else the developer chooses.

2.3   Multilingual Mappings

Because the ML-OntoES architecture ($\mathcal{O} = (\mathcal{A}, \mathcal{L}_1, ..., \mathcal{L}_n)$) includes a central language-agnostic component ($\mathcal{A}$) together with multiple localizations, mappings between $\mathcal{A}$ and the various localizations are key to our approach. These mappings fall into three categories: *Structural Mappings* that resolve differences among conceptualizations with standard schema integration techniques, *Data-Instance Mappings* that maintain correspondences among data instances, and *Commentary Mappings* that require standard language-to-language translation.

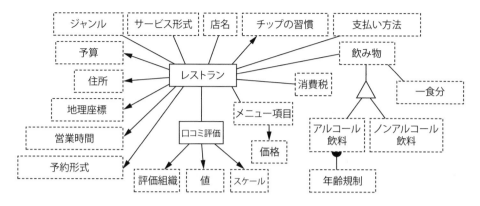

Fig. 5. Japanese Localization of the Restaurant Ontology Figure 4

Structural Mappings

Structural (schema) mappings between $\mathcal{A}$ and $\mathcal{L}_i$ are usually straightforward. For the applications we target, we anticipate most of them to be direct from $\mathcal{L}_i$ to $\mathcal{A}$ and partial from $\mathcal{A}$ to $\mathcal{L}_i$. Fundamentally, this is because applications such as restaurants, items for sale, hotel and airline reservations, and many more all basically include the same concepts in the same relationship to one another. However, as guided by our earlier extensive work on schema mapping [13], we allow a full array of 1:1, 1:n, n:1, and n:m mappings along with operators such as split, merge, select, union, Booleanization, deBooleanization, skolemization, and lexicalization that carry data into structural variations.

Because it is so common to have identical structure, only with a little ingenuity were we able to provide illustrations. To illustrate that a concept in $\mathcal{A}$ sometimes does not appear in some localization, we assumed that *Geo Location* does not appear in $\mathcal{L}_{en-US}$ (as indicated by the gap below *Address* in Figure 4), but does appear in $\mathcal{A}$. And, to illustrate a non-1:1 mapping, we assumed that $\mathcal{L}_{ja-JP}$ has no *Range Min* and *Range Max*, but rather just the more typical "budget" amount. Then, via a complex mapping, the system is able to convert the 予算 values in Figure 1 to the *Price Range* values in Figure 2.

Data-Instance Mappings

Data-instance mappings encode lexical-level snippets of instance information that are largely self-contained in nature and whose lexicalizations tend to be fairly direct across various languages. Various types of language resources serve to mediate these differences. Thus, given some existing language-specific extraction ontologies, $\mathcal{L}_1$, ..., $\mathcal{L}_n$ and their mappings to and from $\mathcal{A}$, we can quickly assemble a new language-specific extraction ontology $\mathcal{L}_{new}$ for ML-OntoES and mappings to and from it and $\mathcal{A}$. We identify four types of data-instance mappings: *Scalar Units Conversions*, *Lexicon Matching*, *Transliteration*, and *Currency Conversions*.

Scalar Units Conversions. One type of data-level correspondence assures conversion between items that are expressed with respect to some scale, for example measurements such as temperature, weight, length, volume, speed, and altitude. Different fixed scales exist for measuring such items, and these scales may vary by locale: much of the world uses the metric system, for example, whereas the U.S. for the most part does not. Conversion routines between measurement units and their associated values are straightforward to implement. A 5-3/8 oz. wine carafe will always have that measurement, and the value of an ounce is constant over time, as is its metric equivalent. We can thus store measurement values and associated units in a language- and locale-agnostic resource and convert it to any other format via simple arithmetic when developing and using a localized ontology. A wide range of such measurements exists across cultures and languages, of course. So the specification of conversion factors between such "exotic" measures (e.g. a stone for weight in English) may be necessary when localizing an ontology, but ML-OntoES supports this functionality.

Lexicon Matching. Another level of data mapping, this one more directly tied to language, has to do with the lexicon. Each language expresses concepts in its own combination of words, phrases, and other expressions. Often these terms correspond fairly closely, though this point has been debated among linguists. In cases where the correspondence or mapping is fairly direct, we can simply maintain a list of the crosslinguistic mappings. So, for example, the English word "meal" is a fairly close translation equivalent to the French word "repas". Of course, there are word sense ambiguities: the English word "meal" in fact has several other senses, including one that means finely ground grain. This may complicate the storage of such correspondences, but for the types of data-rich web application domains we envision, the problem is not nearly as intractable as comprehensive modern dictionaries would suggest. In fact, several available technologies, such as termbase systems, software localization, lexical databases, and statistical machine translation assist in developing and maintaining crosslinguistic correspondences of this type, and the process scales well [14]. ML-OntoES allows us to specify lexical information at this granularity in our ontologies and use them for finding and extracting data.

Transliteration. An even lower level of data mappings is necessary when considering a crosslinguistic context—that of transliteration. Proper nouns such as people's names, place names, and company names generally do not vary much across languages, though language differences in terms of phonetics (i.e. individual sounds) and phonology (e.g. syllable structure and allowable phonetic sequences) are observable. For example, the name of Muhammar Ghadaffi has no less than 39 variant spellings in published English sources, and the surname of President Bill Clinton has been rendered in more than 6 ways into Arabic in newswire. Tracking and identifying all of the proper nouns in any language is an important task, and various machine learning techniques and comprehensive language resources exist for identifying and cataloging them for any one language. Much more substantial, however, is the task of doing this across languages. While maintaining a crosslinguistic lexicon of proper names is possible, we are also able to take advantage of character conversion and phonetic transcription tools, perhaps with fuzzy matching, to compute these correspondences on-the-fly. The restaurant names in Figure 1, for example, were converted for Figure 2 by transliteration, and tools exist for automatic Kanji-to-English transliteration.[5]

Currency Conversions. Because of the evanescent nature of prices, referring to a price with an ontology, particularly a language-agnostic one, is best accomplished by storing the raw extracted value from the web page in question, rather than with respect to some idealized universal standard, which in this case does not exist. We are then confronted with the issue of converting this amount to other languages/locales when the user requires the price in another currency. The task would appear to be difficult, given the temporal variance of the conversion. Fortunately, because this need is so prevalent today, several web services are available that given a date, an amount, and source and target currencies, provide a conversion for the values in question. This precludes the need for developing and maintaining a conversion protocol. Since ML-OntoES supports web services, we are able to execute these conversions at query or retrieval time. When developing a language-specific ontology and retrieving associated information, we can call a currency conversion web service to compute the appropriate value.

Commentary Mappings

Beyond these representational issues that impact how we specify and use correspondences at a linguistic level, there are larger-scale mismatches across cultures that must be addressed. For example, restaurants in different countries may have widely divergent requirements that customers need to be aware of, especially customers from outside the culture: tipping practices, how meals are structured, and even dress codes and the allowableness of pets on the premises. This type of information is best kept as short free-form notes or *commentaries* that are stored in $\mathcal{A}$ and are available for scrutiny and elaboration by developers of language-specific ontologies. For example, the reservation protocol of a typical U.S. fine-dining restaurant might be described as, *"Reservations highly recommended, especially on Friday, Saturday, and holiday evenings."*

When moving from one localization to another, translating commentary such as this can be quite valuable. Since there are web services that provide automatic natural-language translation (e.g. `translate.google.com` or `babelfish.yahoo.com`), it is possible simply to submit the commentary to a web service and request a particular language translation. Unfortunately, even though automatic translation technology has improved considerably in recent years, the quality of automatic translation still varies immensely, and human review with correction generally gives the best results.

Since commentary is written with respect to a local culture and language, there cannot be a language-agnostic version of commentary. Thus, the nature of the problem dictates that commentary mappings (translations) must be provided for each additional localization added to a multilingual ontology. For example, if

---

[5] For example, see `http://nihongo.j-talk.com/kanji` and `http://www.romaji.org`

we start our restaurant ontology by creating a Japanese version and then adding an American localization, the ontology author of the American localization must translate commentary from the Japanese localization into English, and any new commentary from the American version into Japanese. In the worst case, this creates n^2 mappings (where n is the number of localizations), but again since we have automatic translation services readily available, we get a base-level automatic translation essentially for free.

Nonetheless, high-quality mappings of natural-language commentary do require significant effort, often from a multidisciplinary, multilingual team. But as many web sites demonstrate, when the community receives significant value from a shared resource, it is possible to elicit from the community the team needed to create, enhance, and maintain that resource. Prominent examples include Wikipedia articles, Amazon book reviews, and TripAdvisor travel recommendations. We envision a "pay-as-you-go" approach where the system creates initial translations automatically, and experts from the community incrementally supply improved translations. Crucially, this does not adversely impact our extraction because it is not directly used for extraction purposes.

3   Evaluation

To show the feasibility and practicality of cross-language query processing, we describe an implemented early prototype of ML-OntoES and give some results of testing the prototype on independent-user-provided queries in Japanese, Chinese, and English (Section 3.1). To show the accuracy of cross-language information extraction and query processing, we give results for an initial Japanese/-English cross-language application we have implemented for the car-ad domain (Section 3.2).

3.1   Results from an Early Prototype

Based on extraction ontologies, we have developed a preliminary system, called *Pijin* [15]. Pijin accepts free-form, natural-language queries from mobile phone users in English, Japanese, and Chinese; maps queries to a restaurant extraction ontology; and reformulates them as form-based web queries to query four Japanese restaurant recommendation web services: Hotpepper, LivedoorGourmet, Tabelog, and Gournavi. These services return results in Japanese. Pijin also makes use of GPS information, Google maps, and other web services to provide "mashed up" recommendations to users.

For the experiment, we asked five subjects not involved with the project to make 100 queries for each language (Chinese, English, and Japanese). The subjects were asked to write free-form, natural-language queries that could be used to inquire about restaurants where they might like to eat. Typical of many, one of the queries posed was: クーポンのあるヤキニク屋さん、東京駅の近くに、予算は5000円 (loosely translated, "find me a BBQ restaurant that offers coupons near Tokyo station and my budget is under 5000 yen). Pijin interprets this query using the free-form query processor described in [11] and composes the web service query: station=東京駅&coupon=0&food=焼肉&maxBudget=5000 which it then rewrites for each specific web-service API. This query produces a list of restaurants near Tokyo Station that offer menus priced under 5000 yen.

The system was able to correctly interpret and translate to interface form queries 79% of the Japanese queries, 72% of the English queries, and 69% of the Chinese queries. Pijin, for example, was unable to recognize and reformulate as a form query the Japanese query: アルコルの種類が多い居酒屋 (loosely translated: find me a bar that provides a wide variety of alcoholic beverages). Although Pijin recognizes 居酒屋 ("bar") and correctly maps it to the restaurant genre, it can do nothing for アルコルの種類が多い (a "wide variety of alcoholic beverages") because none of the web services has a parameter to accept this kind of search criterion.

3.2   Cross-Language Query Translation and Extraction Accuracy

To experimentally verify the feasibility of cross-language information extraction, we began with OntoES (our current data-extraction system) and made modifications to allow it to behave in accord with ML-OntoES. We call the version we implemented ML-OntoES'. For ML-OntoES' we added UTF-8 encoding, which immediately enabled us to build extraction ontologies in multiple languages and to process free-form queries in multiple languages. We were then faced with the task of constructing extraction ontologies for some domain in some natural language other than English. We chose the car-ads domain and the Japanese language—car ads because it is a challenging domain for information extraction and free-form query processing, but also because we have been able to make On-toES perform successfully in this domain, and Japanese because both the other languages, French and Spanish, for which we have near-native language abilities are too much like English for the testing we wished to do.

Having chosen a test domain and test language, we then took our existing car-ads extraction ontology and replaced the English concept recognizers with Japanese concept recognizers. To simplify crosslinguistic extraction, we limited the extraction ontology to six basic lexical concepts: *Make, Model, Price, Year*, and *Transmission*. To make ML-OntoES' work multilingually, we used the English car-ads extraction ontology as our language-agnostic extraction ontology (as well as its English localization) and we made the Japanese car-ads extraction ontology correspond 1-1 both structurally and for data instances. To make it correspond structurally for data instances, we extracted Japanese instances using Japanese regular-expression recognizers, but immediately converted the

	ExE	ExJ	QiE	QiJ	QrEE	QrJJ	QrEJ	QrJE
Precision	.95	.89	.97	.92	.96	.84	.75	.87
Recall	.94	.91	.94	.82	.95	.84	.72	.85

Fig. 6. Experimental Results

resulting values to English (e.g., H12年 to the year 2000, 日産 to Nissan, and with the exchange rate \$1.00=JPY82.3). These conversions allowed us to further process data, converting it to RDF, and enabling us to query it with SPARQL, for queries generated by our already implemented free-form query engine [11]. Thus, we were able to interpret and process free-form queries such as H12年よ り新しい、50万円未満の車を探してい and 全ての白い日産の車、価格、年式 及び走行距離を見せてください which fared comparably to the English parsed queries to produced generic queries of the form: `Year,>,2000;Price,<,6050` and `Make,=,Nissan;Color,=,White`.

With ML-OntoES′, implemented as explained, we conducted an experiment and obtained the precision and recall results in Figure 6 for Extraction in English on English car ads (ExE), Extraction in Japanese on Japanese car ads (ExJ), Query interpretation for free-form English queries (QiE), Query interpretation for free-form Japanese queries (QiJ), Query results for English queries on English car ads (QrEE), Query results for Japanese queries on Japanese car ads (QrJJ), Query results for English queries on Japanese car ads (QrEJ), and Query results for Japanese queries on English car ads (QrJE). For the experiment, we used a collection of 100 English car ads taken from `craigslist.com` and 30 Japanese car ads taken from `Goo-Net.com`. For queries, we used 200 English free-form car-ad queries, which we had previously gathered from students in two senior-level database courses, and we manually translated 50 of them to Japanese free-form queries (see examples in the previous paragraph). We computed precision and recall for English and Japanese car ads by counting all the matches and mismatches the ML-OntoES′ recognizers labeled for each of the six car-ad attributes in the two collection of car ads and taking an average over the individual attributes. For query interpretation, we counted the matches and mismatches for each ML-OntoES′-generated constraint (e.g., `Year,>,2000`). And, for query results we counted the number of car ads ML-OntoES′ selected that were relevant and irrelevant over the respective document collections.

One of the interesting characteristics of the application we encountered was the problem of multiple years of interest in Japanese car ads. In addition to using 年式 and 製造年, which both translate as "model year," most Japanese car ads on `Goo-Net.com` report 車検 ("*shaken* year"), which is a required and expensive smog, safety, and registration certification that can be transferred to new owners if it has not expired. As a further complication, what would be the year 2008 in an English localization, would be written as 平成20/2008年式 or H20/2008年 in the Japanese localization, where the first number preceded by either 平成 or H represents the year 20 of Heisei, the current Japanese Imperial period. The second number, 2008, followed by 年, the Kanji for "year," is its Julian-year equivalent. We overcame this difficulty partially by tuning ML-OntoES' to recognize a single instance of year from both model year and *shaken* year, and to some extent, for the *shaken* year by recognizing the specific keyword for *shaken*. Application characteristics like these show some of the subtleties of implementing multilingual extraction and semantic search systems.

4   Conclusions

Our proposed multilingual architecture (ML-OntoES), with its central language-agnostic ontology and pay-as-you-go incremental design, along with our proof-of-concept prototypes and our initial cross-language extraction and query results, support the conclusion that cross-language information extraction and semantic search can be successful. Our results (reported in harmonic-mean F-measures) indicate the following: We can accurately extract in multiple languages: English ($F = .94$) and Japanese ($F = .90$). We can accurately interpret queries in multiple languages: English ($F = .95$) and Japanese ($F = .87$). We can query sites written in one language with queries written in another language: English query against Japanese source ($F = .73$) and Japanese query against English source ($F = .86$). The accuracy of these results is somewhat lower than we would like. We expect, however, that with the addition of accurate schema and data-instance mappings to and from localized extraction ontologies and a central language-agnostic ontology we can increase the accuracy. Currently within-language query accuracy indicates that this is achievable: English query against English source ($F = .95$) and Japanese query against Japanese source ($F = .84$).

As for future work, we intend to complete the transformation of ML-OntoES' to ML-OntoES, and we intend to experiment with many different domains and several more languages. The results we have for car-ads English extraction reported here are consistent with previous results for the car-ads domain [9]. And, since we have applied English extraction ontologies to a few dozen other domains with consistently good results (F-measures typically between .80 and .95), we can be reasonably confident that similar results to those reported here are possible. We must, of course, add and make use of instance mappings as defined here, so that we can boost the accuracy of cross-language information extraction and semantic search.

References

1. Sarawagi, S.: Information extraction. Foundations and Trends in Databases 1(3), 261–377 (2008)
2. Turmo, J., Ageno, A., Català, N.: Adaptive information extraction. ACM Computing Surveys 38(2) (July 2006)
3. Grefenstette, G. (ed.): Cross-Language Information Retrieval. Kluwer, Boston (1998)

4. Klavans, J., Hovy, E., Furh, C., Frederking, R.E., Oard, D., Okumura, A., Ishikawa, K., Satoh, K.: Multilingual (or cross-lingual) information retrieval. In: Hovy, E., Ide, N., Frederking, R., Mariani, J., Zampolli, A. (eds.) Multilingual Information Management: Current Levels and Future Abilities. Linguistica Computazionale, vol. XIV–XV, Insituti Editoriali e Poligrafici Internazionali, Pisa (2001)
5. Falaise, A., Rouquet, D., Schwab, D., Blanchon, H., Boitet, C.: Ontology driven content extraction using interlingual annotation of texts in the OMNIA project. In: Proceedings of the 4th International Workshop on Cross Lingual Information Access, Beijing, China (August 2010)
6. Lonsdale, D.W., Franz, A.M., Leavitt, J.R.R.: Large-scale machine translation: An interlingua approach. In: Proceedings of the Seventh International Conference on Industrial and Engineering Applications of Artificial Intelligence and Expert Systems (IEA/AIE 1994), Austin, Texas, USA, pp. 525–530 (May/June 1994)
7. Dorr, B.J., Hovy, E.H., Levin, L.S.: Machine translation: Interlingual methods. In: Natural Language Processing and Machine Translation, Encyclopedia of Language and Linguistics, 2nd edn. Elsevier Ltd., Amsterdam (2004)
8. Murray, C., Dorr, B.J., Lin, J., Hajič, J., Pecina, P.: Leveraging reusability: Cost-effective lexical acquisition for large-scale ontology translation. In: Proceedings of the Association for Computational Linguistics (ACL 2006), Sydney, Australia, pp. 945–952 (July 2006)
9. Embley, D.W., Campbell, D.M., Jiang, Y.S., Liddle, S.W., Lonsdale, D.W., Ng, Y.-K., Smith, R.D.: Conceptual-model-based data extraction from multiple-record web pages. Data & Knowledge Engineering 31(3), 227–251 (1999)
10. Embley, D.W., Liddle, S.W., Lonsdale, D.W.: Conceptual modeling foundations for a web of knowledge. In: Embley, D.W., Thalheim, B. (eds.) Handbook of Conceptual Modeling: Theory, Practice, and Research Challenges, ch. 15, pp. 477–516. Springer, Heidelberg (2011)
11. Al-Muhammed, M., Embley, D.W.: Ontology-based constraint recognition for free-form service requests. In: Proceedings of the 23rd International Conference on Data Engineering (ICDE 2007), Istanbul, Turkey, pp. 366–375 (April 2007)
12. Embley, D.W., Kurtz, B.D., Woodfield, S.N.: Object-oriented Systems Analysis: A Model-Driven Approach. Prentice-Hall, Englewood Cliffs (1992)
13. Xu, L., Embley, D.W.: A composite approach to automating direct and indirect schema mappings. Information Systems 31(8), 697–732 (2006)
14. Lonsdale, D., Mitamura, T., Nyberg, E.: Acquisition of large lexicons for practical knowledge-based MT. Machine Translation 9, 251–283 (1995)
15. Geng, Z., Tijerino, Y.A.: Using cross-lingual data extraction ontology for web service interaction – for a restaurant web service. In: 2010 Workshop on Cross-Cultural and Cross-Lingual Aspects of the Semantic Web, Shanghai, China (November 2010)

Querying Conceptual Schemata
with Expressive Equality Constraints

Andrea Calì[2,3], Georg Gottlob[1,3], and Andreas Pieris[1]

[1] Computing Laboratory, University of Oxford, UK
[2] Dept. of Computer Science and Inf. Systems, Birkbeck University of London, UK
[3] Oxford-Man Institute of Quantitative Finance, University of Oxford, UK
andrea@dcs.bbk.ac.uk,
{georg.gottlob,andreas.pieris}@comlab.ox.ac.uk

Abstract. When querying data through a conceptual schema or ontology, we compute answers entailed by the logical theory constituted by the data plus the conceptual schema. Traditional database constraints like tuple-generating dependencies (TGDs) and equality-generating dependencies (EGDs) are a useful tool for ontology specification. However, their interaction leads to undecidability of query answering even in simple cases. In this paper we exhibit a novel and general class of EGDs that, together with a relevant class of TGDs, ensures decidability of query answering. Our results capture well-known ontology languages as special cases; in particular, they allow us to deal with extended Entity-Relationship schemata enriched with expressive equality constraints.

1 Introduction

Answering queries over ontologies has become an important problem in knowledge representation and databases. In ontology-enhanced database systems, an extensional relational database D is combined with an *ontological theory* Σ describing rules and constraints[1] which derive new intensional data from the extensional data. A query is not just answered against the database D, but against the logical theory $D \cup \Sigma$. The Entity-Relationship (ER) [13] model has recently gained importance in ontology specification, due to the fact that it is natural, well-known to theorists and practitioners, and with high expressive power. Several extensions of the original ER model, grouped in a family of languages known as ER$^\pm$, have been proposed in [2,5,7] in the context of ontology-based query answering; in particular, the ER$^\pm$ language of [7] properly generalizes the fundamentals languages of the DL-lite family [11], a prominent family of tractable languages designed for ontology-based data access. In ER$^\pm$ the complexity of answering conjunctive queries (that is, select-project-join queries) is highly tractable (in particular, in the complexity class AC^0, which is the complexity class of recognizing words in languages defined by constant-depth Boolean circuits with an unlimited fan-in AND and OR gates) in data complexity (that is, considering everything as fixed except the data). This is due to so-called *first-order (FO) rewritability*, that is, the possibility

---

[1] In the following, we will use interchangeably the terms "dependency" and "constraint", the latter being the common term in database theory parlance.

M. Jeusfeld, L. Delcambre, and T.W. Ling (Eds.): ER 2011, LNCS 6998, pp. 161–174, 2011.
© Springer-Verlag Berlin Heidelberg 2011

of answering a query Q against a database D and an ontology Σ by rewriting Q into a *first-order* query Q_Σ, which somehow encodes Σ, and evaluating Q_Σ on D.

In [7] ER schemata are encoded into relational schemata with *inclusion dependencies (IDs)* and *key dependencies (KDs)*, so as to perform reasoning tasks on them. However, in some cases, more expressive constraints are needed for ontology modeling. This need has been recently addressed in a series of works on the Datalog$^\pm$ family, a family of rule-based languages derived from Datalog [3,4,6,8]. In Datalog$^\pm$, an ontological theory is expressed by means of rules of three kinds: *(i) tuple-generating dependencies (TGDs)*, that is, (function-free) Horn rules enhanced with the possibility of having existentially quantified variables in the head; *(ii) equality-generating dependencies (EGDs)*, that is, (function-free) Horn rules with a single equality atom in the head; *(iii) negative constraints (NCs)*, a form of denial constraints expressed as (function-free) Horn rules with the constant "false" in the head. Notice that IDs are a special case of TGDs, and each KD can be expressed by means of a set of EGDs.

Example 1. The TGD $\forall X\ employee(X), leads(X, Y)\ \rightarrow\ \exists Z\ supervises(Z, X)$ expresses that each employee who leads a group has a supervisor. The EGD $leads(X, Z_1)$, $leads(X, Z_2)$, $assigned\_to(Z_1, P)$, $assigned\_to(Z_2, P) \rightarrow Z_1 = Z_2$ asserts that each employee cannot lead two distinct groups assigned to the same project.   ∎

A central notion in ontological query answering is the *chase* [16,18], a procedure for "repairing" a database instance D with respect to a set of constraints Σ (TGDs and EGDs). Notice that the term "chase" is used interchangeably to denote both the chase procedure and its result. In the chase, in the presence of a TGD (resp. EGD) violation (and consequent repair), we say that the TGD (resp. EGD) is *triggered*.

The main notion regarding the interaction of TGDs and EGDs is *separability*. A set Σ_T of TGDs and a set Σ_E of EGDs, expressed on the same relational schema, are *separable* if, for every query Q and for every database instance D, assuming that the theory $D \cup \Sigma_T \cup \Sigma_E$ is satisfiable (that is, it admits at least one model), the answers to Q on $D \cup \Sigma_T \cup \Sigma_E$ coincide with the answers to Q on $D \cup \Sigma_T$. In other words, separability holds if, when the theory is satisfiable, the presence of EGDs does not change the results of query answering. Separability was first introduced in [10], and then adopted in several works [4,5,6,7]. In most cases in the literature, separability is enforced by a syntactic condition which prevents the EGDs to be applied in the chase, that is, no repair of EGD violations is performed. Notable exceptions are the works on ER$^\pm$ [5,7], where EGDs (which are, in fact, key dependencies) can be applied, but without altering the result of query answering.

In this paper we follow the more general approach of [5,7] and propose a separability condition which does not prevent EGD applications in the chase. We focus on general EGDs and their (non)-interaction with TGDs. Our research initiates from the need of expressing more complex equality constraints on ER (or ER$^\pm$) schemata, as in the following simple example.

Example 2. Consider the ER$^\pm$ in Figure 1, where entity and relationship names are self-explanatory – we have omitted attributes to avoid clutter, and numbered roles in relationships. Using the usual (and natural) relational representation of [2], we can express, for example, the following EGD.

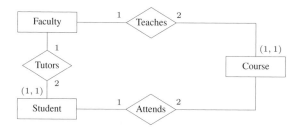

Fig. 1. Figure for Example 2

$$student(S), attends(S, C_1), attends(S, C_2),$$
$$tutors(F, S), teaches(F, C_1), teaches(F, C_2) \rightarrow C_1 = C_2$$

which asserts that each student can attend at most one course taught by his tutor. Obviously, such a constraint is not expressible with $ER^{\pm}$ constructs. ∎

We tackle the more general problem of query answering in the presence of *linear TGDs* [4], that is, TGDs with a single body-atom, and general EGDs. Notice that linear TGDs, of which IDs are a special case, are able to capture (when enriched with KDs and NCs) both the $ER^{\pm}$ family and the DL-lite family.

The contributions in this paper are the following.

(1) We first present a syntactic condition of *non-triggerability* between a set of EGDs and a set of general TGDs. Such a condition ensures that EGDs are never triggered during the chase construction, thus ensuring separability. Non-triggerable EGDs properly extend several conditions for separability in the literature.

(2) Building upon the notion of non-triggerable EGDs, we propose a sufficient *syntactic* condition for separability between a set of EGDs and a set of *linear* TGDs. Our condition, called *non-conflict* condition, is very broad and properly generalizes several known conditions in the literature. Non-conflicting sets of EGDs and linear TGDs guarantee separability without preventing the triggering of EGDs.

(3) We prove that the complexity of the problem whether two sets of EGDs and linear TGDs are non-conflicting is PSPACE-complete.

(4) We show that our results are applicable in several contexts. In particular, we show how non-conflicting EGDs can be added to $ER^{\pm}$ schemata [7] without increasing the complexity of query answering. Moreover, since DL-lite ontologies can be easily expressed by means of linear TGDs with minor additions (which do not affect complexity of answering), we are able to add non-conflicting EGDs to DL-lite languages, thus significantly enhancing their expressive power.

2 Preliminaries

In this section we recall some basics on databases, queries, tuple-generating dependencies, equality-generating dependencies, and the chase procedure.

General. We define the following pairwise disjoint (infinite) sets of symbols: *(i)* a set Γ of *constants* (constitute the "normal" domain of a database), *(ii)* a set Γ_N of *labeled* *nulls* (used as placeholders for unknown values, and thus can be also seen as variables), and *(iii)* a set Γ_V of *variables* (used in queries and dependencies). Different constants represent different values (*unique name assumption*), while different nulls may represent the same value. A lexicographic order is defined on $\Gamma \cup \Gamma_N$, such that every value in Γ_N follows all those in Γ. We denote by $\mathbf{X}$ sequences of variables $X_1, \ldots, X_k$, where $k \geqslant 0$. Also, let $[n]$ be the set $\{1, \ldots, n\}$, for any integer $n \geqslant 1$.

A *relational schema* $\mathcal{R}$ (or simply *schema*) is a set of *relational symbols* (or *predicates*), each with its associated arity. A *position* $r[i]$ (in a schema $\mathcal{R}$) is identified by a predicate $r \in \mathcal{R}$ and its i-th argument (or attribute). A *term* t is a constant, null, or variable. An *atom* has the form $r(t_1, \ldots, t_n)$, where r is an n-ary relation, and $t_1, \ldots, t_n$ are terms. Conjunctions of atoms are often identified with the sets of their atoms. A *database (instance)* D for a schema $\mathcal{R}$ is a (possibly infinite) set of atoms of the form $r(\mathbf{t})$ (a.k.a. *facts*), where r is an n-ary predicate of $\mathcal{R}$, and $\mathbf{t} \in (\Gamma \cup \Gamma_N)^n$.

A *substitution* from one set of symbols S_1 to another set of symbols S_2 is a function $h : S_1 \to S_2$ defined as follows: *(i)* $\varnothing$ is a substitution (empty substitution), *(ii)* if h is a substitution, then $h \cup \{X \to Y\}$ is a substitution, where $X \in S_1$ and $Y \in S_2$, and h does not already contain some $X \to Z$ with $Y \neq Z$. If $X \to Y \in h$ we write $h(X) = Y$. A *homomorphism* from a set of atoms A_1 to a set of atoms A_2, both over the same schema $\mathcal{R}$, is a substitution $h : \Gamma \cup \Gamma_N \cup \Gamma_V \to \Gamma \cup \Gamma_N \cup \Gamma_V$ such that: *(i)* if $t \in \Gamma$, then $h(t) = t$, and *(ii)* if $r(t_1, \ldots, t_n)$ is in A_1, then $h(r(t_1, \ldots, t_n)) = r(h(t_1), \ldots, h(t_n))$ is in A_2.

Conjunctive Queries. A *conjunctive query (CQ)* Q of arity n over a schema $\mathcal{R}$ has the form $q(\mathbf{X}) \leftarrow \varphi(\mathbf{X}, \mathbf{Y})$, where $\varphi(\mathbf{X}, \mathbf{Y})$ is a conjunction of atoms over $\mathcal{R}$, $\mathbf{X}$ and $\mathbf{Y}$ are sequences of variables or constants in Γ, and q is an n-ary predicate that does not occur in $\mathcal{R}$. $\varphi(\mathbf{X}, \mathbf{Y})$ is called the *body* of q, denoted as $body(q)$. A *Boolean CQ (BCQ)* is a CQ of zero arity. The *answer* to an n-ary CQ Q of the form $q(\mathbf{X}) \leftarrow \varphi(\mathbf{X}, \mathbf{Y})$ over a database D, denoted as $Q(D)$, is the set of all n-tuples $\mathbf{t} \in \Gamma^n$ for which there exists a homomorphism $h : \mathbf{X} \cup \mathbf{Y} \to \Gamma \cup \Gamma_N$ such that $h(\varphi(\mathbf{X}, \mathbf{Y})) \subseteq D$ and $h(\mathbf{X}) = \mathbf{t}$. Formally, a BCQ Q has *positive* answer over D, denoted as $D \models Q$, iff $\langle\rangle \in Q(D)$, where $\langle\rangle$ is the empty tuple.

Dependencies. Given a schema $\mathcal{R}$, a *tuple-generating dependency (TGD)* σ over $\mathcal{R}$ is a first-order formula $\forall \mathbf{X} \forall \mathbf{Y} \, \varphi(\mathbf{X}, \mathbf{Y}) \to \exists \mathbf{Z} \, \psi(\mathbf{X}, \mathbf{Z})$, where $\varphi(\mathbf{X}, \mathbf{Y})$ and $\psi(\mathbf{X}, \mathbf{Z})$ are conjunctions of atoms over $\mathcal{R}$, called the *body* and the *head* of σ, denoted as $body(\sigma)$ and $head(\sigma)$, respectively. Henceforth, we will omit the universal quantifiers in TGDs. Such σ is satisfied by a database D for $\mathcal{R}$ iff, whenever there exists a homomorphism h such that $h(\varphi(\mathbf{X}, \mathbf{Y})) \subseteq D$, there exists an extension h' of h (i.e., $h' \supseteq h$) where $h'(\psi(\mathbf{X}, \mathbf{Z})) \subseteq D$.

An *equality-generating dependency (EGD)* η over $\mathcal{R}$ is a first-order formula of the form $\forall \mathbf{X} \, \varphi(\mathbf{X}) \to X_i = X_j$, where $\varphi(\mathbf{X})$ is a conjunction of atoms over $\mathcal{R}$, called the *body* and denoted as $body(\eta)$, and $X_i = X_j$ is an equality among variables of $\mathbf{X}$. Henceforth, for brevity, we will omit the universal quantifiers in EGDs. Such η is satisfied by a database D for $\mathcal{R}$ iff, whenever there exists a homomorphism h such that $h(\varphi(\mathbf{X})) \subseteq D$, then $h(X_i) = h(X_j)$.

Note that *functional dependencies (FDs)* can be identified with sets of EGDs; we assume that the reader is familiar with the notion of FD (see, e.g., [1]).

Example 3. The FD ϕ of the form $r : \{1\} \rightarrow \{2,4\}$, defined on the predicate r of arity four, can be identified with the set of EGDs $\Sigma_E = \{r(X, Y_2, Y_3, Y_4), r(X, Z_2, Z_3, Z_4) \rightarrow Y_i = Z_i\}_{i \in \{2,4\}}$. It is easy to verify that, for every D, it holds that D satisfies ϕ iff D satisfies Σ_E. ∎

CQ Answering under Dependencies. We now define the notion of *query answering* under TGDs and EGDs. Given a database D for $\mathcal{R}$, and a set Σ of TGDs and EGDs over $\mathcal{R}$, the *models* of D w.r.t. Σ, denoted as $mods(D, \Sigma)$, is the set of all databases B such that $B \models D \cup \Sigma$, i.e., $B \supseteq D$ and B satisfies Σ. The *answer* to a CQ Q w.r.t. D and Σ, denoted as $ans(Q, D, \Sigma)$, is the set $\{\mathbf{t} \mid \mathbf{t} \in Q(B), \text{ for each } B \in mods(D, \Sigma)\}$. The *answer* to a BCQ Q w.r.t. D and Σ is *positive*, denoted as $D \cup \Sigma \models Q$, iff $\langle\rangle \in ans(Q, D, \Sigma)$. Note that query answering under general TGDs and EGDs is undecidable. In fact, this is true even in extremely simple cases such that of *inclusion dependencies* and *key dependencies* [10].

We recall that the two problems of CQ and BCQ answering under TGDs and EGDs are LOGSPACE-equivalent [3]. Moreover, it is easy to see that the query output tuple problem (as a decision version of CQ answering) and BCQ evaluation are AC^0-reducible to each other. Henceforth, we thus focus only on the BCQ answering problem.

The Chase Procedure. The *chase procedure* (or simply *chase*) is a fundamental algorithmic tool introduced for checking implication of dependencies [18], and later for checking query containment [16]. Informally, the chase is a process of repairing a database w.r.t. a set of dependencies so that the resulted database satisfies the dependencies. We shall use the term chase interchangeably for both the procedure and its result. The chase works on an instance through the so-called TGD and EGD *chase rules*. The TGD chase rule comes in two different equivalent fashions: *restricted* and *oblivious* [3]. The restricted one, which is defined formally below, repairs TGDs only when they are not satisfied, whereas the oblivious one repairs TGDs even if they are satisfied. Usually, the oblivious chase is used for clarity (see, e.g., [3]). However, for technical reasons, in this paper we employ the restricted chase.

TGD CHASE RULE. Consider a database D for a schema $\mathcal{R}$, and a TGD σ of the form $\varphi(\mathbf{X}, \mathbf{Y}) \rightarrow \exists \mathbf{Z}\, \psi(\mathbf{X}, \mathbf{Z})$ over $\mathcal{R}$. If σ is *applicable* to D, i.e., there exists a homomorphism h such that $h(\varphi(\mathbf{X}, \mathbf{Y})) \subseteq D$, but *there is no* extension h' of h (i.e., $h' \supseteq h$) that maps $\psi(\mathbf{X}, \mathbf{Z})$ to D, then: *(i)* define $h' \supseteq h$ such that $h'(Z_i) = z_i$, for each $Z_i \in \mathbf{Z}$, where $z_i \in \Gamma_N$ is a "fresh" labeled null not introduced before, and following lexicographically all those introduced so far, and *(ii)* add to D the set of atoms $h'(\psi(\mathbf{X}, \mathbf{Z}))$, if not already in D.

EGD CHASE RULE. Consider a database D for a schema $\mathcal{R}$, and an EGD η of the form $\varphi(\mathbf{X}) \rightarrow X_i = X_j$ over $\mathcal{R}$. If η is *applicable* to D, i.e., there exists a homomorphism h such that $h(\varphi(\mathbf{X})) \subseteq D$ and $h(X_i) \neq h(X_j)$, then: *(i)* if $h(X_i)$ and $h(X_j)$ are both constants of Γ, then there is a *hard violation* of η, and the chase *fails*, otherwise *(ii)* replace each occurrence of $h(X_j)$ with $h(X_i)$, if $h(X_i)$ precedes $h(X_j)$ in the lexicographic order, or vice-versa otherwise.

Given a database D and a set of dependencies $\Sigma = \Sigma_T \cup \Sigma_E$, where Σ_T are TGDs and Σ_E are EGDs, the chase algorithm for D and Σ consists of an exhaustive application of the chase rules in a breadth-first fashion, which leads to a (possibly infinite) database. Roughly, the chase of D w.r.t. Σ, denoted as $chase(D, \Sigma)$, is the (possibly infinite) instance constructed by iteratively applying *(i)* the TGD chase rule once, and *(ii)* the EGD chase rule as long as it is applicable (i.e., until a fixed point is reached). A formal definition of the chase algorithm is given, e.g., in [6].

Example 4. Let $\mathcal{R} = \{r, s\}$. Consider the set Σ of TGDs and EGDs over $\mathcal{R}$ constituted by the TGDs $\sigma_1 : r(X, Y) \rightarrow \exists Z \, r(Z, X), s(Z)$ and $\sigma_2 : r(X, Y) \rightarrow r(Y, X)$, and the EGD $\eta : r(X, Y), r(X', Y) \rightarrow X = X'$. Let D be the database $\{r(a, b)\}$ for $\mathcal{R}$. During the construction of $chase(D, \Sigma)$ we first apply σ_1, and we add the atoms $r(z_1, a), s(z_1)$, where z_1 is a "fresh" null of Γ_N. Moreover, σ_2 is applicable and we add the atom $r(b, a)$. Now, the EGD η is applicable and we replace each occurrence of z_1 with the constant b; thus, we get the atom $s(b)$.   ∎

The chase of D w.r.t. Σ is a *universal model* of D w.r.t. Σ, i.e., for each $B \in mods(D, \Sigma)$, there exists a homomorphism from $chase(D, \Sigma)$ to B (see, e.g., [14,15]). Using this fact it can be shown that the chase is a formal tool for query answering under TGDs and EGDs. In particular, the answer to an n-ary CQ Q w.r.t D and Σ, in the case where the chase does not fail, can be obtained by evaluating Q over $chase(D, \Sigma)$, and discarding tuples containing at least one null [15]. If the chase fails, then $mods(D, \Sigma)$ is empty, and thus $ans(Q, D, \Sigma)$ contains all tuples in Γ^n. Notice that the chase is (in general) infinite, and thus not explicitly computable.

3   Separability

In this section we exhibit a sufficient syntactic condition for separability between a set of linear TGDs (LTGDs), i.e., TGDs with just one atom in the body, and a set of EGDs. Before we proceed further, let us first give the formal definition of separability [4,10]. In the rest of the paper, for notational convenience, given a set Σ of dependencies we will denote as Σ_T and Σ_E the set of TGDs and EGDs in Σ, respectively. We start by recalling the notion of separability.

Definition 1. *Consider a set Σ of dependencies over a schema $\mathcal{R}$. We say that Σ is separable if, for every database D for $\mathcal{R}$, either $chase(D, \Sigma)$ fails, or $chase(D, \Sigma) \models Q$ iff $chase(D, \Sigma_T) \models Q$, for every BCQ Q over $\mathcal{R}$.*   □

We now introduce *non-triggerable* EGDs; this syntactic notion ensures separability by preventing the triggering of EGDs during the (restricted) chase. Later, in Subsection 3.2, we will introduce EGDs that are *non-conflicting* with a set of LTGDs; non-conflicting TGDs and EGDs are separable, but it is possible that EGDs are triggered during the construction of the chase.

3.1   Non-triggerable EGDs

Intuitively, we say that a set of EGDs is *non-triggerable* w.r.t. to a set of TGDs, if it is not possible to trigger any of them during the construction of the (restricted) chase, providing that the given database satisfies the EGDs. Clearly, this implies separability since, for query answering purposes, we can consider the TGDs only. Note that in this subsection we consider arbitrary TGDs (and not just LTGDs). Before defining formally non-triggerable EGDs, let us give first some preliminary notions.

Recall that each FD ϕ can be identified with a set Σ_ϕ of EGDs (see Example 3); for each $\eta \in \Sigma_\phi$, we say that η is *associated* to ϕ. An EGD η is associated to a FD iff there exists a FD ϕ and an EGD $\eta' \in \Sigma_\phi$, such that η is the same (up to bijective variable renaming) with η', or, equivalently, η is of the form $r(\mathbf{X}, \mathbf{Y}), r(\mathbf{X}, \mathbf{Z}) \rightarrow Y = Z$, where each $X \in \mathbf{X}$ occurs in both atoms at the same position, $Y \in \mathbf{Y}$, and $Z \in \mathbf{Z}$.

Given an EGD η associated to a FD, we define the set J_η of *joined positions of η* as the set of positions at which a variable that occurs in both atoms of $body(\eta)$ appears. Given a (general) EGD η (not associated to a FD), for each atom $\underline{a} \in body(\eta)$, we define the set $J_{\underline{a},\eta}$ of *joined positions of $\underline{a}$ relative to η* as the set of positions in $\underline{a}$ at which a variable that occurs also in some other atom $\underline{b} \in body(\eta)$, but at a different position, appears. Moreover, for each variable V that occurs in $\underline{a}$, we define the set $P_{\underline{a},\eta}(V)$ of *V-positions of $\underline{a}$ relative to η* as the set of positions in $\underline{a}$ at which the variable V occurs. Finally, for a TGD σ, we define the set U_σ of *universal positions of σ* as the set of positions in $head(\sigma)$ at which a $\forall$-variable occurs.

Example 5. Consider the EGDs $\eta_1 : r(V, W), s(W, X, Y, Z) \rightarrow V = X$, and $\eta_2 : r(U, V), r(U, W) \rightarrow V = W$. Clearly, the sets of joined positions of $\underline{a} = r(V, W)$ and $\underline{b} = s(W, X, Y, Z)$ relative to η_1 are $J_{\underline{a},\eta_1} = \{r[2]\}$ and $J_{\underline{b},\eta_1} = \{s[1]\}$, due to the variable W. Finally, the set of joined positions of η_2 is $J_{\eta_2} = \{r[1]\}$; η_2 is associated to the FD $r : \{1\} \rightarrow \{2\}$. ∎

Note that query answering under (general) TGDs is equivalent to query answering under TGDs with just one head-atom [3]. This was established by providing a LOGSPACE transformation from (general) TGDs into TGDs with singleton atoms in their heads. Henceforth, we assume w.l.o.g. that every TGD has just one head-atom. Let us now define when a set of EGDs, associated to FDs, is non-fd-triggerable w.r.t. a set of TGDs. Note that the following definition coincides with the definition of non-conflicting TGDs and FDs given in [6].

Definition 2. *Consider a set Σ_T of TGDs over a schema $\mathcal{R}$, and a set Σ_E of EGDs over $\mathcal{R}$ associated to FDs. Σ_E is* non-fd-triggerable *w.r.t. Σ_T if, for each pair $\langle \sigma, \eta \rangle \in \Sigma_T \times \Sigma_E$, the following conditions are satisfied: (i) $U_\sigma \not\supseteq J_\eta$, and (ii) if $U_\sigma = J_\eta$, then each $\exists$-variable in σ occurs just once.* □

We now define when a set of arbitrary EGDs (not associated to FDs) is non-egd-triggerable w.r.t. a set of TGDs

Definition 3. *Consider a set Σ_T of TGDs over a schema $\mathcal{R}$, and a set Σ_E of EGDs over $\mathcal{R}$ (not associated to FDs). Σ_E is* non-egd-triggerable *w.r.t. Σ_T if, for each pair $\langle \sigma, \eta \rangle \in \Sigma_T \times \Sigma_E$, and for each atom $\underline{a} \in body(\eta)$, one of the following conditions is satisfied: (i) $U_\sigma \not\supseteq J_{\underline{a},\eta}$, and each $\exists$-variable in σ occurs just once, or (ii) there exists a variable V such that $|P_{\underline{a},\eta}(V)| \geqslant 2$, and there exist two positions $\pi_1, \pi_2 \in P_{\underline{a},\eta}(V)$ such that in $head(\sigma)$ at π_1 and π_2 two distinct variables occur, where at least one of them is an $\exists$-variable.* □

Clearly, a set Σ_E of EGDs can always be partitioned into sets Σ_E^F and Σ_E^G, where Σ_E^F are EGDs associated to FDs, and $\Sigma_E^G = \Sigma_E \setminus \Sigma_E^F$ are general EGDs (not associated to FDs). By exploiting Definitions 2 and 3, we define when a set of EGDs in non-triggerable w.r.t. a set of TGDs.

Definition 4. *Consider a set Σ_T of TGDs over a schema $\mathcal{R}$, and a set Σ_E of EGDs over $\mathcal{R}$. We say that Σ_E is* non-triggerable *w.r.t. Σ_T if Σ_E^F is non-fd-triggerable w.r.t. Σ_T, and Σ_E^G is non-egd-triggerable w.r.t. Σ_T.*   □

Example 6. Consider the TGDs $\sigma_1 : p(W, X), t(X, Y) \rightarrow \exists Z\, s(Z, W, Y, X)$ and $\sigma_2 :$ $s(V, W, X, Y) \rightarrow \exists Z\, r(W, Z)$, and the EGDs η_1 and η_2 given in Example 5. Since $U_{\sigma_1} = \{s[2], s[3], s[4]\} \not\supseteq J_{b,\eta_1}$, and $U_{\sigma_2} = \{r[1]\} \not\supseteq J_{a,\eta_1}$, then $\{\eta_1\}$ is non-egd-triggerable w.r.t. $\{\sigma_1, \sigma_2\}$. Moreover, since $U_{\sigma_2} \not\supseteq J_{\eta_2}$, then $\{\eta_2\}$ is non-fd-triggerable w.r.t. $\{\sigma_1, \sigma_2\}$; recall that η_2 is associated to a FD. We conclude that $\{\eta_1, \eta_2\}$ is non-triggerable w.r.t. $\{\sigma_1, \sigma_2\}$.   ■

It is straightforward to verify that, given a set Σ_T of TGDs and a set Σ_E of EGDs, to decide whether Σ_E is non-triggerable w.r.t. Σ_T is feasible in PTIME. More precisely, we need to perform at most $|\Sigma_T| \cdot |\Sigma_E|$ checks, where each one of them can be carried out in PTIME. The main result of this subsection, namely, given a set Σ of TGDs and EGDs, the property of EGDs being non-triggerable w.r.t. the TGDs is sufficient for separability of Σ, follows.

Theorem 1. *Consider a set Σ of dependencies. If Σ_E is non-triggerable w.r.t. Σ_T, then Σ is separable.*

3.2   Non-conflicting Sets of Linear TGDs and EGDs

In this subsection we focus on the class of LTGDs. We extend the non-triggerabiliy condition by defining when a set of LTGDs and EGDs is *non-conflicting*, and then establish that this condition is indeed sufficient for separability. Note that under non-conflicting sets it is possible to trigger an EGD, during the construction of the chase, unlike non-triggerable EGDs.

Before we proceed further, we need to give some preliminary definitions. First, we recall the notion of *affected positions* of a relational schema w.r.t. a set of TGDs [3]. Given a schema $\mathcal{R}$, and a set Σ_T of TGDs over $\mathcal{R}$, an *affected position* of $\mathcal{R}$ w.r.t. Σ_T is defined inductively as follows. Let π_h be a position in the head of a TGD $\sigma \in \Sigma_T$. If an existentially quantified variable occurs at π_h, then π_h is affected w.r.t. Σ_T. If the same universally quantified variable X appears both in position π_h, and in the body of σ at affected positions *only*, then π_h is affected w.r.t. Σ_T. Intuitively speaking, the affected positions of a schema w.r.t. a set Σ_T of TGDs, are those positions at which a labeled null may occur during the construction of the chase under Σ_T.

A key notion is the well-known query containment under TGDs. In particular, given a set Σ_T of TGDs over a schema $\mathcal{R}$, and two CQs Q_1 and Q_2 over $\mathcal{R}$, we say that Q_1 is contained in Q_2 w.r.t. Σ_T, written $Q_1 \subseteq_{\Sigma_T} Q_2$, if $Q_1(D) \subseteq Q_2(D)$, for every database D for $\mathcal{R}$ that satisfies Σ_T. Notice that the problems of query containment and of query answering (the latter in its decision version, a.k.a. query output tuple problem) are mutually LOGSPACE-reducible [3], and thus they have the same complexity bounds.

We now recall the notion of applicability of a TGD to an atom [9]. Consider a TGD σ over a schema $\mathcal{R}$, and a set A of atoms over $\mathcal{R}$. We say that σ is A-*applicable* to an atom $\underline{a} \in A$ if the following conditions are satisfied: *(i)* $\underline{a}$ and $head(\sigma)$ unify (recall that we consider w.l.o.g. TGDs with just one atom in the head), *(ii)* if the term at position π in $\underline{a}$ is either a constant of Γ, or a variable that occurs in some atom of A other than $\underline{a}$, then the variable at position π in $head(\sigma)$ occurs also in $body(\sigma)$, and *(iii)* if a variable of A occurs only in $\underline{a}$ at positions $\pi_1, \ldots, \pi_m$, for $m \geqslant 2$, then either the variable at position π_i in $head(\sigma)$, for each $i \in [m]$, occurs also in $body(\sigma)$, or at positions $\pi_1, \ldots, \pi_m$ in $head(\sigma)$ we have the same existentially quantified variable.

Consider now a set A of atoms over a schema $\mathcal{R}$, a variable X which occurs in A, called the *watched variable* of A, and a set Σ_T of LTGDs over $\mathcal{R}$. By applying a procedure, called Expansion, which is actually a modified version of the rewriting algorithm given in [9], we construct the *expanded set* of A w.r.t. Σ_T. Formally, Expansion(A, X, Σ_T) consists of the following steps:

1. Let $S = \{\langle A, \text{id} \rangle\}$, where id is the identity substitution on the terms of A.
2. Let $S' = S$.
3. For each pair $\langle A, \lambda \rangle \in S'$ apply the following two steps:
   (a) For each $\underline{a}, \underline{b} \in A$: if $\underline{a}$ and $\underline{b}$ unify, then add to S the pair $\langle \gamma(A), \gamma \circ \lambda \rangle$, where $\gamma = MGU(\underline{a}, \underline{b})$, only if there is no $\langle A', \lambda' \rangle \in S$, and a bijective (renaming) substitution ρ that maps $\gamma(\lambda(X))$ to $\lambda'(X)$, such that $\rho(\gamma(A)) = A'$.
   (b) For each pair $\langle \underline{a}, \sigma \rangle \in A \times \Sigma_T$: if *(i)* σ is A-applicable to $\underline{a}$; in the sequel let $\gamma = MGU(\underline{a}, head(\sigma))$, *(ii)* $\widehat{A}$ contains the variable $\gamma(\lambda(X))$, where $\widehat{A} = \gamma(A')$ and A' is obtained from A by replacing the atom $\underline{a}$ with $body(\sigma)$, and *(iii)* all the occurrences of $\gamma(\lambda(X))$ in $\widehat{A}$ appear at affected positions of $\mathcal{R}$ w.r.t. Σ_T, then add to S the pair $\langle \widehat{A}, \gamma \circ \lambda \rangle$, only if there is no $\langle A', \lambda' \rangle \in S'$, and a bijective (renaming) substitution ρ that maps $\gamma(\lambda(X))$ to $\lambda'(X)$, such that $\rho(\widehat{A}) = A'$.
4. If $S = S'$, then return S; otherwise, goto 2.

Note that at step 3b we assume w.l.o.g. that the TGD σ and the set S' have no variables in common; we can simply rename (or *standardize apart*, in Logic Programming parlance) the variables of σ. This is needed to avoid clutter among variable names introduced during different applications of step 3b. Let us clarify that steps 3a and 3b correspond to *minimization* and *rewriting* steps, respectively, of the rewriting algorithm presented in [9]. We now formally define non-conflicting sets of LTGDs and EGDs.

Definition 5. *Consider a set Σ of LTGDs and EGDs over a schema $\mathcal{R}$. We say that Σ is non-conflicting if Σ_E can be partitioned into two sets Σ'_E and Σ''_E such that Σ'_E is non-triggerable w.r.t. Σ_T, and, for each $\eta \in \Sigma''_E$ of the form $\varphi(\mathbf{X}) \to X_i = X_j$, the following condition holds: for each pair $\langle A, \lambda \rangle \in$ Expansion$(\mu(\varphi(\mathbf{X})), X_i, \Sigma_T)$, for $\mu = \{X_j \to X_i\}$, it holds that $Q_1 \subseteq_{\Sigma_T} Q_2$, where Q_1 and Q_2 are the conjunctive queries $q(\mathbf{Y}) \leftarrow \lambda(\varphi(\mathbf{X}))$ and $q(\mathbf{Y}) \leftarrow A$, respectively, where $\mathbf{Y}$ are the variables that appear both in $\lambda(\varphi(\mathbf{X}))$ and A.* $\qquad \square$

Example 7. Consider the set Σ consisting by $\sigma_1 : s(X_1, Y_1) \to r(Y_1, X_1)$, $\sigma_2 : p(X_2) \to \exists Y_2 \, s(Y_2, X_2)$, $\sigma_3 : t(X_3, Y_3) \to r(X_3, Y_3)$, $\sigma_4 : r(X_4, Y_4) \to s(Y_4, X_4)$, and $\eta : r(X_5, Y_5), r(X_5, Z_5) \rightarrow Y_5 = Z_5$. It is easy to see that Σ_E is not non-triggerable w.r.t. Σ_T. The expanded set S of $\mu(body(\eta))$, where $\mu = \{Z_5 \rightarrow Y_5\}$, consists of the pairs $\langle \{r(X_5, Y_5)\}, \mathsf{id} \rangle$ and $\langle \{s(Y_5, X_5)\}, \{Y_1 \rightarrow X_5, X_1 \rightarrow Y_5\} \rangle$. Note that $\langle \{t(X_5, Y_5)\}, \{X_3 \rightarrow X_5, Y_3 \rightarrow Y_5\} \rangle$ is not added to S since the watched variable Y_5 occurs in $t(X_5, Y_5)$ at a non-affected position, while the pair $\langle \{p(X_5)\}, \{Y_2 \rightarrow Y_5, X_2 \rightarrow X_5, Y_1 \rightarrow X_5, X_1 \rightarrow Y_5\} \rangle$ is not added since $p(X_5)$ does not contain the watched variable Y_5. It is not difficult to verify that $Q_1 \subseteq_{\Sigma_T} Q_2$ and $Q_1 \subseteq_{\Sigma_T} Q_3$, where $Q_1 : q(X_5, Y_5) \leftarrow r(X_5, Y_5), r(X_5, Z_5)$, $Q_2 : q(X_5, Y_5) \leftarrow r(X_5, Y_5)$, and $Q_3 : q(X_5, Y_5) \leftarrow s(Y_5, X_5)$. Consequently, Σ is non-conflicting. ∎

Identifying Non-Conflicting Sets. It is easy to show that the expanded set of the body-atoms of an EGD w.r.t. a set of LTGDs is always finite. Since conjunctive query containment under LTGDs is decidable [4], we immediately get that the non-conflicting condition as defined above is decidable. However, this tells nothing about the complexity of identifying non-conflicting sets. It is possible to show that the decision problem whether a set of LTGDs and EGDs is non-conflicting is PSPACE-complete. The desired upper bound is obtained by exhibiting a simple non-deterministic polynomial space algorithm.

Lemma 1. *Consider a set Σ of LTGDs and EGDs over a schema $\mathcal{R}$. The problem whether Σ is non-conflicting is feasible in PSPACE.*

Proof (sketch). Recall that the problem whether a set of EGDs is non-triggerable w.r.t. a set of TGDs is feasible in PTIME. Therefore, we can identify in PTIME the maximal subset $\Sigma_E' \subseteq \Sigma_E$ which is non-triggerable w.r.t. Σ_T. Since each pair in the expanded set of $\mu(\varphi(\mathbf{X}))$, for some EGD $\varphi(\mathbf{X}) \rightarrow X_i = X_j \in \Sigma_E''$, where $\Sigma_E'' = \Sigma_E \setminus \Sigma_E'$ and $\mu = \{X_j \rightarrow X_i\}$, w.r.t. Σ_T can be represented using polynomial space, and also since CQ containment under LTGDs is in PSPACE (implicit in [16]), we can decide in non-deterministic PSPACE whether Σ_E'' violates the non-conflicting condition. Since PSPACE coincides with NPSPACE we get that the problem whether Σ_E'' violates the non-conflicting condition is feasible in PSPACE, and hence the problem whether Σ is non-conflicting is in coPSPACE. It is well-known that coPSPACE and PSPACE coincide. Hence, the problem whether Σ is non-conflicting is in PSPACE, as needed. □
The desired lower bound can be established by providing a reduction from the CQ containment problem under LTGDs which is PSPACE-hard [16].

Lemma 2. *Consider a set Σ of LTGDs and EGDs over a schema $\mathcal{R}$. The problem whether Σ is non-conflicting is PSPACE-hard.*

Proof (sketch). The proof is by reduction of the query containment problem under LTGDs. Note that the problem is still PSPACE-hard even in the case of atomic queries. Consider an instance of the CQ containement problem, i.e., two queries $Q_1 : q(\mathbf{X}) \leftarrow r(\mathbf{X}, \mathbf{Y})$ and $Q_2 : q(\mathbf{X}) \leftarrow s(\mathbf{X}, \mathbf{Y})$, and a set Σ of LTGDs. We are going to construct a set Σ_T of LTGDs, and an EGD η as follows. Σ_T is the union of Σ with the set of linear TGDs consisting by: $r(\mathbf{X}, \mathbf{Y}) \rightarrow \exists Z \, r^\star(\mathbf{X}, Z)$, $s(\mathbf{X}, \mathbf{Y}) \rightarrow \exists Z \, s^\star(\mathbf{X}, Z)$, and $s^\star(X_1, \ldots, X_n) \rightarrow r^\star(X_1, \ldots, X_n)$, where $r(\mathbf{X}, \mathbf{Y})$ and $s(\mathbf{X}, \mathbf{Y})$ are the body-atoms of Q_1 and Q_2, respectively, and $r^\star, s^\star$ are auxiliary predicates. Moreover, η is the EGD $r^\star(\mathbf{X}, Y), r^\star(\mathbf{X}, Z) \rightarrow Y = Z$. Observe that Expansion($\{r^\star(\mathbf{X}, Y)\}, Y, \Sigma_T$) contains $\langle\{r^\star(\mathbf{X}, Y)\}, \text{id}\rangle$ and $\langle\{s^\star(\mathbf{X}, Y)\}, \lambda\rangle$, where λ maps $\langle X_1, \ldots, X_n\rangle$ to $\langle\mathbf{X}, Y\rangle$. Therefore, $\Sigma_T \cup \{\eta\}$ is not non-conflicting iff the CQ $q(\mathbf{X}, Y) \leftarrow r^\star(\mathbf{X}, Y), r^\star(\mathbf{X}, Z)$ is not contained in the CQ $q(\mathbf{X}, Y) \leftarrow s^\star(\mathbf{X}, Y)$ under Σ_T. This implies that $\Sigma_T \cup \{\eta\}$ is not non-conflicting iff $Q_1 \not\subseteq_\Sigma Q_2$. Since coPSPACE coincides with PSPACE, we immediately get that the problem whether $\Sigma_T \cup \{\eta\}$ is non-conflicting is PSPACE-hard, and the claim follows. $\square$

The following complexity characterization of the problem whether a set of LTGDs and EGDs is non-conflicting follows from Lemma 1 and 2.

Theorem 2. *Consider a set Σ of LTGDs and EGDs over a schema $\mathcal{R}$. The problem whether Σ is non-conflicting is PSPACE-complete.*

Non-Conflicting Sets are Separable. Let us now establish that non-conflicting sets of LTGDs and EGDs are indeed separable. Before we proceed further, let us establish an auxiliary technical lemma.

Lemma 3. *Consider a non-conflicting set Σ of LTGDs and EGDs over $\mathcal{R}$. If chase(D, Σ) does not fail, then there exists a homomorphism that maps chase(D, Σ) into chase(D, Σ_T), for every database D for $\mathcal{R}$.*

Proof (sketch). The proof is by induction on the number of applications of the (TGD or EGD) chase rule. We can show that, for each $k \geqslant 0$, there exists a homomorphism h_k such that $h_k(chase^{[k]}(D, \Sigma)) \subseteq chase(D, \Sigma_T)$, where $chase^{[k]}(D, \Sigma)$ is the part of the chase obtained by applying k times either the TGD or the EGD chase rule. $\square$

Theorem 3. *Consider a set Σ of LTGDs and EGDs over a schema $\mathcal{R}$. If Σ is non-conflicting, then it is also separable.*

Proof. Let D be a database for $\mathcal{R}$ such that $chase(D, \Sigma)$ does not fail. Clearly, by construction, $chase(D, \Sigma)$ satisfies all the dependencies in Σ. Therefore, $chase(D, \Sigma) \in mods(D, \Sigma) \subseteq mods(D, \Sigma_T)$. Since $chase(D, \Sigma_T)$ is a universal model of D w.r.t. Σ_T we immediately get that there exists a homomorphism h such that $h(chase(D, \Sigma_T)) \subseteq chase(D, \Sigma)$. On the other hand, Lemma 3 implies that there exists a homomorphism h' such that $h'(chase(D, \Sigma)) \subseteq chase(D, \Sigma_T)$. Due to the existence of h and h' it holds that, for every BCQ Q over $\mathcal{R}$, $chase(D, \Sigma) \models Q$ iff $chase(D, \Sigma_T) \models Q$. $\square$

Query Answering under Non-Conflicting Sets. We conclude this subsection by investigating the *data* and *combined complexity* of BCQ answering under non-conflicting sets of linear TGDs and EGDs. Recall that the data complexity is calculated by considering only the data as input, while the combined complexity is calculated by considering also the query and the dependencies as part of the input.

Theorem 4. *Consider a BCQ Q over a schema $\mathcal{R}$, a database D for $\mathcal{R}$, and a non-conflicting set Σ of LTGDs and EGDs over $\mathcal{R}$. The problem whether $D \cup \Sigma \models Q$ is in AC^0 in data complexity, and is PSPACE-complete in combined complexity.*

Proof (sketch). Suppose that $chase(D, \Sigma)$ does not fail. By Theorem 3, we get that $D \cup \Sigma \models Q$, or, equivalently, $chase(D, \Sigma) \models Q$ iff $chase(D, \Sigma_T) \models Q$. It is well-known that BCQ answering under LTGDs is in AC^0 in data complexity [4], and PSPACE-complete in combined complexity (implicit in [16]). Since Σ_T is a set of LTGDs, providing that the chase does not fail, the desired complexity follows. Since the problem whether $chase(D, \Sigma)$ fails is tantamount to BCQ answering under LTGDs (see, e.g., [7]), the claim follows.   □

4   Applications

As mentioned in the introduction, the research presented in this paper originated from our recent work on Entiry-Relationship schemata, and in particular on our $ER^{\pm}$ family [5,7], a family of languages derived from the original ER model. More specifically, $ER^{\pm}$ languages are variants of the ER formalism, enriched with is-a (inclusion) among entities and relationships, plus functional and mandatory participation constraints. Interestingly, every $ER^{\pm}$ schema can be encoded in a relational schema by using IDs (a special case of linear TGDs) and KDs. The results in this paper immediately imply that we can add sets of general EGDs to $ER^{\pm}$ schemata, as in Example 2, as long as the EGDs are non-conflicting with the linear TGDs (in fact, IDs) that encode the $ER^{\pm}$ schema. Such an addition will not at all affect the query answering complexity, as EGDs need to be considered only in a preliminary step (see, e.g., [7]), to check whether any hard violation occurs in the chase, thus revealing whether the theory is inconsistent. Query answering can then be done by rewriting queries into first-order queries, which can be translated into SQL and executed by means of a relational DBMS.

As shown in [4], *negative constraints* (a form of denial constraints) can be added to any set of linear TGDs without affecting the complexity of query answering. This was used in [7] to show that negative constraints can be added to $ER^{\pm}$ schemata. The addition of the non-conflicting EGDs presented in this paper turns out to be independent of that of negative constraints, therefore we can express both kinds of constraints in addition to sets of linear TGDs without increasing the complexity of query answering. This leads us to another important application of our results, regarding the well-known DL-lite family of description logics. DL-lite languages have been shown to be useful in ontology-based query answering, especially because, as they are all FO-rewritable, they offer the desirable feature of providing tractable query answering services. As shown in [4], each DL-lite schema (ontology) is expressible with non-conflicting linear TGDs and KDs. Therefore, as for $ER^{\pm}$ languages, we can add non-conflicting EGDs to DL-lite schemas (once we represent them in relational form) and keep the same query answering techniques and complexity.

Complexity. For the above consideration on the applications of our results, the same tight complexity bounds of conjunctive query answering under non-conflicting TGDs and EGDs (Theorem 4) hold for $ER^{\pm}$ schemata with non-conflicting EGDs, and for DL-lite schemata with non-conflicting EGDs.

Extensions. By using a syntactic condition similar to that of Definition 5, we can define sets of EGDs which are non-conflicting with sets of a larger class of TGDs called *sticky sets* of TGDs [6]. Sticky sets of TGDs, while allowing for an arbitrary number of atoms in their bodies, are FO-rewritable; the complexity of CQ answering under sticky sets of TGDs is therefore AC^0 in data complexity, while it is EXPTIME-complete in combined complexity. EGDs which are non-conflicting with sticky sets of TGDs are separable, and thus can be added without affecting the complexity of query answering.

5   Discussion

In this paper we have addressed the problem of separability between TGDs and EGDs in the context of ontological query answering. We have exhibited a sufficient, syntactic condition for separability for the case of LTGDs and general EGDs. The non-conflicting condition can be extended to EGDs in the presence of sticky sets of TGDs [6], a relevant class of ontology constraints. We have shown that non-conflicting EGDs can be added, without adding complexity to query answering, to several tractable ontology representation languages, including the $ER^\pm$ family, and to most languages in the DL-lite family of tractable description logics. Moreover, the complexity of checking whether a set of LTGDs and EGDs is non-conflicting has the same complexity (that is, PSPACE-complete) as the combined complexity of query answering under the same dependencies. The same holds for the most relevant special case of our language, namely the $ER^\pm$ family. While checking the non-conflict condition is hardly done by visual inspection, design tools for ontologies (e.g., for $ER^\pm$ schemata) could alert the designer when the condition is not met. Notice that, since non-conflicting TGDs and EGDs are FO-rewritable, query answering can be done by rewriting each query into a single SQL one, and then having it efficiently executed by a DBMS on the initial data (see, e.g., [4]). This opens the possibility of performing efficient query answering in real-world scenarios, something we are currently experimenting with a prototype system. An important research direction is to reduce the size of the rewriting, possibly in combination with a suitable instance expansion, to further improve efficiency (see, e.g., [17]).

Related Work. Identification constraints, which are similar to EGDs, have been thoroughly studied in the context of Description Logics, Databases and Conceptual Modeling (see for example [12] and references therein). The interaction of such constraints with TGDs easily creates complexity or decidability problems, as shown, for example, in [10] in the case of inclusion and key dependencies. An early separable class of IDs and KDs, called *key-based*, was proposed in the seminal work of Johnson and Klug [16]. In [10], the key-based condition is relaxed and the more general *non-key-conflicting (NKC) IDs* are presented. Notice that NKC IDs capture the well-known class of *foreign key dependencies*. The class of NKC IDs was slightly generalized in [4] to the context of arbitrary (single-head) TGDs by defining the class of *non-key-conflicting TGDs*, which uses a very similar idea. In [6] it was shown that the class of non-key-conflicting TGDs can be effortless extended to treat not just keys, but FDs. The main reason due to which the above classes are separable is because, if the given database satisfies the set of EGDs, we know that it is not possible to apply any EGD during the chase procedure. In fact, all the above conditions are captured by our notion of *non-triggerable EGDs*. The separable classes of IDs and KDs introduced in [5,7] in the context of Entity-Relationship schemata, instead, are such that KDs can be applied during the chase. The separable class of LTGDs and EGDs that we propose is a proper generalization of the classes of IDs and KDs introduced in [5,7]. Moreover, it is built upon the notion of non-triggerability, and also generalizes the conditions in [4,6].

Acknowledgements. The authors acknowledge support by the European Research Council under the European Community's Seventh Framework Programme (FP7/2007–2013) / ERC grant agreement DIADEM no. 246858.

References

1. Abiteboul, S., Hull, R., Vianu, V.: Foundations of Databases. Addison-Wesley, Reading (1995)
2. Calì, A., Calvanese, D., De Giacomo, G., Lenzerini, M.: Accessing data integration systems through conceptual schemas. In: Kunii, H.S., Jajodia, S., Sølvberg, A. (eds.) ER 2001. LNCS, vol. 2224, pp. 270–284. Springer, Heidelberg (2001)
3. Calì, A., Gottlob, G., Kifer, M.: Taming the infinite chase: Query answering under expressive relational constraints. In: Proc. of KR, pp. 70–80 (2008)
4. Calì, A., Gottlob, G., Lukasiewicz, T.: A general datalog-based framework for tractable query answering over ontologies. In: Proc. of PODS, pp. 77–86 (2009)
5. Calì, A., Gottlob, G., Pieris, A.: Tractable query answering over conceptual schemata. In: Laender, A.H.F., Castano, S., Dayal, U., Casati, F., de Oliveira, J.P.M. (eds.) ER 2009. LNCS, vol. 5829, pp. 175–190. Springer, Heidelberg (2009)
6. Calì, A., Gottlob, G., Pieris, A.: Advanced processing for ontological queries. PVLDB 3(1), 554–565 (2010)
7. Calì, A., Gottlob, G., Pieris, A.: Query answering under expressive entity-relationship schemata. In: Parsons, J., Saeki, M., Shoval, P., Woo, C., Wand, Y. (eds.) ER 2010. LNCS, vol. 6412, pp. 347–361. Springer, Heidelberg (2010)
8. Calì, A., Gottlob, G., Pieris, A.: Query answering under non-guarded rules in datalog+/-. In: Hitzler, P., Lukasiewicz, T. (eds.) RR 2010. LNCS, vol. 6333, pp. 175–190. Springer, Heidelberg (2010)
9. Calì, A., Gottlob, G., Pieris, A.: Query rewriting under non-guarded rules. In: Proc. AMW (2010)
10. Calì, A., Lembo, D., Rosati, R.: On the decidability and complexity of query answering over inconsistent and incomplete databases. In: Proc. of PODS, pp. 260–271 (2003)
11. Calvanese, D., De Giacomo, G., Lembo, D., Lenzerini, M., Rosati, R.: Tractable reasoning and efficient query answering in description logics: The DL-lite family. J. Autom. Reasoning 39(3), 385–429 (2007)
12. Calvanese, D., Giacomo, G.D., Lembo, D., Lenzerini, M., Rosati, R.: Path-based identification constraints in description logics. In: Proc. of KR, pp. 231–241 (2008)
13. Chen, P.P.: The entity-relationship model: towards a unified view of data. ACM Trans. Database Syst. 1(1), 124–131 (1976)
14. Deutsch, A., Nash, A., Remmel, J.B.: The chase revisited. In: Proc. of PODS, pp. 149–158 (2008)
15. Fagin, R., Kolaitis, P.G., Miller, R.J., Popa, L.: Data exchange: Semantics and query answering. Theor. Comput. Sci. 336(1), 89–124 (2005)
16. Johnson, D.S., Klug, A.C.: Testing containment of conjunctive queries under functional and inclusion dependencies. J. Comput. Syst. Sci. 28(1), 167–189 (1984)
17. Kontchakov, R., Lutz, C., Toman, D., Wolter, F., Zakharyaschev, M.: The combined approach to query answering in DL-lite. In: Proc. of KR (2010)
18. Maier, D., Mendelzon, A.O., Sagiv, Y.: Testing implications of data dependencies. ACM Trans. Database Syst. 4(4), 455–469 (1979)

A Precious Class of Cardinality Constraints for Flexible XML Data Processing

Flavio Ferrarotti[1], Sven Hartmann[2], and Sebastian Link[1]

[1] Victoria University of Wellington, New Zealand
[2] Clausthal University of Technology, Germany

Abstract. Modern Web developers must often process collections of XML data that are aggregated from potentially thousands of heterogeneous sources. While the semi-structured nature of XML provides a high degree of syntactic flexibility there are significant shortcomings to specify the semantics of its data. For the advancement of XML applications it is therefore an important problem to identify natural classes of constraints that can be utilized effectively by XML data engineers. The problem is challenging given the range of intractability results in the area. In this paper we propose a class of XML cardinality constraints that is sufficiently flexible to process concisely XML data from various sources. The flexibility is a result of the right balance between expressiveness and efficiency of maintenance. In particular, we characterize the associated implication problem axiomatically, and algorithmically by a low-degree polynomial time decision procedure. Our class is precious as small extensions in expressiveness result in intractability.

1 Introduction

Context. The most common format for web accessible data is provided by the eXtensible Markup Language (XML) [5]. It is used for hypertext document collections like Wikipedia, and for data exchange and integration in web applications including web service messaging, blogs, news feeds, and podcasts. Modern Web developers often process XML collections that are aggregated from potentially thousands of heterogeneous sources. For this purpose the semi-structured nature of XML provides a high degree of syntactic flexibility. Unfortunately, XML presents significant shortcomings to specify the semantics of its data.

The Current Conundrum. For the advancement of XML applications it is therefore an important problem to identify useful classes of integrity constraints. XML engineers use these classes to constrain collections of XML data to those considered meaningful for the application domain. This is particularly important for data integration where not only the data but also its properties (e.g. constraints) are integrated to provide a concise customer service [9]. Many classes of constraints can express desirable properties of XML data. However, the delicate interactions between XML data items often mean that these constraint classes cannot be maintained effectively, nevermind efficiently. A huge range of infeasibility and intractability results exists, see [4,16]. For example, the satisfiability

M. Jeusfeld, L. Delcambre, and T.W. Ling (Eds.): ER 2011, LNCS 6998, pp. 175–188, 2011.

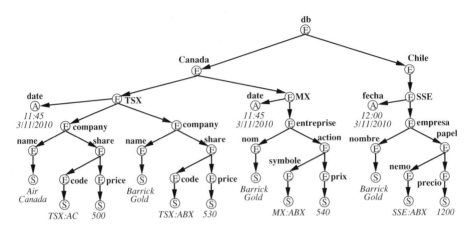

Fig. 1. Tree representation of XML data

problem of the keys and foreign keys in XML Schema is undecidable, and that of XML Schema keys is *NP*-hard [3]. Thus, it is a conundrum to identify classes that are precious, i.e. expressive and tractable.

Motivation. We study cardinality constraints for XML. As bounds occur naturally in everyday life they can express many desirable properties. They have also enjoyed a great deal of popularity in conceptual modeling [10,15,17,18]. Our constraints are inherently different from the *minOccurs* and *maxOccurs* constraints in XML Schema [19]. The latter restrict the number of children element nodes independently of any data values. We define cardinality constraints in the XML tree model as proposed by DOM [2] and XPath [7], but independently from schema specifications such as DTDs [5] or XSDs [19]. Figure 1 shows a tree representation of an XML data fragment in which nodes are annotated by their type: *E* for elements, *A* for attributes, and *S* for text (PCDATA) in XML data.

Cardinality constraints restrict the number of nodes in an XML tree that have the same (complex) values on some selected descendant nodes. To address the tree-like structure of XML data such restrictions can be specified for an entire document or relatively to selected context nodes. As is common in XML data processing, path expressions are used to select the nodes of interest.

For example, consider the XML tree T in Figure 1. The XML document is the result of integrating XML data from different sources, i.e. stock markets around the world. Each market provides, in the local official language, information regarding shares. For instance, the Toronto Stock Exchange (TSX) shows this information in English while the Montréal Exchange (MX) chooses French and the Santiago Stock Exchange (SSE) chooses Spanish. It is assumed that the markets provide the information as XML documents with the structure of the subtrees rooted at the nodes at level three (the *company*-nodes, the *entreprise*-node and the *empresa*-node in our example). Suppose Canada has a policy that a company can list its shares in at most two of the stock markets that operate in the country. Further, each company can list its shares in up to four stock markets globally.

Cardinality constraints have the power to unlock a vast amount of application domains effectively. These include consistency management, query optimization, and view maintenance. Moreover, they can help to predict the number of query answers, updates or de/encryptions. For instance, we would like to provide a service where clients receive up-to-date information regarding company shares that are traded in different stock markets worldwide. Suppose a client is using a smart phone to receive the current value for all shares of the multinational company *Barrick Gold*. Clients will only use the service if the costs are reasonable, but our service provider prefers to integrate data from different sources only when the service has been paid for. If reasoning about cardinality constraints can be automated, then it is likely that we can estimate the maximum number of answers to a client's query and hence the maximum cost for the service. Thus, the client is able to make an informed choice and the service provider has minimized its cost for unpaid services, without querying or integrating data.

Contributions. To unlock applications effectively it is crucial to identify precious classes of cardinality constraints. We will first introduce an expressive class of cardinality constraints. The first source of expressiveness is the ability to specify lower and upper bounds on the number of nodes (called selector nodes) in an XML tree that are value-equal on some of its subnodes (called field nodes). The bounds can be specified with respect to a context node. The second source results from the very general notion of value equality: isomorphic subtrees in contrast to just value equality on leaf nodes for instance. The third source is a result of the path language we use to select nodes. This includes the single label wildcard, child navigation, and descendant navigation, as known from XPath. For our general class of cardinality constraints we will single out three fragments that are likely to be intractable as their associated implication problems are all *coNP*-hard. The fragments direct our attention towards the class of *max-constraints* which allow the specification of upper bounds, our general notion of value-equality, context and target nodes can be selected by our general path language, and field nodes by using single label wildcards and child navigation. Thus, max-constraints can capture many desirable properties of XML data, e.g. the business rules in our example. In contrast to other expressive classes of XML constraints, max-constraints are also tractable. Indeed, we characterize their implication problem axiomatically, and by a shortest path problem on a suitable digraph. This enables us to design a compact low-degree polynomial time algorithm to decide implication efficiently. Hence, we establish a precious class of cardinality constraints that is effective for flexible XML data processing.

Organization. We fix basic notions in Section 2. Cardinality constraints and their implication problem are studied in Section 3. In Section 4 we establish a finite axiomatization for max-constraints, and characterize the implication problem in terms of shortest paths. In Section 5 we design an efficient algorithm for deciding implication. Section 6 concludes our work.

2   Preliminaries

The XML Tree Model. Let $\mathbf{E}$ denote a countably infinite set of element tags, $\mathbf{A}$ a countably infinite set of attribute names, and $\{S\}$ a singleton set denoting text (PCDATA). These sets are pairwise disjoint. The elements of $\mathcal{L} = \mathbf{E} \cup \mathbf{A} \cup \{S\}$ are called *labels*. An *XML tree* is a 6-tuple $T = (V, lab, ele, att, val, r)$ where V is a set of nodes, and lab is a mapping $V \to \mathcal{L}$ assigning a label to every node in V. A node $v \in V$ is an *element node* if $lab(v) \in \mathbf{E}$, an *attribute node* if $lab(v) \in \mathbf{A}$, and a *text node* if $lab(v) = S$. Moreover, ele and att are partial mappings defining the edge relation of T: for any node $v \in V$, if v is an element node, then $ele(v)$ is a list of element and text nodes, and $att(v)$ is a set of attribute nodes in V. If v is an attribute or text node, then $ele(v)$ and $att(v)$ are undefined. The partial mapping val assigns a string to each attribute and text node: for each node $v \in V$, $val(v)$ is a string if v is an attribute or text node, while $val(v)$ is undefined otherwise. Finally, r is the unique and distinguished root node. A *path* p of T is a finite sequence of nodes $v_0, \ldots, v_m$ in V such that (v_{i-1}, v_i) is an edge of T for $i = 1, \ldots, m$. The path p determines a word $lab(v_1). \cdots .lab(v_m)$ over the alphabet $\mathcal{L}$, denoted by $lab(p)$.

Value Equality of Nodes in XML Trees. Two nodes $u, v \in V$ are *value equal*, denoted by $u =_v v$, iff the following conditions are satisfied: (a) $lab(u) = lab(v)$, (b) if u, v are attribute or text nodes, then $val(u) = val(v)$, (c) if u, v are element nodes, then *(i)* if $att(u) = \{a_1, \ldots, a_m\}$, then $att(v) = \{a'_1, \ldots, a'_m\}$ and there is a permutation π on $\{1, \ldots, m\}$ such that $a_i =_v a'_{\pi(i)}$ for $i = 1, \ldots, m$, and *(ii)* if $ele(u) = [u_1, \ldots, u_k]$, then $ele(v) = [v_1, \ldots, v_k]$ and $u_i =_v v_i$ for $i = 1, \ldots, k$.

Path Expressions for Node Selection in XML Trees. We use the path language $PL^{\{.,\_,\_^*\}}$ consisting of expressions given by the following grammar: $Q \to \ell \mid \varepsilon \mid Q.Q \mid \_ \mid \_^*$. Here $\ell \in \mathcal{L}$ is any label, ε denotes the empty path expression, "." denotes the concatenation of two path expressions, "_" denotes the *single-label* wildcard, and "_*" denotes the *variable length don't care* wildcard. Let P, Q be words from $PL^{\{.,\_,\_^*\}}$. P is a *refinement* of Q, denoted by $P \lesssim Q$, if P is obtained from Q by replacing variable length wildcards in Q by words from $PL^{\{.,\_,\_^*\}}$ and single-label wildcards in Q by labels from $\mathcal{L}$. Let Q be a word from $PL^{\{.,\_,\_^*\}}$. A path p in the XML tree T is called a Q-path if $lab(p)$ is a refinement of Q. For nodes $v, w \in V$, we write $T \models Q(v, w)$ if w is reachable from v following a Q-path in T. For a node $v \in V$, let $v[\![Q]\!]$ denote the set of nodes in T that are reachable from v following any Q-path, that is, $v[\![Q]\!] = \{w \mid T \models Q(v, w)\}$. We use $[\![Q]\!]$ as an abbreviation for $r[\![Q]\!]$ where r is the root node of T. For $\mathcal{S} \subseteq \{., \_, \_^*\}$, $PL^{\mathcal{S}}$ denotes the subset of $PL^{\{.,\_,\_^*\}}$ expressions restricted to the constructs in $\mathcal{S}$. $Q \in PL^{\{.,\_,\_^*\}}$ is *valid* if it does not have labels $\ell \in \mathbf{A}$ or $\ell = S$ in a position other than the last one. Let P, Q be words from $PL^{\{.,\_,\_^*\}}$. P is *contained* in Q, denoted by $P \subseteq Q$, if for every XML tree T and every node v of T we have $v[\![P]\!] \subseteq v[\![Q]\!]$. It follows immediately from the definition that $P \lesssim Q$ implies $P \subseteq Q$. For nodes v and v' of an XML tree T, the *value intersection* of $v[\![Q]\!]$ and $v'[\![Q]\!]$ is given by $v[\![Q]\!] \cap_v v'[\![Q]\!] = \{(w, w') \mid w \in v[\![Q]\!], w' \in v'[\![Q]\!], w =_v w'\}$.

3   From Expressive towards Precious Classes

Our expressive notion of cardinality constraints results from the ability to specify both lower and upper bounds, the generality of value-equality and the path language. For more expressive path languages the containment problem becomes at least intractable [16]. Let $\mathbb{N}$ denote the positive integers, and let $\bar{\mathbb{N}} = \mathbb{N} \cup \{\infty\}$.

Definition 1. *A* cardinality constraint φ *for XML is an expression of the form* $card(Q, (Q', \{Q_1, \ldots, Q_k\})) = (\min, \max)$ *where* $Q, Q', Q_1, \ldots, Q_k$ *are* $PL^{\{\cdot, \_, \_*\}}$ *expressions such that* $Q.Q', Q.Q'.Q_1, \ldots, Q.Q'.Q_k$ *are valid, where* k *is a non-negative integer, and where* $\min \in \mathbb{N}$ *and* $\max \in \bar{\mathbb{N}}$ *with* $\min \leq \max$. *Herein,* Q *is called the* context path, Q' *is called the* selector path, $Q_1, \ldots, Q_k$ *are called the* field paths, $\min$ *is called the* lower bound, *and* $\max$ *the* upper bound *of* φ. *If* $Q = \epsilon$, *we call* φ absolute; *otherwise* φ *is called* relative. □

For a cardinality constraint φ, let Q_φ denote its context path, Q'_φ its selector path, $Q_1^\varphi, \ldots, Q_{k_\varphi}^\varphi$ its field paths, $\min_\varphi$ its lower and $\max_\varphi$ its upper bound. Let $\sharp S$ denote the cardinality of a finite set S, i.e., the number of its elements.

Definition 2. *Let* $\varphi = card(Q, (Q', \{Q_1, \ldots, Q_k\})) = (\min, \max)$ *be a cardinality constraint. An XML tree* T *satisfies* φ, *denoted by* $T \models \varphi$, *if and only if for all* $q \in [\![Q]\!]$, *for all* $q'_0 \in q[\![Q']\!]$ *such that for all* $x_1, \ldots, x_k$ *with* $x_i \in q'_0[\![Q_i]\!]$ *for* $i = 1, \ldots, k$, *it is true that*

$$\min \leq \sharp\{q' \in q[\![Q']\!] \mid \exists y_1, \ldots, y_k. \forall i = 1, \ldots, k.\, y_i \in q'[\![Q_i]\!] \wedge x_i =_v y_i\} \leq \max$$

holds. □

Note that $card(Q, (Q', \{Q_1, \ldots, Q_k\})) = (\min, \max)$ enforces the cardinalities imposed by min and max only on those selector nodes $q'_0 \in q[\![Q']\!]$ in T for which for all $i = 1, \ldots, k$ field nodes $x_i \in q'_0[\![Q_i]\!]$ exist in T. Hence, with no such selector node q'_0, T automatically satisfies the constraint.

Examples. Let T be the XML tree in Figure 1. We formalize the constraints from the introduction. The constraint $card(\_^*.\text{Canada}, (\_\_, \{\_\text{S}\})) = (0, 2)$ says that every company that is listed in a Canadian stock market is listed in at most two of the stock markets that operate in the country. This constraint is satisfied by T. Instead of making the constraint relative to the subtree rooted at *Canada*, we can make it absolute: $card(\varepsilon, (\_\_\_, \{\_\text{S}\})) = (0, 2)$. This constraint is violated by T since the company *Barrick Gold* has its shares listed in three stock markets. The following constraint states that each company lists its shares in at least two and at most four stock markets: $card(\varepsilon, (\_\_\_\_, \{\_\text{S}\})) = (2, 4)$. This constraint is also absolute and violated by T since the company *Air Canada* is only listed in the Toronto Stock Exchange. The constraint $card(\_, (\_, \emptyset)) = (2, \infty)$ illustrates the case in which the set of field paths is empty. It states that each country has at least two stock markets or none at all. Again, this constraint is not satisfied by T since *Chile* has only one stock market.

Subsumption of Keys. XML keys as studied in [6,8,11] are covered by cardinality constraints. In fact, a cardinality constraint φ is an XML key precisely when

$\min_\varphi = \max_\varphi = 1$. An example of an XML key is $card(\_..\_, (\_, \{\_.S\})) = (1,1)$ stating that a company cannot be listed more than once in the same stock market. The key $card(\_^*.\text{TSX}, (\_^*.\text{share}, \{\text{code}\})) = (1,1)$ states that in the Toronto Stock Exchange a share is identified by its code; and $(card(\varepsilon, (\_..\_..\_, \{\_.S\})) = (1,1)$ states that a share is identified by the text values of its code and price. Note that the XML keys of [12] are not covered by cardinality constraints.

Implication Problems. In order to take advantage of XML applications effectively it becomes necessary to reason about constraints efficiently. Central to this task is the implication problem. Let $\Sigma \cup \{\varphi\}$ be a finite set of constraints in a class $\mathcal{C}$. We say that Σ *(finitely) implies* φ, denoted by $\Sigma \models_{(f)} \varphi$, if and only if every (finite) XML tree T that satisfies all $\sigma \in \Sigma$ also satisfies φ. The *(finite) implication problem* for the class $\mathcal{C}$ is to decide, given any finite set of constraints $\Sigma \cup \{\varphi\}$ in $\mathcal{C}$, whether $\Sigma \models_{(f)} \varphi$. If Σ is a finite set of constraints in $\mathcal{C}$ let $\Sigma^*_{(f)}$ denote its *(finite) semantic closure*, i.e., the set of all constraints (finitely) implied by Σ. That is, $\Sigma^*_{(f)} = \{\varphi \in \mathcal{C} \mid \Sigma \models_{(f)} \varphi\}$.

Intractability Results. Unfortunately, the price for the general notion of cardinality constraints results in the intractability of the finite implication problem. As the following result shows this is already true for restricted classes [13].

Theorem 1. *The finite implication problem for the following three classes*
$\mathcal{C}_1 = \{card(\varepsilon, (P', \{P_1, \ldots, P_k\})) = (\text{min,max}) \mid P', P_1, \ldots, P_k \in PL^{\{\cdot\}}, k \geq 1, \max \leq 5\}$,
$\mathcal{C}_2 = \{card(\varepsilon, (P', \{P_1, \ldots, P_k\})) = (1,\text{max}) \mid P', P_1, \ldots, P_k \in PL^{\{\cdot\}}, k \geq 0, \max \leq 6\}$,
$\mathcal{C}_3 = \{card(\varepsilon, (Q', \{Q_1, \ldots, Q_k\})) = (1,\text{max}) \mid Q', Q_1, \ldots, Q_k \in PL^{\{\cdot..^*\}}, k \geq 1, \max \leq 4\}$
is coNP-hard.   □

Thus, there are at least three different sources of computational intractability: i) the specification of both lower and upper bounds, ii) an empty set of field paths, and iii) allowing arbitrary $PL^{\{\cdot..^*\}}$ expressions in both target- and key paths.

Max-Constraints. The intractability results direct our attention to the following subclass of cardinality constraints.

Definition 3. *The class* $\mathfrak{M}$ *of* max-constraints *for XML consists of cardinality constraints of the form* $card(Q, (Q', \{P_1, \ldots, P_k\})) = (1, \max)$, *where* Q, Q' *are* $PL^{\{\cdot..^*\}}$ *expressions,* $P_1, \ldots, P_k$ *are* $PL^{\{\cdot..\}}$ *expressions and* k *is a positive integer. We use* $card(Q, (Q', \{P_1, \ldots, P_k\})) \leq \max$ *to denote these constraints.*   □

The class $\mathfrak{M}$ is still very expressive. In particular, it subsumes the class of XML keys [8] for the special case where $\max_\varphi = 1$. We would like to emphasize the significance of including the single label wildcard _ into the path language. In fact, this feature adds expressiveness to the language that has important applications in data integration. We will illustrate this point by the example from the introduction. Let us consider, for instance, the constraints $\varphi_1 = card(\_^*.\text{Canada}, (\_..\_, \{\_.S\})) \leq 2$ and $\varphi_2 = card(\varepsilon, (\_..\_..\_, \{\_.S\})) \leq 4$. That is, every company is listed in at most two of the stock markets that operate in Canada, and every company lists its shares in at most four stock markets. Clearly, these constraints cannot be expressed without the single label wildcard when we consider trees with the structure of T in Figure 1. We could represent the same information in a tree T' different from T. For example, replacing the element nodes *Canada* and *Chile* by element nodes *country* with attribute children *name* where $val(name) = Canada$ and $= Chile$, respectively; replacing the element nodes *TSX*, *MX* and *SSE* by element nodes *market* with attribute children *date* and *name* where $val(name) = TSX$, $= MX$, and $= SSE$, respectively; and replacing all non-English labels of the remaining element nodes by their corresponding English translation, i.e., replacing *empresa* by *company*, *papel* by *share* and so on. Over trees with the structure of T', the constraint $card(\varepsilon, (\text{country.market.company}, \{name.S\})) \leq 4$ (without single label wildcards) is equivalent to φ_2. However, φ_1 is not meaningful in T' and there is no cardinality constraint φ_1' such that for every tree T_i with the structure of T and every corresponding equivalent tree T_i' with the structure of T', $T_i \models \varphi_1$ iff $T_i' \models \varphi_1'$. We can replace the *country*-nodes in T' with the labels they have in T, but then no constraint without a single label wildcard is equivalent to φ_2.

Towards a Precious Class. In conclusion, the class $\mathfrak{M}$ of max-constraints provides XML engineers with an enhanced ability to capture significant properties of XML data. For the remainder of the article we will address the challenging task to show that $\mathfrak{M}$ forms a precious class of cardinality constraints. That is, despite its expressiveness the class $\mathfrak{M}$ can be reasoned about efficiently.

Remaining Outline. To address this challenge, we will first characterize the implication problem associated with $\mathfrak{M}$ by a finite axiomatization. We can speak of *the* implication problem as the finite and unrestricted implication problems coincide for the class $\mathfrak{M}$. This is different for the general class of cardinality constraints. Our axioms provide complete insight into the interaction of max-constraints. This insight allows us to characterize the implication problem by constructive graph properties. This characterization enables us to establish a compact, low-degree polynomial-time algorithm for deciding implication.

4   Axiomatic and Graph-Theoretical Characterization

We devote this section to describe the semantic notion of implication for max-constraints in completely syntactic terms. For this purpose we utilize the syntactic notion of derivability. Indeed, derivability with respect to a set $\mathfrak{R}$ of inference rules, denoted by the binary relation $\vdash_{\mathfrak{R}}$ between a set of max-constraints and a single max-constraint, can be defined analogously to the notion in the relational data model [1, pp. 164-168]. Our aim is to find a set $\mathfrak{S}$ of inference rules which is *sound* and *complete* for the implication of max-constraints. That is, a set $\mathfrak{S}$ of inference rules is sound (complete) for the implication of max-constraints, if for all finite sets Σ of max-constraints we have $\Sigma_{\mathfrak{S}}^+ \subseteq \Sigma^*$ ($\Sigma^* \subseteq \Sigma_{\mathfrak{S}}^+$) where $\Sigma_{\mathfrak{S}}^+ = \{\varphi \mid \Sigma \vdash_{\mathfrak{S}} \varphi\}$ denotes the *syntactic closure* of Σ under derivations by $\mathfrak{S}$.

Sound Rules. Table 1 shows the set $\mathfrak{R}$ of inference rules for the implication of max-constraints. We omit the lengthy, but not very difficult proofs.

Completeness. We will now demonstrate that $\mathfrak{R}$ is also complete for the implication of max-constraints. Completeness means we need to show that for an

Table 1. An axiomatisation for max-constraints

$$\frac{}{card(Q,(Q',S)) \leq \infty}$$
(infinity)

$$\frac{}{card(Q,(\epsilon,S)) \leq 1}$$
(epsilon)

$$\frac{card(Q,(Q',S)) \leq \max}{card(Q,(Q',S)) \leq \max +1}$$
(weakening)

$$\frac{card(Q,(Q',S)) \leq \max}{card(Q,(Q',S \cup \{P\})) \leq \max}$$
(superkey)

$$\frac{card(Q,(Q'.P,\{P'\})) \leq \max}{card(Q,(Q',\{P.P'\})) \leq \max}$$
(subnodes)

$$\frac{card(Q,(Q'.Q'',S)) \leq \max}{card(Q.Q',(Q'',S)) \leq \max}$$
(target-to-context)

$$\frac{card(Q,(Q',S)) \leq \max}{card(Q'',(Q',S)) \leq \max} \, Q'' \subseteq Q$$
(context-path-containment)

$$\frac{card(Q,(Q',S)) \leq \max}{card(Q,(Q'',S)) \leq \max} \, Q'' \subseteq Q'$$
(target-path-containment)

$$\frac{card(Q,(Q',S \cup \{P\})) \leq \max}{card(Q,(Q',S \cup \{P'\})) \leq \max} \, P' \subseteq P$$
(key-path-containment)

$$\frac{card(Q,(Q',S \cup \{\epsilon,P\})) \leq \max}{card(Q,(Q',S \cup \{\epsilon,P.P'\})) \leq \max}$$
(prefix-epsilon)

$$\frac{card(Q,(Q'.P,\{\epsilon,P'\})) \leq \max}{card(Q,(Q',\{\epsilon,P.P'\})) \leq \max}$$
(subnodes-epsilon)

$$\frac{card(Q,(Q',\{P.P_1,\ldots,P.P_k\})) \leq \max, \quad card(Q.Q',(P,\{P_1,\ldots,P_k\})) \leq \max'}{card(Q,(Q'.P,\{P_1,\ldots,P_k\})) \leq \max \cdot \max'}$$
(multiplication)

arbitrary finite set $\Sigma \cup \{\varphi\}$ of max-constraints with $\varphi \notin \Sigma_{\mathfrak{R}}^{+}$ there is some XML tree T that satisfies all members of Σ but violates φ. That is, T is a counter-example tree for the implication of φ by Σ. The general proof strategy is as follows. For T to be a counter-example we i) require a context node q_φ with more than $\max_\varphi$ selector nodes q'_φ that all have value-equal field nodes $p_1^\varphi, \ldots, p_{k_\varphi}^\varphi$, and ii) must for each context node q_σ not have more than $\max_\sigma$ selector nodes q'_σ that all have value-equal field nodes $p_1^\sigma, \ldots, p_{k_\sigma}^\sigma$, for each member σ of Σ. Basically, such a counter-example tree exists if and only if these two conditions can be satisfied simultaneously. In a first step, we represent φ as a finite node-labeled tree $T_{\Sigma,\varphi}$, which we call the *mini-tree*. Then, we reverse the edges of the mini-tree and add to the resulting tree downward edges for certain members of Σ. Finally, each upward edge receives a label of 1 and each downward edge resulting from $\sigma \in \Sigma$ a label of $\max_\sigma$. This final digraph $G_{\Sigma,\varphi}$ is called the *cardinality graph*. A downward edge resulting from σ tells us that under each source node there can be at most $\max_\sigma$ target nodes. Now, if we can reach the selector node of φ from its context node along a dipath of weight (the product of its labels) at most $\max_\varphi$, then there is no counter-example tree T. In other words, if we satisfy condition ii) above, then we cannot satisfy condition i). Otherwise, we can construct a counter-example tree T.

Mini-Trees and Cardinality Graphs. Let $\Sigma \cup \{\varphi\}$ be a finite set of max-constraints. Let $\mathcal{L}_{\Sigma,\varphi}$ denote the set of all labels $\ell \in \mathcal{L}$ that occur in path expressions of members in $\Sigma \cup \{\varphi\}$, and fix a label $\ell_0 \in \mathbf{E} - \mathcal{L}_{\Sigma,\varphi}$. Let O_φ and O'_φ be the $PL^{\{\cdot\}}$ expressions obtained from the $PL^{\{\cdot,\_,*\}}$ expressions Q_φ and Q'_φ, respectively, by replacing each single-label wildcard "$\_$" by ℓ_0 and each variable length wildcard "$\_^*$" by a sequence of $l + 1$ labels ℓ_0, where l is the maximum number of consecutive single label wildcards that occurs in any constraint in Σ. In particular, if there are no occurrences of a single label wildcard, then it is sufficient to replace each variable length wildcard "$\_^*$" by ℓ_0. Further, for each $i = 1, \ldots, k_\varphi$, let O_i^φ be the $PL^{\{\cdot\}}$ expression obtained from the $PL^{\{\cdot,\_\}}$ expression P_i^φ by replacing each single label wildcard "$\_$" by ℓ_0.

Let p be an O_φ-path from a node r_φ to a node q_φ, let p' be an O'_φ-path from a node r'_φ to a node q'_φ and, for $i = 1, \ldots, k_\varphi$, let p_i be a O_i^φ-path from a node r_i^φ to a node x_i^φ, such that the paths $p, p', p_1, \ldots, p_{k_\varphi}$ are mutually node-disjoint. From the paths $p, p', p_1, \ldots, p_{k_\varphi}$ we obtain the *mini-tree* $T_{\Sigma,\varphi}$ by identifying the node r'_φ with q_φ, and by identifying each of the nodes r_i^φ with q'_φ.

The *marking* of the mini-tree $T_{\Sigma,\varphi}$ is a subset $\mathcal{M}$ of the node set of $T_{\Sigma,\varphi}$: if for all $i = 1, \ldots, k_\varphi$ we have $P_i^\varphi \neq \varepsilon$, then $\mathcal{M}$ consists of the leaves of $T_{\Sigma,\varphi}$, and otherwise $\mathcal{M}$ consists of all descendant nodes of q'_φ in $T_{\Sigma,\varphi}$.

We use mini-trees to calculate the impact of max-constraints in Σ on a possible counter-example tree for the implication of φ by Σ. To distinguish max-constraints that have an impact from those that do not, we introduce the notion of *applicability*. Intuitively, when a max-constraint is not applicable, then we do not need to satisfy its upper bound in a counter-example tree as it does not require all its field paths. Let $T_{\Sigma,\varphi}$ be the mini-tree of the max-constraint φ with respect to Σ, and let $\mathcal{M}$ be its marking. A max-constraint σ is said to be *applicable* to φ if there are nodes $w_\sigma \in [\![Q_\sigma]\!]$ and $w'_\sigma \in w_\sigma[\![Q'_\sigma]\!]$ in $T_{\Sigma,\varphi}$ such that $w'_\sigma[\![P_i^\sigma]\!] \cap \mathcal{M} \neq \emptyset$ for all $i = 1, \ldots, k_\sigma$. We say that w_σ and w'_σ *witness* the applicability of σ to φ.

Example 1. Let us consider an XML database for projects of a company. A year is divided into quarters and each quarter contains a sequence of projects. Each project has a list of employees labeled by their role in the project (e.g. manager or consultant). Employees are identified by their employee id. In this context, the max-constraint $\varphi = card(\_^*.\text{year}, (\text{quarter.project}, \{\_.\text{eid.S}\})) \leq 5$ indicates that in a given year an employee cannot be involved in more than 5 projects. Now, suppose that we have a set of max-constraints $\Sigma = \{\sigma_1, \sigma_2, \sigma_3\}$, where

$$\sigma_1 = card(\_^*.\text{year}, (\text{quarter}, \{\text{project.}\_.\text{eid.S}\})) \leq 3, \text{ and}$$

$$\sigma_2 = card(\_^*.\text{year.quarter}, (\text{project}, \{\_.\text{eid.S}\})) \leq 2, \text{ and}$$

$$\sigma_3 = card(\_^*.\text{project}, (\_, \{\text{eid.S}\})) \leq 1.$$

The first constraint σ_1 says that the same employee can be involved in projects in up to three quarters of each year. The constraint σ_2 says that the same employee can work on at most two different projects per quarter, and σ_3 says that no employee can take on more than one role in each project. The left picture

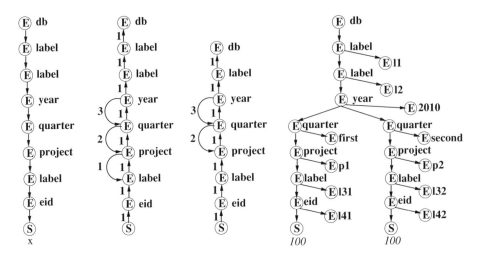

Fig. 2. A mini-tree, two cardinality graphs and a counter-example tree

of Figure 2 shows the mini-tree of φ and its marking (note that leaves are marked by ×). All max-constraints σ_1, σ_2 and σ_3 are applicable to φ. On the other hand, $\sigma_4 = card(\_.year.\_, (project.\_, \{eid.S\})) \leq 2$ is not applicable to φ.   □

We define the *cardinality graph* $G_{\Sigma,\varphi}$ of φ and Σ as the node-labeled digraph obtained from $T_{\Sigma,\varphi}$ as follows: the nodes and node-labels of $G_{\Sigma,\varphi}$ are exactly the nodes and node-labels of $T_{\Sigma,\varphi}$, respectively. The edges of $G_{\Sigma,\varphi}$ consist of the reversed edges from $T_{\Sigma,\varphi}$. Furthermore, for each max-constraint $\sigma \in \Sigma$ that is applicable to φ and for each pair of nodes $w_\sigma \in [\![Q_\sigma]\!]$ and $w'_\sigma \in w_\sigma[\![Q'_\sigma]\!]$ that witness the applicability of σ to φ we add a directed edge (w_σ, w'_σ) to $G_{\Sigma,\varphi}$. We refer to these additional edges as *witness edges* while the reversed edges from $T_{\Sigma,\varphi}$ are referred to as *upward edges* of $G_{\Sigma,\varphi}$. This is the case since for every witness w_σ and w'_σ the node w'_σ is a descendant of the node w_σ in $T_{\Sigma,\varphi}$, and thus the witness edge (w_σ, w'_σ) is a downward edge or loop in $G_{\Sigma,\varphi}$. We now introduce weights as edge-labels: every upward edge e of $G_{\Sigma,\varphi}$ has weight $\omega(e) = 1$, and every witness edge (u, v) of $G_{\Sigma,\varphi}$ has weight $\omega(u,v) = \min\{\max_\sigma \mid (u,v)$ witnesses the applicability of some $\sigma \in \Sigma$ to $\varphi\}$.

We need to use some graph terminology, cf. [14]. Consider a digraph G. A path t is a sequence $v_0, \ldots, v_m$ of nodes with an edge (v_{i-1}, v_i) for each $i = 1, \ldots, m$. We call t a path of length m from node v_0 to node v_m containing the edges (v_{i-1}, v_i), $i = 1, \ldots, m$. A simple path is just a path whose nodes are pairwise distinct. Note that for every path from u to v there is also a simple path from u to v in G containing only edges of the path. In the cardinality graph $G_{\Sigma,\varphi}$ the weight of a path t is defined as the product of the weights of its edges, i.e.,

$$\omega(t) = \prod_{i=1}^{n} \omega(v_{i-1}, v_i),$$ or $\omega(t) = 1$ if t has no edges. The *distance* $d(v,w)$ from a node v to a node w is the minimum over the weights of all paths from v to w, or ∞ if no such path exists.

Example 2. Let Σ and φ be as in Example 1. The cardinality graph of Σ and φ is illustrated in the second picture from the left in Figure 2. Let v denote the unique *year*-node, w the unique *project*-node, and u the unique *eid*-node in the second picture from the left in Figure 2. Then $d(v, w) = 6$ and $d(v, u) = \infty$.   □

The following result is crucial. If the distance $d(q_\varphi, q'_\varphi)$ from q_φ to q'_φ in $G_{\Sigma,\varphi}$ is at most $\max_\varphi$, then $\varphi \in \Sigma_\mathfrak{R}^+$. In other words, if φ is not derivable from Σ, then every path from q_φ to q'_φ in $G_{\Sigma,\varphi}$ has distance at least $\max_\varphi + 1$.

Lemma 1. *Let $\Sigma \cup \{\varphi\}$, where $\varphi = card(Q_\varphi, (Q'_\varphi, \{P_1^\varphi, \ldots, P_{k_\varphi}^\varphi\})) \leq \max_\varphi$, be a finite set of max-constraints. If $d(q_\varphi, q'_\varphi) \leq \max_\varphi$ in the cardinality graph $G_{\Sigma,\varphi}$, then $card(Q_\varphi, (Q'_\varphi, \{P_1^\varphi, \ldots, P_{k_\varphi}^\varphi\})) \leq \max_\varphi \in \Sigma_\mathfrak{R}^+$.*   □

The strategy to prove this lemma is to encode an inference by $\mathfrak{R}$ by witness edges of the cardinality graph. We omit the technical details of this proof and show an example instead.

Example 3. Let $\varphi' = card(\_^*.year, (quarter.project, \{\_.eid.S\})) \leq 6$ and Σ be as in Example 1. The corresponding mini-tree and cardinality graph are shown as first and second picture from the left in Figure 2, respectively. Since $d(q_\varphi, q'_\varphi) \leq 6$, it follows by Lemma 1 that φ' is derivable from Σ. In fact, φ' is clearly derivable by a single application of the *multiplication* rule to σ_1 and σ_2.   □

Next, we illustrate the completeness argument from which the following important result follows.

Theorem 2. *The inference rules in Table 1 are complete for the implication of max-constraints.*   □

Let $\Sigma \cup \{\varphi\}$ be a finite set of max-constraints such that $\varphi \notin \Sigma_\mathfrak{R}^+$. We construct a finite XML tree T which satisfies all max-constraints in Σ but does not satisfy φ. Since $\varphi \notin \Sigma_\mathfrak{R}^+$ every existing path from q_φ to q'_φ in $G_{\Sigma,\varphi}$ has weight at least $\max_\varphi + 1$. For each node n in $G_{\Sigma,\varphi}$ let $\omega'(n) = \omega(D)$ where D denotes the shortest path from q_φ to n in $G_{\Sigma,\varphi}$, or $\omega'(n) = \max_\varphi + 1$ if there is no such path. In particular, we have $\omega'(q_\varphi) = 1$ and $\omega'(q'_\varphi) > \max_\varphi$. Let T_0 be a copy of the path from the root node r to q_φ in $T_{\Sigma,\varphi}$. We extend T_0 as follows: for each node n on the path from q_φ to q'_φ in $T_{\Sigma,\varphi}$ we introduce $\omega'(n)$ copies $n_1, \ldots, n_{\omega'(n)}$ into T_0. Suppose T_0 has been constructed down to the level of $u_1, \ldots, u_{\omega'(u)}$ corresponding to node u in $T_{\Sigma,\varphi}$, and let v be the unique successor of u in $T_{\Sigma,\varphi}$. Then $\omega'(u) \leq \omega'(v)$ due to the upward edges in $G_{\Sigma,\varphi}$. For all $i = 1, \ldots, \omega'(u)$ and all $j = 1, \ldots, \omega'(v)$ we introduce a new edge (u_i, v_j) in T if and only if j is congruent to i modulo $\omega'(u)$. Eventually, T_0 has $\omega'(q'_\varphi) > \max_\varphi$ leaves.

For $i = 1, \ldots, \omega'(q'_\varphi)$ let T_i be a node-disjoint copy of the subtree of $T_{\Sigma,\varphi}$ rooted at q'_φ. We want that for any two distinct copies T_i and T_j a node of T_i and a node of T_j become value equal precisely when they are copies of the same marked node in $T_{\Sigma,\varphi}$. For attribute and text nodes this is achieved by choosing string values accordingly, while for element nodes we can adjoin a new child node with a label from $\mathcal{L} - (\mathcal{L}_{\Sigma,\varphi} \cup \{\ell_0\})$ to achieve this. The counter-example tree

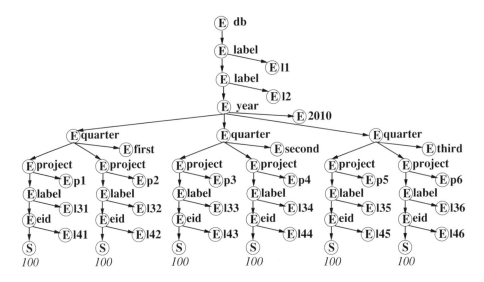

Fig. 3. Counter-example tree for the implication of φ by Σ from Example 4

T is obtained from $T_0, T_1, \ldots, T_{\omega'(q'_\varphi)}$ by identifying the leaf node q'_i of T_0 with the root node of T_i for all $i = 1, \ldots, \omega'(q'_\varphi)$. We conclude that T violates φ since $\omega'(q') > \max_\varphi$, and our construction guarantees that T satisfies Σ.

Example 4. Let Σ and φ be as in Example 1. The counter-example tree T for the implication of φ by Σ is illustrated in Figure 3. In particular, φ is violated since the unique *year*-node has six distinct *project*-descendants whose corresponding *eid*-grandchildren nodes have the same text content.   □

5   Algorithmic Characterization

We will now design a low-degree polynomial time algorithm for deciding the implication problem of max-constraints. It is based on the following characterization of the implication problem in terms of the shortest path problem between two suitable nodes of the cardinality graph.

Theorem 3. *Let* $\Sigma \cup \{\varphi\}$ *be a finite set of max-constraints. We have that* $\Sigma \models \varphi$ *if and only if* $d(q_\varphi, q'_\varphi) \leq \max_\varphi$ *in the cardinality graph* $G_{\Sigma,\varphi}$.   □

Theorem 3 suggests to decide implication by constructing the cardinality graph and applying well-known shortest paths techniques. This establishes a surprisingly compact method.

Algorithm 4 (Max-constraint implication)

    Input: a finite set $\Sigma \cup \{\varphi\}$ of max-constraints in $\mathfrak{M}$
    Output: yes, if $\Sigma \models \varphi$; no, otherwise

Method:
(1) Construct $G_{\Sigma,\varphi}$ for Σ and φ;
(2) Find the shortest path P from q_φ to q'_φ in $G_{\Sigma,\varphi}$;
(3) **if** $\omega(P) \leq \max_\varphi$ **then return**(yes); **else return**(no).

The simplicity of Algorithm 4 enables us to conclude that the implication of max-constraints can be decided in low-degree polynomial time in the worst case.

Theorem 5. *If $\Sigma \cup \{\varphi\}$ is a finite set of max-constraints, then the implication problem $\Sigma \models \varphi$ can be decided in time $\mathcal{O}(|\varphi| \times l \times (\|\Sigma\| + |\varphi| \times l))$, where $|\varphi|$ is the sum of the lengths of all path expressions in φ, $\|\Sigma\|$ is the sum of all sizes $|\sigma|$ for $\sigma \in \Sigma$, and l is the maximum number of consecutive single label wildcards that occur in Σ.* □

It is important to note the blow-up in the size of the counter-example with respect to φ. This is due to the occurrence of consecutive single label wildcards. If the number l is fixed in advance, then Algorithm 4 establishes a worst case time complexity that is quadratic in the input. In particular, if the input consists of XML keys as studied in [11], then the worst-case time complexity of Algorithm 4 is that of the algorithm dedicated to XML keys only [11].

Remark 1. If we simply replace each variable length wildcard "_*" by the single label ℓ_0 and not by a sequence of $l + 1$ labels ℓ_0, then Theorem 3 does not hold. To see this fact, consider $\varphi = card(\_^*.year, (quarter.project, \{\_.eid.S\})) \leq 1$ and $\Sigma = \{\sigma_1, \sigma_2\}$, where $\sigma_1 = card(\_.year, (quarter, \{project.\_.eid.S\})) \leq 3$, and $\sigma_2 = card(\_^*.year.quarter, (project, \{\_.eid.S\})) \leq 2$. A simple replacement of "_*" by ℓ_0 results in the cardinality graph shown on the third picture in Figure 2. But then by Lemma 1, Σ would imply φ, which is clearly incorrect as shown by the counter-example tree on the fourth picture in Figure 2. □

6   Conclusion

Cardinality constraints are naturally exhibited by XML data since they represent restrictions that occur in everyday life. They cover XML keys where the upper bound is fixed to 1, and also generalized participation constraints from conceptual databases. XML applications such as consistency management, data integration, query optimization, view maintenance and cardinality estimation can therefore benefit from the specification of cardinality constraints. We have proposed the class of max-constraints that is sufficiently flexible to advance XML data processing. The flexibility results from the right balance between expressiveness and efficiency of maintenance. While slight extensions result in the intractability of the associated implication problem we have shown that our class is finitely axiomatizable, robust and decidable in low-degree polynomial time. Thus, our class forms a precious class of cardinality constraints that can be utilized effectively by data engineers. Indeed, the complexity of its associated implication problem indicates that it can be maintained efficiently by database systems for XML applications.

Acknowledgement. This research is supported by the Marsden fund council from Government funding, administered by the Royal Society of New Zealand. The second author is supported by a research grant of the Alfried Krupp von Bohlen and Halbach foundation, administered by the German Scholars organization.

References

1. Abiteboul, S., Hull, R., Vianu, V.: Foundations of Databases. Addison-Wesley, Reading (1995)
2. Apparao, V., et al.: Document Object Model (DOM) Level 1 Specification. W3C Recommendation (October 1998),
   http://www.w3.org/TR/REC-DOM-Level-1-19981001/
3. Arenas, M., Fan, W., Libkin, L.: What's hard about XML schema constraints? In: Hameurlain, A., Cicchetti, R., Traunmüller, R. (eds.) DEXA 2002. LNCS, vol. 2453, pp. 269–278. Springer, Heidelberg (2002)
4. Arenas, M., Fan, W., Libkin, L.: On the complexity of verifying consistency of XML specifications. SIAM J. Comput. 38(3), 841–880 (2008)
5. Bray, T., Paoli, J., Sperberg-McQueen, C.M., Maler, E., Yergeau, F.: Extensible Markup Language (XML) 1.0 W3C Recommendation 3 edn. (February 2004),
   http://www.w3.org/TR/2004/REC-xml-20040204/
6. Buneman, P., Davidson, S., Fan, W., Hara, C., Tan, W.: Keys for XML. Computer Networks 39(5), 473–487 (2002)
7. Clark, J., DeRose, S.: XML path language (XPath) version 1.0, W3C Recommendation (November1999), http://www.w3.org/TR/REC-xpath-19991116/
8. Ferrarotti, F., Hartmann, S., Link, S., Wang, J.: Promoting the semantic capability of XML keys. In: Lee, M.L., Yu, J.X., Bellahsène, Z., Unland, R. (eds.) XSym 2010. LNCS, vol. 6309, pp. 144–153. Springer, Heidelberg (2010)
9. Fuxman, A., Miller, R.: Towards inconsistency management in data integration systems. In: IIWeb, pp. 143–148 (2003)
10. Hartmann, S.: On the implication problem for cardinality constraints and functional dependencies. Ann. Math. Art. Intell. 33, 253–307 (2001)
11. Hartmann, S., Link, S.: Efficient reasoning about a robust XML key fragment. ACM Trans. Database Syst. 34(2), Article 10 (2009)
12. Hartmann, S., Link, S.: Expressive, yet tractable XML keys. In: EDBT. ACM Conference Proceedings Series, vol. 360, pp. 357–367. ACM, New York (2009)
13. Hartmann, S., Link, S.: Numerical constraints on XML data. Inf. Comput. 208(5), 521–544 (2010)
14. Jungnickel, D.: Graphs, Networks and Algorithms. Springer, Heidelberg (1999)
15. Liddle, S., Embley, D., Woodfield, S.: Cardinality constraints in semantic data models. Data Knowl. Eng. 11(3), 235–270 (1993)
16. Miklau, G., Suciu, D.: Containment and equivalence for a fragment of XPath. J. ACM 51(1), 2–45 (2004)
17. Thalheim, B.: Fundamentals of cardinality constraints. In: Pernul, G., Tjoa, A.M. (eds.) ER 1992. LNCS, vol. 645, pp. 7–23. Springer, Heidelberg (1992)
18. Thalheim, B.: Foundations of Entity-Relationship Modeling. Springer, Heidelberg (2000)
19. Thompson, H., Beech, D., Maloney, M., Mendelsohn, N.: XML Schema part 1: Structures W3C Recommendation 2 edn.(October 2004),
    http://www.w3.org/TR/REC-xmlschema-1-20041028/

Formal Semantics and Ontological Analysis for Understanding Subsetting, Specialization and Redefinition of Associations in UML

Dolors Costal[1], Cristina Gómez[1], and Giancarlo Guizzardi[2]

[1] Dept. d'Enginyeria de Serveis i Sistemes d'Informació, Universitat Politècnica de Catalunya (UPC), Barcelona (Catalonia)
{dolors,cristina}@essi.upc.edu
[2] Ontology and Conceptual Modeling Research Group (NEMO), Federal University of Espírito Santo (UFES), Vitória-ES, Brazil
gguizzardi@inf.ufes.br

Abstract. The definition of the exact meaning of conceptual modeling constructs is considered a relevant issue since it contributes to their effective and appropriate use by conceptual modelers. This paper studies three related constructs that enhance the expressiveness of the UML language about associations and which still lack a complete and comprehensive study, namely, association *subsetting*, *specialization* and *redefinition*. It formalizes their semantics, analyses them from an ontological perspective and compares them. The semantic formalization is based on mapping the studied constructs to a basic UML layer which have a previous formal definition in the literature. Furthermore, the ontological analysis developed here is based on a formal theory of relations which is part of the Unified Foundational Ontology (UFO).

Keywords: conceptual modelling, ontological analysis, UML associations.

1 Introduction

During the last decade, UML has been widely adopted both in industry and academia, thus contributing to the improvement of information systems engineering practices. However, one drawback of UML that has been frequently pointed out is the lack of clear meaning for some of its constructs. While the UML metamodel [1] gives information about its abstract syntax, its meaning is described in natural language. Thus, many concepts still lack definitions precise enough to be interpreted unambiguously. The version 2.0 of UML has made a significant step towards precise definitions of concepts. But its attempt to increase the expressiveness of the language has introduced new ambiguities and there are still issues that remain open.

Associations (also termed *relationship types* or simply *relations*) are central structural elements in conceptual modelling, in general, and in UML, in particular. UML 2 has improved the expressiveness of the language with respect to associations in several manners. A significant one has been the introduction of the association *redefinition* concept. This concept allows enhancing the definition of an association by means of another association that defines it more specifically in a particular

M. Jeusfeld, L. Delcambre, and T.W. Ling (Eds.): ER 2011, LNCS 6998, pp. 189–203, 2011.
© Springer-Verlag Berlin Heidelberg 2011

context. Association subsetting and association specialization have been included in UML since its earliest versions and share some relevant features with association redefinition. These similarities among the three constructs make it frequently difficult, especially to novice users, to: decide which one of these concepts is the best suited to model a particular situation; systematically justify their modelling choices. This situation is worsened by the fact that, despite its importance, the association construct is often regarded as one of the most problematical in conceptual modelling [2].

It seems also to be generally accepted that redefinition, specialization and subsetting of associations still need to be studied in more detail [3,4]. For instance, [3] notices that *"the distinction between subsetting and specializing an association is not clearly described in the UML2 specification"* and [4] mentions that *"it is not completely clear what else subtyping for associations should really mean"*.

The contributions of this paper are two-fold. Firstly, we provide a precise and complete description of the meaning of subsetting, specialization and redefinition of binary associations in UML, making explicit the similarities and differences that exist among these constructs. The semantic formalization is based on mapping them to a basic UML layer which has a previous formal definition in the literature. The proposed formalization provides an interpretation of the constructs under consideration which is in accordance with the OMG document statements about them [1]. Secondly, as we will demonstrate, the formal characterization of these constructs by itself is insufficient to completely differentiate them. Thus, as a second contribution, we develop here an ontological analysis of these constructs by employing an ontologically well-founded formal theory of relations. By mapping these concepts to this ontological theory we are able to: (i) provide unambiguous real-world semantics to them; (ii) provide some methodological guidelines for helping conceptual modelers to systematically choose how elements in the universe of discourse should be modeled using these concepts; (iii) explain specific characteristics of each of these concepts which are manifested in their syntactical constraints and formal semantics.

The remainder of this paper is organized as follows. The next section gives a brief introduction to these constructs in UML. Section 3 provides the formal semantics of the three constructs. Section 4 conducts the ontological analysis. Section 5 reviews related work and finally, Section 6 presents our final considerations.

2   Background

This section briefly describes the notion and syntax of subsetting, specialization and redefinition of associations according to the UML standard document [1].

Subsetting is a construct specified for association ends. It defines that the instances related by the subsetting end are a subset of the instances related by the subsetted end, taking the same departing instance at the opposite ends. One or both ends of a binary association can be subsetted.

An association specialization is a taxonomic relationship between a more specific and a more general association. The specific association inherits the features of the general one. In contrast to subsetting, specialization is a construct specified for associations themselves and not for association ends.

The purpose of association redefinition is to define an association end more specifically in a particular context. One or both ends of an association can be redefined and redefinitions always involve two associations.

The syntax and the syntactic rules, according to UML, of the three constructs are depicted in Figure 1. Note that, in case of redefinition, class A_1 cannot be the same as class A in contrast to the other constructs.

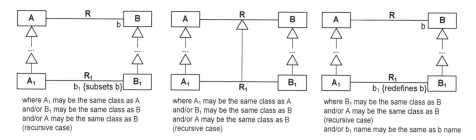

Fig. 1. a-b-c Association subsetting, specialization and redefinition syntax and syntactic rules

3 Formal Semantics

The semantics of a language defines the meaning of each construct of the language. A semantic definition consists of two steps: first, a semantic domain must be defined and then, the semantic definition of a construct is done by mapping the syntax of the construct to concepts of the semantic domain. In general, several notations or languages may be used as semantic domains. Formal languages like mathematical terms (as done in [5]), mathematical structures (as done in [6]) or, even, a subset of the UML itself (as done in [7]) may be used among others.

We use a basic UML layer as a semantic domain. It includes the following basic elements: classes, binary associations, multiplicities, class specializations and general OCL constraints [1,8]. Since its elements are generally well-understood, we think that using this layer contributes to the goal of making the studied constructs understandable for any UML user. The concrete and abstract syntaxes of these basic elements are completely developed in [1,3,8] and their semantics is defined using set theory as a basis [5,8,9]. The mapping of a construct to the UML layer is defined as a translation between a generic schema with the specified construct and another generic schema using only elements of the basic UML layer [7].

3.1 UML Association Subsetting Semantics

The translation of a subsetting into our basic UML layer consists in replacing it by an inclusion constraint between the subsetting and the subsetted ends expressed in OCL.

Definition 1. *Subsetting translation definition*: Consider the schema of Figure 1.a. The translated schema is obtained from the original one by: 1) eliminating from it the adornment which denotes that the end b_1 subsets the end b, and, 2) attaching to it the OCL expression: **context** A_1 **inv:** self.b ->includesAll(self.b$_1$).

Since the instances of an association can be understood as bidirectional links from a conceptual modelling point of view, it is semantically identical to specify a subset between two association ends or between their respective opposite ends [10-12]. This indicates that, although subsetting is specified for association ends, it affects the whole association. The semantics of a subsetting is to establish an inclusion constraint between the subsetting association (that with the subsetting end) and the subsetted association (that with the subsetted end). This constraint implies that each instance of the subsetting association must be an instance of the subsetted one.

Consider the example of Figure 2.a. The end *es* subsets the end *s*. Part (b) gives its translation. The OCL invariant guarantees that the set of instances of *Enrols* is a subset of the set of instances of *HasPreference*.

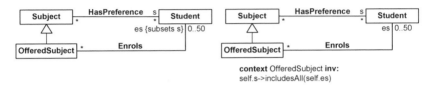

context OfferedSubject inv:
self.s->includesAll(self.es)

Fig. 2. a-b Example of an association subsetting and its translation

3.2   UML Association Specialization Semantics

The semantics of an association specialization is to establish an inclusion constraint between the specific and the general association. Thus, its semantics is identical to the semantics of subsettings.

Definition 2. *Specialization translation definition*: Consider the schema of Figure 1.b. The translated schema is obtained from the original one by: 1) eliminating from it the specialization symbol that relates R and R_1, and, 2) attaching to it the OCL expression:

```
context A1 inv: self.b ->includesAll(self.b1)
```

In Figure 3.a, *PronouncesSentence*, that relates a court and a defendant, is specialized by *Absolves*. The pronouncements of sentences in which the defendant is found not guilty by the court correspond to instances of *Absolves*. The translation (Figure 3.b) ensures that, for all absolutions, there exists the corresponding sentence pronouncement.

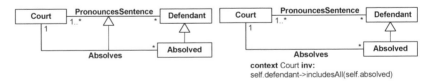

context Court inv:
self.defendant->includesAll(self.absolved)

Fig. 3. a-b Example of an association specialization and its translation

UML Association Redefintion Semantics

The semantics of an association redefinition is to establish a constraint that guarantees that the links involving instances of A_1 (see Figure 1.c) coincide in both associations.

Those links are redefined since they have to encompass not only the specification of the redefined association but also the specification of the redefining association.

Definition 3. *Redefinition translation definition*: Consider the schema of Figure 1.c. The translated schema is obtained from the original one by: 1) eliminating from it the adornment which denotes that the end b_1 redefines the end b, and, 2) attaching to it the OCL expression:

context A_1 **inv:** `self.b = self.b`$_1$ in case b name $\neq b_1$ name

context A_1 **inv:** `self.oclAsType(A).b = self.b`$_1$ in case b name $= b_1$ name

Figure 4.a shows two examples of association redefinitions. The end *participant* is redefined in the context of critical projects and the end *proj* is redefined in the context of junior employees. Their translation is depicted in Figure 4.b. The second invariant translates the *senPart* redefinition and guarantees that the instances that relate critical projects to employees via *Participates* are the same as those that relate them to senior employees through *ParticipatesCritical*.

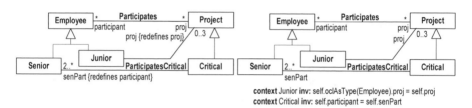

Fig. 4. a-b Examples of association redefinitions and their translations

Although the semantics of a redefinition is different from that of specializations and subsettings, an inclusion constraint is also induced. Indeed, from the translation we can see that all the instances of the redefining association belong to the redefined one. This can be easily proven from the definition 3. In Figure 4, for example, all instances of the *ParticipatesCritical* association are also instances of *Participates*.

An association redefinition has implicit significant semantic effects on the redefined association. These effects are circumscribed to the instances of the redefined association that are also instances of the redefining association. We call them affected instances of the redefinition. In Figure 4, the affected instances of the *senPart* redefinition are the instances of *Participates* that involve critical projects. In the following, we describe all kinds of constraints that may be induced on a redefined association depending on the features of the redefinition.

Type is redefined when the redefining end is connected to a descendant of the class at the redefined end. Considering the Figure 1.c syntax, this occurs when class B_1 is not the same as class B. The effect of a type redefinition is to establish an additional participation constraint on the redefined association [13]. In Figure 4, the *senPart* redefinition establishes that critical projects may only have senior employees as participants and, consequently, not junior employees. This induced effect can be proven from the translation of the association redefinition and the referential integrity constraint that is implicit in the redefining association.

Multiplicity is redefined when the redefining end has a multiplicity which is more restrictive than that of the redefined end. The effect is to establish additional minimum and/or maximum cardinality constraints that restrict the cardinality for the affected instances of the redefinition [13]. In Figure 4, the *senPart* redefinition establishes that critical projects must have at least two participants. This induced effect can be proven from the translation of the association redefinition and the cardinality constraints specified by the multiplicity at the redefining end.

On the other hand, association subsettings/specializations induce minimum cardinality constraints over the subsetted/general associations when the lower bound of a multiplicity specified for the subsetting/specific association is greater than the corresponding lower bound at the subsetted/general association. The reason is the existence of the inclusion constraint between both associations due to the subsetting/ specialization. However, it is never the case that maximum cardinality constraints or participation constraints are induced by a subsetting or a specialization. In Figure 2, although the offered subjects may have at most 50 enrolled students, they may have more than 50 students with a preference for them.

3.4 Comparing Subsetting, Specialization and Redefinition of Associations

Table 1 summarizes the syntactic and semantic relevant features that we have identified. We can observe that: 1) the three constructs have differing syntactic features, 2) the three constructs imply the existence of an inclusion constraint between the involved associations and 3) subsetting and specialization induce the same constraints on the subsetted/specialized association (i.e. minimum cardinality) while redefinition may induce participation and maximum cardinality constraints in addition.

Therefore, subsettings and specializations cannot be distinguished from a formal semantic point of view since they are semantically equivalent. Redefinitions can be semantically distinguished from the other two constructs when they induce participation and/or a maximum cardinality constraints but not when they only induce minimum cardinality constraints.

Table 1. Syntactic and semantic features for assoc. subsetting, specialization and redefinition

		Subsetting	Specialization	Redefinition
Syntactic	**Specified for**	Association end	Association	Association end
	Rules for association end classes	Descendant or same classes	Descendant or same classes	End opp. redefining end: desc. class Redefining end: desc. or same class
Sem.	**Inclusion constr.**	Yes	Yes	Yes
	Induced constr.	Min. card.	Min. card.	Participation Min. & max. card.

We must conclude that the formal semantics analysis contributes to capture relevant aspects of the meaning of each construct but it is not sufficient to completely characterize each one of them. To provide the conceptual modeller the criteria to decide which construct is the most adequate to model a particular domain situation we analyse, in the following section, the constructs from an ontological point of view.

4 An Ontological Analysis of Relations

In [14], we have presented an in depth analysis of domain relations from an ontological point of view. In particular, we have employed the Unified Foundational Ontology (UFO), a formal framework which has been constructed by considering a number of theories from formal ontology in philosophy, but also cognitive science, linguistics and philosophical logics. In a number of papers, UFO has been successfully employed to analyze and provide real-world semantics for conceptual modeling grammars and specifications. Here, we make a very brief presentation of this foundational ontology and concentrate only on the categories which are germane to the purposes of this article. For an in depth discussion on UFO, one should see [15].

A fundamental distinction in this ontology is between the categories of *Objects* and *Tropes*. *Objects* are existentially independent entities. Examples include ordinary objects of everyday experience such as an individual person, an organization, an organ. The word *Trope,* in contrast, denotes, what is sometimes named an individualized (objectified) property or property in particular. A trope is an individual that can only exist in other individuals (in the way in which, for example, electrical charge can exist only in some conductor, or that a covalent bond can only exist if those connecting atoms exist). Typical examples of tropes are a colour, a connection, an electric charge, a symptom, a covalent bond. As discussed in [15], there is solid evidence for tropes in the literature. On one hand, in the analysis of the content of perception, tropes are the immediate objects of everyday perception. On the other hand, the idea of tropes as *truthmakers* underlies a standard event-based approach to natural language semantics. Existential dependence can also be used to differentiate intrinsic and relational tropes: intrinsic tropes or *qualities* are dependent on one single individual (e.g., a symptom, a skill, a belief); relational tropes or *relators* depend on a plurality of individuals. In this paper, we focus on relators.

Another important distinction in the UFO ontology is within the categories of relations. Following the philosophical literature, it recognizes two broad categories of relations, namely, *material* and *formal* relations. *Formal relations* hold between two or more entities directly, without any further intervening individual. In principle, it includes those relations that form the mathematical superstructure of our framework. Examples include historical and existential dependence (*ed*), subtype-of, part-of, subset-of, instantiation, among many others [15]. Domain relations such as *working at*, *being enrolled at*, and *being the husband of* are of a completely different nature. These relations, exemplifying the category of *Material relations*, have material structure of their own. Whilst a formal relation such as the one between Paul and his headache x holds directly and as soon as Paul and x exist, for a material relation of *being treated in* between Paul and the medical unit MU_1 to exist, another entity must exist which *mediates* Paul and MU_1. These entities are termed *relators*.

Relators are individuals with the power of connecting entities. For example, a medical treatment connects a patient with a medical unit; an enrollment connects a student with an educational institution; a covalent bond connects two atoms. The notion of relator is supported by several works in the philosophical literature [16] and, they play an important role in answering questions of the sort: what does it mean to say that John is married to Mary? Why is it true to say that Bill works for Company X but not for Company Y? Again, relators are special types of tropes which, therefore, are existential dependent entities. The relation of *mediation* (holding between a relator *r* and the entities that *r* connects) is a sort of existential dependence relation [15].

An important notion for the characterization of relators (and, hence, for the characterization of material relations) is the notion of *foundation*. Foundation can be seen as a type of *historical dependence* [15], in the way that, for instance, an instance of *being kissed* is founded on an individual *kiss,* or an instance of *being connected to* between airports is founded on a particular flight connection. Suppose that John *is married to* Mary. In this case, we can assume that there is an individual relator m_1 of type *marriage* that mediates John and Mary. The foundation of this relator can be, for instance, a wedding event or the signing of a social contract between the involved parties. In other words, for instance, a certain event e_1 in which John and Mary participate can create an individual marriage m_1 which existentially depends on John and Mary and which mediates them. The event e_1 is the foundation of relator m_1.

The relator m_1 in this case is said to be the *truthmaker* of propositions such as "John is the husband of Mary", and "Mary is the wife of John". In other words, material relations such as *being married to, being legally bound to, being the husband of* can be said to hold for the individuals John and Mary because and only because there is an individual relator marriage m_1 mediating the two. Thus, as demonstrated in [14], material relations are purely linguistic/logical constructions which are founded on and can be completely derived from the existence of relators. In fact, in [14], we have defined a formal relation of derivation (symbolized as *der*) between a relator type (e.g., Marriage) and each material relation which is derived from it.

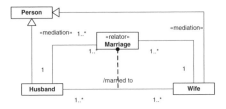

Fig. 5. Model with an explicit representation of: a Relator Type and a Material Relation derived from it.

Figure 5 above depicts a model expressed in the OntoUML language which summarizes our discussion on relators and material relations. OntoUML is a well-founded version of UML whose modelling primitives (stereotypes in this Figure) are derived from the ontological categories underlying UFO [14]. This model captures that the material relation *married to* is derived from the relator type Marriage (the derivation relation *der* is symbolized as ●‑‑‑‑ in the language). As a consequence, we have that a tuple such as <John,Mary> is an instance of this relation iff there is an instance of Marriage m_1 that mediates the elements of the tuple.

The explicit representation of the relator type in OntoUML solves a number of problems associated with the traditional representation of relations in Conceptual Modelling, including the ambiguity of cardinality constraints of material relations (and only material relations!) caused by the so-called problem of collapsing *Single-tuple* and *Multiple-tuple* cardinality constraints [17]. The reader should notice that the relator type is not a UML association class as it actually addresses an ontological problem caused by the Association Class construct termed *non-lucidity at the language level* [18]. These aspects are discussed in depth in [14]. Here we only make use of this representation to make explicit the relevant relator types and the material relations derived from them.

4.1 An Ontological Analysis of Subsetting

Let us start with the example depicted in Figure 2. The relation *Enrolls* is a stereotypical example of a material relation derived from the relator *Enrollment*. So, the truthmaker of the predicate *Enrolls(x,y)* is the existence of a particular enrollment *z* connecting *x* and *y*. What about *HasPreference*? The relevant question again is to inquiry about the truthmaker of *HasPreference(x,y)*, i.e., when is it true to say that a *student x has preference for subject y* in the conceptualization underlying this model? In order for these preferences to become public (and then recorded in an information system), we can imagine an explicit manifestation of interest of Student for a list of Subjects. Notice that, the social object which records this list of interests is indeed a relator (existentially dependent on both a student and on the list of subjects). This situation is depicted in Figure 6.a below.

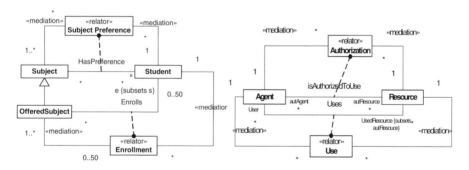

Fig. 6. a-b Explicit representations of the relator types from which the relations in Figure 2 and [12] are derived, respectively

One should notice that the two relations of Figure 6.a are derived from relator types of different kinds and are based on different foundational events (different social speech acts). In other words, there is no necessary connection between the truthmakers of these two relations. It is just a matter of accident that the extension of *Enrolls* is included in the extension of *HasPreference*, and one can easily imagine an alternative conceptualization in which this constraint is abandoned, i.e., in which students are allowed to enroll in subjects regardless of their preferences. This accidental inclusion of the extension of one relation in the extension of the other is intuitively captures in the statement in the UML specification [1, pg.39]: *"subsetting is a relationship in the domain of extensional semantics"*. In summary, we postulate that:

Postulate 1: *a subsetting relation should be defined between two material relations R_2 and R_1 (R_2 subsets R_1) iff these relations are derived from relators of disjoint kinds and there is an inclusion constraint that includes the extension of R_2 in the one of R_1.*

In Figure 6.b, we present another example of the result of an ontological analysis of subsetting extracted from [12]. Here again, our analysis is able to explain the modelling choice adopted by the author. Once more both material relations are founded on relators of disjoint kinds, and once more that it is merely accidental that (in this conceptualization) resources must be authorized before used.

4.2 An Ontological Analysis of Specialization

Now, let us examine the example of Figure 3 with two material relations: *PronouncedSentence* and *Absolves*. The former is derived from a social relator *Sentence* which records the outcome of a given event (the sentence pronunciation). However, a further analysis of this relator type reveals that this type is an *abstract* one, i.e., there is no general instance of *Sentence* which is not one of its specific kinds (e.g., Conviction, Absolution). Thus, we have that the relator type associated with the *Absolves* relation, i.e., *Absolution*, is a specialization of the *Sentence* relator type (Figure 7.a). In other words, to be absolved is a specific kind of being sentenced.

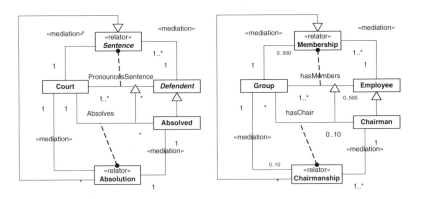

Fig. 7. a-b Explicit representations of the relator types from which the relations in Figure 3 and [12] are derived, respectively

In contrast with subsetting, specialization has an intentional relation between types: an absolution has all the properties of a general sentence (e.g., date of pronunciation) and it is founded on the very same individual event (the sentence pronunciation). This explains the intuition discussed in [12] that: (i) the specializing relation necessarily shares properties with the general one and typically includes additional properties; (ii) there is an analytical connection between these two relations. In fact, if *Sentence* is an abstract type then *Absolution* not only inherits all its properties but should also have at least of property to differentiate it from other (disjoint) kinds of sentences. Moreover, if the definition of to be absolved is to receive a sentence z such that z is an absolution, and the definition of to be sentence is to receive a sentence z (of any kind), then indeed the definition of *being sentenced* is part of the very definition of *being absolved*. Thus, one cannot be absolved without being sentenced in the same way that one cannot be a bachelor without being unmarried. Thus, we postulate that:

Postulate 2: *a specialization relation should be defined between two material relations R_2 and R_1 ($R_1 \Leftarrow R_2$) if these two relations are derived from relator types RR_1 and RR_2 such that RR_2 specializes RR_1 ($RR_1 \Leftarrow RR_2$).*

Another example of specialization is depicted in Figure 7.b. It was taken from [12, pg.242] without any change in the relations except a change in the constraints max_b and max_{b1}, in order to illustrate the following point. Notice that in all these cases there is always the (sometimes implicit) existence of at least one additional type RR_3 (e.g., *RegularMember*, *Conviction*) such that RR_3 is distinct from RR_2 (e.g., *Chairman*, *Absolution*) and RR_3 specializes RR_1. This means that the maximum cardinality constraints of R_1 (max_b) govern relations between individuals, which are mediated by both types of relators (RR_2 and RR_3). For instance, suppose that a group is allowed to have a maximum of 500 members. Thus, the maximum of Chairmen can, in principle, be $\leq$ 500 in that period. However, if there is a limit of 10 chairmen for the Group, there could still be up to 490 regular members. This feature explains why the maximum cardinality constraints of R_2 (max_{b1}) are not imposed on the maximum cardinality constraints of R_1 (max_b - see discussion in section 3.3).

4.3 An Ontological Analysis of Redefinition

We now turn to the example of Figure 4 with three material relations: (i) *Participates* defined between the types *Employee* and *Project*; (ii) *ParticipatesCritical* defined between the types *Senior* and *Critical*; and (iii) *Participates* defined between the types *Junior* and *Project*. In this case, we have that all these relations are derived from the same relator type and the same foundation, namely, an allocation event and the resulting *Allocation* contract. In the situation represented by this model, the different ways of participating in a project (which entail the different relations of participation) are defined by the different types associated with the association end opposite to the redefining end of these relations. In other words, the differences in the ways a junior or senior employee participate in a project are motivated by difference in properties of these different types of employees not by difference in different types of *Allocation*.

For instance, let us suppose the case that the property *"having less than 10 years of experience"* differentiates junior from senior employees. Now, suppose an individual *John* which by virtue of having this *(intrinsic) quality* instantiates *Junior*. It is because of this quality that *John* is constrained to participate in at most 3 critical projects, not because he is connected to these projects by a relator of specific kind of *Allocation*. Moreover, notice that, in this case, *John* instantiates *Junior* (the specializing class) prior to establishing any relation to a project, i.e., the nature of this relation is constrained by the specific type *John* instantiates. In contrast, if one examines the specializing type *Absolved*, one shall realize that an individual instantiates *Absolved* because of the specific type of *Sentence* that mediates him. Thus, in the latter case, it is the specific type this individual instantiates which is determined by the specific nature of the relator that mediates him. In other words, in the case of redefinition, the type the relata (instances connected to the association end) instantiate is defined *a priori* and the participation constraints in the relation follows from that; in the case of specialization, the type the relata instantiates in that relation is defined *a posteriori* entailed by the type of relator binding them. The remodelling of this situation with an explicit representation of the founding relator type is depicted in Figure 8.a. Another

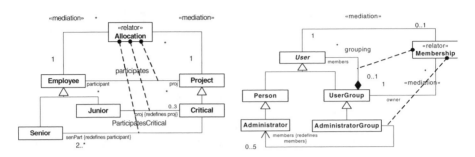

Fig. 8. a-b Explicit representations of the relator types from which the relations in Figure 3 and [19] are derived, respectively

example of association redefinition, taken from [19], is depicted in Figure 8.b where it is also remodelled to represent the founding relator type.

Notice that the ontological differences between these concepts also explains the difference discussed in section 3.3 on how these two relations influence the maximum cardinality constraints of the original (redefined or specialized) relation. As discussed there, only in the case of redefinition, multiplicity is redefined when the redefining end has a multiplicity which is more restrictive than that of the redefined end. This can be observed, for instance, in Figure 8.a when a junior employee can participate in at most 3 critical projects. The reader can contrast it with Figure 7.b in which a Group can have at most 10 chairs and still an upper bound of 500 employees. Again, in the latter case, the way entities participate in these relations is defined by the relator type: to be a Chairman is to have a relational bond to this group of a specific nature, namely, a Chairman Membership (Chairmanship). However, employees can participate in groups in different ways, for instance, as regular members. In the former case, conversely, it is the specific type the employee instantiates which *a priori* determinates her constraints in participating in the relation. For this reason, there is no other manner a junior employee can participate in this relation with a critical project. In other words, the specific (redefining) way of participating in this relation is the only way of participating in the general (redefined) relation. As a consequence, the multiplicity constraints of the former should be valid for the general case.

Finally, notice that this analysis also explains the syntactic constraint depicted in Figure 4 which differentiates redefinition from subsetting and specialization, namely, that in the case of redefinition the type A_1 in the opposite end of the redefining association end of association R_1 must be a subclass of type A. This is due to the fact that the difference in ways that instances of A participate in association R is determined by differences in intrinsic properties of these instances. Thus, if we have at least of property p that some instances of A must have in order to participate in R in a specific way (e.g., R_1) then we can define the type A_1 such that $A_1(x)$ *iff A(x) and (x possesses p)*. Conversely, notice that without a single property that differentiates particular subtypes of A then we cannot explain why they participate in association R in different manners and subject to different constraints. After all, in that case, all instance of A would have exactly the same properties including the specific relator type that binds then to instances of B. As a result of this analysis, we postulate that:

Postulate 3: *a redefinition relation should be defined between two material relations R_2 and R_1 (R_2 $_{redefines}$ R_1) if: (i) these two relations are derived from the same relator type RR; (ii) there is a type A_1 connected to one of the association ends of R_2 such that A_1 is a specialization of A ($A \triangleleft\!\!\!-\!\!\!A_1$) and A is connected to the association end of R_1 equivalent to that of A_1.*

5 Related Work

Some studies attempt to clarify or formalize the meaning of one or more of the three constructs under consideration. They can be classified in two groups: first, works that provide informal definitions, explanations or examples and, second, works that formalize the semantics of one or more of the constructs.

In the first group, we can mention [4] developed by Stevens, that deals with the association specialization of UML 1.4. She points out the difficulty of distinguishing it from subsettings and argues that specializations in UML 1.4 may be used to represent inclusion constraints and participation constraints over associations. We must note that this latter case is better represented in UML 2 as a redefinition. Moreover, Milicev [19] defines the subsetting as an implicit constraint attached to association ends. He also defines that end redefinitions may redefine the type and the multiplicity of the redefined end. Costal and Gómez [20] describe how to use redefinitions and analyze their interactions with taxonomic constraints. Olivé [12] states that inclusion constraints between associations can be represented by means of subsettings or specializations. He indicates that specializations must be used when the specific association has the defining properties of the general one together with others and subsettings in the rest of cases. Olivé indicates that redefinitions can be used to represent participant refinements and to strength cardinality [21]. From this first set of works, the only one that sketches a distinction between subsetting and specialization is that of Olivé [12] by means of intuitive explanations and well-chosen examples.

In the second group, that presents semantic formalizations, [10] by Alanen and Porres, deals with association subsetting. In addition, Kleppe and Rensink [6] formalize subsetting and redefinition as formal extensions of a type graph (not for all scenarios). Amelunxen and Schürr [11] present a set theoretic formalization of graph transformations that is used to define the semantics of a set of UML features including subsetting, specialization and redefinition. Bildhauer [22] describes the semantics of subsetting, redefinition and specialization by providing formal definitions for specific examples. All these works, give consistent interpretations of the constructs, also consistent with our semantic formalization. However, ours is the only one that explicitly characterizes the specific participation, minimum and maximum cardinality constraints implied by the constructs. Moreover, none of these works develops an ontological analysis and, thus, they are not able to distinguish subsetting from specialization and from some cases of redefinition. There exist some ontological analyses of relations, such as [23], but they do not cover subsetting, specialization or redefinition. Hence, to our knowledge, ours is the first contribution presenting a comprehensive view by specifying both the formal semantics and ontology-based semantics and able to differentiate the three constructs.

6   Final Considerations

The purpose of a conceptual model is to support users in tasks such as communication, understanding and problem-solving about a certain universe of discourse. For this reason, two fundamental quality attributes for a conceptual modeling language are: (i) *semantic discrimination*, i.e., users of the language must understand the semantic distinctions between language's constructs and the semantic consequences of applying these constructs; (ii) *ontological clarity*: the users of the language must understand what these constructs represent in terms of phenomena in reality. In this paper, we make a contribution in both these directions by specifying the *formal semantics* and the (ontology-based) *real-world semantics* of three important, yet poorly understood, UML association constructs, namely, subsetting, specialization and redefinition.

As a future work, we intend to test the ontological analysis put forth here by conducting empirical studies. In particular, we would like to further test the ability of this theory to predict the outcome of modeling choices. However, we should point out that one significant challenge of conducting such a study at this point, namely, that, despite their importance, these constructs are still unknown to a large community of modelers. This is specially the case of redefinition, which has only been introduced in the newest version of UML.

Nonetheless, we have conducted a preliminary empirical investigation on this theory using as a benchmark a catalog of models produced by different people using these constructs. This catalog has been obtained from the papers reviewed in our related work section, thus, comprising a set of ten examples produced by different authors (which can be considered experts in the field). The result of this study can be found in [24]. As demonstrated there, our theory was able to predict the modeling choices made by the authors in 90% of the cases. We take this to be preliminary evidence that the ontological theory developed here together with the modeling postulates derived from it constitute a *descriptive theory for explaining and predicting*, as well as a *prescriptive theory for design and action*.

Acknowledgements. This work has been partly supported by the *Ministerio de Ciencia y Tecnologia* and FEDER under projects TIN2008-00444/TIN and TIN2010-19130-C02-01, *Grupo Consolidado*, and by the funding agencies CNPq (Project Grant #481906/2009-6 and Productivity Grant #309382/2008) and FAPES (Project Grant #45444080/09).

References

1. Object Management Group: OMG Unified Modeling Language (OMG UML), Superstructure, V2.3 (formal/May 5, 2010) (2010)
2. Batra, D., Hoffler, J.A., Bostrom, R.P.: Comparing representations with relational and EER models. Communications of the ACM 33, 126–139 (1990)
3. Rumbaugh, J., Jacobson, I., Booch, G.: The unified modeling language reference manual, 2nd edn. Addison-Wesley, Reading (2005)
4. Stevens, P.: On the interpretation of binary associations in the Unified Modelling Language. Software and Systems Modeling 1, 68–79 (2002)

5. Szlenk, M.: Formal Semantics and Reasoning about UML Class Diagram. In: DEPCOS-RELCOMEX, pp. 51–59. IEEE Computer Society, Los Alamitos (2004)
6. Kleppe, A., Rensink, A.: On a Graph-Based Semantics for UML Class and Object Diagrams. Electronic Communications of the EASST 10 (2008)
7. Gogolla, M., Richters, M.: Expressing UML Class Diagrams Properties with OCL. In: Clark, A., Warmer, J. (eds.) Object Modeling with the OCL. LNCS, vol. 2263, pp. 85–114. Springer, Heidelberg (2002)
8. Object Management Group: Object Constraint Language (OCL), Version 2.2. Available Specification (formal/February 1, 2010) (2010)
9. Richters, M., Gogolla, M.: On Formalizing the UML Object Constraint Language OCL. In: Ling, T.-W., Ram, S., Li Lee, M. (eds.) ER 1998. LNCS, vol. 1507, pp. 449–464. Springer, Heidelberg (1998)
10. Alanen, M., Porres, I.: Basic Operations over Models Containing Subset and Union Properties. In: Wang, J., Whittle, J., Harel, D., Reggio, G. (eds.) MoDELS 2006. LNCS, vol. 4199, pp. 469–483. Springer, Heidelberg (2006)
11. Amelunxen, C., Schürr, A.: Formalising model transformation rules for UML/MOF 2. IET Software 2, 204–222 (2008)
12. Olivé, A.: Conceptual modeling of information systems. Springer, Heidelberg (2007)
13. Nieto, P., Costal, D., Gómez, C.: Enhancing the semantics of UML association redefinition. Data Knowl. Eng. 70, 182–207 (2011)
14. Guizzardi, G., Wagner, G.: What's in a Relationship: An Ontological Analysis. In: Li, Q., Spaccapietra, S., Yu, E., Olivé, A. (eds.) ER 2008. LNCS, vol. 5231, pp. 83–97. Springer, Heidelberg (2008)
15. Guizzardi, G.: Ontological Foundations for Structural Conceptual Models. Universal Press, The Netherlands (2005); ISBN 90-75176-81-3
16. Heller, B., Herre, H.: Ontological Categories in GOL. Axiomathes 14, 71–90 (2004)
17. Bock, C., Odell, J.: A More Complete Model of Relations and Their Implementation: Relations as Object Types. Journal of Object-Oriented Programming 10(3) (1997)
18. Gurr, C.A.: Effective Diagrammatic Communication: Syntatic, Semantic and Pragmatic Issues. Journal of Visual Languages and Computing 10, 317–342 (1999)
19. Milicev, D.: Model-Driven Development with Executable UML. Wiley Pub. Inc., Chichester (2009)
20. Costal, D., Gómez, C.: On the Use of Association Redefinition in UML Class Diagrams. In: Embley, D.W., Olivé, A., Ram, S. (eds.) ER 2006. LNCS, vol. 4215, pp. 513–527. Springer, Heidelberg (2006)
21. Costal, D., Olivé, À., Teniente, E.: Relationship Type Refinement in Conceptual Models with Multiple Classification. In: Kunii, H.S., Jajodia, S., Sølvberg, A. (eds.) ER 2001. LNCS, vol. 2224, pp. 397–411. Springer, Heidelberg (2001)
22. Bildhauer, D.: On the Relationships Between Subsetting, Redefinition and Association Sepecialization. In: DB&IS 2010 (2010)
23. Evermann, J.: The Association Construct in Conceptual Modelling – An Analysis Using the Bunge Ontological Model. In: Pastor, Ó., Falcão e Cunha, J. (eds.) CAiSE 2005. LNCS, vol. 3520, pp. 33–47. Springer, Heidelberg (2005)
24. Costal, D., Gómez, C., Guizzardi, G.: On the Meanings of Subsetting, Specialization and Redefinition in UML, Technical Report (2011),
    http://hdl.handle.net/2117/12827

Developing RFID Database Models for Analysing Moving Tags in Supply Chain Management

Wilfred Ng

Department of Computer Science and Engineering,
The Hong Kong University of Science and Technology,
Hong Kong
wilfred@cse.ust.hk

Abstract. The applications of RFID (Radio Frequency Identification) have become more important and diversified in recent years due to the lower cost of RFID tags and smaller tag sizes. One promising area for applying the technology is in Supply Chain Management (SCM) in which the manufacturers need to analyse product and logistic information in order to get the right quantity of products arriving at the right time to the right locations.

In this paper, we present a holistic framework that supports data querying and analysis of raw datasets obtained from different RFID collection points managed by supply chains. First, the framework provides repair mechanisms to preprocess raw RFID data from readers. Second, we present a database model to capture SCM information at various abstraction levels such as items, time and locations, and then discuss the use of SQL query language to manipulate RFID databases. Finally, we present a graph data model called a Tag Movement Graph (TMG) to capture the moving information of tagged objects.

1 Introduction

RFID (*Radio Frequency Identification*) is a technology that allows a sensor (an *RF reader*) to read, from a distance, and without line of sight, a unique EPC (*Electronic Product Code*) associated with a tag [19,20,5,17]. The applications of RFID have become more important and diversified in recent years due to the lower cost of RFID tags and smaller tag sizes. One promising area for applying the technology is in *Supply Chain Management* (SCM) [15] in which the manufacturers need to analyse product and logistic information in order to get the right quantity of products arriving at the right time to the right locations.

However, the amount of RFID data in SCM is noisy and massive (e.g. Walmart's warehouse data can be up to the size of petabytes in scale [17]). There still lacks of a unifying model that is able to capture information arising from multi-level and multi-dimensional RFID data. Importantly, we need to develop a framework that supports managing, querying and analysing the information obtained from different RFID sources. All these new RFID features and requirements bring new challenges for providing seamless integration of techniques of data cleaning, data modeling and data mining.

In this paper, we present a holistic framework that enables the management of RFID information and facilitates advanced analysis of the information. We establish data

M. Jeusfeld, L. Delcambre, and T.W. Ling (Eds.): ER 2011, LNCS 6998, pp. 204–218, 2011.

models for RFID data obtained from SCM in the framework which supports tackling the following RFID data problems:

- How to clean massive RFID raw data and store the data in an effective database?
- How to support storing RFID information arising from SCM?
- How to support querying RFID information arising from SCM?
- How to discover useful tag movement trails and correlated patterns in different levels and dimensions of logistic information?

Figure 1 shows the blueprint of the framework, which can pre-process, repair, and store the data collected from multi-RFID data streams. Within the framework, we use a relational DBMS to store RFID data and develop a query language which is translatable into SQL expressions. This approach is practical to RFID industrials, since they usually have a relational DBMS as one of the SCM infrastructures. The new query language can also be employed to manipulate the scope of the derived RFID graph called *Tag Movement Graphs* (TMGs). The framework supports discovering the tag movement relationships from the TMG and RFID databases. Our proposed notions of *Tag Movement Trails* (TMTs) and *Logistic Correlated Patterns* (LCPs) take data abstraction and the SCM logistic information, such as location topology, object grouping and temporal hierarchies, into consideration.

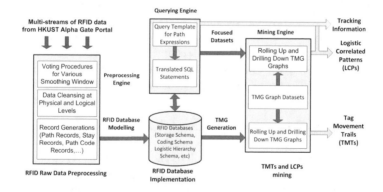

Fig. 1. A system view of our proposed framework to support analysing RFID data

The main contributions of this work are related to many interesting modeling and algorithmic issues arising from our proposed framework.

In the modeling aspect, we design the database model as well as the TMG data model to handle the RFID data obtained from multi-stream RFID readers. Figure 2(a) show the setup of the α-gate portal that we used to detect RFID tags from three different readers, thereby generating three RFID data streams that are collected in the detection system in which the connection of the components are presented in Figure 2(b) [21].

In the algorithmic aspect, we develop the coding schemes that support the execution of RFID queries. The algorithm for finding TMTs is an application of the the state-of-the-art research work of graph mining. However, we enrich the techniques to cater

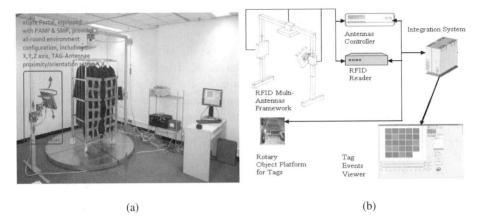

(a)   (b)

Fig. 2. (a) RFID three-stream (x, y, and z axes) data collection by α-gate portal (b) The setup of the detection system (More details can be consulted from [21])

for cases of different abstraction levels in TMG data model. The algorithms for finding LCPs are the interesting application of the research discovering correlated patterns in graph databases [14].

The rest of the paper is organised as follows. Section 2 presents our cleaning strategies to pre-process RFID raw data obtained from our α-gate portal. Section 3 presents the RFID database model and the coding scheme. We illustrate the application of SQL to support various kinds of RFID queries in Section 4 and present the TMG data model that supports mining of TMTs and LCPs in Section 5. We review the related work of handling RFID data in Section 6. Finally, we give our concluding remarks in Section 7.

2   Preprocessing Multi-stream Raw RFID Data

In this section, we present the cleaning methods and illustrate the repairing mechanism that preprocesses multi-stream raw RFID Data collected in the α-gate portal and the detection system shown in Figures 2(a) and (b). The main problem in this task related to the RFID raw data preprocessing module presented in Figure 1 is as follows. Given an SCM environment with possibly RFID signal interferences or noises, we devise effective tactics of cleaning multi-RFID data streams obtained from the portal.

In contrast to most existing approaches that focus mainly on low level data [4,23], we pre-process the data into two phases of physical cleaning and logical cleaning.

Physical cleaning is firstly imposed at the raw data level, in which a smoothing window is employed to remove noises such as *tag jamming* (tag failing to respond to two different reader signals coming at similar time) or *tag blocking* (tag signal is blocked by moisture or metal objects), and logical cleaning is then imposed at the record level to remove multiple, missing or incorrect readings. The challenge is that there is a tension in setting the window size for tracking tags. On the one hand, if we choose a smaller window, we are able to capture the tag movement more accurately. However, it gives rise to more false negatives and undercounting the tags. It is due to the fact that raw data readings can only be picked up by the reader irregularly in the period of tag's presence. On the other hand, if we choose a larger window, we are able to correct more reader's unreliability due to tag jamming or blocking. (c.f. The read rate reported in [12] is roughly 70% of total tag readings in sensor network environments.) However, it gives rise to more false positives and missed tag transitions.

To address the noise problem, we use the α-gate portal shown in Figure 2(a) to develop tactics to clean and repair multi-stream RFID data. We adopt a different approach of "smoothing filter" from SMURF [13], since it is not effective to determine a variable window for all possible RFID data streams. The underlying idea is that we impose a voting system for readings from different window sizes over RFID data streams in order to compensate (i) undercounting tags (missing tag read) and overcounting tags (repeated tag read) and (ii) removing false negatives and false positives.

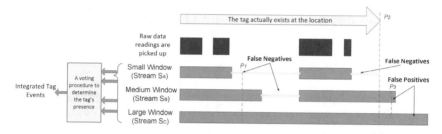

Fig. 3. Using three different smoothing windows for tracking a tag: Stream S_A from a small window avoids most false positives. Stream S_B from a medium window avoids some false positives and some false negatives. Stream S_C from a large window avoids most false negatives. Finally, a voting procedure that obtains "votes" from all streams can effectively remove errors

To illustrate the idea of the voting strategy on the data streams, we show a simplified diagram in Figure 3 that S_A (small window) has a bigger voting weight whenever the conflict of false positives happens (e.g. points P_2 and P_3). However, S_C (large window) has a bigger voting weight whenever the conflict of false negatives happens (e.g. point P_1). S_B (medium window) can be"neutral" such that it carries medium weight on voting. The idea of the voting algorithm is adapted from our earlier work of [16]. We find that the voting strategy is very effective if using more windows of different size that are set on the multi-streams obtained by different antennae configurations (e.g. varying x, y, z and angle settings of the antennas of the α-gate portal in Figure 2).

Logical cleaning following physical cleaning is more interesting. The challenge is how to continue the data cleaning by developing inference rules to repair data (e.g. the EPC is missing in a reader). We classify the logical errors of RFID data into five different classes of (i) missing time - no tracing time data are recorded, (ii) missing location - no location information are recorded, (iii) conflicting path - multiple impossible location location information are recorded, (iv) ambiguous path - multiple possible location information are recorded, and (v) repeated reading - reading are repeatedly recorded. Due to the space limit, we only highlight two interesting scenarios using three repairing classes in Figure 4, where the pattern $\{Time, Sec\}[t_1, t_2]\{Spot, A\}$ denotes the fact that a tag is detected within a time interval "$[t_1, t_2]$" measured in seconds at spot A.

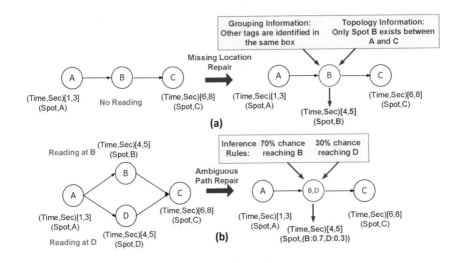

Fig. 4. Logical Cleaning: Repair Schemes for (a) Missing location (b) Ambiguous Path

Missing location repair deals with the following scenario shown in Figure 4(a): When a tag goes through a sequence of readers (or locations) A, B and C, B fails to detect the tag. The error may be due to many reasons such as bad reading angles, blocked signals or signal dead zones, which result in weak or no signal readings that are eliminated by the physical cleaning [12,13]. To repair the error, one rule is to make reference to other location information. For example, by checking the connectivity of the readers, we can deduce that a tag going from A to C must pass B. Another rule is to check the group information. For example, in most SCM settings, tags are moving in groups (e.g. items are contained in boxes or pallets) and thus it is possible to repair some missing tag readings in certain locations if other tags in the same group or a group ID are recorded. Furthermore, *missing time repair* references other tags that go from A to C and then estimates the relative staying time in the detecting region of a reader.

Ambiguous path repair deals with a usual scenario shown in Figure 4(b): A tag goes from A to C passing through B but it is accidentally detected by an abutting reader D placed in another possible path. In this case, we may not be able to decide if the tag passed through B or D. In general, we accommodate the uncertainty in a probability node which represents a possible set of location nodes, each of which is attached a probability as shown in the figure. The assignment of the probability values in the probability nodes is deduced by the rules established by statistical methods that evaluate the sample distribution of the responding tag signal in B and D. An example of such a rule is "if Tag_1 to Tag_{10} passed D, then the probability of Tag_{11} to Tag_{20} going to D is 0.7".

3   RFID Database Model

In this section we develop an RFID database model that supports querying and mining and discuss the implementation issues of database storage.

3.1 RFID Database Modeling

We design an RFID database model and implement a scalable storage system for RFID data to support querying and mining. An RFID system consists of three main objects: tags, antennas and readers. A tag T in a location reflects (if T is a passive tag) or emits (if T is an active tag) RF signals within its detection region. When the antenna detects the signal, the reader analyses the signal and stores the EPC and the current timestamp into the database. We represent paths, tags, times and other information in the model and develop path coding schemes for the movement of T in a stored data model. We also incorporate logistic hierarchies and relevant product information into the product data model and the logistic hierarchy data model respectively, which are depicted in Figure 5. This serves as a foundation for the database implementation.

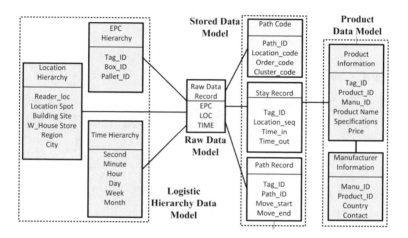

Fig. 5. RFID Database Model with Logistic Hierarchies and Relevant Production Information

To explain the database model in Figure 5, we start by assuming a simple model of RFID raw data in SCM. An RFID reader detects a tag and generates *Raw Data Record* having three attributes (EPC, LOC, TIME) where EPC is a unique ID of a tag and LOC is the location of the (unique) RFID reader and TIME is the time instant of detecting the tag. We then collapse the raw data into the *Stay Record* entity having four attributes (tag_id, loc_code, time_in, time_out) where time_in and time_out are the time instants of the first detection and the final detection of the tag. A stay record represents an RFID tag moving through a location during a specific time interval. However, using a stay record as a stored data model is too simplistic to support the evaluation of path queries that track objects, particularly for those path queries involving many locations, which need to perform self-joining of the table many times. Thus, we develop various sophisticated coding techniques and include *Path Record* and *Path Code* entities into the model.

The basic idea of the coding scheme is that a tag movement path "$L_1 \rightarrow L_2 \rightarrow \cdots \rightarrow L_n$" can be coded by assigning a unique prime number, P_l, to represent all locations (or all readers) and another prime number, P_o, to represent the location order. To generate a unique integer pair (P_l, P_o), we rely on the *Unique Factorization Theorem* for coding locations and the *Chinese Remainder Theorem* for coding their order. However, due to the scarcity of prime numbers, the state-of-the-art method in [15] which supports neither long path coding (e.g. encode a long path of more than 8 locations) nor cyclic path coding (e.g. encode a path in which a tag passed a location twice). The first problem is due to the fact that most programming languages use unsigned integers (32 bits) that only support $2^{32} - 1$, which is less than the product of the first nine prime numbers $2 \times 3 \times 5 \times 7 \times 11 \times 13 \times 17 \times 19 \times 23$. Even for 64 bit unsigned integers (2^{64}-1), it can only support the first 15 prime numbers. In addition, suppose a tag goes through the path "$L_1 \rightarrow L_2 \rightarrow L_3 \rightarrow L_1 \rightarrow L_2 \rightarrow L_3$". In this case, the coding method in [15] fails, since the system of simultaneous *congruences* of Chinese remainder theorem is not applicable here and thus (P_l, P_o) fails to code $2\rightarrow3\rightarrow5\rightarrow2\rightarrow3\rightarrow5$.

3.2   RFID Data Coding Schemes

To tackle the two problems illustrated in Section 3.1, we need to review some important results from number theory, which is the necessary background for understanding our proposed path coding schemes. Theorem 1 summaries all the relevant results.

Theorem 1. *The following theorems are well-established mathematical results [10].*

1. *(**The Fundamental Theorem of Arithmetic**). Any natural number greater than 1 is uniquely expressed by the product of prime numbers.*
2. *(**The Chinese Remainder Theorem**). Suppose that $n_1, n_2, \ldots, n_k$ are pairwise relatively prime numbers. Then, there exists x between 0 and $(n_1 \cdot n_2 \cdot n_3 \cdots n_k - 1)$ by solving the following system of simultaneous congruences*

$$x \mod n_i \equiv a_i \text{ for } 1 \leq i \leq k.$$

3. *(**Euler Formula for Prime Generation**). For every integer x between 0 and 40, $x^2 - x + 41$ is a prime number.*
4. *(**Finite Continued Fraction**). Given a finite sequence of positive integers $\langle x_1, x_2, \ldots, x_n \rangle$, there exists a rational number Y given by*

$$Y = \cfrac{1}{x_1 + \cfrac{1}{x_2 + \cdots \frac{1}{x_n}}}$$

such that Y uniquely expresses $\langle x_1, x_2, \ldots, x_n \rangle$.

To solve the long path coding problem, we first partition the whole set of locations into different clusters having roughly the same number of locations. Using finite continued fraction in Theorem 1 we are able to represent a cluster_code denoted as C (having a unique positive integer as its id) together with its respective (P_l, P_o). Notably, the clustering can be straightforwardly extended into more than one level within each cluster, which therefore removes the constraint of having no more than 8 prime numbers for coding a path in a cluster.

Suppose there are two clusters coded by two positive integers C_1 and C_2. The sub-path in cluster 1 can be computed as loc_code 1 and order_code 1 and similarly notations for the subpath in cluster 2. If a path goes from cluster 1 to cluster 2, we generate the fullpath_code $\mathcal{P}$ as

$$\cfrac{1}{C_1 + \cfrac{1}{loc\_code1 + \cfrac{1}{order\_code1 + \cfrac{1}{C_2 + \cfrac{1}{loc\_code2 + \cfrac{1}{order\_code2}}}}}}.$$

When decoding $\mathcal{P}$, we first check whether it is smaller than 1. If this is the case, then the path covers more than one cluster. We then decompress $\mathcal{P}$ to extract loc_code and order_code in each cluster.

To solve the cyclic path coding problem, we apply Euler's prime number generation formula in Theorem 1. For example, the cyclic path $2{\to}3{\to}5{\to}2{\to}3{\to}5$ is coded as "2 $\to 3 \to 5 \to 43(x{=}2) \to 47(x{=}3){\to} 61(x = 5)$ which can be used to form the system of congruences required by the Chinese remainder theorem of Theorem 1.

We are now ready to present our algorithms to handle long and cyclic paths. For simplicity in presentation, we assume one reader for each location and one level of clustering. We divide the whole set of locations into n clusters, each of which has less than 8 locations. We then code each cluster by an integer and within each cluster a location is coded by a unique prime number n_p. We now represent a path with three integers (loc_code P_l, order_code P_o, cluster_code N_c) only. Loc_code can be computed by using the *Fundamental Theorem of Arithmetic* in Theorem 1, which by definition P_l is the product of all prime numbers associated with the path. Order_code exists according to the *Chinese Remainder Theorem* in Theorem 1 and P_o can be computed by Euclid's algorithm [22]. For example, consider $\{n_1 = 2, n_2 = 3, n_3 = 5\}$ and $(P_o \mod 2) \equiv 1, (P_o \mod 3) \equiv 2, (P_o \mod 5) \equiv 3$, then P_o can be computed as $((1 \times 3 \times 5 + 2 \times 5 \times 2 + 2 \times 3 \times 3) \mod(2 \times 3 \times 5)) \equiv 23$.

As we are not able to make order_code P_o congruent to the same location twice in the Chinese Remainder Theorem, we need to assign more than one prime number to those repeatedly visiting locations. Here is our proposed solution to this problem. First, we code each location with a prime number as said and this number is not an *Euler Formula Prime*. We call this set of location prime numbers the *Fundamental Location Set* and denote the set by $\mathcal{F}$. Given that the *Stay Records* can be sorted by time_in, if a specific location occurs twice, the first occurrence will be the prime code n from $\mathcal{F}$ and then the second occurrence can be coded by applying Euler Formula by putting $x = n$. The new generated Euler prime numbers do not belong to $\mathcal{F}$. We now ready to present the ideas of path coding in Algorithm 1.

The underlying idea of the decoding process is as follows. First, we decompress the fullpath_code (if it is found to be larger than 1) to identify clusters and for each cluster C decompose loc_code into its corresponding list of all locations p. Second, we know whether there is a cycle in an encoded path by comparing p with $\mathcal{F}$. If there are cycles, after sorting p, we decode those prime numbers that are not in $\mathcal{F}$ by reversing Euler Theorem to get their original set of prime numbers. Finally, the path can be constructed by sorting p by using order_code. We now present the ideas in Algorithm 2.

Algorithm 1. Encoding

Input: A fullpath p, Fundamental Location Set $\mathcal{F}_i$ for each cluster c_i
Output: Fullpath_code $\mathcal{P}$

Assign a positive integer n_i to each cluster c_i
for each cluster c_i **do**
    if there are repeated Stay Records in c_i **then**
        Encode these Repeated locations by Euler Theorem
        Update $\mathcal{E}_i$ by including the Euler's prime numbers
    end if
    loc_code := Product of all prime number in $\mathcal{F}_i \cup \mathcal{E}_i$
    order_code := Output by using $\mathcal{F}_i \cup \mathcal{E}_i$ in the Chinese remainder theorem
end for
fullpath_code := Result of a finite continued fraction of $\{n_i,$ loc_code, order_code $\}$ for all c_i

---

Algorithm 2. Decoding

Input: A fullpath_code $\mathcal{P}$, Fundamental Location Set $\mathcal{F}_i$ for each cluster c_i
Output: A full path defined by $p := \bigcup p_i$ for all path segment p_i in the clusters

Decompress $\mathcal{P}$ to identify the ordered set of loc_code and order_code in each cluster
for each cluster c_i where i preserves the order of the decompressed integer sequence from $\mathcal{P}$
do
    for all prime numbers $n_p \leq$ loc_code **do**
        if loc_code % n_p equals to 0 (i.e. the remainder for dividing loc_code by n_p is 0) **then**
            Add n_p into p_i with an order
        end if
    end for
    for all n_p in p_i **do**
        Remainder Set $\mathcal{R} := \mathcal{R} \cup \{$order_code % $n_p\}$
    end for
    Sort p_i according to the order in $\mathcal{R}$
    if there are cycles (i.e. $p_i - \mathcal{F}_i \neq \emptyset$) **then**
        Inverse Euler Theorem to all n_p in $(p_i - \mathcal{F}_i)$
    end if
end for

Example 1. Suppose that a tagged object goes though locations $C \rightarrow B \rightarrow A \rightarrow B \rightarrow C$ in the same cluster. We have $\mathcal{F} = \{1, 2, 3\}$. We use prime numbers to represent these locations as follows: C is denoted as 2, B is denoted as 3, and A is denoted as 5. Then, cluster_code = 1, loc_code = $2 \times 3 \times 5 \times Euler\,(3) \times Euler\,(2) = 2 \times 3 \times 5 \times 47 \times 43 = 60630$, and order_code = 24773. To decode the path, we first decompose loc_code into $\mathcal{P} = \{2, 3, 5, 47, 43\}$. Then we can get their order by dividing order_code by all the elements in $\mathcal{P}$ and the remainder set (in order) are $\{1, 2, 3, 4, 5\}$. We sort $\mathcal{P}$ by this order and thus get $2 \rightarrow 3 \rightarrow 5 \rightarrow 47 \rightarrow 43$. As the numbers 47 and 43 do not belong to $\mathcal{F}$, we decode them by reversing *Euler Theorem* to get original prime numbers 2 and 3.

4 RFID Manipulation Languages

In this section we present RFID Manipulation Languages and discuss their SQL processing. The architecture shown in Figure 1 provides a platform to translate different classes of RFID queries into their corresponding SQL statements.

The language for formulating RFID queries is defined by borrowing the notation of XML path expressions. We consider queries and the results can be expressed by the syntax elements such as parent axis (/), ancestor axis (//) and predicate ([]). Let us consider the following RFID raw data and the corresponding stay records in Table 1.

Table 1. RFID Raw Data and Stay Record

Raw Data Records	$(Tag_1,L_1,1), (Tag_1,L_1,2), (Tag_1,L_2,3), (Tag_1,L_2,4),$ $(Tag_1,L_3,5), (Tag_1,L_3,6), (Tag_2,L_1,3), (Tag_2,L_1,6),$ $(Tag_2,L_2,7), (Tag_2,L_2,8), (Tag_2,L_3,9), (Tag_2,L_3,10)$
Stay Records	$Tag_1: L_1[1, 2] \rightarrow L_2[3, 4] \rightarrow L_3[5, 6]$ $Tag_2: L_1[3, 6] \rightarrow L_2[7, 8] \rightarrow L_3[9, 10]$

SQL is employed to support three types of queries of *tracking queries*, *path-oriented queries*, *containment queries*.

– Tracking queries aim to obtain the path information for a given tag.
– Path-oriented queries aim to obtain information in a given path expression.
– Containment queries aim to obtain information from the relationships between tags, boxes and pallets.

To support processing of above three classes of queries, we rely on the RFID database model presented in Figure 5 for handling the path and tag information. We illustrate the language by using the following RFID queries and their corresponding SQL translation.

We can formulate tracking queries that require tag locations or location history. The query results are given according to Table 1.

Query Q_1: Find the path for tag_id = Tag_1.

Results: $L_1/L_2/L_3$ (decoded from the path code by Algorithm 2).

Tracking queries require tag locations or location history. Q_1 traces Tag_1 and the query can be translated into an SQL statement by assuming the tables corresponding to Figure 5: pathrecord(tag_id, path_id, move_start, move_end), pathcode(path_id, loc_code, order_code, cluster_code) and stayrecord(tag_id, loc_code, time_in, time_out) as the following SQL expression.

SELECT decode(loc_code, order_code, cluster_code)
FROM pathcord P, pathcode C
WHERE tag_id = 'Tag_1' AND P.path_id = C.path_id

We are able to formulate path oriented queries to obtain information in a given path expression. We assume $n_i = Prime(L_i)$ and the MOD function provided by Oracle DBMS in SQL translation.

Query Q_2: Find the tag_ids that go to L_3 via L_1.
Expression: Expressions (based on XPath convention) $\langle //L1//L3 \rangle$
Results: Tag_1, Tag_2

SELECT tag_id
FROM pathrecord P, pathcode C
WHERE MOD(C.loc_code, $n_1 \times n_3$) = 0 AND
MOD(C.order_code, n_1) < MOD(C.order_code, n_3) AND P.path_id = C.path_id

Query Q_3: Find the tag_ids going from L_1 to L_2 where the duration at L_1 is less than 2.
Expression: $\langle //L_1[(\text{EndTime} - \text{StartTime}) \le 2]/ L_2 \rangle$
Results: Tag_1

SELECT S.tag_id
FROM pathrecord P, pathcode C, stayrecord S
WHERE MOD(C.loc_code, $n_1 \times n_2$) = 0 AND
MOD(C.order_code, n_1) + 1 = MOD(C.order_code, n_2) AND P.path_id = C.path_id
AND P.tag_id = S.tag_id AND S.loc_code = n_1 AND (S.Time_in - S.Time_out) < 2

For containment queries that involves product information and manufacturer details, SQL expressions can be formulated in a similar way as usual data warehouse queries [9], which are well-known SQL work and therefore are not detailed here.

5   Tag Movement Graph (TMG) Model

In this section, we present a graph-theoretic data model to capture RFID tag trail information and discuss how to discover *tag movement trails* (TMTs) and *logistic correlated patterns* (LCP) defined within the model.

5.1   Capture Frequent Tag Movement Trails in a TMG

We establish a graph-theoretic data model to capture RFID tag movement information. This can be achieved by decomposing the RFID database into a TMG via adapting some established "tables to graph" algorithms such as BANKS [1]. Based on the logistic hierarchy model in Figure 5, a node in the TMG graph is annotated with SCM information along three dimensions of the object tags (i.e. with an EPC hierarchy: object $\rightarrow$ box $\rightarrow$ case $\rightarrow$ pallet), locations (i.e. with a location hierarchy: spot $\rightarrow$ site $\rightarrow$ store $\rightarrow$ region) and time (i.e. with a temporal hierarchy: minute $\rightarrow$ hour $\rightarrow$ day $\rightarrow$ week).

For example, a node in a TMG at the lowest level of the mentioned three hierarchies is annotated as {(EPC,object), (Loc,Spot), (Time,Sec)} to store the object coded as EPC. A higher level annotation on the node can be formulated as {(EPC,Box), (Loc,Store), (Time,Day)} or a further higher level as {(EPC,Pallet), (Loc,Region), (Time, Month)}. We implement data warehouse operators such as roll up and drill down to control different levels of abstraction in each dimension. In contrast to the RFID Cuboid [9], each node of TMG can be annotated with the data in all the dimensions and each edge with the aggregated information of transitions such as the total number of tag

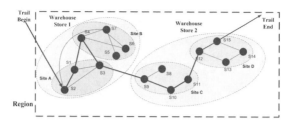

Fig. 6. A TMG Graph viewed at multi-levels of location: Spot → Site → Store → Region

read. We can restrict the TMG on a focused dataset obtained by formulating an RFID manipulation language expression as discussed in Section 4.

We now show a simplified location view of a TMG in Figure 6. Within the TMG graph model, we discover frequent Tag Movement Trails (TMTs) that meet some threshold criteria in various abstraction levels. We can see that a simple form of a TMT trail can be defined as $(E, S_2 \rightarrow S_1 \rightarrow S_4 \rightarrow S_3 \rightarrow S_9 \rightarrow S_{10} \rightarrow S_{11} \rightarrow S_{12} \rightarrow S_{15}, T_{Spot})$ which represents a trajectory of tag E running in different location spots at different times specified by T_{Spot}. The TMT trail can be rolled up to the site level as $(E, Site_A \rightarrow Site_B \rightarrow Site_A \rightarrow Site_C \rightarrow Site_D, T_{Site})$, or to the warehouse level as $(E, Store_1 \rightarrow Store_2, T_{Store})$. The abstraction for tags E and time T (e.g. T_{Spot} in second, T_{Site} in minute, and T_{Store} in hour) can also be rolled up similarly.

The TMTs can be explored by performing a generalization of some standard graph exploration methods such as DFS (depth-first search) or BFS (breadth-first search) [22]. The parameters that judge various approaches are defined in terms of memory consumption and number of iterations. We define a stopping condition of the exploration as follows: using BFS-like algorithm we construct a tree-like structure with the start node as its root wherein each branch of the tree is explored until its probability falls below a cut-point. A branch of the tree having probability above the cut-point is a candidate trail if it still has some expansions to be evaluated. The process continues until a longest TMT can be found. There is also a trade-off between mining more trails by lowering the cut-point and improving the efficiency by reducing the depth of exploration.

5.2   Logistic Correlated Patterns on TMG

A *Logistic Correlated Pattern* (or simply an LCP) is a nonempty set of correlated items having distinct logistic attributes (time, trails and other product quality parameters), which are both multi-level and quantitative in nature [14]. An example item is "(Time, minute)[100, 200]" representing from 100 to 200 minutes and an example of 2-patterns is "(Time, minute)[100, 200](Trail, spot)[S1, S5]" with the logistic attribute set {(Time, minute), (Trail, spot)} and the interval set {[100, 200], $[S_1, S_5]$}.

LCPs reveal the fact that "The time (100 to 200 sec) spent in the trail $S_A \rightarrow S_B$ (coded as 1→2) is too long and makes the milk spoil" or "The number of tags passing through the trail $S_A \rightarrow S_B \rightarrow S_C$ (coded as 1→2→3) is between 1K and 2K in the first day". They can be expressed as LCPs "(Time, minute)[100, 200](Trail, Spot)[1, 2](quality)[spoil]" and "Sum(Object, tag)[1K, 2K](Trail, spot)[1, 3](Time, day)[0, 1]".

Mining the RFID database and the TMG graph together give rise to the discovery of rich hidden SCM information for further analysis.

6   Related Work

Initial studies of RFID technologies focused mainly on the issues arising from low level abstraction such as signal filtering and resolution, RFID sensitivity tuning and RFID benchmarking and standardization [8,2]. As the amount of RFID data becomes extremely large (e.g. Walmart generates RFID data in the petabyte scale each day [17]), the problem of applying database and data mining technologies to handle RFID data is increasingly necessary and important. There are many interesting issues for handling RFID data such as stream processing [24,5,13], managing RFID data [23,9], cleaning raw RFID data and RFID data mining [18,7]. However, there still lacks of an integrated framework to support more advanced data analysis.

The work related to event processing can be found in Wang et al. [24], which considers temporal RFID events and formalizes the specification and semantics of RFID events and rules. Also, they proposed a method to detect RFID complex events efficiently. Bai et al. [4,5] explored the limitation of SQL in supporting the temporal event detection and discussed an SQL-based stream query language to provide comprehensive temporal RFID event detection. The system architecture for managing RFID data is also discussed in [3,6,11].

An important issue for RFID applications is that the collected raw data has different sorts of errors such as duplicate readings and missing readings. To clean the raw data, SMURF [13] was proposed to control the window size of the smoothing filter adaptively using statistical sampling. [4] also proposed several methods to filter RFID data. However, there is still a lack of work to address the errors in high level abstraction and handling multi-streams of raw RFID data.

In the area of RFID data modeling, Wang et al. [23] proposed the Dynamic Relationship ER Model (DRER) which includes a new relationship (dynamic relationship). They also proposed methods to express temporal queries based on DRER. Gonzalez et al. [9] proposed a new data warehousing model for the object transition and a method to process a path selection query. Lee and Chung [15] proposed a storage scheme to aid processing a set of RFID queries such as tracking and path-oriented queries. The coding schemes apply some important results from the prime number theory. Unlike our coding schemes presented in Algorithms 1 and 2, only very few location nodes can be handled due to the scarcity nature of prime numbers and no cycle is allowed to happen in their scheme. There are few works related to mining RFID [7] but still many issues such as analysing patterns and trails that have not been adequately explored.

7   Concluding Remarks

We present a holistic framework that supports collecting and analysing RFID raw data in a SCM setting. Within the framework, we illustrate the techniques of modeling and storing RFID data and discuss how to make RFID queries translatable into SQL expressions. This approach is practical to RFID industrials, since they usually have relational

DBMSs as one of the SCM infrastructures. To discover more interesting SCM information, we also propose the notions of TMTs and LCPs, which take data abstraction and the SCM logistic information, such as location topology, object grouping and logistic hierarchies, into consideration. The proposed framework provides much stronger support to business activities that involve complex movements of goods in large quantities. This work also demonstrates the application of many fundamental research areas such as data warehouse operations and data mining on graphs. Throughout the paper, we have discussed various issues from modeling and system view points. To further demonstrate the feasibility of the framework, we are collaborating with our RFID lab industrial partners (see [20], Partners) to gain user feedback as a future work.

Acknowledgements. This work is partially supported by Hong Kong RGC GRF under project number 617610.

References

1. Aditya, B., et al.: Sudarshan: BANKS: Browsing and Keyword Searching in Relational Databases. In: Proc. of VLDB, pp. 1083–1086 (2002)
2. Angeles, R.: RFID Technologies: Supply-chain Apps. and Implementation Issues (2005)
3. Bornhövd, C., et al.: Integrating Automatic Data Acquisition with Business Processes - Experiences with SAP's Auto-ID Infrastructure. In: Proc. of VLDB (2004)
4. Bai, Y., Wang, F., Liu, P.: Efficiently Filtering RFID Data Streams. In: Proc. of VLDB Workshop on Clean Databases (2006)
5. Bai, Y., Wang, F., Liu, P., Zaniolo, C., Liu, S.: RFID Data Processing With a Data Stream Query Language. In: Proc. of ICDE (2007)
6. Chawathe, S.S., Krishnamurthy, V., Ramachandran, S., Sarma, S.: Managing RFID data. In: Proc. of VLDB (2004)
7. Elio, M.: A Framework for Outlier Mining in RFID data. In: Proc. of IDEAS (2007)
8. EPCGlobal, Inc. http://www.epcglobalinc.org/home
9. Gonzalez, H., Han, J., Li, X., Klabjan, D.: Warehousing and Analysing Massive RFID Data Sets. In: Proc. of ICDE (2006)
10. Hardy, G.H., Wright, E.M.: An Introduction to the Theory of Numbers (1979)
11. Hoag, J.E., Thompson, C.W.: Architecting rfid middleware. IEEE Internet Computing 10(5), 88–92 (2006)
12. Jeffery, S.R., et al.: A Pipelined Framework for Online Cleaning of Sensor Data Streams. In: Proc. of ICDE (2006)
13. Jeffery, S.R., Garofalakis, M.N., Franklin, M.J.: Adaptive Cleaning for RFID Data Streams. In: Proc. of VLDB, pp. 163–174 (2006)
14. Ke, Y., Cheng, J., Ng, W.: Correlated Pattern Mining in Quantitative Databases. ACM Transactions on Database Systems 33(3) (2008)
15. Lee, C.-H., Chung, C.-W.: Efficient Storage Scheme and Query Processing for Supply Chain Management using RFID. In: Proc. of SIGMOD (2008)
16. Ng, W., Deng, L., Lee, D.L.: Spying Out Real User Preferences in Web Searching. ACM Transactions on Internet Technology (2007)
17. Palmer, M.: Principles of Effective RFID data management. Enterprise System (March 2004)
18. Rao, J., Doraiswamy, S., Thakkar, H., Colby, L.S.: A Deferred Cleansing Method for RFID Data Analytics. In: Proc. of VLDB, pp. 175–186 (2006)
19. http://www.hk-rd.com/ Hong Kong RFID

20. `http://www.rflab.org` HKUST RFID Lab
21. `http://www.cse.ust.hk/News/RFIDAward2008` α-Gate Portal Award News
22. Sedgewick, R., Flajolet, P.: An Introduction to the Analysis of Algorithms
23. Wang, F., Liu, P.: Temporal Management of RFID Data. In: Proc. of VLDB, pp. 1128–1139 (2005)
24. Wang, F., Liu, S., Liu, P., Bai, Y.: Bridging physical and virtual worlds: Complex event processing for RFID data streams. In: Ioannidis, Y., Scholl, M.H., Schmidt, J.W., Matthes, F., Hatzopoulos, M., Böhm, K., Kemper, A., Grust, T., Böhm, C. (eds.) EDBT 2006. LNCS, vol. 3896, pp. 588–607. Springer, Heidelberg (2006)

Semi-automatic Conceptual Data Modeling Using Entity and Relationship Instance Repositories

Ornsiri Thonggoom, Il-Yeol Song, and Yuan An

The iSchool at Drexel University, Philadelphia, PA USA
{Ot62,songiy,yuan.an}@drexel.edu

Abstract. Data modelers frequently lack experience and have incomplete knowledge about the application being designed. To address this issue, we propose new types of reusable artifacts called Entity Instance Repository (EIR) and Relationship Instance Repository (RIR), which contain ER modeling patterns from prior designs and serve as knowledge-based repositories for conceptual modeling. We explore the development of automated data modeling tools with EIR and RIR. We also select six data modeling rules used for identification of entities in one of the tools. Two tools were developed in this study: Heuristic-Based Technique (HBT) and Entity Instance Pattern WordNet (EIPW). The goals of this study are (1) to find effective approaches that can improve the novice modelers' performance in developing conceptual models by integrating pattern-based technique and various modeling techniques, (2) to evaluate whether those selected six modeling rules are effective, and (3) to validate whether the proposed tools are effective in creating quality data models. In order to evaluate the effectiveness of the tools, empirical testing was conducted on tasks of different sizes. The empirical results indicate that novice designers' overall performance increased 30.9~46.0% when using EIPW, and increased 33.5~34.9 % when using HBT, compared with the cases with no tools.

Keywords: HBT, EIPW, entity instance repository, relationship instance repository, conceptual data modeling, reuse pattern, ER model.

1 Introduction

Conceptual data modeling is challenging because it requires good understanding of an application domain and an ability to translate requirements into a data model. Novice modelers frequently lack experience and have incomplete knowledge about the application domain being designed. Even expert designers could fail to obtain a quality conceptual model when they lack domain knowledge. Hence, data modelers at any level should benefit from reusing existing modeling knowledge during the modeling process. In addition, concepts that are not explicitly expressed in a requirement but are necessary for the domain are often very difficult to capture. Expertise in domain knowledge to identify entities and relationships hidden in the requirement is therefore also needed [1].

At present, a fully automated conceptual modeling approach seems impossible due to the inherent ambiguities in natural language (NL), context-dependent nature of

M. Jeusfeld, L. Delcambre, and T.W. Ling (Eds.): ER 2011, LNCS 6998, pp. 219–232, 2011.

modeling, and incompleteness of domain knowledge. When complete automation is not possible, it is still desirable to develop a semi-automatic process than an entirely manual modeling process. Therefore, many researchers have proposed knowledge-based systems (KBSs) and tools to support the modelers in developing conceptual models. One of the limitations of the proposed tools is that such tools do not solve the problems that novice modelers are inexperienced and have incomplete knowledge. In addition, they do not address the semantic mismatch issue [2], which represents the inability of novice modelers for translating the requirements literally into conceptual modeling structures.

Most conceptual designs are usually created from scratch, although a similar design might have previously been created. Reuse of existing resources and solutions has become a strategy for cost reduction and efficient improvement in the information system development process. Currently, building a library of reusable artifacts involves explication of human developer's knowledge, which is a major obstacle in facilitating reuse of knowledge [3]. One solution to reduce the efforts and time of human experts comes from extracting artifacts from prior designs. If this could be conducted for various application domains, then it would assist in creating the practically reusable libraries.

In this research, we explore development of automated data modeling tools that help novice modelers develop quality conceptual data models. We propose new types of reusable artifacts that contain knowledge about an application domain, called the entity instance repository (EIR) and the relationship instance repository (RIR), which are repositories of entity instance patterns (EIPs) and relationship instance patterns (RIPs), respectively. An EIP is a pattern of a single entity and its properties. An RIP is a binary relationship with cardinality constraints between two entities. The EIP and RIP can be automatically extracted from prior relational database schemas via reverse engineering. The EIR and RIR are useful for conceptual designs in the following aspects: (1) they contain knowledge about a domain; (2) automatic generation of EIR and RIR overcomes a major problem of inefficient manual approaches; and (3) they are domain-specific and therefore easy to understand and reuse.

Typically, a rule-based approach is a popular technique for conceptual modeling because it could lead modelers to use known heuristics. However, this approach does not provide an optimal solution to many complex requirements because most of the proposed heuristics/rules were built based on syntax of some specific NLs. These rules cannot overcome the inherent ambiguities of NLs. In this research, we test six data modeling rules that have been used in an introductory data modeling class for many years. We evaluate the usefulness of these rules by developing a tool named heuristic-based technique (HBT) that applies these rules to the identification of entities.

Two tools were developed in this study: HBT and EIPW (Entity Instance Pattern WordNet). The tasks of our tools are divided into two subtasks: the entity identification and the relationship identification. The entity identification processes of our tools are different, but the relationship identification processes in them are the same. The entity identification process of HBT incorporates the six domain independent modeling rules and entity categories adopted from Taxonomic Class Modeling (TCM) [1]. TCM identifies entities from three different sources: entities from noun phrases, entities derived from verb phrases, and entities that were not explicitly stated in the requirement (See Section 5 for more details). The entity identification process of EIPW incorporates EIR, hypernym chains in WordNet, and entity categories adopted from TCM. The relationship identification processes of both tools incorporate RIR. WordNet is also used to ensure that the synonyms of EIR's entities and RIR's entities are not missed out. The architectures of each tool are discussed in later sections.

The goals of this study are as follows: (1) to find effective approaches that can improve the novice modelers' performance in developing conceptual models by integrating pattern-based technique and various modeling techniques, (2) to evaluate whether those selected six modeling rules are effective, and (3) to validate whether the proposed tools are effective in creating quality data models.

The remainder of this paper is organized as follows. Section 2 reviews five techniques for developing conceptual models. Section 3 provides a methodology to create EIR and RIR. Section 4 presents our six selected modeling rules. Section 5 presents the architecture of HBT. Section 6 presents the architecture of EIPW. Section 7 discusses the results from empirical experiments. Finally, Section 8 concludes the paper and gives directions for future work.

2   Related Techniques for Conceptual Modeling

There are at least five categories of techniques used for automatically generating conceptual models from NL requirement specifications. They are rule-based, pattern-based, case-based, ontology-based, and multi-techniques-based.

2.1   Rule-Based

Chen [4] proposed eleven rules for translating English sentence structures into ER model's structure. Since then, many studies have tried to refine and extend on this approach. The trend in this technique orients towards the collaboration with huge linguistic dictionaries and common sense ontologies. The domain independence is the strength of this technique. However, the strength of this technique is also its weakness because tools or systems proposed have no domain knowledge incorporated in them. Most of tools proposed for developing conceptual models follow this technique [5].

2.2   Pattern-Based

Recently, analysis patterns [6] have been popular and used in conceptual designs. The advantage of reusable patterns aims not only to reuse schema components, but also to reuse relationships between objects, which is a difficult task for novice modelers. However, building a repository of patterns involves explication of human developers' knowledge, which is a major obstacle in facilitating reuse of knowledge [3]. Another limitation of using this technique is that most of the available patterns in this field are analysis patterns that require manually matching.

2.3   Case-Based

This technique involves storing the whole conceptual models of a large number of applications and providing a keyword mechanism that enables users to search for a conceptual model that is a candidate solution for a requirement [7]. It takes the advantage of reusing previous designs. The limitation in this technique is that if any adjustment is required in the conceptual model, it has to resort to the generic data modeling approach. Another disadvantage is that developing the conceptual model libraries and indexing mechanism are very expensive.

2.4 Ontology-Based

Ontologies have been considered as important components in many applications. Some generic and large scale ontologies such as WordNet, SUMO, and Cyc are available, but most applications require a specific domain ontology to describe concepts and relations in the domain [8]. Some researchers proposed the approaches with the development of conceptual models by refinement of large scale ontologies [9] [10]. However, currently there are no supporting tools or effective APIs to enhance the process. Most studies of ontology development and applications assume manual processes.

2.5 Multi-techniques-Based

From our survey, most tools or systems for conceptual design require users' involvement during the process. And no single technique work best all the times because each technique has some limitations. Ideally, various techniques should be integrated together for a design process. For example, Song et al. [1] proposed a TCM (taxonomic class modeling) methodology used for object-oriented analysis in business applications. This method integrated several class modeling techniques under one framework. Their framework integrates the noun analysis method, class categories, English structures, check lists, and rules for modeling. In our study, we adopted the noun analysis method, class categories and modeling rules from the TCM work.

3   A Methodology for Creating EIR and RIR

This section presents our automatic methodology for creating the Entity Instance Repository (EIR) and the Relationship Instance Repository (RIR), which are the repositories of Entity Instance Patterns (EIPs) and Relationship Instance Patterns (RIPs), respectively. EIR and RIR contain ER modeling patterns from prior designs and serve as knowledge-based repositories for conceptual modeling. An EIP is a pattern of a single entity and its properties. An RIP is a binary relationship with cardinality constraints between two entities. An example of an EIP and an RIP is shown in Figure 1. We propose a method based on database reverse engineering concepts that are inspired by Chiang et al. [11] to automatically extract EIPs and RIPs from relational schemas. In this paper, we use the UML class diagram notation for representing ER models. This methodology employs three assumptions for the characteristics of input schemas for database reverse engineering process:

1) Relational schemas: An input is a DDL (Data Definition Language) schema of an application domain.

2) 3NF relations: There are no non-3NF relations in the input relational schemas. It would simplify the extraction process.

3) Proper primary keys (PK) and foreign keys (FK): Proper PKs and FKs are specified in input DDL schemas.

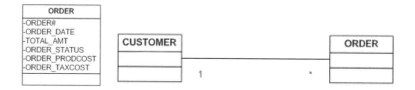

Fig. 1. An example of an EIP and an RIP, respectively

The method for creating EIR and RIR consists of the following three main steps:

INPUT: DDL schemas
OUTPUT: EIR and RIR

(1) Obtaining Information about the Executable Schemas (DDL Schemas)

In order to reverse engineer existing database schemas, the information about the executable schemas must be available. In our study, we use the library of DDL schemas created by Silverston [12] containing 464 relations and 1859 attributes as our first input. Later the lists of EIR and RIR were extended by case studies.

(2) Extracting EIP's Elements

We extracted the EIP's elements from input DDL schemas by storing a relation name as an entity_name and an attribute as an attribute_name in EIR. The metadata model of EIP and RIP is shown in Figure 2.

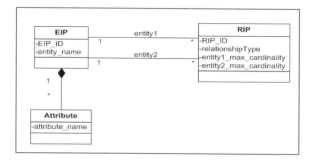

Fig. 2. The metadata model of an EIP and an RIP

(3) Extracting RIP's Elements

We extracted the RIP's elements by identifying relationships between extracted entities from Step (2) above. Most of the ER (Entity-Relationship) methods used in textbooks or CASE tools can be classified as either binary models or n-ary models [13]. In this research, we only specify the maximum cardinality constraints for binary models. Because of the limited semantic expressiveness of DDL schemas, the minimum cardinality cannot be automatically identified. Using a fully automated process, we can identify five binary relationship types:

    3.1 1:N for relationships identified by FK
    3.2 1:N for relationships identified by partial keys
    3.3 N:M for relationships identified by relationship relations
    3.4 Is-a relationships
    3.5 Recursive relationships

Subsequently, these binary relationships are stored in an RIR. The reverse engineering rules used in this step are created by inverting the schema transformation rules based on the EER (Extended Entity-Relationship) approach [14]. The definitions of these transformation rules are described in [15].

4   The Six Domain Independent Modeling Rules

This section presents our selected six modeling rules termed as the six domain independent modeling rules. Our survey shows that one of the difficulties in creating conceptual models is the scattered modeling rules. There is no complete set of rules that help developing conceptual models. In general, rules/heuristics are useful but sometimes they may lead to cognitive errors called bias [2] [16]. Also, there is always trade off in design so that not all rules can work together because some rules are conflicting. We have selected the six domain independent modeling rules based on teaching experiences of over 20 years by one of the authors of this paper. These six rules are considered a minimal set of rules to teach novice designers in identifying entities. These six rules are not based on the syntax of any NLs and thus are domain independent. This means that these rules can be applied to a wide range of applications and domains. In this research, we would like to experiment whether the six rules are indeed useful. The six domain independent modeling rules are:

R1: The ID (Identifier) Rule
IF a concept (noun or verb) needs to have a unique identifier, THEN it is an entity.
R2: The MA (Multiple Attribute) Rule
IF a concept has multiple attributes, THEN it is an entity.
R3: The MVA (Multi-Valued Attribute) Rule
IF a concept has multi-values, THEN it is an entity.
R4: The TDA (Time-dependent attributes) Rule
IF a concept has time-dependent attributes or needs to keep track of history of values, THEN it is an entity.
R5: The SC (Single Concept) Rule
A good entity should represent one and only one concept.
R6: The DI (Domain Importance) Rule
IF a concept is important in its own right within the problem domain whether it has one or multiple attributes, THEN it is an entity.

5   Overview of HBT Architecture

The modules and data flow of HBT are shown in Figure 3. A prototype of HBT was developed by using JAVA applet. First, the system takes a NL requirement specification as an input to a preprocessing module. The main functionality of the preprocessing module is to do the part of speech tagging (POS) in order to list all of the possible candidate entities. We use a well-known open source called LingPipe (http://alias-i.com/lingpipe) to perform POS. In HBT, the entity list can be identified based on noun phrases, verb phrases, and hidden requirements. During the post-parsing analysis, a noun phrase and verb phrase belonging to any of a *discard noun set* and a *discard verb set*, respectively, will be excluded as a candidate entity. The discard noun set and the discard verb set are created based on the history of words discarded by designers and the class elimination rules [1] . The discard noun set and the discard verb set are domain independent.

In the entity identification module, there are three activities performed:

(1) The first activity is to identify the entity list based on noun phrases by using the six domain independent modeling rules, which are the ID, MA, MVA, TDA, SC, and DI rules.

(2) The second activity is to identify the entity list based on verb phrases by using two rules out of six domain independent modeling rules, which are the ID and MA rules.

(3) The third activity is to identify the hidden entities that are not explicitly stated in the requirements but are necessary for the conceptual modeling by applying entity categories. Entity categories are domain knowledge and used as a tip for identifying candidate entities. Our entity categories in business domain are adopted from the class categories developed by Song et al. [1].

After, getting the entity list from Entity Identification Module, relationships between entities are generated by considering the application domain semantics inherent in the RIR. The relationship modeling rules [1] are used to ensure that all of the relationships are identified. WordNet is also used to ensure that the synonyms of RIR's entities are not missed out while preparing a list of the relationships. The lists of EIR and RIR are extended by case studies. Figure 4 shows one of the user interfaces of HBT.

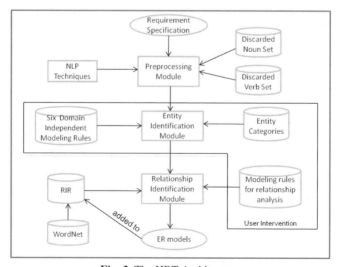

Fig. 3. The HBT Architecture

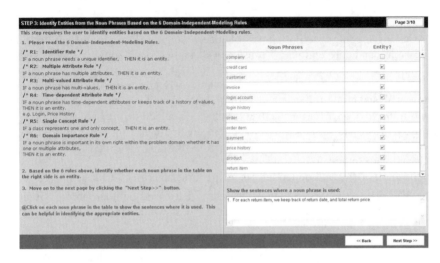

Fig. 4. An example of user interface in HBT

6 Overview of EIPW Architecture

The system modules and data flow of EIPW are shown in Figure 5. A prototype of EIPW was developed by using JAVA Applet. Most of the modules' functions in EIPW are very similar to those in HBT. The only difference is in the entity identification module. In this module, there are three activities performed:

(1) The first activity is to identify the entity list based on EIR. WordNet is also used to ensure that the synonyms of EIR's entities are not missed out while preparing the lists of entities.

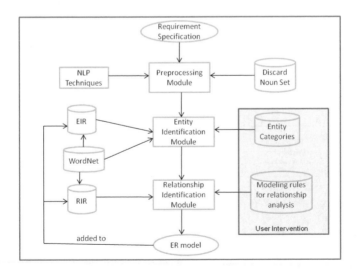

Fig. 5. The EIPW Architecture

(2) The second activity is to identify the entities that are not detected by EIR by applying the top noun categories and hypernym chains in WordNet [5].

(3) The third activity is to identify the hidden entities by applying entity categories.

The user interfaces of EIPW are also similar to those in the HBT as shown in Figure 6. The more details of the EIPW's workflow is presented in [15].

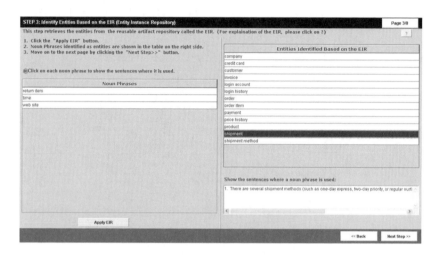

Fig. 6. An example of user interface in EIPW

7 Empirical Evaluation

In this section, we evaluated the quality of the output generated by our proposed tools by using the ANOVA technique. Since the quality of the conceptual models is of interest, the following hypotheses are tested:

H1: Novice Modelers using EIPW will create conceptual models with better quality compared to the models generated by novice designers without using any tools.
H2: Novice Modelers using HBT will create conceptual models with better quality compared to the models generated by novice designers without using any tools.
H3: There is no significant difference between the two tools regarding the quality of the conceptual models.

7.1 Experimental Design

The experimental framework is shown in Figure 7. The two independent variables are the systems and the task sizes. In conceptual modeling, a linear increase in the number of entities can result in a combinatorial increase in the number of possible relationships [2]. As the task size increases, so do the numbers of decisions required in the modeling process. Therefore, our experimental design incorporates two levels of the task size to provide some sensitivity for this factor. The medium task size has 9 entities and 9 relationships, while the moderate task size has 14 entities and 14 relationships. The dependent variable is the quality scores of the ERD. The accuracy of an ER model is evaluated by a scoring schema, which we adopted from Du [5]. It focuses on the correct identification of appropriate entities and relationships based on the given problem statements. The conceptual models created by the subjects are judged by third parties (not the authors of this paper). To take into account differences in task size, the quality scores obtained for each design are normalized in percentage [18].

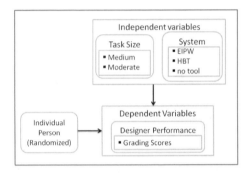

Fig. 7. The framework of experiments

7.1.1 Subjects and Tasks

There were 41 subjects. All of the subjects were students in the iSchool at Drexel University and did not work in conceptual modeling field before. Therefore, we concluded that all of our subjects were novice modelers. Twenty-one were undergraduates and twenty were graduate students. Forty-one subjects were divided into four groups as shown in Table 1. Each subject worked on four problem statements [17]: one medium size and one moderate size problem statements with the aid of our tool, and one medium size and one moderate size problem statements with no tool. The problem statements are in the e-commerce domain. The subjects could take time as long as they wanted to create conceptual models based on the given problem statements.

Table 1. The Experimental Design

Group	Num of subject	Problem1	Problem2	Problem3	Problem4
1	11	No tool	No tool	Using EIPW	Using EIPW
2	10	Using EIPW	Using EIPW	No tool	No tool
3	10	No tool	No tool	Using HBT	Using HBT
4	10	Using HBT	Using HBT	No tool	No tool

Test of Hypothesis 1: EIPW

A *2x2 within-subjects analysis of variance* was performed on quality scores as a function of EIPW (with, no tool) and task size (medium, moderate) as shown in Table 2.

Table 2. An ANOVA analysis of modeling quality

	QUALITY SCORE
System (EIPW, no tool)	$F(1,20) = 97.512$, $p < 0.000$
Task Size (medium, moderate)	$F(1,20) = 2.776$, $p < 0.111$
System x Task Size	$F(1,20) = 1.085$, $p < 0.310$

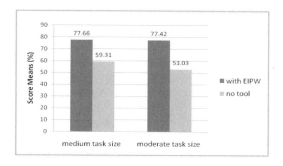

Fig. 8. The plot of the mean quality scores (%)

From the calculated means shown in Figure 8, the conceptual models created by EIPW are better than those created by *no tool cases* for both task sizes. In Table 2, the results show that the main effect of **system** (with EIPW, no tool) is significant ($p < 0.00$). Therefore, this result supports our hypothesis (H1) that the EIPW helps novice designers create better conceptual models than they do without it. There is no significant main effect for **task size** ($p < 0.111$). It shows that the effect of **System x Task Size** is not significant ($p < 0.310$), which means there is no interaction between the system and the task size. We conclude that EIPW improves the novices' performance by 30.9% for the medium task size and 46.0% for the moderate task size.

Test of Hypothesis 2: HBT

A *2x2 within-subjects analysis of variance* was performed on quality scores as a function of HBT (with, no tool) and task size (medium, moderate) as shown in Table 3.

Table 3. An ANOVA analysis of modeling quality

	QUALITY SCORE
System (HBT, no tool)	$F(1,19) = 25.69$, $p < 0.000$
Task Size (medium, moderate)	$F(1,19) = 6.925$, $p < 0.016$
System x Task Size	$F(1,19) = 0.132$, $p < 0.720$

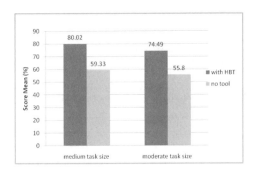

Fig. 9. The plot of the mean quality scores (%)

From the calculated means shown in Figure 9, the conceptual models created by the HBT are better than those created by *no tool cases* for both task sizes. In Table 3, the results show that the main effect of **system** (with HBT, no tool) is significant (p < 0.00). Therefore, this results support our hypothesis (H2) that the HBT helps novice modelers create better conceptual models than they do without it. There is significant main effect for **task size** (p < 0.016). However, it shows that the effect of **System x Task Size** is not significant (p < 0.720), which means there is no interaction between the system and the task size. We conclude that HBT improves the novices' performance by 34.9% for the medium task size and 33.5% for the moderate task size.

Test of Hypothesis 3: EIPW and HBT

A *2x2 mixed model design with system as between-subject and task size as within-subject factors* was used. The two independent variables are **system** (with EIPW, with HBT) and the **task size** (medium, moderate). The dependent variable is the **quality score**. Since the aspects of within-subject factor are not used for analyzing this hypothesis, only the test of between-subject analysis is shown in Table 4.

Table 4. Tests of between-subjects effects with dependent variable QUALITY SCORE

	QUALITY SCORE
System (EIPW, HBT)	F(1,39) = 0.004, p < 0.948

In Table 4, the main effect of system is not significant (p < 0.948). So, this result supports our hypothesis (H3) that there is no significant difference between the two tools regarding the quality of the conceptual models. However, the mean scores of EIPW and HBT suggest that EIPW is better than HBT when the task size is moderate. On the other hand, HBT is slightly better than EIPW when the task size is smaller. This results show that the six domain independent modeling rules are effective in the medium to moderate task sizes.

8   Conclusions and Future Research

In this paper, we have proposed methods for improving the process of automatically developing conceptual data models. We have implemented two knowledge-based data modeling tools: HBT and EIPW. They use different techniques for entity identification, but use the same techniques for relationship identification. HBT uses noun phrases, verb phrases, identification of entities from hidden requirements using entity categories, and the six domain independent modeling rules. EIPW uses noun phrases, an entity instance repository (EIR), entity categories, and WordNet. Relationship identification uses a relationship instance repository (RIR), and WordNet. This study is an initial step to show how domain knowledge stored in the form of instance patterns can be used together with other modeling techniques.

The empirical results indicate that novice modelers' performance increased by 30.9~46% when using EIPW, while the performance increased by 33.5~34.9 % when using HBT, compared with the cases of no tools. The EIPW with EIR and RIR clearly helps the novice modelers in creating better quality conceptual models. These results also imply that the use of EIR and RIR in EIPW is effective by providing us with a library of reusable patterns and by automating the process of finding the most appropriate one for certain situation. In addition, the results of HBT experiments show that the six domain independent rules in HBT are effective in identifying entities. They also minimize the cognitive load on the novices. This study shows that the six domain independent rules can be taught in a beginning database modeling class, and HBT can serve as a learning tool. It provides a smooth head-start to novices. In addition, RIR used in relationship identification process in both tools can ease the identification of relationships.

The study has, so far, been carried out on one domain only, but it provides a theoretical background for research on other domains as well. For future work, we want to test the usability of the tools for different domains and subjects. We plan to make our tools interface module to import the output schema into an ER diagram or a class diagram in commercial graphical CASE tools.

References

1. Song, I.-Y., Yano, K., Trujillo, J., Lujan-Mora, S.: A Taxonomic Class Modeling Methodology for Object-Oriented Analysis. In: Krostige, T.H.J., Siau, K. (eds.) Information Modeling Methods and Methodologies. Advanced Topics in Databases Series, pp. 216–240. Idea Group Publishing, USA (2004)
2. Batra, D.: Cognitive complexity in data modeling: causes and recommendations. Requir. Eng. 12(4), 231–244 (2007)
3. Han, T., Purao, S., Storey, V.: Generating large-scale repositories of reusable artifacts for conceptual design of information systems. Decision Support Systems 45, 665–680 (2008)
4. Chen, P.: English Sentence Structure and Entity-Relationship Diagram. Information Sciences 1(1), 127–149 (1983)
5. Du, S.: On the Use of Natural Language Processing for Automated Conceptual Data Modeling. Ph.D Dissertation, University of Pittsburgh (2008)

6. Purao, S., Storey, V., Han, T.: Improving Analysis Pattern Reuse in Conceptual Design: Augmenting Automated Processes with Supervised Learning. Information Systems Research 14(3), 269–290 (2003)

7. Choobineh, J., Lo, A.: CABSYDD: Case-Based System for Database Design. Journal of Management Information Systems 21(3), 242–253 (2004)

8. Sugumaran, V., Storey, V.: The role of domain ontologies in database design: An ontology management and conceptual modeling environment. ACM Trans. Database System 31(3), 1064–1094 (2006)

9. Conesa, J., Olivé, A.: A method for pruning ontologies in the development of conceptual schemas of information systems. Journal of Data Semantics 5, 64–90 (2006)

10. Conesa, J., Storey, V., Sugumaran, V.: Usability of Upper level ontologies: The case of ResearchSyc. Data & Knowledge Engineering 69(4) (2010)

11. Chiang, R., Barron, T., Storey, V.: Reverse engineering of relational databases: Extraction of an EER model from a relational database. Data & Knowledge Engineering 12, 107–142 (1994)

12. Silverston, L.: The Data Model Resource Book, 1st edn., vol. 2. John Willey & Sons Inc., Chichester (2001)

13. Song, I.-Y., Evans, M., Park, E.: A Comparative Analysis of Entity-Relationship Diagrams. Journal of Computer and Software Engineering 3(4), 427–459 (1995)

14. Elmasri, R., Nevathe, S.: Fundamentals of Database Systems. The Benjamin/Cummings Publishing Co., Inc., Redwood City, CA (2004)

15. Thonggoom, O., Song, I.-Y., An, Y.: EIPW: A Knowledge-based Database Modeling Tool. In: Advanced Information Systems Engineering Workshop on Conceptualization of Modeling Methods (CMM 2011), London, UK, pp. 119–133 (2011)

16. Parson, J., Saunders, C.: Cognitive heuristics in software engineering: applying and extending anchoring and adjustment to artifact reuse. IEEE Trans. Software Engineering 30(12), 873–888 (2004)

17. Coronel, C., Morris, S., Rob, P.: Database Systems: Design, Implementation and Management: Course Technology (2009)

18. Cohen, J., Cohen, P.: Applied Multiple Regression/Correlation Analysis for the Behavior Science. Lawrence Erlbaum Associates, NJ (1983)

Impact of MDE Approaches on the Maintainability of Web Applications: An Experimental Evaluation*

Yulkeidi Martínez[1], Cristina Cachero[2], Maristella Matera[3], Silvia Abrahao[4], and Sergio Luján[2]

[1] Universidad Máximo Gómez Báez de Ciego de Ávila, Cuba
[2] Universidad de Alicante, Spain
[3] Politecnico di Milano, Italy
[4] Universidad Politécnica de Valencia, Spain

Abstract. Model-driven Engineering (MDE) approaches are often recognized as a solution to palliate the complexity of software maintainability tasks. However, there is no empirical evidence of their benefits and limitations with respect to code-based maintainability practices. To fill this gap, this paper illustrates the results of an empirical study, involving 44 subjects, in which we compared an MDE methodology, WebML, and a code-based methodology, based on PHP, with respect to the performance and satisfaction of junior software developers while executing *analysability*, *corrective* and *perfective maintainability* tasks on Web applications. Results show that the involved subjects performed better with WebML than with PHP, although they showed a slight preference towards tackling maintainability tasks directly on the source code. Our study also aims at providing a replicable laboratory package that can be used to assess the maintainability of different development methods.

1 Introduction

It is well known that maintenance is the most expensive phase in the software life cycle, absorbing between 45% and 60% [1] of total management costs. This situation has led many researchers to focus on maintainability from different perspectives. On the one hand, *unstructured maintenance* postulates wading straight into the code of the target application in order to make the necessary changes, normally with the aid of specialized tools. Sometimes this process relies on -automatic- maintainability measures that operate over the code of the target application [2]. On the other hand, *structured maintenance* examines and modifies the design, and then -either manually or automatically- reworks the code to match it. Many authors claim that structured maintenance is a more reliable and efficient process than unstructured maintenance [3].

---

* The authors wish to thank the students who kindly agreed to participate in this empirical study.

M. Jeusfeld, L. Delcambre, and T.W. Ling (Eds.): ER 2011, LNCS 6998, pp. 233–246, 2011.

The Model Driven Engineering (MDE) paradigm goes one step further in the lane of structured maintenance, and advocates the use of models and model transformations to speed up and simplify the maintenance process. The MDE community claims several advantages over code-based maintenance processes, such as short and long term productivity gains, improved project communication and defect and rework reduction [4,5]. Unfortunately, despite all these claims and the fact that MDE practices are maturing by the day, practitioners still lack a body of practical evidence that soundly backs the purported maintainability gains due to the use of this paradigm [5,6]. As Glass says, "We (practitioners) need your help. We need some better advice on how and when to use methodologies" [7]. Such evidence can be provided in the shape of empirical studies - such as surveys, experiments, case studies or postmortem analysis studies - that directly measure the effect of the chosen paradigm on the developer performance and satisfaction [8]. Many authors have written about the importance of providing empirical evidence in Software Engineering (SE) [9,10]. Unfortunately, the percentage of empirical studies on maintainability in MDE approaches is still very low, contrasting with other disciplines and even other areas of SE [11]. This paper tries to fill this gap, and presents the results of a quasi-experiment in which two groups of junior developers performed a set of maintainability tasks on two Web applications.

The paper is structured as follows: Section 2 presents the rationale behind the selection of WebML and PHP as typical examples of the two current paradigms (model-driven and code-based) in Web applications development, as well as the definition of maintainability that we are using all along the paper, and how it has been assessed in the past in MDE methodologies. This background sets the context for the definition of hypotheses and variables in Section 3, together with the experimental design (subjects, instrumentation, operation and data collection mechanisms). Section 4 presents the data analysis and an interpretation of results that takes into account the identified threats to validity. Last, Section 5 concludes the paper and presents some further lines of research.

2   Background

The last years have witnessed a continuous evolution in the scenario of Web application development. A number of technologies have been proposed, fostering the adoption of server-side and client-side languages for the Web. Within this plethora of proposals, some technologies have been largely adopted by practitioners. Server-side scripting is one such technology, through which the generation of HTML markup is achieved by means of languages like JSP, PHP, and ASP.NET. Among them, numbers point at PHP as the most popular server-side scripting language today [12]. Given such diffusion, in our experiment we have chosen it as representative of the programming languages for the Web.

In parallel to the technology innovation line, the Web Engineering community has devoted several efforts to the definition of MDE approaches [13], strongly characterized by the adoption of *conceptual models*. Such approaches offer high-level abstractions, capturing the most salient characteristics of Web applications, which can be used for the definition of application models abstracting from implementation details. MDE also stresses the importance of model transformations, leading to the automatic generation of the application code starting from the high-level conceptual models. One of the arguments most commonly brought forward in favor of MDE approaches is the "ease of maintenance". The commonly accepted (but scarcely proved) claim is that the adoption of model-driven design techniques in the development of a Web application implicitly enhances maintainability: requests for changes can be turned into changes at the conceptual level and then propagated systematically down to the implementation code.

Among the MDE Web development methodologies so far proposed, WebML (Web Modelling Language) [14] outstands, due to its broad adoption both in academia and industry. WebML is a visual language and development method for specifying the content structure of a Web application and the organization and presentation of contents in the form of hypertext. The main contribution of WebML is the proposal of a mix of concepts, notations, and techniques for the construction of data-intensive Web applications, which blends traditional ingredients well known to developers, such as conceptual data design with the Entity-Relationship model, with new concepts and methods for the design of hypertext, which are central to Web development. Therefore, the value of WebML lies not in the individual ingredients, but in the definition of a systematic framework, also equipped with a CASE tool[1] offering support for all the design activities and for the automatic code generation.

2.1   The Maintainability Concept

Although many definitions for maintainability exist, perhaps the most commonly used is the one provided by the ISO [15], that is, "the capability of the software product to be modified". Maintainability can be assessed through measures associated to the following sub-characteristics:

- *Analysability*: Capability of the software product to be diagnosed for deficiencies or causes of failure in the software, or for the parts to be modified to be identified.
- *Changeability*: Capability of the software product to enable the application of a specified modification.
- *Stability*: Capability of the software product to avoid unexpected effects from modifications of the software.
- *Testability*: Capability of the software product to enable modified software to be validated.
- *Compliance*: Capability of the software product to meet the standards or conventions relating to maintainability.

In MDE environments not all these sub-characteristics are equally important, though. Provided that the chosen MDE approach is mature enough (such as

---

[1] WebRatio - http://www.webratio.com

is the case of WebML), we can safely assume testability and compliance: in an automated code generation environment these issues are taken good care of during the code generation process. Therefore, in this paper, we have centered on the first three sub-characteristics: analysability, changeability and stability.

In relation to the changes that can take place during the life cycle of a system, some authors also distinguish among four different modification types [16]:

- *Corrections*: Corrective maintainability refers to the capability to detect errors, diagnose the problems and fix them.
- *Improvements*: Perfective maintainability refers to the capability to extend the software according to new requirements or enhancements.
- *Adaptations*: Adaptive maintainability refers to the capability to modify the software in order to cope with the effects of environmental changes.
- *Preventions*: Preventive maintainability refers to the software capability to support internal reengineering processes without adverse impact.

Some authors use a more coarse classification, and merely distinguish between *corrective tasks* (corrections) and *evolution tasks* (which encompass improvements, adaptations and preventions).

Based on these two characterizations of maintainability, our experiment includes three types of tasks: *analysability tasks*, which cover the analysability subcharacteristic, and *corrective* and *perfective tasks*, which cover the two most common changeability types. These tasks have been assessed both objectively and subjectively. The perceived stability of changes has also been measured.

2.2 Maintainability Assessment

The empirical assessment of maintainability activities in MDE methodologies has been gaining momentum during the last years. This claim is supported by a systematic mapping [17] that gathers the empirical evidence on software productivity and quality gains due to the use of MDE approaches during the period from 2001 to 2010 [18]. In this study, out of the 300 publications related to the impact of the MDE paradigm on the product quality and process productivity, only 9 (that is, barely a 3%) focused on maintainability. One of the conclusions of this systematic mapping is that the bulk of the work on model-driven maintainability lies in the definition of prediction models of the actual maintainability of the applications that are derived from the conceptual artifacts. However, there is little evidence on the impact of model-driven development methodologies on the performance and satisfaction of maintainability tasks. According to our systematic mapping, out of the 9 maintainability papers, only [19] tackled this issue, and concluded that the time to evaluate the impact of a change to the software was significantly shorter (around 37% shorter) in MDE than in code-based development environments[2].

---

[2] Due to space constraints, for a more detailed discussion about the results of the systematic mapping, readers are referred to [18].

3   Description of the Experiment

Following the GQM template [20], our empirical study is aimed at *analyzing* WebML and PHP *for the purpose of* evaluating model-driven against code-based maintenance practices *with respect to* their performance and satisfaction *from the point of view of* young developers and prospective adopters. The context of the study is two advanced SE courses at the University of Alicante and the Politecnico di Milano, where both a code-based Web development process, based on the PHP language, and a model-driven Web development process, based on the WebML methodology, are taught.

The design of the experiment was based on the framework for experimentation in SE suggested by [8]. The study was conducted as a laboratory blocked subject-object quasi-experiment. The broad research questions addressed are:

- **RQ1:** Is the maintainability performance (actual efficiency and actual effectiveness) of the WebML methodology higher than the actual maintainability performance of a traditional, code-based, methodology using PHP?
- **RQ2:** Is the maintainability satisfaction (perceived ease of use and perceived usefulness) of the WebML methodology higher than the maintainability satisfaction of a traditional, code-based methodology using PHP?

These research questions are further explained and decomposed into research hypotheses next.

3.1   Variables and Operational Hypotheses

The independent variable of our study is the methodology used to perform the maintainability tasks: model-driven (WebML methodology) or code-based (tasks performed directly over PHP code). Hence, the experiment defines two treatments: maintainability tasks over WebML models and maintainability tasks over PHP code. The collected experimental data allow comparing the effects of both treatments.

The theoretical model underlying the definition of dependent variables and the formulation of hypotheses of our experiment is presented in Fig. 1 [21]. According to this model, the actual performance of the developers influences their satisfaction, and this in turn contributes to their intention to use the method and, eventually, to its actual usage. The actual performance is made up of two subcomponents: the *actual effectiveness*, which in our experiment is measured through the precision and recall while performing tasks with the methodology, and the *actual efficiency*, which is measured through the time that it takes to fulfill the maintainability tasks. On the other hand, the satisfaction is also made up of two subcomponents: the *perceived ease of use*, which in our experiment is measured through a global satisfaction scale, and the *perceived usefulness*, which is measured through the perceived subjective complexity, certainty and stability experienced by subjects while using the methodology to perform the maintainability tasks. All these measures are further explained below.

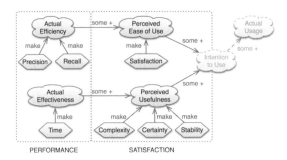

Fig. 1. Theoretical model components and their associated experimental variables (adapted from [21])

It results that in our experiment there are two types of dependent variables for comparing the treatments: *performance-based* (precision, recall and time) and *satisfaction-related* (complexity, certainty and, in the case of corrective and perfective tasks, perceived stability).

Maintainability tasks involve a set of actions on models or code. Some of these actions may be correct while others may be wrong, not contributing to the maintenance problem at hand. Still, the subject may miss some actions that would be needed to completely solve the task. For this reason, inside the group of performance-based variables, we have distinguished between *maintainability precision* (MP) and *maintainability recall* (MR). Precision is defined as the percentage of actions correctly identified by the subjects with respect to the total number of actions reported, while recall refers to the ratio between the percentage of correct actions performed by the subject and the total number of actions needed to completely solve the task. The third performance variable is *maintainability time* (MT), which is the time (in seconds) that it takes a subject to complete each maintainability task.

As perception variables, we have used the *maintainability perceived complexity* (MPCx), the *maintainability perceived certainty* (MPCt), the *maintainability perceived stability* (MPSt) and a *maintainability* (global) *satisfaction* scale (MS). Also, we have defined a global *perceived learnability* (PL).

The hypotheses tested in the experiment, which have been defined based on the existing empirical evidence found during the systematic mapping presented in Section 2, and which cover the performance and satisfaction components of the theoretical model presented in Fig. 1, are:

- **HAA** (Actual Analysability): Analyzing maintainability issues over WebML models allows for a better actual performance than analyzing them over PHP code.
- **HACC** (Actual Corrective Changeability): Correcting errors over WebML models allows for a better actual performance than correcting them over PHP code.
- **HAPC** (Actual Perfective Changeability): Improving a Web application over WebML models allows for a better actual performance than improving it over PHP code.

- **HPA** (Perceived Analysability): Subjects feel that finding errors over WebML models is less complex; they also feel more certain about the results.
- **HPCC** (Perceived Corrective Changeability): Subjects feel that correcting errors over WebML models is less complex and more stable than doing so over PHP code; they also feel more certain about the results.
- **HPPC** (Perceived Perfective Changeability): Subjects feel that introducing improvements over WebML models is less complex and more stable than doing so over PHP code; they also feel more certain about the results.
- **HS** (Satisfaction): Generally speaking, subjects feel more satisfied when performing maintainability tasks with WebML than with PHP.
- **HP** (Learnability): Generally speaking, subjects believe that PHP is easier to learn than WebML.

3.2   Subjects

The experimental subjects of our study were two groups of Computer Science students. The first group included twelve students enrolled in the "Internet Programming" course in Alicante. The second group included thirty-two students enrolled in the "Web Technologies" course in Milano, Italy. All the students aged between 22 and 24 years, and they all had a similar background. The subjects were chosen for convenience, i.e., they were students enrolled in the corresponding courses during the second term of the year 2009-2010. The necessary preparation for the experiment and the experimental tasks themselves fitted well into the scope of the courses, as one of the course objectives was to teach students how to maintain applications in PHP and WebML respectively.

3.3   Design and Instrumentation

The geographical dissemination of students made necessary to design the experiment as a between-subject experiment. Subjects in Milano used the WebML approach to perform the maintainability tasks and subjects in Alicante used PHP to perform the same maintainability tasks over the same applications. For both parts of the experiment we used two different sample applications to test the hypotheses: (1) a Concert application (adaptation of an example used in [22]) and (2) a Bookstore application (used in [23]). Subjects inside each group were randomly assigned to either of these applications. To make the results obtained in Alicante (with PHP) and in Milano (with WebML) comparable, the PHP and the WebML experiment instruments were designed to be as similar as possible in terms of both the layout of the information and the information content. Also, the applications were chosen to be of similar complexity, which was controlled by assuring that both applications had a similar number of lines of code in PHP and, at the same time, a similar number of conceptual constructs in WebML.

The instrumentation of the experiment consisted of:

- WebML Booklet (Instrument 1): for each application, a domain model (ER diagram) and corresponding WebML hypertext schema, describing the Web interface.

– PHP Booklet (Instrument 2): for each application, a domain model (Class diagram), an application storyboard (to understand the file structure of the application) and the PHP source files of the application.

These instruments are included in the replication package available at `http://www.dlsi.ua.es/~ccachero/labPackages/er2011/labPackage.rar`. Prior to the experiment, all the instruments were tested in two pilot studies, one in Alicante and one in Milano, and the obtained feedback was used to improve the understandability of the experimental materials. We also want to stress that the PHP applications exactly corresponded with the applications generated from the hypertext schemas in WebML. Therefore, the results obtained with both procedures can be compared, as both groups received the same applications, albeit in different formats.

The experiment had the following structure:

1. Subject instruction sheet.
2. Pre-experiment questionnaire: it included demographic questions as well as questions about subjects' previous experience with Web application development, Web programming and application modelling.
3. Experimental tasks: For each treatment, two modalities (A and B), each one featuring a different application. Each modality included an analysability, a corrective changeability and a perfective changeability task. Each task was accompanied by a post-task questionnaire which assessed the perceived usefulness of the methodology (see Fig.1) while performing the task (user-satisfaction with the results achieved) through three measures (complexity, certainty and stability), each measured on a 5-point Likert scale. The tasks were exactly the same across treatments (that is, Modality A of the WebML treatment was exactly the same as Modality A of the PHP treatment, except for the treatment).
4. Post-experiment questionnaire: it included a semantic-differential scale that required developers to judge the application on 11 pairs of adjectives describing satisfaction with the development methodology. This scale assessed the perceived ease of use of the methodology (see Fig.1), and showed a high degree of reliability ($\alpha = .861$). Based on this scale, the ease of use index was computed averaging scorings for the items. The post-experiment questionnaire also included an item gathering the subjects' impression on the learnability of the treatment they had applied to perform the tasks.

3.4   Operation and Data Collection Procedures

In both groups, all the subjects performed the experiment during the last session of the course. In this way we controlled that they had received the same amount of training on the treatment they were going to apply. We are conscious that 30 hours of course (many of which are devoted to theoretical issues, not directly related with the treatment) is not enough to master a development process, although it was equal for both groups. Also, most of the students assigned to the PHP treatment in Alicante had worked with PHP before the training course, which was not the case with WebML students in Milano. Therefore, our group of Milano students approaches a sample of novice software modelers, while the group of Alicante students approaches a sample of intermediate programmers. This is an internal threat to the validity to the study that has conditioned our interpretation of the results, as we will see in Section 4.

The operation phase for each group of the experiment was defined as follows. First, the students filled in the pretest questionnaire. They chose a nickname that was used for the remaining parts of the experiment, so that they were sure that the results were not going to be used to grade them in any way. Then, half of the students received the Modality A, where the presented application was the concert application, and half of them received the Modality B, where the presented application was the bookstore application. In both modalities the user had to perform a set of analysability, corrective and perfective changeability tasks. Also, they had to subjectively rate the complexity of each task, as well as their perceived certainty and stability of their solution. Last, they received a post-test questionnaire, where they expressed their satisfaction with the treatment and their general perception of the methodology learnability (based on the training sessions).

To maintain the comparability of the data collected during the experiment, no feedback was given to the subjects on their performance with the tasks. We also controlled that no interaction whatsoever between participants occurred. The experiment had a time limit (2 hours). Although the time needed to complete the experiment was checked with the pilot tests, we are conscious that this time limitation may introduce a ceiling effect that we have also taken into account when interpreting the results.

The performance-based variables were collected using data collection forms. These forms recorded the errors found (for analysability tasks) and the corrective and perfective actions needed (for corrective and perfective changeability). Also, forms included the time spent on each task (controlled by the experiment instructor) and the subjective opinion of the students, both regarding each task and regarding the global methodology.

4   Data Analysis and Interpretation of Results

Due to space constraints, the tables containing the descriptive statistics for the set of measures taken for the different maintainability task types (analysability, corrective changeability and perfective changeability) are available at `http://www.dlsi.ua.es/~ccachero/labPackages/er2011/descrStats.pdf`. In the remainder of the paper particular values from these tables are commented when necessary.

4.1   RQ1: Actual Efficacy of Treatments

For the sake of the reliability of the statistical analysis results, and due to the relatively low number of subjects on the PHP group, we chose to apply the

242   Y. Martínez et al.

Mann-Whitney U non parametric test, which makes no assumptions about normality of distributions. All the analyses were performed with the PASW Statistics application, v18[3]. It is important to note that not all the tasks were filled in by all the subjects, which is the reason why the different hypotheses testing procedures may present different degrees of freedom.

We first tested the HAA hypothesis, which is related to the precision, recall and time of subjects while detecting errors in the systems using each of the two treatments. The result of the test show that both groups differ significantly in precision ($U(41) = 80.5, Z = -3.011, p = 0.003$) and time ($U(41) = 345.5, Z = 4.609, p < 0.001$), and that in both cases the WebML group showed a better performance than the PHP group. However, the analysability recall (that is, the number of actual errors found out of the total number of errors) was not significantly different ($U(41) = 170, Z = -0.286, p = 0.775$). Otherwise stated, performing analysability tasks on WebML seems to speed up the identification of errors, and to avoid misclassifying a feature in the application as an error. However, it does not seem to significantly help to detect the errors in the application.

We then tested the hypothesis HACC, which is related to the precision, recall and time of subjects while correcting actual errors in the systems using each of the two treatments. The result of the test show that, again, both groups differ significantly in precision ($U(40) = 104, Z = -2.163, p = 0.031$) and time ($U(39) = 252, Z = 2.484, p = 0.013$). The WebML group shows again a better performance than the PHP group. However, the corrective changeability recall (that is, the number of actual errors corrected out of the total number of errors) was not significantly different ($U(40) = 132, Z = -1.31 p = 0.19$). Otherwise stated, performing corrective changeability tasks on WebML seems to speed up the correction of errors, and to avoid proposing corrections that do not actually correct anything. However, it does not seem to significantly help to correct the actual errors in the application.

The last hypothesis we tested was HAPC, which related to the precision, recall and time that took subjects to introduce perfective modifications in the applications. There were not significant differences between the mean WebML changeability precision and the mean PHP changeability precision ($U(40) = 137.5, Z = -1.22, p = 0.222$). Similarly, the perfective recall (percentage of actions that actually contributed to successfully implement the change) was not significantly higher in WebML than in PHP ($U(40) = 165, Z = -0.283, p = 0.777$). However, subjects were again significantly quicker performing the improvements in WebML than in PHP ($U(40) = 336, Z = 4.647, p < 0.001$).

Since, as we have aforementioned, WebML subjects were novice developers, while PHP subjects had a higher level of experience, we can rely more heavily on the found significant differences in performance (all pointing at WebML having a higher performance than PHP for maintainability tasks): had WebML subjects had more experience with the methodology, the only natural evolution of the measures would have been towards making differences larger in favor of WebML.

---

[3] PASW - http://www.spss.com/software/statistics/

4.2   RQ2: Perceived Efficacy and Satisfaction of Treatments

For all the statistical analysis, we again performed a non-parametric Mann-Whitney U test.

Regarding HPA, the result of the test shows that both groups differ significantly in subjective complexity assessment ($U(37) = 84, Z = -2.195, p = 0.028$) but not in subjective certainty assessment ($U(37) = 92, Z = -1.871, p = 0,061$). Otherwise stated, the subjects regard working on models as simpler than working on code, but they feel equally (un)secure about the errors they identify.

Regarding HPCC, users felt that changes were slightly less complex when using PHP ($U(36) = 140, Z = -0.179, p = 0.858$), although this difference was not significant. Also, users felt slightly more certain about their changes in WebML ($U(36) = 125, Z = -0.355, p = 0.723$). Last but not least, since in this case users were actually changing the application, we could ask about their feeling of stability. Users felt the stability of the system to be significantly better preserved when using PHP ($U(36) = 224, Z = 3.152, p = 0.002$). Otherwise stated, users seem to feel more sure about what needs to be done when using WebML, but they seem to feel more 'in control' of the changes when they directly work on code.

Regarding HPPC, WebML was considered slightly simpler to introduce perfective changes than PHP, although the statistical test showed no significance ($U(37) = 105, Z = -1.55, p = 0.121$). On the contrary, subjects using PHP felt slightly more confident about the correctness of the changes introduced, although, again, the difference was not significant with respect to WebML subjects ($U(37) = 187, 5Z = 1, 31p = 0, 19$). Regarding stability, both groups showed very similar levels of confidence on the stability of the solution ($U(36) = 136.5, Z = 0.053, p = 0.958$).

Regarding HS, as we have aforementioned, the post-tests questionnaire included a scale of satisfaction with the technique. The satisfaction indexes with both treatments were compared by a t-test. Results showed a non-significant effect of the methodology ($t(38) = -0.208, p = 0.836$). On average, evaluations were moderately positive for both methodologies, with a mean difference of .06 slightly favoring the PHP group.

Last but not least, we tested HP; the global satisfaction index (measured through the satisfaction scale) is highly correlated to the measure (a direct item) assessing learnability of the methodology ($r = 0.663, p < 0.001$). This suggests that the easier the methodology was perceived to be, the better it was evaluated.

4.3   Threats to Validity

The analysis of the threats to validity evaluates under which conditions our experiment is applicable and offers benefits, and under which circumstances it might fail [24].

Threats to Conclusion Validity refer to the relationship between the treatment and the outcome. In our experiment we have used the number of lines of code to control the application size. This measure is generally preferred over functional points due to its higher reliability [8]. Additionally, statistical tests have been chosen conservatively, without making any kind of assumption on variable distributions. However, given the limited amount of time that students had to fulfil the experiment questionnaire, it is possible that the subjects have felt a pressure that may have affected the data. This notwithstanding, since both treatment groups suffered from the same time restrictions, we can assume that such effect, if present, has affected all the levels of the treatment equally.

Threats to Internal Validity are concerned with the possibility of hidden factors that may compromise the conclusion that it is indeed the treatment what causes the differences in outcome. In our case, the students belonged to different countries, which may bias the results. We limited the effect of the lack of randomization of subjects assigned to treatments by assuring that the mean age for the WebML group of students (M=22,47) was not significantly different from the mean age for the PHP group of students (M=23,17). Also, we assured that they had been enrolled in a similar number of courses on related modelling/programming topics, and had developed a similar number of WebApps ($M(WebML) = 3.93, M(PHP) = 4.25, t(27) = -0.183, p = 0.18$). Only the experience with code could not be controlled ($M(WebML) = 7.27, M(PHP) = 69.27$). This difference can be explained by the structure of the degrees in universities, which still today mainly focus on programming more than modelling skills. We tried to diminish the effect of different facilitators running the experiment in the two locations by compiling an instruction sheet that avoided unintended differences in the conditions of the experiment. Another threat to the internal validity of this study is related with the instrumentation. Since precision and recall measures had to be manually computed by different evaluators (each one an expert in WebML and PHP respectively), there is a risk of the criteria being applied differently to each group. We have tried to avoid this risk by defining a clear taxonomy of errors that were agreed upon before the evaluation.

Threats to Construct Validity refer to the relationship between theory and observation. In this sense, both the treatments and the measures used to assess the maintainability have been previously widely used in literature. This notwithstanding, there are still some risks we need to be aware of. First, we have used similar size applications, all belonging to the same domain (monomethod bias). Therefore we cannot generalize the results to applications of different sizes or different domains. Second, we have observed a positive outcome between maintainability and WebML, but we cannot assure that using WebML does not hamper other quality characteristics (restricted generalizability across constructs).

Last but not least, **Threads to External Validity** are concerned with generalization of the results. In our case, the fact that we have used undergraduate students, that is, subjects without experience in business, as well as the particular methodologies and languages we have used, constitute a limited environment. The latter is an unavoidable risk for this kind of experiments, in which subjects need to use a predefined approach to perform the tasks. The easiest way to minimize this threat is through replication of the experiment with different languages and MDE approaches. For this purpose, the replication package of this experiment can be found at `http://www.dlsi.ua.es/~ccachero/labPackages/er2011.rar`.

5   Conclusions

Generally speaking, the use of MDE engineering approaches such as WebML improves the precision and time it takes to perform analysability, corrective and perfective maintainability tasks. Also, junior developers, with a stronger experience in coding rather than on modelling, perceive maintainability tasks over models as simpler. This notwithstanding, subjects still rely more on their maintainability outcomes (certainty and perceived stability of the solution achieved) when they perform the maintainability tasks directly over PHP code. One reason for this result can be still the major confidence about code hold by the users involved in our experiment. This certainty and perceived stability however slightly tips the satisfaction balance in favor of code-based approaches.

Our results augment the repository of empirical data comparing maintainability performance and satisfaction of MDE methodologies with respect to traditional code-based approaches. The laboratory package that accompanies our research allows for replications with the same or different methodologies, languages, applications and subject profiles. Such replication is at the base of our future research.

References

1. Ruiz, F., Polo, M.: Mantenimiento del Software. Grupo Alarcos, Departamento de Informática de la Universidad de Castilla-La Mancha (2007)
2. Coleman, D., Ash, D., Lowther, B., Oman, P.: Using metrics to evaluate software system maintainability. Computer 27(8), 44–49 (2002)
3. Ameller, D., Gutiérrez, F., Cabot, J.: Dealing with non-functional requirements in model-driven development (2010)
4. López, E.D., González, M., López, M., Iduñate, E.L.: Proceso de Desarrollo de Software Mediante Herramientas MDA. In: CISCI: Conferencia Iberoamericana en Sistemas, Cibernética e Informática (2007)
5. Heijstek, W., Chaudron, M.R.V.: Empirical investigations of model size, complexity and effort in a large scale, distributed model driven development process. In: 35th Euromicro Conference on Software Engineering and Advanced Applications, pp. 113–120. IEEE, Los Alamitos (2009)
6. Mohagheghi, P.: An Approach for Empirical Evaluation of Model-Driven Engineering in Multiple Dimensions. In: From Code Centric to Model Centric: Evaluating the Effectiveness of MDD (C2M:EEMDD), pp. 6–17. CEA LIST Publication (2010)
7. Glass, R.L.: Matching methodology to problem domain. Communications of the ACM 47(5), 19–21 (2004)
8. Wohlin, C., Runeson, P., Host, M.: Experimentation in software engineering: an introduction. Springer, Netherlands (2000)
9. Dyba, T., Kitchenham, B.A., Jorgensen, M.: Evidence-based software engineering for practitioners. IEEE Software 22(1), 58–65 (2005)

10. Kitchenham, B., Budgen, D., Brereton, P., Turner, M., Charters, S., Linkman, S.: Large-scale software engineering questions-expert opinion or empirical evidence? IET Software 1(5), 161–171 (2007)

11. Zelkowitz, M.V.: An update to experimental models for validating computer technology. Journal of Systems and Software 82(3), 373–376 (2009)

12. Wikipedia, http://en.wikipedia.org/wiki/PHP

13. Vallecillo, A., Koch, N., Cachero, C., Comai, S., Fraternali, P., Garrigós, I., Gómez, J., Kappel, G., Knapp, A., Matera, M., et al.: MDWEnet: A practical approach to achieving interoperability of model-driven Web engineering methods. In: Workshop Proc. of 7th Int. Conf. on Web Engineering (ICWE 2007). Citeseer, Italy (2007)

14. Ceri, S., Fraternali, P., Bongio, A., Brambilla, M., Comai, S., Matera, M.: Morgan Kaufmann series in data management systems: Designing data-intensive Web applications. Morgan Kaufmann Pub., San Francisco (2003)

15. ISO/IEC FCD 25010: Systems and software engineering - Software product. Requirements and Evaluation(SQuaRE) - Quality models for software product quality and system quality in use (2009)

16. Chapin, N., Hale, J.E., Khan, K.M., Ramil, J.F., Tan, W.G.: Types of software evolution and software maintenance. Journal of Software Maintenance and Evolution: Research and Practice 13(1), 3–30 (2001)

17. Kitchenham, B., Mendes, E., Travassos, G.H.: Cross versus Within-Company Cost Estimation Studies: A Systematic Review. IEEE Transactions on Software Engineering 33(5), 316–329 (2007)

18. Martinez, Y., Cachero, C., Melia, S.: Evidencia empírica sobre mejoras en productividad y calidad mediante el uso de aproximaciones MDD: un mapeo sistemático de la literatura. REICIS (submitted) (2011)

19. Mellegård, N., Staron, M.: Improving Efficiency of Change Impact Assessment Using Graphical Requirement Specifications: An Experiment. In: Product-Focused Software Process Improvement, pp. 336–350 (2010)

20. Perry, D.E., Porter, A.A., Votta, L.G.: Empirical studies of software engineering: a roadmap. In: The Future of Software Engineering, pp. 345–355. ACM, New York (2000)

21. Moody, D.L.: Dealing with Complexity: A Practical Method for Representing Large Entity Relationship Models (PhD Thesis). Melbourne, Australia: Department of Information Systems, University of Melbourne (2001)

22. Abrahão, S., Mendes, E., Gomez, J., Insfran, E.: A model-driven measurement procedure for sizing web applications: Design, automation and validation. In: Engels, G., Opdyke, B., Schmidt, D.C., Weil, F. (eds.) MODELS 2007. LNCS, vol. 4735, pp. 467–481. Springer, Heidelberg (2007)

23. Ceri, S., Fraternali, P., Bongio, A.: Web Modeling Language (WebML): a modeling language for designing Web sites. Computer Networks 33(1-6), 137–157 (2000)

24. Cook, T.D., Campbell, D.T., Day, A.: Quasi-experimentation: Design & analysis issues for field settings. Houghton Mifflin Boston (1979)

From Pattern-Based User Interfaces to Conceptual Schemas and Back

Ravi Ramdoyal and Anthony Cleve

Laboratory of Database Application Engineering - PReCISE Research Centre
Faculty of Computer Science, University of Namur
Rue Grandgagnage 21 - B-5000 Namur, Belgium
{rra,acl}@info.fundp.ac.be
http://www.fundp.ac.be/precise

Abstract. Since the necessity to associate end-users of the future system with its specification and development steps has proven indisputable, it is crucial to define accessible means to express and communicate conceptual requirements between end-users and analysts in the context of Information Systems engineering. For this purpose, we present a simple form-based interface model offering an understandable and expressive graphical counterpart to a rich subset of the Generic Entity-Relationship model (GER). We describe how the elements of the proposed interface model can be translated into GER schema constructs, bearing the semantic characterisation of inter-concept relationships. The exposed principles support the automated translation of user-drawn form-based interfaces into a conceptual schema. The same principles can also serve as a basis to support the inverse translation process that aims at deriving a set of form-based interfaces from a conceptual schema.

Keywords: Information Systems Engineering, Conceptual Modelling, Forms-Based Human-Computer Interactions, Participatory Design.

1 Introduction

The necessity to associate end-users of the future system with its specification and development steps has long been advocated in the realm of Information Systems Engineering [12]. In the specific context of Database Engineering, involving end-users is particularly critical during *conceptual analysis*, as this process defines the semantic core of the future application. The Entity-Relationship (ER) model has long been the most popular medium to express conceptual requirements [13]. Its simplicity, its graphical representation, the availability of numerous CASE tools that include an ER schema editor (should) make it the ideal communication medium between designers and users. However, despite its merits, the ER formalism often fails to meet its objectives as an effective end-users communication medium [8]. On the other hand, most users are quite able to deal with complex data structures, provided they are organised according to familiar layouts. In particular, electronic forms have proved to be more natural

M. Jeusfeld, L. Delcambre, and T.W. Ling (Eds.): ER 2011, LNCS 6998, pp. 247–260, 2011.

and intuitive than usual conceptual formalisms to express data requirements [2], while making the semantics of the underlying data understandable [15].

The RAINBOW approach is precisely a collaborative user-oriented approach to design database conceptual schemas, using a simple form-based interfaces model to transparently convey conceptual requirements in the context of Information Systems engineering [8]. It exploits the expressiveness of user-drawn form-based interfaces and prototypes, and specialises and integrates standard techniques to help acquire and validate data specifications from existing artefacts in order to use such interfaces as a two-way channel to express, communicate and validate static data requirements between end-users and analysts.

The first two steps of the approach focus on the elaboration of a set of form-based interfaces and on their automatic translation into a first set of "raw" conceptual schemas. More precisely, the end-users are first invited to draw and specify a set of form-based interfaces to perform usual tasks of their application domain, using a simple form model. Then, thanks to intuitive mapping rules, the forms are "translated" into the *raw* conceptual schemas that will form the basis of the conceptualisation process (see Figure 1). These raw schemas are semantically and structurally poor, as they only use a minimal subset of the Entity-Relationship model. The following steps of the approach help to acquire additional specifications to analyse, enrich and integrate the schemas.

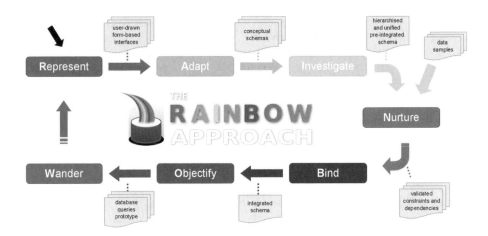

Fig. 1. Overview of the RAINBOW approach

Experimentation highlighted the effectiveness of the RAINBOW approach [7], but user feedback suggested that the overall procedure could be tedious at times. In this paper, we therefore investigate the feasibility of improving this process by integrating the subsequent steps into the drawing process. This improvement implies extending the informational content of the current form model and defining combinations of widgets to support this extension. To solve these issues, we identify critical semantic patterns of conceptual schemas and propose to steer the drawing process using corresponding interface widgets patterns and a dedicated set of heuristics. The remainder of the paper is structured as follows. Section 2 delineates the research context and describes the related works. The problem we are dealing with is formalised in Section 3. Section 4 discusses the mapping from form-based interfaces to the GER model using our new form model, then Section 5 addresses the converse process. Section 6 discusses this proposition and Section 7 concludes this paper.

2   Research Context and State of the Art: Electronic Forms to Convey Conceptual Requirements

Using form-based interfaces as a means to express and capture static database requirements has a long tradition. In 1984, Batini et al. studied paper forms as a means to collect and communicate data in the office environment [1]. Later on, Choobineh et al. explored a form-based approach for database analysis and design, and developed an analyst-oriented Form Definition System and an Expert Database Design System that incrementally produced an ER diagram based on the analysis of a set of forms [2]. Kösters et al. introduced a requirements analysis method combining user interface and domain analysis [5], while Rollinson and Roberts studied the problem of non-expert customisation of database user interfaces and developed a set of graph-oriented transformations to extract an Extended Entity-Relationship schema describing an interface's informational content [11]. More recently, Terwilliger et al. defined the formal GUAVA (GUi As View) framework to use the user interface directly as a conceptual model, by exploiting the hierarchical nature of forms-based user interfaces to provide a simple representation of their informational content, including the relationships between forms [15]. Rode et al. investigated the feasibility of end-user web engineering for webmasters without programming experience and developed a

Widget	ER Counterpart	Widget	ER Counterpart
FORM	Entity Type	Fieldset	Monovalued Compound Attribute
		Input *	Mandatory Monovalued Simple Attribute
Table Column 1 Column 2 Column 3 Add Edit Delete Reset	Multivalued Compound Attribute	Selection (radiobuttons) ○ Option1 ○ Option2 ○ Option3 Selection (checkboxes) □ Option1 □ Option2 □ Option3 Selection (list) Option2 Option3 Option4	Mono/Multi-valued Simple Attribute with Value Domain
		Click to > Button	Procedural Unit

Fig. 2. Available graphical widgets with their mapping rules to data structures

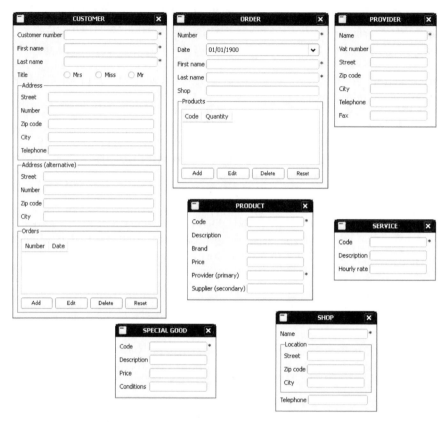

Fig. 3. User-drawn form-based interfaces for the management of a small company that offers services and sales products

prototypical tool for the end-user development of web application involving non professional programmers [10]. Yang et al. also inquired about the WYSIWYG user-driven development of Data Driven Web Applications, while transparently generating their underlying application model on the fly [16].

Two main limitations must be underlined in these approaches. On the one hand, the underlying form models are problematic. Since they are intended to express rich and complex interfaces, layouts and behaviours, their structure becomes complex and difficult to read, and furthermore, end-users tend to be overwhelmed by their superabundance of available widgets and compositions. Paradoxically, on the other hand, the schemas obtained using these approaches are poor, as they notably ignore, among others, hierarchies, existence constraints and functional dependencies. The RAINBOW approach successfully answered these issues by defining a simple form-based model as starting input and a structured procedure to gather and validate additional specifications using the user-drawn form-based interfaces as a communication means.

In order to focus on simple interface widgets that can allow end-users to simply express concepts, while casting away the technical aspects of layout, the

RAINBOW approach offers a simplified form model based on the most primitive and usual form widgets. This model avoid the mentioned drawbacks of existing (too) rich User Interface Description Languages (UIDL) enabling to model form-based interfaces. In particular, in order to make the development of the interfaces more accessible and focus the drawing on the content rather than the appearance, the available graphical elements are restricted to the most commonly used ones (*forms*, *fieldsets* and *tables*, *inputs*, *selections* and *buttons*) and limited the layout of forms as a vertical sequence of elements, which also simplifies the transition from the form model to the ER model (see Figure 2).

Intuitively, the "raw" transposition associates each form with an entity type, each fieldset or table with a compound attribute, each input or selection with a simple attribute, and buttons with procedural units. These data structures are a subset of the Generic Entity-Relationship (GER) model, which is a wide-spectrum model used to describe database schemas in various abstraction levels and paradigms [4].

Let us consider the following example to illustrate the process. The context is the development of a tailored IT solution to manage a small company that offers **Services** and sales **Products**, including **Special goods**, through different **Shops**. They wish to store information on their **Providers** and **Customers**, including the **Orders** that the latter submitted. Figure 3 illustrates forms that the end-users might draw for this purpose. For instance, for each customer, personal information including his main and alternative addresses are stored, as well as the list of orders that he issued. Each of these orders mention information on the context of its creation, and list the associated list of products, and so on. For the sake of further discussion, we consider that the forms do not initially mention any unique, existence or prerequisite constraint.

The direct transposition of these forms are the "raw" entity types of Figure 4. Given the mapping rules of Figure 2, the structure of these individual schemas

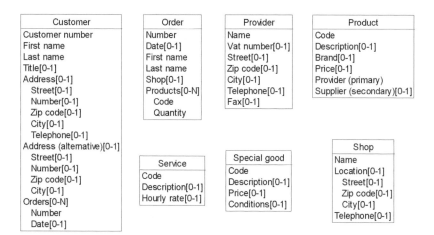

Fig. 4. The translation of the forms depicted in Figure 3 into "raw" conceptual schemas

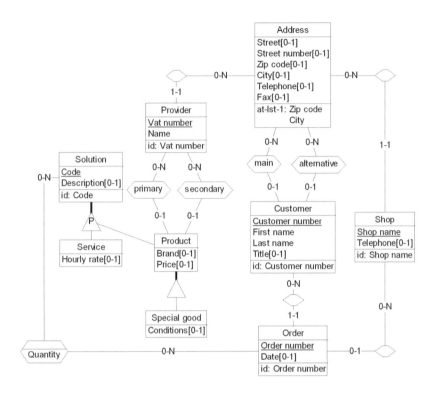

Fig. 5. The underlying data model of the forms depicted in Figure 3

is poor, as it consists in entity types, compound and simple attributes. To obtain the rich integrated schema of Figure 5, it is necessary to proceed with an interactive and therefore non deterministic analysis of the forms and their underlying schema. Though the final schema originates from the original forms, the latter are not representative of this schema any more. Besides, despite its modularity, the RAINBOW process remains sequential: whereas the labels are analysed on-the-fly to suggest alternative labels during the drawing step, the structural similarities and possible constraints are analysed later on. Could these subsequent steps be integrated in the drawing step so that the set forms can directly be mapped to a schema using rich structures of the ER model?

3   Formalising the Problem

3.1   Overview

Let $\mathcal{M}_{HCI}$ be the current form-based interface model used in the RAINBOW approach, and $\mathcal{M}_{ER}$ be the Entity Relationship model, as illustrated in Figure 6. The current RAINBOW process relies on the following sequence of mapping and transformations:

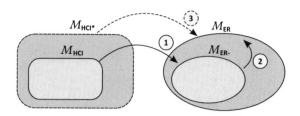

Fig. 6. Instead of using (1) a surjective mapping followed by (2) a non-deterministic interpretation to express the current form model $\mathcal{M}_{HCI}$ using the ER model $\mathcal{M}_{ER}$, we propose to define $\mathcal{M}_{HCI*} \supseteq \mathcal{M}_{HCI}$ so that we can directly define (3) a surjective mapping to $\mathcal{M}_{ER}$

- First a (1) surjective mapping: $\mathcal{M}_{HCI} \rightarrow \mathcal{M}_{ER-}$ (with $\mathcal{M}_{ER-} \subset \mathcal{M}_{ER}$) associates a set of forms to a set of "poor" conceptual schemas;
- Then a (2) non-deterministic interpretation: $\mathcal{M}_{ER-} \rightarrow \mathcal{M}_{ER}$ enables to integrate these schemas into a "rich" integrated conceptual schema.

To simplify the process and make it systematic, we want to define:

- A new form model $\mathcal{M}_{HCI*} \supseteq \mathcal{M}_{HCI}$
- A new (3) surjective mapping: $\mathcal{M}_{HCI*} \rightarrow \mathcal{M}_{ER}$ so that we can directly associate a set of forms to a single "rich" conceptual schema
- A set of heuristics $\mathcal{H}$ to automatically process semantic and structural redundancies in $\mathcal{M}_{HCI*}$ in order to manage the integration on the fly.

3.2 Identifying Missing Constructs

In this paper, we focus on managing critical structures of the GER model that are present in Fig. 5 but missing in Fig. 4, namely binary *relationship types* and *IS-A hierarchies*. Note that we leave aside the issue of eliciting constraints and dependencies, for which principles such as those presented in [9] are intended to be integrated later on. The IS-A hierarchies actually emerge from the analysis of redundancies that occur in raw schemas such as the ones of Fig. 4. Indeed, entity types sharing a set of components can be handled according to the nature of their relationship, as illustrated in Fig. 7: (a) difference, (b) equality, (c) union, (d) specialisation or (e) reference, which means that a binary relationship type exists between them. Binary relationship types can be classified into four classes: 1:N, N:1, N:N and 1:1, as illustrated in Fig. 8.

Beyond their mere structure, a semantic layer can be considered to characterise the exact *nature* of the relationship types. As illustrated in Fig. 9, we distinguish four typical *patterns*, based on the interpretation of the link that holds between the entity types E_1 (on the left) and E_2 (on the right) involved in the relationship type:

- *complementary structures*: E_2 provides *additional information* about E_1. For example, a `Criminal Record` serves as an informational complement specific to a `Person`, while a `Main Work Address` can serve as an informational complement to different `Persons`.

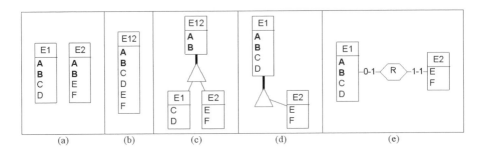

Fig. 7. Most common cases of structural redundancy

Fig. 8. Binary relationship types of classes 1:N, N:1, N:N and 1:1

- *compositions*: E_2 can be seen as a *component* of E_1. A typical case is the relationship between Book and Chapter. Another classic example is the cyclic composition of Product.
- *aggregations*: any instance of E_1 gathers a set of instances of E_2. Such a semantic pattern holds, among others, between Team and Person or between School and Student.
- *materialisations*: an instance of E_2 constitutes a *concrete instance* of an abstract entity type E_1. A famous example is a book Copy, that actually materialises a Book.

Note that the very same relationship type may involve *two* semantic patterns, depending on the entity type considered as E_1. For instance, a Book complements a book Copy, while a book Copy materialises a Book.

4   From Form-Based Interfaces to GER Schemas

4.1   A New Pattern-Based Form Model

As discussed above, the current form-based user interface model $\mathcal{M}_{HCI}$ falls short in supporting the representation (or the detection) of IS-A relationships and relationship type patterns. A richer user interface model $\mathcal{M}_{HCI*}$ is therefore required. This $\mathcal{M}_{HCI*}$ model obviously includes the interface constructs of $\mathcal{M}_{HCI}$:

- *Form* containers, for top level entity types;
- *Inputs*, for monovalued simple attributes;

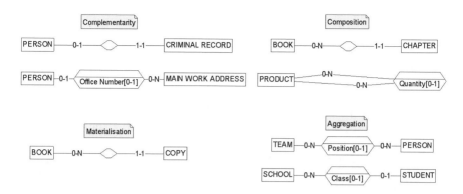

Fig. 9. Examples of complementarity, composition, aggregation and materialisation of concepts

- *Selections*, for mono/multivalued simple attributes;
- *Buttons*, for procedural units.

In addition to those basic constructs, $\mathcal{M}_{HCI^*}$ also recombines fieldsets and tables to offer the following containers:

- *Composed fields*, to represent monovalued compound attributes;
- *Category containers*, to represent IS-A hierarchies;
- Pattern containers to handle multivalued compound attributes and relationship types between entity types:
  - *Complementary containers*, to manage occurrences of complementary concepts relative to the current container;
  - *Component containers*, to visualise compositions;
  - *Contributor containers*, to support aggregations;
  - *Specimen containers*, to depict materialisations.

Pattern containers typically hold a (set of) field(s) used as referential keys to a counterpart concept that must be expressed by a form, as well as a set of elements representing the attributes of the underlying relationship type, and a navigational button to view and set associated instances of the counterpart concept.

4.2   A Heuristic-Driven Drawing Process

In addition, a set of heuristics $\mathcal{H}$ is used to automatically detect and process semantic and structural similarities between distinct user interface fragments. In the RAINBOW approach [8], built on top of $\mathcal{M}_{HCI}$, similarity detection was carried out *offline*, in support to *view integration*. In contrast, the use of $\mathcal{M}_{HCI^*}$ as user interface model allows detection of similarities *on-the-fly*, i.e., while the forms are being drawn by the user. Whenever a new field or container is added to a form, a similarity check is performed and, if relevant, a specific interaction takes place between the drawing tool and the user:

- if the new element is semantically equivalent to a previously used element, the user is invited to arbitrate and uniform the terminology;
- if a container is identified as structurally equivalent to another previously drawn container, the user is invited to characterise the equivalence and to adapt the structure of the current forms (for instance, regrouping entity types involved in the same IS-A hierarchy within a single form, replacing referential elements with the adequate pattern container, or transforming a composed field into a pattern container if the other container is a form);
- whenever a new container B is inserted into a container A in order to manage a given pattern p between A and B:
  1. the user is asked to define the converse semantic pattern p' existing between concepts B and A;
  2. if there no form currently associated with B, such a form is created and the user is asked to provide the elements to be used as referential keys;
  3. the pattern p' is inserted in B, and the user is asked if it should be set visible or hidden.

Those heuristics notably ensures that the underlying relationship types between two entity types is always available in the forms associated to these entity types, and that it can be hidden or unhidden for navigational purposes.

Besides, the combination of the new form model and these heuristics allows to obtain forms that are representative of their underlying conceptual schema, as illustrated in Fig. 10. It also permits to accelerate both the drawing of the interfaces and their automated translation into GER schemas. For instance, if the drawing of the forms of Fig. 10 was done from scratch, a realistic scenario would include phases such as the following:

- the user starts by drawing the `Customer` form, then adds fields `Customer Number`, `First Name`, `Last Name`, `Title`. Next, the user inserts a composed field `Main Address`, while specifying that the same value of `Main Address` can be used by different `Customers`. When the next composed field `Alternative Address` is inserted, the user is asked to arbitrate these similar concepts, and she decides to merge their underlying data structure. This implies that both composed fields will now contain the same elements, some of which may be hidden for convenience.
- when the user draws the `Order` and adds fields `First Name` and `Last Name` (which were defined in the form `Customer`), she is asked to arbitrate the relationship between `Order` and `Customer`. The user consequently specifies that an `Order` can be described thanks to a `Customer` (complementarity), and that conversely a `Customer` gathers `Orders` (aggregation). She also specifies that the latter pattern should be visible in the form `Customer`, and that the referential key is `Order Number`.
- the user then adds a complementary container `Shop` to `Order`. As there is no form `Shop` yet, it is automatically created, and the user provides the `Shop Name` as referential key. She also specifies that conversely, a `Shop` aggregates `Orders`, but that this pattern should remain hidden. It can however be unhidden later on if required.

Fig. 10. New representation of the forms of Fig. 3 in order to convey the specifications of Fig. 5. One may for instance notice, among others, the IS-A hierarchy contained in the form `Solution` and the aggregation/complementarity pattern which is visible for `Customer/Order`

- after drawing the form `Service`, the user starts drawing the form `Product` and adds fields `Code` and `Description` (which are already defined in the form `Service`). The user is therefore asked to arbitrate these similar concepts, and chooses to define a union. Consequently, the forms are merged into a single form: the user provides the unifying term `Solution` for the new form, which now includes the fields `Code` and `Description` and a category container requiring to choose between `Service` and `Product`. The user then proceeds by adding the subcategory `Special Good` to `Product`, before carrying on with the addition of the fields `Brand` and `Price`, followed by the complementary containers `Primary Provider` and `Secondary Provider`.

5   From GER Schemas to Form-Based Interfaces

These principles also serve as a basis to support the reverse translation process that consists in deriving a set of form-based interfaces from a conceptual schema. On the one hand, transformational and generative techniques allow to automate the production of logical and physical counterparts of the conceptual schema [4], as well as applicative artefacts [6] (such as interface forms, database code and program fragments). On the other hand, constraining the regeneration of forms from a conceptual schema obtained using the proposed approach is straightforward, as we already possess all the additional semantic specifications described in Section 3.2. However, the converse process of generating forms from a conceptual schema developed independently from the proposed approach is less trivial. Indeed, in order to ensure a bijective translation between the schema and its form representation, it is necessary to analyse and semantically annotate the schema, notably to:

- ensure that the inter-concept relationships are restricted to (or transformed into) binary relationship types and IS-A hierarchies;
- specify which entity types should explicitly appear as forms (e.g. `Customer`) or not (e.g. `Address`);
- identify semantic patterns and specify the nature of the roles played by the involved entity types (e.g. a `Product` is complemented by a `Primary Provider`, while a `Primary Provider` aggregates `Products`);
- specify which fields and patterns that should be hidden in the forms (e.g. the "primary" `Provider` should be visible in a `Product`, but the "primary" `Products` should be hidden in the `Provider`).

By annotating the schema accordingly, we can generate forms that respect the form model described in Section 4, hence offering an alternative and bijective representation of the original schema to ease further collaboration with end-users.

6   Discussion

The approach developed in this paper generalises the principles of the RAINBOW approach, while offering an integrated and iterative process instead of a sequential procedure. In addition to managing the direct coevolution of the interfaces and their associated conceptual schema, the proposed approach also reduces the articulatory distance of an already proven and tool-supported process. Indeed, the RAINBOW approach was experimented and evaluated using the RAINBOW Toolkit, which is developed on top of the DB-Main CASE Tool [3], as well as a validation protocol based on *Participant-Observer* and *Brainstorming/Focus group* principles, as defined in [14]. Experiments analysis notably highlighted that the RAINBOW approach and tool support did help end-users and analysts to communicate static data requirements to each other, inclusive of inter-concept relationships, constraints and dependencies. Since the validation aspect of the proposed approach cannot be addressed more extensively in this paper, the interested reader may refer to [7] for further details on the validation process and methodology.

7   Conclusion

In this paper, we presented a simple form-based interface model offering an understandable and expressive graphical counterpart to conceptual schemas.

Considering this interface model as an alternative pattern-based representation model for entity-relationship schemas, we show how the interface model constructs translate as conceptual schema constructs. The exposed principles allow the automated, direct translation of a conceptual schema from user-drawn form-based interfaces. This translation process involves, in particular, the on-the-fly semantic characterisation of underlying relationships between schema concepts using a specific set of heuristics. As a positive side effect, the same principles can also serve as a basis to support the inverse translation process that aims at deriving a set of form-based interfaces from a conceptual schema.

Building on these findings, our short-term research agenda will focus on four main tasks. First of all, we intend to integrate the principles presented in [9] in order to directly include the specification of constraints and dependencies in the drawing process. Secondly, since the exposed principles are currently implemented as a proof-of-concept on top of the DB-Main CASE Tool to support the transition from forms to GER schemas, we plan to implement the converse process to come full circle with the tool support. Thirdly, a special effort will be devoted to study and enhance the usability and user-friendliness of the tool support in order to improve the user experience of this participatory approach to conceptual analysis. Finally, we expect to conduct comparative experiments in real-life settings to study the qualitative and quantitative benefits of using this approach, both from the analyst and the end-user perspective, notably in comparison to the RAINBOW approach.

References

1. Batini, C., Demo, G.B., Leva, A.D.: A methodology for conceptual design of office data bases. Information Systems 9(3/4), 251–263 (1984)
2. Choobineh, J., Mannino, M.V., Tseng, V.P.: A form-based approach for database analysis and design. Communications of the ACM 35(2), 108–120 (1992)
3. DB-Main: The DB-Main CASE Tool (2010), http://www.db-main.be
4. Hainaut, J.-L.: The transformational approach to database engineering. In: Lämmel, R., Saraiva, J., Visser, J. (eds.) GTTSE 2005. LNCS, vol. 4143, pp. 95–143. Springer, Heidelberg (2006)
5. Kösters, G., Six, H.W., Voss, J.: Combined analysis of user interface and domain requirements. In: ICRE 1996: Proceedings of the 2nd International Conference on Requirements Engineering (ICRE 1996), p. 199. IEEE Computer Society, Washington, DC, USA (1996)
6. Pizano, A., Shirota, Y., Iizawa, A.: Automatic generation of graphical user interfaces for interactive database applications. In: CIKM 1993: Proceedings of the Second International Conference on Information and Knowledge Management, pp. 344–355. ACM, New York (1993)
7. Ramdoyal, R.: Reverse Engineering User-Drawn Form-Based Interfaces for Interactive Database Conceptual Analysis. Ph.D. thesis, University of Namur, Namur, Belgium (December 2010), electronic version,
   http://www.info.fundp.ac.be/libd/rainbow
8. Ramdoyal, R., Cleve, A., Hainaut, J.L.: Reverse engineering user interfaces for interactive database conceptual analysis. In: Pernici, B. (ed.) CAiSE 2010. LNCS, vol. 6051, pp. 332–347. Springer, Heidelberg (2010)

9. Ramdoyal, R., Hainaut, J.L.: Interactively eliciting database constraints and dependencies. In: Mouratidis, H., Rolland, C. (eds.) CAiSE 2011. LNCS, vol. 6741, pp. 184–198. Springer, Heidelberg (2011)

10. Rode, J., Bhardwaj, Y., Pérez-Quiñones, M.A., Rosson, M.B., Howarth, J.: As easy as "Click": End-user web engineering. In: Lowe, D.G., Gaedke, M. (eds.) ICWE 2005. LNCS, vol. 3579, pp. 478–488. Springer, Heidelberg (2005)

11. Rollinson, S.R., Roberts, S.A.: Formalizing the informational content of database user interfaces. In: Ling, T.-W., Ram, S., Li Lee, M. (eds.) ER 1998. LNCS, vol. 1507, pp. 65–77. Springer, Heidelberg (1998)

12. Rosson, M.B., Carroll, J.M.: Usability Engineering: Scenario-Based Development of Human-Computer Interaction (Interactive Technologies). Morgan Kaufmann, San Diego (2001)

13. Shoval, P., Shiran, S.: Entity-relationship and object-oriented data modeling-an experimental comparison of design quality. Data & Knowledge Engineering 21(3), 297–315 (1997)

14. Singer, J., Sim, S.E., Lethbridge, T.C.: Software engineering data collection for field studies. In: Shull, F., Singer, J., Sjøberg, D.I. (eds.) Guide to Advanced Empirical Software Engineering, pp. 9–34. Springer, Heidelberg (2008)

15. Terwilliger, J.F., Delcambre, L.M.L., Logan, J.: The user interface is the conceptual model. In: Embley, D.W., Olivé, A., Ram, S. (eds.) ER 2006. LNCS, vol. 4215, pp. 424–436. Springer, Heidelberg (2006)

16. Yang, F., Gupta, N., Botev, C., Churchill, E.F., Levchenko, G., Shanmugasundaram, J.: WYSIWYG development of data driven web applications. Proceedings of the VLDB Endowment 1(1), 163–175 (2008)

Automatically Mapping and Integrating Multiple Data Entry Forms into a Database

Yuan An, Ritu Khare, Il-Yeol Song, and Xiaohua Hu

College of Information Science and Technology, Drexel University, USA
{yan,ritu,isong,thu}@ischool.drexel.edu

Abstract. Forms are a standard way of gathering data into a database. Many applications need to support multiple users with evolving data gathering requirements. It is desirable to automatically link dynamic forms to the back-end database. We have developed the FormMapper system, a fully automatic solution that accepts user-created data entry forms, and maps and integrates them into an existing database in the same domain. The solution comprises of two components: *tree extraction* and *form integration*. The tree extraction component leverages a probabilistic process, Hidden Markov Model (HMM), for automatically extracting a semantic tree structure of a form. In the form integration component, we develop a merging procedure that maps and integrates a tree into an existing database and extends the database with desired properties. We conducted experiments evaluating the performance of the system on several large databases designed from a number of complex forms. Our experimental results show that the FormMapper system is promising: It generated databases that are highly similar (87% overlapped) to those generated by the human experts, given the same set of forms.

1 Introduction

Using forms as the front-end interface mapping to a back-end database is a standard way for data collection. For building form-based applications, Do-It-Yourself (DIY) [18] and What You See Is What You Get (WYSIWYG) [28] are popular paradigms in the Cloud or in supporting non-technical users. Applications in these paradigms automatically translate forms into underlying databases and shield users from the technical details for database creation and code generation. There are a number of online systems that provide commercial services for users to create custom forms on their own. Example systems include Formassembly [1], Zoho [4], Jotform [2], and Wufoo [3]. In a previous study [16], we also developed a system that allows non-technical clinicians to create high-quality databases through forms. Despite the effort, we find that *mapping and integrating multiple forms into an existing structured database* remains largely unexplored. We call the problem *form2db* problem which is the focus of this paper. The following example illustrates the problem.

Example 1. Figure 1 (a) shows an existing form and an associated back-end database. The application maintains a mapping between the form and the back-end database.

Suppose that the form in Figure 1 (b) is a newly created one and will be used to collect data into the same database. It may be required to link the elements on the

M. Jeusfeld, L. Delcambre, and T.W. Ling (Eds.): ER 2011, LNCS 6998, pp. 261–274, 2011.
© Springer-Verlag Berlin Heidelberg 2011

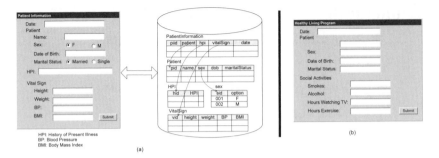

Fig. 1. Data Entry Forms and the Associated Database

form to elements in the database. For example, if the patient information is linked between the form and the database, then patient information could be filled up through auto-completion and integrated automatically. To map and integrate the new form to the existing database, a technical developer would first manually link the Name, Sex, Date of Birth, and Marital Status items on the form to the existing Patient table in the database. He/she would then extent the existing database appropriately to collect the new data items under Social Activities on the form in Figure 1 (b).

In such a manual process, the technical developer needs to directly access the database system and write the application code. However, some applications may not provide such an environment to users, for example, creating databases in the Cloud or supporting non-technical users to create forms on their own. In these applications, either **the database system is not directly exposed to the user** or **the user does not possess the necessary technical skills for generating the code**. It is desirable to develop an automatic approach that could map and integrate forms into an existing database without user intervention. Such an approach would greatly reduce human effort in system building and would benefit to many applications. ∎

We have developed the FormMapper system, a fully automatic solution that accepts user-created data entry forms, and maps and integrates them into an existing database. The FormMapper system is built on our previous work [15,16] and extends it in many aspects: First, the FormMapper integrates multiple forms into a single database instead of creating individual database for each form. Second, we have attempted to implement the following requirements in the FormMapper: (i) the system can accept sophisticated forms as input, (ii) the system automatically captures the semantic relationships among form elements, (iii) the system automatically links form elements to the elements in the hidden database, (iv) the system automatically extends the hidden database for unmatched form elements, and (v) the system automatically generates mapping expressions between the form and the hidden database.

There are many challenges in developing such an automatic system. To address the challenges, we first propose a formal hierarchical model that represents the semantic relationships among elements of a form; then we develop a solution comprising of two components: a *tree extraction* component and a *form integration* component. The tree extraction component leverages a machine learning technique, Hidden Markov Model (HMM) [25], for automatically extracting a tree structure from a data entry form. In a previous study, we have applied the HMM model to the problem of segmenting search interfaces [15]. To address the *form2db* problem, we extend the method to automatically extract a complete tree structure from a form. In the form integration component, we develop a merging procedure that maps and integrates a form tree into an existing database and extends the database as needed. Specifically, the merging procedure includes a *birthing algorithm* that creates a relational database from a form tree and a *megring algorithm* that integrates the form tree into an existing database.

In summary, we make the following contributions in this paper:

1. We identify the *form2db* problem and study related issues in developing a fully automatic approach.
2. We develop an initial solution which leverages an advanced machine learning technique for form tree extraction and takes the classic database design principles into consideration for database merging and extension.
3. We implemented the solution and conducted experimental studies. Empirically, the results generated by the system are highly similar to expert designed databases (87% overlapped). Overall, the automated system saves a great deal of human effort (seconds vs. hours) while generating results that are comparable to what human experts produced.

The remainder of this paper is organized as follows. Section 2 discusses related work. Section 3 presents the formal models and the problem definition. Section 4 describes the tree extraction component. Section 5 studies the merging process. Section 6 presents the experiments. Finally, Section 7 concludes the paper.

2   Related Work

There is a broad array of related work including *form-driven database generation* [11], *DIY web services for form creation* [1] *schema mapping* [20], *view integration* [7], *schema evolution* [26], and *automatic understanding of Deep Web search interfaces* [17]. However, the problem that we address here is a new and has not been addressed before in totality. An automatic solution to the problem including its subproblems has not been developed yet.

The earlier form-driven database creation techniques were designed for IT professionals to develop databases using "form structures;" users have to specify the exact semantics of the underlying database schemas through "forms" [11,22,19]. Recent DIY web services for form creation can hide the underlying data storage details from the users. However, each form is stored individually without semantic integration [1,28].

Our problem is different from schema mapping and integration in several aspects. Schema mapping aims to discover meaningful relationships between database schemas [20,21,23,5], while view/schema integration builds a database schema by unifying a set of views/schemas [7]. Both problems primarily focus on schema elements and do not consider database extension. Also, solutions to schema mapping and view integration are semi-automatic, requiring the user to examine the final results. Our problem is a continuous and dynamic process which does not ask the user to examine the results. Schema evolution focuses on maintaining the consistency of a database when its schema is modified [26]. Our problem focuses on how to extend a database when new data needs to be collected.

There are techniques proposed for modeling and understanding search interfaces [17]. In particular, Wu et al. [27] and Dragut et al. [12] model a search interface as a hierarchical structure call *schema tree*. To extract schema trees, Dragut et al. in [12] develop a rule-based approach exploiting Web browser rendering. We develop a model-based machine learning technique for extracting a tree structure from a data entry form. Our approach does not reply on specific browser rendering and extracts information from sophisticated form structures.

3 Formal Preliminaries and Problem Definition

A form consists of a collection of form elements laid out in a particular way. Example form elements include text label, text box, radio buttons, select list, and check boxes. The underlying relationships among the elements are naturally captured by a tree structure [27,12]. Here, we formally define a *form tree* as follows.

Definition 1 (Form Tree). *A form tree is defined as a labeled, directed and ordered tree, $\mathcal{FT} = (N, E, <_{sib}, root)$, where $N = \mathcal{I} \cup \mathcal{E} \cup \mathcal{V}$ is a finite set of nodes, E is a finite set of edges, $<_{sib}$ is the next-sibling relation between children of a tree node, and $root \in N$ is the root of the tree. Moreover,*

- *$\mathcal{I}$ is a finite set of input elements (or inputs), where items of $\mathcal{I}$ are drawn from the following set of input fields:* {text box, text area, radio buttons, check boxes, drop-down list, calendar} ;
- *$\mathcal{E}$ is a finite set of logical elements. Each $e \in \mathcal{E}$ has a label $l = \lambda(e)$, a data type $t = \tau(e)$, and a constraint $k = \kappa(e)$, where the function $\lambda(e)$ returns the label l of e, the function $\tau(n)$ returns the data type t of e, and the function $\kappa(e)$ returns the constraint k of e.*
- *$\mathcal{V}$ is a finite set of values;*
- *For an edge $(n_i \longrightarrow n_j) \in E$, $n_i, n_j \in N$, n_i is called* **parent** *and n_j is called* **child***.*

Figure 2 shows the form tree model of the form in Figure 1 (a). Graphically, we use different shapes to represent the different types of nodes. The data type of an element can be extracted from the source code of a form, for example, Date for calendar input. Furthermore, the source code of a form often provides constraint information about whether an input is required or optional.

Database. A (relational) database $\mathcal{D} = (I, R, \Sigma)$ is a 3-tuple, where I is a set of relational tables, R is the schemas of the tables, and Σ is a set of integrity constraints imposed on the tables.

Definition 2 (The *form2db* Problem). *Given a set of data entry forms $\{\mathcal{F}_i, i = 1..n\}$ and a relational database $\mathcal{D} = (I, R, \Sigma)$, the form2db problem is to (1) discover the semantic mappings between the elements in a from $\mathcal{F}_i, i = 1...n$ and the elements in the database $\mathcal{D}$ and (2) extend the database to cover the unmapped elements in the form. The following is a set of desired properties for a solution:*

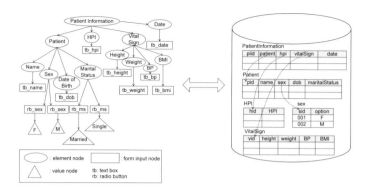

Fig. 2. The Form Tree for the Patient Information Form

- **correctness:** *a mapping linking a form element to a data element indicates that both elements represent the same concept in the application domain.*
- **completeness:** *every form element is mapped to a database element.*
- **compactness:** *every form element is mapped to at most one database element.*
- **normalization:** *the extended database should respect the normalization principles with regard to the functional dependencies that can be identified on the forms.*
- **optimization:** *the extended database should be optimized in terms of query efficiency (e.g., minimizing joins) and storage (e.g., minimizing **NULL** values.)*

For multiple forms $\{\mathcal{F}_i, i = 1..n\}$, we consider the problem of mapping and integrating them in a sequential order $\mathcal{F}_1$, $\mathcal{F}_2$, ..., $\mathcal{F}_n$. An individual form $\mathcal{F}_i$ is mapped and integrated to a database $\mathcal{D}$ that has already integrated the forms $\mathcal{F}_1$ to $\mathcal{F}_{i-1}$. With this consideration, in the rest of the paper, we focus on developing methods for mapping and integrating a single form to an existing database. Our solution first extracts a form tree from a form, and then maps and integrates the tree to an existing database.

4   Extracting Form Trees

Tree extraction is the process of clustering the elements on a form into semantically related groups and organizing the groups into parent-child hierarchical relationships. We have developed an effective and efficient method for segmenting form elements into semantically related groups [15]. To address the *form2db* problem, we extend the previous segmentation technique to a tree extraction method. The core of the method is a probabilistic process, Hidden Markov Model (HMM), that simulates the process of designing a data entry form. In general, an HMM [25] can model a probabilistic process that generates a sequence of observations. Particularly, an HMM consists of a set of states that satisfy the Markov assumption, i.e., the state of the process only depends on the previous states of the process. In a first order Markov model, which we assume for our problem, a current state only depends on the previous state and not on any earlier states. At each state, e.g., corresponding to an object in a domain conceptual model, the process generates an observable value, e.g., a form element, based on a fixed

Table 1. Observation Space T_HMM

Code	Description
σ_0^T	textbox/textarea
σ_1^T	select group
σ_2^T	radiobutton
σ_3^T	checkelement
σ_4^T	long text(more than 4 words)
σ_5^T	lower case non-colon-ending multi-character text
σ_6^T	colon ending text
σ_7^T	special character text
σ_8^T	uppercase text
σ_9^T	uppercase colon-ending text
σ_{10}^T	paranthesized text

probability distribution. In an HMM, an observer can observe a sequence of observable values emitted by a (first order) Markov process, but cannot see which states emit which values. An important inference problem is: *given a sequence of observed values, to find the sequence of states that is most likely to have generated those observations.*

We model the process of designing forms as a Markov process where a designer creates form elements when moving from object to object in a conceptual model following the relationship links. An object in a conceptual model could be an entity, attribute, relationship, or value. At each object, the designer decides whether to create a logical element, an input field, a nested element, etc. We simulate this design process into 2-layered HMM. The first layer T_HMM is aimed to tag the elements of the forms (observations) with their semantic roles (states), and the second layer S_HMM is used to segment the forms into groups (and sub-groups) of elements. Formally, an HMM is specified as a 3-tuple (Π, A, B) over a set of states $Q = \{q_i, i = 1..n\}$ and a set of observable values $\Sigma = \{\sigma_j, j = 1..m\}$, where $\Pi = \{\pi_i\}$, $\pi_i = Pr(q_i)$, is a vector of initial state probability, $A = \{a_{ij}\}$, $a_{ij} = Pr(q_j|q_i)$, is a matrix of transition probability among the states, and $B = \{b_{ij}\}$, $b_{ij} = Pr(\sigma_i|q_j)$, is a matrix of emission probability between states and observations. Tables 1 presents the observable values of the T_HMM, while Table 2 and Table 3 describe the states of T_HMM and S_HMM. In the 2-layered HMM, the states of T_HMM also become the observable values of the S_HMM.

In the tagging phase, the T_HMM automatically tag the elements of a form with states q_0^T - q_6^T. These states indicate whether a form element is labeled as an Entity, Attribute, or Value. In addition, a form may contain other types of elements such as Value Separator, Value Data Type, Instructions, and Misc. Text. For example, a Value Separator is a piece of text with special characters. A Value Separator separates two input fields which collect data for the same attribute. For instance, blood pressure is often collected on a patient encounter form using BP : ⬜/⬜, where the text labels "BP" and "/" are followed by text boxes, respectively. The text "/" is a Value Separator rather than an attribute. In the next grouping phase, the S_HMM accepts the output of the T_HMM and assigns new states q_0^S - q_3^S. These states indicate which set of elements should be grouped into a segment.

Table 2. State Space T_HMM (Also Observation Space S_HMM)

Code	Description
q_0^T	Entity
q_1^T	Attribute
q_2^T	Value
q_3^T	Value Separator
q_4^T	Value Data Type
q_5^T	Instructions
q_6^T	Misc. Text

Table 3. State Space S_HMM

Code	Description
q_0^S	Begins a segment
q_1^S	Inside a segment
q_2^S	Begins a subsegment
q_3^S	Inside a subsegment

After a form is tagged and segmented, the tree is derived by the segmentation information. The topology of nodes within a branched segment is determined based on the semantic tags. The tree branching structure is determined in the following manner. Each segment is represented by a tree node. The root is the container segment that represents the entire form. A sub-segment within a segment becomes the child of the node represented by the segment. After the initial branching, each segment node is elaborated into a segment tree based on the semantic tags associated with the segment elements using the following rules.

- The entity becomes the root of the segment tree.
- A attribute node becomes the child of the segment root
- The value nodes associated with a given attribute node become the children of the attribute node.
- Some value nodes (radio, check, select) may need to be extended to contain the value text nodes as their children.
- A subsegment becomes the child of the root of the container segment.

The main tasks for the tree extraction include learning the parameters, Π, A, B, of the model by acquiring training examples, and applying the model to new instances. We train the HMMs by the Expectation Maximization algorithm [25] using a set of manually labeled examples. We solve the inference problem of finding the most likely explanation by the Viterbi algorithms [25]. In the Experiments section, we show that the accuracy of extraction is 96% based on a number of example forms we collected and manually labeled.

5   Mapping and Integrating Form Trees

Given a form tree $\mathcal{FT}$ and a database $\mathcal{D}$, our solution to the *form2db* problem first discovers initial element correspondences (or matchings) between the atomic elements in the tree and the database. Then it integrates the form into the database by discovering valid correspondences and extending the database. For element correspondences, we employ an element matching function $\delta(\mathcal{FT}, \mathcal{D})$ (e.g., a schema matching program [8]) which returns a set of correspondences $\mathcal{M} = \{\mathcal{FT}:\text{P}/\text{e} \rightsquigarrow \mathcal{D}:\text{d}\}$, which relates an

atomic element P/e reached by a simple path
P in the form tree with an atomic element d in
the database. The element matching function
$\delta(\mathcal{FT}, \mathcal{D})$ returns a similarity (≥ 0 and ≤ 1)
between every pair of elements in the tree and
the database. We set up a high threshold value
(e.g., 0.99) and take all pairs of elements that
have similarity above the threshold as an initial set of correspondences.

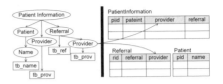

Fig. 3. Ambiguous Correspondences

Having the initial set of element correspondences, the merging process needs to address two challenges: First, there may be one-to-many or many-to-one initial correspondences. For example, Figure 3 shows a case where the form element Provider is linked
to two different columns in the database. The merging process needs to resolve the ambiguities by cleaning up the set of initial correspondences. Second, in general, there
could be several modeling alternatives for the same concept. For example, the relationship Patient ----- Provider could be modeled as Patient ----- Hospital
----- Provider in a database. Consequently, an automatic method would not be able
to resolve the heterogeneity without human expert's intervention.

To develop a fully automatic approach, we take a *syntactic and structural* approach
by assuming there is a well-defined forward engineering method for creating databases
from form trees. Consequently, the mapping part in our solution is to discover "equivalent" structures between two databases generated by the forward engineering method;
and the extension part is to merge two databases generated by the forward engineering
method. By "equivalent", we mean the syntactically same. In the following sections, we
first present a forward engineering method – the birthing algorithm. Next, we describe
a merging algorithm that integrates a database generated by the birthing algorithm into
an existing database. Overall, we develop our merging process into the following steps:

1. Discover a set of initial element correspondences.
2. Derive a new database from the given form tree.
3. Clean up the initial correspondences.
4. Extend the existing database for the unmapped elements.

5.1 Birthing Algorithm

The birthing algorithm takes as input a form tree and creates new database tables.
Consider a form tree $\mathcal{FT} = (N, E, <_{sib}, root)$ as a conceptual model. An internal
logical element $e \in \mathcal{E}$ corresponds to an entity and an edge between two logical elements $(n_i \longrightarrow n_j) \in E$, $n_i, n_j \in \mathcal{E}$ corresponds to a relationship in an ER model.
The birthing algorithm creates tables corresponding to logical elements and associated
edges. However, a form tree is different from a traditional ER model in many ways.
A form tree contains *input fields* and *values* which can be organized in complex and
messy ways. Figure 4 shows a complex data-entry form in which an input check box
with a value, e.g., Obesity, is extended by another input text box. Moreover, the hierarchical relationships between form elements capture important semantics regarding

the information collected on the form. For example, the hierarchy **Health Problems** – **Diagnosed** – **Depression** indicates that the value **Depression** is a diagnosed problem, rather than a concerned symptom.

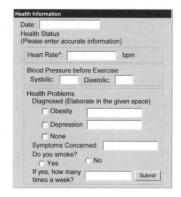

To achieve largely the desired properties specified in Definition 2, we consider the following requirements when developing the birthing algorithm:

Requirement 1: *All the user-specified elements and values should be captured in the database.*

Requirement 2: *All the hierarchical relationships among logical and value elements should be maintained in the database.*

Fig. 4. A Complex Form

Requirement 3: *Requirements 1 and 2 considered, tables should be merged for query efficiency.*

A form tree is pre-processed for extracting the data type $\tau(e)$ and identifying constraint $\kappa(e)$ of an element e. For example, the element **Heart Rate** is a required field (i.e., **NOT NULL**) and has a data type **bpm** in Figure 4. In addition, we also consider extension of an input filed, e.g. the **check box** *Obesity* extended by a **text box**. The birthing algorithm creates a relational database in a top-down fashion. In particular, the procedure starts with the root of the original form tree and implements the key patterns illustrated in Figure 5 (the full implementation catches all the rare exceptions.)

Pattern (a): The root of the form tree is mapped to a table representing an n-ary relationship.

Pattern (b): If n's children are **text boxes** and n has a parent, then n is mapped to a column named after n in the parent table. The **text boxes** are concatenated and mapped to the values of the column.

Pattern (c): An edge between two logical elements (except for Patterns (d) and (e)) is mapped to a many-to-many relationship table connecting two tables corresponding to the two elements.

Pattern (d): The values of a set of radio button are stored in the database as a lookup table. The logical element covering

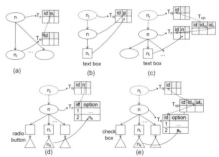

Fig. 5. Mapping Form Tree Patterns to Database

a set of radio buttons is linked by a functional relationship from the parent logical element.

Pattern (e): The values of a set of check boxes are stored in the database as a lookup table. The logical element covering a set of check boxes is linked by a many-to-many relationship from the parent logical element.

An extension field is added as an extra column of the table referencing the extended field. To meet the **Requirements 1 and 3**, the procedure works as follows: (1) It stores values in individual lookup tables; (2) It merges root's children to an n-ary relationship table; and (3) It inlines an element with only text box children to the element's parent. To verify **Requirement 2**, we turn a relational database into a *database graph* where the nodes are tables, columns, and values; and edges are table-column, column-value, table-table (foreign key referencing) relationships. For a foreign key column, we replace the table-column relationship with a referencing relationship between two tables. Let $\mathcal{FT}' = (N', E', <'_{sib}, root)$ be the tree that is obtained from the original form tree by removing *input nodes* and reconnecting value nodes to logical nodes. Then, for an edge $(n_i \longrightarrow n_j) \in E'$ in the tree $\mathcal{FT}'$, there are corresponding two nodes, v_i and v_j, in the database graph, such that, either v_i and v_j are linked by an edge or they are linked by a path passing through an intermediate node v_k, where v_k is a many-to-many relationship table.

5.2 Merging Algorithm

The merging algorithm takes as input a new database $\mathcal{D}'$, an existing database $\mathcal{D}$, and a set $\mathcal{M}$ of correspondences between $\mathcal{D}'$ and $\mathcal{D}$. It aims to merge the two databases. Traditional schema integration [9,24] finds a unified representation from a set of source schemas. However, existing approaches to schema integration require substantial amount of human feedback during the integration process. It has been shown that there can be multiple possible schemas that integrate data in different ways and each may be valuable in a given scenario [10]. In our case, we focus on developing a fully automatic solution that only uses the structural information for merging. We assume that the existing database was also generated by the birthing algorithm. The method first cleans up the correspondences by checking whether the linked two elements are compatible in terms of types and constraints (e.g., NOT NULL). It then extends the existing database by comparing two partially matched databases and adding the missing elements in the existing one. *The current method considers different structures as having different semantics even though the structures may model the same concepts.* (We will develop an ontology-based approach for fully automatically resolving semantic heterogeneity in the future work.)

Cleaning up Correspondences. Besides ambiguous correspondences, an invalid correspondence may link two elements that are incompatible in terms of types or constraints. We develop a procedure cleanup($\mathcal{D}', \mathcal{D}, \mathcal{M}$) that removes invalid correspondences. For each correspondence, the procedure first ensures that the pairs of elements linked by the correspondence are compatible in terms of their types, i.e., tables are linked to tables, columns are linked to columns, and values are linked to values. Second, for a correspondence linking two columns, the procedure checks their data types if available. Third, for two foreign keys linked by a correspondence, the procedure ensures the referenced tables are linked by a correspondence. Finally, the procedure removes correspondences that cannot be used to insert data due to relevant NOT NULL constraints. For example, if a correspondence $\mathcal{FT}$:P/e $\rightsquigarrow \mathcal{D}$:T.$c_i$ links the element P/e (P is a simple path in the tree) to the column c_i of the table T(c_1,..., c_i, ...c_j,..., c_m). If the column c_j has a constraint NOT NULL and there are no other correspondence from the form tree to the column c_j, then the correspondence $\mathcal{FT}$:P/e $\rightsquigarrow \mathcal{D}$:T.$c_i$ is prevented by the NOT NULL constraint of c_j, because a tuple that only contains the data about P/e cannot be inserted in the table T.

Extending Database. Let $\mathcal{M}'$ be the set of correspondences returned by the procedure cleanup($\mathcal{D}'$, $\mathcal{D}$, $\mathcal{M}$). If there is an element $d \in \mathcal{D}'$ that is not covered by any correspondences in $\mathcal{M}'$, we need to extend $\mathcal{D}$ to accommodate d.

We develop a procedure extendDB($\mathcal{D}'$, $\mathcal{D}$, $\mathcal{M}'$) which returns an extended database and new mappings. The issues we consider in extending database are optimizations for data storage and query processing (as proposed in Definition 2.) It is desirable to minimize the number of columns that have NULL values. However, adding a column to an existing table may bring in a lot of NULL values to the table. Consider two tables $T'(a_1, a_2, ..., a_n) \in \mathcal{D}'$ and $T(b_1, b_2, ..., b_m) \in \mathcal{D}$ such that $T' \rightsquigarrow T$ and there are h correspondences between the columns of T' and T, that is, $a_{i_1} \rightsquigarrow b_{j_1}$, $a_{i_2} \rightsquigarrow b_{j_2}$, ..., and $a_{i_h} \rightsquigarrow b_{j_h}$. If $m > h$ or/and $n > h$, then there are dangling columns in the tables that are not matched. If we add a new column to T, then all the existing tuples as well as all the new tuples inserted by other forms will have NULL values under the column. However, if we create a new table for new columns in order to reduce the number of NULL values, the number of tables is increased. To balance the trade-off between reducing the number of tables (joins) and reducing NULL values, two of the fundamental concerns in database design, we employ a user-defined *quality tuning factor*(qf) $(0 \le qf \le 1)$. $qf = 0$ indicates a high preference to reducing NULL values, while $qf = 1$ indicates a high preference to reducing the number of tables. When merging two tables, we compare the tuning factor with a numeric metric *null value ratio* (nvr) to make decision. The *null value ratio* ($nvr = \frac{(m-h)+(n-h)}{h}$) reflects the possibility of having NULL value columns if the two tables are merged together. If the nvr is lower than qf, we merge the two tables, otherwise, we create a new table.

6 Experiments

We conducted experiments on evaluating the performance of the FormMapper system. The goal of the experiments is two-fold: (1) to evaluate the effectiveness of the tree extraction component and (2) to evaluate whether the merging process can generate "good" results while dynamically and continuously mapping and integrating user-created forms.

6.1 Testing the Tree Extraction Component

Testing tree extraction consists of two parts: (1) training the HMM models and (2) applying the models to test data. We collected 52 data-entry forms in the healthcare domain and manually labeled them with semantic tags as training examples. Because the limited number of examples, we conducted a k-fold cross-validation for training and testing. That is, we divided the entire set into k sets (folds). For each fold, we trained the model on the other folds and test on the fold. The smallest form has 50 elements and the largest form has 183 elements. The average size of form happens to be 100. For measuring the effectiveness, we define the *extraction accuracy* as the percentage of the correctly extracted patient-child relationships. Our experiments on the 52 examples showed the average accuracy was 96%. The average time for generating a tree structure was within one second.

6.2   Evaluating the Merging Process

We conducted comparative experiments on evaluating the performance of the merging process. We used sets of complex and overlapping forms to incrementally build databases in the **FormMapper** system. We manually examined the resultant databases and compared them with "gold standard" databases created by human experts. The experimentation was carried out as follows. For a set of forms, we put the forms in a random order and applied the system to them one by one. We started with an empty database. The system generated a new database from the first form and sequentially integrated other forms. We were concerned with the following two questions: (i) did the resultant database have the desired properties? and (ii) was the resultant database comparable to the "gold standard" databases?

Datasets and Benchmarks. We selected 3 sets with total 16 forms (among the 52 forms) belonging to 3 different healthcare institutions. The average form size is 61. We asked two human experts to manually generate databases from the 3 sets of forms. These manually generated databases serve as "gold standard" for comparison. Both experts have more than 10 years of experience in designing databases for various enterprises. We were informed that the experts required *several hours* to prepare the "gold standard".

Implementation and Experiment Setting. The system is implemented in a IBM x3400 server with 8 GB memory. In all the experiments, the *quality tuning factor* qf (defined in Section 5.2) which is used in the database extension process is set to 0.5. For discovering element correspondences, we developed our own solution by exploiting linguistic and structural information.

Experimental Results. First of all, the system took on average 3 seconds to create a new database or integrate a form to an existing database. On an average, the databases contain 56 tables, 172 columns, 98 values, and 61 foreign key references. Next, we manually examined the resultant databases and compared them with the "gold standard" databases for evaluating desired properties and quality. Our examination showed that all the resultant databases are *complete*. In addition, the system built *normalized* databases based on the functional dependences deduced from the many-to-one relationships. Figure 6 shows a summary of the comparison between the system generated databases and the "gold standards" in terms of the total number of database elements.

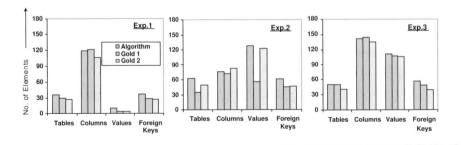

Fig. 6. Total Elements - Algorithm Vs Gold

On an average, 87% of system generated databases are considered to be "matched" to the "gold standard" databases.

We are more interested in the discrepancies. A small portion of the discrepancies is due to missing correspondences. For discrepancies under the same set of correspondences, we analyzed the results and identified 7 form patterns where the result differed between the algorithm and the gold standards. We found that the algorithm resulted in a superior result in 3 out of the 7 cases, and also both the gold standards resulted in superior results in 3 cases each. For the superior cases in the "gold standards", we found that they were mainly due to human judgement based on a personal understanding of the domain semantics. For example, a human expert extracted many-to-one relationships from the category-subcategory relationships on forms based on personal domain knowledge. Considering the algorithms generate databases with "good" properties by only taking as input the forms, we would conclude that the algorithms are promising and have the potential to replace human developers.

7 Conclusions

Jagadish et al. recently illustrated 5 painful issues in database usability [13]. Among them, the birthing pain is related to the difficulties of creating a database and putting information into a database. We are motivated to study an easy and flexible way for users to use a database for storing information. Forms are a user-friendly way for interacting with databases. We develop a solution for automatically generating databases from data-entry forms. In terms of form creation, our problem is an inverse process of that studied in [14], where query forms are automatically generated from databases. For our problem, we show that with the fully automatic solution, users do not need a clear knowledge of the final structure of a database. As users create more forms for evolving needs, the structure of the database grows automatically, however, in a principled way with predictive characteristics. The limitations of our approach include the missing correspondences and syntactic nature of the merging process. In future, we intend to exploit more sophisticated schema matching techniques [6] and apply an ontology to resolving semantic heterogeneity.

References

[1] Form Assembly, http://www.formassembly.com
[2] Jotform, http://www.jotform.com/
[3] Wufoo, http://wufoo.com/
[4] Zoho Creator, http://creator.zoho.com
[5] An, Y., Borgida, A., Miller, R.J., Mylopoulos, J.: A Semantic Approach to Discovering Schema Mapping Expressions. In: ICDE 2007, pp. 206–215 (2007)
[6] Aumueller, D., Do, H.-H., Massmann, S., Rahm, E.: Schema and ontology matching with coma++. In: SIGMOD (2005)
[7] Batini, C., Lenzerini, M., Navathe, S.B.: A comparative analysis of Methodologies for database schema integration. ACM Computing Surveys 18(4), 323–364 (1986)

[8] Bellahsene, Z., Bonifati, A., Rahm, E. (eds.): Schema Matching and Mapping (Data-Centric Systems and Applications). Springer, Heidelberg (2011)

[9] Buneman, P., Davidson, S.B., Kosky, A.: Theoretical aspects of schema merging. In: Pirotte, A., Delobel, C., Gottlob, G. (eds.) EDBT 1992. LNCS, vol. 580, pp. 152–167. Springer, Heidelberg (1992)

[10] Chiticariu, L., Hernández, M.A., Kolaitis, P.G., Popa, L.: Semi-automatic schema integration in clio. In: VLDB, pp. 1326–1329 (2007)

[11] Choobineh, J., Mannino, M.V., Tseng, V.P.: A form-based approach for database analysis and design. Commun. ACM 35(2), 108–120 (1992)

[12] Dragut, E.C., Kabisch, T., Yu, C.T., Leser, U.: A hierarchical approach to model web query interfaces for web source integration. PVLDB 2(1), 325–336 (2009)

[13] Jagadish, H.V., Chapman, A., Elkiss, A., Jayapandian, M., Li, Y., Nandi, A., Yu, C.: Making database systems usable. In: SIGMOD 2007, pp. 13–24. ACM, New York (2007)

[14] Jayapandian, M., Jagadish, H.V.: Automated creation of a forms-based database query interface. Proc. VLDB Endow. 1(1), 695–709 (2008)

[15] Khare, R., An, Y.: An empirical study on using hidden markov model for search interface segmentation. In: Proceedings of 18th ACM Conference on Information and Knowledge Management (CIKM), pp. 17–26 (2009)

[16] Khare, R., An, Y., Hu, X., Song, I.-Y.: Can clinician create high-quality databases? a study on a flexible electronic health record (fehr) system. In: The Proceedings of the 1st ACM Health Informatics Symposium (IHI 2010), Washington, DC, USA (2010)

[17] Khare, R., An, Y., Song, I.-Y.: Understanding search interfaces: A survey. SIGMOD Record 39(1), 33–40 (2010)

[18] Kowalczykowski, K., Ong, K.W., Zhao, K.K., Deutsch, A., Papakonstantinou, Y., Petropoulos, M.: Do-it-yourself custom forms-driven workflow applications. In: CIDR 2009 (2009)

[19] Luković, I., Mogin, P., Pavićević, J., Ristić, S.: An approach to developing complex database schemas using form types. Softw. Pract. Exper. 37(15), 1621–1656 (2007)

[20] Madhavan, J., Bernstein, P.A., Rahm, E.: Generic schema matching with cupid. In: VLDB 2001, pp. 49–58 (2001)

[21] Miller, R.J., Haas, L.M., Hernandez, M.A.: Schema Mapping as Query Discovery. In: VLDB, pp. 77–88 (2000)

[22] Pavicevic, J., Lukovic, I., Mogin, P., Govedarica, M.: Information system design and prototyping using form types. In: ICSOFT (2), pp. 157–160 (2006)

[23] Popa, L., Velegrakis, Y., Miller, R.J., Hernández, M.A., Fagin, R.: Translating web data. In: VLDB, pp. 598–609 (2002)

[24] Pottinger, R., Bernstein, P.A.: Merging models based on given correspondences. In: VLDB, pp. 826–873 (2003)

[25] Rabiner, L.R.: A tutorial on hidden markov models and selected applications in speech recognition. Proceedings of the IEEE, 257–286 (1989)

[26] Rahm, E., Bernstein, P.: An on-line bibliography on schema evolution. SIGMOD Record 35(4), 30–31 (2006)

[27] Wu, W., Yu, C., Doan, A., Meng, W.: An interactive clustering-based approach to integrating source query interfaces on the deep web. In: SIGMOD 2004, pp. 95–106. ACM, New York (2004)

[28] Yang, F., Gupta, N., Botev, C., Churchill, E.F., Levchenko, G., Shanmugasundaram, J.: Wysiwyg development of data driven web applications. Proc. VLDB Endow. 1(1), 163–175 (2008)

External Variability of Software: Classification and Ontological Foundations

Iris Reinhartz-Berger[1], Arnon Sturm[2], and Yair Wand[3]

[1] Department of Information Systems, University of Haifa, Haifa 31905, Israel
iris@is.haifa.ac.il
[2] Department of Information Systems Engineering,
Ben-Gurion University of the Negev, Beer Sheva 84105, Israel
sturm@bgu.ac.il
[3] Sauder School of Business, University of British Columbia, Canada
yair.wand@ubc.ca

Abstract. Software variability management deals with the adaptation of reusable artifacts, such as models, specifications, and code, for particular requirements. External variability, which refers to software functionality as visible to users, deserves a special attention as it is closely linked to requirements and hence to early development stages. Errors or inaccuracies in these stages are relatively inexpensive to detect and easy to correct, yet can lead to expensive outcomes if not corrected. Nevertheless, the analysis of external variability in the literature is done ad-hoc and requires improvement.

In this paper we introduce a framework for classifying external variability types based on ontological principles. The framework defines the external view of software in terms of the behavior of the application domain. Behavior is formalized as state changes in response to external stimuli. Based on this view we classify the possible similarities and differences among applications and identify an integrated similarity measurement. We demonstrate the usage of this classification framework for feasibility studies in system development.

Keywords: domain engineering, software product line engineering, domain analysis, variability management.

1 Introduction

In the context of software engineering, *variability* is the ability of a core asset to be efficiently extended, changed, customized, or configured for use in a particular context [18]. Variability is of particular importance in different software engineering fields, one of which is software product line engineering [8, 17]. In this context, Weiss and Lai [21] define variability as an assumption about how members of a family may differ from each other. Identifying the commonality of a family of software products or applications is important as it describes the main concepts and rules of the domain under consideration. However, Gomaa [11] states that identification of the differences that can exist among artifacts is even more important, as it relates to a variety of possible ways of reuse. In that respect, Kim et al. [15]

M. Jeusfeld, L. Delcambre, and T.W. Ling (Eds.): ER 2011, LNCS 6998, pp. 275–289, 2011.
© Springer-Verlag Berlin Heidelberg 2011

claim that "to carry out domain analysis effectively and design widely reusable components, precise definitions of variability related terms and a classification of variability types must be made. Without an appropriate level of formal view, modeling and realizing variability are neither feasible nor practical."

Several studies have addressed classification of variability into types (e.g., [12] and [17]). Pohl et al. [17] divide variability into *external variability* which is the "variability of domain artifacts that is visible to customers", and *internal variability* which is the "variability of domain artifacts that is hidden from customers." Both external and internal variability are important to the success of developing software artifacts. However, external variability deserves special attention as it is visible to users and relates to requirements defined at early development stages where errors or inaccuracies are relatively inexpensive and easy to detect and correct.

Variability in general and external variability in particular are mostly analyzed either from practical points of view or in terms of taxonomies and metamodels (see, for example, [1] and [16]). However, the usability of these works for analyzing the similarity and differences between complete applications or software products is limited, as they are primarily designed for specification purposes.

The aim of this work is to present a *general classification framework* for external variability. Such classification can serve to better understand variability types and analyze their implications in various contexts. The main premise that underlies our approach is that from a user's point of view, what mainly matters is *the behavior of the implemented system*. In that respect, various artifacts produced during software development serve to identify and specify this behavior. Therefore, our framework takes a view which defines an application as a set of intended changes in a given domain. We term such changes – *application behaviors*. Thus, we will focus on application behaviors as specified in functional requirements. We will not refer to the ways to realize and implement these behaviors, as these aspects are usually less relevant to the customers (users) of the resulting software system. In particular, we will not refer to the actual composition of the system (e.g., in terms of objects and their interactions).

To formalize behaviors we use an ontological model. Specifically, we adapt Bunge's work [6, 7] to define formally domains, applications, and behaviors. This formalization enables us to define similarities and differences of behaviors and operationalize the notion of user's points of view. We chose Bunge's ontology since it places an emphasis on the notion of systems, defines the concepts of states and events in an axiomatic, well-formalized way, and has been adapted to conceptual modeling in the context of systems analysis and design [19, 20]. These aspects of Bunge's ontology made it appropriate for modeling external software behavior.

The rest of the paper is organized as follows. Section 2 reviews relevant concepts of Bunge's ontology and their adaptation to information systems. Section 3 sets the ground for comparing applications and defines similarities between states and events. Section 4 identifies eight classes of external variability of behaviors, explains their essence, and suggests measures for defining similarity between applications. Section 5 elaborates on one possible use of the framework: supporting formal feasibility studies during the requirements analysis stage of system development. Finally, Section 6 summarizes the work and suggests future research directions.

2   Bunge's Systems Ontology

Bunge's ontology describes the world as made of things that possess properties. The main Bunge's concepts that are relevant to our work are summarized in Table 1, along with explanations and notations. The following uses these concepts for defining additional ones required for analyzing external variability.

Table 1. Summary of relevant Bunge's concepts

Ontological Construct	Explanation	Notation
(substantial) Thing	The elementary unit in Bunge's ontology. Something that exists in time and space.	
Property	All things possess properties. Properties are always attached to things. A property can be intrinsic to a thing or mutual to several things.	
Composite thing	A thing comprised of other things (components). A composite thing inherits properties from its components, but must also possess emergent properties not possessed by its components.	
Attribute	A characteristic assigned to things by humans. Properties are only known via attributes.	
State variable (attribute function)	A function which assigns to an attribute of a thing a value (out of a specific range) at a given time.	x_k
Functional schema	A set of attribute functions used for modeling similar things.	$X=\{x_k\}$
State	The vector of values of state variables of a thing at a particular point in time.	$s=<v_1,\dots v_n>$, $s.x_k=v_k$ $k=1..n$
Event	A change in the state of a thing (from s_1 to s_2)	$<s_1, s_2>$
External event	A change in the state of a thing as a result of an action of another thing.	
Internal event	A change which arises due to an internal transformation in the thing.	
Transition laws	The specification of what might and what might not happen by transformations.	$L:S{\rightarrow}S$, where S is the possible states of a thing
Stable state	A state in which a thing remains unless forced to change by an external event. A state of a composite thing is stable if all its components are stable.	$L(s)=s$
Unstable state	A state that can be changed to another state by internal events which are governed by transition laws. A state of a composite thing is unstable if at least one of its components is unstable.	$L(s)\neq s$
Interaction	Two things interact if at least one of them affects the states the other progresses through. The existence of interactions is manifested via mutual properties (modeled as mutual attributes).	
Environment of a thing	All things that are not components of the thing but may interact with its components.	

We will assume that external events can affect a thing only when it or at least one of its components is in a stable state. If all components are in unstable states, they all undergo state transitions. Hence we term this the *no interruption assumption* as it requires that state transitions will not be interrupted by external events.

Based on the no interruption assumption, we define input sensitive states:

Definition 1. An *input sensitive state* is a state that can change due to an occurrence in the environment of the thing, i.e., due to an external event.

According to the no interruption assumption, an input sensitive state of a simple thing must be stable. For a composite thing, in every input sensitive state at least one component must be in a stable state (and can handle the external event).

We define a behavior of a thing as a sequence of external events which begins on an input sensitive state and ends at a stable state of the thing.

Definition 2. Given an input sensitive state s_1 and a sequence of external events $<e_i>$, *a behavior* is a triplet (s_1, $<e_i>$, s^*), where s^* is the first stable state the thing reaches when it is in state s_1 and the sequence of external events $<e_i>$ occurs. s_1 is termed the *initial state* of the behavior and s^* – the *final state* of the behavior.

Note that for a given input sensitive state and a given sequence of external events, a "swarm" of behaviors is possible as different combinations of events and interim states are possible (leading to different interim transitions). However, we assume that all simple things we deal with in practice will eventually reach some kind of stability (*stability assumption*). In other words, we assume that a thing will always have a way to complete processing a sequence of events, before starting processing the next sequence of external events.

As an example, consider a warehouse, which is a (composite) thing that includes *workers*, a *manager*, and *inventory*. External to the warehouse are *clients* who request orders, and *technicians*, who may help fix different types of problems. Orders are represented by mutual properties of the client and the warehouse employees (i.e., the manager and/or the workers), as these are the two parties that exchange information while ordering. The manager first decides on whether to approve orders or not. Orders are then processed by workers. Orders can be canceled due to internal warehouse problems or clients' requests.

In the context of order processing, relevant state variables of the warehouse are client input (indicating a new order, cancellation of order, or resumption of cancelled order), description of the requested item, order size, inventory level, worker status (processing an order or not), manager's status (considering an order or not), manager's decision (approving or declining the order), and the outcome of worker actions related to orders (e.g., successfully completed, canceled, and failed).

Each state in the warehouse is defined in terms of values of state variables. Two examples of such definition are given in Table 2. The "Ready to Receive Orders" state is stable: the warehouse will not change its state as long as no external event occurs. When the external event "client order arrives" occurs, the warehouse will change its state to "Request is being Created". This change will be followed by more changes of states, depending on internal laws and occurrences of additional external events.

Three possible behaviors of the warehouse are depicted in Figure 1. Two behaviors differ due to internal laws: in the first behavior the client's request is fully satisfied, while in the second behavior the warehouse fails to supply the requested item, due to internal problems (e.g., lack of inventory). The third behavior differs from the first two due to an additional external event that occurs before the whole warehouse reaches a stable state. Note that the time when the second event, "client cancels", occurs is important, as according to the no interruption assumption, at least one of the warehouse's components should be stable in that time. In other words, the client can cancel an order only when a worker is available to receive this request. Handling this sequence of the two events, the warehouse eventually reaches a stable state, following the stability assumption.

Table 2. Definition of two states in the Warehouse example

State → Variable State ↓	manager status	manager decision	worker status	worker outcome	requested item	order size	inventory level	client input
Ready to Receive Orders	'available'	'none'	'available'	'none'	null	null	L	'none'
Request is being Created	'notified'	'none'	'available'	'none'	item_id	q>0	L	'ordering'

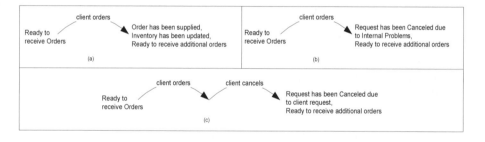

Fig. 1. Possible behaviors of order processing in a warehouse (text before and after arrows represents states, arrows represent external events)

Note that the behaviors in Figure 1 may seem similar or different depending on the point of view. The two first behaviors, a and b, for example, can be considered similar if we are only interested in the ability to react to all ordering events generated by clients, independent of the outcome (order is supplied or canceled).

We turn now to the definitions of application domains and applications.

Definition 3. An *application domain* (a *domain* for short) is a set of things where the states or the behaviors of these things are of interest for some stakeholders.

Definition 4. Given a domain D, *an application over the domain* D is a sub-set of behaviors of interest in the domain.

Consider the warehouse as a domain. Examples of applications are order processing, billing, and order delivery. Examples of states, external events, and behaviors in an order processing application are depicted in Figure 1. A billing application may be interested in other behaviors, such as paying by cash and paying by credit card.

Applications over the same domain can be described at various levels of abstraction. The right choice of abstraction can enable handling wide domains and comparing different behaviors. In the warehouse example, we can define an application that refers only to whether the order is handled or not, while another application can refer to this aspect as well as to whether the order is successfully processed or not (the second case will require more state variables than the first one). We denote by X^D the state variables of the domain and by X^A – the sub-set of state variables of the domain that affect or are affected by behaviors in application A.

3   Comparing Application Behaviors – The Similarity Anchor

In order to explore ways to compare applications, we first define similarity between behaviors. Variability will be viewed as the opposite of similarity. We will operationalize similarity by asking the question: can a given behavior be substituted by another and to what extent. The rationale for this approach is that the purpose of analyzing artifacts for their similarity is to examine whether one can be used instead of the other, at least in some circumstances. In the same vein, variability will address the limits of when one application behavior can be substituted by another.

While comparing applications (or particular behaviors), we will assume that they are defined over the same domain (the union of the application domains). However, in order to compare application behaviors, it is not enough that the applications are both over the same domain. It should also be possible to compare their states.

Definition 5. We will say that A_1 and A_2, which are defined over the same domain D, are *state-comparable* if and only if their sets of state variables are not disjoint, i.e., $X^{A_1} \cap X^{A_2} \neq \varnothing$.

In the following, we will assume that A_1 and A_2 are state comparable. Furthermore, A_1 and A_2 may be the same application and then we will compare different behaviors of that application.

The comparison of behaviors will be in terms of states (initial and final ones) and external events. Since external events are defined as occurrences in the domain and the two state-comparable applications are defined over the same domain, we will define similarity of external events in terms of equality. In other words, two external events are similar if they appear to be the same in the application domain.

Similarity of states is defined in terms of equivalence with respect to a set of state variables. The choice of state variables manifests the view of interest, as formalized in the following definitions.

Definition 6. Let s and t be states in A_1 and A_2, respectively, and X be a set of state variables common to the two applications ($\varnothing \neq X \subseteq X^{A_1} \cap X^{A_2}$). We will say that s and t *are equivalent with respect to X*, iff $\forall x \in X$ s.x = t.x.
Notation: $s \overset{x}{=} t$. X will be termed the *view of interest*.

State equivalence is actually an equivalence relationship, i.e., it is (1) reflexive: $s \overset{x}{=} s$, (2) symmetric: $t \overset{x}{=} s \rightarrow s \overset{x}{=} t$, and (3) transitive: $t \overset{x}{=} s \wedge s \overset{x}{=} r \rightarrow t \overset{x}{=} r$.

As an example, consider the two following states of the warehouse (Figure 1):

Request has been Canceled due
to Internal Problems,
Ready to receive additional orders

Request has been Canceled due
to client request,
Ready to receive additional orders

From an inventory point of view, these states are equivalent: both do not change the inventory level. However, from a client point of view, these states may be different, since in the left case the client remains with the wish to receive the requested item, while in the right case the client gave up this opportunity (by an explicit cancellation request). Thus, in the client's view of interest these states cannot be considered equivalent.

4 Classifying External Variability

We now turn to using the similarity of states and external events as defined above to the identification of the types of differences between behaviors. In principle, for an external observer of a system a behavior is defined in terms of three elements: an initial state, a set of external events, and a final state. Hence, when comparing two behaviors, there are eight possible cases, where for two given behaviors each of the three elements can be the same or different. Table 3 summarizes these classes of variability and exemplifies them. All these variability classes are identified with respect to a specific view of interest, X, which reflects and specifies an external point of view of some stakeholders. Examples of such views of interest are given in the right column of each row. The differences between the examples in each row of the table appear in bold. Note that for completeness we specify in this table all categories of variability, even when the degree of similarity is very low (e.g., in row 7) or there is no similarity (i.e., in row 8). Such cases can still be useful in indicating that two applications behave completely differently with respect to some views of interest and some behaviors.

The aforementioned analysis addressed the comparison of two specific behaviors. We now turn to comparing applications. This requires taking into account many possible behaviors. We therefore need to define similarity measurements that take into consideration all the behaviors of interest. Such measurements can be used to indicate the degree to which one application can be used instead of the other.

Different approaches have been suggested for evaluation of reusability of artifacts, especially in the area of software product line engineering (e.g., [13]), and for estimating the effort required for developing particular systems from reusable artifacts (e.g., [4]). The development of reusable artifacts might be a very demanding task that requires wide knowledge in the application domain and analysis at high abstraction levels. Here we suggest an approach based on measuring the similarity of two particular (state comparable) applications. Performing such measurements on different applications in the domain, can be the first step in identifying commonality and variability of the domain and defining its scope.

Definition 7. Let A_1 and A_2 be two applications and b a particular behavior in A_1. We define the *similarity of the application A_1 and A_2 with respect to the behavior b, a view of interest X, and a variability class c*, as $\mathrm{sim}(A_1, A_2|\, b, X, c) = 1$ if there exists a behavior of A_2, b', such that b and b' are in the same variability class c with respect to the view of interest X. $\mathrm{sim}(A_1, A_2|\, b, X, c) = 0$ otherwise.

Table 3. External variability classes in application behaviors

#	s_1	$<e_i>$	s^*	Class Name	Examples	Explanation of the Examples
1.	$\underset{\sim}{X}$	$=$	$\underset{\sim}{X}$	Completely similar behaviors	$ready \xrightarrow{client\ orders} succeeded$ $ready \xrightarrow{client\ orders} handled$	View: orders are handled[*]. Result: The behaviors are completely similar.
2.	$\underset{\sim}{X}$	$\neq$	$\underset{\sim}{X}$	Similar cases and responses, different interactions	$ready \xrightarrow{client\ orders\ by\ phone} succeeded$ $ready \xrightarrow{client\ orders\ by\ fax} \xrightarrow{technician\ fixes} succeeded$	View: orders are successfully processed. Result: The order is processed even though the events are different.
3.	$\underset{\sim}{X}$	$=$	$\underset{\not\sim}{X}$	Similar triggers, different responses	$ready \xrightarrow{client\ orders} succeeded$ $ready \xrightarrow{client\ orders} failed$	View: the warehouse is ready to receive orders. Result: Although having the same start and interactions, the behaviors end differently.
4.	$\underset{\sim}{X}$	$\neq$	$\underset{\not\sim}{X}$	Similar cases, different behaviors	$ready \xrightarrow{client\ orders\ by\ phone} succeeded$ $ready \xrightarrow{client\ orders\ by\ fax} \xrightarrow{technician\ cancels} failed$	View: the warehouse is ready to receive orders. Result: Behaviors start similarly, but different sets of events yield different responses.
5.	$\underset{\not\sim}{X}$	$=$	$\underset{\sim}{X}$	Different cases, similar behaviors	$opened \xrightarrow{client\ orders} succeeded$ $closed \xrightarrow{client\ orders} handled$	View: orders are handled. Result: Behaviors end similarly with the same set of events occurring at different initial states
6.	$\underset{\not\sim}{X}$	$\neq$	$\underset{\sim}{X}$	Different triggers, similar responses	$opened \xrightarrow{client\ orders} succeeded$ $closed \xrightarrow{client\ orders} \xrightarrow{client\ cancels} handled$	View: orders are handled. Result: Behaviors end similarly with different sets of events occurring at different initial states.
7.	$\underset{\not\sim}{X}$	$=$	$\underset{\not\sim}{X}$	Different cases and responses, similar interactions	$opened \xrightarrow{client\ orders} succeeded$ $closed \xrightarrow{client\ orders} failed$	View: the warehouse receives client orders. Result: Behaviors react to the same set of events that arrives at different initial states and yields different responses.
8.	$\underset{\not\sim}{X}$	$\neq$	$\underset{\not\sim}{X}$	Completely different behaviors	$opened \xrightarrow{client\ orders} succeeded$ $closed \xrightarrow{client\ orders} \xrightarrow{client\ cancels} failed$	View: the warehouse handles ordering processes. Result: The behaviors react to different sets of events that arrive at different initial states and yield different responses.

[*] Here and in the following – "handled" mean that the request has been processed, whether ending successfully or not.

Since the different behaviors and different variability classes may have different importance to some stakeholders, we enable the association of weights to behaviors (bw_i) and to the variability classes (vcw_k, k=1,...,8) to reflect their importance; $\sum_{i=1}^{|A_1|} bw_i = 1$ and $0 \leq vcw_k \leq 1$. The different weights can be assigned in discussion between the analyst and the stakeholders to mirror the customer preferences.

Definition 8. The *similarity between application A_1 and application A_2* with respect to *the view of interest X* takes into consideration the highest similarity of the different behaviors in the various variability classes. Formally, this is defined as:

$$\text{sim}(A_1, A_2 | X) = \sum_{i=1}^{|A_1|} bw_i * (\max_{k=1}^{8}(vcw_k * sim(A_1, A_2 | X, b_i, c_k)))$$

Note that similarity as defined above is not a symmetric relationship, meaning that the similarity between A_1 and A_2 may be different than the similarity in the other direction (for example, when the functionality of one application completely includes the functionality of the other). In the next section, we demonstrate the application of the proposed framework in general and the use of the similarity metric between applications in particular in the context of feasibility studies in system development.

5 Framework Usage: Conducting Feasibility Studies

The purpose of the *feasibility study* in system development is to analyze the strengths and weaknesses of possible solutions to given problems [22]. In its simplest form, the two criteria to judge feasibility are cost required and value to be attained. *Operational feasibility* is a measure of how well a given system satisfies the requirements identified in the requirements analysis phase [3]. Existing operational feasibility techniques are limited in explaining to customers the preferred or recommended solutions and lack the ability to examine the behaviors of these solutions at different points of view (manifested at different level of granularity of analysis).

To overcome the above limitations, we suggest using our external variability classification framework to conduct a formal operational feasibility analysis in a 5-stage process, depicted in Figure 2.

As a first stage, the analyst has to define, together with the customer who requests the system, the *view of interest*. This can be done by choosing a sub-set of the already revealed state variables of the domain, to reflect the requirements and preferences of the customer. As the domain may be specified by a large set of state variables, some of which have not been explored while developing previous applications in the domain, the view of interest (X) may refer to new state variables relevant to the domain and, thus, both X and X^D may be modified while defining the exact requirements for the requested system (stage 2).

After defining the view of interest, the requirements for the system to be developed need to be elicited and collected, taking into consideration the view of interest. As these requirements are usually not described using the concepts of states, events, and behaviors, the application of our approach would require that the information about the applications will be translated to these concepts. We do not deal with this issue here, but we demonstrate how such translation can be done for one common method used in requirements modeling – use case modeling. The translation from other requirements engineering approaches is a subject for future research.

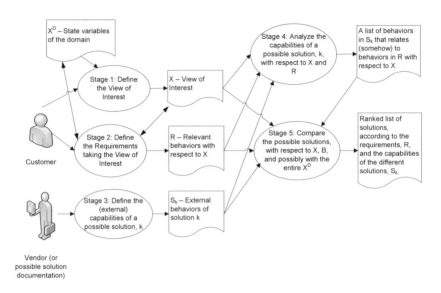

Fig. 2. Using the suggested classification framework for conducting operational feasibility analysis

In use case modeling, different templates exist for documenting required scenarios or desired behaviors of an application. We exemplify our approach using a simplified template with three fields: *pre-conditions* that specify the initial state of the scenario, *interactions* that correspond to the sequences of external events, and *post-conditions* that describe the final state when the scenario completes.

As an example, consider requirements for a warehouse application that includes ordering and inventory management. The system is required to enable receiving orders and cancellations only through phone or fax. The warehouse worker enters incoming orders and cancellations into the system. The warehouse cannot process in parallel more than 10 orders. Inventory can be updated only if no orders are being processed. The state variables of the domain include the warehouse status, the way orders are requested (by phone, by fax, or via the internet), the way order cancellation is requested, description of the requested item, order size, inventory level, processed orders, opened orders, required payment, payment type, and requested delivery details. However, according to requirements of the system customer[1], the relevant functionality is ordering items, canceling orders, and inventory update. Consequently, the relevant state variables selected in the first stage – *define the view of interest* – are:

X={warehouse status (open/closed), inventory level, opened orders, order status, order request type (phone/fax/internet), cancellation request type (phone/fax/internet)}

In the second stage – *define requirements* – a use case model, such as the one depicted in Figure 3, is created. This model, denoted "Requirements Model", reflects

---

[1] The word "customer" is used in this section to depict the orderer of the requested system, while the word "client" is used for describing a type of a user in the warehouse example.

the requirements from the proposed system. Additional relevant state variables may be extracted from the use case templates (e.g., notification in our example).

In the third stage – *define external capabilities* – which can also be performed via use case modeling, the analyst is required to model the external behaviors of systems that (partially) satisfy the requirements. This can be done by focusing on the view of interest (X) only, thus minimizing effort in conducting the feasibility study. Alternatively, the analysis can be conducted with respect to the full set of state variables of the domain (X^D), in order to provide a more in-depth analysis. Such analysis can support the selection of appropriate view of interest. The second possibility also supports selecting between applications that similarly satisfy the requirements, but are different in aspects that were not included in the more limited chosen view of interest, which reflects the customer's minimal requirements.

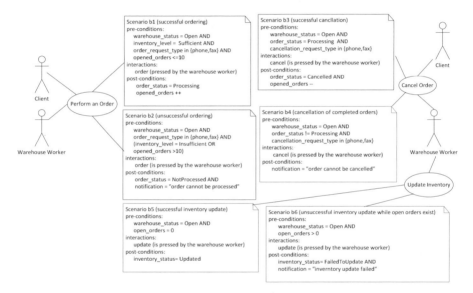

Fig. 3. The requirements model of an ordering and inventory update application in the warehouse domain

As an example for this stage, consider adapting an existing OrdSys, with the following capabilities. OrdSys handles orders received directly from the client via the internet. Orders can be received at any time, even when the warehouse is closed. This will enable the warehouse to begin preparing the order (e.g., replenishing inventory). However, the orders will be processed for fulfillment only if a signed confirmation with the same order details arrives by fax within three days of the original order. If the inventory is not sufficient for fulfilling the order, the order details are stored for future fulfillment. No cancellation by the client is allowed, but the warehouse worker can cancel orders, even if they have been already initially processed (and the client will be reimbursed if payment has been already made). The system does not have the functionality to update the inventory status. The model of OrdSys is depicted in Figure 4. Note that the scenarios refer to the included or extending use cases.

Scenarios b_1' and b_2', for example, refer to the included use cases through the additional "received fax" event in the interactions section.

In the fourth stage – *analyze capabilities of the proposed solution* – the solution as specified in stage 3 is examined with respect to the view of interest (X) and the (functional) requirements that were specified in stage 2 (via use cases). The analysis is done in terms of the predefined variability classes with respect to the specified view of interest.

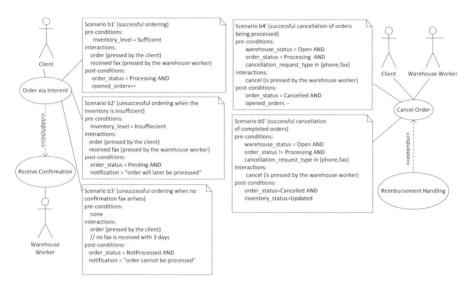

Fig. 4. The use case model of OrdSys

An example of an outcome of this stage for OrdSys is given in Figure 4. We weighted the different behaviors to reflect the customer's opinion that ordering is the most important functionality (received 0.5 for all its scenarios), then canceling (receiving the overall weight of 0.3), and finally the inventory update (receiving the overall weight of 0.2). Perceiving the variability classes as providing some kind of estimate for the effort required for changing the system in order to satisfy the given requirements model with a certain solution, we assigned relative weights to the variability classes as follows. The completely similar behaviors class (c_1) – 1, behaviors which differ only in their (external) interactions (c_2) – 0.75, behaviors which differ only in some aspects that refer to cases or responses (c_3, c_5, and c_7) – 0.25, and behaviors which differ in both external interactions and cases or response (c_4, c_6, and c_8) – 0 (as they require too much effort to be considered similar for feasibility study). Table 4 presents all the relevant similarity calculations. Note that we compared only behaviors that are comparable according to a specific view of interest, namely behaviors that refer to the same functionality.

The resultant overall similarity measurement, which range between 0 and 1, may indicate on the effort required in order to modify a system to fulfill the given requirements. Thus, the fifth stage of the suggested process – *compare possible solutions* – enables examining other options and comparing them with respect to their similarity measurements to the requirements model. Based on the outcome of this stage, the preferable solution is selected and further adapted and modified to fulfill all the given requirements.

Table 4. Evaluating OrdSys with respect to the given Requirements model

Behavior in Req.	Behavior Weight	Behavior in OrdSys	Similarity Concerns	Sim
b_1 – successful ordering	0.25	b'_1	Different triggers (both initial state and external events), similar responses – belong to c_6	0.25
		b'_2	Completely different behaviors (although dealing with receiving orders and thus may seem similar from some points of view) – belong to c_8	
		b'_3	Different cases and responses, but similar interactions, assuming that the source of the events is of no importance – belong to c_7	
b_2 – unsuccessful ordering	0.25	b'_1, b'_2	Completely different behaviors (although dealing with receiving orders and thus may seem similar from some points of view) – belong to c_8	0.25
		b'_3	Different cases and responses, although similar interactions – belong to c_5	
b_3 – successful cancellation	0.15	b'_4	Completely similar behaviors – belong to c_1	1
		b'_5	Different cases and responses, but similar interactions – belong to c_7	
b_4 – cancellation of completed orders	0.15	b'_4	Different cases and responses, but similar interactions – belong to c_7	0.25
		b'_5	Similar triggers, but different responses belong to c_3	
b_5 – successful inv. update	0.1	---		0
b_6– unsuccessful inv. update	0.1	---		0
Overall				**0.3125**

6 Summary and Future Work

The prevalence of variability in various engineering fields indicates that it is important to further understand and formalize it for software-based systems. Presently, in software engineering, formalization of variability in general and external variability in particular usually reflects technical or ad-hoc considerations. To formally define and analyze external variability which is tied to functional requirements, we suggest a framework based on an ontological model of application domain in terms of states and events. The approach enables us to operationalize the notion of a stakeholder view and to reflect the degree of similarity among applications. Based on the assumption that if fewer differences exist, less effort is needed to adjust a system to the requirements, we suggested how this framework can be applied during an operational feasibility study.

We consider this work the first step towards a more complete approach and plan to extend the work in several ways. First, to test usability, we will conduct practical case studies. Second, testing usefulness would require empirical work, such as experimenting with the guidance provided by the framework to identify similarities and differences between applications; comparing the measures of similarity calculated analytically to answers provided by domain experts as to how willing they would be to substitute one application for the other; and comparing the average similarity value to application adaptation effort as assessed by experts. Third, uses of the approach need to be developed, such as the evaluation of variability modeling methods. Fourth, the framework can be extended to include additional behavioral considerations such as the times and order of external events. Finally, it might be possible to extend the approach to include (some) aspects of internal variability, reflecting structural and non-behavioral characteristics (e.g., variability related to quality [12]).

References

1. Asikainen, T., Männistöa, T., Soininena, T.: Kumbang: A domain ontology for modelling variability in software product families. Advanced Engineering Informatics 21(1), 23–40 (2007)
2. Becker, J., Delfmann, P., Knackstedt, R.: Adaptive Reference Modeling: Integrating Configurative and Generic Adaptation Techniques for Information Models. In: Becker, J., Delfmann, P. (eds.) Reference Modeling – Efficient Information Systems Design through Reuse of Information Models, pp. 27–58. Physica-Verlag HD, Heidelberg (2006)
3. Bentley, L., Whitten, J.: System Analysis and Design for the Global Enterprise, 7th edn. (2007)
4. Böckle, G., Clements, P., McGregor, J.D., Muthig, D., Schmid, K.: A Cost Model for Software Product Lines. In: van der Linden, F.J. (ed.) PFE 2003. LNCS, vol. 3014, pp. 310–316. Springer, Heidelberg (2004)
5. Brocke, J.: Design Principles for Reference Modelling - Reusing Information Models by Means of Aggregation, Specialisation, Instantiation, and Analogy. In: Fettke, P., Loos, P. (eds.) Reference Modeling for Business Systems Analysis, pp. 47–75 (2007)
6. Bunge, M.: Treatise on Basic Philosophy, Ontology I: The Furniture of the World, vol. 3. Reidel, Boston (1977)
7. Bunge, M.: Treatise on Basic Philosophy, Ontology II: A World of Systems, vol. 4. Reidel, Boston (1979)
8. Clements, P., Northrop, L.: Software Product Lines: Practices and Patterns. Addison-Wesley, Reading (2007)
9. Coplien, J., Hoffman, D., Weiss, D.: Commonality and Variability in Software Engineering. IEEE Software 15(6), 37–45 (1998)
10. Czarnecki, K., Eisenecker, U.W.: Generative Programming - Methods, Tools, and Applications. Addison-Wesley, Reading (2000)
11. Gomaa, H.: Designing Software Product Lines with UML: From Use Cases to Pattern-Based Software Architectures. Addison-Wesley Professional, Reading (2004)
12. Halmans, G., Pohl, K.: Communicating the Variability of a Software-Product Family to Customers. Software and Systems Modeling 2(1), 15–36 (2003)
13. Her, J.S., Oh, S.H., Rhew, S.Y., Kim, S.D.: A framework for evaluating reusability of core asset in product line engineering. Information and Software Technology 49(7), 740–760 (2007)
14. Jacobson, I., Griss, M., Jonsson, P.: Software Reuse-Architecture. Process and Organization for Business Success. ACM Press, New York (1997)

15. Kim, S.D., Her, J.S., Chang, S.H.: A Theoretical Foundation of Variability in Component-Based Development. Information and Software Technology 47, 663–673 (2005)
16. Moon, M., Yeom, K., Chae, H.S.: An Approach to Developing Domain Requirements as a Core Asset Based on Commonality and Variability Analysis. IEEE Transactions on Software Engineering 31(7), 551–569 (2005)
17. Pohl, K., Böckle, G., van der Linden, F.: Software Product Line Engineering: Foundations, Principles, and Techniques. Springer, Heidelberg (2005)
18. Svahnberg, M., van Gurp, J., Bosch, J.: A taxonomy of variability realization techniques. Software – Practice and Experience 35(8), 705–754 (2006)
19. Wand, Y., Weber, R.: On the deep structure of information systems. Journal of Information Systems 5(3), 203–223 (1995)
20. Wand, Y., Weber, R.: An Ontological Model of an Information System. IEEE Transactions on Software Engineering 16, 1282–1292 (1990)
21. Weiss, D., Lai, R.: Software Product-Line Engineering: A Family-Based Software Development Process. Addison-Wesley, Reading (1999)
22. Young, G.I.M.: Feasibility studies. Appraisal Journal 38(3), 376–383 (1970)

Context Schema Evolution in Context-Aware Data Management[*]

Elisa Quintarelli, Emanuele Rabosio, and Letizia Tanca

Politecnico di Milano, Dipartimento di Elettronica e Informazione
{quintare,rabosio,tanca}@elet.polimi.it

Abstract. Pervasive access – often by means of mobile devices – to the massive amount of available (Web) data suggests to deliver, anywhere at any time, exactly the data that are needed in the current specific situation. The literature has introduced the possibility to describe the context in which the user is involved, and to tailor the available data on its basis. In this paper, after having formally defined the context schema – a representation for the contexts which are to be expected in a given application scenario – a strategy to manage context schema evolution is developed, by introducing a sound and complete set of operators.

1 Introduction

The current technological scenario is characterized by an extremely large variety of information sources, which constitutes an unprecedented opportunity for the users but at the same time risks to overwhelm them, especially when portable devices with limited memory are used. One viable solution is to tailor the data on the basis of the user context, that is, a set of properties characterizing the user, the system and the environment the user is interacting with. This set of characterizing parameters is modeled by means of context models (see [1,5,14] for surveys), allowing the reduction of large datasets on the basis of some perspectives (dimensions) that describe the situation (i.e., the *context*) in which the user is involved. We call the activity of selecting the relevant information for a target application, in a specific context, *data tailoring* [6], where the system allows a user to access only the view (over a global database schema) that is relevant for his/her context.

We use the expression *context model* to indicate the set of constructs and constraints to represent the useful dimensions of context and their values. A *context schema* exploits the constructs provided by a context model to describe the set of dimensions and values relevant for a certain application. Finally, a *context instance*, or simply a *context*, represents a particular situation, described according to a context schema.

Running Example: we consider a company offering services of video on demand and reservation of cinema tickets, relying on a global database schema.

---

[*] This research is partially supported by the European Commission, Programme IDEAS-ERC, Project 227977-SMScom.

M. Jeusfeld, L. Delcambre, and T.W. Ling (Eds.): ER 2011, LNCS 6998, pp. 290–303, 2011.

Useful context dimensions are: the kind of user (e.g., adult, teenager or family with children), the interest topic (e.g., cinemas or movies), the situation (e.g., alone or with friends), the time (e.g., daytime or night) and the location. Figure 1(a) shows the context schema of this example, formally described in Section 3.

The dimensions for data tailoring depend on the application requirements, that are intrinsically dynamic and thus can evolve; the evolution of requirements can be due to various reasons, including changing business needs or market and technology developments [16], therefore the context schema used to perform the tailoring process should be adapted in a way as seamless as possible to this evolution. Consider the movie example above. The company might change its business policy, deciding to remove the distinction between the daytime and evening schedules: this would lead to deleting the time dimension in the context schema. Again, at a certain point marketing researches could reveal that adult customers and teenagers show the same behavior, thus making the distinction between them useless: the designer may simplify the representation of the user type, merging the two categories adult and teenager together. The above changes may become out-of-synch w.r.t. the previously envisaged contexts, known by the users or by the context-aware applications at a given moment; thus the system must be able to respond to the applications in a seamless way, that is, a way as similar as possible to the context-aware behavior the applications expect. This problem is very similar to a problem of database schema evolution, where the queries designed to run on old schema versions should be maintained to be valid "through" the database schema changes. However, we will show in this paper that specific problems encountered in the scenario of context schema evolution cannot be solved within that of classical schema evolution.

Context schema evolution is relevant when an update of the available context-aware data is necessary, as well as when the user (or application) context changes and the system must provide the new context-aware portion of data. If the context schema has evolved, in both situations it may happen that the context detected by the user's device conforms to an obsolete context schema; in order to deliver the appropriate data, the system has to determine the context which (i) conforms to the new schema and (ii) is the closest to the one detected by the user's device. Studying context schema evolution is also preliminary to understanding context sharing, a need that may arise in P2P scenarios.

This work proposes strategies to support the evolution of context schemas in a semi-automatic way. The hierarchical context model of [6] is re-formulated in terms suitable to deal with context schema evolution; then, a set of operators to evolve context schemas is introduced along with the necessary modifications to make the instances compliant with the new schemas. Soundness and completeness properties are studied. The paper is organized as follows. Section 2 describes the related work, while Section 3 introduces the employed context model. Section 4 outlines a framework for managing context schema evolution and Section 5 formalizes the evolution operators. Finally, Section 6 concludes the paper.

2   Related Work

The problem of context schema evolution has not been much explored in the literature yet. An exception is [11], which defines a general framework supporting the representation and management of context information based on the notions of *profile schema* and *profile instance*, and sketches a method to manage profile schema and instance evolution which however is very onerous for the designer.

Schema evolution has been studied in various fields: for example, in the web domain [21,7] propose two frameworks to manage the evolution of conceptual schemas. However, such an issue is typical of the database research area: in object-oriented [3,12] and relational [10,9] databases, ontologies [17,18] and XML [19,13], the focus is on the introduction of operators able to modify the entities that, in the specific scenarios, are the objects of the evolution and on the reactions the various systems have to enact to comply with the performed changes. Here we discuss the proposals on XML evolution since they are the most relevant for our work, based on a hierarchical context model that can be simply implemented in XML. Paper [20] defines some evolution primitives, without tackling schema update problems, while [2,4,8] introduce updating primitives for XML documents in order for efficient incremental validation with respect to a fixed schema. These approaches consider changing instances w.r.t. to fixed schemas, whereas our problem requires to study instance evolution when the schema changes. The evolution of XML DTDs is considered by Su et al. [19], who define a set of modification primitives; for each of them preconditions and results of the application are described. Moreover, the DTD modification primitives are also associated with the changes necessary to guarantee that the XML documents remain valid w.r.t. the modified DTD. Also Klettke [15] introduces evolution operations to evolve schemas, this time represented through a conceptual model; changes are then propagated to the XML documents. While these proposals provided us with interesting intuitions, they do not supply a formal framework, which is one of our objectives in this paper.

A formal characterization of operators is introduced by Guerrini et al. in [13]. They propose modification primitives for XSD describing their preconditions and semantics; algorithms for partial revalidation and adaptation of documents dependent on the applied primitives are also defined. We were inspired by this approach, however it is, on the one hand, too general to take into account the specific semantics of context schemas and instances, and on the other hand, the proposed preconditions and semantics — as well as the related document adaptation algorithms — should be heavily revised to comply with the requirements of context schema evolution.

3   Context Model

We formalize the context model of [6], called Context Dimension Tree (CDT), for the purpose of context schema evolution. The CDT model represents context schemas as trees with nodes of two kinds: dimensions (black nodes) and their values, or *concepts* (white nodes). A visual representation of a CDT for the movie scenario is shown in Figure 1(a). Dimensions and concepts can have attributes (square nodes), that are parameters whose values are provided by the users at execution time. A dimension can be connected to at most one attribute (e.g. the zone id), and in this case it does not have any concept child; the attribute is used when it is impractical to enumerate all the dimension children. Concept attributes are used to further specify a concept, for instance, to indicate the age of a teenager.

The set $\mathcal{N}$ of node identifiers is thus partitioned into two subsets: *concept node identifiers* ($\mathcal{N}^\circ$) and *dimension node identifiers* ($\mathcal{N}^\bullet$). $\mathcal{A}$ is the set of attribute identifiers and $\mathcal{L}$ a set of strings. All these sets are pairwise disjoint. We start by defining the *context semischema*:

Definition 1 (Context semischema). *A context semischema is a tuple $S = (N, E, r, Att, \alpha, \lambda)$ such that:*

(i) *$N \subseteq \mathcal{N}$, with $N = N^\circ \cup N^\bullet$, $N^\circ \subseteq \mathcal{N}^\circ$ and $N^\bullet \subseteq \mathcal{N}^\bullet$. $E \subseteq N \times N$ is a set of directed edges, $r \in N$ is a node identifier such that (N, E) is a tree with root r and $Att \subseteq \mathcal{A}$.*

(ii) *Every generation contains node identifiers of the same type and different from the immediately previous and following generations, i.e., for each $(n_1, n_2) \in E$, $n_1 \in N^\circ \Rightarrow n_2 \in N^\bullet$ and $n_1 \in N^\bullet \Rightarrow n_2 \in N^\circ$.*

(iii) *$\alpha : Att \to N$ is a function assigning a node identifier to each attribute. For $n \in N^\bullet$, if n is a leaf then $|\alpha^{-1}(n)| = 1$, otherwise $\alpha^{-1}(n) = \emptyset$.*

(iv) *$\lambda : N \cup Att \to \mathcal{L}$ is a function assigning a unique label to node and attribute identifiers. Two distinct siblings cannot have the same label, i.e for all $(n_1, n_2) \in E$ and $(n_1, n_3) \in E$ such that $n_2 \neq n_3$ it holds that $\lambda(n_2) \neq \lambda(n_3)$. Two distinct attributes associated with the same node cannot have the same label, i.e. if $a_1 \in \alpha^{-1}(n)$, $a_2 \in \alpha^{-1}(n)$ and $a_1 \neq a_2$ then $\lambda(a_1) \neq \lambda(a_2)$.*

The set E of edges constitutes a binary relation on the set of node identifiers; its transitive closure is indicated by E^+.

Definition 2 (Context schema). *A context schema is a context semischema $(N, E, r, Att, \alpha, \lambda)$ in which r is a concept node and $\lambda(r) = $ `context`.*

In an instance, i.e., a *context*, the value of at least one dimension must be specified, possibly along with a value for its attributes (if any). A context instance too can be represented as a tree, for example the instance (of the schema in Figure 1(a)) depicted in Figure 1(b) describes an adult aged 35, who is currently with friends, interested in romantic comedies, at night time, located in a zone whose ZIP code is 20133.

Let $\mathcal{V} = \mathcal{L} \cup \{ALL\}$, where ALL is a special string indicating that no values have been provided. Formal definitions about instances are:

Definition 3 (Context semi-instance). *A context semi-instance is a pair $I = (S, \rho)$ where: (i) $S = (N, E, r, Att, \alpha, \lambda)$ is a context semischema such that*

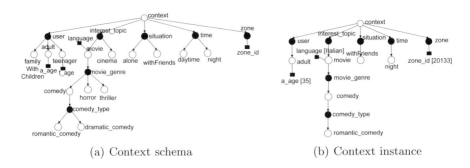

(a) Context schema   (b) Context instance

Fig. 1. Context schema and an instance related to the movie running example

*every dimension node identifier with no attributes has exactly one child, i.e.,
for each $n \in N^{\bullet}$ such that $|\alpha^{-1}(n)| = 0$, there is exactly one $n' \in N$ such that
$(n, n') \in E$. (ii) $\rho : Att \to V$ is a function assigning a value to the attribute
identifiers of S.*

Definition 4 (Context instance). *A context instance is a context semi-
instance $I = (S, \rho)$ such that S is a context schema.*

Definition 5 (Schema-instance relationship). *Let $I = (S_I, \rho_I)$ be a context
instance, where $S_I = (N_I, E_I, r_I, Att_I, \alpha_I, \lambda_I)$, and let $S = (N_S, E_S, r_S, Att_S, \alpha_S,
\lambda_S)$ be a context schema. I is said to be an* instance of S *iff there exist an in-
jective function $h_N : N_I \to N_S$, and an injective function $h_A : Att_I \to Att_S$
satisfying the following conditions:*

(i) $h_N(r_I) = r_S$
(ii) for all $(n_1, n_2) \in E_I$, $(h_N(n_1), h_N(n_2)) \in E_S$
*(iii) for all $n \in N_I$, $a \in Att_S$ if $\alpha_S(a) = h_N(n)$ then there exists $a_1 \in \alpha_I^{-1}(n)$
   such that $a = h_A(a_1)$*
*(iv) for all $n \in N_I$ it holds that $\lambda_I(n) = \lambda_S(h_N(n))$, and for all $a \in Att_I$ it
   holds that $\lambda_I(a) = \lambda_S(h_A(a))$*

Note that both context schemas and their instances can be represented as XML
documents, the latter containing a subset of the elements of the former.

In the rest of the paper, we indicate by $\mathcal{S}$ the set of all possible context
schemas, $\mathcal{SS}$ the set of all possible semischemas, $\mathcal{I}$ the set of all possible context
instances and $\mathcal{SI}$ the set of all possible semi-instances. The components of a
context semischema S_X are denoted by $(N_X, E_X, r_X, Att_X, \alpha_X, \lambda_X)$, while those
of a semi-instance I_X by (S_{IX}, ρ_{IX}). Given a context semischema $S = (N, E,
r, Att, \alpha, \lambda)$ and a node identifier $n \in N$, $father(S, n)$ indicates a node $n' \in N$
such that $(n', n) \in E$. In addition, the following shorthands denote useful sets:
$children(S, n) = \{n' \in N : (n, n') \in E\}$, $siblings(S, n) = \{n' \in N : n' \neq
n \wedge father(S, n) = father(S, n')\}$, $desc(S, n) = \{n' \in N : (n, n') \in E^+\}$ and
$\widetilde{desc}(S, n) = desc(S, n) \cup \{n\}$.

4   Framework for Context Evolution

We describe a reference architecture for context schema evolution for the purpose of data tailoring, relying on a global database[1] managed by a server. There are three actors: the user device, the server and the designer. The device provides the server with the current context instance and requests the related data, while the server manages the context schema and global data schema, and performs all the activities needed to administer the context, including data tailoring and evolution management. Data tailoring consists in associating every context instance with the view representing the relevant data for that context; this is realized by assigning a view to each concept node and to each dimension node with attribute, and then appropriately combining these views [6]. During system life-time, the designer may modify the context schema, but only by using certain evolution operators defined below; the sequence of the modifications is logged. The application of the operators modifies the context schema, obliging the designer to redefine the views related to some nodes. When the context schema changes, or when the associations between context instances and views, or the global database schema, vary over time, it is reasonable to suppose that the context/view associations be kept updated only for the instances of the most recent schema. Thus, it is not possible to deal with obsolete instances: if the device communicates an outdated context instance, the server must convert it into an instance of the current schema relying on the information contained in the log. The evolution strategy proposed in the next sections is thought to enable the designer to use the appropriate schema update operators, according to the effect he/she desires on the instances: in this way, he/she will also be aware of the nodes affected by an update. After an evolution from a context schema to a new one the designer has only to revise or add the (few) views related to the nodes that are involved in that operation, yielding a high degree of flexibility.

5   Evolution Operators

We now describe the evolution operators that the designer uses to update the context schema, along with the transformations that the instances undergo after the application of each operator. We first introduce the *update operations*: each operation *op* is implemented by a *schema evolution operator* SU_{op} and an *instance evolution operator* IU_{op}. The schema evolution operator describes the features of the resulting schema in terms of the source one and of some other parameters. The instance evolution operator adapts the instances to the new schema, trying to preserve as much information as possible. The schema operators are characterized by a set of preconditions expressed through first-order formulae.

Given a context schema S_S and a context instance I_S legal for S_S, the execution of an update operation with input parameters $p_1, \ldots, p_n$ produces — if

---

[1] Note that the fact that the database itself be centralized or not is irrelevant w.r.t. this discussion.

Table 1. Preconditions and semantics of Delete

Delete	
$SU_{Delete} : \mathcal{S} \times \mathcal{N} \to \mathcal{S}$	$IU_{Delete} : \mathcal{S} \times \mathcal{S} \times \mathcal{I} \times \mathcal{N} \to \mathcal{I}$
$SU_{Delete}(S_S, n) = S_T$	$IU_{Delete}(S_S, S_T, I_S, n) = I_T$

$\vdash N_T = N_S \setminus \widetilde{desc}(S_S, n)$

$\vdash E_T = E_S \setminus \{(n_1, n_2) \in E_S : n_2 \in \widetilde{desc}(S_S, n)\}$

$\vdash r_T = r_S$

$\vdash Att_T = Att_S \setminus \{a_1 \in Att_S : \alpha_S(a_1) \in \widetilde{desc}(S_S, n)\}$

$\vdash \alpha_T(a_1) = \alpha_S(a_1)$ if $a_1 \in Att_T$

$\vdash \lambda_T(n_1) = \lambda_S(n_1)$ if $n_1 \in N_T \cup Att_T$

$- N_{IT} = \{n_1 \in N_{IS} : h_N(n_1) \in N_T \wedge (n_1 \in N_{IS}^{\bullet}) \Rightarrow (\nexists n_2 \in children(S_{IS}, n_1))(h_N(n_2) = n))\}$

$- E_{IT} = \{(n_1, n_2) \in E_{IS} : (h_N(n_1), h_N(n_2)) \in E_T \wedge (n_2 \in N_{IS}^{\bullet} \Rightarrow (\nexists n_3 \in children(S_{IS}, n_2))(h_N(n_3) = n))\}$

$- r_{IT} = r_{IS}$

$- Att_{IT} = \{a_1 \in Att_{IS} : h_A(a_1) \in Att_T\}$

$- \alpha_{IT}(a_1) = \alpha_{IS}(a_1)$ if $n_1 \in Att_{IT}$

$- \lambda_{IT}(n_1) = \lambda_{IS}(n_1)$ if $n_1 \in N_{IT} \cup Att_{IT}$

$- \rho_{IT}(a_1) = \rho_{IS}(a_1)$ if $a_1 \in Att_{IT}$

Preconditions

1) $n \in N_S$, 2) $n \in N_S^{\circ} \Rightarrow siblings(S_S, n) \neq \emptyset$, 3) $n \neq r_S$

the preconditions are fulfilled — a new schema $S_T = SU_{op}(S_S, p_1, \ldots, p_n)$ and a new instance $I_T = IU_{op} (S_S, S_T, I_S, p_1, \ldots, p_n)$.

In this paper we define *atomic evolution operators*, which have the following features: i) **soundness**: every operator guarantees to produce a well-formed context schema and instance and to maintain the consistency between context instances and context schemas; ii) **completeness**: evolution operators allow to evolve to any valid target context schema; iii) **minimality**: each atomic operator cannot be obtained as combination of other atomic operators either on schemas or on instances. The set of schema atomic operators is denoted by $\mathbb{SOP}$, and the set of associated instance operators by $\mathbb{IOP}$. Moreover, our atomic operators can be used as building blocks to obtain composed, high-level ones. In the following, h_N and h_A denote the injective functions connecting the S_{IS} component of the source instance I_S with the source schema S_S.

5.1   Basic Atomic Evolution Operators

In the following we describe the first atomic operations, Delete and Insert. Due to space reasons, Table 1 reports preconditions and semantics only of the Delete.

Delete: The operator SU_{Delete} eliminates the subtree rooted in a node n from the source schema S_S. Since a dimension must have either an attribute (when it is a leaf) or at least a concept child, SU_{Delete} can be applied to remove either a dimension node and its sub-tree, or a concept node — if it has at least another sibling — and its sub-tree. The effect of SU_{Delete} on an instance is IU_{Delete}, which eliminates from the instance the subtree rooted in the node whose identifier corresponds to n in the function h_N, if such a node is present; moreover, if n is a concept, in order to not have a leaf dimension, in the instance also the node corresponding to the father of n must be eliminated, together with the edge connecting it with the node corresponding to n.

Table 2. Application of Delete and Insert

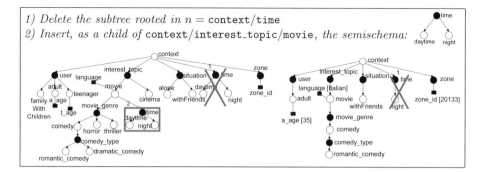

1) *Delete the subtree rooted in* $n =$ context/time
2) *Insert, as a child of* context/interest_topic/movie, *the semischema:*

Insert: Given a source schema S_S, the operator SU_{Insert} inserts a semischema R as a child of a specified node identified by n. The identifiers contained in the semischema must be different from the ones in S_S, and the correct type alternation among the generations must be preserved; moreover, the root of the semischema must have a label different from the ones of the children of n, in order to not introduce label conflicts. Since SU_{Insert} does not alter the existing nodes and attributes, the instances are not affected at all.

Example 1 (Atomic operations). Table 2 shows the application of the atomic schema operators to the context schema of Figure 1(a) (left-hand side), and the resulting modifications of the instance depicted in Figure 1(b) (right-hand side). For readability reasons, in the figures we denote each node by means of its path from the root, like in XPath.

Completeness of the Basic Atomic Operators. The set of basic atomic operators is enough to express all the possible schema modifications, i.e., it is *complete*. Our notion of completeness is similar to that in [3,19,13]. This notion is applied only to schemas because the evolution of an instance is *a possible consequence of that of the schema* and in general we do not apply the operators to change an arbitrary context instance into another, arbitrary one; rather, instances must be automatically updated when the schema changes, according to the meaning attached by the designer to that change. For example, when the schema operations on the left hand side of Table 2 are applied, the context instance representing an adult interested in cinema is not influenced, and thus remains unchanged.

Theorem 1 (Completeness). *Given two arbitrary context schemas S_1 and S_2, it is possible to find a finite sequence of operators belonging to $\{\mathsf{SU}_{Insert}, \mathsf{SU}_{Delete}\}$ that transforms S_1 into S_2.*

5.2   Methodological Considerations and Further Atomic Operators

Consider the schema and the instance obtained after the operations described in Example 1. Suppose first that the designer deletes from the schema the nodes adult and teenager — children of user —, triggering the removal of the user dimension from the associated instance; then, he/she inserts a *new* node `person` under the same dimension `user`. According to the IU_{Insert} semantics, the instance remains unaltered, because the instance where IU_{Insert} is applied now does not carry any information about the new node. Nevertheless, such a sequence of changes might intuitively represent a "replace" operation, that is, in the designer's aims, the added node is intended as a substitute for both `adult` and `teenager`; the sequence of deletions and insertions, though able to modify the schema according to the designer's intentions, did not modify the instance as intended. Therefore it turns out that, even if $\{SU_{Insert}, SU_{Delete}\}$ is enough to achieve completeness, this set needs to be extended if the designer needs updating operations inducing useful behaviors *on the instances* and not obtainable as combinations of insertion and deletion. To cope with this problem and similar ones, we add other atomic operators to $\mathbb{SOP}$, and the corresponding ones to $\mathbb{IOP}$. The set of operators we are presenting has been determined according to our intuition about the changes that may take place as consequences of the dynamism of the requirements; therefore, it may be further widened.

Replace: The operator $SU_{Replace}$ substitutes a set of concept siblings $\{m_1, \ldots, m_p\}$ with a unique node labeled ℓ; the new node carries all the attributes previously connected to the replaced nodes. The root cannot be replaced. The label ℓ must not be in conflict with the labels of other possible siblings of $\{m_1, \ldots, m_p\}$, and label conflicts must not arise neither among the children of the replaced nodes (now all children of the new node) nor among the attributes of the replaced nodes (now all assigned to the new node). If an instance contains a node corresponding to one of the replaced ones, $IU_{Replace}$ substitutes it with a new node labeled ℓ. Note that this operator is atomic (and thus minimal), because on instances $IU_{Replace}$ cannot be obtained by combining IU_{Delete} and IU_{Insert}.

ReplaceSubtreesWithAttribute: $SU_{RepSubWithAttr}$ replaces all the subtrees rooted in the (concept) children of a dimension node identified by n with an attribute labeled ℓ; the application of $SU_{RepSubWithAttr}$ indicates that the designer deems the hierarchy underlying the dimension node no more interesting. The operator $IU_{RepSubWithAttr}$ updates an instance if it contains a node identifier k corresponding to one of the children of n; in such a situation the subtree rooted in k is replaced by the new attribute, whose value will be the label of k. This operator is atomic for the same reason of the previous one. Table 3 shows the application of these additional atomic schema operators to the context schema obtained after the operations described in Example 1.

Let us now analyze Example 1 in more detail: at step 1, the subtree rooted in the dimension named `time` is eliminated from the schema, thus causing the same deletion on the instance. At step 2 a subtree identical — syntactically and semantically — to the one that had been deleted is inserted under the concept node `movie`; however, according to the IU_{Insert} semantics, the instance remains unaltered, because the instance where IU_{Insert} is applied now does not carry any information about the new subtree. Nevertheless, such a sequence of changes might intuitively represent a "move" operation, that is, in the designer's intention, the time information has probably become relevant only for those users

Table 3. Application of Replace and ReplaceSubtreesWithAttribute

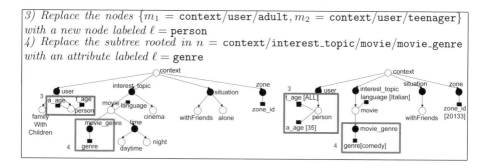

Table 4. Schema and instance cache operators

Delete: cache operators

$SC_{Delete} : S \times S \times N \rightarrow SS$ $IC_{Delete} : S \times S \times SS \times I \times I \times N \rightarrow SI$

$SC_{Delete}(S_S, S_T, n) = S_{TM}$ $IC_{Delete}(S_S, S_T, S_{TM}, I_S, I_T, n) = I_{TM}$

- $N_{TM} = N_S \setminus N_T$
- $E_{TM} = E_S \setminus E_T$
- $r_{TM} = n$
- $Att_{TM} = Att_S \setminus Att_T$
- $\alpha_{TM}(a_1) = \alpha_S(a_1)$ if $n_1 \in Att_{TM}$
- $\lambda_{TM}(n_1) = \lambda_S(n_1)$ if $n_1 \in N_{TM} \cup Att_{TM}$

- $N_{ITM} = N_{IS} \setminus N_{IT}$
- $E_{ITM} = E_{IS} \setminus E_{IT}$

$$- r_{ITM} = \begin{cases} \begin{rcases} n_1 \in N_{IS} : (\exists n_2 \in N_{IS}) \\ (n_1 = father(S_{IS}, n_2) \\ \wedge n_2 = h_N(n)) \end{rcases} & \begin{array}{l} \text{if } (\exists n_1 \in N_{IS}^\circ) \\ (h_N(n_1) = n) \end{array} \\ \begin{rcases} n_1 \in N_{IS} : \\ h_N(n_1) = n \end{rcases} & \begin{array}{l} \text{if } (\exists n_1 \in N_{IS}^\bullet) \\ (h_N(n_1) = n) \end{array} \\ \text{undefined} & \text{otherwise} \end{cases}$$

- $Att_{ITM} = Att_{IS} \setminus Att_{IT}$
- $\alpha_{ITM}(a_1) = \alpha_{IS}(a_1)$ if $a_1 \in Att_{ITM}$
- $\lambda_{ITM}(n_1) = \lambda_{IS}(n_1)$ if $n_1 \in N_{ITM} \cup Att_{ITM}$
- $\rho_{ITM}(a_1) = \rho_{IS}(a_1)$ if $a_1 \in Att_{ITM}$

who are interested in movies. The initial instance indicates both the interest in movies and the time but, when the time information is deleted, this aspect is completely lost in the context instance and does not influence the successive insertion. Therefore the application of the operators at the instance level results in the loss of the information related to time, due to the fact that the evolution process "forgets" the deleted subtree, taking care only of the information contained in the most recent schema and instances.

To solve the problem we store the eliminated subtrees in order to facilitate, if necessary, a later reintegration. In more detail, we redefine the *Delete* operation incorporating two additional operators: the *schema cache* SC_{Delete} and the *instance cache* IC_{Delete} (Table 4). The former describes the cached content after the schema deletion, while the latter does the same after the instance deletion. Now, *Delete* entails the caching of the semischema $S_{TM} = SC_{Delete}(S_S, S_T, p_1, \ldots, p_n)$ and of the semi-instance $I_{TM} = IC_{Delete}(S_S, S_T, S_{TM}, I_S, I_T, p_1, \ldots, p_n)$. We remark that SC_{Delete} and IC_{Delete} do not realize any schema or instance modification: they only define the information to be cached after that schema and instances have been

Table 5. Preconditions and semantics of InsertFromMemory

InsertFromMemory Given $R = (N, E, r, Att, \alpha, \lambda)$

$\mathsf{SU}_{InsertFM} : \mathcal{S} \times \mathcal{SS} \times \mathcal{SS} \times \mathcal{N} \to \mathcal{S}$

$\mathsf{SU}_{InsertFM}(S_S, S_{SM}, R, n) = S_T$

$\vdash N_T = N_S \cup N$
$\vdash E_T = E_S \cup E \cup \{(n, r)\}$
$\vdash r_T = r_S$
$\vdash Att_T = Att_S \cup Att$

$- \alpha_T(a_1) = \begin{cases} \alpha_S(a_1) & \text{if } a_1 \in Att_S \\ \alpha(a_1) & \text{otherwise} \end{cases}$

$- \lambda_T(n_1) = \begin{cases} \lambda_S(n_1) & \text{if } n_1 \in N_S \cup Att_S \\ \lambda(n_1) & \text{otherwise} \end{cases}$

$\mathsf{IU}_{InsertFM} : \mathcal{S} \times \mathcal{S} \times \mathcal{SS} \times \mathcal{I} \times \mathcal{SI} \times \mathcal{SS} \times \mathcal{N} \to \mathcal{I}$

$\mathsf{IU}_{InsertFM}(S_S, S_T, S_{SM}, I_S, I_{SM}, R, n) = I_T$

Let h_{NM}, h_{AM} be the injective functions relating nodes and attributes of S_{ISM} with the nodes and the attributes of the schema associated with the instance from which the semischema S_{ISM} has been eliminated.

Let $e_1, \dots, e_k$ be the system-assigned identifiers for the attributes $f_1, \dots, f_k$ of the inserted semischema defined as follows: $f_i \in Att : (\exists n_1 \in N_{ISM})(\alpha_{TM}(f_i) = h_{NM}(n_1) \wedge (\nexists a_1 \in Att_{ISM})(f_i = h_{AM}(a_1)))$

$\vdash N_{IT} = \begin{cases} N_{IS} \cup N_{ISM} & \left. \begin{array}{l} \text{if } N_{ISM} \neq \emptyset \wedge ((n \in N_T^\circ \\ \wedge (\exists n_1 \in N_{IS})(h_N(n_1) = n)) \vee h_N(r_{ISM}) = n) \end{array} \right. \\ N_{IS} & \text{otherwise} \end{cases}$

$\vdash E_{IT} = \begin{cases} \left. \begin{array}{l} E_{IS} \cup E_{ISM} \cup \\ \{(n_1, r_{ISM}) : h_N(n_1) = n\} \end{array} \right\} & \begin{array}{l} \text{if } N_{ISM} \neq \emptyset \\ \wedge n \in N_T^\circ \wedge (\exists n_1 \in N_{IS})(h_N(n_1) = n) \end{array} \\ \left. \begin{array}{l} E_{IS} \cup E_{ISM} \cup \\ \{(n_1, n_2) : h_{NM}(n_2) = n \wedge \\ h_N(n_1) = father(S_S, n)\} \end{array} \right\} & \text{if } N_{ISM} \neq \emptyset \wedge h_{NM}(r_{ISM}) = n \\ E_{IS} & \text{otherwise} \end{cases}$

$\vdash r_{IT} = r_{IS}$

$\vdash Att_{IT} = \begin{cases} \left. \begin{array}{l} Att_{IS} \cup \{a_1 \in Att_{ISM} : \\ (\exists n_1 \in N, a_2 \in Att) \\ (a_2 = h_{AM}(a_1) \wedge \alpha_{SM}(a_1) = \\ \alpha(a_1) = n_1)\} \cup \{e_1, \dots, e_k\} \end{array} \right\} & \begin{array}{l} \text{if } N_{ISM} \neq \emptyset \wedge ((n \in N_T^\circ \wedge \\ (\exists n_1 \in N_{IS})(h_N(n_1) = n)) \\ \vee h_{NM}(r_{ISM}) = n) \end{array} \\ Att_{IS} & \text{otherwise} \end{cases}$

$\vdash \alpha_{IT}(a_1) = \begin{cases} \alpha_{ISM}(a_1) & \text{if } a_1 \in Att_{ISM} \\ \{n_1 \in N_{IS} : \alpha_{TM}(f_i) = h_{NM}(n_1)\} & \text{if } a_1 = e_i, e_i \in \{e_1, \dots, e_k\} \\ \alpha_{IS}(a_1) & \text{otherwise} \end{cases}$

$\vdash \lambda_{IT}(n_1) = \begin{cases} \lambda_{ISM}(n_1) & \text{if } n_1 \in N_{ISM} \cup Att_{ISM} \\ \lambda(f_i) & \text{if } n_1 = e_i, e_i \in \{e_1, \dots, e_k\} \\ \lambda_{IS}(n_1) & \text{otherwise} \end{cases}$

$\vdash \rho_{IT}(a_1) = \begin{cases} \rho_{ISM}(a_1) & \text{if } a_1 \in Att_{ISM} \\ ALL & \text{if } a_1 \in \{e_1, \dots, e_k\} \\ \rho_{IS}(a_1) & \text{otherwise} \end{cases}$

Preconditions

1) $n \in N_S$, 2) $N = N_{SM}$, 3) $E = E_{SM}$, 4) $Att \cap Att_S = \emptyset$, 5) $(\forall n_1 \in children(S_S, n))(\lambda_S(n_1) \neq \lambda(r))$, 6) $n \in N_S^\circ \Rightarrow r \in N^\bullet$, 7) $n \in N_S^\bullet \Rightarrow r \in N^\circ$

---

updated with SU_{Delete} and IU_{Delete}. For the sake of simplicity the stored content is available only if an insertion is executed immediately after the deletion, then it is purged.

Table 6. Application of the Delete operation and of InsertFromMemory

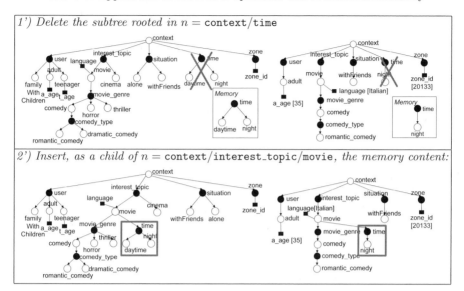

In order to exploit the content stored during the deletion, also the insert operation has to be memory-aware; therefore, the set of atomic operations is enriched with *InsertFromMemory* (Table 5). The related operators take as additional input the cached semischema S_{SM} and semi-instance I_{SM}: $S_T = \mathsf{SU}_{InsertFM}(S_S, S_{SM}, p_1, \ldots, p_n)$, $I_T = \mathsf{IU}_{InsertFM}(S_S, S_T, S_{SM}, I_S, I_{SM}, p_1, \ldots, p_n)$. The operator $\mathsf{SU}_{InsertFM}$ behaves exactly as SU_{Insert} does, but the semischema R inserted under the node n is retrieved from the cache; it is allowed to modify attributes and labels, while nodes and edges have to remain the same of the semischema stored in the memory. If n is a concept node, the memory contains a semi-instance, and the source instance contains the node corresponding to n, then $\mathsf{IU}_{InsertFM}$ reinserts the stored semi-instance. On the contrary, if n is a dimension node, the semi-instance is reintegrated only if the semischema has been reinserted exactly in the same position, thus simply rolling back the previous deletion; in fact, if the stored semischema were moved, the reinsertion would cause the presence of concept siblings in the instance.

Table 6 revises steps 1 and 2 of Example 1 taking into account the memory functionality: step 1' considers the new formulation of the *Delete* operation, extended with the cache operators. Step 2' mimics step 2 of Example 1, but applying *InsertFromMemory* instead of *Insert*.

Complexity Considerations. The computational complexity of schema and instance update is not an issue in our framework. In fact, all the operations can be implemented exploiting well-known tree search algorithms to locate the nodes involved in the transformations. Moreover, the size of context schemas is supposed to be of few tens of nodes, and the instances are even smaller.

Soundness of the Atomic Operators. A fundamental property of the evolution process is soundness. If a schema evolution operator is applied to a legal context schema fulfilling the preconditions, it should produce a legal context schema according to Definition 2. Moreover, the corresponding instance evolution operator must be such that its outcome is: 1) a legal context instance according to Definition 4 and 2) an instance of the schema produced by the related schema evolution operator, according to Definition 5 [12].

Theorem 2 (Soundness of schema evolution). *Let S_S be a context schema,* $\mathsf{SU}_{op} \in \mathbb{SOP}$ *and* $p_1, \ldots, p_n$ *the additional parameters required by* SU_{op}, *then* $\mathsf{SU}_{op}(S_S, p_1, \ldots, p_n)$ *gives as result a context schema* S_T.

Theorem 3 (Soundness of instance evolution). *Let S_S be a context schema,* I_S *an instance of S_S,* $\mathsf{IU}_{op} \in \mathbb{IOP}$, $\mathsf{SU}_{op} \in \mathbb{SOP}$, $p_1, \ldots, p_n$ *the additional parameters required by* SU_{op}, $q_1, \ldots, q_m$ *the additional parameters required by* IU_{op}, S_T *the context schema result of* $\mathsf{SU}_{op}(S_S, p_1, \ldots, p_n)$. *The result I_T of* $\mathsf{IU}_{op}(S_S, S_T, I_S, q_1, \ldots, q_m)$ *is an instance of S_T.*

6   Conclusions and Future Work

In this paper we have investigated the problem of context schema evolution. A set of atomic schema evolution operators has been introduced; we have also shown the soundness and the completeness of the evolution process. Our atomic operators are suitable to be composed for obtaining high-level ones, expressing common evolution needs; e.g, to move subtrees, rename nodes and attributes, insert and delete attributes. We plan to refine our proposal exploring techniques to optimize the sequence of operators applied to migrate from the initial instance to the instance of the target schema. Another, orthogonal interesting problem we will tackle is the one of *instance update*: it arises because, after a context switch from I_1 to I_2 (derived from a change in the environment), knowing the sequence of operators that leads from I_1 to I_2 allows graceful and automatic derivation of the I_2-aware views to be provided to the user. Thus, given two instances of the same schema, we want to study minimal and complete sets of operators that lead from I_1 to I_2. Finally, we are implementing a tool realizing the context schema evolution process.

Acknowledgments. The authors wish to thank Jan Hidders for the helpful discussions on the formalization of the context model.

References

1. Baldauf, M., Dustdar, S., Rosenberg, F.: A survey on context-aware systems. Int. Journal of Ad Hoc and Ubiquitous Computing 2(4), 263–277 (2007)
2. Balmin, A., Papakonstantinou, Y., Vianu, V.: Incremental validation of XML documents. ACM Transactions on Database Systems 29(4), 710–751 (2004)
3. Banerjee, J., Kim, W., Kim, H.-J., Korth, H.F.: Semantics and implementation of schema evolution in object-oriented databases. In: Proc. of SIGMOD, pp. 311–322. ACM Press, New York (1987)

4. Barbosa, D., Mendelzon, A.O., Libkin, L., Mignet, L., Arenas, M.: Efficient incremental validation of XML documents. In: Proc. of ICDE, pp. 671–682. IEEE Computer Society, Los Alamitos (2004)
5. Bolchini, C., Curino, C., Quintarelli, E., Schreiber, F.A., Tanca, L.: A data-oriented survey of context models. SIGMOD Record 36(4), 19–26 (2007)
6. Bolchini, C., Quintarelli, E., Rossato, R.: Relational data tailoring through view composition. In: Parent, C., Schewe, K.-D., Storey, V.C., Thalheim, B. (eds.) ER 2007. LNCS, vol. 4801, pp. 149–164. Springer, Heidelberg (2007)
7. Bossung, S., Sehring, H.-W., Hupe, P., Schmidt, J.W.: Open and dynamic schema evolution in content-intensive web applications. In: Proc. of WEBIST, pp. 109–116. INSTICC Press (2006)
8. Bouchou, B., Halfeld Ferrari Alves, M.: Updates and Incremental Validation of XML Documents. In: Lausen, G., Suciu, D. (eds.) DBPL 2003. LNCS, vol. 2921, pp. 216–232. Springer, Heidelberg (2004)
9. Curino, C., Moon, H.J., Zaniolo, C.: Graceful database schema evolution: the PRISM workbench. PVLDB 1(1), 761–772 (2008)
10. De Castro, C., Grandi, F., Scalas, M.R.: Schema versioning for multitemporal relational databases. Inf. Syst. 22(5), 249–290 (1997)
11. De Virgilio, R., Torlone, R.: A framework for the management of context data in adaptive web information systems. In: Proc. ICWE, pp. 261–272. IEEE, Los Alamitos (2008)
12. Grandi, F., Mandreoli, F.: A formal model for temporal schema versioning in object-oriented databases. Data and Knowledge Engineering 46(2), 123–167 (2003)
13. Guerrini, G., Mesiti, M., Sorrenti, M.A.: XML schema evolution: Incremental validation and efficient document adaptation. In: Barbosa, D., Bonifati, A., Bellahsène, Z., Hunt, E., Unland, R. (eds.) XSym 2007. LNCS, vol. 4704, pp. 92–106. Springer, Heidelberg (2007)
14. Hong, J., Suh, E., Kim, S.: Context-aware systems: A literature review and classification. Expert Syst. Appl. 36(4), 8509–8522 (2009)
15. Klettke, M.: Conceptual XML schema evolution - the CoDEX approach for design and redesign. In: Proc. of BTW Workshops, pp. 53–63. Verlagshaus Mainz (2007)
16. Lehman, M.M.: Software's future: Managing evolution. IEEE Software 15(1), 40–44 (1998)
17. Papavassiliou, V., Flouris, G., Fundulaki, I., Kotzinos, D., Christophides, V.: On detecting high-level changes in RDF/S kBs. In: Bernstein, A., Karger, D.R., Heath, T., Feigenbaum, L., Maynard, D., Motta, E., Thirunarayan, K. (eds.) ISWC 2009. LNCS, vol. 5823, pp. 473–488. Springer, Heidelberg (2009)
18. Plessers, P., De Troyer, O.: Ontology change detection using a version log. In: Gil, Y., Motta, E., Benjamins, V.R., Musen, M.A. (eds.) ISWC 2005. LNCS, vol. 3729, pp. 578–592. Springer, Heidelberg (2005)
19. Su, H., Kramer, D., Chen, L., Claypool, K.T., Rundensteiner, E.A.: XEM: Managing the evolution of XML documents. In: Proc. of RIDE-DM, pp. 103–110. IEEE Computer Society, Los Alamitos (2001)
20. Tatarinov, I., Ives, Z.G., Halevy, A.Y., Weld, D.S.: Updating XML. In: Proc. of SIGMOD, pp. 413–424 (2001)
21. Wienberg, A., Ernst, M., Gawecki, A., Kummer, O., Wienberg, F., Schmidt, J.W.: Content schema evolution in the coreMedia® content application platform CAP. In: Jensen, C.S., Jeffery, K.G., Pokorný, J., Saltenis, S., Bertino, E., Böhm, K., Jarke, M. (eds.) EDBT 2002. LNCS, vol. 2287, pp. 712–721. Springer, Heidelberg (2002)

Modeling the Propagation of User Preferences

Paolo Ciaccia[1] and Riccardo Torlone[2]

[1] Dip. di Elettronica, Informatica e Sistemistica, Università di Bologna, Italy
paolo.ciaccia@unibo.it
[2] Dip. di Informatica e Automazione, Università Roma Tre, Italy
torlone@dia.uniroma3.it

Abstract. User preferences are a fundamental ingredient of personalized database applications, in particular those in which the user context plays a key role. Given a set of preferences defined in different contexts, in this paper we study the problem of deriving the preferences that hold in one of them, that is, how preferences *propagate* through contexts. For the sake of generality, we work with an abstract context model, which only requires that the contexts form a poset. We first formalize the basic properties of the propagation process: *specificity*, stating that more specific contexts prevail on less specific ones, and *fairness*, stating that this behavior does not hold for incomparable contexts. We then introduce an algebraic model for preference propagation that relies on two well-known operators for combining preferences: Pareto and Prioritized composition. We study three alternative propagation methods and precisely characterize them in terms of the fairness and specificity properties.

1 Introduction

The information available in digital form is growing so fast that today the availability of methods for automatically filtering the accessible data according to the real needs of the users has become a compelling need. In this framework, context awareness [5] and user preferences [6] have emerged as viable solutions to this problem. The former refers to the ability of selecting data according to features of the environment in which the application is used, such as the location, the time, and the device. The latter refers to the ability of evaluating the relevance of data for a given user on the basis of a set of preferences settled on such data.

In this paper we consider both aspects together and study the problem of selecting the most relevant data in a situation in which preferences are defined in different contexts and queries are posed in one of them. The scenario we refer to is illustrated in the following example.

Example 1. Assume that we have fixed some contextual preferences for food such as "In Italy, a dish of pasta is preferable to one of beef, but if you are in Naples you should taste the world-famous pizza instead of pasta. In summer, however, a fresh salad is preferable to a hot dish of pasta". Assume now that it is summer, we are in Naples and we would like to have some suggestion for food. All of such preferences should be taken into account since they refer to contexts that are

M. Jeusfeld, L. Delcambre, and T.W. Ling (Eds.): ER 2011, LNCS 6998, pp. 304–317, 2011.
© Springer-Verlag Berlin Heidelberg 2011

more general than the current one. However, it is evident that the preferences defined in "Naples" and "Italy in summer" should take precedence on those in the more generic context "Italy". Moreover, the preference in "Naples" should not take precedence on the preference in "Italy in summer", and vice versa, since, in general, one does not apply to the other. It turns out that, in the current context, pizza and salad are both the best alternatives among the mentioned foods and should be returned first by a data filtering system since, on the basis of the given preferences, no other food is preferable to them.

As shown in the example, a generalization hierarchy can be usually defined over contexts and preferences defined in different contexts *propagate* along this hierarchy. Thus the problem can be rephrased as the investigation of preference propagation in a hierarchy of contexts and its impact on database querying. Recently, this issue has been studied extensively [1,11,14,15,16,18] but always resorting to pragmatic, operational approaches. Conversely, we intend to tackle the problem in a principled way with the goal of providing a solid basis to the issue of context-aware preferences in database applications.

With this goal in mind, we consider a very general framework in which the only requirement is that the contexts form a *poset*, that is, a set with a partial order relationship on its elements. Actually, in order to provide concrete examples we introduce a formalism (the CT model) for the representation of contexts, but our results apply to the general notion of context poset. Moreover, we express user preferences in terms of a *partial* order relation over the tuples of interest [6,8], a general approach that includes the case in which preferences are expressed by associating a numerical score with tuples [2,10].

We then start by formalizing the basic properties of the propagation process, which are also implicitly at the basis of earlier approaches to the problem [14,15,16] and correspond to the observations made in Example 1: *(i)* preferences over a pair of incomparable contexts c_1 and c_2 do not take precedence on each other (*fairness*), and *(ii)* preferences over a context c_1 take precedence on the preferences over a context c_2 when c_1 is more specific than c_2 (*specificity*).

Building on these notions, we introduce an algebraic model for expressing preference propagation based on two binary operators: (i) $\oplus$, which combines preferences defined in two unordered contexts, and (ii) $\circledast$, which combines preferences in two ordered contexts. Interestingly, it turns out that these operators can be captured by two popular methods for combining preferences: Pareto and Prioritized composition [6,8]. We then adopt their semantics for $\oplus$ and $\circledast$ and call a composition thereof a PC (Preference Composition) expression.

Example 2. An example of PC-expression computing the propagation of preferences to the context "Naples in summer" discussed in Example 1 is the following:

$$\succ_{\text{Naples,summer}} \circledast ((\succ_{\text{Naples}} \oplus \succ_{\text{Italy,summer}}) \circledast \succ_{\text{Italy}})$$

where $\succ_c$ denotes a set of preferences defined in the context c and, e.g., $\succ_{\text{Italy}} =$ {pasta $\succ$ beef}. In this expression the preferences in "Naples" and those in "Italy in summer" are combined with $\oplus$, since the corresponding contexts are incomparable. The result is combined with the preferences in "Italy" using ⊛, since this context is more general than both "Naples" and "Italy in summer". Finally, the result is combined with the preferences for "Naples in summer" using ⊛, since it is the most specific context.

We identify a "natural" form of PC-expression and prove that it is unable to enforce specificity. This leads us to introduce two alternative approaches to preference propagation. It turns out that the latter is indeed well-behaved since it satisfies all the desirable properties for preference propagation.

In sum, our main contributions are: (i) the identification and formalization of the desirable properties of preference propagation in a poset of contexts; (ii) the definition of an algebra for preference propagation based on Prioritized and Pareto composition; and (iii) the formal analysis of three propagation methods. To our knowledge, these are the first results that can provide a theoretical foundation to the management of contextual preferences in database systems.

The rest of the paper is organized as follows. In Section 2, we introduce the notion of context poset and present a specific context model that is used in the examples. In Section 3 we introduce the algebraic model for combining preferences and, in Section 4, we investigate different methods for computing preference propagation. In Section 5 we compare our work with the related literature and finally, in Section 6, we draw some conclusions.

2   Contexts in Databases

2.1   A General Notion of Context

Our aim is to investigate the problem of contextual preference queries independently of the specific formalism used to represent contexts (and preferences as well). We only focus on a fundamental characteristic of context models: the ability to represent contexts at different levels of detail [4]. We will therefore rely on the general notion of context that follows.

We recall that a *partial order* $\leq_V$ on a domain of values V is a binary relation on V that is reflexive ($v \leq_V v$ for all $v \in V$), antisymmetric (if $v_1 \leq_V v_2$ and $v_2 \leq_V v_1$ then $v_1 = v_2$), and transitive (if $v_1 \leq_V v_2$ and $v_2 \leq_V v_3$ then $v_1 \leq_V v_3$). A partially ordered set, or *poset*, is a set S on which a partial order $\leq_S$ is defined.

Definition 1 (Context). *A context c is an element of a poset C, called* context poset. *If $c_1 \leq_C c_2$ and $c_1 \neq c_2$, written $c_1 <_C c_2$, we say that c_1 is* more specific *than c_2 and that c_2 is* more generic *than c_1.*

2.2   The CT Model

The CT (ConTextual) model is a possible refinement of the deliberately general notion of context poset introduced above. In CT a context is represented by means of a finite set of *contextual dimensions*, which represent aspects that may influence the relevance of data, such as time and location. Each dimension is described by means of a set of *levels* representing the dimension at different degrees of granularity.

Definition 2 (Contextual dimension). *A (CT) contextual dimension d is composed of: (i) a finite poset L of levels; each level l in L is associated with a set of values $M(l)$, called the* members *of level l; and (ii) a family* CM *of containment mappings* $\text{CMAP}_{l_1}^{l_2} : M(l_1) \rightarrow M(l_2)$ *for each $l_1 \leq_L l_2$.*

For instance, day, week, month, and year are possible levels for the time dimension. A possible member of the day level is 23/07/2011, which is mapped by the containment mappings to the member 07/2011 of the level month.

A partial order $\leq_M$ can also be defined on the members M of a dimension d: given a pair of members m_1 and m_2 of levels l_1 and l_2 of d, respectively, we have that $m_1 \leq_M m_2$ if $\text{CMAP}_{l_1}^{l_2}(m_1) = m_2$. We are now ready to introduce the notion of context poset in the CT model.

Definition 3 (Context poset in the CT model). *Let D be a finite set of dimensions. A (CT)* context *c over D is a tuple over $l_1, \ldots, l_n$, where each l_i is a level of a dimension in D. A CT* context poset *C over D is a set of contexts c_j over some $D_j \subseteq D$, such that $c_1 \leq_C c_2$ if, for each dimension $d \in D_2$: (i) c_1 is defined on d, and (ii) $c_1[d] \leq_M c_2[d]$, where $c[d]$ denotes the member of d occurring in a context c.*

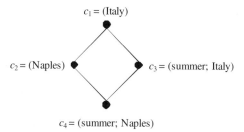

Fig. 1. A context poset in the CT model

Example 3. A simple example of CT context poset, which refers to the scenario discussed in Example 1, is shown in Figure 1.[1] In this example, c_1 is a context over the dimension Location at the level Country, whereas c_2 is a context over the same dimension at level City. Similarly, c_3 and c_4 are contexts over dimensions Time and Location at the levels {Season, Country} and {Season, City}, respectively. Then, we have for instance that $c_4 \leq_C c_3$ since summer $\leq_M$ summer and Naples $\leq_M$ Italy.

3   Preferences in Contexts

3.1   Qualitative Preferences

According to a general and widely accepted approach [6,8], preferences over tuples of a relation scheme $R(A_1, \ldots, A_k)$ are expressed by a binary relation

---

[1] We represent the poset with its *Hasse diagram*, in which the edges represent the partial order (transitively reduced), and x is drawn lower than y if $x \leq y$.

over the *tuple domain* of R, that is, over the set $\prod_{i=1}^{k} D_i$, where D_i is the value domain of attribute A_i. We recall that a *strict* partial order on a set S is an asymmetric (we never have both $s_1 <_S s_2$ and $s_2 <_S s_1$) and transitive binary relation on S.

Definition 4 (Preference relation). *A preference relation $\succ$ over a scheme $R(X)$ is a strict partial order on the tuple domain of R. Given a pair of tuples t_1 and t_2 in the tuple domain of R, if $t_1 \succ t_2$ then t_1 is preferable to t_2. If neither $t_1 \succ t_2$ nor $t_2 \succ t_1$, then t_1 and t_2 are* indifferent, *denoted by $t_1 \sim t_2$.*

A refinement of the indifference relation $\sim$ associated to a preference relation $\succ$ allows some indifferent tuples to be also *equivalent*, which, as we will see, is a key property for the composition of preference relations [9].

Definition 5 (Equivalent tuples). *Given a preference relation $\succ$, t_1 and t_2 are* equivalent under $\succ$, *written $t_1 \approx t_2$, if $t_1 \sim t_2$ and, for all t in the tuple domain such that $t_1 \succ t$ ($t \succ t_1$), it is $t_2 \succ t$ ($t \succ t_2$), and vice versa. If $t_1 \sim t_2$, but $t_1 \not\approx t_2$, we say that t_1 and t_2 are* incomparable.

Example 4. Let us consider the relation over the scheme R(Food, Calories, Fat) made of the following tuples:

$t_1 = (\text{pasta}, 221, 1.3)$ $t_2 = (\text{beef}, 63, 2.5)$ $t_3 = (\text{salad}, 15, 0.1)$ $t_4 = (\text{pizza}, 160, 3.2)$

A possible set of preferences over this scheme is $t_1 \succ t_2$ and $t_3 \succ t_2$. In words, pasta and salad are both preferable to beef. It follows that pasta and salad are equivalent, whereas pizza is incomparable with all other foods.

The best tuples in a relation r over the scheme $R(X)$ according to the preferences $\succ$ can be selected by the *Best* operator [17]: $\beta_\succ(r) = \{t \in r \mid \nexists t' \in r, t' \succ t\}$.[2] The restriction of Definition 4 to strict partial orders guarantees that, for any $r \neq \emptyset$, $\beta_\succ(r)$ is never empty [6]. A *preference query* is any expression of the relational algebra augmented with the Best operator.

3.2   Contextual Preferences and Their Propagation

Throughout the paper we consider a context poset C and a relation scheme $R(X)$, and denote by BP a function that associates with each context $c \in C$ a preference relation $\mathsf{BP}(c) = \succ_c$ over $R(X)$.[3] If no preferences have been defined for a context c in C, then $\mathsf{BP}(c) = \emptyset$. We call $\succ_c$ the *base* preferences in c and BP a *preference configuration* over C. Since, as we have seen, preferences *propagate* along the poset C, we call *complete* preferences in c, denoted by $\succ_c^+$, the result of combining $\succ_c$ with the base preferences defined in the other contexts in C, and denote by CP the function that associates with each context $c \in C$ the complete preferences $\mathsf{CP}(c) = \succ_c^+$ over $R(X)$. We call CP the *propagation* (function) of a preference configuration BP over a context C.

---

[2] This operator is also called *winnow* [6] and *preference selection* [8].

[3] We assume that BP is given by the user or somehow derived from the application.

Let us now try to capture the basic ideas underlying earlier, practical approaches on preference propagation [14,15,16]. The first issue is the *scope* of propagation. It is apparent that, for each context c, all and only the base preferences in the contexts c' such that $c \leq_C c'$ (denoted by $C\lfloor c \rfloor$) are needed to determine $\succ_c^+$. This is made precise by the following definition.

Definition 6 (Propagation scope). *The propagation scope of a context $c \in C$ is $C\lfloor c \rfloor$. For each c' in the scope of c, if $t_1 \succ_{c'} t_2$ and $t_1 \approx_{c''} t_2$ for each $c'' \in C\lfloor c \rfloor$ different from c', then $t_1 \succ_c^+ t_2$.*

The second part of the definition specifies that a preference between two tuples in a context c', belonging to the scope of c, has to be propagated in c if such tuples are equivalent in all the other contexts in the scope of c.

As discussed in Example 1, two further basic properties should be satisfied by preference propagation. Specifically, given a context c: (1) for each pair of unordered contexts c_1 and c_2 in the scope of c, the base preferences in c_1 and c_2 should not take precedence on each other in determining $\succ_c^+$; in this case we say that the propagation is *fair*; (2) for each pair of ordered contexts $c_1 <_C c_2$ in the scope of c, the base preferences in c_1 should take precedence on those in c_2 in determining $\succ_c^+$; in this case we say that the propagation is *specific*. A precise characterization of the above principles can be given as follows.

Definition 7 (Fairness). *A propagation CP is fair if, for each context c in C, each pair of unordered contexts c_1 and c_2 in $C\lfloor c \rfloor$, and each preference configuration BP over C such that: (i) $t_1 \succ_{c_1} t_2$, (ii) $t_2 \succ_{c_2} t_1$, (iii) $t_1 \approx_{c_i} t_2$ for each $c \leq_C c_i <_C c_1$, and (iv) $t_1 \approx_{c_j} t_2$ for each $c \leq_C c_j <_C c_2$, it is: $t_1 \not\succ_c^+ t_2$ and $t_2 \not\succ_c^+ t_1$.*

Definition 8 (Specificity). *A propagation CP is specific if, for each context c in C, each pair of ordered contexts $c_1 <_C c_2$ in $C\lfloor c \rfloor$, and at least one preference configuration BP over C such that: (i) $t_1 \succ_{c_1} t_2$, (ii) $t_2 \succ_{c_2} t_1$, (iii) $t_1 \approx_{c_i} t_2$ for each $c \leq_C c_i <_C c_1$, it is: $t_1 \succ_c^+ t_2$.*

Basically, Definition 7 asserts that if c_1 and c_2 disagree on how to order t_1 and t_2 while such tuples are equivalent in all more specific contexts, then t_1 and t_2 are not ordered in $\succ_c^+$. Conversely, Definition 8 says that if t_1 is preferred to t_2 in c_1 and such tuples are equivalent in all more specific contexts, then this preference might propagate to context c (and it actually propagates if no conflict arises with other contexts in BP incomparable with c_1).

3.3   PC-Expressions

The properties of specificity and fairness suggest that the complete preferences can be computed by means of an expression involving two basic binary operators that, given two base preference relations $\succ_{c_1}$ and $\succ_{c_2}$, return a new preference relation: one applies when c_1 and c_2 are unordered, the other one when $c_1 <_C c_2$. Clearly, the former is commutative whereas this is not the case for the latter. Both operators are associative, since their composition should not depend on the order in which preferences are considered. Also, they are both idempotent since the combination of the same preferences should not have any effect. Finally, they both have the empty set of preferences, $\emptyset$, as identity element since contexts without base preferences should not influence the result.

Incidentally, there are two popular ways to combine preference relations that meet all the requirements above: Pareto and Prioritized composition [6,8].

Definition 9 (Pareto and Prioritized composition). *Let $\succ_1$ and $\succ_2$ be two preference relations over a scheme $R(X)$. The Prioritized composition of $\succ_1$ and $\succ_2$, written $\succ_1 \circledast \succ_2$, is defined as:*

$$t_1 \succ_1 \circledast \succ_2 t_2 \Leftrightarrow (t_1 \succ_1 t_2) \vee (t_1 \succ_2 t_2 \wedge t_1 \approx_1 t_2)$$

and their Pareto composition, written $\succ_1 \oplus \succ_2$, is:

$$t_1 \succ_1 \oplus \succ_2 t_2 \Leftrightarrow (t_1 \succ_1 t_2 \wedge t_1 \succ_2 t_2) \vee (t_1 \succ_1 t_2 \wedge t_1 \approx_2 t_2) \vee (t_1 \approx_1 t_2 \wedge t_1 \succ_2 t_2)$$

Intuitively, Prioritized composition gives precedence to preferences in $\succ_1$, while preferences in $\succ_2$ are used only if two tuples are equivalent according to $\succ_1$. Conversely, Pareto considers the two preference relations equally important.

Example 5. Given the two preference relations

$$\succ_1 = \{t_1 \succ_1 t_2, t_1 \succ_1 t_3\} \quad \succ_2 = \{t_2 \succ_2 t_1, t_2 \succ_2 t_3\}$$

it is $t_2 \approx_1 t_3$ and $t_1 \approx_2 t_3$. Then, the Prioritized composition $\succ_1 \circledast \succ_2$ yields the preferences $t_1 \succ t_2$, $t_1 \succ t_3$, and $t_2 \succ t_3$, whereas the Pareto composition $\succ_1 \oplus \succ_2$ leads to have $t_1 \succ t_3$ and $t_2 \succ t_3$.

Actually, both Prioritized and Pareto composition preserve strict partial orders [9], whereas this is not guaranteed by replacing in their definition $\approx$ with $\sim$ [6]. It is known that $\oplus$ is commutative and associative and that $\circledast$ is associative [9] (but obviously not commutative). It is also evident that both operators are idempotent (that is, $\succ \oplus \succ = \succ$ and $\succ \circledast \succ = \succ$) and have $\emptyset$ as the identity.

We are now ready to introduce the main tool for expressing preference propagation in our framework.

Definition 10 (PC-expression). *A preference composition expression, or PC-expression, is any expression E of the form: $E ::= \succ_c| E \oplus E | E \circledast E | (E)$.*

Because of Definition 6, any PC-expression computing the complete preferences in a context c must include all and only the base preferences in contexts in $C\lfloor c \rfloor$.

Example 6. Consider the context poset in Figure 1. The complete preferences for context c_4 could be expressed by the following PC-expression:

$$\succ_{c_4} \circledast ((\succ_{c_2} \circledast \succ_{c_1}) \oplus (\succ_{c_3} \circledast \succ_{c_1}))$$

Both $\succ_{c_2}$ and $\succ_{c_3}$ are first combined with $\succ_{c_1}$ using the $\circledast$ operator, since the corresponding contexts are ordered. These sub-expressions are then combined with the $\oplus$ operator, since c_2 and c_3 are unordered. Finally, $\succ_{c_4}$ is added using the $\circledast$ operator, since c_4 is the most specific context.

4   Computing the Propagation of Preferences

4.1   The Complete-Cover Propagation

The first way of using a PC-expression for computing preference propagation, which we call $\mathcal{CC}$ (Complete Cover), is based on an intuitive argument: the complete preferences in a context c can be obtained recursively by composing the base preferences in c, $\succ_c$, with the complete preferences that hold in the contexts that, in the context poset C, *cover* c. We remind that c_i covers c if $c <_C c_i$ and there is no other context c_j such that $c <_C c_j <_C c_i$. The *covering* of c in the poset C, denoted $\mathrm{COV}_C(c)$, is the set of contexts in C that cover c.

Definition 11. *Let c be a context in C with covering $\mathrm{COV}_C(c) = \{c_1, \ldots, c_k\}$. The complete preferences in c under the $\mathcal{CC}$ propagation are computed as:*

$$\succ_c^{+\mathcal{CC}} = \begin{cases} \succ_c \circledast \left(\succ_{c_1}^{+\mathcal{CC}} \oplus \succ_{c_2}^{+\mathcal{CC}} \oplus \ldots \oplus \succ_{c_k}^{+\mathcal{CC}} \right) & \text{if } \mathrm{COV}_C(c) \neq \emptyset \\ \succ_c & \text{if } \mathrm{COV}_C(c) = \emptyset \end{cases} \quad (1)$$

From Equation 1 we can derive a "canonical" PC-expression. For this, the following preliminary result is fundamental.

Lemma 1. *Prioritized composition left-distributes (but not right-distributes) over Pareto composition, that is, for any preference relations $\succ_1, \succ_2, \succ_3$ it is:*

$$\succ_1 \circledast (\succ_2 \oplus \succ_3) = (\succ_1 \circledast \succ_2) \oplus (\succ_1 \circledast \succ_3)$$

For the following result we remind that a *chain* $H = \langle c_1, \ldots, c_k \rangle$ of poset C is a sequence of contexts such that $c_1 <_C c_2 <_C \ldots <_C c_k$, and that H is *maximal* if it is not included into another chain.

Corollary 1. *Let c be a context in C and $\mathrm{COV}_C(c) = \{c_1, \ldots, c_k\}$ be the covering of c in C. The complete preferences in c under the $\mathcal{CC}$ propagation can also be computed by the canonical PC-expression:*

$$\succ_c^{+\mathcal{CC}} = \circledast(H_1) \oplus \circledast(H_2) \oplus \ldots \oplus \circledast(H_l) \quad (2)$$

where $\{H_1, H_2, \ldots, H_l\}$ are all the maximal chains in $C\lfloor c \rfloor$ (the set of contexts c' such that $c \leq_C c'$), and, for $H_i = \langle c_1, c_2, \ldots, c_h \rangle$, $\circledast(H_i)$ is shorthand for the expression $(\succ_{c_1} \circledast \succ_{c_2} \circledast \ldots \circledast \succ_{c_h})$.

The result easily follows by unfolding Equation 1 and then applying the left-distributive property.

Example 7. For the context poset in Figure 1 consider the preferences in Table 1, which mimic those in Example 1.[4] In context $c_1 = (\texttt{Italy})$, pasta is preferred to beef and beef to salad. On the other hand, in context $c_2 = (\texttt{Naples})$, pizza is preferred to both pasta and beef. It follows that in c_2 it is pasta $\approx_{c_2}$ beef, thus such foods can be ordered using the preferences valid in c_1, as shown

---

[4] For simplicity in the table we just show the key of each tuple.

Table 1. Base and complete preferences under the $\mathcal{CC}$ propagation for the context poset in Figure 1

c	$\succ_c$	$\succ_c^{+\mathcal{CC}}$
c_1	{pasta $\succ$ beef, beef $\succ$ salad, pasta $\succ$ salad}	{pasta $\succ$ beef, beef $\succ$ salad, pasta $\succ$ salad}
c_2	{pizza $\succ$ pasta, pizza $\succ$ beef}	{pizza $\succ$ pasta, pizza $\succ$ beef, pasta $\succ$ beef}
c_3	{salad $\succ$ pasta, salad $\succ$ beef}	{salad $\succ$ pasta, salad $\succ$ beef, pasta $\succ$ beef}
c_4	$\emptyset$	{pasta $\succ$ beef}

in the right-most column of the table. Conversely, a salad is preferred to both pasta and beef in $c_3 =$ (summer;Italy). In the most specific context $c_4 =$ (summer; Naples), for which no base preferences are given, Pareto composition is applied to $\succ_{c_2}^{+\mathcal{CC}}$ and $\succ_{c_3}^{+\mathcal{CC}}$. These both agree on preferring pasta to beef, whereas other foods stay unordered due to the semantics of Pareto composition. Thus, the best alternatives in c_4 are pizza, pasta, and salad. This can be expressed by the PC-expression $\succ_{c_4} \circledast ((\succ_{c_2} \circledast \succ_{c_1}) \oplus (\succ_{c_3} \circledast \succ_{c_1}))$, which is the unfolding of Equation 1, or equivalently by the canonical PC-expression $(\succ_{c_4} \circledast \succ_{c_2} \circledast \succ_{c_1}) \oplus (\succ_{c_4} \circledast \succ_{c_3} \circledast \succ_{c_1})$.

In spite of the intuitive form of Eq. 1, we have the following negative result:

Theorem 1. *The $\mathcal{CC}$ propagation is fair but not specific.*

Proof. To prove fairness, let c_1 and c_2 be two unordered contexts in $C\lfloor c \rfloor$, with $t_1 \succ_{c_1} t_2$ and $t_2 \succ_{c_2} t_1$, and let $t_1 \approx_{c_i} t_2 \; \forall c_i : (c \leq_C c_i <_C c_1) \vee (c \leq_C c_i <_C c_2)$. Let $c_{k,1}$ $(c_{k,2})$ be a context in $\text{cov}_C(c)$ such that $c <_C c_{k,1} \leq_C c_1$ $(c <_C c_{k,2} \leq_C c_2$, respectively). Due to the semantics of Pareto operator, either t_1 is still better than t_2 in the complete preferences in $c_{k,1}$, or the two tuples are incomparable in this context. Similar arguments hold for $c_{k,2}$, from which it is derived that t_1 and t_2 are incomparable in c. To see why $\mathcal{CC}$ violates specificity, consider the poset in Figure 1 and any preference configuration BP such that: $t_1 \succ_{c_3} t_2$, $t_2 \succ_{c_1} t_1$, $t_1 \approx_{c_2} t_2$, and $t_1 \approx_{c_4} t_2$. To show that for no such BP it is $t_1 \succ_{c_4}^{+\mathcal{CC}} t_2$, thus violating specificity, it is enough to observe that $t_1 \succ_{c_3}^+ t_2$ and $t_2 \succ_{c_2}^+ t_1$, which, according to Pareto composition, leads to have t_1 and t_2 incomparable in c_4.

Example 8. Let us slightly revise the base preferences in Table 1 assuming now that there are no base preferences in c_2. By proceeding as in Example 7 it is still derived that $\succ_{c_4}^{+\mathcal{CC}} =$ {pasta $\succ$ beef}, since the complete preferences in c_2 coincide with those of c_1 while stay unchanged in c_3. This contradicts the specificity principle, for which the complete preferences in c_4 should coincide with those in c_3, thus making pizza and salad the only best alternatives.

4.2   The Active-Cover Propagation

Since Example 8 shows that contexts with no base preferences, such as c_2, might invalidate the specificity property of the whole propagation process, it is interesting to study the effect of not considering at all such contexts. For this, given a preference configuration BP, let us say that a context c is *active* if $\text{BP}(c) \neq \emptyset$.

Table 2. Base and complete preferences under the $\mathcal{AC}$ propagation for the context poset in Figure 1

c	$\succ_c$	$\succ_c^{+\mathcal{AC}}$
c_1	{pasta $\succ$ beef, beef $\succ$ salad, pasta $\succ$ salad}	{pasta $\succ$ beef, beef $\succ$ salad, pasta $\succ$ salad}
c_2	$\emptyset$	{pasta $\succ$ beef, beef $\succ$ salad, pasta $\succ$ salad}
c_3	{salad $\succ$ pasta, salad $\succ$ beef}	{salad $\succ$ pasta, salad $\succ$ beef, pasta $\succ$ beef}
c_4	$\emptyset$	{salad $\succ$ pasta, salad $\succ$ beef, pasta $\succ$ beef}

The *Active Cover* ($\mathcal{AC}$) *propagation* just considers the covering of c with respect to the poset $A \subseteq C$ of all active contexts, rather than C. More precisely, let $\mathrm{COV}_A(c) = \{c_1, \ldots, c_l\}$. Under the $\mathcal{AC}$ propagation the complete preferences in context c, $\mathsf{CP}_{\mathcal{AC}}(c) = \succ_c^{+\mathcal{AC}}$, are now computed as:

$$\succ_c^{+\mathcal{AC}} = \succ_c \circledast (\succ_{c_1}^{+\mathcal{AC}} \oplus \succ_{c_2}^{+\mathcal{AC}} \oplus \ldots \oplus \succ_{c_l}^{+\mathcal{AC}}) \tag{3}$$

Note that if c itself is inactive, above Equation still correctly applies by considering the poset $A \cup \{c\}$.

Table 2 shows how Example 8 change under the $\mathcal{AC}$ propagation, with the complete preferences in c_4 now consistent with what observed in the Example. However, in spite of being insensitive to the side-effects of contexts with no base preferences, even $\mathcal{AC}$ cannot always guarantee specificity.

Theorem 2. *The $\mathcal{AC}$ propagation is fair but not specific.*

Proof. Fairness follows from the same arguments used in the proof of Theorem 1. The same counterexample used in the proof of Theorem 1 applies here to show that $\mathcal{AC}$ violates specificity, with the only additional hypothesis that $t_1 \approx_{c_2} t_2$, yet $\mathsf{BP}(c_2) \neq \emptyset$ (i.e., c_2 is active).

4.3   The Tuple-Specific Cover Propagation

The rationale under the third propagation we introduce, called *Tuple-specific Cover* ($\mathcal{TC}$), is that the arguments used for discarding inactive contexts can be refined so as to drop, when comparing tuples t_1 and t_2, also those contexts for which there is no specific preference relating t_1 and t_2 (thus, for each pair of tuples t_1 and t_2, a specific subset of the active context poset A is considered).

Given a preference configuration BP, we say that a context c is (t_1, t_2)-*active* if $t_1 \not\approx_c t_2$. Let A_{t_1, t_2} be the poset of (t_1, t_2)-active contexts and $\mathrm{COV}_{A_{t_1, t_2}}(c) = \{c_1, \ldots, c_m\}$ be the covering of context c in the A_{t_1, t_2} poset. In the $\mathcal{TC}$ propagation, tuples t_1 and t_2 are compared using the following equation, in which the observation that t_1 and t_2 are either ordered or incomparable in all contexts in $\mathrm{COV}_{A_{t_1, t_2}}(c)$ is exploited to avoid recursion:

$$t_1 \succ_c^{+\mathcal{TC}} t_2 \iff t_1[\succ_c \circledast (\succ_{c_1} \oplus \succ_{c_2} \oplus \ldots \oplus \succ_{c_m})]t_2 \tag{4}$$

Example 9. Consider the poset in Figure 1 and the BP configuration:

$$\succ_{c_1} = \{t_2 \succ t_1, t_2 \succ t_3\} \quad \succ_{c_2} = \{t_1 \succ t_3, t_2 \succ t_3\} \quad \succ_{c_3} = \{t_1 \succ t_2, t_1 \succ t_3\} \quad \succ_{c_4} = \emptyset$$

It is $A_{t_1,t_2} = \{c_1, c_3\}$, $A_{t_2,t_3} = \{c_1, c_2\}$, and $A_{t_1,t_3} = \{c_2, c_3\}$. Thus, $\mathrm{COV}_{A_{t_1,t_2}}(c_4) = \{c_3\}$, $\mathrm{COV}_{A_{t_2,t_3}}(c_4) = \{c_2\}$, and $\mathrm{COV}_{A_{t_1,t_3}}(c_4) = \{c_2, c_3\}$. According to both $\mathcal{AC}$ and $\mathcal{CC}$ propagation, tuples t_1 and t_2 are incomparable in context c_4, since $\succ_{c_2}^{+\mathcal{CC}} = \succ_{c_2}^{+\mathcal{AC}}$ includes the preference $t_2 \succ t_1$, as inherited from c_1, whereas $t_1 \succ t_2$ is an element of $\succ_{c_3}^{+\mathcal{CC}} = \succ_{c_3}^{+\mathcal{AC}}$. Instead, the $\mathcal{TC}$ propagation *does not* consider context c_2 for ordering t_1 and t_2, since c_2 is not (t_1, t_2)-active $(t_1 \approx_{c_2} t_2)$, thus $t_1 \succ_{c_4}^{+\mathcal{TC}} t_2$. The complete preferences for all the three propagations in context c_4 are as follows (preferences coincides in the other contexts):

- $\succ_{c_4}^{+\mathcal{CC}} = \succ_{c_4}^{+\mathcal{AC}} = \{t_1 \succ t_3, t_2 \succ t_3\}$
- $\succ_{c_4}^{+\mathcal{TC}} = \{t_1 \succ t_2, t_2 \succ t_3, t_1 \succ t_3\}$

The following result shows that $\mathcal{TC}$ can be indeed considered the "ultimate" semantics for preference propagation.

Theorem 3. *The $\mathcal{TC}$ propagation is both fair and specific.*

Proof. Fairness stems directly from the definition of $\mathrm{COV}_{A_{t_1,t_2}}(c)$. Specificity is also guaranteed, since when the three conditions of Definition 8 hold for any $c_1 <_C c_2$, $c_1, c_2 \in A\lfloor c \rfloor$, namely: $t_1 \succ_{c_1} t_2$, $t_2 \succ_{c_2} t_1$, and $t_1 \approx_{c_i} t_2 \; \forall c_i : c \leq_C c_i <_C c_1)$, the definition of $\mathrm{COV}_{A_{t_1,t_2}}(c)$ guarantees that $c_2 \notin \mathrm{COV}_{A_{t_1,t_2}}(c)$. Thus, there exists a preference configuration BP for which it is $t_1 \succ_{c_j} t_2 \; \forall c_j \in \mathrm{COV}_{A_{t_1,t_2}}(c)$, which implies $t_1 \succ_c^{+\mathcal{TC}} t_2$.

Apparently, the $\mathcal{TC}$ propagation requires a distinct covering for each pair of tuples. However this is not true, since *there exists a PC-expression, the same for all pairs of tuples, that implements $\mathcal{TC}$ propagation*. The intuition behind this result is that specificity needs to avoid that a preference $t_1 \succ t_2$, for which a conflicting preference exists in a more specific context, propagates along a chain that does not order t_1 and t_2 (which is the reason why both $\mathcal{CC}$ and $\mathcal{AC}$ violate specificity). Algebraically, this requires a PC-expression, which we denote $E_A^{\mathcal{TC}}(c)$, that is maximally "grouped on the right", so that this pass-through phenomenon is inhibited. The following provides a formal definition of $E_A^{\mathcal{TC}}(c)$.

Definition 12 (PC-expression for $\mathcal{TC}$ propagation). *Let c' be a context in $A\lfloor c \rfloor$ and let $\{c_1, \ldots, c_k\}$ be the contexts in $A\lfloor c \rfloor$ that are covered by c'. The "right-grouped" expression $E_A^{RG}(c, c')$ is recursively defined as follows:*

$$\begin{cases} E_A^{RG}(c, c') = (E_A^{RG}(c, c_1) \oplus \ldots \oplus E_A^{RG}(c, c_k)) \circledast \succ_{c'} \\ E_A^{RG}(c, c) = \succ_c \end{cases}$$

Let $\{\hat{c}_1, \ldots, \hat{c}_n\}$ be the set of maximal elements in $A\lfloor c \rfloor$ (i.e., the contexts $\hat{c}_i$ in $A\lfloor c \rfloor$ such that there is no context $c' \in A\lfloor c \rfloor$ for which $\hat{c}_i <_C c'$). Then:

$$E_A^{\mathcal{TC}}(c) = E_A^{RG}(c, \hat{c}_1) \oplus \ldots \oplus E_A^{RG}(c, \hat{c}_n) \tag{5}$$

Example 10. Consider the poset in Figure 1, and assume that all contexts are active. The PC-expression $E_A^{\mathcal{TC}}(c_4)$ is $((\succ_{c_4} \circledast \succ_{c_2}) \oplus (\succ_{c_4} \circledast \succ_{c_3})) \circledast \succ_{c_1}$. For convenience, this can also be more compactly rewritten, by applying the left-distributive property of $\circledast$, as $\succ_{c_4} \circledast (\succ_{c_2} \oplus \succ_{c_3}) \circledast \succ_{c_1}$.

Intuitively, $E_A^{TC}(c)$ can be obtained from the canonical expression by first grouping chains on maximal elements and factoring them out, then recursively applying this process to the so-reduced chains until no more factors can be extracted.

Theorem 4. *The PC-expression $E_A^{TC}(c)$ correctly computes the TC propagation, i.e., $t_1 \succ_c^{+TC} t_2$ iff $t_1 \ E_A^{TC}(c) \ t_2$.*

Proof. If $t_1 \not\approx_c t_2$ the result is obvious, since in both cases only $\succ_c$ is considered. Then, assume $t_1 \approx_c t_2$. We show that $E_A^{TC}(c)$ propagates downward to context c all and only the preferences concerning tuples t_1 and t_2 for those contexts $c_j \in \text{COV}_{A_{t_1,t_2}}(c)$, from which the result follows. If $c_j \in \text{COV}_{A_{t_1,t_2}}(c)$, it is $t_1 \not\approx_{c_j} t_2$ and $t_1 \approx_{c_i} t_2$ holds for any context c_i such that $c \leq_C c_i <_C c_j$. From the definition of $E_A^{RG}(c, c_j)$ it is immediate to derive that $E_A^{TC}(c)$ propagates the preference of c_j to c. By contradiction, assume now that $c_k \notin \text{COV}_{A_{t_1,t_2}}(c)$, $t_1 \not\approx_{c_k} t_2$, yet this preference is propagated by $E_A^{TC}(c)$ to context c. From the hypothesis, there exists a context $c_j \in \text{COV}_{A_{t_1,t_2}}(c)$ such that $c_j <_C c_k$. From the definitions of $E_A^{TC}(c)$ and $E_A^{RG}(c, c_k)$, it turns out that $E_A^{TC}(c)$ includes the sub-expression $(\ldots \succ_{c_j} \ldots) \circledast \succ_{c_k}$, and this is the case for every occurrence of $\succ_{c_k}$. Since the left operand includes $\succ_{c_j}$, for which t_1 and t_2 are not equivalent, the preference of c_k on these tuples does not propagate to c, proving the assert.

We conclude with a major result establishing a precise relationship among the three propagations we have analyzed so far.

Theorem 5. *Let c be a context in the context poset C. Then, the complete preferences in c under the three propagations, CC, AC and TC, satisfy the following relationships: $\succ_c^{+CC} \subseteq \succ_c^{+AC} \subseteq \succ_c^{+TC}$ and $\approx_c^{CC} = \approx_c^{AC} = \approx_c^{TC}$.*

Proof (sketch). $(\approx_c^{CC} = \approx_c^{AC} = \approx_c^{TC})$: Due to the semantics of Pareto and Prioritized composition, two tuples t_1 and t_2 are equivalent according to $\succ_c^+$ iff this holds in all contexts whose base preferences appear in the PC-expression computing $\succ_c^+$. These are clearly the same for AC and TC. Since the additional contexts used by CC are all inactive, all tuples are equivalent in such contexts, from which the result follows.

$(\succ_c^{+CC} \subseteq \succ_c^{+AC})$: Both propagations compute $\succ_c^+$ using a PC-expression that is equivalent to the canonical form, i.e., Pareto composition of all the "products" $\circledast(H_i)$, where H_i is a maximal chain (of the context poset C in the case of CC, and of the active poset A in the case of AC). If H_1 and H_2 are two chains, with $H_2 \subseteq H_1$, it is simple to see that $\circledast(H_1) \oplus \circledast(H_2) \subseteq \circledast(H_1)$. A repeated application of this yields the result, after observing that each $\circledast(H_i)$ in Equation 2 is equivalent to an expression $\circledast(H_i^-)$, $H_i^- \subseteq H_i$, obtained by discarding inactive contexts from H_i (since such contexts are uninfluential to the result of $\circledast(H_i)$). $(\succ_c^{+AC} \subseteq \succ_c^{+TC})$: The proof follows similar arguments.

Example 11. The preferences in Table 2 lead to have only one maximal chain in $A\lfloor c_4 \rfloor$, i.e., $\langle c_3, c_1 \rangle$. Thus, $\succ_{c_4}^{+AC} = \succ_{c_3} \circledast \succ_{c_1}$. On the other hand, since the maximal chains in $C\lfloor c_4 \rfloor$ are $\langle c_4, c_3, c_1 \rangle$ and $\langle c_4, c_2, c_1 \rangle$, yet c_2 and c_4 are inactive, we can equivalently consider the chains $\langle c_3, c_1 \rangle$ and $\langle c_1 \rangle$. It follows that $\succ_{c_4}^{+CC} = \succ_{c_1} \oplus (\succ_{c_3} \circledast \succ_{c_1}) \subseteq \succ_{c_3} \circledast \succ_{c_1} = \succ_{c_4}^{+AC}$.

5 Related Works

Preferences in databases have been extensively investigated in recent years following two main approaches: in the *quantitative* approach a numerical score is associated with tuples [2,10], while in the *qualitative* one a (strict) partial order relation is defined on tuples [6,8]. We have adopted the latter, which is more general from an order-theoretic point of view. Moreover, our approach is parametric with respect to the context model used since we only exploit the ability to relate different contexts according to a partial order between them, a feature common to the majority of the models proposed [4].

Recently, a number of papers have focused on the management of contextual preferences [1,14,15,16,18]. The main difference with the present paper is that all of them follow a pragmatic approach based on specific heuristics and then focus on implementation issues. More in detail, the works by van Bunningen et al. [18] and Agrawal et al. [1] do not address the issue of combining preferences defined in different contexts. Agrawal et al. [1] introduce a technique for the management of contextual preferences, based on the qualitative approach, but they do not consider any generalization relationship between contexts. Stefanidis and Pitoura [16] consider quantitative preferences in a hierarchical context model. Preferences in a context c are computed from preferences defined in context c' that generalizes c and is at "minimal distance" from c in the hierarchy. With respect to the propagation properties introduced in Section 3, this approach is specific, but it is not fair and does not respect the propagation scope. Miele et al. [14] also consider numerical preferences and distances between contexts, but preferences defined on contexts at a distance from c that is not minimal are also considered, provided they are not *overwritten* by some other preference. Since a smaller context distance does not imply $c_1 \leq_C c_2$, this approach respects the propagation scope, it is specific, but it is not fair.

Mindolin and Chomicki [13] have recently introduced *p-skylines*, a particular case of PC-expressions in which each preference relation (i) is used only once, and (ii) is a total order over an attribute of interest. Taken together, these two restrictions simplify the problem of determining equivalence and containment of expressions, but this comes at the price of a reduced expressive power. In particular, p-skyline expressions (i) cannot be used for arbitrary context posets, and (ii) limits the kind of preferences we can define.

Contextual preferences could be considered as a particular case of *conditional preference networks* (CP-nets), a tool largely investigated in the AI field [3] and used for database querying [7,12]. Behind the surface, there are important differences between our work and that on CP-nets. With CP-nets one defines, for each attribute of interest, a set of total orders that are conditionally dependent on some other attribute(s). The resulting preferences are then defined as the transitive closure of the union of such orders [12] (this might not be an order since cycles might arise). Conversely, we start with a set of arbitrary strict partial orders and study how to compose them in a context poset, ensuring that the result is always a strict partial order.

6   Conclusions

In this paper we have considered the problem of how database preferences propagate when they depend on the context of the user. Unlike previous approaches, which are based on heuristic arguments, we have tackled the problem in a principled way and have proposed an algebraic model for expressing preference propagation, based on the well-known Pareto and Prioritized composition rules. We have then analyzed with this model three alternative propagation methods and shown that one of them satisfies all the desirable propagation properties.

As future work we plan to investigate specialized optimization techniques for contextual preference queries on large databases and to study how our results apply to numerical preference models.

References

1. Agrawal, R., Rantzau, R., Terzi, E.: Context-Sensitive Ranking. In: SIGMOD, pp. 383–394 (2006)
2. Agrawal, R., Wimmers, E.L.: A Framework for Expressing and Combining Preferences. In: SIGMOD, pp. 297–306 (2000)
3. Boutilier, C., Brafman, R.I., Domshlak, C., Hoos, H.H., Poole, D.: CP-nets: A Tool for Representing and Reasoning with Conditional Ceteris Paribus Preference Statements. Journal of Art. Intell. Research 21, 135–191 (2004)
4. Bolchini, C., Curino, C., Quintarelli, E., Schreiber, F.A., Tanca, L.: A Data-Oriented Survey of Context Models. SIGMOD Record 36(4), 19–26 (2007)
5. Bolchini, C., Curino, C., Orsi, G., Quintarelli, E., Rossato, R., Schreiber, F.A., Tanca, L.: And what Can Context Do for Data? Com. of ACM 52(11), 136–140 (2009)
6. Chomicki, J.: Preference Formulas in Relational Queries. ACM Trans. on Database Systems 28(4), 427–466 (2003)
7. Ciaccia, P.: Querying Databases with Incomplete CP-nets. In: M-PREF (2007)
8. Kießling, W.: Foundations of Preference in Database Systems. In: VLDB, pp. 311–322 (2005)
9. Kießling, W.: Preference Queries with SV-Semantics. In: COMAD, pp. 15–26 (2005)
10. Koutrika, G., Ioannidis, Y.E.: Personalization of Queries in Database Systems. In: ICDE, pp. 597–608 (2004)
11. Li, X., Feng, L., Zhou, L.: Contextual Ranking of Database Querying Results: A Statistical Approach. In: Roggen, D., Lombriser, C., Tröster, G., Kortuem, G., Havinga, P. (eds.) EuroSSC 2008. LNCS, vol. 5279, pp. 126–139. Springer, Heidelberg (2008)
12. Mindolin, D., Chomicki, J.: Hierarchical CP-nets. In: M-PREF (2007)
13. Mindolin, D., Chomicki, J.: Discovering Relative Importance of Skyline Attributes. In: VLDB (2009)
14. Miele, A., Quintarelli, E., Tanca, L.: A Methodology for Preference-Based Personalization of Contextual Data. In: EDBT, pp. 287–298 (2009)
15. Stefanidis, K., Pitoura, E., Vassiliadis, P.: Adding Context to Preferences. In: ICDE, pp. 846–855 (2007)
16. Stefanidis, K., Pitoura, E.: Fast contextual preference scoring of database tuples. In: EDBT, pp. 344–355 (2008)
17. Torlone, R., Ciaccia, P.: Which Are My Preferred Items? In: RPEC, pp. 217–225 (2002)
18. van Bunningen, A.H., Fokkinga, M.M., Apers, P.M.G., Feng, L.: Ranking Query Results Using Context-Aware Preferences. In: DBRank, pp. 269–276 (2007)

Towards a Theory of Refinement for Data Migration

Bernhard Thalheim[1] and Qing Wang[2]

[1] Department of Computer Science, Christian-Albrechts-University Kiel, Germany
thalheim@is.informatik.uni-kiel.de
[2] Department of Information Science, University of Otago, Dunedin, New Zealand
qing.wang@otago.ac.nz

Abstract. We develop a theoretical framework for refining transformations occurring in the process of data migration. A legacy kernel can be discovered at a high-level abstraction which consolidates heterogeneous data sources in a legacy system. We then show that migration transformations are specified via the composition of two subclasses of transformations: property-preserving transformations and property-enhancing transformations at flexible levels of abstraction. By defining a refinement scheme with the notions of correct refinements for property-preserving and property-enhancing transformations, we are able to stepwise refine migration transformations and to prove the correctness of refinements. The result of this paper lays down a formal foundation for investigating data migration.

1 Introduction

Modernising legacy systems is one of the most challenging problems we often face when engineering information systems [2,3,10,12]. With new technologies emerging and application domains evolving, legacy systems need to be migrated into new systems at some point, to support enhanced functionality and re-engineered business models. Data migration, as a fundamental aspect of projects on modernising legacy systems, has been recognised to be a difficult task that may result in failed projects as a whole [8,19]. Industry survey results [8] reveal that the data migration market is rapidly growing and business companies annually invest billions of dollars in data migration tasks (e.g., over 5bn from the top 2000 global companies in 2007); nevertheless, only 16% projects have their data migration tasks be successfully accomplished (i.e. being delivered on time and on budget). One of main reasons for time and budget overrun is the lack of a well-defined methodology that can help handle the complexity of data migration tasks.

Data migration moves data sources from legacy systems into new systems in which data sources have different structures. There are several issues that can considerably complicate this process. First, legacy systems may have a number of heterogeneous data sources that are interconnected but designed by using different data modelling tools or interpreted under different semantics. Second,

M. Jeusfeld, L. Delcambre, and T.W. Ling (Eds.): ER 2011, LNCS 6998, pp. 318–331, 2011.

legacy systems may have inaccurate, incomplete, duplicate or inconsistent data, and new systems may also require additional semantic constraints on data after being migrated. Thus, bringing the quality of data up to standard of new systems can be costly and time-consuming. Third, many data migration tasks such as data profiling, discovery, validating, cleansing, etc. need to be iteratively executed in a project and specification changes frequently happen in order to repair detected problems. It is estimated [1] that 90% of the initial specifications change and over 25% of the specifications change more than once during the life of a data migration project. These issues highlight the importance of methodology for data migration, in particular, the need of a refinement theory for data migration that can link conceptual modelling of specifications to executable code in a way practitioners can verify properties of data migration.

This paper aims at establishing a theoretical framework of refinement for data migration that allows us to refine a high-level specification of migration transformations into ones at an implementation level. This framework provides answers to the following questions arising from data migration in practice.

- How can we react to specification changes in a way of keeping track of all relevant aspects the changes may impact on such as inconsistencies between specifications, interrelated data and correctness of implementation?
- How can we compare legacy data sources with the migrated data in new systems to ensure data was migrated properly in terms of desired data semantics and integrity?

From a traditional perspective, the process of data migration involves three stages: Extract, Transform, and Load (ETL). However, different from conventional ETL used for data warehousing that deals with analytic data, ETL in data migration is more complicated in which operational data has to be handled. Our first contribution is the formal development of the ETL processes for data migration as described below.

- A legacy kernel is first "extracted" at a high-level of abstraction, which consolidates heterogeneous data sources in a legacy system. The links between abstract and more concrete models can be further exploited by using Galois connections in abstract interpretation [7,16].
- We then "transform" the legacy kernel into a new kernel by specifying migration transformations in which data cleansing methods are described for "dirty" data, and "clean" data is mapped into an abstract model. A specific migration strategy [2,3,10] can be chosen and applied at this stage.
- As "loading" an abstract model (i.e., the new kernel) into a more concrete model has been well studied (e.g., [13,17,20]), we will omit the discussion of this stage in this paper.

Our second contribution is a refinement scheme specifying the refinement of migration transformations in terms of two types of refinement correctness. Using our refinement scheme, the above ETL processes can be stepwise refined into a

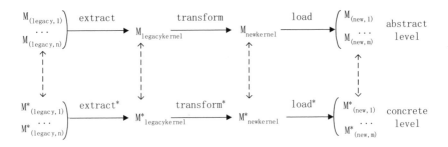

Fig. 1. ETL in data migrations

real-life implementation. As illustrated in Fig.1, the models in an abstract computation (e.g., $M_{legacykernel}$ and $M_{newkernel}$) can be refined into more concrete models (e.g., $M^*_{legacykernel}$ and $M^*_{newkernel}$) of the corresponding computation at a concrete level, and similarly, computation segments of interest (e.g., *extract*, *tranform* and *load*) at an abstract level refined into the corresponding computation segments (e.g., *extract**, *tranform** and *load**) at a concrete level. With our notions of refinement correctness, the generic proof method proposed by Schellhorn [14] can be used to verify the correctness of these refinements.

We present basic definitions for schema and model in Section 2. In Section 3 we discuss an approach of discovering a legacy kernel. Section 4 gives the formal definitions for migration transformations and two important subclasses in data migration. We further exploit the refinement correctness of migration transformations and their subclasses in Section 5, along with a general discussion on how to verify the correctness of refinements for migration transformations. In Section 6 we briefly conclude the paper.

2   Schemata, Models and Level of Abstraction

For simplicity, we take an object-based view on models in this paper. In data migration, data sources of legacy and new systems may be designed by using different data modelling approaches. Nevertheless, components supported by many data modelling approaches can be viewed as objects, for example, entities and relationships in the entity-relationship model, tuples in the relational data model, elements in XML, etc. This simplified but generic view gives us the flexibility to relate models residing at different levels of abstraction to each other.

Let us fix a family $\mathcal{D}$ of basic data types and a set $\mathcal{C}$ of constructors (e.g., record, list, set, multiset, array, etc). Then a set of *object types* over $(\mathcal{D}, \mathcal{C})$ can be inductively defined by applying constructors in $\mathcal{D}$ over basic data types in $\mathcal{C}$. Similarly, given an object type τ, the set of *objects* of type τ can be inductively defined according to the types and constructors that constitute τ. In order to capture additional semantic restrictions on object types, we also need a suitable

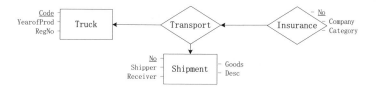

Fig. 2. An ER schema of legacy data source RDM$_A$

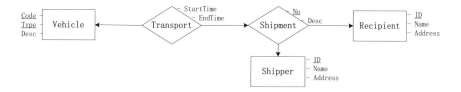

Fig. 3. An ER schema of legacy data source OO$_B$

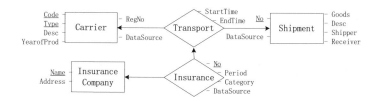

Fig. 4. An ER schema of legacy kernel

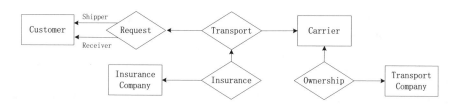

Fig. 5. An ER schema of new kernel

logic[1] L for expressing constraints. As a convention, the notations $\mathcal{F}(T)$ (omit L for simplicity) refer to the set of formulae of L defined over a set T of object types, and $fr(\varphi)$ refer to the set of free variables in formula φ . A formula φ with $fr(\varphi) = \emptyset$ is called *Boolean formula*.

---

[1] The suitable logic is determined by what kinds of constraints we want to capture. For example, first-order logic can express many integrity constraints but not cardinality constraints. However, cardinality constraints can be captured by a more expressive logic such as fixed point logic with counting quantifiers or counting terms [9,11]. We may also use Monadic second-order logic [6] to define constraints of XML tree structures.

A constraint $\varphi \in \mathcal{F}(T)$ defined on T is a Boolean formula. A *schema* $S = (T, \Sigma)$ consists of a finite, non-empty set T of object types and a finite (possibly empty) set Σ of constraints such that $\Sigma \subseteq \mathcal{F}(T)$. A model over a set T of object types consists of objects of types in T. We use $\llbracket \varphi \rrbracket^M$ referring to the interpretation of formula φ over the objects in a model M. A Boolean formula $\varphi \in \mathcal{F}(T)$ is said to be *satisfied* by the objects of a model M over schema (T, Σ), denoted as $M \models \varphi$, iff $\llbracket \varphi \rrbracket^M$ is true. A *model* over schema (T, Σ) is a model over T in which objects satisfy every constraint in Σ. For convenience, we use the notations $\mathcal{M}(S)$ to denote the set of all models over schema S and $\mathcal{M}(T)$ to denote the set of all models over object types T. Clearly, $\mathcal{M}(S) \subseteq \mathcal{M}(T)$ for $S = (T, \Sigma)$.

A model represents the structure of a data source at a certain level of abstraction. Since a legacy system is often associated with a number of heterogeneous data sources, and in real-life situations, it commonly happens that the design information of a legacy system (including its data sources) is unavailable, out-of-date, etc. due to historic reasons, the initial stage of data migration involves the process of reverse engineering to recover the original design information of legacy data sources and then present them as approximate abstract models at a high level abstraction. In doing so, we are able to utilise these abstract models as a bridge to analyse various representations of heterogeneous legacy data sources in a unified environment. The notions of abstract and concrete are relative, depending on chosen levels of abstraction. The linkages between abstract and concrete models can be described by an *abstraction map* $\alpha : \mathcal{M}_C \to \mathcal{M}_A$ and a *concretization map* $\gamma : \mathcal{M}_A \to \mathcal{M}_C$ as defined in abstract interpretation [7,16], where $\mathcal{M}_A$ (resp. $\mathcal{M}_C$) is a set of abstract (resp. concrete) models, α maps a concrete model in $\mathcal{M}_C$ to its most precise approximation in $\mathcal{M}_A$ and γ maps an abstract model in $\mathcal{M}_A$ to its most general refinement in $\mathcal{M}_C$.

Example 1. Consider a shipping company that migrates two legacy transport applications into a new transport application, in which their data sources are referred as $M^*_{(legacy,1)} = \text{RDM}_A$ with a relational schema and $M^*_{(legacy,2)} = \text{OO}_B$ with an object-oriented schema. As insurance information in legacy transport applications is neither complete nor accurate, there are also three legacy data sources $M^*_{(legacy,3)}$, $M^*_{(legacy,4)}$ and $M^*_{(legacy,5)}$ (different data formats) provided by external insurance companies and used for data cleansing. Assume that we choose the ER modelling to build abstract models. Then RDM_A is reversely engineered to $M_{(legacy,1)} = \text{ER}_A$ with the ER schema in Fig.2 and OO_B to $M_{(legacy,2)} = \text{ER}_B$ with the ER schema in Fig.3. Fig.4 and Fig.5 present the ER schemata of the legacy kernel $M_{legacykernel}$ from the legacy data sources and the new kernel $M_{newkernel}$ for the new transport application, respectively.

The schema of ER_A has the object types SHIPMENT, TRUCK, INSURANCE and TRANSPORT, and the constraints such as

- the unique constraint φ_1 on RegNo of TRUCK:

$$\forall x_1, x_2, x_3, y_1, y_2, y_3.((\text{TRUCK}(x_1, x_2, x_3) \wedge \text{TRUCK}(y_1, y_2, y_3) \\ \wedge x_1 \neq y_1) \Rightarrow x_3 \neq y_3),$$

– the foreign key constraint φ_2 on INSURANCE:

$$\forall x_1, x_2, x_3, x_4, x_5.(\text{INSURANCE}(x_1, x_2, x_3, x_4, x_5) \Rightarrow \text{TRANSPORT}(x_4, x_5)).$$

□

3   Legacy Kernel

In this section we discuss how to discover a legacy kernel that consolidates legacy data sources while preserving constraints of interest. For a number of abstract models built at the same level of abstraction, the problem left is how to compare them to ensure that the re-structuring of data into different models is what we expect. In general, these models can be defined over different schemata, and thus have different structures. We approach this problem by a) first identifying constraints that need to be preserved between models, then b) basing the comparison of models on these constraints of interest.

Definition 1. *Let M_1 and M_2 be two models over the schemata $S_1 = (T_1, \Sigma_1)$ and $S_2 = (T_2, \Sigma_2)$, respectively, and $\Phi \subseteq \mathcal{F}(T_2)$ be a set of constraints of interest. Then M_1 is said to* reflect *M_2 with respect to Φ (denoted as $M_2 \preceq_\Phi M_1$) iff, for any formula $\varphi_2 \in \Phi$ with $fr(\varphi_2) = \{x_1, ..., x_n\}$, if $M_2 \models \exists x_1, ..., x_n.\varphi_2$, then there exists a formula $\varphi_1 \in \mathcal{F}(T_1)$ with $fr(\varphi_1) = \{x_1', ..., x_n'\}$ such that $[\![\varphi_1]\!]^{M_1} = [\![\varphi_2]\!]^{M_2}$ holds.*

In this approach, the first step has significant impacts on finding an appropriate legacy kernel. Identifying constraints of interest in a model require a thorough understanding of data from various aspects such as relationships across object types, data quality (for determining data that needs to be selected for migration, especially when data can be found from multiple sources) and application domain knowledge. According to the statistics [8], only 1 in 10 data migration projects used data profiling tools to understand their data, and it may explain why the success rate of data migration projects is currently so low (i.e., 16%).

In terms of a reflecting relation $\preceq_\Phi$, a set of abstract models can be regarded to be partially ordered, i.e., M_2 precedes M_1 if $M_2 \preceq_\Phi M_1$; otherwise incomparable. A legacy kernel can thus be defined as the least upper bound of a set of abstract models in terms of the reflecting relation, i.e, an abstract model that can reflects the abstract model of every legacy data source.

Definition 2. *Let $\mathcal{M} = \{M_1, ..., M_n\}$ be a set of abstract models reversely engineered from legacy data sources and $W = \{\Phi_1, ..., \Phi_n\}$ be a set of sets of constraints Φ_i corresponding to the models $M_i(i = 1, ..., n)$. Then the* legacy kernel *M_L of $\mathcal{M}$ with respect to W is the least upper bound of models in $\mathcal{M}'$, where $\mathcal{M}' = \{M_1', ..., M_n'\}$, in terms of the reflecting relation $M_i \preceq_{\Phi_i} M_i'$ for each $\Phi_i \in W$ and $M_i \in \mathcal{M}$.*

Example 2. The ER schema shown in Fig. 4 could be the schema of a legacy kernel for the two ER models ER_A and ER_B. The attribute DataSource appearing in CARRIER, INSURANCE and SHIPMENT is used to record from which legacy data source each object is extracted.   □

Remark 1. Data semantics reconciliation is a key task in the process of data cleansing and will be handled at the "transform" stage. Thus, when "extracting" a legacy kernel from legacy data sources, any conflicting constraints across different models should be automatically eliminated from the constraints used for defining reflecting relations.

4   Migration Transformations

We consider a migration transformation as a deterministic computation executed at a flexible but fixed level of abstraction, in the same spirit of Abstract State Machine and its variants [5,18,15].

Definition 3. *A transformation $(\mathcal{M}, M_0, M_n, \delta)$ consists of a non-empty set $\mathcal{M}$ of models together with an initial model $M_0 \in \mathcal{M}$ and a final model $M_n \in \mathcal{M}$, and a one-step transition function δ over $\mathcal{M}$, i.e., $\delta : \mathcal{M} \mapsto \mathcal{M}$.*

The one-step transition function δ is determined by a transition rule that is inductively defined by

- *update rule:* the object $\tau(t_1, \ldots, t_n)$ is updated to t_0,
$$\tau(t_1, \ldots, t_n) := t_0$$
- *conditional rule:* if φ is true, then execute the rule r; otherwise do nothing,
if φ then r endif
- *block rule:* the rules $r_1,\ldots,r_n$ are executed in parallel,
par $r_1 \ldots r_n$ endpar
- *sequential rule:* the rules $r_1,\ldots,r_n$ are executed sequentially,
seq $r_1 \ldots r_n$ endseq
- *forall rule:* the rule r is executed in parallel for each x satisfying φ.
forall x with φ do r enddo

Applying a transition rule r over a model M yields a set $\Delta(r, M)$ of updates on objects. If $\Delta(r, M)$ is consistent, i.e., it does not contain conflicting updates, then updates in $\Delta(r, M)$ lead a transformation from the current model M to its successor model $\delta(M)$. A *run* is a finite sequence $M_0, \ldots, M_n$ of models with $M_i \neq M_n$ for $0 < i < n$, and $\delta(M_i) = M_{i+1}$ for all $i = 0, \ldots, n-1$.

In the following, we will discuss two subclasses of transformations that constitute the building blocks of transformations in data migrations.

4.1   Property-Preserving Transformations

The first subclass of transformations is property-preserving transformations that transform data and their description from one model (i.e., the initial model) to another model (i.e., the final model), in which the schema of the final model is different from the schema of the initial model, however, data properties specified over the schema of the initial model must be preserved in the final model. Two typical examples of property preserving transformations are the transformations used for "extracting" a legacy kernel and for "loading" a new kernel. In both cases a set of properties of interest needs to be preserved in transformations.

Definition 4. *A* property-preserving transformation *(PPT) is a transformation* $\Pi = (\mathcal{M}, M_0, M_n, \delta)$, *where* $M_0 \in \mathcal{M}(S_0)$ *for* $S_0 = (T_0, \Sigma_0)$ *and* $M_n \in \mathcal{M}(S_n)$ *for* $S_n = (T_n, \Sigma_n)$, *satisfying the conditions:*

 – *for each* $\tau_i \in T_0 (i = 1, \ldots, k)$, *there exists a formula* $\varphi_i \in \mathcal{F}(T_n)$ *such that* $[\![\tau_i]\!]^{M_0} = [\![\varphi_i]\!]^{M_n}$, *and*
 – *for the set* $\Phi \subseteq \mathcal{F}(T_n)$ *of constraints that is equivalent to* Σ_0, *i.e.,* $\Phi = \Sigma_0[\tau_1 \leftarrow \varphi_1, \ldots, \tau_k \leftarrow \varphi_k]$, $\Sigma_n \Rightarrow \bigwedge_{\phi \in \Phi} \phi$ *holds.*

If Ψ is a set of formulae, then $\Psi[\tau_1 \leftarrow \varphi_1, \ldots, \tau_k \leftarrow \varphi_k]$ is also a set of formulae in which each k-ary object type $\tau_i(x_1, \ldots, x_k)$ is substituted by a formula φ_i with $fr(\varphi_i) = \{x_1, \ldots, x_k\}$.

Example 3. A high-level PPT with an initial model over the schema in Fig. 2 and a final model over the schema in Fig. 4 may have a transition rule as follows, where objects are mapped between the models based on their object types.

> **par forall** x **with** $x \in$ TRUCK **do**
>   MAPPEDTOCARRIER
>   **enddo**
>   **forall** x **with** $x \in$ SHIPMENT **do**
>   MAPPEDTOSHIPMENT
>   **enddo**
>   **forall** x **with** $x \in$ TRANSPORT **do**
>   MAPPEDTOTRANSPORT
>   **enddo**
>   **forall** x **with** $x \in$ INSURANCE **do**
>   MAPPEDTOINSURANCECOMPANYANDINSURANCE
>   **enddo endpar**   □

4.2   Property-Enhancing Transformations

The second subclass of transformations we capture is property-enhancing transformations that transform models violating a certain set of properties into models satisfying these properties. Thus, a set of targeted properties first needs to be determined. When imposing a property φ on a model M, we can obtain a number $\{M_1, \ldots, M_k\}$ of *greatest valid submodels* of M. Each M_i $(i = 1, \ldots, k)$ satisfies the following conditions: 1) M_i consists of a subset of objects in M, 2) $M_i \models \varphi$, and 3) $M_i' \not\models \varphi$ if M_i' is obtained by combining M_i with any objects that are in M but not in M_i. We define the *valid* part of M against φ, denoted as M^φ, to contain objects that appear in every greatest valid submodel of M and thus do not violate φ in any case. Given a set Φ of properties, we use the notation M^Φ to represent $\bigcap_{\varphi_i \in \Phi} M^{\varphi_i}$.

Definition 5. *Let* Ψ *be a set of constraints. Then a* property-enhancing transformation *(PET) over* Ψ *is a transformation* $\Lambda = (\mathcal{M}, M_0, M_n, \delta)$, *where* $\mathcal{M} \subseteq \mathcal{M}(T)$, $M_0 \in \mathcal{M}(S_0)$ *for* $S_0 = (T, \Sigma)$ *and* $M_n \in \mathcal{M}(S_n)$ *for* $S_n = (T, \Sigma \cup \Psi)$, *satisfying the conditions:*

– *for each* $\tau_i \in T (i = 1, \ldots, k)$, *we have* $[\![\tau_i]\!]^{M_0^{\Psi}} \subseteq [\![\tau_i]\!]^{M_n^{\Psi}}$, *and*
– $\Sigma_0 \Rightarrow \neg (\bigvee_{\psi \in \Psi} \psi)$ *and* $\Sigma_n \Rightarrow \bigwedge_{\psi \in \Psi} \psi$ *hold.*

In data migration, PETs are widely used to specify transformations that execute data cleansing tasks in terms of business rules (i.e., expressed as constraints). For each business rule φ, a specific data cleansing strategy needs to be chosen so as to eliminate "dirty" data (i.e. the invalid part of a model against φ) in a transformation. The following example illustrates such a data cleansing transformation at a high-level abstraction.

Example 4. Consider the following PET that cleanses insurance data when migrating from the schema in Fig. 2 to the schema in Fig. 4.

> **seq forall** x **with** $x \in$ INSURANCE $\wedge$ INVALID(x) **do**
> > DELETEINSURANCE
> **enddo**
> **forall** x **with** $x \in$ TRANSPORT $\wedge$ MISSEDINSURANCE(x) **do**
> > **seq**
> > > SEARCHRECORD
> > > **if** FOUNDRECORD **then**
> > > > ADDINTOINSURANCECOMPANYANDINSURANCE
> > > **endif**
> > **endseq**
> **enddo endseq**

INVALID(x) and MISSEDINSURANCE(x) indicate whether an insurance is invalid or a transport has missed the insurance information, respectively, by comparing the model with three data sources from insurance companies. SEARCH- RECORD searches for an insurance in external insurance data sources.   □

4.3   Migration Strategies

Since data migration includes both the cleansing and the mapping of data to ensure that the data being migrated is correct and in the proper format for use by the new system, a migration transformation is the composition of a finite sequence of PPTs and PETs. For two transformations $P_1 = (\mathcal{M}_1, M_0, M_m, \delta_1)$ and $P_2 = (\mathcal{M}_2, M_m, M_n, \delta_2)$, the *composition* of P_1 and P_2 is a transformation $P_1 \circ P_2 = (\mathcal{M}_1 \cup \mathcal{M}_2, M_0, M_n, \delta)$ where $\delta : \mathcal{M}_1 \cup \mathcal{M}_2 \to \mathcal{M}_1 \cup \mathcal{M}_2$ such that, if $M \in \mathcal{M}_1$, then $\delta(M) = \delta_1(M)$; if $M \in \mathcal{M}_2$, then $\delta(M) = \delta_2(M)$. Both PPTs and PETs are closed under composition, which means that a combination of several PPTs (resp. PETs) is another PPT (resp. PET). In the following we discuss transformations under different migration strategies [3,10].

Big Bang. The strategy of big bang transforms all data from the legacy system into a new data source and takes over all operational data at one time. There are many approaches to implement this strategy in data migration projects. Fig. 6.a illustrates one of approaches in which a migration transformation $\Lambda_1 \circ \Pi_1$ starts with Λ_1 to cleanse data in the legacy system and then continue with Π_1 to map data into the new data source. Alternatively, a transformation $\Pi_2 \circ \Lambda_2$ can achieve the same effect by swapping the order of data cleansing and mapping.

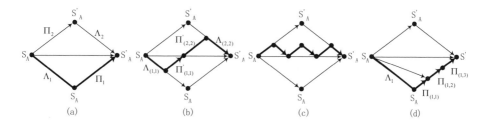

Fig. 6. Refinement of transformations under different migration strategies

Chicken Little. The strategy of chicken little divides a legacy system (including its legacy data) into modules. As few as possible dependencies between modules are remained, and migration takes place by migrating modules step by step. Fig. 6.b shows a two-step data migration process consisting of a transformation $P_1 = \Lambda_{(1,1)} \circ \Pi'_{(1,1)}$ and a transformation $P_2 = \Pi'_{(2,2)} \circ \Lambda_{(2,2)}$. The whole data migration process is the composition of P_1 and P_2. Fig. 6.c shows a three-step data migration in which each step is a transformation that first cleanses the data in a legacy data source and then maps the data into a targeted data source.

Butterfly. The strategy of butterfly uses a crystalliser to transform data from the legacy system to the new system in steps: first transforming data of the read-only legacy data source and then successively temporary data stores. Thus, transformations of data migration in butterfly are similar to ones in chicken little, with the only difference in separating data sources involved in each step of data migration processes. Fig. 6.d describes a transformation P of butterfly that transforms the read-only legacy data source by $\Lambda_1 \circ \Pi_{(1,1)}$, and two temporary data stores by $\Pi_{(1,2)}$ and $\Pi_{(1,3)}$ during the data migration process, i.e., $P = (\Lambda_1 \circ \Pi_{(1,1)}) \circ \Pi_{(1,2)} \circ \Pi_{(1,3)}$. For simplicity, the two temporary data stores are assumed to be clean without violating any constraints in the new system.

5   Refinement

In general a refining process is to refine an abstract transformation over abstract models into a concrete transformation over concrete models. In this section, we define the notions of refinement correctness for PPTs and PETs, and discuss the approach of proving properties of a transformation via verifying the correctness of refinements.

5.1   Refinement of PPTs

We use the notion of *path* to describe a sequence of states of interest in a run of transformations. Let $(\mathcal{M}, M_0, M_n, \delta)$ be a transformation and δ^k be the k-fold composition of δ for $k \geq 1$. Then a *path* of the run $M_0, M_1, ..., M_n$ is a sequence $\langle M_{k_1}, ..., M_{k_m} \rangle$ of states satisfying the conditions: $M_{k_1} = M_0$, $M_{k_m} = M_n$ and $\delta^k(M_{k_i}) = M_{k_{i+1}}$ for $k_{i+1} = k_i + k$. The *length* of a path $\langle M_{k_1}, ..., M_{k_m} \rangle$ is the number (i.e. m) of states in the path. The shortest path of a run is the pair $\langle M_0, M_n \rangle$ of initial and final states with the length 2.

Let us discuss a translation from abstract objects and their properties to more concrete representations. Let $\mathcal{S}_A$ and $\mathcal{S}_C$ be two sets of schemata defined over two different model kinds, and relatively, we consider $\mathcal{S}_C$ as "concrete" schemata and $\mathcal{S}_A$ as "abstract" schemata. Then a *concretization translation* $\varsigma :$ $\mathcal{S}_A \to \mathcal{S}_C$ translate an abstract schema to a concrete schema such that $\varsigma(S_A) = (\varsigma(T_A), \varsigma(\Sigma_A)) = (T_C, \Sigma_C) = S_C$ for $S_A = (T_A, \Sigma_A)$. This translation can be further extended to models, i.e., $\varsigma : \mathcal{M}(S_A) \to \mathcal{M}(S_C)$ in a canonical way. Note that, between two fixed levels of abstractions, we may have several different concretization translations but only one concretization map that is the upper bound of all concretization translations.

Let M and M^* be two models respectively defined over the schemata $S_A \in \mathcal{S}_A$ and $S_C \in \mathcal{S}_C$. A *location invariant* between M and M^*, denoted as $M \approx^{(\varsigma)} M^*$, describes that the model M is similar to M^* because objects in M are translated into M^*, i.e.,

$$M \approx^{(\varsigma)} M^* \equiv M \in \mathcal{M}(S) \wedge M^* \in \mathcal{M}(\varsigma(S))$$
$$\wedge M^* = \varsigma(M).$$

Definition 6. *Let Π be a PPT. Then Π^* is a* correct refinement *of Π, denoted as $\Pi \hookrightarrow \Pi^*$, iff Π^* is a PPT and for any run of Π^* with a path $\langle M_{i_1}^*, ..., M_{i_m}^* \rangle$ of interest, there exists a run of Π with a path $\langle M_{j_1}, ..., M_{j_n} \rangle$ of the same length n such that, for $k = 1, \ldots, n$,*

- $M_{j_k} \approx^{(\varsigma)} M_{i_k}^*.$

Definition 6 states that for any model of interest in the run of a refined PPT Π^* there is a corresponding model in the run of the abstract PPT Π. Each pair of the corresponding states is considered to be equivalent in terms of a location invariant $\approx^{(\varsigma)}$ defined on a concretization translation ς between abstract and concrete models. A general description of the refinement of PPTs is illustrated in Fig. 7(a). Π transforms a model over schema (T_0, Σ_0) to another model over schema (T_n, Σ_n), and correspondingly, Π^* transforms a model over schema (T_0^*, Σ_0^*) to another model over schema (T_n^*, Σ_n^*). If we describe the mapping from (T_0, Σ_0) to (T_n, Σ_n) as f and the mapping from (T_0^*, Σ_0^*) to (T_n^*, Σ_n^*) as f^*, then we have $\varsigma(f(T_0)) = f^*(\varsigma(T_0))$ and $\varsigma(f(\Sigma_0)) \Leftrightarrow f^*(\varsigma(\Sigma_0))$.

5.2   Refinement of PETs

For the refinement of PETs we need the notion of constraint invariant to capture the invariant of constraints between two models. Given a schema S and a set Ψ of constraints defined over S. A coupling *constraint invariant* between two models M and M^* with respect to Ψ (denoted as $M \approx^{(\varsigma, \Psi)} M^*$) describes that models M and M^* are semantically similar in the sense that both models satisfy constraints in Ψ. Formally, it is defined as

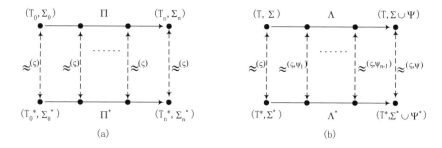

Fig. 7. (a) Refinement of PPTs and (b) Refinement of PETs

$$M \approx^{(\varsigma,\Psi)} M^* \equiv M \in \mathcal{M}(S) \wedge M^* \in \mathcal{M}(\varsigma(S))$$
$$\wedge M^* = \varsigma(M)$$
$$\wedge M \models \bigwedge_{\varphi \in \Psi} \varphi \wedge M^* \models \bigwedge_{\varphi \in \varsigma(\Psi)} \varphi.$$

Definition 7. *Let Ψ be a set of constraints and Λ be a PET over Ψ. Then Λ^* is a correct refinement of Λ, denoted as $\Lambda \hookrightarrow \Lambda^*$, iff Λ^* is a PET and for any run of Λ^* with a path $\langle M_{i_0}^*, ..., M_{i_m}^* \rangle$ of interest, there exists a run of Λ with a path $\langle M_{j_0}, ..., M_{j_n} \rangle$ of the same length n such that, for $k = 1, ..., n$, $\bigwedge_{0 \leq p < q \leq n} \Psi_p \subseteq \Psi_q$, $\Psi_0 = \emptyset$ and $\Psi_n = \Psi$,*

- *$M_{i_k}^* \approx^{(\Psi_k, \varsigma)} M_{j_k}$,*
- *$(M_{i_{k-1}}^*)^{\varsigma(\Psi_k)} \subseteq (M_{i_k}^*)^{\varsigma(\Psi_k)}$ and $(M_{j_{k-1}})^{\Psi_k} \subseteq (M_{j_k})^{\Psi_k}$.*

Definition 7 also states that for any model of interest in the run of a refined PET Λ^* there is a corresponding model in the run of the abstract PET Λ. Each pair of corresponding models is equivalent with respect to a subset $\Psi_k \subseteq \Psi$ of constraints and a concretization translation ς. The subset of constraints satisfied by a pair of models of interest should also be satisfied by the pair of successor models of interest. Eventually, the final models of both transformations satisfy all the constraints in Ψ. The valid part of each model in terms of the subset of constraints specified for its successor model must be remained in the successor model in both Λ^* and Λ. Fig. 7(b) illustrates this refinement process in which Λ transforms a model over schema (T, Σ) to another model over schema $(T, \Sigma \cup \Psi)$, and correspondingly, Λ^* transforms a model over schema (T^*, Σ^*) to another model over schema $(T^*, \Sigma^* \cup \Psi^*)$ for $\varsigma(T) = T^*$, $\varsigma(\Sigma) = \Sigma^*$ and $\varsigma(\Psi) = \Psi^*$.

For data cleansing, the refinement of PETs can be considered as modular refinement on each data cleansing strategy. The obligations of data cleansing strategies are first described at a high-level abstraction, and then are realised through stepwise refinements into more detailed specification.

5.3 Discussion

Given two refinements $P_1 \hookrightarrow P_1^*$ and $P_2 \hookrightarrow P_2^*$. If P_1 and P_2 can be composed and respectively P_1^* and P_2^* can be composed, then $P_2^* \circ P_1^*$ is a refinement of

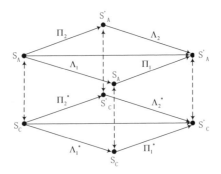

Fig. 8. A refinement scheme for migration transformations

$P_2 \circ P_1$. Fig.8 presents a general refinement scheme for migration transformations. The transformation $\Lambda_1 \circ \Pi_1$ (resp. $\Pi_2 \circ \Lambda_2$) can be refined to $\Lambda_1^* \circ \Pi_1^*$ (resp. $\Pi_2^* \circ \Lambda_2^*$), where $\Lambda_1 \hookrightarrow \Lambda_1^*$ and $\Pi_1 \hookrightarrow \Pi_1^*$ (resp. $\Lambda_2 \hookrightarrow \Lambda_2^*$ and $\Pi_2 \hookrightarrow \Pi_2^*$).

In [14] Schellhorn presented a generic proof method for the correctness of refinements of ASMs, in which invariants are established based on the notion of commuting diagrams. This approach can be adopted to verify the correctness of refinements defined for transformations in data migration. As it has been well studied [4,5] that the ASM refinement is a practically useful method for proving properties in system design, the theory we developed here also provides a general scheme for proving the properties of a migration transformation from a legacy system that may have a number of heterogeneous data sources to a unified new system. To prove that a migration transformation P^* at the implementation level has certain property, we take the following steps:

- specify the abstract transformation P that migrates data from the legacy system to an abstract model of the new system, which is the composition of a number of PPTs and PETs;
- prove that an appropriate abstract form of the property in question holds on the abstract transformation P;
- prove the transformation P^* in question to be a correct refinement of P that preserves correctness, i.e., each PPT Π^* or PET Λ^* included in P^* is a correct refinement of the corresponding PPT Π or PET Λ included in P.

6   Conclusion

In this paper, we developed a refinement theory for data migration. This theory can be further extended to database or application migrations in a broader sense, in which functionality transformation, wrapping of old applications, etc. will bring in additional complexity into the refinement scheme. We will investigate these problems in the future.

References

1. Rapid application development (RAD) for data migration – white paper solutions by Premier International (2004),
   `http://www.premier-international.com/pdf/Applaud_White_Paper.pdf`
2. Bisbal, J., Lawless, D., Wu, B., Grimson, J.: Legacy information systems: Issues and directions. IEEE Software 16(5), 103–111 (1999)
3. Bisbal, J., Lawless, D., Wu, B., Grimson, J., Wade, V., Richardson, R., O' Sullivan, D.: A survey of research into legacy system migration (1997)
4. Börger, E.: The ASM refinement method. In: FAC, vol. 15(2), pp. 237–257 (November 2003)
5. Börger, E., Stärk, R.F.: Abstract State Machines: A Method for High-Level System Design and Analysis. Springer, Heidelberg (2003)
6. Comon, H., Dauchet, M., Gilleron, R., Löding, C., Jacquemard, F., Lugiez, D., Tison, S., Tommasi, M.: Tree automata techniques and applications (2007), `http://www.grappa.univ-lille3.fr/tata`
7. Cousot, P., Cousot, R.: Abstract interpretation: a unified attice model for static analysis of programs by construction or approximation of fixpoints. In: Principles of Programming Languages, pp. 238–252. ACM, New York (1977)
8. Howard, P., Potter, C.: Data migration in Global 2000, research, forecasts and survey results – a survey paper by Bloor Research (2007), `http://www.bloorresearch.com/research/survey/876/data_migrtaion_survey.html`
9. Immerman, N.: Expressibility as a complexity measure: results and directions. In: Second Structure in Complexity Conference, pp. 194–202 (1987)
10. Klettke, M., Thalheim, B.: Evolution and migration of information systems. In: The Handbook of Conceptual Modeling: Its Usage and Its Challenges, ch. 12, pp. 381–420. Springer, Berlin (2011)
11. Otto, M.: The expressive power of fixed-point logic with counting. Journal of Symbolic Logic 61(1), 147–176 (1996)
12. Parnas, D.: Software aging. In: Proceedings of the 16th International Conference on Software Engineering, pp. 279–287. IEEE Computer Society Press, Los Alamitos (1994)
13. Rahm, E., Bernstein, P.: A survey of approaches to automatic schema matching. The VLDB Journal 10(4), 334–350 (2001)
14. Schellhorn, G.: Verification of ASM refinements using generalized forward simulation. Journal of Universal Computer Science 7(11), 952–979 (2001)
15. Schewe, K.-D., Wang, Q.: A customised ASM thesis for database transformations. Acta Cybernetica 19(4), 765–805 (2010)
16. Schmidt, D.A.: Binary relations for abstraction and refinement. In: Workshop on Refinement and Abstraction. Elsevier Electronic (1999)
17. Thalheim, B.: Entity-Relationship Modeling: Foundations of Database Technology. Springer, Heidelberg (2000)
18. Wang, Q.: Logical Foundations of Database Transformations for Complex-Value Databases. Logos Verlag, Berlin (2010)
19. Wu, B., Lawless, D., Bisbal, J., Grimson, J., Wade, V., O'Sullivan, D., Richardson, R.: Legacy system migration: A legacy data migration engine. In: DATASEM 1997, pp. 129–138 (1997)
20. Xiao, R., Dillon, T., Chang, E., Feng, L.: Modeling and transformation of object-oriented conceptual models into XML schema. In: Mayr, H.C., Lazanský, J., Quirchmayr, G., Vogel, P. (eds.) DEXA 2001. LNCS, vol. 2113, pp. 795–804. Springer, Heidelberg (2001)

Design by Selection: A Reuse-Based Approach for Business Process Modeling

Ahmed Awad[1], Sherif Sakr[2], Matthias Kunze[1], and Mathias Weske[1]

[1] Hasso Plattner Institute
University of Potsdam, Germany
{ahmed.awad,matthias.kunze,mathias.weske}@hpi.uni-potsdam.de
[2] National ICT Australia (NICTA)
University of New South Wales, Australia
ssakr@cse.unsw.edu.au

Abstract. During business process design, working procedures in organizations are represented by process models. It is an important task in any process improvement project, yet time consuming and error prone. While many organizations maintain large process model repositories, we observe that the information these repositories carry is not fully exploited during process modeling. In this paper, we present a novel approach to business process design called *Design by Selection*, which takes advantage of process repositories during design and facilitates reuse of process model components. These components can be static or flexible. Static ones represent the specific aspects of the process model, while flexible components realize *re-use*: They are defined by visual queries, which return matching process model components to be embedded in the overall process. Thus, process models can be designed in a more efficient, higher quality, and less error-prone way.

1 Introduction

Designing a new business process model is a tedious and error-prone task. The design requires determining the activities that need to be performed, ordering of their execution, handling exceptional cases that can occur, etc. In any organization, business process models represent a main source of business knowledge which is scattered among several IT systems, business documents and the minds of involved people. This knowledge is reused each time a process model is created or updated, however, in an *ad-hoc* and generally uncontrolled fashion. Moreover, process design usually involves different perspectives, e.g., from business experts, top managers, compliance officers, etc. This makes the integration of these different views a time consuming and a tedious task. Nevertheless, it can be the case that a similar situation has been addressed before in the design of business processes. Thus, it would be of great value to have a systematic way to access and *reuse* existing process models in order to cut down the design cost of a new process model.

Imagine a financial institution that aims at extending its services through the offering of checking accounts in combination with a credit card. The institution is likely to already have several processes in place, which 1) validate the trust in the customer to balance its account after withdrawal through the credit card, e.g., the approval of loans

M. Jeusfeld, L. Delcambre, and T.W. Ling (Eds.): ER 2011, LNCS 6998, pp. 332–345, 2011.

or overdraft limits, and 2) obtain all required information to open a bank account, e.g., setting up a savings account. Reusing existing processes reduces the risk of neglecting steps required by the institution's policies and leverages existing resources and skills. Instead of designing a process model from scratch and validating it against existing guidelines, a process designer expresses new process fragments in a detailed way and highlights those parts of the process that shall stem from reuse in a declarative way. This intentional process description will then be used to query existing process definitions, e.g., from a process repository, for a set of adequate process fragments and to propose them to the designer who completes the process design by selection from this set.

Business process repositories have been developed along with techniques to access models, and associate them with metadata [6,13,21]. While search and retrieval of process models are largely based on keyword and full text search, certain approaches to effectively *query* process models according to their contents have been proposed recently [2,4,14]. Amongst the use cases motivating the development of query languages was the support for process model reuse. However, corresponding work mainly discussed the languages and the technical details on matching queries to processes without providing a vision on how reuse could be supported.

In this paper, we present a novel approach that supports convenient reuse of process model fragments during modeling. Our approach is built on top of existing components, namely the open modeling platform *Oryx* [6], an open process modeling platform and repository, and the *BPMN-Q* query language [2,19], as a means to access and retrieve process components from the repository. We call this approach *Design by Selection*, by which users design so called *partial process models* that comprise both, a process modeling language and a process model query language, in an embedded fashion. The process model query language is similar to the process modeling language with regards to its notation, and thus, although being declarative, eases expressing a certain intention in the partial process model. To come up with suggestions, embedded queries will be matched against models stored in a repository to extract matching components. These components will be composed along with process model parts in the original partial model to provide complete process models and to present them to the process designer as a ranked list, of which the designer can accept one as is or modify it arbitrarily. In particular, we summarize the main strengths of our approach as follows:

- It effectively reduces the time and effort of the process modeling task.
- It enables *reuse* on a process fragment level and precomposes a potential completion.
- A partial process model may contain several embedded queries; each could represent a view on the developed process model, which relaxes the learning curve, particularly for novices in a business domain.
- It improves the quality and maturity of the newly developed process models.
- Redundancy between several process models can be reduced, especially in case of process variants [16].

The remainder of this paper is structured as follows: preliminaries are introduced in Sect. 2. Sect. 3 presents our proposed concept of *partial process models*. Sect. 4 describes our mechanism for composing and ranking the results of completions found in process model repositories. Prototypical implementation of our approach is presented

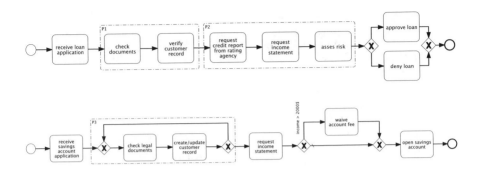

Fig. 1. Process Models and Potential Process Model Components

in Sect. 5. Experimental evaluation is presented in Sect. 6. We discuss related work in Sect. 7, before concluding the paper with a prospect on future work in Sect. 8.

2 Preliminaries

This section formally introduces process modeling and querying, which forms the groundwork for *partial process models*, which are described later.

2.1 Business Process Modeling

Currently, there is a number of graph-based business process modeling languages (e.g. BPMN, EPC, YAWL, and UML Activity Diagram). Despite their variance in expressiveness and modeling notation, they all share the common concepts of tasks, events, gateways (or routing nodes), artifacts, and resources, as well as relations between them, such as control flow [18]. Without loss of generality, we can abstract from particular node types as their execution semantics are not vital to structural query matching, which is rather based on the concept of a process graph.

Definition 1 (Process Model). *A process model P is a connected graph (N, E), where $N = N_C \cup N_A \cup N_E$ is a set of nodes with disjoint sets N_C (a set of* control flow routing nodes*), N_A (a nonempty set of* activities*), and N_E (a nonempty set of* events*), and a set of edges $E \subseteq (N \times N)$ a nonempty set of directed* control flow edges*) where $\bullet n$ ($n \bullet$) stands for the set of immediate predecessor (successor) nodes of $n \in N$.*

A process model has at least one start event $n_{start} \in N_E$ with no incoming and at least one outgoing control flow edge, i.e., $|\bullet n_{start}| = 0 \wedge |n_{start} \bullet| \geq 1$, and at least one end event $n_{end} \in N_E$ with at least one incoming and no outgoing control flow edge, i.e., $|\bullet n_{end}| \geq 1 \wedge |n_{end} \bullet| = 0$. Each other control flow node $n \in (N \setminus \{n_{start} : |\bullet (n_{start})| = 0\}) \setminus \{n_{end} : |(\bullet n_{end})| = 0\}$ is on a path from some n_{start} to some n_{end}.

Definition 2 (Process Model Component). *A connected subgraph (N', E') of a process model (N, E), where $N' \subseteq N, E' \subseteq E$, is a process model component PC.*

Fig. 1 illustrates two process models found in a business process model repository. The notation used is BPMN [1]: Rounded rectangles describe an activity, or a unit of work, and arcs between them define sequence flow and thus causal relationships among the activities. Diamond shapes express gateways, where + denotes that all outgoing branches need to be activated, x denotes that one path must exclusively be chosen, and ○ denotes that a subset of the outgoing branches needs to be followed according to the specified conditions. Empty circles represent start and end event of a process, respectively. Artifacts are illustrated with dog-eared paper sheets.

2.2 Business Process Model Querying

Based on the definition of process models and process model components, we introduce the concept of process model queries, as a means to obtain business process components from a collection of business processes by structurally matching a query to each of them. BPMN-Q is a visual process model query language designed to help business process designers access repositories of business process models [2]. The language supports querying the control flow aspects of business process models. Moreover, it introduces a set of new *abstraction* concepts that are useful for different querying scenarios.

Definition 3 (BPMN-Q Query). A BPMN-Q query is a tuple
$Q = (QC, QCF, QP, isAnonymous)$ *where:*
- QC *is a finite set of* control flow nodes *in a query,*
- $QCF \subseteq QC \times QC$ *is the* control flow relation *between control nodes in a query,*
- $QP \subseteq QC \times QC$ *is the* path *relation between control nodes in a query,*
- $isAnonymous : QC \cup QD \rightarrow \{true, false\}$ *is a functions that determines whether control flow nodes of a query are anonymous.*

BPMN-Q Constructs. A BPMN-Q model is called a query. A query declaratively describes a structural connectivity that must be satisfied by a matching process model. In addition to the core business process modeling concepts, BPMN-Q introduces new concepts which serve its querying purpose.
- **Path edges** connecting two control flow nodes represent an abstraction over an arbitrary set of control flow nodes that could be in between the matching process model.
- **Anonymous activities** can be used if no restriction should be put on the labels of matched process model activities. In such cases elements of a query become labeled with the character @ to declare it as an anonymous activity.

Matching Queries to Processes. A BPMN-Q query is matched to a candidate process model via a set of refinements to the query. With each refinement, nodes (edges) in a query are replaced with the corresponding nodes (edges) of the matching process model. If one node can have more than one possible replacement within the process model, a new refined copy of the query is created for each possible replacement. We call the replacement a resolution of an element of the query.

Since BPMN-Q is designed to match queries to process models in a repository, it is necessary to identify a candidate set of process models that can have the chance to provide a match to the query, rather than scanning the whole repository. To evaluate path edges, we rely on the transitive closure of nodes regarding the control flow relation. A path $(source, target)$ evaluates, if any, to a subgraph (N', E') in which every node $n \in N'$ is on a path from $source$ to $target$. Fig. 2 shows a sample BPMN-Q query along with a match to a process model, highlighted in grey.

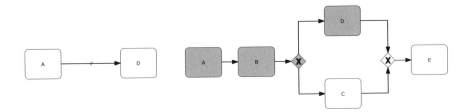

Fig. 2. An example BPMN-Q query with a match to a process model

Basically, the BPMN-Q query processor looks for exact matches to labels of activities in a query with those in the candidate process model. However, in practice, process modelers do not follow a strict naming scheme for activity labels. Thus, the query would find a small set of matching processes. To tackle this problem, we employed information retrieval techniques to automate the discovery of *semantically* similar activities [3]. The BPMN-Q query gets modified by substituting each of its activities with similar ones. With such a substitution step, new BPMN-Q query graphs are generated to constitute the expanded BPMN-Q query set. Fig. 3 illustrates an example of a BPMN-Q query and its possible semantic expansions.

Process components matching a query model will have a similarity score assigned ranging from 0 to 1. A similarity score of 1 indicates an exact match between the query and

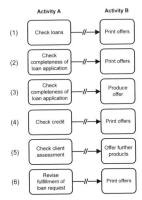

Fig. 3. An example query and its semantic expansions

the process. Similarity scores between 1 and 0 indicate that a match was found between a semantically similar query and the process model. Users are given the opportunity to attribute their search with a threshold, ranging from 0 to 1, that controls the minimum similarity accepted in queries. For more details about the BPMN-Q query language and its similarity matching mechanism, we refer the reader to [2,3].

3   Partial Process Models

The approach presented in this paper—*Design by Selection*—is based on the notion of *partial process models* that describe a desired process model through a combination of process model fragments and process model queries.

Definition 4 (Partial Process Model). *A partial process model* $\mathfrak{P} = (\mathfrak{F}, \mathfrak{Q}, \mathfrak{E})$ *is a connected graph that consists of disjoint sets of process model fragments $\mathfrak{F}$ and process model queries $\mathfrak{Q}$ connected through directed edges $\mathfrak{E} \subseteq \mathfrak{F} \times \mathfrak{Q} \cup \mathfrak{Q} \times \mathfrak{F}$, where each outgoing boundary control flow node $n_{out} \in N$ of a process model fragment $F \in \mathfrak{F}$ is connected to exactly one incoming boundary control flow node $n_{in} \in QC$ of a process model query $Q \in \mathfrak{Q}$ and vice versa.*

Fig. 4 shows a partial process model corresponding to the use case illustrated in Sect. 1. The first intention, to validate trust in the customer, is represented by BPMN-Q query

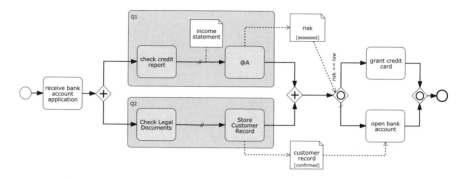

Fig. 4. Partial Process Example, consisting of process model fragments and process model queries

$Q1$, i.e., a set of actions that take the *income statement* of a client into account and an anonymous activity that produces a context artifact *risk* in the state *assessed*. The query in the lower part addresses the second intention, i.e., the creation of a customer record, and matches process components that contain activities labeled similar to *check legal documents* and *store customer record*, yielding a *complete customer record*, cf., $Q2$. The right part of the process model illustrates how artifacts from the queries are incorporated into the remaining process model, e.g., the assessed risk will have an influence on the decision, whether the customer will be granted a credit card. Such relationships make up the context of queries in a partial process model. Fig. 5 shows an example of a composed process model based on the defined partial process model in Fig. 4. In this composed model, the process model components $P2$ and $P3$ are extracted from the process models of Fig. 1 where $P2$ represents the matching element of $Q1$ and $P3$ represents the matching element of $Q2$.

Evaluation of a process model query $Q \in \mathfrak{Q}$ returns zero or more process model components. Obviously, each process model query in the partial process model PM can be replaced by one of its matching process components which results in a complete business process model. In addition, we ensure that there is *no overlap* between the resulting process fragments of different embedded queries if they are originating from the same process model in order to avoid meaningless compositions. In practice, each business process query can return a potentially large number of matched business process components, from which one needs to be chosen. This issue is addressed by the term "selection", i.e., the users who developed the partial process model are supposed to choose from a ranked list of alternatives that comply with the given business process queries. To achieve this, the results of the single business process queries need to be combined into a complete process model, as discussed previously, and a meaningful ranking must be established to support the user in selecting a process model proposal.

4 Ranking of Model Compositions

The main task of a query processor is to evaluate the BPMN-Q queries of the defined partial process model against the process model repository. For each BPMN-Q query, a result set is returned comprising *matched* process model components. These matched

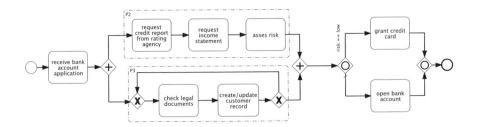

Fig. 5. Complete Process Example, composed of proposals P2 and P3, cf., Fig. 1

components could represent exact or similar matches for the query models (Sect. 2.2). In case of similar matches, each matched process model component is then attached with its similarity score (SS) which is computed during the query evaluation process. In case of an exact match, the value of this similarity score is equal to 1 for each matched component of the result set.

In principle, having different matched components for each query model, which usually belong to different process models, yields that we can have several possible compositions that originate from distinct process models. Each possible composition needs to include exactly one component from the answer set of each query in the partial process model. Hence, the number of the possible compositions is equal to the product of the number of returned results for each query. Clearly, it is inconvenient for process designers to go through this potentially very large list of compositions to select from. Therefore, the set of possible compositions is *ranked* according to various criteria, applying a ranking process that starts by initially ranking the matched process model components inside the answer set of each query based on their similarity scores. Then, it computes a ranking score for each possible composition model. This ranking score is obtained by *fusing* the intermediately computed scores of different scoring elements, which are described as follows.

- **Combined Similarity Matching Score (CS):** Computing this scoring element for a candidate composition model *ccp* is achieved by multiplying the similarity scores of its individual components.

$$CS(ccp) = \prod_{i=1}^{n} SS(mc_i)$$

  where n represents the number of the model components and $SS(mc_i)$ refers to the similarity score of the individual model components, cf., Sect. 2.2.
- **Homogeneity Score (HS):** The process model components of each candidate composition model can belong to the same or to distinct original process models. Having different model components of the candidate composition belonging to the same original process model increases its homogeneity, which leads to an increase in its chances of being more meaningful and highly appealing so as to be accepted by the process designer. For example, the combination between the process model components $P1$ and $P2$ (Fig. 1) will be more homogeneous than the combination between the process model components $P2$ and $P3$. Thus, we start by computing the homogeneity between each *unique different* pair (PHS) of the model components as follows

$$PHS(mc_i, mc_j) = \begin{cases} 0 \text{ if the original models of the pair are different} \\ 1 \text{ if the original models of the pair are the same} \end{cases}$$

where mc_i and mc_j represent a unique different pair of model components. In general, the number of unique different pairs n is equal to $\frac{c(c-1)}{2}$ where c is the number of process model components. The homogeneity score of a candidate model composition ccp is then computed as follows.

$$HS(ccp) = \frac{\sum_{i=1}^{n} PHS(udp_i)}{n}$$

where udp represents a unique pair of model components (mc_i, mc_j) and n represent the total number of unique different pairs.

– **Metadata Matching Score (MS)**: As mentioned above, process model repositories store metadata (descriptive attributes about process models). Clearly, the homogeneity between model components which originate from *different* process models increases if there is an *overlap* in their metadata. For example, model components that have been developed by the same user or in the same department have a higher chance of being more similar or meaningful. Therefore, the metadata matching score (MS) is considered to be complementary to the general homogeneity score (HS). Here, we also start by computing the metadata homogeneity score (MHS) for each *unique different pair* of model components as follows.

$$MHS(mc_i, mc_j) = \frac{T(mc_i) \cap T(mc_j)}{c}$$

where mc_i and mc_j represent a unique different pair of model components, T represents the set of values for the metadata attributes of a model component and c represents the total number of the metadata attributes. The metadata matching score of a candidate model composition ccp is then computed as follows.

$$MS(ccp) = \frac{\sum_{i=1}^{n} MHS(udp_i)}{n}$$

where udp represents a unique pair of model components (mc_i, mc_j) and n represents the total number of unique different pairs. It should be noted that for this scoring element we consider only those pairs of model components which originate from *different* process models. The key reason behind this is that those pairs of components, which originate from the *same* process model, have already had their score increased on the homogeneity scoring element (HS).

– **Reusing Popularity Score (RS)**: For different reasons, e.g., clarity, simplicity, completeness, reputation of the designer, one process model can be more reusable than another. To make use of this fact, for each process model in a repository, we keep track of its *reuse ranking* (RR). This ranking gets automatically increased when any of its components is reused in a newly composed model. Thus, this scoring element can make effective use of the "wisdom of the crowd" in the context of social systems. Based on the reuse ranking of the stored process models, we then compute the reusing popularity score for each candidate composed model ccp as follows.

$$RS(ccp) = \sum_{i=1}^{n} RR(mc_i.originalModel)$$

where *mc* refers to a model component, *originalModel* refers to the original process model from which the process model component originated and n represents the total number of model components.

The *final ranking score* of a candidate composed model (*ccp*) is computed by fusing the values of its scoring elements using the following weighted function.

$$FinalScore(ccp) = w_1 * CS(ccp) + w_2 * HS(ccp) + w_3 * MS(ccp) + w_4 * RS(ccp)$$

where w_i represents a weighting factor for a scoring element which can be configured and adjusted by the end-user, while $\forall w_i \in \mathbb{R} : w_i \geq 0$ and $\sum_{i=1}^{4} w_i = 1$. Initially, process designers can rely on a uniform regression parameter where all weighting factors have the same value, i.e., $w_i = 1/4$. With the continuous usage of the system, workload data can be gathered to generate significant training datasets that can be used as an input for a regression analysis process to deduce optimized weighting factors [11].

In practice, the set of the possible compositions generated by the combination of the matched process model components for the BPMN-Q queries can be large. Therefore, *filtering* mechanisms are needed in order to avoid overwhelming the process designer with less valuable possible compositions such as: 1) The model composer needs to ignore the matched process model components for the BPMN-Q queries with a similarity score (SS) that is less than a user-defined threshold t_1. Similarly, the possible compositions with combined similarity matching scores (CS) that are less than another a user-defined threshold t_2 can be ignored. Moreover, the composer may return only the top K possible compositions based on their final ranking score (*FinalScore*), where the value of K is user-defined. 2) The composition environment needs to allow the process designer to specify some *constraints* on the composition scheme. For example, the process designer can describe that matched process model component of Q_1 and Q_2 must belong to the same original process model or must have an overlap in a particular subset of their metadata.

5   Implementation

In this section, we describe the architecture of our implementation for the *Design By Selection* framework for business process modeling, illustrated in Fig. 6, which consists of the following main components.

- **Process Modeling, Querying, and Composition Environment** provides the process designer with a graphical *modeling interface* [6]. Users express their intention by means of a partial process model. The *query interface* extracts the set of process model queries from the partial process model, and passes them on to the query processor. The returned set of queries will then be *composed* with the model fragments from the partial model and *ranked* through the *model composer*, cf., Sect. 4.
- **Process Model Repository.** Instead of building the Design by Selection framework on top of a proprietary repository, it shall be connected to several, potentially disparate repositories, obtain and maintain process models stored remotely. Repositories do not only store models [5], but also a set of metadata, which is used to control the composition and ranking process.

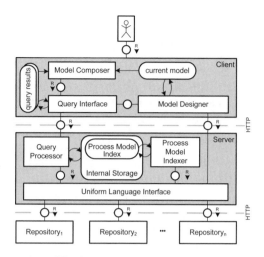

Fig. 6. Framework Architecture

- **Uniform Language Interface** translates process models of specific languages, cf.,
  Sect. 2.1, to a common representation suitable to process model querying, i.e., complying with Definition 1. This allows querying a larger set of process models and
  can further be used to unify the query interface and processor toward different process definition languages [18].
- **Query Processor & Process Model Indexes.** The *query processor* evaluates the
  queries received from the query interface [19]. It provides support for relaxation and
  refinement of user queries. In case the queries do not return sufficient results, the
  query processor is able to relax the query according to some similarity notions [3,8].
  Similarly, if a query returns too many results, the user needs to be provided with a
  possibility of refining and improving their request. In order to further improve the
  searching, process models could be *indexed* upfront to expedite query evaluations.

The *model designer* component of our framework is the Oryx editor[1], an extensible
process modeling platform for research, designed to model and manage process models online [6]. The *query interface* and *query processor* for BPMN-Q [2] components
have been implemented as plugins to the Oryx editor and are able to run process model
queries against the Oryx process model repository. We have implemented a *uniform
language interface* based on the work done by La Rosa et al. [18], who propose a
generic process model representation for an advanced process model repository. The
model composer component is implemented as another plugin to the Oryx editor that
uses the BPMN-Q query processor to evaluate the results of each query in the partial
process model and then returns the ranked compositions to the end-user. Our architecture acknowledges the existence of a multitude of different process model repositories,
which is the rationale behind decoupling process modeling, querying, and composition
system from any particular process model repository.

---

[1] http:/oryx-project.org/research

6 Experimental Evaluation

Our framework is mainly designed and built to help business process designer accelerate and improve the quality of their process models. To evaluate the impact of our framework, we conducted an experiment where we recruited 10 volunteers who have good knowledge of the modeling constructs of BPMN [1] and little background in database query languages. A brief tutorial about the query language (BPMN-Q) was given to the volunteers and a discussion of 5 prepared business process models using the BPMN notations was undertaken. A set of 6 business process models has been designed as user-test process models for our experiment. These process models vary in their domain and their complexity[2]. For each experimental process model, we had at least one model in the Oryx online repository[3] that is similar to the target process model and can be reused to reduce the modeling time (most similar process model needed at least adding/removing three nodes/edges to fit with the scenario of the target model).

We compared the speed and the correctness of the volunteers in designing each process model using the standard Oryx editor environment (*design from scratch*) and using the components of our *Design by Selection* framework. Table 1 summarizes the results of our experiment. For each user, we gave time to understand the model scenario before we started to measure the process design time, when the user decided that the process model was fully understood and they were ready to start their design. For the experiment results, if users were not able to design the process model on the allocated time (the maximum modeling time for each process model was set to 10 minutes) or they finished the design with a wrong result, we considered their result as unsuccessful. The results of our experiment show that our *Design by Selection* framework has accelerated the process models' design times with an average percentage of 33% while the correctness of the designed process models has been improved with an average percentage of 16%. We computed the percentage of speedup improvement of the design time for each process model using the following formula:

$$\frac{DFSDT - DBSDT}{DFSDT}$$

where $DFSDT$ represents the average design time of the design from scratch run and $DBSDT$ represents the average design time of the Design by Selection run.

We computed the percentage of improvement of the design correctness for each process model using the following formula:

$$\frac{DFSCD - DBSCD}{10}$$

Where $DFSCD$ represents the number of correct designs for each process model in the design from scratch run, $DBSCD$ represents the number of correct designs in the Design by Selection run and 10 represents the total number of user designs.

In general, the time improvement varied for each user based on the time to design the process model from scratch in the first run and their ability to formulate the right query for retrieving the nearest process model quickly in the second run. We noticed that the

---

[2] Due to the space limitation, we could not include our experimental queries in the paper. However, they are available on `http://bpmnq.sourceforge.net/EXPQueries.html`

[3] `http://oryx-project.org/try`

Table 1. Experimental Evaluation of Design by Selection Framework

Process Model	M1	M2	M3	M4	M5	M6	Average
Design From Scratch - Average Design Time (in Seconds)	338	291	261	492	283	342	334.5
Design by Selection - Average Design Time (in Seconds)	216	203	173	320	161	268	223.5
Percentage of Average Speed Improvement (%)	36%	30%	34%	35%	43%	22%	33%
Design From Scratch - Number of Correct Designs (Out of 10)	7	9	8	6	8	8	7.6
Design by Selection - Number of Correct Designs (Out of 10)	9	10	8	9	10	10	9.3
Percentage of Correctness Improvement (%)	20%	10%	0%	30%	20%	20%	16.5%

generic BPMN-Q query constructs, e.g., variable activities, generic split, path edge, beside the semantic query expander component of BPMN-Q, have played an important role to help the user retrieve their target models. In addition, the speed improvement for the design of each process model is affected by the level of the similarity of the retrieved models for reuse. In our framework, the precision of the retrieved semantically-similar process models for each query is controlled by a distance threshold parameter. The higher the value of the threshold, the more result models are returned with less precision quality. It could be expected that receiving many process model with less precision quality for individual queries may affect the precision of the composed models. However, our threshold control parameter for the *Combined Similarity* scoring element (CS) has played a significant role in getting rid of most false positive compositions. The results of our experiment show an average 82% user satisfaction with the first five models proposed by our model composer. However, we acknowledge that the improvement percentages of speed, correctness, or composed models could be further improved by incorporating label suggestion mechanisms for the label of query activities during the BPMN-Q query design time, cf. [20], which we will address in future work.

7   Related Work

The issue of accelerating business process design has attracted many researchers. In [15] Mendling and Simon propose to use schema integration approaches from database research to come up with a unified process model that satisfies the different perspectives of the stakeholders, obtained by interviews. Later on, these perspectives are merged and some restructuring rules are applied to refine the final model. Compared to our approach, a view could even be declaratively represented as a query. Moreover, we can contribute to the creation of the view by letting the designer query the repository for similar situations and then discuss the result with the respective stakeholders. Unlike the approach by Mendling and Simon, it is not necessary to state semantic relations between the different views. This can be achieved by the composition and ranking components.

Several approaches have been proposed to measure the similarity between business process models. Ehrig et al. [9] have presented an approach for measuring the similarity between business process models semantically modeled with the Web Ontology Language (OWL). The approach relies on detecting *synonyms* and *homonyms* of process element names, where the degree of similarity between process models correlates positively with the number of used synonyms and negatively with the number of used homonyms. Dijkman et al. [8,17] have described another lexical technique called *N-to-M* label matching which matches any node in one model with any node in the other model as long as the *string edit distance* between their labels is above a given threshold value. The authors have also described two *structural* matching techniques named as *greedy graph* matching and *A-star* graph matching. These algorithms are considered to be variants of the *graph edit distance* similarity measure. In principle, our framework is fully agnostic with respect to integrating and reusing any similarity matching technique for process models into the query processor component.

Pascalau et al. [16] have presented an approach for dealing with *redundancy* in process model repositories. In particular, they described an automated mechanism for maintaining the consistency between process model variants. In this approach, they maintain the *link* between the variant process models by means of defining *process model views* using the BPMN-Q query language [2]. Hence, dynamic evaluation for the defined queries of the process views guarantees that the process modeler is able to get up-to-date and a consistent state of the process model in case of changes in the *related* process model by other modelers.

Our approach further covers the topic of assisted completion of process models, in that it takes one or several fragments of a model and proposes a set of completions that satisfy the modeler's intention, which they describe via queries. A similar problem has been addressed by Koschmider et al. [10,12], who propose a semi-automatic completion framework for a special type of petri nets. A collection of petri nets, a query petri net and a set of textually defined rules that characterize the desired completion are transposed into an ontology. Automatic inference techniques are used to match the query model and rules structurally against the existing model collection. The result is ordered solely by the degree of similarity of a matched model to the query. Our approach is significantly different, in that 1) BPMN-Q proposes a graphical query language that is very similar to the process definition language in notation and semantics, 2) allows several points of inserting queries in a partial process model, and 3) offers a comprehensive ranking model that does not only take the syntax of a process model into account, but also relations between matches found and metadata stored along with models in a repository.

8 Conclusion and Outlook

In this paper, we introduced a new approach to accelerate business process design by querying repositories of business process models. By means of a partial process model, the user can define certain process logic imperatively and specify fragments to be looked up declaratively with process model queries. With this, the designer can focus on new process logic—the innovative part of the process—and just retrieve the common parts from other models in the repository. The results of each embedded query are composed and ranked in order to provide the user with the closest result. This approach provides several benefits by reusing business knowledge materialized in existing process models. The reuse is not only on the level of a whole process model, but rather on a finer grain level which is in the form of process model components. Moreover, the approach collects components from different process models. Another benefit is that each query could represent a view on the process design. Thus, we also address the issue of collaborative process design in a simple way.

For future work, we shall extend the implementation of our query matching process to include different similarity metrics [8,7,17]. We are planning to investigate the effect of applying these different similarity metrics on the quality of the returned ranked list of process model compositions to the end user. Also, we intend to conduct comparative experiments between our approach and design approaches depending on other process retrieval techniques.

References

1. Business Process Model and Notation 2.0 (BPMN 2.0) Specification, Final Adopted Specification, technical report, OMG (2011)
2. Awad, A.: BPMN-Q: A Language to Query Business Processes. In: EMISA (2007)
3. Awad, A., Polyvyanyy, A., Weske, M.: Semantic Querying of Business Process Models. In: EDOC, pp. 85–94 (2008)
4. Beeri, C., Eyal, A., Kamenkovich, S., Milo, T.: Querying business processes. In: VLDB (2006)
5. Bernstein, P., Dayal, U.: An overview of repository technology. In: VLDB (1994)
6. Decker, G., Overdick, H., Weske, M.: Oryx – sharing conceptual models on the web. In: Li, Q., Spaccapietra, S., Yu, E., Olivé, A. (eds.) ER 2008. LNCS, vol. 5231, pp. 536–537. Springer, Heidelberg (2008)
7. Dijkman, R., Dumas, M., van Dongen, B., Käärik, R., Mendling, J.: Similarity of business process models: Metrics and evaluation. Inf. Syst. 36(2) (2011)
8. Dijkman, R., Dumas, M., García-Bañuelos, L.: Graph Matching Algorithms for Business Process Model Similarity Search. In: Dayal, U., Eder, J., Koehler, J., Reijers, H.A. (eds.) BPM 2009. LNCS, vol. 5701, pp. 48–63. Springer, Heidelberg (2009)
9. Ehrig, M., Koschmider, A., Oberweis, A.: Measuring Similarity between Semantic Business Process Models. In: APCCM (2007)
10. Hornung, T., Koschmider, A., Oberweis, A.: Rule-based autocompletion of business process models. In: CAiSE Forum (2007)
11. Hwang, C., Hong, D.H., Seok, K.: Support vector interval regression machine for crisp input and output data. Fuzzy Sets and Systems 157(8) (2006)
12. Koschmider, A., Blanchard, E.: Automatic user assistance for business process modeling. In: RCIS (2007)
13. Ma, Z., Wetzstein, B., Anicic, D., Heymans, S.: Semantic business process repository. In: SBPM (2007)
14. Markovic, I.: Advanced querying and reasoning on business process models. In: BIS (2008)
15. Mendling, J., Simon, C.: Business process design by view integration. In: Eder, J., Dustdar, S. (eds.) BPM Workshops 2006. LNCS, vol. 4103, pp. 55–64. Springer, Heidelberg (2006)
16. Pascalau, E., Awad, A., Sakr, S., Weske, M.: On maintaining consistency of process model variants. In: Muehlen, M.z., Su, J. (eds.) J.1, H.4, D.2. Lecture Notes in Business Information Processing, vol. 66, pp. 289–300. Springer, Heidelberg (2011)
17. Dijkman, R., Dumas, M., García Bañuelos, L., Krik, R.: Aligning Business Process Models. In: EDOC (2009)
18. Rosa, M.L., Reijers, H., Aalst, W., Dijkman, R., Mendling, J., Dumas, M., Garcia-Banuelos, L.: Apromore : An advanced process model repository (2009), http://eprints.qut.edu.au/27448/
19. Sakr, S., Awad, A.: A Framework for Querying Graph-Based Business Process Models. In: WWW (2010)
20. Smirnov, S., Weidlich, M., Mendling, J., Weske, M.: Action Patterns in Business Process Models. In: ICSOC/ServiceWave (2009)
21. Vanhatalo, J., Koehler, J., Leymann, F.: Repository for business processes and arbitrary associated metadata. In: BPM Demo (2006)

System Identification for Adaptive Software Systems: A Requirements Engineering Perspective

Vítor E. Silva Souza[1], Alexei Lapouchnian[2], and John Mylopoulos[1]

[1] Dep. of Information Eng. and Computer Science, University of Trento, Italy
{vitorsouza,jm}@disi.unitn.it
[2] Department of Computer Science, University of Toronto, Canada
alexei@cs.toronto.edu

Abstract. Control Theory and feedback control in particular have been steadily gaining momentum in software engineering for adaptive systems. Feedback controllers work by continuously measuring system outputs, comparing them with reference targets and adjusting control inputs if there is a mismatch. In Control Theory, quantifying the effects of control input on measured output is a process known as *system identification*. This process usually relies either on detailed and complex system models or on system observation. In this paper, we adopt a Requirements Engineering perspective and ideas from Qualitative Reasoning to propose a language and a systematic system identification method for adaptive software systems that can be applied at the requirements level, with the system not yet developed and its behavior not completely known.

1 Introduction

In Control Theory (e.g., [8]), *system identification* is the process of determining the equations that govern the dynamic behavior of a system. White box models describe a system from first principles, e.g., a model for a physical process that consists of Newton equations. In most cases, such models are overly complicated or even impossible to obtain due to the complex nature of many systems and processes (natural or artificial).

A much more common approach is therefore to start from partial knowledge of the behavior of the system and its external influences (inputs), and try to determine a mathematical relation between inputs and outputs without going into the details of what is actually happening inside the system. Two types of models are built using this approach:

1. Gray box models: although the peculiarities of system internals are not entirely known, a certain model based on both insight into the system and experimental data is constructed. This model, however, comes with a number of free parameters (control variables) which can be estimated using system identification. Thus, parameter estimation is an important activity here;

M. Jeusfeld, L. Delcambre, and T.W. Ling (Eds.): ER 2011, LNCS 6998, pp. 346–361, 2011.

2. Black box models: no prior model is available here, so everything has to be constructed from scratch, through observation and experimentation. Most system identification algorithms are of this type.

We are interested in employing this control-theoretic framework for the design of adaptive software systems. In this paper, we adopt a Requirements Engineering (RE) perspective and assume that a goal-based requirements model is available for the system. At the requirements level, the system is not yet implemented and its behavior is not completely known. With this incomplete information, we are unable to fully identify how system configuration parameters affect outputs. Thus, quantitative approaches cannot be applied. Therefore, we base our approach on ideas from Qualitative Reasoning [10] and propose a systematic way of identifying target outputs and system configuration parameters as well as qualitative relations between these parameters and measured outputs, all using models. Our proposed technique is both qualitative and flexible in the sense that it can accommodate multiple levels of precision in specifications depending on available information.

According to our proposal, the output of system identification for a software system is an extended and parametrized requirements model. Each assignment of parameter values represents a different behavior (configuration) that the system might adapt to fulfill its requirements. Some of the parameters ("variation points") come directly from the model. For instance, for a meeting scheduling system that needs to collect timetables from all participants when a meeting is scheduled, there is a choice of collecting these directly from meeting participants (e.g., through email) or from a central repository of timetables. The behaviors are also determined by a set of control variables that influence system execution, its success rate, performance, or quality of service. For instance, the "Collect timetables" goal is influenced by a parameter "From how Many" (FhM) that determines from what percentage of the participants we need to collect timetables before the goal is deemed to have been fulfilled. If we need to collect from all, i.e., FhM $= 100$, then the success rate for the goal may be low and its completion time may be high, compared to the FhM $= 80$ setting.

The main objective of this paper is to propose a systematic process for conducting system identification. This process requires some new concepts, notably the notion of differential relations between control variables and indicators (monitored variables). We illustrate the proposed process with an example and validate the proposal with experiments on it.

The rest of the paper is structured as follows: section 2 summarizes research results used as the baseline in our proposal; section 3 presents a language for the modeling of qualitative information on the relation between system parameters and output; section 4 describes a systematic process for system identification using that language; section 5 discusses the validation of the proposal; section 6 compares it to related work; section 7 describes future research directions; and, finally, section 8 concludes the paper.

2   Research Baseline

The following sub-sections briefly present research results on top of which we build our proposal: Goal-Oriented RE (§2.1) and Qualitative Reasoning (§2.2).

2.1   Goal-Oriented Requirements Engineering (GORE)

Goal-oriented approaches to RE model requirements in terms of goals, softgoals, quality constraints (QCs) and domain assumptions (DAs) [9]. As running example for this paper, figure 1 shows a goal model for a Meeting Scheduler system.

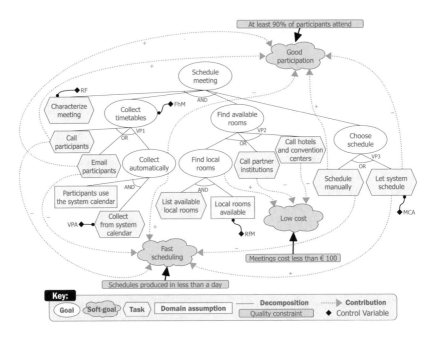

Fig. 1. Goal model for a Meeting Scheduler system

In our example, the main goal of the system is to *Schedule meeting*. **Goals** can be decomposed using Boolean decompositions with obvious semantics. For instance, to *Schedule meeting*, one has to *Characterize meeting*, *Collect timetables*, *Find available rooms* and *Choose schedule*. On the other hand, to *Collect timetables*, it is enough either to *Email participants*, *Call participants* or to *Collect from system calendar*. Goals are decomposed until they reach a level of granularity where there are **tasks** an actor (human or system) can perform to fulfill them.

Softgoals are special types of goals that represent non-functional requirements (qualities) that do not have clear-cut satisfaction criteria. Goals and tasks contribute to the satisfaction of softgoals through positive or negative contribution links. Softgoals need to be refined into **quality constraints** (QCs) which offer concrete metrics for measuring how well the system is fulfilling a softgoal [9]. For example, *Good participation* is a desired quality for our system, receiving positive contribution from *Schedule manually* and negative from *Let system schedule*. A clear-cut satisfaction criteria for this softgoal is specified by the QC *At least 90% of participants attend*.

Goal models may also contain **domain assumptions** (DAs), which are statements that we assume to be true in order for the system to work. In the example, we assume there are *Local rooms available* in order to *Find local rooms*. If the assumption turns out to be false, its parent goal will not be satisfied.

Finally, figure 1 also illustrates **system parameters** that were identified for the meeting scheduler example. Monitored and controlled parameters have long been proposed as a way to implement reconciliation for adaptive systems at runtime [5]. However, in our proposal these are intentional parameters which are introduced much earlier in the development process, at the level of requirements. The example shows five *control variables* as black diamonds connected to other elements of the model.

OR-decompositions in goal models also represent intentional variability in the system. Choosing a different path at such *variation points* has been proposed as a way to configure systems [13] or to reconcile the behavior of adaptive systems at runtime in previous works such as [19]. In figure 1 we label the three existing OR-decompositions as `VP1`, `VP2` and `VP3` in order to be able to reference them in our language.

In section 3.1 we discuss in more depth the role of such parameters in our proposal.

2.2   Qualitative Reasoning

The key feature of qualitative reasoning (QR) methods (e.g., [10]) is that while frequently there is not enough information to construct quantitative models, qualitative models can cope with uncertain and incomplete knowledge about systems. They do not require assumptions beyond what is known. Most QR approaches can be seen as having two types of abstraction.

Domain abstraction abstracts the real domain values of variables into a finite number of ordered symbols that describe qualitative values, *landmarks*, that are behaviorally significant. Landmarks can be numeric or symbolic and can include the values such as 0 and $\pm\infty$. A qualitative variable value is either a landmark or an interval between adjacent landmarks. The finite, totally ordered set of all the possible qualitative values of a variable is called its *quantity space*.

Qualitative *functional abstraction*, which gives the ability to represent incompletely known functional relationships between quantities, complements domain abstraction in QR. E.g., signs $(+,-,0)$ can be used to describe and reason about the direction of change in variables — one can state that there exists some monotonically increasing function relating two quantities, without elaborating further. Merging qualitative information frequently results in ambiguity, such as when combining positive and negative influences without knowing their magnitudes. Ranges of techniques and notations are available within QR, their applicability depending on the precision of the available information. E.g., one can reason about orders of magnitude, if they are known, possibly resolving said ambiguity.

3   Parameters and Qualitative Differential Relations

In this section, we further discuss system parameters and indicators of system output, as well as propose a language based on qualitative modeling [10] to augment our (goal-oriented) requirements model with information that captures the relationships among the these parameters in a qualitative way.

3.1   System Parameters and Indicators

As previously discussed, our proposal consists of a language and a systematic process to identify and model qualitative relations between *configuration parameters* and *measured outputs of the system*. Given our Requirements Engineering perspective, we propose to augment goal models of system requirements by recognizing *variation points* and *control variables* (collectively called *parameters*) and identifying *indicators* (of *system output*).

Variation points (VPs) are the OR-decompositions already present in the goal model. As we have mentioned in §2.1, selecting a different path at a VP at runtime is one way of reconfiguring the system in order to adapt to failures. Our proposal adds labels to VPs in the goal model (e.g., VP1, VP2 and VP3 in figure 1) in order to refer to them when modeling qualitative relations (see §3.3).

In this paper we introduce *control variables* (CVs), which represent another powerful mechanism for system (re)configuration. CVs are part of the system input. They can be applied to goals, tasks, and domain assumptions (DAs) and are used as abstractions over goal/domain model fragments. In particular, CVs are derived from families of related, but slightly different goal/task or DA alternatives, as in figure 2, where the goals *Collect timetables from 10% of participants*, *Collect timetables from 20% of participants*, etc. are shown as alternative ways to achieve the parent *Collect timetables* goal.

Here, we identify variations that differ in some value (usually, but not necessarily numeric) and abstract that value as a parameter to be attached to the appropriate goal model element as a CV (e.g., the FhM, *From how Many* variable in figure 2). Figure 1 shows more examples of CVs, such as: RF (*required fields*

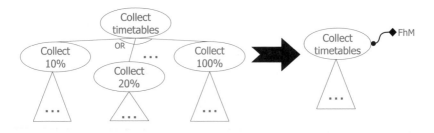

Fig. 2. Using a CV as an abstraction over families of subtrees

when characterizing a meeting), RfM (number of *rooms for meeting* available — note that this CV applies to a DA), etc.

The benefits of having CVs include the ability to represent large number of model variations in a compact way as well as the ability to concisely analyze how changes in CV values affect the system's success rate and/or quality of service when, e.g., scheduling meetings. As any parameter in software design, a CV needs to be taken into consideration (i.e., propagated) when refining the goal model element that it applies to and later when designing and implementing the system. In this proposal, we are interested in analyzing the effect of values of CVs on system output and thus omit the details of CV refinement and implementation.

Finally, *indicators* are essential to control systems as these are monitored system output values that feedback loops need to compare to the output targets in order to calculate the control error and to determine how the system's control input needs to be adjusted. Indicators are similar to *gauge variables*, proposed by van Lamsweerde in [11].

Indicators need to be measurable quantities. In goal models, quality constraints (QCs) as well as the success rates for hard goals and tasks can be used as indicators. Since the number of potential indicators is large, we need to select as indicators the important values that the adaptive system should strive to achieve. *Awareness Requirements* (*AwReqs*) [18] are requirements that talk about the success or failure of other requirements, e.g., "*Find available rooms should never fail*" or "*Schedules produced in less than a day* should succeed 75% of the time". *AwReqs* are formalized and come with a monitoring infrastructure. They can be attached to QCs, hard goals, etc. (i.e., potential indicators) and capture the *reference input* of the system as well as specify the target success rates or other requirements about them. In our system identification approach (§4), we use *AwReqs* as the indicators in goal models. In the next sub-sections, however, we use *cost* and *speed* to refer to the QCs attached to softgoals *Low cost* and *Fast scheduling*, respectively.

Given the above definitions for system parameters and indicators and taking the *Find local room* goal of figure 1 as an example, we would like to model information such as: "upon increasing the value of RfM, the success rate of *Find local room* also increases" and "at VP2, when choosing *Call hotels and convention centers* over *Call partner institutions*, your cost will increase". This kind of information is very important for a feedback controller in its task of deciding how to adapt the system to fulfill its requirements.

In the remainder of the section we describe the qualitative approach for capturing and analyzing this information. Our approach does not differentiate between *control variables* and *variation points* and, thus, we hereafter refer to them generally as **system parameters** or simply **parameters**.

3.2 Numeric Parameters

Numeric parameters, such as *Rooms for Meetings* (RfM), *From how Many* (FhM) and *Maximum Conflicts Allowed* (MCA) (see figure 1), can assume any integer or real value at runtime. There could be, however, some domain-related constraints, e.g., `RfM` can obviously assume only positive integer values, `FhM` ranges between 0% and 100%, etc.

Changing the value of a numeric parameter affects many aspects of system performance, which, as explained in the previous sub-section, are measured through *indicators*. Taking the parameter `RfM` as an example, and assuming the success rate of *Find local room* is affected by changes in `RfM`, we could define this indicator as a function of the parameter (clearly a simplification):

$$success\ rate\ of\ Find\ local\ room = f(RfM) \qquad (1)$$

We could then say how changes in `RfM` affect the success rate of the goal by declaring if the derivative of f is positive or negative. Using Leibniz's notation:

$$\frac{\Delta \langle success\ rate\ of\ Find\ local\ room \rangle}{\Delta RfM} > 0 \qquad (2)$$

Relation 2 tells us that if we increase the value of `RfM`, the success rate of *Find local room* also increases. Of course, the analogous decrease-decrease relation is also inferred. The $\Delta y / \Delta x$ notation is used instead of dy/dx because `RfM`, as previously mentioned, assumes only discrete values. Furthermore, in practice we use a simplified linearized notation to improve writability:

$$\Delta (\langle success\ rate\ of\ Find\ local\ room \rangle / RfM) > 0 \qquad (3)$$

Suppose there is a limit to which this relation holds: after a given number, adding more rooms will not help with the success rate of *Find local room*. For this case, we use the concept of *landmark values* (see §2.2) and specify an interval in which the relation between the parameter and the indicator holds. Since we are dealing with qualitative information, we might not know exactly how many rooms are enough, so we define a landmark value called `enoughRooms`: $\Delta (\langle success\ rate\ of\ Find\ local\ room \rangle / RfM) [0, enoughRooms] > 0$. Although specifying this interval intuitively tells us that adding extra rooms after there are already enough of them available does not change the success rate of the goal, one could formalize this information, making it explicit: $\Delta (\langle success\ rate\ of\ Find\ local\ room \rangle / RfM) [enoughRooms, \infty] = 0$.

This gives us the general form for differential relations in our proposal, shown in (4), where Δ can be replaced with d in case of a continuous parameter, the interval $[a, b]$ is optional, with default value $[-\infty, \infty]$, $\langle op \rangle$ should be substituted by a comparison operator ($>, \geq, <, \leq, =$ or $\neq$) and C is any constant, not just zero as in previous examples.

$$\Delta (indicator/parameter) [a, b] \langle op \rangle C \qquad (4)$$

Non-zero values for C are useful for expressing different rates of change. When facing a decision on how to improve an indicator I, given the information $\Delta (I/P_1) > 0$ and $\Delta (I/P_2) > 0$ the controller will arbitrarily choose to either increase P_1 or P_2; on the other hand, $\Delta (I/P_1) > 2$ and $\Delta (I/P_2) > 7$ could help it choose P_2 in case I needs to be increased by a larger factor.

If we replace the constant C by a function $g(parameter)$, we will be able to represent nonlinear relations between indicators and parameters, for instance, $\Delta(cost/RfM) = 2 \times RfM$ (cost increases by the square of the increase of RfM). However, linear approximations greatly simplify the kind of modeling we are proposing and are enough for our objectives. Moreover, it is very hard to obtain such precise qualitative values before the system is in operation.

3.3   Enumerated Parameters

In addition to numeric parameters, parameters that constrain their possible values to specific enumerated sets are also possible. *Variation points* are clear examples of this type of parameter, as their possible values are constrained to the set of paths in the OR-decomposition. *Control variables*, however, can also be of enumerated type (in effect, as discussed in section 3.1, *control variables* are abstractions over families of goal models in an OR-decomposition).

Figure 1 shows five enumerated parameters elicited for the meeting scheduler, two enumerated *control variables* and three *variation points*:

- *Required fields* (RF) in the task *Characterize meeting* can assume the values: *participants list only, short description required* or *full description required*;
- *View private appointments* (VPA) in the task *Collect from system calendar* can be either *yes* or *no*.
- At *Collect timetables*, VP1 can assume values *Email participants, Call participants* or *Collect automatically*;
- At *Find available rooms*, VP2 can assume values *Find local rooms, Call partner institution* or *Call hotels and convention centers*;
- At *Choose schedule*, VP3 can assume values *Schedule manually* or *Let system schedule*.

Unlike numeric parameters, the meaning of "increase" and "decrease" is not defined for enumerated types. However, we use a similar syntax to specify how changing from one value (α) to another (β) affects a system indicator:

$$\Delta(indicator/parameter)\{\alpha_1 \to \beta_1, \alpha_2 \to \beta_2, \ldots, \alpha_n \to \beta_n\}\ \langle op \rangle\ C \quad (5)$$

By performing pair-wise comparisons of enumerated values, stakeholders can specify how changes in an enumerated parameter affect the system. For example, the relations below show how changes in VP2 affect, respectively, the indicators *cost* and *speed* (both increase if you do the changes listed between curly brackets).

$$\Delta(cost/VP2)\{local \to partner, local \to hotel, partner \to hotel\} > 0 \quad (6)$$
$$\Delta(speed/VP2)\{partner \to local, hotel \to local, partner \to hotel\} > 0 \quad (7)$$

Often, however, an order among enumerated values w.r.t. different indicators can be established. For instance, analyzing the pair-wise comparisons shown in relations 6 and 7, we conclude that w.r.t. *cost, local $\preceq$ partner $\preceq$ hotel*, while for *speed, partner $\preceq$ hotel $\preceq$ local*. Depending on the size of the set of values for an enumerated parameter, listing all pair-wise comparisons using the syntax specified in (5) may be tedious and verbose. If it is possible to specify a total order for the set, doing so and using the general syntax presented for numeric parameters in equation (4) can simplify elicitation and modeling.

3.4   Extrapolations

Differential relations always involve one indicator, but may involve more than one parameter. For example, "increasing" VP1 and VP3 (considering the order of the alternatives in *variation points* to be based on their position in the model, ascending left-to-right) contributes positively to indicator I_{FS} = *Fast schedul-ing* both separately — $\Delta(I_{FS}/VP1) > 0$ and $\Delta(I_{FS}/VP3) > 0$ — and in combination — $\Delta(I_{FS}/\{VP1, VP3\}) > 0$.

When we are not given any relation that differentially relate two parameters P_1 and P_2 to a single indicator I, we may still be able to extrapolate such a relation on the basis of simple linearity assumptions. E.g., if we know that $\Delta(I/P_1) > 0$ and $\Delta(I/P_2) > 0$, it would be reasonable to extrapolate the relation $\Delta(I/\{P_1, P_2\}) > 0$. More generally, our extrapolation rule assumes that homogeneous impact is additive (figure 3). Note that in cases where P_1 and P_2 have opposite effects on I, nothing can be extrapolated because of the qualitative nature of our relations.

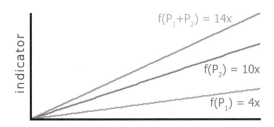

Fig. 3. Combining the effects of different CVs on the same indicator

Generalizing, given a set of parameters $\{P_1, P_2, \ldots, P_n\}$, if $\forall i \in \{1, \ldots, n\}$, $\Delta(I/P_i)[a_i, b_i] \langle op \rangle C_i$, our extrapolation rule has as follows:

$$\Delta(I/\{P_1, P_2, \ldots, P_n\}) \bigcap_{i=0}^{n} [a_i, b_i] \langle op \rangle \sum_{i=0}^{n} C_i \qquad (8)$$

If it is known that two parameters cannot be assumed to have such a combined effect, this should be explicitly stated, e.g., $\Delta(I/\{P_1, P_2\}) < 0$.

From differential calculus we extrapolate on the concept of the second derivative. If $y = f(x)$, we can say that y grows linearly if $f'(x) > 0$ and $f''(x) = 0$ (it "has constant speed"). However, if we have $f''(x) > 0$, then y's rate of growth also increases with the value of x (it "accelerates"). Qualitative information on second derivatives can be modeled in our language using the following notation:

$\Delta^2 (I/P) [a, b] \ \langle op \rangle \ C$. Thus, if we say that $\Delta^2 (I/P_1) > 0$ and $\Delta^2 (I/P_2) = 0$, the controller may conclude that P_1 is probably a better choice than P_2 for large values. Other concepts, such as *inflection* and *saddle points*, *maxima* and *minima*, etc. could also be borrowed, although we believe that knowing information on such points in a $I = f(P)$ relation without knowing the exact function $f(P)$ is very unlikely.

4   System Identification Process

In this section, we describe a systematic process for system identification. **Process Input:** a requirements model G (such as the one in figure 1). **Process Output:** a parametrized specification of the system behavior $S = \{G, I, P, R(I, P)\}$, where G is the goal model, I is the set of indicators identified by *AwReqs* in the model, P is the set of parameters, and $R(I, P)$ is the set of relations between indicators and parameters. At runtime, a feedback-loop controller receives S as input in order to adapt the system pro-actively or in case of failures.

The following are the steps of the process. They can be applied iteratively, gradually enriching the model with each iteration.

Step 1. Identify indicators: Introduce *AwReqs* into the goal model G specifying target success rates for QCs, hard goals or tasks. **Output:** the set of indicators I.

Step 2. Identify parameters: Identify possible variations in the goal model affecting the indicators, which, therefore, can be manipulated to adjust the performance of the system. These are captured by *control variables* and *variation points* (see §3.1). **Output:** the set of parameters P.

Step 3. Identify differential relations: For each indicator from the set I the requirements engineer asks: which parameters from P does this indicator depend on? Alternatively, iterate through set P and ask, for each parameter, which indicator in I is affected by it. Either way, one should end up with a many-to-many association between the sets. There are heuristics that help in answering these questions:

Heuristic 1: if provided, softgoal contribution links capture these dependencies for *variation points*. E.g., in figure 1, the choices in VP1 contribute to the softgoal *Fast scheduling* and thus VP1 affects the success rate of *Schedules produced in less than a day*, a QC derived from that softgoal. Any *AwReq*-derived indicator involving that QC is therefore also affected.

Heuristic 2: another heuristic for deriving *potential* parameter-indicator relations is to link indicators to parameters that appear in the subtrees of the nodes the indicators are associated with. The rationale for this is the fact that parameters in a subtree rooted at some goal G, which models how G is achieved, change the subtree, thus potentially affecting the indicators associated with the goal. E.g., the parameter RfM is below the goal *Find available rooms* in the tree and thus can be (and actually *is*) affecting its success rate, an indicator.

Heuristic 3: yet another way to identify potential parameter-indicator relations is to look at the non-functional concerns that these parameters/indicators address and to match the ones with the same concern. [18] describes how NFRs such as robustness, criticality, etc. lead to the introduction of *AwReqs* into goal models. The already-mentioned softgoal contributions explicitly link *variation points* with NFRs. Similar analysis should be done for *control variables*.

The modeling of the parameter-indicator relations is done using the language of section 3. **Output:** $R(I, P)$, the initial set of relations between indicators and parameters.

Step 4. Refine relations: The initial set of parameter-indicator relations produced in Step 3 should be refined by comparing and combining those that refer to the same indicator. When comparing two relations, say $\Delta(I_1/RfM) > 0$ and $\Delta(I_1/VP2) > 0$ (where I_1 might represent $\langle success\ rate\ of\ Find\ local\ room \rangle$), the modeler can investigate whether either of these adaptation strategies is better than the other and by how much. This may result in the model being refined into, e.g., $\Delta(I_1/RfM) > \Delta(I_1/VP2)$, which would help the controller facing the choice between these alternatives. The analysis of whether selecting an alternative makes the value of an indicator match its reference input is to be addressed in future work.

Combining relations also refers to what has been discussed in section 3.4: if a positive change in both parameters results in a positive change in the indicator, should we expect the default behavior in which $\Delta(I_1/\{RfM, VP2\}) > 0$ or should we explicitly specify that this is not the case? Such questions should be asked for any set of relations that refer to the same indicator.

Note that when combining relations to analyze alternatives, care must be taken to only look at the parameters/indicators relevant in the current system configuration. E.g., in figure 1, the parameter *View Private Appointments* (VPA) cannot affect any indicator if the value of VP1 is not *Collect automatically*. **Output:** $R(I, P)$, the updated set of relations between indicators and parameters.

5   Validation

To validate our proposal, we applied the system identification process described in section 4 to the meeting scheduler example presented throughout this paper, identifying 9 indicators (in the form of *AwReqs*), 8 system parameters (5 *control variables* and 3 *variation points* as shown in figure 1) and a total of 24 differential relations among the identified indicators and parameters.

For instance, one of the identified indicators refers to the goal *Find available rooms* as a critical requirement that should never fail, which is modeled in *AwReq* AR5: NeverFail(G-FindAvailRooms). During parameter identification, *Rooms for Meeting* (RfM) and VP2 were identified, along with other parameters that are not relevant to AR5. In the next phase, two relations were identified: $\Delta(AR5/RfM) > 0$ (increasing the number of local rooms helps), $\Delta(AR5/VP2) > 0$ (changing from *local* → *partner* → *hotel* helps). During refinement, analyzing RfM and VP2 in combination provided $\Delta(AR5/\{RfM, VP2\})$

$= \Delta\,(AR5/VP2)$ (increasing the number of local rooms and then not using them does not make sense) and $\Delta\,(AR5/RfM) = \Delta\,(AR5/VP2)$ (changing RfM or VP2 is equally effective).

Then, we developed a simulation that reads the above system information as well as events reporting *AwReq* failures (which could be provided by the framework we have presented in [18]) in order to identify possible adaptivity actions that could be taken by the controller during reconciliation. For example, when an event representing the failure of AR5 is received during the simulation, the program replies with the choices of parameter changes that have positive effect on AR5 based on the above qualitative relations:

```
* AwReq AR5 has failed! To reconcile, the controller could:
   - Current value of VP2 = local. Change it to one of: [partner, hotel]
   - Current value of RfM = 3. Increase it.
   - Note: VP2 and RfM should not be changed in combination.
```

With the information given by the differential relations, the program was able to identify available alternatives to adapt the system in case of failure. More sophisticated algorithms to analyze all the possibilities and select the best course of action (considering also the effect on NFRs, for example) are in our future plans for developing a complete framework for system adaptivity based on feedback loops. We are also currently working on a larger controlled experiment, conducting system identification on the London Ambulance System [6].

6   Related Work

There is growing interest in Control Theory-based approaches for adaptive systems and many of the proposed approaches include some form of system identification stage, in which the adaptive capabilities of the system are elicited and modeled. In [7], modeling is done by representing *system* and *environment actions* as well as *fluents* that express properties of the environment. In GAAM [17], measurable/quantifiable properties of the system are modeled as *attributes*, a *preference matrix* specifies the order of preference of *adaptation actions* towards goals (similarly to what we proposed in section 3.3) and an *aspiration level matrix* determines the desired levels of *attributes* of each *goal*. Our work differs from these by providing qualitative information on the relation between *system parameters* and run-time *indicators*.

In [14], Letier & van Lamsweerde augment KAOS with a probabilistic layer in order to allow for the specification of partial degrees of goal satisfaction, thus quantifying the impact of alternative designs in high-level system goals. In the approach, domain-specific *quality variables* (QVs) associated with goals are modeled and *objective functions* (OFs) define domain-specific, goal-related quantities to be maximized or minimized. Proposed heuristics for identifying QVs and OFs could be useful in the elicitation of *control variables* in our approach. However, unlike our work, their models do not contain a clear relation between these variables and *indicators* measured in the target system.

Approaches such as $i*$ [16], the work by Elahi & Yu [4] and other proposals on design-time trade-off analysis can be adapted to provide information for run-time adaptivity (i.e., removing the need for stakeholder intervention in the analysis). For instance, contribution links in $i*$ can provide qualitative relations between *variation points* and indicators, although they lack the means of differentiating between links with the same label (e.g., see *Call participants* and *Email participants* in figure 1). GRL [1] could be used for this purpose, if cardinal contribution values $(1, 2, ...)$ were changed to ordinal ones $(1^{st}, 2^{nd}, ...)$, thus providing a graphical representation of enumerated value orders (§3.3). Our proposal provides such run-time trade-off information with a syntax that is more concise (*control parameters* abstract what would have to be represented as large goal sub-trees), uniform (can relate any system parameter to indicators) and flexible (the precision of the specification depends on the available information).

The proposal by Brake et al. [2] automates the discovery of software tuning parameters at the code level using reverse engineering techniques. A taxonomy of parameters and patterns to aid in their automatic identification provides some sort of qualitative relation among parameters, which may be "tunable" or just observed. While their work targets existing and legacy software, our proposal takes a Requirements Engineering perspective and, thus, can refer to higher level parameters, such as the success rate of a functional requirement or a quality constraint imposed over a non-functional one.

Finally, our proposal clearly differs from quantitative approaches (e.g., [1,3,11,15]) in that we are using qualitative information, based on the premise that quantitative estimates at requirements time are usually unreliable [4] (assuming a domain with high uncertainty or incomplete knowledge of the behavior of the system-to-be). Our approach allows the modeler to start with minimum information available and add more as further details about the system become available (either by elicitation or through run-time analysis once the system is executing).

7   Discussion and Future Work

In this paper so far, we have overlooked an important modeling dimension, contextual variability. In this section, we sketch how it can be taken into consideration in the system identification process of section 4. We then discuss other research directions that we plan to pursue in the future.

Properties of the environment can affect the requirements for and the operation of a system, but, unlike the parameters we have discussed previously (CVs and VPs), context parameters cannot be directly manipulated, only monitored. *Contexts* are abstractions of such properties [12]. For instance, the type of a meeting can be viewed as a context for the meeting scheduling system, as can be the importance of a meeting organizer within the company. From the point of view of Control Theory, context most closely corresponds to a *disturbance input* that cannot be manipulated, but influences the output and thus must be accounted for. Contexts are organized using (possibly many) inheritance hierarchies that refine general contexts (e.g., *Regular meeting*) into more specific ones

(*Mandatory meeting* or *Information session*) with descendants inheriting the properties of their ancestors. Each hierarchy structures contexts along a context dimension — some variable aspect of the domain (e.g., meeting importance) — with leaf-level elements directly monitorable. Multiple inheritance is supported.

In [12], (soft)goals and contribution links are identified as context-dependent goal model elements. *Contextual annotations* capture the effects of contexts on these elements and thus on software requirements by stating in which contexts the elements are visible. Unless explicitly overridden, the effects of ancestor contexts are inherited by their descendants. So, by default, the requirements for *Regular meeting* are inherited by *Mandatory meeting*.

As discussed in [12], varying properties of the environment can have significant effect on goal models — namely, goal/task/softgoal addition/removal, changes in VP choices and different evaluations of these choices w.r.t. softgoals. Given a context-parametrized (i.e., with contextual annotations) goal model, the algorithm for producing *context-specific* versions of it for particular sets of active contexts is also described. It removes model elements invisible in the current context. The goal modeling notation presented here is more complex compared to the notation of [12], thus requiring a modified algorithm. The additional elements — DAs, QCs, *AwReqs*, and CVs — are all context-dependent, i.e., can change from context to context. E.g., the success rate for the goal *Find available rooms* can be set to 95% in a *Regular meeting* context and to 70% in a less important *Information session* context by using the appropriate *AwReqs*. Each *AwReq* will be visible in its respective context. Similarly, variations in possible values for VPs/CVs can be represented by different VP/CV variants, each visible in their appropriate context(s).

Clearly, these goal model variations need to be reflected in the system identification process. When we do it in the particular context c, we produce the model $S_c = \{G_c, I_c, P_c, R_c\,(I_c, P_c)\}$, where G_c is context-specific goal model (a subset of the context-parametrized goal model G) generated by the modified algorithm from [12]. Then, $I_c \subseteq I$ and $P_c \subseteq P$ since some of the indicators and parameters may not be visible in c. Moreover, R_c — the set of relations between the relevant parameters and indicators in C — should be restricted to the elements of I_c and P_c (i.e., $r\,(i,p) \in R_c \Rightarrow i \in I_c \wedge p \in P_c$). While being a necessary condition, this expression does not define the relations in R_c. It is up to the modeler to identify which relations exist in the particular contexts and how they are defined using the language of section 3. Once a relationship $r\,(i,p) \in R_c$ is defined for the context c, it also applies for all the descendant contexts of c unless overridden and provided that both i and p exist in the descendant contexts.

A complete analysis of the role of contextual information on the system identification process as well as validating the ideas briefly discussed above is subject of future work. Other possible future work also include investigating: means of estimating during RE whether a particular behavior change will match the desired targets for the system's output; the effect indicators can have on one another and how to model such a qualitative relation during system identification; what other methods and concepts from the Control Theory body of knowledge could be applied in our approach; how does this approach affect traditional Requirements Engineering activities (e.g., stakeholder negotiation during requirements elicitation); how can our proposal contribute to requirements evolution (i.e., changing the goal model because it does not properly represent current stakeholder requirements, despite the system's adaptive capabilities); etc.

Finally, the full potential of the proposal presented in this paper will be realized in the next steps of our research, which includes the development of a framework that implements adaptivity in a target system using feedback loops. With *AwReqs* [18] and qualitative relations in the requirement model, it is now possible to develop such a framework that will provide reconciliation (attempt to satisfy the requirements after failures) and compensation (resolve any inconsistencies that failures might produce) at runtime. Once we have developed such a framework, more experiments are needed to assess to what extent this approach helps in designing adaptive systems as opposed to traditional GORE methods.

In particular, we are currently working on different strategies for reconciliation. With the information that is added to the models by using the approach proposed in this paper, two basic strategies to be executed when a failure is detected are: **parameter tuning** — if there are any parameters that could be modified in order to reconcile, analyze the qualitative information available and select the best course of action w.r.t. other indicators — and **abort** — if there are no parameters or the ones that exist have already been tried, tell the target system to gracefully fail or degrade performance. Other reconciliation strategies can be devised by analyzing existing proposals in the area of adaptive systems and other fields of computer science, such as fault-tolerant computing, artificial intelligence, distributed systems, etc.

8   Conclusion

In this paper, we argue that current requirements models lack an essential information needed by feedback loop controllers in order to adapt their target systems: how changes in parameters affect relevant monitored indicators. We propose a systematic approach for System Identification and, by taking a RE perspective, we use ideas from Qualitative Reasoning to cope with uncertain and incomplete knowledge about systems. Our language allows modeling of parameter-indicator relations varying precision, based on available information. We also briefly discuss the role of contextual information on this process and conduct experiments to validate our ideas.

References

1. Grl website, http://www.cs.toronto.edu/km/grl/
2. Brake, N., Cordy, J.R., Dancy, E., Litoiu, M., Popescu, V.: Automating discovery of software tuning parameters. In: SEAMS 2008: Proceedings of the 2008 International Workshop on Software Engineering for Adaptive and Self-managing Systems. ACM Press, New York (2008)

3. Cornford, S.L., Feather, M.S., Hicks, K.A.: DDP: a tool for life-cycle risk management. IEEE Aerospace and Electronic Systems Magazine 21(6), 13–22 (2006)
4. Elahi, G., Yu, E.: Requirements Trade-offs Analysis in the Absence of Quantitative Measures: A Heuristic Method. In: SAC 2011: 26th Symposium On Applied Computing. ACM, New York (2011)
5. Feather, M.S., Fickas, S., Van Lamsweerde, A., Ponsard, C.: Reconciling System Requirements and Runtime Behavior. In: IWSSD 1998: 9th International Workshop on Software Specification and Design, Washington, DC, USA, p. 50 (1998)
6. Finkelstein, A., Dowell, J.: A comedy of errors: the london ambulance service case study. In: IWSSD 1996: 8th International Workshop on Software Specification and Design, pp. 2–4 (March 1996)
7. Heaven, W., Sykes, D., Magee, J., Kramer, J.: A Case Study in Goal-Driven Architectural Adaptation. In: SEAMS 2009: 2009 ICSE Workshop on Software Engineering for Adaptive and Self-Managing Systems, vol. 2, pp. 109–127. Springer, Vancouver (2009)
8. Hellerstein, J.L., Diao, Y., Parekh, S., Tilbury, D.M.: Feedback Control of Computing Systems. John Wiley & Sons, Chichester (2004)
9. Jureta, I.J., Mylopoulos, J., Faulkner, S.: Revisiting the Core Ontology and Problem in Requirements Engineering. In: RE 2008: 16th IEEE International Requirements Engineering Conference, Barcelona, Spain, pp. 71–80. IEEE, Los Alamitos (2008)
10. Kuipers, B.: Qualitative reasoning: Modeling and simulation with incomplete knowledge. Automatica 25(4), 571–585 (1989)
11. Lamsweerde, A.V.: Reasoning About Alternative Requirements Options, ch. 20, pp. 380–397. Springer, Heidelberg (2009)
12. Lapouchnian, A., Mylopoulos, J.: Modeling domain variability in requirements engineering with contexts. In: Laender, A.H.F., Castano, S., Dayal, U., Casati, F., de Oliveira, J.P.M. (eds.) ER 2009. LNCS, vol. 5829, pp. 115–130. Springer, Heidelberg (2009)
13. Lapouchnian, A., Yu, Y., Mylopoulos, J.: Requirements-Driven Design and Configuration Management of Business Processes. In: Alonso, G., Dadam, P., Rosemann, M. (eds.) BPM 2007. LNCS, vol. 4714, pp. 246–261. Springer, Heidelberg (2007)
14. Letier, E., van Lamsweerde, A.: Reasoning about partial goal satisfaction for requirements and design engineering. In: FSE 2004: 12th ACM SIGSOFT International Symposium on Foundations of Software Engineering, pp. 53–62 (2004)
15. Ma, W., Liu, L., Xie, H., Zhang, H., Yin, J.: Preference Model Driven Services Selection. In: van Eck, P., Gordijn, J., Wieringa, R. (eds.) CAiSE 2009. LNCS, vol. 5565, pp. 216–230. Springer, Heidelberg (2009)
16. Mylopoulos, J., Chung, L., Yu, E.S.K.: From object-oriented to goal-oriented requirements analysis. Communications of the ACM 42(1), 31–37 (1999)
17. Salehie, M., Tahvildari, L.: Towards a Goal-Driven Approach to Action Selection in Self-Adaptive Software. Software Practice and Experience (2011)
18. Souza, V.E.S., Lapouchnian, A., Robinson, W.N., Mylopoulos, J.: Awareness Requirements for Adaptive Systems. In: SEAMS 2011: 6th International Symposium on Software Engineering for Adaptive and Self-Managing Systems, Honolulu, USA. ACM, New York (2011)
19. Wang, Y., Mylopoulos, J.: Self-repair Through Reconfiguration: A Requirements Engineering Approach. In: ASE 2009: 24th IEEE/ACM International Conference on Automated Software Engineering, Auckland, New Zealand (2009)

Using UML Profiles for Sector-Specific Tailoring of Safety Evidence Information

Rajwinder Kaur Panesar-Walawege[1,2], Mehrdad Sabetzadeh[1,2], and Lionel Briand[1,2]

[1] Simula Research Laboratory, Lysaker, Norway
[2] University of Oslo, Oslo, Norway
{rpanesar,mehrdad,briand}@simula.no

Abstract. Safety-critical systems are often subject to certification as a way to ensure that the safety risks associated with their use are sufficiently mitigated. A key requirement of certification is the provision of evidence that a system complies with the applicable standards. The way this is typically organized is to have a generic standard that sets forth the general evidence requirements across different industry sectors, and then to have a derived standard that specializes the generic standard according to the needs of a specific industry sector. To demonstrate standards compliance, one therefore needs to precisely specify how the evidence requirements of a sector-specific standard map onto those of the generic parent standard. Unfortunately, little research has been done to date on capturing the relationship between generic and sector-specific standards and a large fraction of the issues arising during certification can be traced to poorly-stated or implicit relationships between a generic standard and its sector-specific interpretation. In this paper, we propose an approach based on UML profiles to systematically capture how the evidence requirements of a generic standard are specialized in a particular domain. To demonstrate our approach, we apply it for tailoring IEC61508 – one of the most established standards for functional safety – to the Petroleum industry.

Keywords: Safety Certification, UML Profiles, Evidence Information Models, IEC61508.

1 Introduction

Safety-critical systems are typically subject to safety certification, whose aim is to ensure that the safety risks associated with the use of such systems are sufficiently mitigated and that the systems are deemed safe by a certification body. A key requirement in safety certification is the provision of evidence that a system complies with one or more applicable safety standards. A common practice in defining standards for certification is to have a generic standard and then derive from it sector-specific standards for every industry sector that the generic standard applies to. The idea behind such a tiered approach is to unify the commonalities across different sectors into the generic standard, and

M. Jeusfeld, L. Delcambre, and T.W. Ling (Eds.): ER 2011, LNCS 6998, pp. 362–378, 2011.

then *specialize* the generic standard according to contextual needs. The generic standard is sometimes referred to as a *metastandard* [19].

A notable example in safety certification is the specialization of IEC61508 [10] – a generic standard that deals with the functional safety of electrical / electronic / programmable electronic safety-critical systems. In the process industry, this standard is adapted as IEC61511 [9], in railways as EN 50129 [8], in the petroleum industry as OLF070 [5], and in the automotive industry as the forthcoming ISO 26262 [4].

For specialization to be effective, it is important to be able to precisely specify how the evidence requirements stated in a generic standard map onto those stated in a derived standard. Unfortunately, there has been little work to date on systematizing the specification of the relationship between generic and sector-specific standards. This has led to a number of problems. In particular, Feldt et. al. [11] cite the lack of agreed-upon relationships between generic and derived standards as one of the main reasons behind certification delays, caused by ambiguities in the relationships and the need for subjective interpretations by the certification body and system supplier. Furthermore, Nordland [12] notes the lack of a well-formulated process for showing that a derived standard is consistent with a generic standard. This too is directly attributable to the lack of precise and explicitly-defined relationships between the standards.

In this paper, we propose a novel approach based on UML profiles [3] to capture the relationship between the evidence requirements of a generic standard and those of a sector-specific derivation. Briefly, our approach works by (1) building conceptual models for the evidence requirements of both the generic and sector-specific standards, (2) turning the conceptual model of the generic standard into a profile, and (3) using the profile for stereotyping the elements in the conceptual model of the sector-specific standard. Our approach offers two main advantages: First, it provides a systematic and explicit way to keep track of the relationships between a generic and a derived standard in terms of their evidence requirements. And second, it enables the definition of consistency constraints to ensure that evidence requirements are being specialized properly in the derived standard.

While the overall ideas behind our approach are general, we ground our discussions on a particular safety standard, IEC61508, and a particular derivation, OLF070 (used in the petroleum industry). On the one hand, this addresses a specific observed need in safety certification of maritime and energy systems; and on the other hand, it provides us with a concrete context for describing the different steps of our approach and how these steps fit together. The conceptual model characterizing the IEC61508 evidence requirements has been described in our earlier work [18]. The one for OLF070 has been developed as part this current work. Excerpts from both conceptual models will be used for exemplification throughout the paper.

The remainder of this paper is structured as follows: In Section 2, we review background information for the paper. In Section 3, we describe our UML profile for IEC61508 and in Section 4 we discuss how the profile can be used for specialization of safety evidence. Section 5 compares our work with related work. Section 6 concludes the paper with a summary and suggestions for future work.

2   Background

In this section, we provide a brief introduction to safety certification (based on IEC61508), how safety evidence requirements can be structured through conceptual modeling, and UML profiles.

2.1   IEC61508-Based Certification

Safety-critical systems in many domains, e.g., the avionics, railways, and maritime and energy, are subject to certification. One of the most prominent standards used for this purpose is IEC61508. The standard sets forth the requirements for the development of electrical, electronic or programmable electronic systems containing safety critical components. This standard is concerned with a particular aspect of overall system safety, called functional safety, aimed at ensuring that a system or piece of equipment functions correctly in response to its inputs [10]. The standard defines requirements for hardware development, software development, and the development process that needs to be followed. The standard applies to systems with different required safety margins. This is encoded in the standard in the form of Safety Integrity Levels (SILs). The levels range from SIL 1 to SIL 4 and indicate the level of risk reduction measures that need to be in place based on the failure rate of the implementation and the acceptability of the risks involved. A number of sector-specific standards specialize IEC61508. These include IEC61511 in the process industry [9], EN 50129 [8] for railways, OLF070 [5] for the petroleum industry, and the upcoming ISO26262 [4] for the automotive industry.

2.2   Conceptual Modeling of Compliance Evidence Information

In general, standards, irrespective of the domains they are targeted at, tend to be expressed as textual requirements. Since the requirements are expressed in natural language, they are subject to interpretation by the users of the standards. To make the interpretation explicit and develop a common understanding, we develop a conceptual model that formalizes the evidence requirements of a given standard. Such a model can be conveniently expressed in the UML class diagram notation [3].

For illustration, we show in Fig. 1 a small fragment of the conceptual model that we have built in our previous work on IEC61508 [18]. Concepts are represented as classes and concept attributes – as class attributes. Relationships are represented by associations. Generalization associations are used to derive more specific concepts from abstract ones. When an attribute assumes a value from a predefined set of possible values, we use enumerations. Finally, we use the package notation to make groupings of concepts and thus better manage the complexity.

The diagram in Fig. 1 presents the concepts for describing the development process, packaged as `Process Concepts`, and how these relate to concepts in the `Issue Concepts`, `Artifact Concepts` and `Requirements Concepts` packages. From these other packages, we show only the concepts that related to those in `Process Concepts`. The central concept in the diagram of Fig. 1 is the notion of `Activity`, representing a unit of behavior with specific input and output. An activity can be further decomposed into sub-activities. A (life-cycle) phase is made up of a set of activities that are carried out during the lifetime of a system. Each activity utilizes certain techniques to arrive at its desired output, given its input. The selection of techniques is related to the safety integrity level that needs to be achieved. For example, if the activity in question concerns software verification, constructing formal proofs of correctness is usually unnecessary for low integrity levels, whereas, formal proofs are highly recommended for the highest integrity level. Each activity requires certain kind of competence by the agents performing it. The agent itself can be either an individual person or an organization. In either case, the agent is identified by the type of role it plays, for example the agent may be the supplier of a system or the operator. Agents can be made responsible for certain development artifacts. Further detail about the other packages shown can be found in [18].

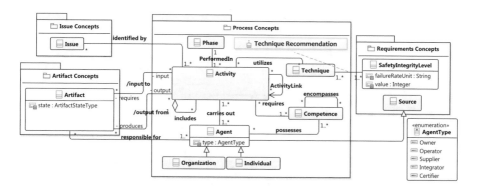

Fig. 1. IEC61508 Process Concepts and Their Links

2.3 UML Profiles

UML profiles [3] aim at providing a lightweight solution for tailoring the UML metamodel for a specific domain. The same mechanisms used by UML profiles for tailoring the UML metamodel can also be effectively used for tailoring standards compliance evidence according to domain-specific needs.

Briefly, UML profiles enable the expression of new terminology, notation and constraints by the introduction of context-specific stereotypes, attributes and constraints. Stereotypes are a means of extending a base metaclass. We extend the `Class`, `Property` and `Association` metaclasses, creating stereotypes for the concepts, their attributes and their relationships respectively. Moreover, constraints can be defined in a profile by using the Object Constraint Language

(OCL) [13] to ensure that certain semantics are maintained in the new models
to which the profile is applied. By using profiles the new models that employ the
profile are still consistent with the UML metamodel.

As we describe in the subsequent sections, we use this mechanism to create a
profile of the IEC61508 conceptual model (Section 3) and then use it to specialize
the IEC61508 standard for the petroleum industry (Section 4).

3   UML Profile of the IEC61508 Standard

Our approach for specializing a generic standard is through the use of a UML
profile. In Fig. 2, we show the methodology we propose for this purpose. The
methodology consists of four main steps: (1) creating a conceptual model of the
generic standard, we do this using a UML class diagram; (2) creating a UML
profile based on the generic conceptual model; (3) creating a conceptual model of
the sector-specific standard and applying the stereotypes from the UML profile
of the generic standard; and (4) validating the OCL constraints of the profile
over the sector-specific conceptual model to ensure that it is consistent with
the generic standard. We apply this methodology for specializing the generic
IEC61508 standard to the OLF070 standard for the petroleum industry.

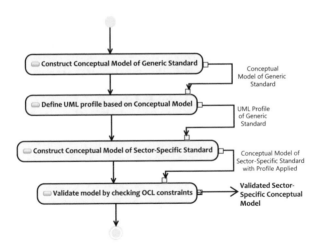

Fig. 2. The Methodology for Specialization of a Generic Standard

Using profiles for specialization offers the following key advantages:

- We can incorporate the specific terminology used by a generic standard and
  still allow the use of context-specific terminology. For example, in IEC61508,
  we have the general concept of `ProgrammableElectronicSystem` (PES). OLF070
  instead refers to very specific types of PESs in the petroleum industry, e.g.,
  Fire and Gas system (F&G), Process Shut-Down system (PSD), Emergency
  Shut-Down system (ESD). These sector-specific concepts can all be stereotyped as `ProgrammableElectronicSystem` to capture the correspondence. It is

of course possible to directly extend the conceptual model of a generic standard for a specific domain by adding new elements to it. However, this makes it hard to keep track of which concepts are from the generic standard and which are from the sector-specific one. When a profile is used, all the stereotypes are known to be from the generic standard, hence a clear distinction is made between the terminologies.

– Stereotypes establish an explicit and rigorous mapping between the generic and sector-specific standards. This mapping can be used to ensure that, for a specific project, all the necessary evidence for demonstrating compliance has been collected. Further, the existence of such an explicit mapping makes it possible to define pairwise consistency rules between the generic and derived standards (using UML's rich constraint language, OCL), and to provide guidance to the users about how to resolve any inconsistencies detected.

As shown in Fig. 2, the basis of our profile of IEC61508 is the conceptual model of the IEC61508 standard. The process of creating a conceptual model of the evidence requirements of a given standard involves a careful analysis of the text of the standard. It requires skills in modelling, systems development and knowledge of the process of certification beyond merely reading the standard. To some extent, this can be viewed as a process of qualitative data analysis, where the data is the text of the standard and it is being analysed to identify from it, all the salient concepts and their relationships. This retrieved information from the text is used to create a common understanding of the standard and as a means of explicitly showing the relationships that exist between the salient concepts.

We exemplify the process of creating the conceptual model of IEC61508 by showing an excerpt of the standard, and the concepts and relationships that have been gleaned from the excerpt. Fig. 3 shows a section of the IEC61508 standard that is dedicated to requirements applicable to the software of a safety-related system. In Fig. 3, we can see the salient concepts and relationships identified in the text - these have been highlighted by enclosing the relevant text in a box and numbering the identified section. Box 1 shows that the concepts Phase and Activity are of importance during the software development lifecycle (in Fig. 3 we have used the concept names shown earlier in Fig. 1). Box 2 identifies some key relationships between phases and activities. An activity is performed during a phase and has specified inputs and outputs. Box 3 indicates that a generic life cycle is prescribed by the standard while not precluding deviations in terms of phases and activities. Box 4 presents the concepts: technique, safety integrity level and techniques recommendation - indicating that activities utilize certain techniques based on the safety integrity level. The same concepts and relationships may be found in several places in the standard. Once the text has been marked up in this manner, a glossary is created to ensure that consistent terms are used to refer to the same concepts and relationships. A part of this glossary, describing the most important concepts is shown in Table 1. The conceptual model is created from this set of concepts and their relationship and serves as the metamodel of the profile.

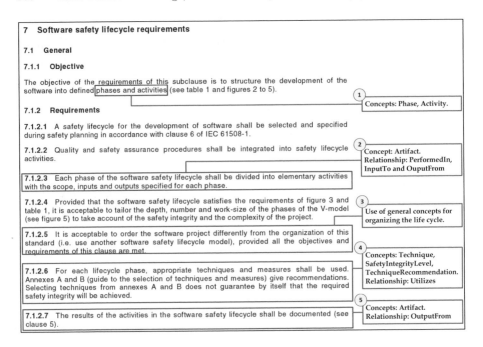

Fig. 3. An Excerpt of IEC61508 showing the textual source of some of the Process elements

Fig. 4 shows a bird-eye's view of the different packages that make up the metamodel for our IEC61508 UML profile. The packages contain abstractions for modelling of the main concepts of IEC61508. We briefly explain each package. For more details, see [18]. The System Concepts package describes the breakdown of the system at a high level; the Hazard Concepts package contains the abstraction for describing the hazards and risks for the system; the Requirements Concepts package for the different types of requirements, including safety requirements; the Process Concepts package for describing the development process (details given in Section 2.2); the Artifact Concepts package for describing the different types of artifacts created as supporting evidence; the Guidance package for describing the other standards and recommended practices that will be used to develop the system, the Issue Concepts package for describing the defects or enhancements that may have given rise to changes; the Configuration Management Concepts package for describing the unique versions for all the components that make up the system, the Justification Concepts package to capture the assumptions and rationale behind the various decisions that are made during development; and the Domain-Specific Concepts package for capturing the enumerations for concept attributes in other packages (e.g., requirement type, system operating mode). The elements of the conceptual model are mapped almost directly into the profile. The concepts become stereotypes that extend the metaclass Class, the relationships become stereotypes that extend the metaclass Association and the attributes of these two extend the metaclass Property.

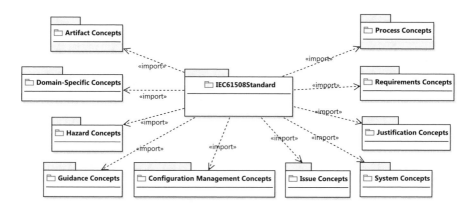

Fig. 4. Packages of the IEC61508 Metamodel

Table 1. Description of Main Concepts from the IEC61508 Metamodel

Stereotype	Description
Activity	A unit of behaviour in a process.
Agent	A person or organization that has the capability and responsibility for carrying out an activity.
Artifact	One of the many kinds of tangible by-products produced during the development of a system.
Assumption	A premise that is not under the control of the system of interest, and is accepted as true without a thorough examination. Assumptions can, among other things, be related to the environment of the system, the users, and external regulations.
Block	Entity of hardware or software, or both, capable of accomplishing a specified purpose.
Change	A modification made to the PES, Block or Artifact.
Competence	The ability to perform a specific task, action or function successfully.
ControlledItem	A PES, Block or Artifact for which meaningful increments of change are documented and recorded.
Defect	An error, failure, or fault in a system that produces an incorrect or unexpected result, or causes it to behave in unintended ways.
Description	A planned or actual function, design, performance or activity (e.g., function description).
DesignatedState	The state of the EUC related to safety, the EUC is either in a safe state or an unsafe state.
Diagram	Specification of a function by means of a diagram (symbols and lines).
Enhancement	Provision of improved, advanced, or sophisticated features.
Error	Discrepancy between a computed, observed or measured value or condition and the true, specified or theoretically correct value or condition.
Event	A single occurence in a series of occurences that cause a hazard to occur.
Failure	Termination of the ability of a functional unit to perform a required function.
Fault	Abnormal condition that may cause a reduction in, or loss of, the capability of a functional unit to perform a required function.
GeneralStandard	A standard that provides generic recommendations on a specific subject to a number of related domains.
HardwareBlock	Any entity of hardware – this may be mechanical, electrical or electronic that is used in the composition of the system.
HazardousElement	The basic hazardous resource creating the impetus for the hazard, such as a hazardous energy source such as explosives being used in the system.
Hazard	Any real or potential condition that can cause injury, illness, or death to personnel damage to or loss of a system, equipment or property or damage to the environment.

Continued on next page ...

Stereotype	Description
	Continued from previous page ...
Individual	Refers to a person.
Initiating-Mechanism	The trigger or initiator event(s) causing the hazard to occur. The IM causes actualization or transformation of the hazard from a dormant state to an active mishap state.
Instruction	Specifies in detail the instructions as to when and how to perform certain jobs (for example operator instruction).
Interface	An abstraction that a block provides of itself to the outside. This separates the methods of external communication from internal operation.
Issue	A unit of work to accomplish an improvement in a system.
List	Information in a list form (e.g., code list, signal list).
Log	Information on events in a chronological log form.
Mistake	Human action or inaction that can produce an unintended result.
NonProgrammable-HardwareBlock	Electro-mechanical devices (electrical) solid-state non-programmable electronic devices (electronic).
OperatingMode	The different modes that a system can be operating in, e.g. normal, maintenance, test, emergency.
Organization	A social arrangement which pursues collective goals, which controls its own performance, and which has a boundary separating it from its environment.
Phase	A set of activities with determined inputs and output that are carried out at a specific time during the life of a system.
Plan	Explanation of when, how and by whom specific activities shall be performed (e.g., maintenance plan).
Programmable-ElectronicSystem	System for control, protection or monitoring based on one or more programmable electronic devices, including all elements of the system such as power supplies, sensors and other input devices, data highways and other communication paths, and actuators and other output devices.
Programmable-HardwareBlock	Any physical entity based on computer technology which may be comprised of hardware, software, and of input and/or output units.
Rationale	The fundamental reason or reasons serving to account for something.
Recommended-Practice	Sound practices and guidance for the achievement of a particular objective.
Report	The results of activities such as investigations, assessments, tests etc. (e.g., test report).
Request	A description of requested actions that have to be approved and further specified (e.g., maintenance request).
Requirement	A necessary attribute in a system; a statement that identifies a capability, characteristic, or quality factor of a system in order for it to have value and utility to a user.
ResidualRisk	Risk remaining after protective measures have been taken.
Risk	Combination of the probability of occurrence of harm and the severity of that harm.
SafeState	The state of the EUC when safety is achieved.
SafetyIntegrity-Level	The probability of a safety-related system satisfactorily performing the required safety functions under all the stated conditions within a stated period of time.
SafetyRequirement	A prescriptive statement that ensures that the system carries out its functions in an acceptably safe manner.
SectorSpecific-Standard	A standard that provides recommendations for a specific industrial sector (e.g., the energy sector).
SoftwareBlock	Any entity of software that may be used for controlling the system – this may be embedded or application software or even different levels of software such as module, component, subsystem, system.
SoftwareLevel	The different levels into which a software system can be decomposed, e.g. System, subsystem, component and module.
Source	An abstract concept that can represent a person, organization or standard that can be a source of requirements to a system.
Specification	Description of a required function, performance or activity (e.g., requirements specification).
Standard	An established norm or requirement, typically provided as a formal document that establishes uniform engineering or technical criteria, methods, processes and practices.
	Continued on next page ...

Continued from previous page ...	
Stereotype	**Description**
Technique-Recommendation	A particular technique recommended based on the safety integrity level of the requirements that have been allocated to the block in question.
Technique	A procedure used to accomplish a specific activity or task.
UnsafeState	The state of the EUC when safety is compromised.
UserRole	An aspect of the interaction between a PES and the human elements.

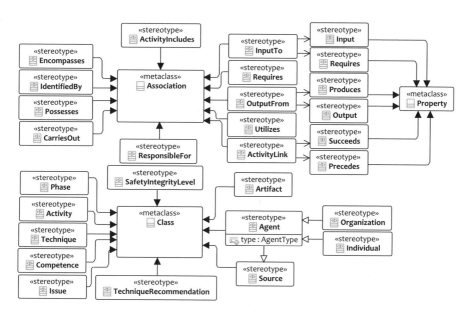

Fig. 5. IEC61508 Profile Fragment for the System Development Process

Our IEC61508 profile consists of:

- 57 stereotypes that extend the metaclass Class, used to characterize the evidence elements
- 53 stereotypes that extend the metaclass Association, used to characterize the traceability links amongst the various evidence elements.
- 6 stereotypes extend the metaclass Property, used on the role names of the corresponding associations.

Besides these stereotypes, stereotypes extending the Class and Association metaclasses have OCL constraints to ensure they are used consistently. We will discuss these constraints and provide examples later in this section.

Since the profile is quite large and cannot be fully explained in this paper, as an example, in Fig. 5, we show the stereotypes created to manage the development process. These are the stereotypes derived from the partial conceptual model shown in Fig. 1. The IEC61508 standard does not mandate a specific development life-cycle such as the waterfall or iterative lifecycle; it does however state that a number of specific activities should be carried out. We have the stereotype Activity to model this. An Activity can itself include other sub activities and this is modelled by the association stereotype `ActivityIncludes`. Certain activities may precede or succeed others and this is modelled via the association stereotype `ActivityLink` along with its properties `Precedes` and `Succeeds`.

In safety-critical systems, it is very important to ensure that all work is carried out by personnel with the required knowledge and skills. IEC61508 mandates that this information be part of the compliance evidence. Hence, for each activity, we model both the required competence and that of the agent performing the activity via the stereotypes `Agent` and `Competence` along with `CarriesOut`, `Requires` and `Possesses`. An activity may have certain artifacts that are needed in order to carry it out and it will produce certain artifacts upon its completion. These concepts are modelled using the stereotypes `Artifact`, `InputTo`, `OutputFrom`, `Requires`, `Produces`, `Input` and `Output`. Finally, each activity will use certain techniques to create its output. These techniques are chosen based on the level of safety required and hence we have the stereotypes `Technique` and `TechniqueRecommendation`.

As stated earlier, there are OCL constraints for the class and association stereotypes. These constraint enforce the structural consistency of the evidence information in the sector-specific derivations. Specifically, for any association stereotyped with X, we must check that the endpoints of the association are stereotyped correctly according to the endpoints of X in the profile metamodel. For example, consider the `CarriesOut` stereotype. We need a constraint to ensure that any association with this stereotype connects two elements stereotyped `Agent` and `Activity`, respectively. This constraint is shown in Table 2. A similar constraint is shown for `OutputFrom`, to ensure that any association having this stereotype has endpoints that are stereotyped `Artifact` and `Activity`.

For stereotypes extending the `Class` metaclass, we need to verify that any stereotyped element respects the multiplicity constraints of the profile metamodel. We show an example in Table 2: we have constraints to ensure that an element with the `Activity` stereotype is linked to at least one element with the `Artifact` stereotype and at least one element with the `Agent` stereotype.

The profile only needs to be created once per standard, and then can be reused for specializing the generic standard to any number of domains. Once the profile is created, the stereotypes of the profile are applied to the conceptual model of the domain-specific standard, also expressed as a UML class diagram. For the derived standard there are three things to bear in mind to ensure its consistency with the generic standard: (1) which concepts will be used directly from the generic standard (possibly with different terminology), (2) which concepts are specific to the domain and thus new, and (3) which concepts, from the generic standard, have been deliberately left out as they may not be applicable to the domain, in which case this omission is clearly noted and explained. The conceptual model of the derived standard is created in a manner similar to the generic standard, except that, the profile stereotypes are applied and the OCL constraints are checked to enforce the semantics of the specialization and guide the user in creating a structurally sound information model for a derived standard.

Table 2. OCL Constraints on Stereotypes

Stereotype	Constraint
| CarriesOut | ```
self.base_Association.memberEnd->
      select(p:Property | not (p.class.getAppliedStereotype(
      'IEC61508Profile::Activity').oclIsUndefined())))->size()=1
and
self.base_Association.memberEnd->
      select(p:Property | not (p.class.getAppliedStereotype(
      'IEC61508Profile::Agent').oclIsUndefined())))->size()=1
``` |
| OutputFrom | ```
self.base_Association.memberEnd->
      select(p:Property| not (p.class.getAppliedStereotype(
       'IEC61508Profile::Activity').oclIsUndefined() ))->size()=1
and
self.base_Association.memberEnd->
      select(p:Property| not (p.class.getAppliedStereotype(
      'IEC61508Profile::Artifact').oclIsUndefined() ))->size()=1
``` |
| Activity | ```
1:  self.base_Class.ownedAttribute->collect(
    c:Property  | c.association)->select(
    a:Association | not a.getAppliedStereotype(
    'IEC61508Profile::OutputFrom').oclIsUndefined())->size()>0
2:  self.base_Class.ownedAttribute->collect(
    c:Property|c.association)->select(
    a:Association | not a.getAppliedStereotype(
    'IEC61508Profile::CarriesOut').oclIsUndefined())->size()>0
``` |

4   Specializing IEC61508 for the Petroleum Industry

OLF070 is a derivation of IEC61508, elaborating the safety concerns that are specific to control systems in the petroleum industry. We discuss at a high level how OLF070 refines IEC61508. Recall the packages shown in Fig. 4: the Artifact Concepts, the Configuration Management Concepts, the Issue Concepts, the Guidance, and the Justification Concepts are the same in OLF070 as in IEC61508. The Hazard Concepts are the same, apart from the fact that in OLF070, the most common hazards have been defined in the standard already. The change in the System Concepts is that in addition to specifying the breakdown of the system, a particular component can be specified as either being part of a local safety function (e.g., process shutdown) or a global safety function (e.g., emergency shutdown). The Requirements Concepts specify that the SIL level of most common components can be obtained from a table provided in the standard unless there is a deviation in the component from what is described in the standard, in which case the SIL level is calculated using the procedures specified by IEC61508. The Process Concepts and the Domain-Specific Concepts are different in that there are specific processes and specific terminology used in the petroleum industry for developing the systems. In this section, we illustrate the specialization process by showing how the profile described in the previous section can be used for tailoring the evidence required by the OLF070 standard [5].

To preserve the continuity of our examples from the previous section, we focus on the development process aspects of OLF070, and more precisely on one of the phases envisaged in the standard, called the Pre-Execution Phase. This phase is
```

concerned with developing a Plan for Development and Operation (PDO) of an oilfield. The PDO contains the details of all the systems that need to be created to make the oilfield functional. The phase ends with the creation of the PDO document that is then sent to the authorities to get permission for the project and used to select the main engineering contractor. In this phase, a number of activities are carried out: (1) all the equipment to be installed at the field and all the safety instruments systems (SIS) are defined; (2) hazards are identified; (3) a risk analysis is performed to gauge the extent of the risks that need to be mitigated; (4) safety functions (such as fire detection, gas detection, process shut-down) and the safety integrity levels are specified based on the results of the risk analysis.

In Fig. 6, we present a small excerpt of the OLF070 conceptual model and show the concepts we have just described as the different activities that take place during the Pre-Execution Phase. The stereotypes from our IEC61508 profile have already been applied. The phase is documented in the artifact called PlanForDevelopmentAndOperation. This is in compliance with IEC61508, whereby each phase should have a plan documenting it. For some of the activities, we show the relevant inputs and outputs and the agents that need to perform them. We use the stereotypes from our IEC61508 profile to show how this OLF070 model excerpt relates to IEC61508. Some of the stereotype we have already explained in Section 3. The four new ones here are DocumentedIn for the result of a phase, BasedOn to show whether an artifact is based on a standard, Standard to indicate a type of material used to create an artifact and PerformedIn for indicating which phase an activity is performed in. Note that stereotypes can have attributes, e.g the attribute type for the stereotype Agent, shown in Fig. 6, has the value Owner to indicate that the Safety Engineer is employed or commissioned by the owner of the system to be developed. For linking to artifacts and facilitating navigation to them, we can include URLs and file references in the conceptual model. An example is shown in the figure, where we link the OLF070 element to the actual document for the standard.

As discussed in Section 3, we use OCL constraints for enforcing consistent use of the profile. Once the stereotypes have been applied to the modelled elements, we can validate the model using an OCL checker, e.g. the Rational Software Architect OCL tool [1] that we use here. In Fig. 6, we can see that five of the elements have a red cross in their upper right-hand corner. These element have failed the OCL validation. The errors generated are shown in Fig. 7. The first five errors concern the constraint that an activity should have an agent performing it. The model elements EquipmentUnderControlDefinition, SafetyInstrumentedSystemDefinition, RiskAnalysis, SafetyFunctionsDefinition, and SILRequirementsDevelopment do not have a corresponding agent element. For EquipmentUnderControlDefinition, a further constraint has been violated: there is no output specified from that activity, indicated by the last error in the snapshot of Fig. 7. Thus, in addition to providing a means to explicitly show the relationships between the generic and sector-specific standard, the profile enables users to check whether the requirements of the generic standard are maintained in the sector-specific one.

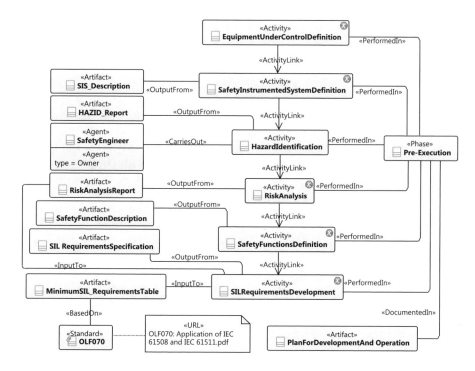

Fig. 6. An example phase from OLF070

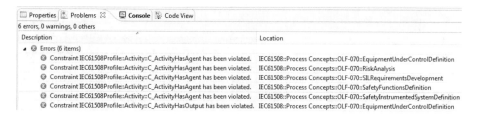

Fig. 7. Error Report showing violated OCL Constraints

5   Related Work

Using UML profiles to adapt UML to a specific context is very common. The Object Management Group have so far standardized three profiles: the UML Profile for Modeling and Analysis of Real-time and Embedded Systems (MARTE) [16], the UML Profile for Modeling QoS and Fault Tolerance Characteristics and Mechanisms (QFTP) [15], and the UML Profile for Schedulability, Performance and Time (SPT) [14]. All three include safety-relevant concepts. However, in contrast to our work, none of these were designed for characterizing the evidence required for compliance to safety standards.

Zoughbi et. al. [20] propose a UML profile for the RTCA DO-178B standard[2] used in commercial and military aerospace software. This profile enables software engineers to directly add certification information to software models. The concepts modeled are targeted at addressing a major requirement of RTCA DO-178B having to do with traceability between requirements and design and eventually code. This information together with evidence of other quality assurance activities would form the basis of full compliance to the standard. The approach we propose in this paper differs from [20] in the following ways: Firstly, we focus on a different and broader standard; secondly, our profile includes a wide range of concepts related to the management of the development process in safety-critical systems, whereas [20] deals primarily with requirements and design; and thirdly and most importantly, we use profiles as a basis for sector-specific specialization – specialization is not tackled in [20].

The Software Assurance Evidence Metamodel (SAEM) [17] is a proposal from the OMG, concerned with managing assurance evidence information. A main distinction between our work and SAEM is that we aim at characterizing the evidence that needs to be collected for certification based on a standard. Instead, SAEM is standard-independent and mainly directed towards linking the evidence to claims and the evaluation of the claims in light of the evidence. An abstract specification of evidence such as the one given by SAEM will therefore need to be complemented with an evidence conceptual model for a specific standard, e.g., our IEC61508 conceptual model. Indeed, just as we use profiles for specializing IEC61508 for a specific sector, one can use profiles to incorporate SAEM into the conceptual model of a given standard and create a metamodel that captures both the evidence requirements for compliance, and also the evaluation of whether the evidence is sufficient to substantiate the claims.

Chung et. al. [7] study the problem of compliance of a user-defined workflow with the activities envisaged in IEC61508. Their approach is to check (process) compliance by comparing user-defined activities in an organization against models of the activities in the standard. Our work is close to [7] in its goal to model compliance information; however, we go beyond the process aspects of IEC61508 and provide an evidence information model for the entire IEC61508, which can in turn be specialized to sector-specific needs through the use of profiles.

6   Conclusion and Future Work

In this paper we presented a methodology for ensuring that a generic standard can be specialized in a systematic manner for a particular domain. We do this by capturing the generic standard as a conceptual model using a UML class diagram and use this as a basis for creating a UML profile. The profile is then applied to the conceptual model of a sector-specific standard and used as an explicit means of keeping track of the relationships between the two. We exemplify our methodology by showing excerpts of the IEC61508 conceptual model that we have created, the UML profile based on this model and how we apply this profile to a conceptual model of the OLF070 standard which is a sector-specific derivation of IEC61508 for the petroleum industry.

Our approach offers two key benefits: (1) It incorporates the specific concepts used by a generic standard into the sector-specific standard whilst making a clear distinction between the two; and (2) It explicitly captures the mapping between two standards and defines consistency rules between them, which can be automatically verified and used for providing guidance to the users about how to resolve any inconsistencies.

Having established a means to capture the evidence required for a specific standard, we are now working on a means to create instantiations of these conceptual models such that we can create repositories of evidence for safety certification. Subsequently, we plan to carry out case studies to assess the cost-effectiveness of our methodology in the context of certification. Another prime concern is the ability to certify a system to multiple and often overlapping standards. For example, in the petroleum industry, it is quite common to certify a system to both OLF070 and to one of the NORSOK standards such as the NORSOK I-002 for Safety Automation Systems [6]. In future work, we plan to extend our methodology so that we can express how a repository of evidence information addresses each standard in a collection of inter-related standards. Finally, to aid the certification process from the perspective of a certification body, we would like to extend our work to the evaluation of evidence as proposed by the SAEM. This would lay the groundwork for a complete certification infrastructure based on industry standards.

References

1. IBM Rational Software Architect, http://www.ibm.com/developerworks/rational/products/rsa/
2. DO-178B: Software considerations in airborne systems and equipment certification (1982)
3. UML 2.0 Superstructure Specification (August 2005)
4. Road vehicles – functional safety. ISO draft standard (2009)
5. The Norwegian Oil Industry Association. Application of IEC61508 and IEC61511 in the Norwegian Petroleum Industry (2004)
6. Norwegian Technology Centre. Safety and automation system (SAS) (2001)
7. Chung, P., Cheung, L., Machin, C.: Compliance flow - managing the compliance of dynamic and complex processes. Knowledge-Based Systems 21(4), 332–354 (2008)
8. International Electrotechnical Commission. Railway Applications Safety-related electronic railway control and protection systems(1999)
9. International Electrotechnical Commission. Functional safety - safety instrumented systems for the process industry sector(IEC 61511) (2003)
10. International Electrotechnical Commission. Functional safety of electrical / electronic / programmable electronic safety-related systems (IEC 61508) (2005)
11. Feldt, R., Torkar, R., Ahmad, E., Raza, B.: Challenges with software verification and validation activities in the space industry. In: ICST 2010, pp. 225–234 (2010)
12. Nordland, O.: A critical look at the cenelec railway application standards (2003), http://home.c2i.net/odd_nordland~SINTEF/tekster/Acriticallookatrail_standards.htm
13. Object Management Group (OMG). OMG Object Constraint Language (2006), http://www.omg.org/spec/OCL/2.0/

14. Object Management Group (OMG). UML profile for schedulability, performance and time (2006), http://www.omg.org/spec/SPTP/
15. Object Management Group (OMG). UML profile for modeling quality of service and fault tolerance characteristics and mechanisms specification (2008), http://www.omg.org/spec/QFTP/1.1/
16. Object Management Group (OMG). UML profile for modeling and analysis of real-time and embedded systems (MARTE) (2009), http://www.omg.org/spec/MARTE/1.0/
17. Object Management Group (OMG). Software Assurance Evidence Metamodel (SAEM) (2010), http://www.omg.org/spec/SAEM/
18. Panesar-Walawege, R.K., Sabetzadeh, M., Briand, L., Coq, T.: Characterizing the chain of evidence for software safety cases: A conceptual model based on the IEC 61508 standard. In: ICST 2010, pp. 335–344 (2010)
19. Uzumeri, M.: Iso 9000 and other metastandards: Principles for management practice? Academy of Management Executive 11 (1997)
20. Zoughbi, G., Briand, L., Labiche, Y.: Modeling safety and airworthiness (RTCA DO-178B) information: conceptual model and uml profile. Software and Systems Modeling, 1–31 (2010)

Merging Relational Views: A Minimization Approach

Xiang Li and Christoph Quix

Informatik 5 (Information Systems), RWTH Aachen University, 52056 Aachen, Germany
{lixiang,quix}@dbis.rwth-aachen.de

Abstract. Schema integration is the procedure to integrate several inter-related schemas to produce a unified schema, called the mediated schema. There are two major flavors of schema integration: data integration and view integration. The former deals with integrating multiple data sources to create a mediated query interface, while the latter aims at constructing a base schema, capable of supporting the source schemas as views. Our work builds upon previous approaches that address relational view integration using logical mapping constraints. Given a set of data dependencies over the source schemas as input, our approach produces a minimal information-preserving mediated schema with constraints, and it generates output mappings defining the source schemas as views. We extend previous approaches in several aspects. First, schema minimization is performed within a scope of Project-Join views that are information preserving and produce a smaller mediated schema than in existing work. Second, the input schema mapping language is expressive enough for not only query containment but also query equivalence. Third, source integrity constraints can be seamlessly incorporated into reasoning. Last but not least, we have evaluated our implementation over both real world data sets and a schema mapping benchmark.

1 Introduction

Integration multiple schemas can be valuable in many contexts. Building a data integration system requires integrating the local schemas to create a global schema for queries. In database design, a database schema can be obtained by integrating a set of desired user views [6,21]. Bernstein and Melnik describe in [5] a scenario of schema evolution, in which an existing view is merged with another view representing newly incorporated information to construct an augmented view over an evolved database. In data warehousing, multiple data marts can be merged into a single materialized view to reduce maintenance costs.

Schema integration is the process of consolidating multiple related heterogeneous input schemas to produce a mediated schema. A typical schema integration procedure consists of three phases: schema matching, schema merging, and post-integration. The first phase identifies interschema relationships in the form of schema mappings. The second phase performs schema restructuring and transformation to construct a mediated schema and output mappings. The last phase performs cleaning up and etc. This paper focus on the schema merging phase.

As clarified in [16], there are two semantically distinct flavors of schema merging, view integration [7,6,22,14,15,3] and data integration [17,8,19,20,12]. From a model theoretic perspective, a main distinction is that the former flavor assumes the input

M. Jeusfeld, L. Delcambre, and T.W. Ling (Eds.): ER 2011, LNCS 6998, pp. 379–392, 2011.
© Springer-Verlag Berlin Heidelberg 2011

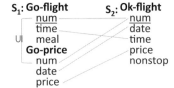

Keys are underlined and $\subseteq$ indicates foreign key constraints, while value correspondences across schemas are illustrated via solid lines. A mapping constraint between the two schemas can be expressed as $\pi_{num,date,time,price}$(Ok-flight) $=$ $\pi_{num,date,time,price}$(Go-flight $\bowtie$ Go-price).

Fig. 1. Running Example

schemas are views of a base schema and hence satisfy constraints on the instance level, while the latter need to integrate autonomous input schemas which do not necessarily conform to any instance level constraints. [16] also analyzed the different operational goals of the two types of schema merging. We study in this paper view integration, while our previous work[12] deals with data integration.

A possible result of a schema mapping discovery process, i.e., the first phase of schema integration, is described in Example 1 (adapted from [17]). Several challenges can be observed there. First, interschema relationships are captured by complex expressions involving multiple relations, and they are in the form of query equivalence instead of query containment. This requires a mapping language more expressive than that in data exchange [10]. Second, integrity constraints encoded in the source schemas provide significant information about the inner structure and hence they should not be ignored. Third, as the input has a non-ambiguous model theoretic semantics, the view integration process also needs to be backed by a rigorous instance level interpretation. Last but not least, in order to be executable, the output should include not only a mediated schema but also mappings defining input schemas as views and constraints over the mediated schema to restrict the instance scope of the mediated schema.

Example 1. Two travel agents *Go-flight* and *Ok-flight* have different schemas of flight information, as illustrated in Figure 1. The attribute *num* denotes flight numbers; *time* and *date* describe the departure time and date of a flight; *price* stands for the price of an air ticket; *meal* and *nonstop* are two boolean attributes indicating whether meals are offered on the flight and whether the flight is non-stop.

To address such challenges, we propose in this paper a novel approach to relational view integration. Our contributions include:

Formulation of Minimal Merge: The formal definition of a valid *Merge* as in [15,3] requires the mediated schema to retain *all and only* the information of the source schemas. They do not consider minimizing schema size, and produce a mediated schema of the same size of the input. The formalism is extended in this paper to incorporate considerations on the size of the mediated schema, resulting in a characterization of *Minimal Merge*. We presented in [12] a merging algorithm that removed redundant columns from the source schemas in a data integration context. The approach described here considers, in addition, collapsing of relations, which leads to an even smaller schema.

Expressive Logical Mapping Language: Most of the early approaches (as surveyed in surveyed in [4]) to view integration focused more on the conceptual design of the mediated schema and used conceptual alignment of entities as input mappings. Logical constraints were first used in [6,7], but the joins are not allowed. However, schema mappings resulting from an automatic process, either mapping discovery or other mapping manipulation operations, are complex expressions such as in Fig. 1. Therefore, an expressive mapping language is crucial for a merging approach to be applicable in a model management workflow. In view of this, the input mapping language in our approach are specified in tuple-generating dependencies (tgds) and equality generating dependencies (egds), with the only restriction that the input mapping constraints admit a terminating chase [1]. Chase termination is in general undecidable, but there are sound syntactic conditions ensuring it (e.g., see [10]). With such an expressive language, we are able to make use of not only query containment constraints, but also query equivalence constraints and integrity constraints (ICs) shipped with the input schemas.

Algorithms for Constructing Minimal Merge: We present algorithms for merging relational schemas, including schema minimization under dependencies, mediated schema construction, output view definition mapping generation, and rewriting input constraints to the mediated schema.

Evaluation on Real World Data Sets: Last but not least, we have implemented and tested our framework on real world data sets and a workload generated from a schema mapping benchmark which summarizes several most common mapping scenarios in practice.

The rest of the paper is organized as follows: section 2 presents a formal definition of *Minimal Merge*; section 3 describes schema minimization under dependencies; section 4 details how to generate the mediated schema and the output mappings from a minimized Project-Join view; the evaluation is presented in section 5; related work is discussed in section 6, and conclusion and outlook are in section 7.

2   The View Integration Problem

2.1   Modeling View Integration

A *relational schema* is a set of relation symbols, each of which has a fixed arity. Let $\mathbf{S}$ be a relational schema, $Inst(\mathbf{S})$ be the set of all instances, a schema mapping $\mathcal{M}$ between two schemas $\mathbf{S}$ and $\mathbf{T}$ can be syntactically represented by a triple $(\mathbf{S}, \mathbf{T}, \Sigma)$, with Σ being a set of data dependencies over $\mathbf{S} \cup \mathbf{T}$. The instances of the mapping $Inst(\mathcal{M})$ is a subset of the cartesian product $Inst(\mathbf{S}) \times Inst(\mathbf{T})$. We also denote by $dom(\mathcal{M})$ and $range(\mathcal{M})$ the domain and range of a mapping $\mathcal{M}$.

In order to define the semantics of view integration, we introduce first the notion of *confluence* of two mappings, which is also adopted in [3,15]. Let $\mathbf{S}$, $\mathbf{S}_1$ and $\mathbf{S}_2$ be schemas where $\mathbf{S}_1$ and $\mathbf{S}_2$ share no common relation symbol. $\mathcal{M}_1$ ($\mathcal{M}_2$) is a mapping from $\mathbf{S}$ to $\mathbf{S}_1$ ($\mathbf{S}_2$ respectively). Then the confluence of $\mathcal{M}_1$ and $\mathcal{M}_2$, denoted by $\mathcal{M}_1 \oplus \mathcal{M}_2$ is $\{(I, J \cup K) | (I, J) \in \mathcal{M}_1, (I, K) \in \mathcal{M}_2\}$. Intuitively, the confluence of two mappings maps each source instance to a concatenation of the two target instances under the original mappings. We now define the *merge* operator.

Definition 1. *Let* $\mathcal{M}$ *be a schema mapping between* $\mathbf{S}_1$ *and* $\mathbf{S}_2$. $(\mathbf{S}, \mathcal{M}_1, \mathcal{M}_2)$ *is a* merge *of* $\mathcal{M}$ *if: 1)* $dom(\mathcal{M}_1) = dom(\mathcal{M}_2)$; *2)* $\mathcal{M}_1 \oplus \mathcal{M}_2$ *is an injective function; and 3)* $range(\mathcal{M}_1 \oplus \mathcal{M}_2) = \{J \cup K | (J, K) \in Inst(\mathcal{M})\}$.

The first condition requires that the two output mappings are views over the same scope of databases. Condition 2) states the output mappings are view definitions and injectiveness guarantees the mediated schema does not carry any extra information not contained in the sources. Condition 3) ensures that every unified instance in the range of the confluence respect the input mapping constraints, that is, a mutually consistent pair of views can be retrieved.

The definition of *merge* does not concern the mapping language. We introduce now tgds and egds. A *tuple generating dependency (tgd)* [1], is a constraint in the form of: $\forall X [\exists Y \phi(X, Y) \rightarrow \exists Z \psi(X, Z)]$, where ϕ and ψ are conjunctions of atoms and X, Y and Z are mutually disjoint sets of variables. It is *full*, if there are no existential variables on the right hand side, otherwise it is an *embedded* tgd. An *equality-generating dependency (egd)* [1] has the form $\forall X [\phi(X) \rightarrow (X_i = X_j)]$, where $\phi(X)$ is a conjunction of atoms, and X_i, X_j are variables in X. When emphasizing the direction of a schema mapping between a designated pair of source and target schemas, we use the term *source-to-target* tgds (s-t tgds). A *closure* of a set of full s-t tgsd Σ, denoted by Σ^*, is the set of dependencies replacing each containment constraint in Σ by an equivalence constraint. Intuitively, closure *closes* the scope of target instances to be exactly the unique view instance computed from a given source instance.

For a schema $\mathbf{S}$, we denote by $\hat{\mathbf{S}}$ a replica schema with each relation renamed. We also denote by $\hat{R}$ the replica relational symbol of R, and by $\hat{\Gamma}$ the dependencies obtained through renaming relational symbols in Γ to their replicas. An identity mapping Id is the mapping $\{(I, J) | I \subseteq J \wedge I \in Inst(\mathbf{S}) \wedge J \in Inst(\hat{\mathbf{S}})\}$. In the theorem below, we denote by Id_1 (resp. Id_2) the mapping copying $\hat{\mathbf{S}}_1$ to $\mathbf{S}_1$ (resp. $\hat{\mathbf{S}}_2$ to $\mathbf{S}_2$). The theorem states that a union of the replicas of the input schemas together with an identity mapping is a valid *merge*.

Theorem 1 ([14]). *Let* $\mathcal{M}$ *be a mapping specified by data dependencies* Γ *in first order logic over* $\mathbf{S}_1$ *and* $\mathbf{S}_2$, *then* $(\hat{\mathbf{S}}_1 \cup \hat{\mathbf{S}}_2, \hat{\Gamma} \cup Id_1^*, \hat{\Gamma} \cup Id_2^*)$ *is a merge of* $\mathcal{M}$.

Example 2 (Example 1 cont.). Following Theorem 1, a valid merge could be $(\hat{\mathbf{S}}_1 \cup \hat{\mathbf{S}}_2, \hat{\Gamma} \cup Id_1, \hat{\Gamma} \cup Id_2)$. $\hat{\Gamma}$ contains two parts: the integrity constraints including all key constraints and inclusion dependencies over $\hat{\mathbf{S}}_1$ and $\hat{\mathbf{S}}_2$, and the rewritten mapping constraints $\pi_{num,date,time,price}(\text{Ok-f\^{l}ight}) = \pi_{num,date,time,price}(\text{Go-f\^{l}ight} \bowtie \text{Go-price})$. The identity mapping Id_2 can be expressed by full s-t tgds $\text{Ok-f\^{l}ight}(n, d, t, p, s) \rightarrow \text{Ok-flight}(n, d, t, p, s)$. Mapping Id_1 is similar.

The result in example 2 is not minimal as *time, date, price* are stored more than once.

Arenas et al. [3] propose a merging algorithm taking full s-t tgds as input and admitting denial constraints over the mediated schema. We show their merge algorithm[1] on an adapted version of Example 2 that confines the input mapping to full s-t tgds.

---

[1] Example 3 slightly extends the original algorithm in [3] , as source integrity constraints are not treated there.

Example 3 (Example 2 cont.). The input is adapted by stating *num* is a key of Go-price, and replacing the interschema constraint by Ok-flight$(n, d, t, p, s) \to$ Go-price(n, d, p). A valid merge can be $(\hat{\mathbf{S}}_1 \cup \hat{\mathbf{S}}_2, \hat{\Gamma}' \cup \Sigma_1^*, \hat{\Gamma}' \cup Id_2^*)$, in which Id_2 is the same as in Example 2, and Σ_1 and $\hat{\Gamma}'$ are specified below. Σ_1 contains the full s-t tgds Go-flight(n, t, m) $\to$ Go-flight(n, t, m), Go-price$(n, d, p) \to$ Go-price(n, d, p), and Ok-flight(n, d, t, p, s) $\to$ Go-price(n, d, p). $\hat{\Gamma}'$ is a union of rewritten source ICs as in Example 2 and a denial constraint $\neg$(Ok-flight$(n, d, t, p, s) \wedge$ Go-price(n, d, p)), which ensures that the relation Go-price does not store tuples which are already in Ok-flight.

Example 3 is also not minimal, as storing *date* and *price* in Ok-flight is unnecessary.

2.2 Minimality of Mediated Schema

The *merge* definition ensures that the mediated schema incorporates *all and only* the information in the input mapping system, but it does not restrict how the information is organized in the mediated schema. In this section, we present a merge requirement that aims at reducing redundant representations of the same piece of information on the mediated schema.

Given a schema with dependencies, we consider a set of schemas resulting from two types of transformations: 1) collapsing fragmented relations representing the same entity, and 2) projecting out unnecessary columns of a schema.

Definition 2. *A bidirectional inclusion dependency (BIND) is a mapping constraint* $\pi_{\mathbf{A}_1}(R_1) = \pi_{\mathbf{A}_2}(R_2)$, *where R_1 and R_2 are two relations, and $\mathbf{A}_1$ ($\mathbf{A}_2$ resp.) is a list of non-repeating attributes in R_1 (R_2 resp.).*

In Example 1, a BIND implied by the input mapping constraint and the integrity constraints is $\pi_{num,date,price}(\text{Go-price}) = \pi_{num,date,price}(\text{Ok-flight})$.

Existence of a BIND is a hint of fragmented entities. Joining the fragments over shared attributes in the BIND will be information preserving, if the join is lossless. However, a lossless join on a Key-ForeignKey relationship may lead to denormalization. In order not to degrade the quality of the mediated schema as a base schema, we confine the minimization scope to fragmented entities implied by BINDs via a key, i.e., the shared attributes are a super key for both relations.

A column in a schema is *redundant*, if removing it does not lose information. More formally, the mapping removing it (expressed in full s-t tgds) is tgd invertible [9]. That is, there exists a backward mapping in full tgds recovering the unprojected database. We refer interested readers to [12] for more details.

Definition 3. *A merge is* minimal *if there is neither a BIND via key nor a redundant column in the mediated schema.*

3   Schema Minimization under Data Dependencies

Assuming the input source schemas share no relation symbol, we refer to the union of them as *the source schema* (denoted by **S**), and the union of interschema constraints and innerschema ICs as *input constraints* (denoted by Γ). Γ is assumed to admit a terminating chase. A *collapse-configuration* is a partial function mapping pairs of relations to a BIND via key that is implied by Γ. A *project-configuration* is a set of columns that are redundant under Γ. A *merge-configuration* is then a collapse-configuration plus a project-configuration. In this section we describe the schema minimization procedure, taking **S** and Γ as input and producing merge-configurations representing *minimal* Project-Join views.

3.1 Collapse-Minimization Using Maximal BINDs

A BIND is *maximal*, if there is no other BIND with the same relations and a superset of attribute pairs. We present in Algorithm 1 a procedure to find all maximal BINDs implied by Γ using the chase procedure [1] for reasoning over data dependencies. The algorithm starts by finding all inclusion dependencies (INDs) implied by Γ. For each relation R in the schema, a singleton tableau containing a single R-tuple with distinct variables is taken as a starting database. The singleton tableau is then chased against Γ. For each T-tuple in the chase result with a set of variables overlapping with the original R-tuple, an IND is recorded. In a second phase, all INDs are "joined" to produce BINDs. Finally, we prune those BINDs that are not maximal.

Input : A source schema **S**, a set of dependencies Γ over **S** with terminating chase.
Output: A set of all maximal BINDs.

1   Initialize IND $\leftarrow \emptyset$
2   **for** *each relation* $R \in \mathbf{S}$ **do**
3   Let I_R be a singleton R-tuple with all different variables
4   Let I_R^{Γ} be the chase of I_R against Γ
5   **for** *each relation* $T \in \mathbf{S}/\{R\}$ **do**
6   **if** *there is a T-tuple* $t \in I_R^{\Gamma}$ *containing variables in* I_R **then**
7              $L \leftarrow \emptyset$
8   **for** *each variable* $x \in dom(I_R)$ **do**
9   If x appears in position j in t and position i in the R-tuple of I_R, add
                 (i, j) to L
10   **end**
11   add (R, T, L) to IND
12   **end**
13   **end**
14   **end**
15   BIND $\leftarrow \emptyset$
16   **for** *each pair of relations R and T* **do**
17   **for** *each* $(R, T, L_{rt}) \in$ IND **do**
18   **for** *each* $(T, R, L_{tr}) \in$ IND **do**
19              $L \leftarrow \emptyset$
20   For each $(i, j) \in L_{rt}$ and $(j, i) \in L_{tr}$, add (i, j) to L.
21   If L is not empty, add (R, T, L) to BIND
22   **end**
23   **end**
24   **end**
25   Remove from BIND those that are non-maximal
26   Return BIND

Algorithm 1. $DiscoverMaximalBINDs(\mathbf{S}, \Gamma)$: find max-BINDs implied by Γ

To simplify the discovery process, we assume that there are no redundant columns within one relation, that is, there are no two distinct attributes A and B of a relation R such that $\Gamma \models \pi_A(R) = \pi_B(R)$. A simple preprocessing phase can easily remove redundant columns within one relation. Even without preprocessing, they will be removed anyway in the later project-minimization phase (section 3.2).

Theorem 2. *If there are no redundant columns within a relation, the algorithm* DiscoverMaximalBINDs *finds all and only the maximal BINDs implied by* Γ.[2]

Having discovered all maximal BINDs, we can easily prune those that are not via keys. Testing key dependencies can be also performed using chase [1]. If we denote the maximal BINDs via key of each pair of source relations as a set, then enumeration of maximal collapse-configurations can be done via enumerating elements of the cartesian product of these (non-empty) sets.

Example 4. Consider the input mapping system in Example 1. Chasing with a singleton Go-flight tuple does not produce any other fact, which means there is no IND originating from Go-flight. Chasing with Go-price(n, d, p) produces two other tuples Go-flight$(n, \perp_1, \perp_2)$ and Ok-flight$(n, d, \perp_1, p, \perp_3)$, which correspond to the INDs Go-price$[num] \subseteq$ Go-flight$[num]$ and Go-price$[num, date, price] \subseteq$ Ok-flight[num, date, price]. In our data structure, we record (Go-price, Go-flight, $\{(1, 1)\}$) and (Go-price, Ok-flight, $\{(1,1), (2,2), (3,4)\}$). Similarly, chasing with a singleton Ok-flight tuple reveals INDs Ok-flight$[num, time] \subseteq$ Go-flight$[num, time]$ and Ok-flight$[num, date, price] \subseteq$ Go-price$[num, date, price]$, corresponding to (Ok-flight, Go-flight, $\{(1,1), (3,2)\}$) and (Ok-flight, Go-price, $\{(1, 1), (2, 2), (4, 3)\}$). A join on the INDs outputs only one BIND (Ok-flight, Go-price, $\{(1, 1), (2, 2), (4, 3)\}$). The only maximal collapse-configuration contains this BIND.

3.2   Project-Minimization over Collapsed Schemas

We have described in [12] a procedure to test redundancy of a set of columns on the source schema with constraints, which is based on testing query rewritability of identity queries of source relations over the projected schema. The procedure can be extended to test redundancy of columns in a collapsed schema. We first define the lineage of a column in a collapsed schema: the *lineage* of column c is the set of source columns that are collapsed into c. Suppose we collapse Go-price and Ok-flight on $num, date, price$ into Ok-flight$'$, the lineage of $price$ in Ok-flight$'$ is $\{$Go-price.$price$, Ok-flight.$price\}$, while the lineage of Ok-flight$'$.$nonstop$ is $\{$Ok-flight.$nonstop\}$.

Proposition 1. *A column on a collapsed schema is redundant if and only if all columns in its lineage are redundant.*

With the above result, we can extend the project-minimization algorithm in [12] to be over collapsed schemas, through replacing the redundancy test by testing redundancy of the lineage over the source schemas. The procedure is presented in Algoirthm 2.

---

[2] Proofs of this theorem and the following are in the appendix, accessible at
http://dbis.rwth-aachen.de/cms/staff/li/er11

Input : A source schema **S**, a set of dependencies Γ over **S** with terminating chase, a target schema **T** that is a collapsing result, a set of s-t tgds Σ_{st} between **S** and **T** representing the collapsing, and a set of columns in **T**

Output: A list of maximal sets of redundant columns.

1 Initialize isMaximal to TRUE
2 **for** *each extension of the redundant columns* $P' \in Enum(P, \mathbf{T})$ **do**
3   **if** IsRedundant $(\mathbf{S}, \Gamma, \Sigma_{st}, P')$ **then**
4   isMaximal $\leftarrow$ FALSE
5   ProjectMinimize($\mathbf{S}, \Gamma, \mathbf{T}, \Sigma_{st}, P'$)
6   **end**
7 **end**
8 **if** isMaximal **then**
9   Add P to result
10 **end**

Algorithm 2. $ProjectMinimize(\mathbf{S}, \Gamma, \mathbf{T}, \Sigma_{st}, P)$: p-min over collapsed schema

Two sub-procedures are used in the algorithm: *IsRedudant* and *Enum*. The former is the column redundancy test, while the latter is a depth-first procedure enumerating all possible sets of columns over the collapsed schema **T** with a-priori pruning. For brevity, we refer interested readers to [12] for more details on the two sub-procedures.

Example 5 (Example 4 cont.). After collapsing, there are two relations Go-flight(num, $time$, $meal$) and Ok-flight'(num, $date$, $time$, $price$, $nonstop$). Only the column $time$ in Ok-flight' is redundant, since the data dependencies imply $\pi_{num,date,price,nonstop}$ (Ok-flight')$\bowtie \pi_{num,time}$(Go-flight) $\equiv$ Ok-flight'.

4   Generating Minimal Merge

A merge-configuration describes how a minimal mediated schema can be constructed as a view over the source schema. We address now how to generate a minimal merge, including constraints over the mediated schema and output mappings.

4.1   Constructing Mediated Schema

Given a merge-configuration, constructing a mediated schema is straightforward. We show that via the running example. The minimization algorithm will produce a collapse-configuration consisting of the BIND (Ok-flight, Go-price, $\{(1,1),(2,2),(4,3)\}$) as computed in Example 4, and the set of redundant columns {Go-flight.$time$}. Following the collapse-configuration, we can join together Ok-flight and Go-price on num, $date$, $price$ and removing the $time$ column, while the relation Go-flight is copied. The mediated schema consists of two relations Ok-flight' and Go-flight', which is a result of transformations defined by a set of full s-t tgds: Go-flight(num, $time$, $meal$) $\rightarrow$ Go-flight'(num, $time$, $meal$) and Ok-flight(n, d, t, p, s), Go-price(n, d, p) $\rightarrow$ Ok-flight' (n, d, p, s). We denote the transformation mapping by Σ.

4.2   Constructing Output Mappings

We can show that the transformation mapping Σ in the previous section is tgd invertible.

Proposition 2. *Let Σ be the transformation mapping corresponding to a merge configuration, Γ_s be the input mapping constraints over the source schema $\mathbf{S}$, $\mathbf{T}$ be the mediated schema, then the mapping $(\mathbf{S}, \mathbf{T}, \Gamma_s \cup \Sigma)$ is tgd invertible.*

The output mapping supporting source schemas as views can be computed as a tgd-inverse of Σ. It is shown in [9] that a tgd-inverse of s-t tgds can be expressed in *full* tgds. Here we describe the procedure following [9]. Let $\mathbf{S}$ be a source schema, Γ_s a set of finitely chaseable tgds and egds over $\mathbf{S}$, Σ a set of tgd invertible full s-t tgds. We can create a tgd inverse Σ^{-1} in full s-t tgds as follows. For each source relation R, we denote by I_R the singleton instance of all distinct variables for each column of R, $I_R^{\Gamma_s}$ the result of chasing I_R against Γ_s, J_R the result of chasing $I_R^{\Gamma_s}$ against Σ, add to Σ^{-1}:
$J_R \to I_R^{\Gamma_s}$.

Let's consider the running example. The procedure above creates a tgd inverse consisting of the following tgds : Go-flight$'(n, t, m) \to$ Go-flight(n, t, m), Ok-flight$'(n, d, p, s)$, Go-flight$'(n, t, m) \to$ Go-price(n, d, p), and Ok-flight$'(n, d, p, s)$, Go-flight$'(n, t, m) \to$ Ok-flight(n, d, t, p, s).

4.3   Rewriting Input Constraints to the Mediated Schema

In order to maintain one-to-one instance level mapping between the mediated schema and the source schema, the input constraints have to be rewritten over the mediated schema. It is easy to see that a conjunctive query (CQ) over the source schema can always be rewritten as a CQ over the mediated schema under the tgd-inverse. Let $rewrite(.)$ be the procedure rewriting each CQ over the source schema $\mathbf{S}$ to a CQ over the mediated schema $\mathbf{T}$, while leaving the CQ over $\mathbf{T}$ and equalities intact. For each tgd $\phi(\mathbf{x}) \to \psi(\mathbf{x})$ in $\Sigma^* \cup \Gamma_s$, add to Γ_t: $rewrite(\phi(\mathbf{x})) \to rewrite(\psi(\mathbf{x}))$. Egds are handled similarly. Rewriting of Γ_s ensures that the view instances computed from the mediated schema always respect the input constraints, while rewriting Σ^* ensures the mediated schema can be computed as a view from the consistent view instances.

Taking the running example as an input, constraint rewriting produces Γ_t as a set of tgds and egds, which can be simplified to: Go-flight$'(n, t_1, m_1)$, Go-flight$'(n, t_2, m_2) \to$ $t_1 = t_2, m_1 = m_2$, Ok-flight$'(n, d_1, p_1, s_1)$, Ok-flight$'(n, d_2, p_2, s_2) \to d_1 = d_2, t_1 = t_2, p_1 = p_2, s_1 = s_2$, and Ok-flight$'(n, d, p, s) \to$ Go-flight$'(n, t, m)$. We can show that the rewriting procedure is information preserving.

Proposition 3. *The constraint rewriting procedure satisfies $\Gamma_t \cup (\Sigma^{-1})^* \equiv \Sigma^* \cup \Gamma_s$.*

Now we can conclude on the correctness of our merging algorithm. Let Γ_s be the input mapping constraints, c be a merge configuration resulting from the schema minimization procedure. Let $\mathbf{T}$, Γ_t and Σ^{-1} be respectively, the mediated schema, rewritten constraints, and generated output mapping according to c. As Σ^{-1} is in full tgds, it can be split to full tgds with only a single predicate in the head. We denote by Σ_1^{-1} (resp. Σ_2^{-1}) the subset of Σ^{-1} with head predicates only from $\mathbf{S}_1$ (resp. $\mathbf{S}_2$).

Theorem 3. $(\mathbf{T}, \Gamma_t \cup (\Sigma_1^{-1})^*, \Gamma_t \cup (\Sigma_2^{-1})^*)$ *is a minimal merge.*

5   Evaluation

The system is developed using Java SE 6 and SWI-Prolog 5.8.0. A chase procedure is implemented in Prolog for reasoning over data dependencies. The experiments have been carried out on a 2.5GHz dual core computer, with a maximal heap size of 512M. Disk I/O costs are excluded from profiling, while communication costs between Java and Prolog are included. Two collections of data sets are used in our experiments: data sets from the Illinois Semantic Integration Archive[3], which include five real world data sets (*Courses, Real Estate II, Inventory, Faculty* and *Real Estate I*), and a workload generated by a schema mapping benchmark *STBenchmark* [2]. The schemas are defined as XML schemas, which are flattened to relational schemas beforehand.

5.1   Expressiveness over Real World Mapping Scenarios

All five data sets in the Illinois archive are able to be represented by tgds and egds. Complex relationships involving joins of relations arise frequently in the data sets, which confirms the necessity of an expressive language such as tgds. Furthermore, we see it is crucial to be able to specify integrity constraints of source schemas. Without the presence of keys in the source no attribute is redundant, even if many attributes are asserted to be equivalent. This is in line with information preservation: when there is no functional dependency, a tuple is only retrievable when all components are kept.

Eight out of ten basic mapping scenarios of STBenchmark are expressible in our mapping language: *Copy, Flattening, Nesting, Denormalization, SelfJoin, SurrogateKey, AtomicValueManagement* and *VerticalPartitioning*. The scenario *Fusion* is not able to be expressed because it requires a language of disjunctive tgds, which is beyond the scope of our current implementation. The scenario *HorizontalPartitioning* cannot be expressed perfectly as it requires expressing selection in the head of a tgd. This requires a representation system like *conditional tables* [11], while the database with labelled nulls used in our approach is in essence *v-tables* [11].

Value conversion functions arising in the data sets (e.g., in *Real Estate II* and *AtomicValueManagement*) are handled by skolem functions and invertible functions are handled with helper predicates and rules as explained in [12].

5.2   Scalability of Schema Minimization

Though there are multiple possible minimal mediated schemas, enumerating all is very costly. There are cases, e.g., project-minimization in the *Copy* scenario, that have an exponential number of possibilities. We focus on the scalability of finding one minimal mediated schema. For each scenario of STBenchmark, we generate 10 input mappings of various sizes. Three strategies of minimizations, project-minimization (p-min), collapse-minimization (c-min) and collapse-project-minimization (c-p-min), are tested over the generated workload. Fig. 2 depicts the running time. The x-axis is the size of the schema (i.e., the sum of the arities of all relations in the schema), while the y-axis

---

[3] http://pages.cs.wisc.edu/~anhai/wisc-si-archive/

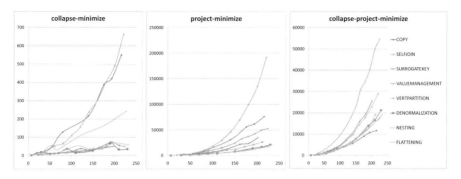

Fig. 2. Running Time (ms) vs Schema Size Categorized by Scenarios of STBenchmark

is the time in milliseconds. A cross comparison among the three minimization strategies reveals that *c-min* is the fastest, while *c-p-min* is faster than *p-min*. *C-min* is fastest as it requires only invoking reasoning procedures in so many times as the number of relations in the input. *P-min* is the most expensive, as it invokes reasoning procedures in proportional to the number of columns in the input. *C-p-min* is faster than *p-min* because the collapsing phase merges columns and hence decreases the input size for *p-min*. *C-min* scales quite well regarding schema size, less than 1 second even for the largest input. *Copy* and *SelfJoin* require a longer time than the other scenarios. This is due to two factors: 1) the portion of attributes identified as overlapping via BINDs in these two scenarios is high; and 2) they have the longest dependency length under a given size of schema. *AtomicValueManagement* also has a long dependency length, but there is no BIND in this scenario since values undergo conversions in the form of a function. Therefore, *c-min* for this scenario is faster. *Nesting* is slightly more costly than the rest as, for the same schema size, the number of relations is larger in this scenario with many leaf relations from normalizing a tree. In *p-min* the reasoning procedure invocations are proportional to the schema size, and the complexity of dependencies is a dominating factor. This explains why the three scenarios *Copy*, *SelfJoin* and *AtomicValueManagement* with the longest dependency take more time than others. *C-p-min* is more scalable than *p-min* because the collapsing minimization phase greatly reduce the input size of the project-minimization phase. Interestingly, now *AtomicValueManagement* is the most expensive scenario. This is because no reduction of schema is achieved during *c-min* for the scenario and hence the cost is almost the same as direct *p-min*.

5.3   Effectiveness of Minimization

We evaluated the effectiveness of our approach using the real world data sets from Illinois archive. We perform three strategies of minimization and present in Fig. 3 the effects of minimization. We measure the ratio of reduced columns to the input schema size, i.e., $1 - \frac{|\mathbf{T}|}{|\mathbf{S}|}$, which indicates how much redundancy has been removed through minimization. As a comparison, [14] and [3] do not head for reducing schema size and have a constantly 0% reduction ratio. [17] considers retaining incompleteness in data integration and may result in a negative reduction ratio, i.e., a schema larger than the input. The reduction ratio is the highest for *Faculty*, in which 80% of the input schema

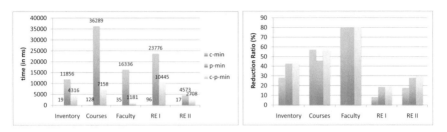

Fig. 3. Schema Reduction Ratio and Running Time of Illinois Data Sets

is redundant. A close look into the data set reveals that this input consists of five replicas of the same schema. *C-p-min* gives the highest reduction ratio, while whether *c-min* or *p-min* achieves a higher reduction ratio depends on the input scenario.

6   Related Work

Batini et al. [4] provide an early survey covering classical view/data integration approaches, in which schemas are usually modeled in a variant of the ER model. Interschema assertions [22,18] are a popular language specifying set-based relationships (e.g., inclusion, disjoint, and equal) between extensions of concepts across schemas. The approaches usually undergo a collapse-resolve procedure: first, collapse equivalent concepts and then resolve the conflicts arising in collapsing. This line of work does not focus on creating output mappings, but on designing the mediated schema.

Logical constraints are first used for view integration in [6] and [7] targeting at a minimal mediated schema. Their interschema assertions are one-to-one relation-wise constraints; key constraints have also to be present. Except for the disjoint constraints stating two relations are disjoint on the instance level, the mapping language is strictly less expressive than the language considered in this paper.

Melnik (Theorem 4.2.4 in [14]) proposes a straightforward algorithm for view integration. The mediated schema is taken to be a disjoint union of the source schemas, with source integrity constraints (ICs) and input mappings encoded as constraints over the mediated schema. Output mappings are identity mappings copying part of the mediated schema to the source schemas. Arenas et al. [3] extend the work to achieve a smaller instance for the mediated schema by adding denial constraints to the mediated schema, while confining input mappings to full source-to-target tgds (full s-t tgds). Similar to the previous approaches, we also require a one-to-one mapping between input schemas and mediated schema on the instance level; output view definition mappings are also in full tgds; and constraints are constructed over the mediated schema. However, we go one step further on schema minimization. We find minimal mediated schemas within a class of Project-Join views of the source schemas, resulting in smaller mediated schemas than those created in [3] and [14]. Our input mapping language is (finitely chaseable) tgds and egds, which is neither restricted to be source-to-target, nor restricted to deny existential variables. Constraints over the mediated schema are expressed in tgds and egds, which are more common than the denial constraints used in [3].

Merging schemas in the data integration context differs from view integration, as instances of the source schemas do not necessarily satisfy any mapping constraints. Pottinger and Bernstein [17] use pairs of conjunctive queries (CQs) to specify overlapping information between two schemas. Source integrity constraints are not used in their approach. Chiticariu et al. [8] propose an interactive schema merging approach taking attribute correspondences as input. Logical entities (chases of singleton relations) are extracted from the source schemas as concepts. The space of plausible collapsing of concepts is navigated by the user in an interactive manner. Since each extracted concept has a particular join path in the source schemas, two concepts and value correspondences between them comprise an implicit Global-Local-As-View mapping. However, when deemed as such, the mapping is still more restricted than tgds in the sense that all joins are performed only along referential constraints, e.g., Key-ForeignKey constraints. The work is extended in [19] to generate top-k mediated schemas, with a ranking of candidate mediated schemas, which is a topic not explored in this paper.

In previous work [12,13], we presented a merging algorithm for data integration, which takes finitely chaseable tgds and egds as input mapping language. The constraints are not regarded as hard constraints over the stored extensions of the data sources (extensional database, EDB), but as intended relationships over an integrated global database (intensional database, IDB). Instead of requiring the mediated schema to preserve the EDB, we require preserving the IDB. We ensure that every source CQ has a rewritten CQ over the mediated schema so that the certain answer of the query in the IDB is the same as the certain answer of the rewriting under the output mapping. We consider removing redundant columns from the source schema. The output mapping created is a mapping representing computing the IDB from EDB composed with the mapping removing redundant columns. The output mapping language needed is second order data dependencies. In this paper, we extend the schema minimization raised there to allow both collapsing and projection. Due to the difference in merge requirements, our formulation of minimal merge for view integration is also different from the requirements of a minimal query interface described there.

7 Conclusion and Outlook

We presented a novel view integration approach which aims at minimizing the mediated schema while still maintaining information preservation. We extend existing work by admitting a more expressive input mapping language consisting of finitely chaseable tgds and egds, and produce output view definition mappings in full s-t tgds. Source integrity constraints are seamlessly incorporated as part of the input constraints. Schema minimization is performed within a class of information preserving Project-Join views, to achieve smaller mediated schemas than in existing solutions. Input constraints are rewritten as tgds and egds over the mediated schema.

We see several possibilities of future work. First, we studied merging relational views and it would be interesting to see how the approach extends to nested structures like XML. Second, we focussed on collapsing relations, but the approach can be extended to collapsing logical entities, i.e., chases of singleton relations. Third, recent results on disjunctive chase suggest that the input mapping language can be extended to disjunctive tgds.

Acknowledgements. This work is supported by the DFG Research Cluster on Ultra High-Speed Mobile Information and Communication (UMIC, http://www.umic.rwth-aachen.de).

References

1. Abiteboul, S., Hull, R., Vianu, V.: Foundations of Databases. Addison-Wesley, Reading (1995)
2. Alexe, B., Tan, W.C., Velegrakis, Y.: STBenchmark: towards a benchmark for mapping systems. PVLDB 1(1), 230–244 (2008)
3. Arenas, M., Pérez, J., Reutter, J.L., Riveros, C.: Foundations of schema mapping management. In: Proc. PODS, pp. 227–238 (2010)
4. Batini, C., Lenzerini, M., Navathe, S.B.: A comparative analysis of methodologies for database schema integration. ACM Computing Surveys 18(4), 323–364 (1986)
5. Bernstein, P.A., Melnik, S.: Model management 2.0: Manipulating richer mappings. In: Proc. SIGMOD, Beijing, China, pp. 1–12 (2007)
6. Biskup, J., Convent, B.: A formal view integration method. In: Proc. SIGMOD, Washington, D.C, pp. 398–407 (1986)
7. Casanova, M.A., Vidal, V.M.P.: Towards a sound view integration methodology. In: Proc. PODS, Atlanta, GA, pp. 36–47. ACM, New York (1983)
8. Chiticariu, L., Kolaitis, P.G., Popa, L.: Interactive generation of integrated schemas. In: Proc. SIGMOD, pp. 833–846 (2008)
9. Fagin, R.: Inverting schema mappings. ACM Transactions on Database Systems 32(4) (2007)
10. Fagin, R., Kolaitis, P., Miller, R.J., Popa, L.: Data exchange: Semantics and query answering. Theoretical Computer Science 336, 89–124 (2005)
11. Imielinski, T., Lipski Jr., W.: Incomplete information in relational databases. J. ACM 31(4), 761–791 (1984)
12. Li, X., Quix, C., Kensche, D., Geisler, S.: Automatic schema merging using mapping constraints among incomplete sources. In: Proc. CIKM, pp. 299–308. ACM, New York (2010)
13. Li, X., Quix, C., Kensche, D., Geisler, S., Guo, L.: Automatic mediated schema generation through reasoning over data dependencies. In: Proc. ICDE (2011)
14. Melnik, S.: Generic Model Management: Concepts and Algorithms. PhD thesis, Universität Leipzig (2004)
15. Melnik, S., Bernstein, P.A., Halevy, A.Y., Rahm, E.: Supporting executable mappings in model management. In: Proc. SIGMOD, pp. 167–178. ACM Press, New York (2005)
16. Miller, R.J., Ioannidis, Y.E., Ramakrishnan, R.: The use of information capacity in schema integration and translation. In: Proc. VLDB, pp. 120–133 (1993)
17. Pottinger, R., Bernstein, P.A.: Schema merging and mapping creation for relational sources. In: Proc. EDBT (2008)
18. Quix, C., Kensche, D., Li, X.: Generic schema merging. In: Krogstie, J., Opdahl, A.L., Sindre, G. (eds.) CAiSE 2007 and WES 2007. LNCS, vol. 4495, pp. 127–141. Springer, Heidelberg (2007)
19. Radwan, A., Popa, L., Stanoi, I.R., Younis, A.A.: Top-k generation of integrated schemas based on directed and weighted correspondences. In: Proc. SIGMOD, pp. 641–654 (2009)
20. Sarma, A.D., Dong, X., Halevy, A.Y.: Bootstrapping pay-as-you-go data integration systems. In: Proc. SIGMOD, pp. 861–874 (2008)
21. Spaccapietra, S., Parent, C.: View integration: A step forward in solving structural conflicts. IEEE Transactions on Knowledge and Data Engineering 6(2), 258–274 (1994)
22. Spaccapietra, S., Parent, C., Dupont, Y.: Model independent assertions for integration of heterogeneous schemas. VLDB Journal 1(1), 81–126 (1992)

Ontology Evolution in Data Integration:
Query Rewriting to the Rescue

Haridimos Kondylakis and Dimitris Plexousakis

Information Systems Laboratory, FORTH-ICS
{kondylak,dp}@ics.forth.gr

Abstract. The evolution of ontologies is an undisputed necessity in ontology-based data integration. In such systems ontologies are used as global schema in order to formulate queries that are answered by the data integration systems. Yet, few research efforts have focused on addressing the need to reflect ontology evolution onto the underlying data integration systems. In most of these systems, when ontologies change their relations with the data sources, i.e., the mappings, are recreated manually, a process which is known to be error-prone and time-consuming. In this paper, we provide a solution that allows query answering under evolving ontologies without mapping redefinition. To achieve that, query rewriting techniques are exploited in order to produce equivalent rewritings among ontology versions. Whenever equivalent rewritings cannot be produced we a) guide query redefinition or b) provide the best "over-approximations". We show that our approach can greatly reduce human effort spent since continuous mapping redefinition on evolving ontologies is no longer necessary.

1 Introduction

The development of new scientific techniques and the emergence of high throughput tools have led to an information revolution. The amount, diversity, and heterogeneity of the information now available have led to the adoption of data integration systems in order to manage it and further process it. However, the integration of several data sources raises many semantic heterogeneity problems.

By accepting an ontology as a point of common reference, naming conflicts are eliminated and semantic conflicts are reduced. Ontologies are used to identify and resolve heterogeneity problems, usually at schema level, as a means for establishing an explicit formal vocabulary to share. During the last years, ontologies have been successfully used in database integration [1, 2].When using ontologies to integrate data, one is required to produce *mappings* [3], to link similar concepts or relationships from the ontology/ies to the sources by way of an equivalence. In practice, this process is done manually with the help of graphical user interfaces and it is a *time-consuming*, *labour-intensive* and *error-prone* activity [4].

Despite the great amount of work done in ontology-based data integration, an important problem that most of the systems tend to ignore is that ontologies are living artifacts and subject to change [3]. Due to the rapid development of research, ontologies are frequently changed to depict the new knowledge that is acquired. The

M. Jeusfeld, L. Delcambre, and T.W. Ling (Eds.): ER 2011, LNCS 6998, pp. 393–401, 2011.

problem that occurs is the following: when ontologies change, the mappings may become invalid and should somehow be updated or adapted.

However, as this evolution might happen too often, the overhead of redefining the mappings each time is significant. The approach, to recreate mappings from scratch each time the ontology evolves, is widely recognized to be problematic [4, 5], and instead, previously captured information should be reused. A nice overview of approaches trying to tackle similar problems can be found on [6] and [7]. The most relevant approaches that could be employed for resolving the problem of data integration with evolving ontologies is mapping adaptation [4] and mapping composition and inversion [8, 9] where mappings are changed automatically each time the ontology evolves. However, in mapping adaptation there is no guarantee that after repeatedly applying the algorithm, the semantics of the resulting mappings will be the desired ones and in mapping composition and inversion complex language of mappings should be employed (second-order dependencies) where the inversion is not guaranteed [8].

The lack of an ideal approach leads us to propose a new mechanism that builds on the current theoretical advances on the areas of ontology change [10] and query rewriting [2, 11] and incorporates and handles ontology evolution efficiently and effectively. More specifically:

- We present a data integration system, named *Evolving Data Integration (EDI)* system [12] that allows the evolution of the ontology used as global schema. Query answering in our system proceeds in two phases: a) query rewriting from the latest to the earlier ontology versions and b) query rewriting from one ontology version to the local schemata. Since query rewriting to the local schemata has been extensively studied [2, 11, 13], we focus on a layer above and we present only the query rewriting between ontology versions. The query processing in the first step consists of: i) *query expansion* that considers constraints coming from the ontology, and ii) *valid query rewriting* that uses the changes between two ontology versions to produce rewritings among them.

- In order to identify the changes between the ontology versions we adopt a high-level language of changes. The sequence of changes between the latest and the other ontology versions is produced automatically at setup time and then those changes are translated into logical *GAV mappings*. This translation enables *valid query rewriting* by *unfolding*.

- Despite the fact that query rewriting always terminates, the rewritten queries issued to other ontology versions might fail. This is because non-information preserving changes may have occurred (such as the deletion of a queried class). To tackle this problem, we propose two solutions: a) either to provide best "over-approximations" by means of *minimally-containing* and *minimally-generalized* queries, or b) to provide insights for the failure by means of *affecting change operation*, thus driving query redefinition.

The rest of the paper is organized as follows: Section 2 introduces the problem by an example and presents related work. Section 3 presents our system and elaborates on the aforementioned query rewriting among ontology versions. Finally, Section 4 provides a summary and an outlook for further research.

2 Evolving Data Integration

Consider the example RDF/S ontology shown on the left of Fig. 1. This ontology is used as a point of common reference, describing persons and their contact points ("*Cont.Point*"). We also have two relational databases DB1 and DB2 mapped to that version of the ontology. Assume now that the ontology designer decides to move the domain of the "*has_cont_point*" property from the class "*Actor*" to the class "*Person*", and to delete the literal "*gender*". Moreover, the "*street*" and the "*city*" properties are merged to the "*address*" property, and the literal "*name*" is renamed to the "*fullname*". Then, one new database DB3 is mapped to the new version of the ontology leading to two data integration systems that work independently. In such a setting we would like to issue queries formulated using any ontology version available. Moreover, we would like to retrieve answers from all underlying databases.

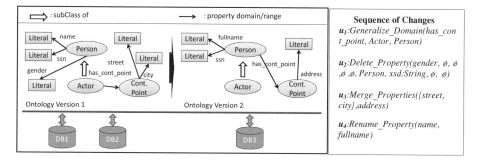

Fig. 1. The motivating example of an evolving ontology

We conceive an *Evolving Data Integration* (EDI) system as a collection of data integration systems, each one of them using a different ontology version as global schema. Therefore, we extend the traditional formalism [13] and define an EDI as:

Definition 2.1 (Evolving Data Integration System): *An EDI system I is a tuple of the form $((O_1, S_1, M_1), ..., (O_m, S_m, M_m))$ where O_i is a version of the ontology, S_i is a set of local sources and M_i is the mapping between S_i and O_i ($1 \leq i \leq m$)*

Next we discuss how the specific components are specialized in the context of an EDI. Considering O_i we restrict ourselves to *valid RDF/S knowledge bases*. The validity constraints [10] that we consider in this work concern mostly the *type uniqueness*, i.e., that each resource has a unique type, the *acyclicity* of the *subClassOf* and *subPropertyOf* relations and that the subject and object of the instance of some property should be correctly classified under the domain and range of the property, respectively. Those constraints are enforced in order to enable *unique* and *non-ambiguous* detection of the changes among the ontology versions.

Moreover, we consider as underlying data integration systems, those that integrate relational databases using an ontology as global schema. We choose such systems as the majority of information currently available is still stored on relational DBs[1].

For modeling ontology evolution we use a high-level language of changes that describes how an ontology version was derived from another ontology version. A high-level language is preferable than a low-level one [10], as it is more *intuitive, concise, closer to the intentions* of the ontology editors and *captures more accurately* the semantics of change. As we shall see later on, a high-level language is beneficial for our problem for two reasons: First, because the produced change log has a smaller size and most important because such a language yields logs that contain a smaller number of individual low-level deletions (which are non-information preserving) and this affects the effectiveness of our rewriting. In our work, a change operation is defined as follows:

Definition 2.2 (Change Operation): *A change operation u over O, is any tuple (δ_a, δ_d) where $\delta_a \cap O = \emptyset$ and $\delta_d \subseteq O$. A change operation u from O_1 to O_2 is a change operation over O_1 such that $\delta_a \subseteq O_2 \backslash O_1$ and $\delta_d \subseteq O_1 \backslash O_2$.*

Change	Rename_Property(a,b)	Split_Property(a,B)	Generalize_Domain(a,b,c)
δ_a	[(b, type, property)]	$\forall b_i \in B$: [(b_i, type, property)] ($1 \le i \le n$)	[(a, domain, c)]
δ_d	[(a, type, property)]	[(a, type, property)]	[(a, domain, b)]
Inverse	Rename_Property(b,a)	Merge_Properties(B, a)	Specialize_Domain(a, c, b)
GAV Mapping	$\forall x, y, a(x, y) \rightarrow b(x, y)$	$\forall x, y, a(x, y) \rightarrow \exists y_1, ..., y_n, b_1(x, y_1) \wedge ... \wedge b_n(x, y_n) \wedge\ concat(y, y_1, ..., y_n)\}$	$\forall x, a(b, x) \rightarrow a(c, x)$

Fig. 2. The definition of three change operations of our high-level language of changes

Obviously, δ_a and δ_d are sets of triples. For simplicity we will denote $\delta_a(u)$ the *added* and $\delta_d(u)$ the *deleted* triples of a change u. Several languages with high level change operations exists [10]. However, in order to be able to use such a language for query rewriting as we shall see in the sequel it is necessary the sequence of changes among two ontology versions to be *unique. Composition* and *inversion* are desirable but not obligatory properties that enhance the quality of the solution proposed. Such a high-level language of changes and the corresponding detection algorithm is presented in [10]. It contains over 70 types of change operations and the complete list can be found there. Hereafter, whenever we refer to a change operation, we mean a change operation from those proposed in [10]. The definition for some of the change operation under consideration, used also in Fig. 1, is presented in Fig. 2.

2.1 Query Processing

Queries to *I* are posed in terms of the global schema O_m. For querying, we adopt the SPARQL query language [14]. We chose SPARQL since it is currently the standard query language for the semantic web and has become an official W3C recommendation. In this paper, we do not consider *OPT* and *FILTER* operators since we leave it for future work. The remaining SPARQL fragment we consider here corresponds to union of conjunctive queries [14]. Continuing our example, assume that we would like to know the "*ssn*" and the "*fullname*" of all persons stored on our DBs and their corresponding address. The SPARQL query, formulated using the latter version of our example ontology is:

q_1: select ?SSN ?NAME ?ADDRESS where {?X type Person.   ?X ssn ?SSN.   ?X fullname ?NAME.
?X has_cont_point ?Y.   ?Y type Cont.Point.   ?Y address ?ADDRESS}

Using the semantics from [14] the algebraic representation of q_1 is equivalent to:

q_1: $\pi_{?SSN,?NAME,?ADDRESS}$((?X, type, Person) $\wedge$ (?X, ssn, ?SSN) $\wedge$ (?X, fullname, ?NAME) $\wedge$ (?X, has_cont_point, ?Y) $\wedge$ (?Y, type, Cont.Point) $\wedge$ (?Y, address, ?ADDRESS))

The query is submitted to the *"Evolution Module"* and query rewriting techniques are employed in order to rewrite queries among ontology versions. For more information on the used techniques, formal proofs, and more examples please refer to [7]. So, query rewriting is performed in two steps, namely: a) *query expansion* and b) *valid rewriting*.

In the first step, the query is expanded to take into account the constraints coming from the ontology. Query expansion amounts to rewriting the query q posed to the ontology version O_m into a new query $exp_{Om}(q)$, so that all the knowledge about the constraints in ontology has been "compiled" into $exp_{Om}(q)$. This is performed by constructing the *perfect rewriting* of q. Algorithms for computing the perfect rewriting of a query q w.r.t to a schema, have been presented in [2, 11]. In our work, we use the *QuOnto* system [2] in order to produce the perfect rewriting of our initial query. The time complexity of the algorithm is $O(S*(M+1)^2)^M$ [2], where S is the number of classes and properties in O_m and M is the number of triple patterns in q. For example, expanding q_1 by considering the transitive constraint of the *subClass* relation among the classes *"Person"* and *"Actor"* we get:

q_2: $\pi_{?SSN,?NAME,?ADDRESS}$ ((?X, type, Person) $\wedge$ (?X, ssn, ?SSN) $\wedge$ (?X, fullname, ?NAME) $\wedge$ (?X, has_cont_point, Y) $\wedge$ (?Y, type, Cont.Point) $\wedge$(?Y, address, ?ADDRESS))   U $\pi_{?SSN,?NAME,?ADDRESS}$ ((? (X, type, **Actor**) $\wedge$ (?X, ssn, ?SSN) $\wedge$ (?X, fullname, ?NAME) $\wedge$ (?X, has_cont_point, ?Y) $\wedge$ (?Y, type, Cont.Point) $\wedge$ (?Y, address, ?ADDRESS))

After query expansion, the query is transformed again to a new query called *valid rewriting*, i.e., $valid(exp_{Om}(q))$. To do that a) we first have to automatically construct the sequence of changes $E^{O2, O1}$ from O_2 to O_1 and then b) to interpret those changes as sound GAV mappings. To automatically get $E^{O2, O1}$ we can either use the algorithm from [10], or invert the $E^{O2, O1}$ since our language of changes possesses the property of inversion. Each one of those changes is then interpreted as sound GAV mappings. The $E^{O2, O1}$ of our example and the corresponding mappings are shown in Fig. 3.

$E^{O2, O1}$	Corresponding GAV Mappings
$inv(u_4)$:Rename_Property(fullname, name)	$inv(u_4)$:$\forall x, y, fullname(x, y) \rightarrow name(x, y)$
$inv(u_3)$:Split_Property(address, {street, city})	$inv(u_3)$:$\forall x, y, address(x, y) \rightarrow$
$inv(u_2)$:Add_Property(gender, $\emptyset$, $\emptyset$, $\emptyset$, $\emptyset$, Person, xsd:String, $\emptyset$, $\emptyset$)	$\exists y1, y2, street(x, y1) \wedge city(x, y2) \wedge concat(y, \{y_1, y_2\}$
	$inv(u_2)$: $\emptyset$
$inv(u_1)$:Specialize_Domain(has_cont_point, Person, Actor)	$inv(u_1)$:$\forall x, has\_cont\_point(Person, x) \rightarrow$
	$has\_cont\_point(Actor, x)$

Fig. 3. The sequence of changes from O2 to O1 and the corresponding GAV mappings

Note, that for the $inv(u_2)$ there is no GAV mapping constructed since we do not know where to map the deleted element. It becomes obvious that the lower the level of the language of changes used the more change operations won't have corresponding GAV mappings (since more low-level individual additions and deletions will appear).

When GAV mappings are used, as in our case, query rewriting is simply performed using *unfolding* [2]. This is a standard step in data integration [13] which trivially terminates and it is proved that it preserves soundness and completeness 11.

Moreover, due to the disjointness of the input and the output alphabet in a change operation, each GAV mapping acts in isolation on its input to produce its output. So we only need to scan the GAV mappings once in order to unfold the query and the time complexity of this step $O(N*M)$ where N is the number of change operations in the evolution log and M is the number of triple patterns in the query. Continuing our example, unfolding the query q_2 using the mappings from Fig. 3 will result to the following query:

q_3: $\pi_{?SSN, ?NAME, ?ADDRESS}$ ((?X, type, Actor) $\wedge$ (?X, ssn, ?SSN) $\wedge$ (?X, name, ?NAME) $\wedge$ (?X, has_contact_point, ?Y) $\wedge$ (?Y, type, Cont.Point) $\wedge$ (?Y, street, ?ADDRESS) $\wedge$ (?Y, city, ?ADDRESS))

Finally, our initial query will be rewritten to the union of q_3 (issued to the data integration system that uses O_1) and q_2 (issued to the data integration system that uses O_2). The queries will be issued to the underlying data integration systems and answers will be collected and returned to the user.

2.1.1 Non-Information Preserving Changes

Despite the fact that both query expansion and unfolding always terminate in our setting, problems may occur. Consider as an example the query q_4 that asks for the "*gender*" and the "*name*" of an "*Actor*", formulated using the ontology version O_1.

q_4: $\pi_{?NAME, ?GENDER}$ ((?X, type, Actor) $\wedge$ (?X, name, ?NAME) $\wedge$ (?X, gender, ?GENDER))

Trying to rewrite the query q_4 to the ontology version O_2 our system will first expand it. Then it will consider the GAV mappings produced from the sequence of changes as they have been presented in Fig. 1. So, the query q_5 will be produced by unfolding using the mapping: $\forall x, y, name(x, y) \rightarrow fullname(x, y)$.

q_5: $\pi_{?AME, ?GENDER}$ ((?X, type, Actor) $\wedge$ (?X, **fullname**, ?NAME) $\wedge$ (?X, gender, ?GENDER))

However, it is obvious that the query produced will not provide any answers when issued to the data integration system that uses O_2 since the "*gender*" literal no longer exists in O_2. This happens because the u_2 change operation is not *information preserving change* among the ontology versions. It deletes information from O_1 without providing the knowledge that this information is transferred on another part of the ontology. This is also the reason that low-level change operations (simple triple addition or deletion) are not enough to dictate query rewriting.

Although, this might be considered as a problem, actually it is not, since if we miss the literal "*gender*" in version O_2 this would mean that we have no data in the underlying local databases for that literal. But even then, we provide two solutions to the users.

The first option is to notify the user that some underlying data integration systems were not possible to answer their queries and present the reasons for that. For our example query q_5, our system will report that the data integration system that uses O_2 will fail to produce an answer because the literal "*gender*" does not exist in that ontology version. To identify the change operations that lead to such a result we define the notion of *affecting change operations*.

Definition 2.3 (Affecting change operation): *A change operation $u \in E^{O1,O2}$ affects the query q, denoted by $u \Diamond q$, iff: 1)$\delta_d(u)=\phi$ and 2) there exists triple pattern $t \in q$ that can be unified with a triple of $\delta_d(u)$.*

The first condition ensures that the operation deletes information from the ontology without replacing it with other information, thus the specific change operation is not information preserving. However, we are not interested in general for the change operations that are not information preserving. We specifically target those change operations that change the ontology part which corresponds to our query (condition 2). In order to identify those change operations that affect user query, we have to scan the evolution log once for each query triple pattern. Users can use that information in order to re-specify the input query if desired. Besides providing an explanation for the failure, we can also provide the best *"over-approximations"*. The first solution here is the *minimally-containing rewriting*.

Definition 2.4 (Minimally-Containing Rewriting): *A query q' is a minimally-containing rewriting of a conjunctive query q using a set of mappings E if and only if (1) q' is a containing rewriting of q (q $\subseteq$ q') and (2) there exists no containing rewriting q'' of q using E, such that the expansion of q'' contains the expansion of q'.*

It is thus the best *"over-approximation"* of q and it is dual to the *"maximally-contained rewriting"* [15] which is the best *"under-approximation"* of q. The algorithm for identifying the minimally-containing rewriting for a conjunctive query q and it is an extension of the simplified version of *Chase/Backchase* [15]. It runs by deleting the conjuncts that do not belong to the current vocabulary of the ontology and its correctness is proved in [7].In our example the algorithm for producing the minimally-containing query would produce query q_6 by deleting the triple pattern *(?X, gender, ?GENDER)* which in not included in the vocabulary of O_2.

q_6: $\pi_{?NAME,?GENDER}(\ (?X, type, Actor) \wedge (?X, fullname, ?NAME))$

However, the resulted query is not safe, since the variable *?GENDER* does not exist in the query body, thus a minimally-containing rewriting cannot be produced in this case. Cases like the previous one, led us to search for another aspect of over-approximation. Our solution here is that when a change operation *affects* a query rewriting, we can check if there is a *parent* triple $t\Box$ in the current ontology version which is not deleted in the next ontology version. If such a triple exists, we can ask for that triple instead, thus providing *a generalized query*.

Definition 2.5 (Generalized query): *Let q a conjunctive query expressed using O_1. We call q_{GEN} a generalized query of q over $E^{O1,O2}$ iff: 1) q is contained in q_{GEN} (q $\subseteq q_{GEN}$) and 2)it does not exist $u \in E^{O1,O2}$ such that $u \Diamond q_{GEN}$.*

Definition 2.6 (Minimally-Generalized query): *A generalized query q_{GEN} of q over $E^{O1,O2}$ is called minimal if there is not q_{GEN}' such that q $\subseteq q_{GEN}'$ and $q_{GEN}' \subseteq q_{GEN}$.*

The idea of minimally-generalized query is that it is a query that can be answered on the evolved ontology version after applying the minimum number of *"repairs"* on the query in order to achieve that. However, in this case the repairs are applied using only the knowledge of the current ontology version and the change log. We have to note, that minimally-generalized queries may not be unique since a deleted property might have several *superProperties*. Assuming a ordering between them (lexicographical for example) identifying a minimally-generalized rewriting requires a slight extension of the algorithm for retrieving the affecting change operations and is not presented due to space limitations. Consider for example, an alternative ontology version O_1, where the *"personal_info"* is a *superProperty* of the *"gender"* property. Assume also the same sequence of changes $E^{O1,O2}$ as shown in Fig. 3. Then, if q_8 previously described is issued, we are able to identify that the triple *"Actor, gender, xsd:String"* has been deleted and look for a minimally q_{GEN} that is:

$$q_{11}: \pi_{?NAME,?GENDER} (\; (?X, type, Actor) \wedge (?X, fullname, ?NAME) \wedge (?X, personal\_info, ?GENDER)$$

3   Conclusion

In this paper, we argue that ontology evolution is a reality and data integration systems should be aware and ready to deal with that. To that direction, we presented a novel approach that allows query answering under evolving ontologies without mapping redefinition. Our architecture is based on a module that can be placed on top of any traditional ontology-based data integration system, enabling ontology evolution. The great benefit of our approach is the *simplicity*, *modularity* and the *short deployment* time it requires. It is only a matter of providing a new ontology version to our system to be able to use it to formulate queries that will be answered by data integration systems independent of the ontology version used.

As future work, several challenging issues need to be further investigated. For example, local schemata may evolve as well, and the ontologies used as global schema may contain inconsistencies. An interesting topic would be to extend our approach for OWL ontologies or to handle the full expressiveness of the SPARQL language. It becomes obvious that ontology evolution in data integration is an important topic and several challenging issues remain to be investigated in the future.

References

1. Calvanese, D., De Giacomo, G., Lembo, D., Lenzerini, M., Poggi, A., Rodriguez-Muro, M., Rosati, R.: Ontologies and databases: The *DL-lite* approach. In: Tessaris, S., Franconi, E., Eiter, T., Gutierrez, C., Handschuh, S., Rousset, M.-C., Schmidt, R.A. (eds.) Reasoning Web. LNCS, vol. 5689, pp. 255–356. Springer, Heidelberg (2009)
2. Poggi, A., Lembo, D., Calvanese, D., Giacomo, G.D., Lenzerini, M., Rosati, R.: Linking data to ontologies. Journal on data semantics X, 133-173 (2008)
3. Flouris, G., Manakanatas, D., Kondylakis, H., Plexousakis, D., Antoniou, G.: Ontology change: Classification and survey. Knowl. Eng. Rev. 23, 117–152 (2008)
4. Velegrakis, Y., Miller, J., Popa, L.: Preserving mapping consistency under schema changes. The VLDB Journal 13, 274–293 (2004)
5. Curino, C.A., Moon, H.J., Ham, M., Zaniolo, C.: The PRISM Workwench: Database Schema Evolution without Tears. In: ICDE, pp. 1523–1526 (2009)
6. Kondylakis, H., Flouris, G., Plexousakis, D.: Ontology and schema evolution in data integration: Review and assessment. In: Meersman, R., Dillon, T., Herrero, P. (eds.) OTM 2009. LNCS, vol. 5871, pp. 932–947. Springer, Heidelberg (2009)

7. Kondylakis, H.: Ontology Evolution in Data Integration. PhD Thesis, Computer Science Department. University of Crete, Heraklion (2010)
8. Fagin, R., Kolaitis, P.G., Popa, L., Tan, W.-C.: Schema Mapping Evolution through Composition and Inversion. Schema Matching and Mapping. Springer, Heidelberg (2011)
9. Curino, C.A., Moon, H.J., Zaniolo, C.: Graceful database schema evolution: the PRISM workbench. PVLDB 1, 761–772 (2008)
10. Papavassiliou, V., Flouris, G., Fundulaki, I., Kotzinos, D., Christophides, V.: On detecting high-level changes in RDF/S kBs. In: Bernstein, A., Karger, D.R., Heath, T., Feigenbaum, L., Maynard, D., Motta, E., Thirunarayan, K. (eds.) ISWC 2009. LNCS, vol. 5823, pp. 473–488. Springer, Heidelberg (2009)
11. Cali, A., Gottlob, G., Lukasiewicz, T.: Datalog+-: a unified approach to ontologies and integrity constraints. In: ICDT, pp. 14–30. ACM, St. Petersburg (2009)
12. Kondylakis, H., Dimitris, P.: Exelixis: Evolving Ontology-Based Data Integration System. In: SIGMOD, pp. 1283-1286 (2011)
13. Lenzerini, M.: Data integration: a theoretical perspective. In: PODS (2002)
14. Perez, J., Arenas, M., Gutierrez, C.: Semantics and complexity of SPARQL. ACM Trans. Database Syst. 34, 1–45 (2009)
15. Deutsch, A., Popa, L., Tannen, V.: Query reformulation with constraints. SIGMOD Rec 35, 65–73 (2006)

Object-Oriented XML Keyword Search

Huayu Wu and Zhifeng Bao

School of Computing, National University of Singapore
{wuhuayu,baozhife}@comp.nus.edu.sg

Abstract. Existing LCA-based XML keyword search approaches are not aware of the significance of using semantics of object to improve search efficiency and quality during LCA-based computation. In this paper, we propose a novel object-oriented approach for XML keyword search. In each step of our approach, i.e., labeling an XML document, constructing related indexes and searching for relevant LCA nodes, we use the semantics of object. We theoretically and experimentally show the superiority our semantic approach over existing approaches.

1 Introduction

XML keyword search is a user-friendly way to query XML database. The most common way to process XML keyword queries is adopting inverted lists to index data nodes in an XML document and perform *lowest common ancestor* (*LCA*) [4] based computation with the inverted lists. There are many subsequent works to either improve the search efficiency of LCA-based approach (e.g., [6]), or improve the search quality (e.g., [5]). However, all the LCA-based search algorithms only focus on checking the structural relationship between query keywords, but do not consider the semantic relationship between them, i.e., the relationship among object, property and value. Without noticing such information, the LCA-based computation may perform redundant searches and return less meaningful result, as discussed in Section 2.2.

In this paper, we propose an Object-Oriented Keyword Search approach, named *OOKS*, to process XML keyword queries in data-centric XML data. The core idea of our approach is to incorporate semantic information, i.e., object, property and value, into LCA-based keyword search. In particular, we construct indexes, i.e., inverted lists and relational tables, in an object-oriented manner, and process XML keyword queries with those indexes in an OO manner as well.

2 Background and Motivation

2.1 Background

The Lowest Common Ancestor (LCA) of a set of nodes S is the common ancestor of the nodes in S, and does not have a descendant node to also be a common ancestor of these nodes. In an XML tree, normally we assign a Dewey ID [1]

M. Jeusfeld, L. Delcambre, and T.W. Ling (Eds.): ER 2011, LNCS 6998, pp. 402–410, 2011.
© Springer-Verlag Berlin Heidelberg 2011

to each node and the LCA of a set of nodes has the Dewey ID of the longest common prefix of the Dewey IDs for these nodes.

For each keyword k, the Dewey IDs of the nodes matching k are stored in an inverted list. XML keyword search focuses on finding the relevant LCAs of the inverted lists of all query keywords. A node is an LCA of a set of inverted lists $\{I_1,..., I_m\}$ if this node is the LCA of $\{u_1,...,u_m\}$ where $u_i \in I_i$ for $1 \leq i \leq m$.

Example 1. The inverted lists for the keywords in the query {book, XML, author} are shown in Fig. 3(a). The LCAs of the three lists include 1, 1.1.2, and 1.1.2.19 etc. In particular, node 1 is the LCA of *book* 1.1.2.1, *XML* 1.1.2.19.1.1 and *author* 1.2.2.1.2.   □

Intuitively the correct answer to the query in Example 1 is book 1.1.2.19, but LCA returns a lot of false answers. To achieve a good search quality, many improved semantics based on LCA are proposed (e.g., [3][10]). In our approach we propose a new semantics SLCOA (discussed later) by incorporating object into SLCA [10]. The SLCA of a set of inverted lists is the LCA node of these inverted lists which has no descendant to also be an LCA of these lists. In Example 1, the SLCA of the inverted lists only returns the correct answer 1.1.2.19.

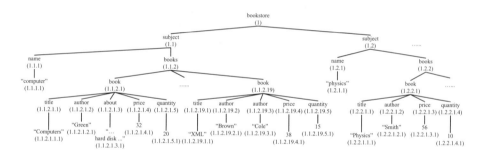

Fig. 1. An example XML document with Dewey IDs for all nodes

2.2   Motivation

We discuss the problems in existing LCA-based XML keyword search approaches which motivate our research.

Efficiency Problems
The LCA-based approach may involve redundant inverted list search. For the example document in Fig. 1, every "book" node corresponds to an object that contains a property "title". To process the query {book, title} which finds all book titles, we actually do not need to scan the inverted list for "title" during LCA-based computation. For another example, consider a query {book, title, XML} to find the books with title of "XML". Suppose there are 100 *title* elements, then we have to consider all 100 Dewey IDs in the inverted list of *title* during LCA searching, though only one of them matches the value of "XML".

Search Quality Problems

Many keyword queries have different interpretations, or say search intentions. A query {physics} may search for a book with title of "Physics", or a subject with name of "physics". Most existing XML keyword search approaches mix different interpretations during query processing, and a user may have difficulty in filtering the mixed results based on his/her search intention. Also using inverted lists, the existing XML keyword search algorithms cannot perform advanced search efficiently, such as range search and phrase search.

3   Object-Oriented Indexes

In this section, we present the OO-based indexes used in our approach. The discussion of object semantics can be found in our technical report [8].

3.1   OO-Dewey ID and Object Tables

Different from existing LCA-based approaches that assign Dewey ID to every document node, OOKS assigns Dewey ID to object nodes (as well as the root) only, thus we also call it OO-Dewey ID[1]. All non-object internal nodes inherit the Dewey ID of the its lowest ancestor object node. Fig. 2 is the OO-Dewey ID assignment for the document in Fig. 1, which contains only two object classes, *subject* and *book*. Using OO-Dewey ID labeling, we can significantly reduce the number of labeled nodes, as shown by comparing Fig. 1 and Fig. 2.

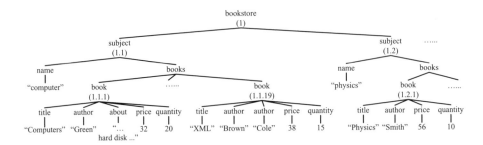

Fig. 2. Document with OO-Dewey ID assignment (only object nodes are labeled)

We only put the Dewey IDs for non-value document nodes into inverted lists, and all the inverted lists are built in object-oriented fashion. The object-oriented inverted lists for "book", "author" and "about" are shown in Fig. 3(b), where the traditional inverted lists are shown in Fig. 3(a). Since we only use object labels, many properties with cardinality of 1 or + to its object, e.g. "author", have the same inverted list as the object.

---

[1] For convenience, we still use *Dewey ID* for *OO-Dewey ID* in later explanations.

book	→	1.1.2.1, ..., 1.1.2.19, 1.2.2.1, ...
XML	→	1.1.2.19.1.1
author	→	1.1.2.1.2, ..., 1.1.2.19.2, 1.1.2.19.3, 1.2.2.1.2, ...

(a) Normal inverted list

book	
book/author	
book/about	→	1.1.1, ...

1.1.1, ..., 1.1.19, 1.2.1, ...

(b) OO inverted list

Fig. 3. Inverted lists in normal LCA-based approaches and in our OO approach

Values are put into relational tables. The relational tables are also object-oriented. For each object class we maintain a table with columns of Dewey ID and its single-valued properties. We call it *object table*. For multi-valued property, e.g., "author", we maintain an object/property table. The example tables for "book" in the document in Fig. 2 are shown in Fig. 4(a). The details of object table construction and problem handling are discussed in [9].

3.2   Other Object-Based Indexes

We assign each type of object and property a numeric ID. We have a hash table to check whether a keyword refers to an object or a property, and return the numeric ID correspondingly. We also maintain Object Attachment Bitmap (OAB) to quickly find by which object classes a given property type is contained, and Containment Index (CI) to match each value to the objects and properties containing it. The details of OAB and CI can be found in [8].

R_{book}

OO-Dewey	Title	About	Price	Quantity
1.1.1	Computers	... hard disk ...	32	20
...	...	...	...	...
1.1.19	XML	null	38	15
...	...	...	...	...
1.2.1	Physics	null	56	10
...	...	...	...	...

$R_{book/author}$

OO-Dewey	Value
1.1.1	Green
...	...
1.1.19	Brown
1.1.19	Cole
...	...
1.2.1	Smith
...	...

$R_{subject}$

OO-Dewey	Name
1.1	computer
...	...

(a) Tables for *book*

(b) Tables for *subject*

Fig. 4. Object tables for *book* and *subject*

4   OO Keyword Query Processing

The object-oriented keyword query processing in our approach has four steps:

1. Partition the keywords in the query based on different objects. Ambiguous queries with different keyword attaching ways are handled.
2. In each partition, filter the Dewey IDs in the corresponding inverted list using object tables, based on property and value constraints in the partition.

3. Find the smallest lowest common object ancestor (SLCOA) of the inverted lists for different partitions.
4. Identify output information and return result using object tables.

4.1   Step 1: Keyword Partitioning

Definition 1. *(**Keyword Partition**) A partition is a group of keywords in a keyword query that contains one object[2], together with a set of properties or property/value pairs that belong to the object. We use (*object, [property$_1$[/value$_1$], property$_2$[/value$_2$]...]*) to represent each partition.*

In a keyword query, we create a partition for each object involved. E.g., there are two partitions for the query {subject, XML}, as there are two objects, *subject* and *book*, involved. Then we put the query keywords into the corresponding partitions. This process is called keyword partitioning. The partitioned query in this example becomes {(subject), (book, title/XML)}. We design a model-driven mechanism (shown in our technical report [8]) to partition query keywords.

Generally, there are two phases when we partition the keywords in a query: attaching each value keyword to properties and objects, and attaching each unattached property keyword to objects. The keyword attaching is performed with the *CI* and *OAB*. The details of keyword partitioning can be found in our technical report [8]. It is possible that a query is ambiguous with different attaching ways for a value keyword or a property keyword. We discuss such ambiguous cases in our technical report as well.

Example 2. The query {subject, physics} to the document in Fig. 2 is unambiguous. We attach the value keyword *physics* to the object *subject* with the implicit property *name*. The final partition is {(subject, name/physics)}.   □

A special case is that multiple value keywords correspond to the same property type of the same object class. Then we consider both cases of using one partition and using multiple partitions for multiple property/value pairs.

Example 3. In the query {Brown, Cole}, both value keywords belong to book/author. The query is partitioned as {(book, author/Brown, author/Cole)} and {(book, author/Brown), (book, author/Cole)}. The first interpretation finds the book co-authored by the two people, while the second interpretation finds the common information (i.e., subject) of the books written by the two authors.   □

For ambiguous queries, we design an algorithm to rank different interpretations in [8].

4.2   Step 2: Inverted List Filtering

For a query with keywords partitioned based on objects, we filter the Dewey IDs in the inverted list for each partition. We consider the three cases regarding the occurrences of properties and values in each partition separately.

---

[2] We simply refer to object (or property) keyword as object (or property), for short.

- Case (1): The partition contains only the object. We use the inverted list of that object.
- Case (2): The partition contains both the object and properties, but no value. If there is only one property, we use the inverted list for that property. Otherwise, we take the intersection of the inverted lists for the properties.
- Case (3): Both properties and values appear with the object in the partition. For the object *obj* in this partition, we get the Dewey IDs from the object table R_{obj} based on the constraints on the properties and values.

Inverted list filtering can reduce the size of relevant inverted lists, which makes later operations on inverted lists more efficient. When there are value keywords in a query, which frequently happens in practice, the inverted list reduction for relevant objects is more significant, due to the high selectivity of value keywords on specific properties.

Example 4. The query {book, XML, subject, name} contains two partitions after keyword partitioning: {(book, title/XML), (subject, name)}. The first partition has both property *title* and value *XML* with the object *book*, so by Case (3) we select the Dewey IDs from R_{book} based on *title="XML"*. For the second partition, we just use the inverted list for subject/name. Now we only use two inverted lists to process this query, while other approaches use five inverted lists for the five keywords. Furthermore, the inverted list for *book* contains only a few Dewey IDs due to the high selectivity on the property *title*. □

4.3   Step 3: SLCOA Processing

When a keyword query involves two or more objects, after simplifying the query with only objects left, we still need to perform an LCA-based computation among the query objects in the document. We propose a Smallest Lowest Common Object Ancestor (SLCOA) semantics based on our OO document labeling. The rationale of finding SLCOA is that we ensure all the relevant LCA nodes found are object nodes, which are more meaningful as return nodes.

Definition 2. *(**LCOA of nodes**) Given m nodes u_1, u_2,..., u_m, node v is called a Lowest Common Object Ancestor (LCOA) of these m nodes, iff (1) v is a common ancestor of all these nodes, (2) v is an object node, and (3) v does not have any descendant object node w which is also a common ancestor of all these nodes. We denote v as $LCOA(u_1, u_2,..., u_m)$.*

Proposition 1. *The LCA of a set of nodes has the same Dewey ID as the LCOA of these nodes.*

Based on our labeling scheme, each non-object node inherits the Dewey ID of its lowest ancestor object node. Thus the Proposition 1 holds (detailed proof is omitted). In the document in Fig. 2, the LCA of two *book* nodes 1.1.1 and 1.1.19 is the node *books* 1.1, while the LCOA of the two *book* nodes is *subject* 1.1. Obviously the LCOA is more meaningful than the LCA as a result node.

Definition 3. *(**LCOA of sets of nodes**) Given m keywords k_1, k_2,..., k_m, and m sets of nodes I_1, I_2,..., I_m such that $\forall 1 \leq i \leq m$, I_i stores a list of nodes matching k_i. Node v belongs to the LCOA of the m sets iff $\exists u_1 \in I_1$, $u_2 \in I_2$,..., $u_m \in I_m$, such that $v = LCOA(u_1, u_2,..., u_m)$. We denote $v \in LCOA(I_1, I_2,..., I_m)$.*

Definition 4. *(**SLCOA of sets of nodes**) A Smallest Lowest Common Object Ancestor (SLCOA) v of m sets of nodes I_1,..., I_m is defined as (1) $v \in LCOA(I_1,..., I_m)$, and (2) v does not have any descendant $w \in LCOA(I_1,..., I_m)$.*

In this step, we find the SLCOA of the reduced inverted lists for the partitions in a query. We can use all the existing efficient SLCA computation algorithms to compute SLCOA, because of Proposition 1.

4.4   Step 4: Result Return

Output Information Identification. Normally a query aims to find the information of a certain object(s), so we infer the meaningful output information based on object. We propose rules in [8] to determine what information should be returned for a keyword query. Generally, we reuse the concept of SLCOA for output information inference. We check the SLCOA of query objects in the structural summary of the XML document. If the SLCOA belongs to a new object class from the objects involved in the query, we will return that SLCOA object. Otherwise, we will return the object in the query partition without property or value, or return the object property containing no value in its partition.

Value Extraction. When the output is an object, we access the object table for that object, and select all the properties and corresponding values based on the Dewey IDs. If the output is a property, we access the corresponding object table and get the property value based on both the Dewey ID and the property name.

4.5   Advanced Search

Inefficient support to *range search* is a shortcoming for most inverted list based algorithms. For example, to process a query to find the book with price less than 50, one possible way for existing works is to find all the numeric keywords with values less than 50 and combine their inverted lists. Obviously it is inefficient. To perform *Phrase search* in XML data, existing works have to adopt a similar technique as in IR [7] to index all phrases, which is very space costly.

OOKS stores values in relational tables. Then the range queries and the phrase queries can be easily performed by SQL selection.

5   Experiments

5.1   Experimental Settings

All algorithms were performed on a dual-core 2.33GHz processor with 3.5G RAM. We use three data sets: DBLP (91MB), XMark (6MB), and a real-life course data set (2MB)[3]. We compare OOKS to several existing algorithms, as mentioned later. We use eight unambiguous meaningful queries for each data set to evaluate efficiency and search quality. We also test the ability of OOKS to return results based on different search intentions for ambiguous queries (including our ranking method). In this paper, we only show the experimental result for unambiguous queries in this paper. The query details and the result for ambiguous query test and index analysis can be found in our technical report [8].

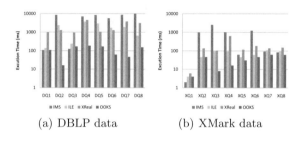

(a) DBLP data   (b) XMark data

Fig. 5. Query processing efficiency comparison

5.2 Efficiency

We compare OOKS with two LCA-based algorithms: Incremental Multiway-SLCA (IMS) [6] and Indexed Lookup Eager (ILE) [10] for efficiency test. IMS introduces anchor node semantics to skip redundant node search, while ILE introduces index to accelerate inverted list scans. They are two representative approaches to improve SLCA search. We also compare to an IR-style algorithm XReal [2]. We choose a larger data set (DBLP) and a smaller data set (XMark) for evaluation. The result is shown in Fig. 5(a) and 5(b). In OOKS, we use ILE to compute SLCOA.

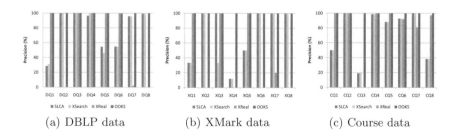

(a) DBLP data   (b) XMark data   (c) Course data

Fig. 6. Search precision comparison

5.3 Search Quality

We evaluate the search quality of OOKS in comparison with other approaches: SLCA, XSEarch [3] and XReal. Especial to be mentioned is XReal, which is a ranking based keyword search algorithm. We take top k results from XReal, where k is the number of expected answers. If there is only 1 expected answer and the first returned result from XReal is not that answer, we use top 5 results from XReal to compute precision, instead of returning 0. The recall value is very high for all approaches, or say all approaches can find the correct answers, but may introduce false positives as noises. Then we only compare the precision, as shown in Fig. 6. More explanations of the result are presented in [8].

6 Conclusion

We propose OOKS, a novel object-oriented approach for XML keyword search. In our approach, we label an XML document, construct related indexes and process XML keyword queries in an object-oriented way. Compared to some existing approaches, both query processing efficiency and search quality are improved in OOKS, as shown in our experiments. Furthermore, by introducing relational table for values, our approach can perform advanced search more efficiently.

Acknowledgement. The work of Zhifeng Bao was in part supported by the Singapore Ministry of Education Grant No. R252-000-394-112 under the project name of UTab.

References

1. http://www.mtsu.edu/~vvesper/dewey2.htm
2. Bao, Z., Ling, T.W., Chen, B., Lu, J.: Efficient XML keyword search with relevance oriented ranking. In: ICDE, pp. 517–528 (2009)
3. Cohen, S., Mamou, J., Kanza, Y., Sagiv, Y.: XSEarch: A semantic search engine for XML. In: VLDB, pp. 45–56 (2003)
4. Guo, L., Shao, F., Botev, C., Shanmugasundaram, J.: XRANK: Ranked keyword search over XML documents. In: SIGMOD Conference, pp. 16–27 (2003)
5. Li, Y., Yu, C., Jagadish, H.V.: Schema-free XQuery. In: VLDB, pp. 72–83 (2004)
6. Sun, C., et al.: Multiway SLCA-based keyword search in XML data. In: WWW, pp. 1043–1052 (2007)
7. Williams, H.E., et al.: Fast phrase querying with combined indexes. ACM Trans. Inf. Syst. 22(4), 573–594 (2004)
8. Wu, H., Ling, T.W., Bao, Z., Xu, L.: Object-oriented XML keyword search. TRA7/10, Technical Report, School of Computing, National University of Singapore (July 2010)
9. Wu, H., Ling, T.-W., Chen, B.: VERT: A semantic approach for content search and content extraction in XML query processing. In: Parent, C., Schewe, K.-D., Storey, V.C., Thalheim, B. (eds.) ER 2007. LNCS, vol. 4801, pp. 534–549. Springer, Heidelberg (2007)
10. Xu, Y., Papakonstantinou, Y.: Efficient keyword search for smallest LCAs in XML databases. In: SIGMOD Conference, pp. 537–538 (2005)

A Hidden Markov Model Approach to Keyword-Based Search over Relational Databases*

Sonia Bergamaschi[1], Francesco Guerra[1], Silvia Rota[1], and Yannis Velegrakis[2]

[1] Università di Modena e Reggio Emilia
firstname.lastname@unimore.it
[2] University of Trento
velgias@disi.unitn.eu

Abstract. We present a novel method for translating keyword queries over relational databases into SQL queries with the same intended semantic meaning. In contrast to the majority of the existing keyword-based techniques, our approach does not require any a-priori knowledge of the data instance. It follows a probabilistic approach based on a Hidden Markov Model for computing the top-K best mappings of the query keywords into the database terms, i.e., tables, attributes and values. The mappings are then used to generate the SQL queries that are executed to produce the answer to the keyword query. The method has been implemented into a system called KEYRY (from KEYword to queRY).

1 Introduction

Keyword searching is becoming the de-facto standard for information searching, mainly due to its simplicity. For textual information, keyword query answering has been extensively studied, especially in the area of information retrieval [14]. However, for structured data, it has only recently received considerable attention [5,12]. The existing techniques for keyword searching over structured sources heavily rely on an a-priori instance-analysis that scans the whole data instance and constructs some index, a symbol table or some structure of that kind which is later used during run time to identify the parts of the database in which each keyword appears. This limits the application of these approaches to only cases where direct a-priori access to the data is possible.

There is a great deal of structured data sources that do not allow any direct access to their own contents. Mediator-based systems, for example, typically build a virtual integrated view of a set of data sources. The mediator only exposes the integrated schema and accesses the contents of the data sources at query execution time. Deep web databases are another example of sources that do not generally expose their full content, but offer only a predefined set of queries that can be answered, i.e., through web forms, or expose only their schema information. Even when the access to the data instance is allowed, it is not practically feasible in a web-scale environment to retrieve all the contents of the sources in order to build an index. The scenario gets even worst

---

* This work was partially supported by project "Searching for a needle in mountains of data"
http://www.dbgroup.unimo.it/keymantic

M. Jeusfeld, L. Delcambre, and T.W. Ling (Eds.): ER 2011, LNCS 6998, pp. 411–420, 2011.
© Springer-Verlag Berlin Heidelberg 2011

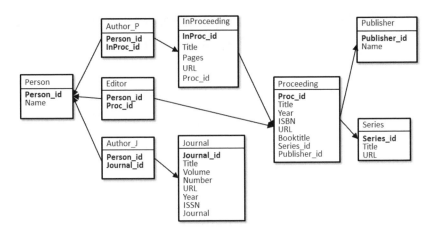

Fig. 1. A fragment of the DBLP schema

when the data source contents are subject to frequent updates, as it happens, for instance, in e-commerce sites, forums/blogs, social networks, etc.

In this paper we present an approach, implemented in the KEYRY (from KEYword to queRY) prototype system, for keyword searching that does not assume any knowledge about the data source contents. The only requirement is for the source to provide a schema, even a loosely described, for its data. Semantics, extracted directly from the data source schema, are used to discover the intended meaning of the keywords in a query and to express it in terms of the underlying source structures. The result of the process is an interpretation of the user query in the form of a SQL query that will be executed by the DBMS managing the source. Notice that there are many interpretations of a keyword query in terms of the underlying data source schemas, some more likely and other less likely to capture the semantics that the user had in mind when she was formulating the keyword query. As usual in keyword based searching systems, assigning a ranking is a critical task since it avoids the users to deal with uninteresting results. One of the innovative aspects of our approach is that we adopt a probabilistic approach based on a Hidden Markov Model (HMM) for mapping user keywords into database terms (names of tables and attributes, domains of attributes). Using a HMM allows us to model two important aspects of the searching process: the order of the keywords in a query (this is represented by means of the HMM *transition probabilities*) and the probabilities of associating a keyword to different database terms (by means of the HMM *emission probabilities*). A HMM typically has to be trained in order to optimize its parameters. We propose a method providing a parameter setting not relying on any training data. In particular, we developed some heuristic rules that applied to the database schema provide the transition probabilities. Moreover, we approximated the emission probability by means of similarity measures (we use string similarity for measuring the distance between keywords and schema elements and regular expressions for evaluating the domain compatibilities, but our approach is independent of the measure adopted). Finally, we developed a variation of the HITS algorithm [9], typically exploited for ranking web pages on the basis of the links among them, for computing an authority score for each database term. We consider these scores as the *initial state probabilities* required by the HMM.

More specifically, our key contributions are the following: (i) we propose a new probabilistic approach based on a HMM for keyword based searching over databases that does not require to build indexes over the data instance; (ii) we develop a method for providing a parameter setting allowing keyword searching without any training data and (iii) we exploit the List Viterbi algorithm that decodes the HMM in order to obtain the top-K results.

The remainder of the paper is as follows. Section 2 is an overview of our approach for keyword-based searching over databases. The problem is formalized in Section 3 and our proposal is described in Section 4. Section 5 describes related work and we conclude in Section 6 with a brief wrap up and some suggestions for future work.

2   KEYRY at a Glance

A keyword in a keyword query may in principle be found in any database term (i.e., as the name of some schema term (table or attribute) or as a value in its respective domain). This gives rise to a large number of possible mappings of each query keyword into database term. These mappings are referred to as *configurations*. Since no access to the data source instance is assumed, selecting the top-K configurations that better represents the intended semantics of the keyword query is a challenging task.

Figure 1 illustrates a fragment of a relational version of the DBLP database[1]. The keywords in a query may be associated to different database terms, representing different semantics of the keyword query. For instance, a user may be interested in the papers written by Garcia-Molina published in a journal on 2011 and poses the query consisting of the three keywords `Garcia-Molina`, `journal` and `2011`. The keyword `journal` should be mapped into the table *Journal*, `2011` into the domain of the attribute *Year* in the *Journal* table, and `Garcia-Molina` should be an element of the domain of the attribute *Name* in the table *Person*. If we do not know the intended meaning of the user query, we may attribute different semantics to the keywords, e.g. `2011` might be the number of a page or part of the ISSN journal number. Not all the keywords may be mapped into all the database terms: certain mappings are actually more likely than other. Since KEYRY does not have any access to the data instance, we exploit the HMM *emission probabilities* to rank the likelihood of each possible mapping between a keyword and a database term. In our approach, we approximate the emission probabilities by means of similarity measures based on semantics extracted from the source schema (e.g. names of attributes and tables, attribute domains, regular expressions).

Moreover, based on known patterns of human behavior [8], we know that keywords related to the same topic are typically close to each other in a query. Consequently, adjacent keywords are typically associated to close database terms, i.e. terms that are part of the same table or belong to tables connected through foreign keys. For example, in the previous query the mapping of the keyword `journal` into the table *Journal* increases the likelihood that `2011` is mapped into the domain of an attribute of the table *Journal*. The HMM *transition probabilities*, that we estimate on the basis of heuristic

---

[1] `http://www.informatik.uni-trier.de/~ley/db/`

rules applied to the database schema, allows KEYRY to model this aspect. Section 4 describes how KEYRY computes the top-K configurations that better approximate the intended meaning of a user query.

Then, the possible paths joining the database terms in a configuration have to be computed. Different paths correspond to different *interpretations*. For example, let us consider the query "Garcia-Molina proceedings 2011" and the configuration that maps proceeding into the table *Proceeding*, 2011 into the domain of the attribute *Year* in the same table, and Garcia-Molina into the domain of the attribute *Name* in the table *Person*. Two possible paths may be computed for this configuration, one involving the tables *InProceeding* and *Author_P*, with the meaning of retrieving all the proceedings where Garcia-Molina appears as an author, and the second involving the table *Editor* and returning the proceedings where Garcia-Molina was an editor. Different strategies have been used in the literature to rank the interpretations. One popular option is the length of the join path, but other heuristics [12] can also be used. In KEYRY we compute all the possible paths and we rank them on the basis of their length. However, this is not the main focus of the current work and we will not elaborate further on it.

3   Problem Statement

Definition 1. *A database D is a collection V_t of relational tables $R_1, R_2, \ldots, R_n$. Each table R is a collection of attributes $A_1, A_2, \ldots, A_{m_R}$, and each attribute A has a domain, denoted as $dom(A)$. Let $V_a=\{A \mid A \in R \wedge R \in V_t\}$ represent the set of all the attributes of all the tables in the database and $V_d=\{d \mid d=dom(A) \wedge A \in V_a\}$ represents the set of all their respective domains. The* database vocabulary *of D, denoted as V_D, is the set $V_D=V_t \cup V_a \cup V_d$. Each element of the set V_D is referred to as a* database term.

We distinguish two subsets of the database vocabulary: the *schema vocabulary* $V_{SC} = V_t \cup V_a$ and the *domain vocabulary* $V_{DO} = V_d$ that concerns the instance information. We also assume that a keyword query KQ is an ordered l-tuple of keywords (k_1, k_2, $\ldots, k_l$).

Definition 2. *A configuration $f_c(KQ)$ of a keyword query KQ on a database D is an injective function from the keywords in KQ to database terms in V_D. In other words, a configuration is a mapping that describes each keyword in the original query in terms of database terms.*

The reason we consider a configuration to be an injective function is because we assume that: (i) each keyword cannot have more than one meaning in the same configuration, i.e., it is mapped into only one database term; (ii) two keywords cannot be mapped to the same database term in a configuration since overspecified queries are only a small fraction of the queries that are typically met in practice [8]; and (iii) every keyword is relevant to the database content, i.e., keywords always have a correspondent database term. Furthermore, while modelling the keyword-to-database term mappings, we also assume that every keyword denotes an element of interest to the user, i.e., there are no stop-words or unjustified keywords in a query. In this paper we do not address query cleaning issues. We assume that the keyword queries have already been pre-processed using well-known cleansing techniques.

Answering a keyword query over a database D means finding the SQL queries that describe its possible semantics in terms of the database vocabulary. Each such SQL query is referred to as an *interpretation* of the keyword query in database terms. An interpretation is based on a configuration and includes in its clauses all the database terms that are part of the image[2] of the query keywords through the configuration. In the current work, we consider only select-project-join (SPJ) interpretations that are typically the queries of interest in similar works [2,7], but interpretations involving aggregations [11] are part of our future work.

Definition 3. *An* interpretation *of a keyword query* $KQ = (k_1, k_2, \ldots, k_l)$ *on a database D using a configuration* $f_c^*(KQ)$ *is an SQL query in the form*
select $A_1, A_2, \ldots, A_o$ from R_1 JOIN R_2 JOIN $\ldots$ JOIN R_p where $A_1' = v_1$ AND $A_2' = v_2$ AND $\ldots$ AND $A_q' = v_q$
such that the following holds:

- $\forall A \in \{A_1, A_2, \ldots, A_o\}$: $\exists k \in KQ$ *such that* $f_c^*(k) = A$
- $\forall R \in \{R_1, R_2, \ldots, R_p\}$: *(i)* $\exists k \in KQ$: $f_c^*(k) = R$ *or (ii)* $\exists k_i, k_j \in KQ$: $f_c^*(k_i) = R_i \wedge f_c^*(k_j) = R_j \wedge$ *exists a join path from* R_i *to* R_j *that involves* R
- $\forall$ *"$A' = v$"* $\in \{A_1' = v_1, A_2' = v_2, \ldots, A_o' = v_o\}$: $\exists k \in KQ$ *such that* $f_c^*(k) = dom(A') \wedge k = v$
- $\forall k \in KQ$: $f_c^*(k) \in \{A_1, A_2, \ldots, A_o, R_1, R_2, \ldots, R_p, dom(A_1'), \ldots, dom(A_q')\}$

The existence of a database term in an interpretation is justified either by belonging to the image of the respective configuration, or by participating in a join path connecting two database terms that belong to the image of the configuration. Note that even with this restriction, due to the multiple join paths in a database D, it is still possible to have multiple interpretations of a keyword query KQ given a certain configuration $f_c^*(KQ)$. We use the notation $\mathcal{I}(KQ, f_c^*(KQ), D)$ to refer to the set of these interpretations, and $\mathcal{I}(KQ, D)$ for the union of all these sets for a query KQ.

Since each keyword in a query can be mapped into a table name, an attribute name or an attribute domain, there are $2\sum_{i=1}^{n} |R_i| + n$ different mappings for each keyword, with $|R_i|$ denoting the *arity* of the relation R_i and n the number of tables in the database. Based on this, and on the fact that no two keywords can be mapped to the same database term, for a query containing l keywords, there are $\frac{|V_D|!}{(|V_D|-l)!}$ possible configurations. Of course, not all the interpretations generated by these configurations are equally *meaningful*. Some are more likely to represent the intended keyword query semantics. In the following sections we will show how different kinds of meta-information and interdependencies between the mappings of keywords into database terms can be exploited in order to effectively and efficiently identify these meaningful interpretations and rank them higher.

---

[2] Since a configuration is a function, we use the term image to refer to its output.

4   Computing Configurations Using a HMM

In a first, intuitive attempt to define the configuration function we can divide the problem of matching a whole query to database terms into smaller sub-tasks. In each sub-task the best match between a single keyword and a database term is found. Then the final solution to the global problem is the union of the matches found in the sub-tasks. This approach works well when the keywords in a query are independent of each other, meaning that they do not influence the match of the other keywords to database terms. Unfortunately, this assumption does not hold in real cases. On the contrary, inter-dependencies among keywords meanings are of fundamental importance in disambiguating the keyword semantics.

In order to take into account these inter-dependencies, we model the matching function as a sequential process where the order is determined by the keyword ordering in the query. In each step of the process a single keyword is matched against a database term, taking into account the result of the previous keyword match in the sequence. This process has a finite number of steps, equal to the query length, and is stochastic since the matching between a keyword and a database term is not deterministic: the same keyword can have different meanings in different queries and hence being matched with different database terms; vice-versa, different database terms may match the same keyword in different queries. This type of process can be modeled, effectively, by using a Hidden Markov Model (HMM, for short), that is a stochastic finite state machine where the states are hidden variables.

A HMM models a stochastic process that is not observable directly (it is hidden), but it can be observed indirectly through the observable symbols produced by another stochastic process. The model is composed of a finite number N of states. Assuming a time-discrete model, at each time step a new state is entered based on a *transition probability distribution*, and an observation is produced according to an *emission probability distribution* that depends on the current state, where both these distributions are time-independent. Moreover, the process starts from an initial state based on an *initial state probability distribution*. We will consider first order HMMs with discrete observations. In these models the *Markov property* is respected, i.e., the transition probability distribution of the states at time $t + 1$ depends only on the current state at time t and it does not depend on the past states at time $1, 2, \ldots, t - 1$. Moreover, the observations are discrete: there exists a finite number, M, of observable symbols, hence the emission probability distributions can be effectively represented using *multinomial distributions* dependent on the states. More formally, the model consists of: (i) a set os states $S = \{s_i\}, 1 \leq i \leq N$; (ii) a set of observation symbols $V = \{v_j\}, 1 \leq j \leq M$; (iii) a transition probability distribution $A = \{a_{ij}\}, 1 \leq i \leq N, 1 \leq j \leq N$ where

$$a_{ij} = P(q_{t+1} = s_j | q_t = s_i) \text{ and } \sum_{0 < j < N} a_{ij} = 1$$

(iv) an emission probability distribution $B = \{b_i(m)\}, 1 \leq i \leq N, 1 \leq m \leq M$ where

$$b_i(m) = P(o_t = v_m | q_t = s_i) \text{ and } \sum_{0 < m < M} b_i(m) = 1$$

and (v) an initial state probability distribution $\Pi = \{\pi_i\}$, $1 \leq i \leq N$ where

$$\pi_i = P(q_1 = s_i) \text{ and } \sum_{0 < i < N} \pi_i = 1$$

Based on the above, the notation $\lambda = (A, B, \Pi)$ will be used to indicate a HMM. In our context, the keywords inserted by the user are the observable part of the process, while the correspondent database terms are the unknown variables that have to be inferred. For this reason, we model the keywords as observations and each term in the database vocabulary as a state.

4.1 Setting HMM Parameters

In order to define a HMM, its parameters have to be identified. This is usually done using a training algorithm that, after many iterations, converges to a good solution for the parameter values. In our approach we introduce some heuristic rules that allow the definition of the parameter values even when no training data is available. The HMM parameter values are set by exploiting the semantics collected from the data source metadata. In particular:

The transition probabilities are computed using heuristic rules that take into account the semantic relationships that exist between the database terms (aggregation, generalization and inclusion relationships). The goal of the rules is to foster the transition between database terms belonging to the same table and belonging to tables connected through foreign keys. The transition probability values decrease with the distance of the states, e.g. transitions between terms in the same table have higher probability than transitions between terms in tables directly connected through foreign keys, that, in turn, have higher probability than transitions between terms in tables connected through a third table.

The emission probabilities are computed on the basis of similarity measures. In particular two different techniques are adopted for the database terms in V_{SC} and V_{DO}. We use the well known *edit distance* for computing the lexical similarity between the keywords and each term (and its synonyms extracted from Wordnet[3]) in the schema vocabulary V_{SC}. On the other side, the similarity between keywords and the terms in the domain vocabulary V_{DO} is based on domain compatibilities and regular expressions. We use the calculated similarity as an estimate for the conditional probability $P(q_t = s_i | o_t = v_m)$ then, using the Bayes theorem, we calculate the emission probability $P(o_t = v_m | q_t = s_i)$. Note that the model is independent of the similarity measure adopted. Other more complex measures that take into account external knowledge sources (i.e., public ontologies and thesauri) can be applied without modifying the model.

The initial state probabilities are estimated by means of the scores provided by the HITS algorithm [9]. The HITS algorithm is a link analysis algorithm that calculates two different scores for each page: *authority* and *hub*. A high authority score indicates

---

[3] http://wordnet.princeton.edu

that the page contains valuable information with respect to the user query, while a high hub score suggests that the page contains useful links toward authoritative pages. This algorithm has been adapted to our context in order to rank the tables in a database based on their authority scores. The higher the rank, the more valuable is the information stored in the tables. For this reason, the authority score is used as an estimate of the initial state probabilities.

Adapted HITS Algorithm. In order to employ the HITS algorithm, we build the database graph $G_D = (V_t, E_{fk})$ which is a directed graph where the nodes are the database tables in V_t and the edges are connections between tables through foreign keys, i.e., given two tables R_i, R_j there exists an edge in E_{fk} from R_i to R_j, denoted as $R_i \rightarrow R_j$, if an attribe in R_j is referred by a foreign key defined in R_i. Let A be the n x n adjacency matrix of the graph G_D

$$A = [a_{ij}], a_{ij} = 1 \text{ iff } e_{ij} \in E_{fk}, a_{ij} = 0 \text{ iff } e_{ij} \notin E_{fk}$$

In our approach we use the modified matrix B that takes into account the number of attributes minus the number of foreign keys in a table (foreign keys are considered as links).

$$B = [b_{ij}], b_{ij} = a_{ij} \cdot (|R_i| - ||\{R_i \rightarrow R_j, 1 \leq j \leq n\}||)$$

Let us define the authority weight vector $auth$ and the hub weight vector hub

$$auth^T = [u_1, u_2, \ldots, u_n] \text{ and } hub^T = [v_1, v_2, \ldots, v_n]$$

The algorithm initializes these vectors with uniform values, e.g., $\frac{1}{n}$, then the vectors are updated in successive iterations as follows

$$\begin{cases} auth = B^T \cdot hub \\ hub = B \cdot auth \end{cases}$$

At each iteration a normalization step is performed to obtain authority and hub scores in the range $[0, 1]$. After few iterations the algorithm converges and the authority scores are used as estimate for the initial state probabilities.

Example 1. Let us consider the database in Figure 1. This database generates 53 states[4], one for each database term. Concerning the transition probability distribution, the heuristic rules foster transitions between database terms of the same table or in tables connect via foreign key. According to this, the most probable states subsequent to the state associated to the table *Journal* are the states associated to the names and the domains of the attributes *Title*, *Volume*, *Number*, etc., then, the state associated to the table *Author_J*, subsequently, the states associated to the table *Person* and so on. We use different similarity measures for computing the emission probability distribution. Domain compatibility and regular expressions are used for measuring the probabilities of the values associated to states of terms in the V_{DO}, e.g., the possible values associated to the state representing the *Year* of the table *Journal* are numeric values between

---

[4] Since in this schema the primary key values are not meaningful for the user, we removed the states associated to these database terms.

1900 and 2100. The probabilities of values associated to states if terms in the V_{SC} is computed on the basis of lexical similarity computed on the term and on its synonyms, hypernyms and hyponyms. For example, we consider "article" as synonym of journal. In our experiments we noticed that, by applying the adaptation of the HITS algorithm, the states corresponding to the database terms in the tables *Journal* and *Inproceeding* obtain the highest authority scores.

4.2   Decoding the HMM

Once the parameters A, B, and Π have been defined, the resulting HMM is used to compute the top-K configurations by applying the *List Viterbi* algorithm [10], which is a generalization of the well known Viterbi algorithm [6]. The algorithm has also been applied, using a different formulation, to HMMs in order to solve the following problem:

Given a HMM λ and an observation sequence $O_l = (o_1, o_2, \ldots, o_T)$ find the ordered list of the K state sequences $\hat{Q}_l^k = (q_1^k, q_2^k, \ldots, q_T^k), 1 \leq k \leq K$ which have the highest probability of generating O_l

In other words, the algorithm generalizes the well-known Viterbi algorithm finding the top-K maximum likelihood state sequences (MLSSs) instead of the single MLSS found by the original algorithm.

Example 2. The top-2 results of the keyword query "proceeding ER 2011" are the ones mapping the keyword proceeding into the table *proceeding*, ER into the domain of the attribute *Title* of the table *proceeding*, and 2011 into the domains of the attributes *Year* and *ISBN*, respectively. Both the solutions have the same transition probabilities but different emission probabilities since the likelihood of the mapping of 2011 into the attribute *Year* is higher than the one into *ISBN*. Other mappings are possibles: for example the configuration that maps the keyword proceeding into the table *proceeding*, ER into the domain of the attribute *Title* of the table *proceeding*, and 2011 into the domain of the attribute *Year* of the table *Journal* has rank 9.

5   Related Work

There has been already a number of different systems that consider keyword searching over structured or semi-structured data. Specifically, well-known systems of the former include BANKS [1], DISCOVER [7], DBXplorer [2], QUICK [13], SQAK [11] and many others presented in various surveys [5,12]. Their typical approach is to perform an off-line pre-prosessing step that scans the whole data instance and constructs an index, a symbol table or some structure of that kind which is later used at run time to identify the parts of the database in which each keyword appears. After that, they perform a path discovery algorithm to find the different ways in which these tables are connected. The algorithms range from finding minimal joining networks [7] to Steiner trees [1]. In contrast to all these approaches, KEYRY is able to achieve similar results without the need of accessing and scanning the data. QUICK guides the users into a series of query refinements to find the one that describes their intended semantics, but it assumes that there is only one such semantics, while practice has shown that there may be different alternatives. Keymantic [3,4] has goals similar to ours but it follows a fundamentally different approach. It handles the keyword search as a bipartite graph assignment problem and finds the solutions using an extended version of the Hungarian algorithm.

6   Conclusion and Future Work

We described KEYRY, a probabilistic keyword-based searching system for relational databases that is based on a HMM for computing the top-K best mappings of the query keywords into the database terms. The use of HMM allows the efficient modeling of the order of the keywords in a query and the probabilities of associating them to different database terms. Although a HMM typically has to be trained to optimize its parameters, we propose a method that does not rely on any particular training.

References

1. Aditya, B., Bhalotia, G., Chakrabarti, S., Hulgeri, A., Nakhe, C., Parag, Sudarshan, S.: Banks: Browsing and keyword searching in relational databases. In: VLDB, pp. 1083–1086 (2002)
2. Agrawal, S., Chaudhuri, S., Das, G.: Dbxplorer: A system for keyword-based search over relational databases. In: ICDE, pp. 5–16. IEEE Computer Society, Los Alamitos (2002)
3. Bergamaschi, S., Domnori, E., Guerra, F., Lado, R.T., Velegrakis, Y.: Keyword search over relational databases: a metadata approach. In: SIGMOD. ACM, New York (2011)
4. Bergamaschi, S., Domnori, E., Guerra, F., Orsini, M., Lado, R.T., Velegrakis, Y.: Keymantic: Semantic keyword-based searching in data integration systems. PVLDB 3(2), 1637–1640 (2010)
5. Chakrabarti, S., Sarawagi, S., Sudarshan, S.: Enhancing search with structure. IEEE Data Eng. Bull. 33(1), 3–24 (2010)
6. Forney Jr., G.D.: The Viterbi algorithm. Proceedings of the IEEE 61(3), 268 (1973)
7. Hristidis, V., Papakonstantinou, Y.: Discover: Keyword search in relational databases. In: VLDB, pp. 670–681 (2002)
8. Kumar, R., Tomkins, A.: A Characterization of Online Search Behavior. IEEE Data Engineering Bulletin 32(2), 3–11 (2009)
9. Li, L., Shang, Y., Shi, H., Zhang, W.: Performance evaluation of hits-based algorithms. In: Hamza, M.H. (ed.) Communications, Internet, and Information Technology, pp. 171–176. IASTED/ACTA Press (2002)
10. Seshadri, N., Sundberg, C.-E.W.: List viterbi decoding algorithms with applications. IEEE Transactions on Communications 42(234) (1994)
11. Tata, S., Lohman, G.M.: SQAK: doing more with keywords. In: SIGMOD, pp. 889–902. ACM, New York (2008)
12. Yu, J.X., Qin, L., Chang, L.: Keyword Search in Databases. Synthesis Lectures on Data Management. Morgan & Claypool Publishers, San Francisco (2010)
13. Zenz, G., Zhou, X., Minack, E., Siberski, W., Nejdl, W.: From keywords to semantic queries-incremental query construction on the semantic web. Journal of Web Semantics 7(3), 166–176 (2009)
14. Zobel, J., Moffat, A.: Inverted files for text search engines. ACM Computing Surveys 38(2) (2006)

A Modularization Proposal for Goal-Oriented Analysis of Data Warehouses Using I-Star

Alejandro Maté[1], Juan Trujillo[1], and Xavier Franch[2]

[1] Lucentia Research Group
Department of Software and Computing Systems
University of Alicante
{amate,jtrujillo}@dlsi.ua.es
[2] Universitat Politécnica de Catalunya (UPC)
franch@essi.upc.edu

Abstract. The success rate of Data Warehouse (DW) development is improved by performing a requirements elicitation stage in which the users' needs to be fulfilled by the DW are modeled. Currently, among the different proposals for modeling requirements, there is a special focus on Goal-Oriented models, and in particular on the i* framework. In order to adapt this framework for DW development, a UML profile for DWs was proposed. However, as the general i* framework, the proposal lacks modularity. This has a specially negative impact for DW development, since the business strategy plans tend to include a huge number of elements with many crossed relationships between them. In turn, the readability of the models is decreased, harming their utility and increasing the error rates and development time. In this paper, we propose an extension of the i* profile for DWs considering the modularization of goals. We also provide a set of guidelines in order to correctly apply our proposal. Furthermore, we have performed an experiment in order to validate our proposal. The great benefits of our proposal are an increase in the modularity and scalability of the models which, in turn, increases the error correction capability, and makes complex models easier to understand by both DW developers and non expert users.

Keywords: Data Warehouses, modules, user requirements, i-star.

1 Introduction

Nowadays, there is an increasing importance of the Business Intelligence (BI) in the enterprise environment. Organizations manage huge amounts of information, and wish to take informed decisions by using that information. In fact, the Gartner Group showed that, during the recent recession period, the BI market not only did not decrease, but instead it grew a 4% [3].

At the core of the BI, among other technologies, is the Data Warehouse (DW). DWs integrate several heterogeneous data sources in multidimensional structures in support of the decision-making process [4]. Therefore, the modeling of user needs is a very important aspect of DWs, which can be accomplished by means

M. Jeusfeld, L. Delcambre, and T.W. Ling (Eds.): ER 2011, LNCS 6998, pp. 421–428, 2011.

of goal-oriented models. Among the goal-oriented approaches, the i* framework [9], is currently one of the most widespread goal modeling frameworks and has been applied for modeling organizations, and business processes, as well as for modeling DW requirements [6].

Nevertheless, as pointed in [2], the i* framework lacks scalability due to the absence of modularity. As DW requirements models may become very complex, they become difficult to correct and update as requirements change. We have experienced this drawback ourselves, as some of our real projects had over 16 goals, 15 tasks and 53 resources for a single actor. These models became huge for correction, validation, and communication with the users, presenting elements repeated in the same model with different structures, since designers forgot which elements were already defined.

In this work, we propose an extension of our i* profile [6], in order to improve its modularity. We include *Decision*, *Information*, and *Hierarchy* modules, thus increasing the scalability of the models. With these modifications, the communication between users and developers is improved, leading to higher success rates. Furthermore, we provide a set of guidelines to correctly apply the proposal. Moreover, we have performed an experiment in order to validate our proposal.

The rest of the paper is structured as follows. Section 2 presents the related work in this area. Section 3 proposes the different types of modules for our i* profile. Section 4 presents an example of application and the experiment performed. Finally, Section 5 summarizes the conclusions and future work.

2   Related Work and Background

When dealing with scalability issues, other works have focused on i* modularity in general [2]. However, these modules do not have meaningfull semantics for a specific domain, which could favor the understandability of the modularization process. Therefore, before performing any kind of adaptation, a study of the target domain must be performed. The study, and the ontology mapping between i* and DWs, is provided in [1]. After this ontology mapping is performed, the necessary modules should be defined accordingly to how the target domain is structured.

In our previous work, we developed a UML profile for modeling DWs at conceptual level [5], where the importance of packages was shown. These packages allow the developer to analyze the model at different levels of detail, hiding those elements on which the developer has no interest, lowering the complexity of the model and increasing its readability. In turn, this aspect makes designing the schemata less error prone.

However, since the conceptual level is closer to developers than to users, we included a RE phase in our methodology [6,7]. Now, in this work, we complement our approach, by improving the modularity and scalability of our i* profile. We include modules for the decision and information goals, as well as for hierarchies of contexts. By improving the modularity, the models are easier to read and less error prone, thus increasing user satisfaction.

3   Definition of Modules and Guidelines

In this section, we will present the extension to our i* profile for DWs, defining the proposing modules and the extended metaclasses, and presenting some guidelines for the application of modules.

3.1   Definition of Modules

First, we will define our proposed modules, in order to decrease the complexity of the goal models. The modules which we will define (see figure 1) are strongly related with the identified concepts in the DW domain. Therefore, each module has a specific semantic associated adapted for the DW domain. We have not included a module for strategic goals since typically there is only a few of them.

- **Decision modules** include the elements related to a given *decision goal*. They can include *decision goals, information goals, requirements, contexts, measures, other decision modules, information modules*, and *hierarchy modules*. They contain all the necessary information to take a given decision, which helps achieving a *strategic goal*.
- **Information modules** include the elements related to a given information goal. They can include *information goals, requirements, contexts, measures, other information modules*, and *hierarchy modules*. They aggregate all the information which is necessary to satisfy a given information goal.
- **Hierarchy modules** include the elements which constitute a hierarchy. They are formed by the different contexts which represent the different levels of aggregation of a dimension. They can only include *contexts*. These modules help with the reusability of the dimensions at the requirements level, and hide the complexity of hierarchies when it is unnecessary.

These modules are loosely coupled with the core i* elements and extend from the *Package* element, as shown in figure 1, and include an intermediate element

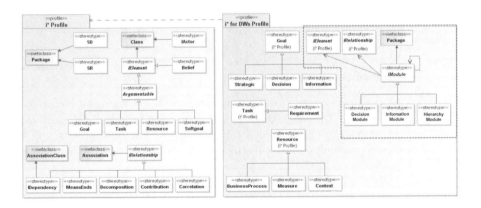

Fig. 1. Modules extension for DW

iModule in order to help with the definition of OCL constraints. After having defined the modules, we will present a set of guidelines to apply them while minimizing the drawbacks.

3.2   Guidelines

In this section, we will give some guidelines to use the provided modules, in order to maximize their benefits. It is not mandatory to package every element, although it is recommended for the sake of uniformity and to provide different abstraction levels, which is a more intuitive approach (G1). However, if some parts of the goal tree have a low complexity, it might not be necessary to group them in a separate package (G2). For each package created, there should be a single root element, corresponding to the type of package, which acts as a connection for higher level elements. This element should have no dependencies to other elements inside the same package (G3). The name of the package should be the same as the root element, in order to help with the identification of the corresponding packaged subtree (G4). This helps keeping in mind which lower level elements support each higher level goals. For each decision goal a *Decision module* should be created (G5). Inside a decision module there should be an *Information module* for each information goal which supports the decision goal (G6). If included in a CASE tool, elements should not be repeated, but instead imported from packages where they were first defined (G7). *Information modules* should include all the elements related to the information goal, importing elements where necessary, and always including a *Hierarchy module* for each different hierarchy of contexts present (G8). These *Hierarchy modules* represent the lowest level of abstraction in the strategic rationale, and should be always separated from the goal tree, in order to hide the details of the hierarchies of contexts unless they are necessary (G9).

4   Example of Application and Experimental Results

In this section we will present the application of our proposal to an example, as well as the results of an experiment performed in order to analyze how users and developers perceive the modularized models.

4.1   Example of Application

The following example presents a simple goal tree, while contexts and hierarchies are better defined, and the scope of each element may be hard to identify. In this case, the contexts can be aggregated at different levels of detail, presenting market and electronic product contexts as the lowest level, which can be aggregated up to state and section levels.

This example can be modularized using the proposed packages, decreasing its complexity and providing different levels of detail. In this sense, now there is a first level providing an overview of the strategies related to the business process and their corresponding decisions. In this case, the goal tree presents the

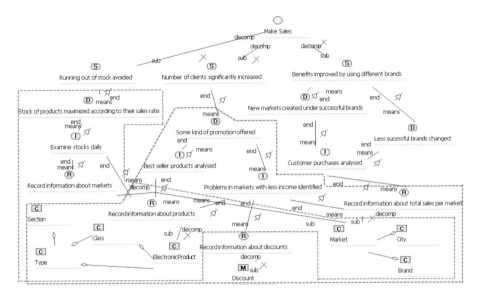

Fig. 2. Part of the requirements model for Sales analysis with the scope of the decision goal *Some promotion offered* marked in red, and the scope of *Stock of products* in blue

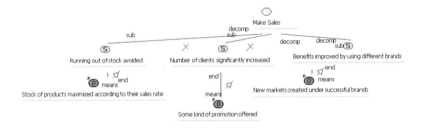

Fig. 3. Strategy level for Sales analysis

different decision packages as its leaves, which are further detailed in their corresponding models. The following model presents the previous business process with 3 related strategies and the corresponding 3 decision packages.

For each decision, we have a different package which includes their related information goals and presents the intermediate level of detail. The elements corresponding to each information goal are also modularized in their own packages, which are the leaves of the decision models. Finally, for each information goal, we have a package which includes their related information requirements, presenting the corresponding hierarchy packages and measures.

4.2   Experimental Results

In order to evaluate the impact of our proposal, we have performed an experiment, with participants ranging from non-expert people to DW designers and experts on i* modeling. This experiment is part of a family of experiments for validating the proposal, following the same methodology as in [8]. There were two rounds of questionnaires presenting two examples, one small (omitted due to space constraints, *Example 1*), and one bigger (see figure 2, *Example 2*). Both examples were presented in generic i* notation. Monolitic models were presented in a single sheet, whereas modularized models were presented in multiple sheets. These examples were presented in four combinations, in order to prevent the order of the questions from altering the results.

A total of 28 participants filled the questionnaire. Each participant was given one type of questionnaire. The tasks were to identify and mark a series of elements on each model, and the answer could not be modified. After the identification tasks, participants had to assign scores (from 0 to 3) for a series of characteristics. The hypothesis for our experiment are:

Null hypothesis, H_{01}: There is no statistically significant correlation between the modularization of models and the time required for different tasks and the characteristics perceived.

Hypothesis H_{11}: $\neg H_{01}$

The results are shown in table 1 for the first round, and in table 2 for the second round. As the experiment results results proved H_{01}, we did not calculate further values like efficiency and effectiveness. Therefore, the results will be discussed in terms of trends. Time is measured in seconds.

In order to obtain the results, first, outliers were identified and filtered. Then, the second step was to perform a variance analysis of the data, in order to identify significant differences between the models. The significance analysis ($\rho < 0.05$) revealed that the reading time for the modularized Sales model was significantly inferior than when built in a monolitic way, while the scalability of both examples was notably increased.

Table 1. Tasks performed (left) and independent (top) variables for experiment 1

	Monolitic	Modularized
Avg. reading time Sales	299.31	210.31
Identif. task 1 Sales	190.08	278.62
Identif. task 2 Sales	190.94	165.08
Avg. reading time Contracts	162.73	181.33
Identif. task 1 Contracts	150.07	211.5
Identif. task 2 Contracts	124.33	161.00
Avg. errors per questionnaire Sales	0.82	0.47
Avg. errors per questionnaire Contracts	0.33	0.36
Readability score Sales	2	1,93
Scalability score Sales	1,41	2,26
Comprehension score Sales	1,5	1,87
Modificability score Sales	1,5	2,06
Readability score Contracts	2,27	2,33
Scalability score Contracts	1,67	2,41
Comprehension score Contracts	2,13	2,05
Modificability score Contracts	1,73	2,17

Table 2. Tasks performed (left) and independent (top) variables for experiment 2

	Monolitic	Modularized
Modif. task 1 Sales	202	154,27
Modif. task 2 Sales	223,6	290
Modif. task Contracts	128,73	197,6
Avg. Time drawing	1306,67	1891,44
Avg. Time/element	50,10	44,34
Avg. number of elements	25,67	42,89
Avg. unique non package elements	25,67	27,67

In terms of trends, we perceive an increase in time spent in order to identify modularized elements, which can be consequence of marking a higher number of elements. On the other hand, the number of wrong answered questions notably diminished in the Sales example when modularized. This is specially relevant, since identifying elements in the modularized example required to correctly identify the detail level of a package in the next sheet. Finally, most participants chose a modularized approach to organize new elements. Out of 27 participants 17 chose to package the decision goals and their related elements, 16 packaged the information goals, and 19 chose to package hierarchies.

After the first round, a second round was performed with 21 participants, including modification tasks over existing models, as well as the creation of a new model. The examples were the same as in the previous round. The results of this round are shown in table 2.

As previously, in terms of trends, we perceive a decrease in time spent when the model is big and modifications are made on a single module (task 1), whereas there is an increase when modifications affect multiple modules (task 2). Finally, the creation of a new model from the scratch had a sample of 15 questionnaires, with a significant correlation between the structure of the model created and the measured variables. Time spent was notably superior for models created with a modularized approach, while time spent per element drawn was inferior when the model was modularized. Most importantly, the average number of elements identified from the description was superior when modules were applied. Additionally, some monolitic models (filtered in the outliers analysis), presented repeated elements, which should not be created, and tend to increase in number as the model gets bigger.

5   Conclusions and Future Work

Traditionally, i* models lack any modularity, suffering from scalability and readability issues. Therefore, although the profile presented in [6] is adapted for the semantics present in DWs, it suffers from the same issues, since it provides no additional modularity. In turn, when real project models become huge, they turn from a useful tool for communicating with the user into a burden which requires effort to correct, use and modify. Therefore, an improve in modularity is required in order to maintain the quality of the requirement analysis for DWs.

In this work, we have presented a proposal for applying modules, specially designed for DWs. We have provided some guildelines on how to correctly apply the proposal and we also have shown an example of application. The experimental results show an increase in the scalability of the models, and a reduced error rate when identifying the scope of an element. Furthermore, modules help to create richer goal models. Since we could not establish a significant correlation between the modularization and some of the variables, we pretend to perform further experiments.

Acknowledgments. This work has been partially supported by the ProS-Req (TIN2010-19130-C02-01), MESOLAP (TIN2010-14860) and SERENIDAD (PEII-11-0327-7035) projects from the Spanish Ministry and the Junta de Comunidades de Castilla La Mancha respectively. Alejandro Maté is funded by the Generalitat Valenciana under an ACIF grant (ACIF/2010/298).

References

1. Franch, X., Maté, A., Trujillo, J.: On the joint use of i* with other Modelling Frameworks: a Vision Paper. In: Proceedings of the 19th International Conference on Requirements Engineering. IEEE, Los Alamitos (in Press)
2. Franch, X.: Incorporating Modules into the i* Framework. In: Pernici, B. (ed.) CAiSE 2010. LNCS, vol. 6051, pp. 439–454. Springer, Heidelberg (2010)
3. Group, G.: Gartner Group BI Revenue Analysis (2009),
   http://www.gartner.com/it/page.jsp?id=1357514
4. Kimball, R.: The data warehouse toolkit. Wiley-India (2009)
5. Luján-Mora, S., Trujillo, J., Song, I.-Y.: A UML profile for multidimensional modeling in data warehouses. DKE 59(3), 725–769 (2006)
6. Mazón, J.-N., Trujillo, J.: A model driven modernization approach for automatically deriving multidimensional models in data warehouses. In: Parent, C., Schewe, K.-D., Storey, V.C., Thalheim, B. (eds.) ER 2007. LNCS, vol. 4801, pp. 255–264. Springer, Heidelberg (2007)
7. Mazón, J.-N., Trujillo, J.: A hybrid model driven development framework for the multidimensional modeling of data warehouses. SIGMOD Record 38(2), 12–17 (2009)
8. Serrano, M., Trujillo, J., Calero, C., Piattini, M.: Metrics for data warehouse conceptual models understandability. Information and Software Technology 49(8), 851–870 (2007)
9. Yu, E.S.K.: Modelling strategic relationships for process reengineering. Ph.D. thesis, Toronto, Ont., Canada, Canada (1995)

Strategic Models for Business Intelligence

Lei Jiang[1], Daniele Barone[1], Daniel Amyot[2], and John Mylopoulos[1,3]

[1] Department of Computer Science, University of Toronto, Canada
[2] EECS, University of Ottawa, Canada
[3] DISI, University of Trento, Italy
{leijiang,barone}@cs.toronto.edu, damyot@eecs.uottawa.ca,
jm@cs.toronto.edu

Abstract. Business Intelligence (BI) promises a range of technologies for using information to ensure compliance to strategic and tactical objectives, as well as government laws and regulations. These technologies can be used in conjunction with conceptual models of business objectives, processes and situations (aka business schemas) to drive strategic decision-making about opportunities and threats. This paper focuses on three key concepts for strategic business models – *situation*, *influence* and *indicator* – and how they are used, in the context of goal modeling, to build and analyze business schemas based on goal and probabilistic reasoning techniques.

Keywords: Business Intelligence, Goal, Situation, Indicator, Influence Diagram.

1 Introduction

Business Intelligence (BI) promises a range of technologies for using information within organizations to ensure compliance to strategic and tactical objectives, as well as government laws and regulations. As a research field, BI encompasses data and knowledge management, modeling of processes and policies, data quality, data privacy and security, data integration, data exchange, data cleaning, inconsistency management, information retrieval, data mining, analytics, and decision support.

The past decade has seen unprecedented interest in BI technologies and services, and a corresponding growth of the BI market. By now, most competitive organizations have a significant investment in BI, much of it technology-related, based on software tools and artifacts. But business people – be they executives, consultants, or analysts – are in general agreement that what helps them the most is not new gadgets producing a dizzying array of statistics. Instead, they are interested in having their business data analyzed in their terms, which are strategic objectives, business models and strategies, business processes, markets, trends and risks. This gap between the worlds of business and data remains today the greatest barrier to the adoption of BI technologies, as well as the greatest cost factor in their application to specific projects.

We propose to bridge this gap by extending the notion of conceptual schema to include concepts beyond entities and relationships. In particular, we are working on the design of a business modeling language (the *Business Intelligence Model*, or simply *BIM*) [25] as a business-level counterpart to the Entity-Relationship Model, so

M. Jeusfeld, L. Delcambre, and T.W. Ling (Eds.): ER 2011, LNCS 6998, pp. 429–439, 2011.

that strategic objectives, business processes, risks and trends can all be represented in a business schema, for purposes of analysis and monitoring. Users can query a business schema, much like conventional database schemas, but in terms of business terms. Such queries are to be translated through schema mappings into queries defined over databases and data warehouses, and the answers are to be translated back into business-level concepts [26].

This paper focuses on three key concepts in BIM, those of *situation, influence* and *indicator,* and how they are used, in the context of goal modeling, to build and analyze business schemas based on goal and probabilistic reasoning techniques. The rest of the paper is organized as follows. Section 2 introduces BIM concepts and our view on instantiating a business schema. Sections 3 present various ways to analyze a business schema, using a running example built from real-world analysis reports. We discuss related work in Section 4, and conclude and point out to future work in Section 5.

2   Strategic Business Models

This section introduces the three key concepts (situation, influence and indicator) for building business schemas. In this paper, we present these concepts informally with intuitive examples. These concepts have been formalized using the DOLCE+ [1] upper ontology. We refer interested readers to [25] for a detailed discussion on this formalization.

The concepts to be introduced in this section are intended to be used in the context of goal modeling. Given its wide popularity in Requirements Engineering, we only give a brief introduction to the notion of goal here. A *goal* represents an objective of a business, defined during strategic planning, and pursued during subsequent business operation. The basic characteristics of a goal include: (i) it may be (AND/OR) refined into subgoals so that its satisfaction depends on that of its subgoals; (ii) a goal may be satisfied in more than one way if it or its subgoals are OR-refined, in which case a choice needs to be made among alternatives; and (iii) a goal's satisfaction may be affected by that of goals other than its subgoals. Goal analysis produces a goal model consisting of an AND/OR refinement tree with additional positive/negative contributions. The satisfaction of a goal can be inferred from that of others in the same goal model using a label propagation algorithm [7-8].

In addition to goals, we also model *domain assumptions* that assume properties of the domain in pursuing satisfaction of a goal. For example, the goal "*to schedule meeting*" may be AND-refined into subgoals "*to collect timetables*" and "*to choose timeslots*" assuming "*there are meeting rooms available*". A domain assumption may, in fact, be false (broken), in which case goal fulfillment is not possible.

2.1   Situation

During strategic planning, SWOT (<u>S</u>trengths (internal, favorable), <u>W</u>eaknesses (internal, unfavorable), <u>O</u>pportunities (external, favorable), and <u>T</u>hreats (external, unfavorable)) analysis [2] is often used to identify internal and external factors that may influence the fulfillment, favorable or unfavorable, of strategic goals. We propose to model these in terms of the notion of situation. Intuitively, a *situation* defines a partial state of the world in terms of things that exist in that state, their properties, and interrelations among them [22]. For example, the partnership between a company and a research network would be an external, unfavorable situation for the company's competitor with respect to maintaining its technological superiority.

Since we are interested in strategic business models, we focus on organizational situations. The organization in question is the *viewpoint* of the situation. Note that the same situation may be favorable from one viewpoint, but unfavorable from others. In particular, we say an organizational situation is *internal* (analogously *external*) to its viewpoint if all (analogously none of) its components are related to the viewpoint through parthood relations.

2.2   Influence

To reason about goal fulfillment under the influence of situations, we extend the contribution relation from goals to situations. Traditionally in goal modeling, one goal is said to contribute to the other one if its satisfaction/denial implies (partial) satisfaction/denial of the other. Such relations also hold between situations and goals. We call this type *logical influence*.

To support probabilistic reasoning, we also support *probabilistic influences* among situations, goals and domain assumptions. In this case, situations and domain assumptions are represented by random variables whose values are their possible states; each state is assigned a probability of that situation or domain assumption being. In Section 3.4, we show how this type of influence is used to support decision-theoretic analysis.

Following [20], a logical influence is characterized along the following dimensions: (i) *direction*: a positive (resp. negative) influence exists from a situation to a goal if it (when being true) increases (resp. decreases) the chance of the goal being satisfied; and (ii) *degree*: an influence is full if it is a casual relation (i.e., 100% chance); otherwise, it is partial. We say an organizational situation is *favorable* for an organization for achieving a goal if has a positive logical influence on that goal; It is *unfavorable* if it has a negative one.

2.3   Indicator

A successful business depends both on its initial strategic planning and subsequent business operations. Performance measures play an important role in helping businesses align their daily activities with the strategic objectives. Generally speaking, performance measures quantify various aspects of business activities, including their input, execution and output, for monitoring, control and improvement purposes [21]. We model performance measures in terms of indicators.

Performance measures employed in a business environment often form an aggregation hierarchy -- a higher-level measure is defined in terms of lower-level ones. Top level measures (e.g., satisfaction of service, quality of care) usually give a clear picture whether a business is moving towards fulfilling its strategic objectives, while leaf level measures (e.g., patient length of stay, emergency room wait time) are usually tied to specific actions and responsibilities.

More specifically, we say an indicator is *composite* if it refers to other indicators in its definition; otherwise, it is an *atomic* indicator. An atomic indicator that inheres directly to a single individual. For example, *"admission wait time"* is a temporal indicator inheres to the *"admission service"* whose participants include a particular person and a hospital. A composite indicator may inhere indirectly to (possibly more than) one individual through its parts. For example, *"wait time"* is a composite indicator that defined in terms of *"admission wait time"*, *"test wait time"*, *"procedure wait time"*, etc., which inhere to different hospital services.

2.4   Instantiation of Business Schemas

As with any other modeling framework, it is necessary to distinguish between instances (particulars) of a concept (goal, situation, etc.) in the application domain and the concept itself (universal). For example, *"to reduce wait time"* is a goal class (universal) that describes many instances to reduce wait time pursued by particular hospitals at specific times. Our models consist of concepts and we call such models *business schemas*. A long term objective of our work is to connect a business schema to data sources that store (partial) information about its instances, and use it as an interface to query the underlying data.

A business schema is instantiated by instantiating its elements. A goal instance is created whenever an organization decides to pursue it (i.e., to make it at least partially satisfied). Of course, an organization may pursue a goal many times (e.g., *"to sell a type of a product"*). A goal instance is *initiated* upon creation, and maybe be *satisfied*, *denied* or *abandoned*. It may also be *inactive* (*suspended*) if it is not being pursued currently. Finally, an indicator instance is created whenever a value is *obtained* (*measured / calculated*) for that indicator at a particular time point. Thus, indicator instances represent concrete measurements. Notice that by definition, an indicator instance must inhere to some other entity (e.g., a goal instance). The inherence link therefore represents a measurement relation.

3   Reasoning with Business Schemas

A business schema, once constructed, can be analyzed in various ways. Strategic planning [6] usually starts with the definition of an organization's mission, followed by the specification of the goals toward the mission and the strategies to achieve these goals. For a given goal, it is not uncommon that alternative strategies exist. Therefore, analyzing those alternative strategies is an important element in any strategic planning process. In this section, we discuss a number of ways to analyze alternative strategies, using goal reasoning techniques [5]. In addition, during strategic planning, a strategy is normally produced by making decisions at a number of decision points. At each point, one decision option is chosen from a pool of available ones. We show how this decision-making process can be supported using probabilistic decision analysis.

3.1   Running Example

We use a running example (see Figure 1) to help elaborate different reasoning techniques. This example is built from real-world analysis reports, published by

DataMonitor[1], a company that specializes in industry analysis for a number of industry sectors.

When building strategic business models, all modeling concepts are relative to (business) goals. Accordingly, we build a business schema by starting with a goal modeling phase, based on the Tropos methodology [20]. In our example, we have two root goals: "*to main revenue growth*" and "*to reduce risks*". To achieve the first one, we need achieve both "*to increase sales*" and "*to maintain competitive advantage*". Lateral influences are also identified among sub-goals. For example, one alternative way to maintain competitive advantage is to "*acquire technology through partnership*". This alternative helps to reduce financial risk, but increases the dependence on external partners. A goal can be decomposed into both sub-goals and domain assumptions. For example, in addition to achieving the goals "*to increase sales volume*" and "*to main gross margin*", the domain assumption "*high demand*" (for our products/services) need to be true, in order fulfill the goal "*to increase sales*" (in dollar amount).

After goal modeling, we identify the internal and external factors that may influence fulfillment of the goals identified previously. Specifically, we start with domain assumptions in the schema, and ask the question: what observable evidence could potentially support or challenge these assumptions. In our example, "*high R&D expenditure*" (strength) positively contributes to the domain assumption "*strong R&D capability*", while "*healthy balance sheet*" (strength) suggests high degree of certainty that there are "*sufficient funds*" available to make strategic investment. Situations may also influence goals directly. For example, the fact "*increased competition*" (threat) may hinder the fulfillment of the goal "*to open new sales channels*". Influences may also occur among situations. For example, "*low cost financing*" (opportunity), caused by "*economic slowdown*", positively contributes to "*high R&D expenditure*" and "*healthy balance sheet*".

Modeling indicator (especially composite ones) is a highly domain-specific process, and is dealt with in a companion paper [23]. In our example, we assume that a set of indicators is already in place (which is true in practice in many organizations); so the task of the modeler is to associate them with the elements in the schema. In our example, some indicators are associated with the goals under "*to increase sales*". Note that these indicators are composite indicators, and may be further decomposed in practice. For example, "*sales volume*" may be broken by the types of products/services, fiscal periods, or geographical locations. Also notice that although not shown, "*total sales*" (in dollar amount) can be mathematically determined by "*sales volume*" and "*gross margin*", entailing a hierarchical relation among these indicators.

3.2 Exploration of Possible Strategies

Goal-Oriented Requirements Engineering [19] has long studied the problem of systematic exploration of alternative plans for achieving specified goals. Given a goal model and an assignment of desired satisfaction values (either qualitative or quantitative) to its root goals, a top-down/backward reasoning algorithm [7] find *all*

---

[1] http://www.datamonitor.com/

possible assignments (or strategies) to others goals that leads to the assigned satisfaction values of those root goals.

In our example, two root goals are "*to maintain revenue growth*" and "*to reduce risks*". Let us assume the input assignment is *fully satisfied (FS)* for the first goal and *partially satisfied (PS)* for the second one. A top-down goal reasoning (supported by tools such as the Goal Reasoning Tool[2]) generates all possible *strategies* that make the input assignment true, including the one depicted in Figure 1. The root goals with input assignment are shaded; other goals in the model are annotated with *fully satisfied (FS), partially satisfied (PS), partially denied (PD)* or *fully denied (FD)*. In this strategy, for example, goal "*to establish strategic partnership*" is preferred to "*to invest in new technologies*", while the goal "*to offer promotion*" is preferred to "*to open new sales channels*". Also note that, although not shown in Figure 1, a goal being satisfied means that its processes are carried out successfully and its domain assumptions are true.

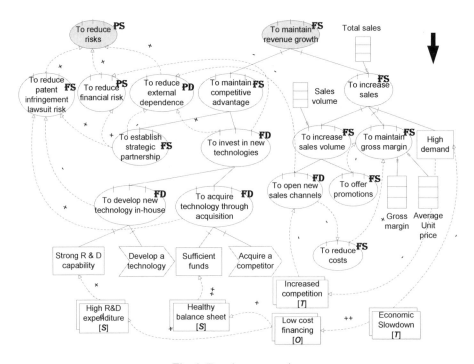

Fig. 1. Top-down reasoning

3.3   Evaluation of Specific Strategies

In some cases, a manager is not interested in all possible strategies for fulfilling given goals. Rather, she has specific strategies and she wants to compare them relative to given root goals (in order to eventually select one). A *bottom-up/forward reasoning*

---

[2] http://www.troposproject.org/tools/grtool/

algorithm [8] starts with an assignment of satisfaction values to some goals in a goal model. Such an assignment corresponds to a particular strategy to fulfill root goals. It then forward propagates these input values to the root goals, according to a set of pre-defined propagation rules.

In our example, evaluation of a specific strategy amounts to answering the question: if we pursue it, will the two root goals "*to maintain revenue growth*" and "*to reduce risks*" be satisfied at desire levels? Consider the input assignment depicted in Figure 2, where we choose "*to maintain competitive advantage*" by partially fulfilling the goal "*to develop new technology in-house*"; we also assume that we fully satisfy the goal "*to increase sales*". As before, goals with input assignment are shaded. A bottom-up reasoning (supported by tools such as jUCMNav tool[3]) propagates these input labels up the goal hierarchy all the way to the two root goals. As we can observe from the result (also shown in Figure 2), this strategy leads to "*to maintain revenue growth*" being partially satisfied, while "*to reduce risks*" being partially denied.

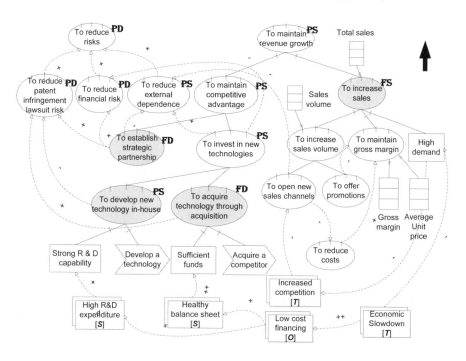

Fig. 2. Bottom-up goal reasoning

3.4   Probabilistic Evaluation of Strategies

Decision analysis techniques rest on an empirically verified assumption that humans are capable of framing a decision problem, listing possible decision options, and quantifying uncertainty, but are rather weak in combining information into a rational

---

[3] http://jucmnav.softwareengineering.ca/jucmnav/

decision. An influence diagram [4] is decision model that supports decision-making by computing the expected utility value of each decision option; the option with the highest utility value is optimal and should be chosen by the decision maker.

To carry out decision analysis, a goal model needs to be projected into an influence diagram. Such projections are automated using a set of translation rules. We omit their details in this paper.

In our example, we focus on a subset of the goal model, namely the one rooted at the goal *"to increase sales"*, as shown in Figure 3. The nodes directly involved in the decision analysis (supported by tools such as GeNIe[4]) is shaded. In particular, to pursue the goal *"to increase sales volume"*, two decision options are available (according to the OR decomposition in the original goal model): either by pursuing the goal *"to open new sales channels"* or *"to offer promotions"*. Notice that the goal *"to maintain gross margin"* and the domain assumption *"high demand"* are also involved here through influence links. A decision analysis amounts to answer the question: which of these two sub-goals should be pursued in order to maximize expected gain for the indicators *"sales volume"* and *"gross margin"* (which could then be combined into *"total sales"*).

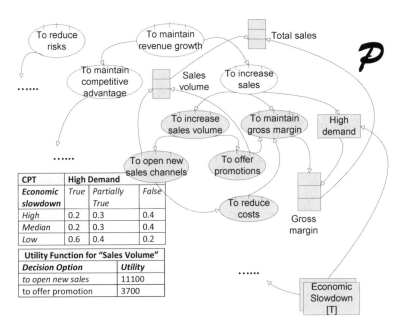

Fig. 3. Decision analysis

To reason with an influence diagram, we need to estimate conditional probabilities of various events, such as high demand for a certain product given economic slowdown, or high sales volume given we open new sales channel vs. we offer promotion; these events directly or directly affect the outcome of a decision. These

---

[4] http://genie.sis.pitt.edu/

probabilities are represented by a conditional probability tables (CPTs) for each event; the one for the event "*high demand*" given its parent event "*economic slowdown*" is shown the Figure 3. The resulting utility function for "*sales volume*" is also shown here. As we can see, the option "*to open new sales channels*" is preferable over "*to offer promotions*" as far as "*sales volume*" is concerned.

4   Related Work

The use of business-level concepts, such as business objects, rules and processes, has been researched extensively for more than a decade [9-11]. These efforts have more recently resulted in standards, such as the Business Process Modeling Notation (BPMN) [12]. These proposals focus on modeling business objects and processes, with little attention paid to business objectives. One exception is the Business Motivation Model (BMM) [8], which proposes an extensive vocabulary for modeling business objectives (among other things). What differentiate our work from BMM is that we give formal semantics to our modeling concepts by aligning them to the upper ontology DOLCE+, while concepts in BMM are only defined informally. For example, BMM includes several intentional concepts, such as vision, goal and objective; in our case, all these are modeled as goals.

   Modeling of goals has a long tradition within Requirements Engineering [14, 16-18]. However, these models lack primitive constructs for situation, influence and indicator which are important to Business Intelligence applications. A recent proposal has extended URN [18] to include indicators [15], but our concept of indicator is more general than that defined in URN: it covers both atomic and composite indicators, and pays special attention to the definition of composite indicators and the construction of indicator hierarchies.

   Modeling of situations, especially unfavorable ones (e.g., weaknesses or threats), has received much attention in Security Engineering under the topic of vulnerability. For example, [24] proposed a vulnerability-centric modeling ontology. More specifically, it identified the basic concepts for modeling and analyzing vulnerabilities, and proposed criteria to compare and evaluate security frameworks based on vulnerabilities. Inspired by SWOT analysis, our proposal supports a more comprehensive classification of situations, covering both favorable and unfavorable ones, also internal or external to an organization.

5   Conclusion

As a first step towards bridging the gap between the worlds of business and data in the adoption of BI technologies, we are working on the design of a business modeling language as a business-level counterpart to the Entity-Relationship Model. In this paper, we have introduced three key concepts for building business schemas, which are intended to capture the internal and external factors that affect the strategic goals of an organization, as well as the performance measures on their fulfillment. We have shown how they are used, in the context of goal modeling, to build and analyze business schemas based using existing formal analysis techniques supported by off-the-shelf tools.

As for our future work, on one direction, we are planning to carry out a real-world case study to evaluate the proposed concepts. The plan is to use our concepts during the requirements elicitation and analysis phase in a Business Intelligence project of a local Toronto hospital, in parallel to its actual development effort. Our objective is to evaluate our proposal by modeling and analyzing the project requirements in terms of the concepts and tools we have presented here. On another direction, we intend to develop tools to connect business schema to underlying data sources. Part of this work is being carried within the context of the Strategic Network for Business Intelligence[5].

References

1. Masolo, C., Borgo, S., Gangemi, A., Guarino, N., Oltramari, A.: Ontology Library (ver. 1.0, 31-12-2003). WonderWeb Deliverable D18. Laboratory for Applied Ontology (2003)
2. Dealtry, T.R.: Dynamic SWOT Analysis: Developer's Guide. Intellectual Partner (1992)
3. Hellerstein, J.L., Diao, Y., Parekh, S., Tilbury, D.M.: Feedback Control of Computing Systems. John Wiley & Sons, Chichester (2004)
4. Howard, R.A., Matheson, J.E.: Influence diagrams. Strategic Decision Group, Menlo Park (1984)
5. Giorgini, P., Mylopoulos, J., Sebastiani, R.: Goal-Oriented Requirements Analysis and Reasoning in the TROPOS Methodology. Engineering Application of Artificial Intelligence 18(2) (2005)
6. Uchil, A.: Goals-Based Strategic Planning: A No-Nonsense Practical Guide to Strategy. Outskirts Press (2009)
7. Sebastiani, R., Giorgini, P., Mylopoulos, J.: Simple and Minimum-Cost Satisfiability for Goal Models. In: Persson, A., Stirna, J. (eds.) CAiSE 2004. LNCS, vol. 3084, pp. 20–35. Springer, Heidelberg (2004)
8. Giorgini, P., Nicchiarelli, E., Mylopoulos, J., Sebastiani, R.: Formal Reasoning Techniques for Goal Models. Journal of Data Semantics (October 1, 2003)
9. Sutherland, J.: Business Objects in Corporate Information Systems. ACM Comput. Surv. 27(2), 274–276 (1995)
10. Loucopoulos, P., Katsouli, E.: Modelling Business Rules in an Office Environment. SIGOIS Bull. 13(2), 28–37 (1992)
11. Jablonski, S.: On the Complementarily of Workflow Management and Business Process Modeling. SIGOIS Bull. 16(1), 33–38 (1995)
12. Object Management Group: Business Process Modeling Notation (BPMN). (January 2009) version 1.2., http://www.omg.org/spec/BPMN/1.2/
13. Gangemi, A., Mika, P.: Understanding the Semantic Web through Descriptions and Situations. In: Chung, S., Schmidt, D.C. (eds.) CoopIS 2003, DOA 2003, and ODBASE 2003. LNCS, vol. 2888, pp. 689–706. Springer, Heidelberg (2003)
14. van Lamsweerde, A.: Requirements Engineering: From System Goals to UML Models to Software Specifications. John Wiley & Sons, Chichester (2009)
15. Pourshahid, A., Amyot, D., Peyton, L., Ghanavati, S., Chen, P., Weiss, M., Forster, A.J.: Business Process Management with the User Requirements Notation. Electronic Commerce Research 9(4), 269–316 (2009)

---

[5] http://bin.cs.toronto.edu/home/index.php

16. Dardenne, A., van Lamsweerde, A., Fickas, S.: Goal-directed requirements acquisition. Sci. Comput. Program. 20(1-2), 3–50 (1993)
17. Yu, E.: Towards Modelling and Reasoning Support For Early-phase Requirements Engineering. In: Proc. 3rd IEEE Int. Symp. on Requirements Engineering (1997)
18. International Telecommunication Union. Recommendation Z.151: User Requirements Notation (URN) - Language definition, http://www.itu.int/rec/TREC-Z.151/en
19. Giorgini, P., Mylopoulos, J., Sebastiani, R.: Goal-oriented requirements analysis and reasoning in the TROPOS methodology. Eng. Apps. of Artificial Intelligence 18(2) (2005)
20. Bresciani, P., Perini, A., Giorgini, P., Giunchiglia, F., Mylopoulos, J.: TROPOS: An agent-oriented software development methodology. Autonomous Agents and Multi-Agent Systems 8(3), 203–236 (2004)
21. Parmenter, D.: Key Performance Indicators: Developing, Implementing, and Using Winning KPIs, 2nd edn. John Wiley and Sons, Chichester (2009)
22. Wetzel, T.: States of Affairs. The Stanford Encyclopedia of Philosophy (Fall 2008 Edition), http://plato.stanford.edu/archives/fall2008/entries/states-of-affairs/
23. Barone, D., Jiang, L., Amyot, D., Mylopoulos, J.: Composite Indicators for Business Intelligence. In: 30th Int. Conf. on Conceptual Modeling (ER), Springer, Heidelberg (to appear)
24. Elahi, G., Yu, E., Zannone, N.: A Vulnerability-Centric Requirements Engineering Framework. Requirements Engineering Journal (2009)
25. Barone, D., Mylopoulos, J., Jiang, L., Amyot, D.: Business Intelligence Model, version 2.0. Technical Report CSRG-607. University of Toronto (March 2010), ftp://ftp.cs.toronto.edu/csri-technicalreports/INDEX.html
26. Barone, D., Peyton, L., Rizzolo, F., Amyot, D., Mylopoulos, J.: Towards Model-Based Support for Managing Organizational Transformation. In: Babin, G., Stanoevska-Slabeva, K., Kropf, P. (eds.) MCETECH 2011. Lecture Notes in Business Information Processing, vol. 78, pp. 17–31. Springer, Heidelberg (2011)

Evolving Requirements in Socio-Technical Systems: Concepts and Practice

Anna Perini, Nauman Qureshi, Luca Sabatucci*, Alberto Siena, and Angelo Susi

Fondazione Bruno Kessler - IRST, Center for Information Technology (CIT)
Via Sommarive, 18, 38050 Trento, Italy
{perini,qureshi,sabatucci,siena,susi}@fbk.eu

Abstract. Changes in requirements are inevitable in the context of socio-technical systems (STS) that involve human organizations with their rules, as well as individuals and software systems. In these complex systems need for changes may emerge once software components come into operation, due to undesirable behavior of the STS, or due to variations in organization rules, laws, resources and STS's components themselves. This leads to a problem of continuous analysis of evolving requirements in a traceable way. Our work is motivated by experience in a real project in the health-care domain, and in analysis practices based on participatory design methods (scenarios and personas) and on techniques for law-compliant requirements analysis. We revisit this experience and generalize it into a novel framework that provides concepts and practices to support an evolutionary and "participatory" process for requirements evolution in STS.

Keywords: Evolving Requirements, Participatory Design, Law Compliance.

1 Introduction

The increasing use of software systems in our daily life results into stronger and stronger integration of human and systems tasks, leading to form the so called socio-technical systems (hereafter, STS). Such systems incorporate different components, such as application domain's stakeholders (humans and organization), software system and resources, each playing its own roles to achieve common objectives. For instance, in the health-care domain, a *Social Residence STS* is defined by the patients and their relatives, doctors, nurses and software systems, each playing pre-defined roles and collaborating to support patients lives.

In STS, requirements do change overtime. Such changes may be caused by a variety of factors, which may be broadly classified as changes in: the operational environment (e.g. new or alternative technology or new usage conditions); in the organization within which the system is used (e.g. new organizational structure and procedures, new regulations); and in user's needs (e.g. new functional feature, new class of users as well as new users' preferences or way to do things). This leads to the problem of managing changes in requirements that emerge once the STS is in operation, and to the more general problem of software evolution.

---

* L. Sabatucci has been partially supported by the ACube project founded by the Autonomous Province of Trento, Italy.

M. Jeusfeld, L. Delcambre, and T.W. Ling (Eds.): ER 2011, LNCS 6998, pp. 440–447, 2011.

A rich research agenda for requirements evolution has been recently proposed [2]. It includes the need of *(i)* defining infrastructures for requirements evolution that accommodate other kinds of artifacts beside code; *(ii)* revising taxonomies for root causes for change, taking into account new challenges posed by today socio-technical systems; *(iii)* defining evolution mechanisms, both manual and automated; *(iv)* defining new viable frameworks at support of design for evolution and *(v)* evolutionary design.

Our work builds around the points *(i)*, *(iii)* — *(v)*, and is motivated by experience in a real project in the health-care domain, called *Ambient Aware Assistance - ACube*[1] and by experience in analysis practice based on participatory design methods for the active involvement of stakeholders in design decisions [1,6] and on techniques for the analysis of law-compliant requirements [10]. Needs for requirements change and system evolution in ACube emerged when focusing on the trade-off between having the STS behaving in a law-compliant way and satisfying the ultimate goal of the *Social Residence STS* itself, that is to create an environment which is more responsive and appropriate to their inhabitants' and users' cultural, emotional, spiritual and practical needs. We investigate methods that can be used to support the analysis of these types of requirements changes and ultimately on system evolution, with the involvement of key stakeholders.

In this paper, we revisit this experience and generalize it into a novel framework, we call it *CAFfE* (Concepts and Analysis Framework for Evolving requirements), which provides concepts and analysis techniques to support an evolutionary and "participatory" process for requirements evolution in STS. Novelty in our framework stems from the fact that: *(i)* we adopt a participatory design approach as process backbone, to enable the participation of stakeholders in design activities [1,6,5], including the software systems (within the STS). Participatory design provides peculiar techniques for engaging participants, such as scenarios and of "persona" (sort of fictional user) or ethnographic study techniques; *(ii)* we allow for the integration of specialized techniques, which are suitable for the analysis of particular concerns, as for instance law-compliance; and *(iii)* we aim at ensuring traceability across heterogeneous artifacts.

The rest of the paper is organized as follows: in Section 2, we present the context of our work. In section 3, we detail our conceptual analysis framework for evolving requirements. In section 4, we instantiate this framework using participatory design methods (e.g. focus group workshops) and the law-compliant requirements modeling framework *Nomos* [10]. Related work is discussed in section 5. Conclusion and future work are outlined in section 6.

2   Context

Ambient Aware Assistance: ACube is an ambient aware middleware, which is integrated into a *Social Residence STS*. It provides monitoring and event detection capabilities, which support the caregivers activities in the physical environment of the social residence, where patients with cognitive problems (some more severe than others, namely Alzheimer) live, assisted by caregivers.

---

[1] See http://acube.fbk.eu/fordetailsabouttheproject.

The *Social Residence STS* is characterized by the strong integration of social and technological dimensions. The social dimensions encompass the organizational setting with rules and humans, each one playing a role (patients, caregivers, nurses, doctors and managers). The technological dimension concerns software and hardware systems of the ACube middleware, e.g. sensors, video cameras, automatic doors. A first version of ACube system (ACube1 hereafter) is currently in operation.

Emerging Requirements: there are particular situations where, in spite of ACube1, human efforts to perform activities and relative time consumption are still relevant. For example, in case of emergencies, where a patient requires an immediate medication and caregivers or nurses are not authorized unless the doctor is present, or, in cases of monitoring, when crucial issues related to law compliance (e.g. privacy) can arise. More generally, undesirable behaviors of the *Social Residence STS* may occur, leading to the emergence of new requirements that call for an evolution of the technological components (ACube1), or of the whole STS.

3   Towards a Conceptual and Analysis Framework for Evolving Requirements (*CAFfE*)

Elaborating our experience in the ACube project, we identified a set of concepts, analysis methods and process steps that all together define a general framework for requirements evolution in STS, called *CAFfE*. *CAFfE* aims at supporting the analysis of the problem and of the solution space for the purpose of enabling requirements evolution. When need for requirements change emerges, the system analysts are involved for understanding causes of changes (by analyzing the problem space) and to identify possible evolutions of system requirements and associated solutions (within the solution space), through a "participatory" process that involves all the STS elements and the engineers who developed the technological elements.

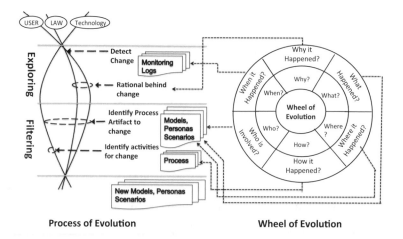

Fig. 1. Process for Evolution and Wheel of Evolution

Being a fragment of a real world, STS are characterized by many dimensions which need to be abstracted into a lower number along with analysis may be feasible. For instance in the case of our *Social Residence STS*, we consider three dimensions (or perspectives), namely **end-users perspective**, which includes goals and preferences; the **technological (hardware/software) perspective**, which can be characterized along the objectives i.e. the reason they have been designed for or the features these devices can control, and the **legal perspective** that governs the overall STS e.g. norms, policies or regulations that determines the roles and procedures in an STS. This abstraction provides the reference dimensions with respect to the problem space and the solution spaces can be defined. The solution space will include instances of artifacts produced exploiting specific analysis techniques, such as requirements models and scenarios.

As depicted in Fig. 1, this process is shaped in consecutive iterations in which **exploring** and **filtering** phases alternate until converging towards an ultimate solution spaces analysis. The process is composed as a sequence of iterations in which we distinguish two different phases: exploration and filtering. During the **exploration** the analysts study the "problem space" opening the analysis to all details including significant and less significant features of the domain. During the **filtering** phase, the analysis is restricted by selecting only the significant aspects for leading the following design sessions, by returning a restricted space as output in which some research directions are drafted. The "wheel of evolution" (right part of Fig. 1) guides the analysis of the problem and solution spaces. It is composed of "why" and "how" questions whose answers address real domain instances, in the case of problem space analysis, and respectively instances of the solution space.

Main concepts of the *CAFfE* framework are grounded on questions (why, when, who, what, how, where) from the "wheel of evolution". Those concepts are used to define a set of guidelines, recommendations and activities for generating the evolution process. The **participatory** design techniques have a relevant role in the process: domain experts own the (often implicit) knowledge to be considered in the study. Their involvement is fundamental in the exploration phase for defining boundaries of the space under analysis. The identification of relevant elements, during the "filtering", involves the participation of domain experts, who validate the value of the selected elements e.g. new scenarios. The following iteration starts on a smaller problem space, with respect to the previous one, thus ensuring a convergence driven by the validation of the participating stakeholders. Below we summarize activities that are typically performed in these phases:

Exploration. *Observing:* aims at identifying the need for the evolution. Changes are detected as chain of events that the STS monitors during its execution at runtime by logging the information. This provides a proof of external changes that helps the analyst in exploring the context, in which the evolution is necessary by addressing the (*WHEN*) question along the (*WHO*) question.

Analysis and Envisioning: relates the reasoning over the monitored data i.e. reading through the logs maintained by the STS. Decision criteria help in addressing the (*WHAT*) and (*WHY*) questions. Addressing such questions provides rationale to evolve the existing requirements. The activities related to the decision are supported by taxonomy of changes, such as those described in [4],which proposes four main contexts of changes, namely environment, requirements, viewpoints and design.

Filtering. *Assessing:* is a direct consequence of the decision analysis conducted in previous activity. It contains a set of activities and guidelines, from which it is possible to restrict and select the candidate solution by addressing the (*HOW*) question. Activities may regard different threads of specific analysis to evolve the overall STS.

Participatory Filtering and Validation: leads to decisions for selecting candidate artifacts to be changed/evolved. The target artifacts that are required to be evolved in order to satisfy the required external changes enable to answer (*WHERE*) questions. The situational context for the changes are closely linked with the artifacts to be affected. During this activity, the main concern is to keep the traceability among the key artifacts that were produced before the system was introduced in an operational environment.

Revising/Adapting: leads to mechanisms that enable the STS to alter its behavior during its execution.

4   Instantiating the Framework

The evolving requirements of ACube1 system to ACube2 were discussed with project managers, requirement engineers, directors of social residences, lawyers and developers. Three workshops took place for envisioning, assessing, filtering and validating the results. In Table 2, we summarize the application of the *CAFfE* framework along four aspects: Process phases, Process activity, Who is involved and Process artifacts.

Observing. The need for evolution arises from real situations in the environment. These were partly observed by the stakeholders and analysts and by the running system that monitors deviations between expected behavior and concrete flows of events, e.g., interventions made by nurses out of the control of the system, thus dis-aligned with the designed course of actions.

Analysis and Envisioning. Episodic knowledge (collected as logs) about the critical situations mentioned in section 2 was collected and organized before the meetings. To motivate the discussion during the workshop this knowledge was presented as scenarios/personas and models depicting the system as it is. The scenario/persona technique is used in interaction design to engage domain stakeholders during analysis [1]. Personas are concrete representations of fictional users, with their names, characteristics, aptitudes, and motivations. A scenario with personas may be easily presented to non technical people. *Nomos* [10] is a goal-oriented approach that provides the capability to model law prescriptions and the link between intentional elements and legal elements models to analyze their impact with respect to law compliance (e.g. regulations and norms). During the first exploratory workshop, contributors discussed shortcoming of the existing system. Scenarios highlights situation in which the system could be evolved. Participation of personnel of social residence was critical, such as the director, who prospected legal issues of evolution. For instance, the authorization management for health care interventions (what, who, why) were identified as cause of change. In this situation, the patient depends on the nurse to receive life-critical assistance. The nurse is able to provide the assistance, but she has to comply with the law, which protects the rights of the patient: the nurse has to be legally entitled to decide about the right

Phases		Process Activity	Who is Involved	Process Artifact Used
Exploration	Observing (when)	The system monitors changes with respect to designed courses of actions (as shown in initial *Nomos* Models [7]) For instance, real situation in the environment i.e. interventions made by nurses out of the control of the system, so, out of the designed course of actions (when)	ACube1 Tracking Subsystem	System Log reports Nomos Models
	Analysis & Envisioning (what, who, why)	Early analysis of changes in the domain envisioning of the causes of change are detected by the system. Later during the exploratory workshop individual analysis sessions (user, technology and legal analysis); for instance the **authorization management** for health care interventions (what, who, why) were identified as cause of change. New envisioned personas were identified.	Stakeholders (Director of the Social Residence, Lawyer) Designers (Project Manager, Requirements engineer, Software architect)	Personas & Scenarios (describing the functionalities of ACube1) Nomos Models - to analyze the impact of the changes on the ACube1 models
Filtering	Assessing (how, where)	In response to the changes, among several candidate alternatives for ACube1 evolution. Scenarios related to **authorization management** were assessed during second workshop [7] (How and where)	Stakeholders (Director of the Social Residence, Lawyer) Designers (Project Manager, Requirements engineer, Software architect)	Personas & Scenarios (describing the functionalities of ACube2) Nomos Models - to analyze the impact of the changes on the ACube2 models
	Participatory Filtering and Validation (how)	Possible alternatives were discussed to understand the impact on the current system of the chosen solutions via Nomos models informal analysis techniques; Personas and Scenarios related to **authorization management** were filtered. Solutions for authorization management during the third workshop. Early validation was obtained during this session.	Stakeholders (Director of the Social Residence, Lawyer) Designers (Project Manager, Requirements engineer, Software architect)	Personas & Scenarios (describing the functionalities of ACube2) Nomos Models - to analyze the impact of the changes on the ACube2models
	Revising/ Adapting (how)	Iterative revision of the requirements models via Nomos modeling. By incorporating new persona and scenarios.	Designers (Project Manager, Requirements engineer, Software architect)	Evolved Nomos Models Acube 2 Tracking Subsystem (Role management sub-system)

Fig. 2. Activity, artifacts and responsible stakeholder, in the process of requirements evolution between two system versions: from ACube1 to ACube2. They are detailed in [7].

assistance, or she must receive a proper authorization from a doctor. This is represented in the Nomos model by a "realization relationship" between the law Authorization to intervene and the goal Have Authorization. Consequently, the nurse depends on the doctor to have the authorization, although she has the experience to provide the assistance autonomously. This solution can fail if the stakeholders do not own the necessary rights. For example, if the nurse is not able to obtain the authorization (the doctor could be not reachable or is not possible for a doctor to give the authorization remotely), she fails in providing assistance to the patient, and the patient could die.

As post-analysis of the meeting, new envisioned personas were identified and consequently scenarios were evolved. For example, the manager Carla is one of the *personas* identified when analyzing possible evolutions of the system. The identified scenarios and personas describe hypothesis for evolving the existing ACube1 system and its short comings.

Assessing. New personas/scenarios (i.e. those related to authorization management) were assessed during second workshop (How and where). We discussed several candidate alternatives for ACube1 evolution, analyzing the legal impact, which can support identifying possible cause of change in the environment and ultimately help in identifying causes for system requirements evolution (we follow here the change taxonomy proposed in [4]). This leads to produce a set of revised models, on which selection upon critical review, will be operated during the "Filtering" phase. For example, a possible change in the requirements set is identified, to incorporate an answer to the above mentioned law-compliance problem. In the revised Nomos model (see [7]), since the nurse's goal Have authorization can not be removed (since a law prescribes it). It is further refined into the sub-goal Have direct authorization , which enables nurse the responsibility to obtain the authorization by the doctor, if present. Alternatively, if this goal fails, the nurse can ask for authorization remotely by using the multimedia services. This way, the achievement of the main goal is not inhibited, and assistance can be given.

Participatory Filtering and Validation. After the selected solutions are exploited via Nomos models informal analysis techniques, a third workshop was organized. The selected solution were presented via personas/scenarios and discussed to understand the impact on the current domain, including a risk and cost/benefit analysis. The goal of the workshop was to validate the analysts' work. For instance some scenarios were filtered during the meeting, whereas the Authorization management scenarios obtained a general consensus.

Revising/Adapting. During this activity, Nomos models and the requirements were updated to include new scenarios; new personas are transformed into new roles in the system e.g. Manager.

5   Related Work

The importance of requirements evolution is investigated, both theoretically and empirically, and a state-of-the art is provided in [3]. Evolution is considered inherent to software production but it is recognized that requirements engineering methodologies provide limited support to capture it. As a result, the need for Requirements Evolution Engineering is outlined, which involves analysis, modeling and practice of requirements evolution. Among the theoretical works, Zowghi and Offen [12] propose a model of requirements evolution based on a combination of monotonic and nonmonotonic reasoning. Requirements evolve through a systematic process that starts from an incomplete set of sentences and ends with a complete requirements model, validated through the intervention of stakeholders.

Considering approaches that aim at defining practices for evolution, in [4] it is illustrated the EVE (EVolution Engineering) project that proposes a framework for evolution based on a meta-model and an associated process model. The EVE meta-model includes the concepts of change (4 types: environment, requirements, design, viewpoint), impact, risk, violation, etc. The process aims at supporting the analysis of changes in either user's needs (requirements changes or R-Changes) or the environment (E-Changes). In [11] two quantitative techniques are presented, for dealing with requirements change in a maintenance environment based on data collected from one organization on several product releases. Several types of analysis are described.

6   Conclusion and Future Work

We proposed the *CAFfE* framework that aims at facilitating the evolution of requirements, with the involvement of key stakeholders, including the software system itself. Key elements of our framework are the adoption of participatory design techniques (e.g. workshop, 'persona'), which can be integrated with specialized analysis techniques (e.g. law-compliant requirements modeling). Another peculiarity of *CAFfE* is the evolution process that mixes exploratory phases, in which all possible alternatives are identified and analyzed, with filtering phases in which a subset of the alternatives are selected. This form of process helps managing evolving requirements and satisfying changing needs in a continuous way by revising and adapting the designed solutions.

We illustrated the framework on a real case study in the health-care domain, i.e. a *Social Residence STS*, in which the main problem consisted in managing the evolution of the software system artifacts (requirements and law models, personas, scenarios) corresponding to the current version of the system, into new artifacts describing the requirements of an new version of the system, in a continuous manner. Further instantiation of *CAFfE* on other scenarios of requirements evolution, which concern other specific aspects, will be necessary to consolidate and validate the framework. A formalization of the framework is ongoing, as well as the investigation of its integration with the recently proposed approach for supporting requirements engineering at run-time for self-adaptive systems [9,8].

References

1. Cooper, A., Reimann, R., Cronin, D.: About Face 3. Wiley, Chichester (2007)
2. Ernst, N., Mylopoulos, J., Wang, Y.: Requirements Evolution and What (Research) to Do about It. In: Design Requirements Engineering: A Ten-Year Perspective. Design Requirements Workshop, Cleveland, OH, USA, June 3-6, vol. 14, pp. 186–214 (2009); Revised and Invited Papers
3. Felici, M.: Observational Models of Requirements Evolution. Ph.D. thesis, University of Edinburgh (2004)
4. Lam, W., Loomes, M.: Requirements Evolution in the Midst of Environmental Change: A Managed Approach. In: CSMR 1998. IEEE Computer Society, Los Alamitos (1998)
5. Leonardi, C., Sabatucci, L., Susi, A., Zancanaro, M.: Design as intercultural dialogue: coupling human-centered design with requirement engineering methods. In: Proceedings of INTERACT 2011(to appear, 2011)
6. Nielsen, L.: Engaging personas and narrative scenarios. A study how a user-centered approach influenced the perception of the design process in the e-business group at AstraZeneca. Copenhagen Business School Editor, Fredriksberg, Denmark (2004)
7. Perini, A., Qureshi, N.A., Sabatucci, L., Siena, A., Susi, A.: On evolving requirements in socio-technical systems: Concepts and practice, SE Research Group Technical Report (TR-FBK-SE-2011-6), FBK, Trento, Italy (2011),
http://se.fbk.eu/files/TR-FBK-SE-2011-6.pdf
8. Qureshi, N.A., Jureta, I.J., Perini, A.: Requirements engineering for self-adaptive systems: Core ontology and problem statement. In: Mouratidis, H., Rolland, C. (eds.) CAiSE 2011. LNCS, vol. 6741, pp. 33–47. Springer, Heidelberg (2011)
9. Qureshi, N.A., Perini, A.: Requirements engineering for adaptive service based applications. In: 18th IEEE Int. Requirements Eng., Sydney, Australia, pp. 108–111 (2010)
10. Siena, A., Mylopoulos, J., Perini, A., Susi, A.: Designing law-compliant software requirements. In: Laender, A.H.F., Castano, S., Dayal, U., Casati, F., de Oliveira, J.P.M. (eds.) ER 2009. LNCS, vol. 5829, pp. 472–486. Springer, Heidelberg (2009)
11. Stark, G.E., Oman, P., Skillicorn, A., Ameele, A.: Journal of Software Maintenance: Research and Practice 11(5), 293–309 (1999)
12. Zowghi, D., Offen, R.: A Logical Framework for Modeling and Reasoning About the Evolution of Requirements. In: RE, pp. 247–257. IEEE Computer Society, Los Alamitos (1997)

Composite Indicators for Business Intelligence

Daniele Barone[1], Lei Jiang[1], Daniel Amyot[2], and John Mylopoulos[1]

[1] Department of Computer Science, University of Toronto, Toronto, ON, Canada
{barone,leijiang,jm}@cs.toronto.edu
[2] EECS, University of Ottawa, Ottawa, ON, Canada
damyot@eecs.uottawa.ca

Abstract. Business organizations continuously monitor their environments, looking out for opportunities and threats that may help/hinter the fulfilment of their objectives. We are interested in strategic business models that support such governance activities. In this paper, we focus on the concept of composite indicator and show how it can be used as basic building block for strategic business models that support evaluation and decision-making. The main results of this paper include techniques and algorithms for deriving values for composite indicators, when the relationship between a composite indicator and its component indicators cannot be fully described using well-defined mathematical functions.

Keywords: Business intelligence, Business model, Conceptual modeling languages, Key performance indicators, Strategic planning.

1 Introduction

A Key Performance Indicator (KPI), or simply *indicator* in this paper, is an industry term for a measure or metric that evaluates performance with respect to some objective. Indicators are used routinely by organizations to measure both success and quality in fulfilling strategic goals, enacting processes, or delivering products/services. For example, the indicator "Percentage increase of customer-base" may be appropriate for the goal "Increase market share", while "Average number of defects" may be a suitable indicator for software product quality.

Indicators constitute an important element of business modelling as they offer criteria for determining whether an organization is fulfilling its objectives, be they strategic goals, quality requirements, or production targets. They increasingly see applications in other areas. For example, in Requirements Engineering (RE), indicators have been used to evaluate the degree of fulfillment of goals [8], and in self-adaptive software systems they serve as monitored variables that determine whether a system is doing well relative to its mandate, or whether it should adapt its behaviour [13].

To choose the right indicators for a given object (goal/process/product), one must have a good understanding of what is important to the organization. Moreover, this importance is generally contextual, e.g., indicators useful to a finance team may be inappropriate for a sales force. Because of the need to develop

M. Jeusfeld, L. Delcambre, and T.W. Ling (Eds.): ER 2011, LNCS 6998, pp. 448–458, 2011.

a good understanding of what is important, performance indicators are closely associated with techniques for assessing the present state of the business.

A very common method for choosing indicators is to apply a management framework such as the Balanced Scorecard [6], whereby indicators measure a range of factors in a business, rather than a single one (e.g., profits).

The objects that indicators assess – be they goals, processes or products – are generally composite, consisting of hierarchies of elements. For instance, goals are usually modelled as AND/OR tree hierarchies of sub-goals to reflect a reductionist view of problem solving. Likewise, processes are usually defined in terms of sub-processes ultimately reduced to atomic actions that an agent can perform, and products are modelled as aggregates of simpler parts that are themselves composite objects amenable to further decomposition. Alternatively – and orthogonally to the examples above – a process/product may be a root node of a taxonomy tree that defines specializations (e.g., the process "Loan application" might be specialized to "Small loan application" and "Large loan application"). Of course, the value of an indicator for a composite object should depend on the values of indicators for objects one level lower in the hierarchy. Unfortunately, there are no guidelines on what this dependency is and how to define it consistently for a given business model.

In this paper, we focus on *composite* indicators, which are indicators whose values are obtained from those of their *components*. These components themselves may also be composite indicators, leading to a hierarchy of indicators. We are interested in the problem of propagating values of indicators from lower to higher levels, much like label propagation in goal reasoning [1,4]. This type of analysis is essential for calculating / deriving values for composite indicators. This is a non-trivial problem since, in many cases, there is no well-defined mathematical function that relates a composite indicator to its components. This might be simply due to lack of knowledge about the indicators, or the intrinsic nature of the indicators at hand. Our main contribution consists in proposing different techniques and algorithms for deriving values of composite indicators, when the relationship between a composite indicator and its component indicators cannot be fully described using well-defined mathematical functions.

This research is conducted in the context of the Business Intelligence Network, a Canada-wide strategic research network. Our long-term objective within the network is to develop a conceptual modelling language, called Business Intelligence Model (BIM)[2], for modelling business objectives, processes and objects in order to support business intelligence activities.

The rest of the paper is structured as follows. Sections 2 presents key concepts for strategic business models. Section 3 introduces the concept of indicator and how it can be used to evaluate goals and situations. Section 4 presents in detail three techniques to derive values of composite indicators using different estimation / approximation approaches. Finally, Sections 5 and 6 discuss related work and conclusions, respectively.

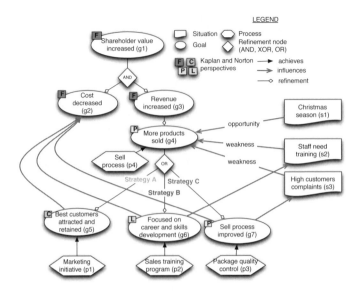

Fig. 1. Examples of goals, situations and influences

2 Strategic Business Models

In this section, we review some of the key concepts used in BIM [2] to support strategic business modelling and reasoning about strengths, weaknesses, opportunities and threats (popularly known as SWOT). Technical details about these concepts are presented in a companion paper [5].

A *goal* (also intention, objective, vision, mission) represents a desired state-of-affairs, defined during strategic planning and pursued (hopefully successfully) during business operation. The most basic characteristics of goals include: i) a goal may be AND/OR-refined into subgoals so that its *satisfaction* level depends on that of its subgoals; ii) a goal may be satisfied in more than one way if it or any of its refinements are OR-refined, in which case a choice needs to be made among alternative subgoals in deciding how to fulfill the root-level goal; and iii) a goal's satisfaction may be affected by that of goals other than its subgoals. Goal analysis produces a goal model consisting of an AND/OR refinement tree with additional positive/negative *contributions*. The satisfaction level of a goal can be inferred from that of others in the same goal model using a label propagation algorithm [4,1]. Examples of goals are shown in Figure 1. Notice how the "Shareholder value increased" goal is AND-decomposed into the sub-goals "Cost decreased" and "Revenue increased"; similarly, the "More Products sold" goal is OR-decomposed in three different alternative sub-goals (strategies), namely "Best customers attracted and retained", "Focused on career and skills development", and "Sell process improved". An example of influence among goals is represented by the one existing from the "Sell process improved" goal towards the "Cost decreased" goal.

In addition to goals, we model partial states of the world as *situations*. For strategic business models, we need the notion of organizational situation, such as "Christmas season", an opportunity for a sales organization, or "Competitor buys key technology", a potential threat. Analogously to satisfaction levels for goals, we have *occurence* levels for situations, which define the degree to which a situation occurs in the current state-of-affairs. The situations "Christmas season", "Staff need training", and "High customers complaints", described in Figure 1, are some examples of partial states of the world that can occur within a business context.

To reason about goal satisfaction under the influence of situations, we extend the contribution relation so that it can be used to relate any combination of goals and situations. Hereafter, we refer to this concept using the term *influence*. For example, the situation "Christmas season" positively influences the goal "Increase sales", while the situation "Booming economy" positively influences the situation "Growing inflation". We call such influence relations logica,' to distinguish them from probabilistic ones. Figure 1 shows some examples of such influences. For instance, the "Staff need training" situation, representing an internal weakness for the company, influences negatively the "More products sold" goal. We characterize influences along two dimensions: i) *direction*: a positive (resp. negative) influence exists from a situation/goal to another if the occurence/satisfaction of the source increases (resp. decreases) the occurence/satisfaction of the target; and, ii) degree or *strength*: an influence is full if it is a causal relation (i.e., 100% effect on the target), otherwise it is partial.

3   Indicators

An *indicator* is a measure, quantitative or qualitative, on the progress or degree of fulfillment of organization goals. The subject of an indicator is a particular *feature* or *quality* of an element in the business environment, e.g., the *workload* of an employee, or the *compliance* of an internal process with respect to external regulations.

To express *why* an indicator is needed and *what* it is measuring, we rely on two relations, *evaluates* and *measures*, as illustrated in Figure 2. In this figure, the indicator "Number of products sold" is needed (why) to evaluate the goal "More products sold" by measuring the task "Sell products".

Each indicator, being composite or component, has a *current value* which is evaluated against a set of parameters: *target (value)*, *threshold (value)* and *worst (value)* [9]. The result of such evaluation is a normalized value (ranging in $[-1, 1] \in \mathbb{R}$), which is often referred to as the *performance level*. Note that a current value can be assigned by: i) extracting it at run-time from back-end data sources[1], ii) supplying it interactively to explore "what-if" scenarios, or iii) calculating it with a *metric* expression (see Section 4.1).

---

[1] *Dimensions* and *levels* [9] can be used to filter data from datawarehouses.

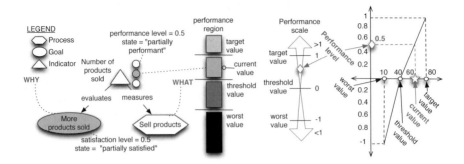

Fig. 2. An example of an indicator to evaluate a goal

Fig. 3. Example of interpolation [11] to calculate performance levels

The above parameters can be combined in different ways to define *performance regions*. Figure 2 shows an example of a *lower* region, but *upper* and *merged* regions can be defined in a similar way.

The relative position of indicator current values within such regions leads to indicator performance levels, as shown by Figure 3. Notice how the worst and target values are mapped respectively to -1 and +1 on the performance scale, while the threshold value is mapped to 0. A linear interpolation[2] is used to approximate performance levels, as also described by System equation 1 [11]. For instance, the performance level (pl) for Figure 3 is $pl(60) = \frac{|60-40|}{|80-40|} = 0.5$.

$$pl(\text{current } v.) = \begin{cases} \frac{|\text{current } v. - \text{threshold } v.|}{|\text{target } v. - \text{threshold } v.|}, & \text{if } \text{current } v. \geq \text{threshold } v. \\[2ex] -\frac{|\text{current } v. - \text{threshold } v.|}{|\text{threshold } v. - \text{worst } v.|}, & \text{if } \text{current } v. < \text{threshold } v. \end{cases} \quad (1)$$

Performance levels are, in turn, propagated to the corresponding goals to evaluate satisfaction levels. For example, in Figure 2, the performance level 0.5 is propagated to the satisfaction level of the corresponding goal which, in turn, is mapped to a "partial satisfied" state (orange colour[3]).

As shown in the following section, indicators can be used to evaluate situations in a similar way we do for goals, by propagating a performance level to the occurence level of the situation under evaluation. For example, the indicator "Number of products returned" can evaluate the situation "Low number of returned products".

4   Reasoning with Indicators

In a business strategy model, indicators are associated with various business elements. These elements in general are composite, consisting of hierarchies of

---

[2] Other forms of interpolation can be used, e.g., polynomial, spline, etc.
[3] BIM provides mapping tables to map satisfaction, occurence and performance levels to corresponding states of business elements.

sub-elements. Such structure implies hierarchies for indicators. For example in Figure 6, the goal hierarchy results in a hierarchy for associated indicators. More specifically, "Number of special package" is a component indicator of "Number of products sold", since it evaluates the goal "Sell process improved',' which is a sub-goal of "More products sold".

We are interested in algorithms that propagate values of indicators at a lower level in a hierarchy to the ones at a higher level, much like the label propagation in goal reasoning [1,4]. To accomplish this, we classify such propagation into four categories, as described in Figure 4, based on what is known about the relation between a composite indicator and its components.

		Knowledge	Outcome	
More ↑	Quantitative (accurate)	component current values, component strength influences, composite (well-defined) mathematical function.	composite current values, composite performance level.	More ↑
	Quantitative (heuristic)	component current values, component strength influences, component conversion factors, composite (approx.) metric.	composite (approx.) current value, composite (approx.) performance level.	Accurate
Less	Quantitative (normalized)	component current values, component performance levels, normalizing function, composite (approx.) metric.	composite (approx.) performance level	Less
	Qualitative	component current values and/or label state values, propagation rules.	composite label state value, composite conflict.	

Knowledge (left vertical axis label)

Fig. 4. Techniques classification

In the simplest case, a relation is fully described using a mathematical function. In this case, there is no problem in computing values for the composite indicator. For example, profits can be calculated directly from revenues and costs. In other cases, when such a mathematical relation does not exist, indicator values have to be derived using estimation or approximation techniques. In what follows, we present three techniques to derive values of composite indicators using conversion factors, range normalization, and qualitative reasoning.

4.1 Quantitative Reasoning

When a composite indicator does not share that same unit of measure as its components' units, a necessary condition for finding a metric that computes its values is that there is a suitable conversion factor for each component indicator that has a different unit of measure.

For example, consider the two indicators "Employee cost" and "Working time". In particular, Employee cost can be defined as a composite indicator whose value relies on the component indicator Working time. According to our requirement, we need to convert the current value of Working time values measured in hours into Employee cost units. One possible conversion factor is to take the average of the wage per hour for all employees[4]. Assuming that such an average is 20 and that the current value for Working time is 160 hours, we can calculate an approximated current value for Employee cost as:

1. 20 dollars $= 1$ hours $\rightarrow 20\frac{\text{dollars}}{\text{hours}} = 1$, where 20 is the conversion factor;

---

[4] This value can be also defined as an "Average hourly wage" indicator and, in turn, as a related indicator for the Employee cost.

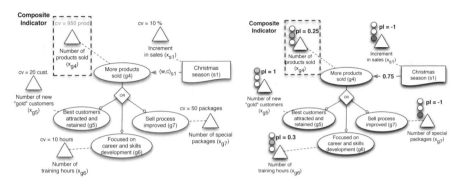

Fig. 5. Examples of reasoning with conversion factors

Fig. 6. Examples of reasoning with performance levels of indicators

2. $160 \text{ hours} \cdot 20\frac{\text{dollars}}{\text{hours}} = 3,200 \text{ dollars}.$

Notice that in many cases a conversion factor is an estimate based on previous experience / statistics. For example, the average wage per hour could be 30 instead of 20 for a different company. When conversions are impossible, e.g., it is not possible to convert gallons to square feet, we have to fallback to a "normalized" approach, described further in this section, or to a "qualitative" one, presented in Section 4.2.

Now supposing that suitable conversion factors are available, we are able to define valid metric expressions which contain: i) current values for component indicators, ii) influence strengths, and iii) conversion factors. With this aim, we adopt and use off-the-shelf the grammar of the Jep Java Library[5], which allows us to express rich and flexible expressions to meet user requirements. An example of such an expression is $x_{g_4} = x^e_{g_4} + w_{s_1} \cdot c_{s_1} \cdot x_{s_1} + \sum_{j=5}^{j=7} w_{g_j} \cdot c_{g_j} \cdot x_{g_j}$[6], which is used in Figure 5 to calculate the current value of the "Number of products sold" indicator.

Another form of quantitative conversion is needed when we do not have a conversion factor to relate component indicators to a composite one. This conversion is based on "range normalization'," which takes values spanning a specific range and represents them in another range. Indeed, when we calculate the performance level of an indicator (by using its current value and parameters as described in Section 3), we are producing a "normalized value" in a range within $[-1, +1] \in \mathbb{R}$. As show in Figure 6, this technique calculates the performance level for each component indicator and combines them to calculate the performance level of the composite one. We have defined a BNF grammar to build the qualitative metrics used to combine performance levels. Due to space limitations, we omit its description, but the interested reader can find further details in [2].

---

[5] http://www.singularsys.com/jep/

[6] $x^e_{g_4}$ is the expected value of products sold while the different w_m and c_n are, respectively, influence strengths and conversion factors of the component indicators.

4.2 Qualitative Reasoning

Inspired by [4], we augment the techniques of the previous section with a qualitative reasoning technique. In this case, instead of propagating indicator performance levels, we propagate the category label assigned to indicators. This technique has long been used for qualitative goal reasoning in RE.

A major difference between this technique and ones presented in the previous sections is that conflicts are allowed, i.e., an indicator can be at the same time "fully performant" and "fully non-performant" (see Figures 7 and 8). This is analogously to [4], where goals have *satisfiability* values but also *deniability* ones: during label propagation, a goal can be both "partially satisfied" and "partially denied". In this case, we associate each indicator I_i with two variables, namely, positive performance (per^+) and negative performance (per^-). Ranging in {F,P,N} ("full", "partial", "none"), such that $F > P > N$. These variables represent the current evidence of performance or non-performance of an indicator I_i. For instance, $per^+(I_i) \geq P$ states that there is at least partial evidence that I_i is performant. To assign "evidence" and, therefore, values to the variables per^+ and per^-, we use the mapping rules described in Figure 7. When the current value of an indicator I_i lies among its target value and the middle point M (a value that is equally distant from the target t and from the threshold th), we conclude that $per^+ =$ "*partial*" and $per^- =$ "*none*".

Indicators colour (per⁺, per⁻)	Evidence	Mapping rule	Variables (per⁺, per⁻)
	fully performant (green)	$cv \geq t$	$per^+ =$ "full" $per^- =$ "none"
	partially performant (green-orange)	$M \leq cv < t$	$per^+ =$ "partial" $per^- =$ "none"
	partially non-performant (red-orange)	$th \leq cv < M$	$per^+ =$ "none" $per^- =$ "partial"
	fully non-performant (red)	$w \leq cv < th$	$per^+ =$ "none" $per^- =$ "full"

Fig. 7. Mapping rules, where: cv = current value, th = threshold value, w = worst value, and M = middle value among the target t and threshold th

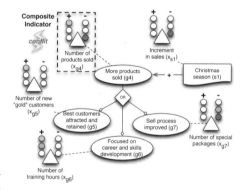

Fig. 8. Examples of qualitative reasoning

Propagation of the values from component indicators to a composite indicator relies on the axioms and (adapted) propagation rules from [4], which are summarized in Table 1. For example, the rule $(I_2^r, I_3^r) \overset{and}{\longmapsto} I_1^c$ states how labels are propagated when there is an AND-decomposition relation between goal G_1 and sub-goals G_2 and G_3 (here we refer to goal nodes, but they can also be situation nodes, or a mix of both), with associated indicators I_1^c, I_2^r and I_3^r. Analogously, $I_2^r \overset{-S}{\longmapsto} I_1^c$ states how labels are propagated when there exists an influence relation between goals G_2 and G_1, with associated indicators I_2^r and I_1^c. The strength of this influence is equal to $-S$, which means that if G_2 is

Table 1. Propagation rules in the qualitative framework. The (or), (+D), (-D), (++D), (--D) cases are dual w.r.t. (and), (+S), (-S), (++S), (--S) respectively. See [4], for details.

	$(I_2^r, I_3^r) \xmapsto{and} I_1^c$	$I_2^r \xmapsto{+S} I_1^c$	$I_2^r \xmapsto{-S} I_1^c$	$I_2^r \xmapsto{++S} I_1^c$	$I_2^r \xmapsto{--S} I_1^c$
$per^+(I_1^c)$	$min\begin{cases} per^+(I_3^r) \\ per^+(I_2^r) \end{cases}$	$min\begin{cases} per^+(I_2^r) \\ P \end{cases}$	N	$per^+(I_2^r)$	N
$per^-(I_1^c)$	$max\begin{cases} per^-(I_3^r) \\ per^-(I_2^r) \end{cases}$	N	$min\begin{cases} per^+(I_2^r) \\ P \end{cases}$	N	$per^+(I_2^r)$

satisfied, then there is some evidence that G_1 is denied, but if G_2 is denied, then nothing is said about the satisfaction of G_1, see [4] for further details.

Figure 8 provides an example of our qualitative approach. For each indicator, the per^+ variable is represented by a traffic light with a plus symbol on the top, while the per^- variable by the one with a minus symbol on the top. The colours for the traffic lights are those described in Figure 7. Propagating the values of the component indicators by using Table 1, we obtain a conflict for the composite indicator "Number of products sold". When such conflicts appear in a schema, although undesirable, they do help to highlight particular aspects of a business that need user attention because of possible inconsistencies.

5   Related Work

The use of business-level concepts—such as goals, processes and resources—has been researched widely for at least 15 years and is already practiced to some extent in both Data Engineering and Software Engineering. In the literature, different modeling proposals exist that are related to our work, such as i* [14], URN/GRL [1] and KAOS [3,8], all from the general area of Goal-Oriented Requirements Engineering. From these we have adopted intentional and social concepts. However, these models lack primitive constructs for influence relationships, (composite) indicators, and various types of situations integrated in the BIM modeling framework. Recent proposals have extended URN to include indicators [12]. We share ideas with this work; however: i) our indicators are more general and they can be used to measure any model object, including other indicators; ii) we provide more guidelines to distinguish "what" is measured and "why" it is measured; and iii) our indicators can be used to evaluate situations which, from our perspective, are fundamental for strategic reasoning.

In [10], the authors propose a formal framework for modelling goals (and for evaluating their satisfaction) based on performance indicators. Our work shares similar intentions but focuses more on the concept of composite indicator and a way to define metric expressions to calculate their values.

From a business perspective, our business schemas can capture what is commonly found in Strategic Maps [7] and Balanced Scorecards [6], but we also support reasoning and we include the concept of situation which is a fundamental concept for supporting SWOT analysis. In fact, as we show in [5], we can map our approach to SWOT analysis and other languages that enable goal analysis techniques [4,1], including probabilistic ones.

6 Conclusions

In this paper, we presented a model-based approach to design and reason about an organization's business environment and strategies. Specifically, we provided qualitative and quantitative techniques to analyze the impact of strategies on organization goals, by relying on different types of knowledge.

To validate our proposal, we are currently involved in a Business Intelligence project at a Toronto-area hospital, where we are building a global picture of patient flow in order to identify sources of bottlenecks within and beyond the hospital. We are also evolving a tool prototype to support the modeling and analysis techniques described in this paper.

Acknowledgments. This work was supported by BIN and NSERC. We are grateful to E. Yu, L. Peyton and many others for useful discussions.

References

1. Amyot, D., Ghanavati, S., Horkoff, J., Mussbacher, G., Peyton, L., Yu, E.S.K.: Evaluating goal models within the goal-oriented requirement language. Int. J. Intell. Syst. 25(8) (2010)
2. Barone, D., Mylopoulos, J., Jiang, L., Amyot, D.: Business Intelligence Model, ver. 1.0. Tech. Rep. CSRG-607. University of Toronto (March 2010), ftp://ftp.cs.toronto.edu/csri-technical-reports/INDEX.html
3. Dardenne, A., van Lamsweerde, A., Fickas, S.: Goal-directed requirements acquisition. Sci. Comput. Program. 20(1-2), 3–50 (1993)
4. Giorgini, P., Mylopoulos, J., Nicchiarelli, E., Sebastiani, R.: Reasoning with goal models. In: Proc. of the 21st Intern. Conf. on Conceptual Modeling (2002)
5. Jiang, L., Barone, D., Amyot, D., Mylopoulos, J.: Strategic models for business intelligence: Reasoning about opportunities and threats. In: Jeusfeld, M., Delcambre, L., Ling, T.W. (eds.) ER 2011. LNCS, vol. 6998, pp. 448–458. Springer, Heidelberg (2011)
6. Kaplan, R.S., Norton, D.P.: Balanced Scorecard: Translating Strategy into Action. Harvard Business School Press, Boston (1996)
7. Kaplan, R.S., Norton, D.P.: Strategy maps: Converting intangible assets into tangible outcomes. Harvard Business School Press, Boston (2004)
8. van Lamsweerde, A.: Reasoning About Alternative Requirements Options. In: Borgida, A.T., Chaudhri, V.K., Giorgini, P., Yu, E.S. (eds.) Conceptual Modeling: Foundations and Applications. LNCS, vol. 5600, pp. 380–397. Springer, Heidelberg (2009)
9. Parmenter, D.: Key Performance Indicators. John Wiley & Sons, Chichester (2007)
10. Popova, V., Sharpanskykh, A.: Formal modelling of organisational goals based on performance indicators. Data & Knowledge Engineering (2011)

11. Pourshahid, A., Amyot, D., Peyton, L., Ghanavati, S., Chen, P., Weiss, M., Forster, A.J.: Business Process Management with the User Requirements Notation. Electronic Commerce Research 9(4), 269–316 (2009)
12. Pourshahid, A., Richards, G., Amyot, D.: Toward a goal-oriented, business intelligence decision-making framework. In: Babin, G., Stanoevska-Slabeva, K., Kropf, P. (eds.) MCETECH 2011. LNBIP, vol. 78, pp. 100–115. Springer, Heidelberg (2011)
13. Souza, V., Lapouchnian, A., Mylopoulos, J.: System identication for adaptive software systems: a requirements-engineering perspective. In: Jeusfeld, M., Delcambre, L., Ling, T.W. (eds.) ER 2011. LNCS, vol. 6998, pp. 448–458. Springer, Heidelberg (2011)
14. Yu, E.: Towards modelling and reasoning support for early-phase requirements engineering. In: RE 1997, Washington, USA (1997)

Incorporating Traceability in Conceptual Models for Data Warehouses by Using MDA

Alejandro Maté and Juan Trujillo

Lucentia Research Group
Department of Software and Computing Systems
University of Alicante
{amate,jtrujillo}@dlsi.ua.es

Abstract. The complexity of the Data Warehouse (DW) development process requires to follow a methodological approach in order to be successful. A widely accepted approach for this development is the hybrid one, in which requirements and data sources must be accommodated to a new DW model. The main problem is that the relationships between conceptual elements coming from requirements and those coming from data sources are lost in the process, since no traceability is explicitly specified, consuming additional time and resources. Previously, we have defined a trace metamodel in order to trace user requirements to DW conceptual models. In this paper, we complement our approach by including traceability along the successive refinements performed at the conceptual level. Therefore, we preserve the existing relationships between elements, eliminating additional costs derived from performing the matching process multiple times. We provide an example of how Query/View/Transformation rules can automate trace generation, and we also provide a set of guidelines for connecting conceptual elements coming from requirements with those coming from the data sources.

Keywords: Data warehouses, traceability, conceptual models, user requirements, data sources, MDA.

1 Introduction

Data Warehouses (DW) integrate several heterogeneous data sources in multi-dimensional structures (i.e. facts and dimensions) in support of the decision-making process [5]. Therefore, the development of the DW is a complex process which must be carefully planned in order to meet user needs. In order to develop the DW, three different approaches, similar to the existing ones in Software Engineering were proposed: bottom-up, top-down, and hybrid [3].

The first two approaches ignore at least one source of information for the DW, leading to failure in DW projects [3]. On the other hand, the third approach (hybrid) makes use of both data sources and user requirements [9], solving the incompatibilities by acommodating both requirements and data sources in a single conceptual model. Nevertheless, the acommodation process introduces modifications, causing the existing traceability by name matching to be lost. Once

M. Jeusfeld, L. Delcambre, and T.W. Ling (Eds.): ER 2011, LNCS 6998, pp. 459–466, 2011.
© Springer-Verlag Berlin Heidelberg 2011

traceability is lost, the effort required for validating requirements or performing changes is increased, and the quality of the result is decreased [12]. The reason is that the developer must repeatedly track down each element through the different layers involved in the development process, which is time consuming and error prone. Despite this drawback, aside from our previous contribution in [7], where we defined a trace metamodel to trace DW requirements to their corresponding conceptual elements, the traceability aspect has been overlooked in DW development. By incorporating traceability, these time consuming and error prone tasks are minimized, allowing the developer to focus on the conceptual design of the DW, and improving the quality of the final product.

In this paper, we complement our previous works by including support for the traceability of conceptual elements through the different Platform Independent Models (PIM) up to the final conceptual model. We also provide an example of how trace generation can be automated where possible.

The remainder of the paper is structured as follows. Section 2 presents related work about traceability and DWs. Section 3 introduces the necessary trace semantics in order to include traceability at the conceptual level in DWs. Section 4 presents the QVT rules for automatic derivation of traces. Section 5 presents an example of application, in order to show the benefits of our proposal. Finally, Section 6 outlines the conclusions and further work to be done.

2   Related Work

In this section, we will briefly discuss the existing traceability research, its benefits and problems, and its current status in the DW field. Due to space constraints we will only describe the most important aspects.

Traditionally, traceability is focused on requirements. Either coming from the traditional RE [4,10] or following a MDD approach [1,2], requirements are traced to their lower abstraction level counterparts. Therefore, traceability helps assesing the impact of changes in requirements and rationale comprehension, by identifying which parts of the implementation belong to each requirement [2]. However, the effort required to manually record the traces, and the lack of standarization, make it difficult to apply traceability to projects. Therefore, there is a special interest on automating traces.

Our approach, presented in [9], applies MDD, and is sensitive to generate traces by exploiting transformation logic, thus being less error prone than manual recording. Therefore, by generating traces simultaneously as conceptual models are transformed, we provide support for requirements validation, impact change and automated analysis, while minimizing the drawbacks. While our approach applies MDA for DW development, other development proposals [3,11] make use of similar layers, so they could benefit from this approach.

In order to maintain all this information, elements coming from both requirements and data sources must be traced while maintaining the semantics of their relationships, allowing us to support automatic operations over the models.

3   Traceability from PIM to PIM DW Models

As previously stated, we require to trace information from both user requirements and data sources up to the final conceptual implementation. First, we will
introduce the trace metamodel and the concepts used for tracing elements along
the PIM models. Then we will describe how these elements will be traced.

In order to trace conceptual elements, up to the final PIM, we require to
include different semantics, in order to differentiate the relationships between elements and support further automatic operations. These semantics are included
in the trace metamodel (we refer the reader to [7] for more information) depicted
in figure 1. The semantic types on which we will focus are:

– **Evolution** links are included to handle horizontal traceability which takes
  care of element changes at the same layer. In our case these links will track
  the different versions of each element at each PIM model.
– **Overlap** and **Conflict** are used for relating elements coming from both requirements and data sources in different shape. In this case, the developer
  will decide which is the correct solution to the conflict. These links are crucial for enabling traceability support, as they record the semantics between
  elements coming from data sources and those coming from requirements.
– **Rationalization** links are included as means of enabling the user to record
  his own annotations in the trace model about changes or decisions taken and
  provide reconciliated solutions for existing conflicts.

These trace types will be recorded in the different trace models included in our
proposal, as shown in figure 2. In our proposal, first we derive an initial PIM

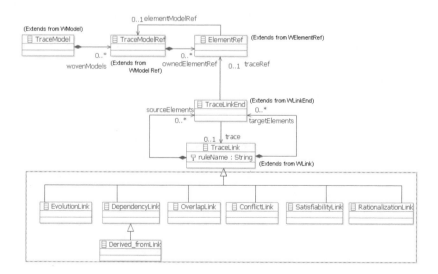

Fig. 1. Trace metamodel with semantic links for DWs

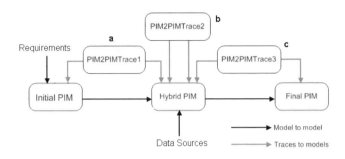

Fig. 2. Trace models linking the different PIM models in our DW approach

model from the user requirements represented in the requirements model. This
PIM is refined with the necessary additions, not present at requirements level,
and then it is derived into a mixed, hybrid PIM. The first trace model, labeled as
"a" in figure 2, connects the initial PIM to the hybrid PIM in a pretty straightforward manner by means of *Evolution* traces. This trace model "a" is included
in order to support automatic operations which require to track information
related to requirements.

After we have derived the initial PIM, we first obtain a Platform Specific
Model (PSM) from the data sources, which serves as basis to create a hybrid
PIM model [8]. The hybrid PIM includes conceptual elements from both requirements and data sources and is characterized by representing the same concepts
in different versions. In order to relate the different versions, their relationships
are recorded by means of traces in trace model "b". These traces must be manually added because typically there is no knowledge about which element coming
from the data sources is the counterpart to an element coming from user requirements. Therefore, we provide a set of guidelines in order to correctly relate
elements in the hybrid PIM: whenever an element coming from requirements is
complementary with its representation coming from data sources, they are related by means of *Overlap* links (G1). On the other hand, whenever an element
coming from requirements is contrary to its representation coming from data
sources, they are related by means of *Conflict* links (G2). In order to solve this
situation, either one of the elements in conflict can be marked as solution, if
it fits the user needs (G3) or, alternatively, the developer can provide a new,
reconciling element (G4), by means of *Rationalization* links.

Once the hybrid model has been refined, the desired elements which will be
part of the final implementation are marked, as proposed in [9], and derived
into the final PIM. Evolution traces, recorded in trace model "c" as part of the
derivation into the final PIM, show which elements from the hybrid PIM were
chosen to define the final conceptual model. This way, we can trace which parts
of the final model come from either requirements or data sources, allowing us to
perform impact change analysis as well as other automatic analysis tasks.

After having defined which trace models record the evolution of conceptual elements at PIM level, we will provide an example of how trace generation can be automated by means of transformations.

4   Automatic Derivation of Traceability Models in Data Warehouses

In this section, we will provide an example of how the necessary transformations can be formally defined to automatically generate the necessary traces. Due to paper constraints, we will only show one transformation rule as example.

According to our proposal for developing DWs [9], we use a hybrid approach, transforming models up to the final implementation by means of QVT rules. QVT rules specify a transformation by checking for a defined pattern in the source model. Once the pattern is found, a QVT rule transforms elements from the source metamodel into the target metamodel. In our case, a QVT which creates the *Evolution* link, from the hybrid to the final PIM, between overlapping bases in the hybrid PIM, is shown in figure 3.

In this QVT, two overlapping bases from the hybrid conceptual model, "b1" and "b2", are derived into a base "b3" in the final conceptual model.

On the left hand of the transformation rule, are the source metamodels. In our case, the sources are the multidimensional profile and the trace metamodel for DWs. On the upper left hand, we have a dimension "d1" and a base "b1", as well as the base level counterpart coming from the data sources, "b2". On the lower left hand, we have the traces which record the relationship between

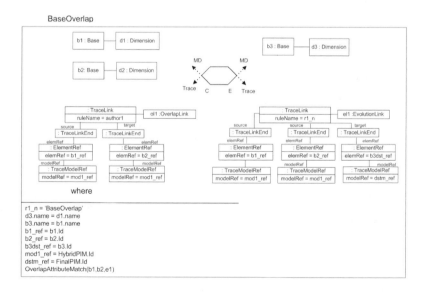

Fig. 3. QVT rule for deriving overlapping bases and creating their *Evolution* trace link

multidimensional elements coming from requirements, and those coming from the data sources. In this case, there is an overlap link between the two previously mentioned bases, which represents that both bases are complementary.

On the right hand of the transformation rule, are the target metamodels. On the upper right hand, we have our multidimensional profile, composed by the resulting dimension and base level. Since the relationship between the bases was defined as overlap, "b3" will present a combination of attributes from both "b1" and "b2". This merge will be performed by the *OverlapAttributeMatch* rule, called from the "Where" clause. On the lower right hand, we also have the trace metamodel, composed by the trace link which tracks the different elements used for composing the solution. In this case, as the original relationship between bases was an overlap, both bases are linked as sources of the new base level in the final PIM and its corresponding attributes.

The "C" at the center of the figure means that the source model is only checked, whereas the "E" means that the target models are enforced (generated). With QVT transformations, we can generate the associated traces simultaneously as the models are derived, avoiding the introduction of errors due to manual recording.

Once we have presented how to automate trace generation, we will present a case study for our proposal.

5   Case Study

In this section, we will present a case study for our proposal, showing how the traces can be used to relate the different elements in the hybrid PIM. This case study is inspired from a real world project with another university, and describes the basic process of our proposal, while making it easier to read the data source model. Note that the diagrams are presented with our iconography for DWs [6].

A university wishes to improve its educative process. In order to do so, a DW is designed to store the necessary information for the decision making process. The initial PIM, part of which can be seen at the left hand in figure 4, is derived from the users' requirements and refined with the expected attributes. This PIM includes 4 dimensions and a single measure. On the one hand, we have the *Subject* dimension. A subject is expected to include its code, a name, the credits and a description of the subject. Furthermore, subjects can be aggregated by their *Type*. On the other hand, is the *Teacher* dimension. A teacher includes a code, a name and the years of experience he has. Furthermore, teachers can be aggregated according to their *Department*, their *Faculty* or their job *Type*. The omitted dimensions in the figure, due to space constraints, are the *Student* and the *AcademicPeriod* dimensions.

As opposed to this initial PIM, the model created from the data sources (restricted to the most relevant tables) presents a higher number of attributes and lower readability. Part of this PIM can be seen at the right hand in figure 4. The first dimension is *TH_SUBJ*, which would correspond to the previous *Subject* dimension. This dimension includes a code for the subject, as expected,

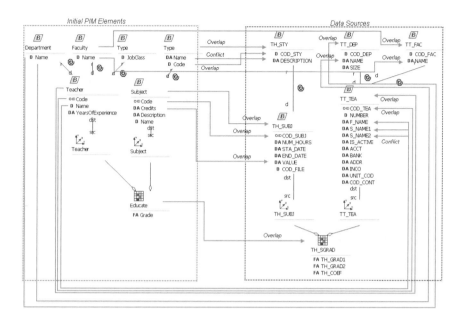

Fig. 4. Intra-model PIM traces relating conceptual elements from requirements (left) with elements from data sources (right)

the number of hours of the subject, a starting date, an ending date, a value which could correspond to the number of credits, and a code for the file of the subject. Subjects may also be grouped by type, as expected. The next dimension is *TT_TEA*, corresponding to information about the teachers. The information recorded for a teacher includes his name and surname, a mark for indicating if he is active or not, his bank information, address, unit code and a code related to the accounting. According to the data sources, teachers can be grouped either by department or by faculty. In this case, if we wished to group them by their job position, additional elements would be required.

Once we have both models in the hybrid PIM diagram, we can manually record the traces relating their elements, as sketched in figure 4. By recording only once these relationships, we do not require to repeatedly match each element coming from the requirements with those in the data sources, avoiding the introduction of errors in the process.

6   Conclusions and Future Work

In this paper, we have proposed a traceability approach in order to explicitly specify the relationships between elements at the conceptual level in DWs. We have shown the necessary trace semantics to record these relationships and have proposed a set of guidelines, in order to aid with the identification of these relationships. Furthermore, we have shown how trace derivation and recording would be automated and have exemplified the application of the proposal by means of the case study. The great benefit of our proposal is that the reconciliation task is only performed once per element and is preserved for further derivations. Therefore, we avoid repeatedly inspecting the data sources in order to match conceptual elements coming from requirements with those coming from data sources, diminishing time and resources spent.

Our plans for the immediate future are defining the complete set of QVT transformations to derive alternative final PIM models and to explore the relationships between the PSM and PIM levels.

Acknowledgments. This work has been partially supported by the MESO-LAP (TIN2010-14860) and SERENIDAD (PEII-11-0327-7035) projects from the Spanish Ministry of Education and the Junta de Comunidades de Castilla La Mancha respectively. Alejandro Maté is funded by the Generalitat Valenciana under an ACIF grant (ACIF/2010/298).

References

1. Aizenbud-Reshef, N., Nolan, B., Rubin, J., Shaham-Gafni, Y.: Model traceability. IBM Systems Journal 45(3), 515–526 (2006)
2. Antoniol, G., Canfora, G., Casazza, G., De Lucia, A., Merlo, E.: Recovering traceability links between code and documentation. IEEE Transactions on Software Engineering 28(10), 970–983 (2002)
3. Giorgini, P., Rizzi, S., Garzetti, M.: GRAnD: A goal-oriented approach to requirement analysis in data warehouses. DSS 45(1), 4–21 (2008)
4. Gotel, O.C.Z., Morris, S.J.: Macro-level Traceability Via Media Transformations. In: Rolland, C. (ed.) REFSQ 2008. LNCS, vol. 5025, pp. 129–134. Springer, Heidelberg (2008)
5. Kimball, R.: The data warehouse toolkit. Wiley-India (2009)
6. Luján-Mora, S., Trujillo, J., Song, I.Y.: A UML profile for multidimensional modeling in data warehouses. DKE 59(3), 725–769 (2006)
7. Maté, A., Trujillo, J.: A Trace Metamodel Proposal Based on the Model Driven Architecture Framework for the Traceability of User Requirements in Data Warehouses. In: Mouratidis, H., Rolland, C. (eds.) CAiSE 2011. LNCS, vol. 6741, pp. 123–137. Springer, Heidelberg (2011)
8. Mazón, J., Trujillo, J.: A model driven modernization approach for automatically deriving multidimensional models in data warehouses. In: Parent, C., Schewe, K.-D., Storey, V.C., Thalheim, B. (eds.) ER 2007. LNCS, vol. 4801, pp. 56–71. Springer, Heidelberg (2007)
9. Mazón, J.N., Trujillo, J.: An MDA approach for the development of data warehouses. DSS 45(1), 41–58 (2008)
10. Ramesh, B., Jarke, M.: Toward reference models for requirements traceability. IEEE Transactions on Software Engineering 27(1), 58–93 (2001)
11. Vassiliadis, P.: Data Warehouse Modeling and Quality Issues. Ph.D. thesis, Athens (2000)
12. Winkler, S., von Pilgrim, J.: A survey of traceability in requirements engineering and model-driven development. Software and Systems Modeling 9, 529–565 (2010)

Lightweight Verification of Executable Models

Elena Planas[1], Jordi Cabot[2], and Cristina Gómez[3]

[1] Universitat Oberta de Catalunya (Spain)
eplanash@uoc.edu
[2] École des Mines de Nantes - INRIA (France)
jordi.cabot@inria.fr
[3] Universitat Politècnica de Catalunya (Spain)
cristina@essi.upc.edu

Abstract. Executable models play a key role in many development methods by facilitating the immediate simulation/implementation of the software system under development. This is possible because executable models include a fine-grained specification of the system behaviour.

Unfortunately, a quick and easy way to check the correctness of behavioural specifications is still missing, which compromises their quality (and in turn the quality of the system generated from them). In this paper, a lightweight verification method to assess the strong executability of fine-grained behavioural specifications (i.e. operations) at design-time is provided. This method suffices to check that the execution of the operations is consistent with the integrity constraints defined in the structural model and returns a meaningful feedback that helps correcting them otherwise.

1   Introduction

Executable models play a cornerstone role in the Model-Driven Development (MDD) approach, in which models must be fine-grained specified in order to be used to (semi)automatically implement the software system. Executable models are now increasing its popularity. As a relevant example, the OMG has recently published the first version of the fUML [15] standard, an executable subset of the UML [13] that can be used to define, in an operational style, the structural and behavioural semantics of systems.

In MDD the quality of the final system implementation depends on the quality of the initial specification, so the existence of methods to verify the correctness of executable models is becoming crucial. In this sense, the goal of this paper is to propose a lightweight verification method for executable models. Our method focuses on the verification of the *strong executability* correctness property of action-based operations. An operation is *Strongly Executable* (SE) if it is guaranteed that every time the operation is invoked, the set of modifications the operation performs on the system´s data evolves the system to a new state fully consistent with all integrity constraints. This is one of the most fundamental correctness properties for behavioural specifications. When we know that all operations are SE, we can avoid checking at the end of each operation execution if all constraints are satisfied which improves the efficiency of the system.

M. Jeusfeld, L. Delcambre, and T.W. Ling (Eds.): ER 2011, LNCS 6998, pp. 467–475, 2011.
© Springer-Verlag Berlin Heidelberg 2011

In this paper we assume structural models are written in UML/OCL and operations are specified in Alf Action Language [14], although our method could be used with models written in other languages.

Paper Organization. The rest of the paper is structured as follows. Section 2 presents the state of the art. Section 3 introduces several preliminary concepts. Section 4 presents our method and describes the feedback it provides. Finally, Section 5 presents our conclusions and further work.

2   State of the Art

There is a broad set of research proposals devoted to the verification of (UML) behavioural models, focusing on state machines [11] [12], sequence diagrams [3] [9], activity diagrams [1] [6], operations [4] [18] [16], or the consistent interrelationship between them and/or the class diagram [8], among others.

Table 1 classifies the most representative works and positions our method wrt them. For each approach we indicate the kind of behavioural model targeted, the integrity constraints that are considered when evaluating the models, whether actions can be added to specify the model, the main correctness properties addressed by the method, the basic technique employed during the verification and if the approach returns some kind of feedback beyond a simple yes/no answer.

Only few works [8] [1] (and also our previous work [16]) allow inclusion of actions in their diagrams, which is precisely the focus of our method, but they do not check their strong executatibility. Works dealing with the executability of operations [4] [18] depart from declarative operations specified by means of pre and postconditions contracts, instead of using imperative specifications.

The above works simulate the behavioural models by translating them into Model Checking [2], Constraint Programming [10] or Query Containment [7], and thus, do not scale properly and compromise the efficiency of the method.

Table 1. Related methods comparison. *Abbreviations: AD(Activity Diagram), SqD(Sequence Diagram), StD(Statechart Diagram), decl-OP(Declarative Operation), imp-OP (Imperative Operation), MC(Model Checking), CP(Constraint Programming), QC (Query Containment)*

Refs	Behavioural Model	Supported Constraints	Include Actions?	Main Properties	Technique	Repairing Feedback?
[8]	AD,SqD,StD	None	Yes	Consistency	MC	No
[1]	AD	None	Yes	Deadlocks	MC	No
[11]	StD	None	No	Safety Liveness	MC	No
[12]	StD	Associated to states	No	Deadlocks Livelocks	MC	No
[4]	decl-OP	All	No	SE et al.	CP	No
[18]	decl-OP	Subset	No	Weak Execu- tability et al.	QC	No
our work	imp-OP	Subset	Yes	SE	Static Analysis	Yes

Instead, our method performs an static analysis, thus, it does not require to simulate the behaviour in order to determine their executability.

On the other hand, most of the above methods do not provide a valuable feedback but just provide a binary response and, at most some provide example execution traces that do (not) satisfy the property. None clearly identify the source of the problems nor assist the designer to repair them.

As a trade-off, our method supports a restricted set of integrity constraints. Once the model passes our first analysis, designers may choose to use more expressive (but more time expensive) methods.

3 Preliminary Concepts

This section introduces some preliminary concepts to facilitate the comprehension of our method and presents a running example to illustrate these concepts.

3.1 Structural Model

Class Diagram. A UML Class Diagram (CD) consists of a set of classes (i.e. entity types), attributes, associations (i.e. relationship types) among classes, generalizations among classes and integrity constraints.

Integrity Constraints. When verifying executability of operations, our method covers the constraints that most frequently appear in the structural models (a detailed list of the addressed constraints is provided in [17]).

Example. Figure 1 shows an excerpt of the class diagram and integrity constraints in an e-commerce system. It includes information about its *customers*, which can acquire *orders*. An *order* is composed of one or more *order lines*, each of them related to exactly one *product*. A product may be in offer as denoted by the value of the *special price* attribute. A product may have several substituted products, which are suggested to the customer when the desired product is sold out. Additional identifier, value comparison and symmetric constraints are expressed in OCL. The derivation rule for *totalPrice* attribute is not showed here since it has no relevance in our analysis.

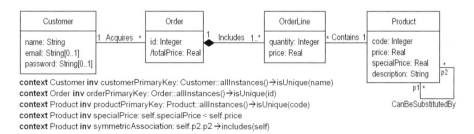

Fig. 1. Excerpt of a e-commerce system class diagram

3.2   Behavioural Model

In UML there are several alternatives to represent the behaviour of a system but the basic way is using operations (attached into classes) that the user may execute to query and/or modify the information modeled in the structural model.

Our method is focused on operations specified by means of *"Action Language for fUML"* (Alf) [14], a beta standard published recently by the OMG. Alf provides a concrete syntax conforming to the fUML abstract syntax, defining the basic actions to specify the fine-grained behaviour of systems and a set of statements to coordinate these actions in action sequences, conditional blocks or loops. As any action language, the expressiveness of Alf is comparable to that of the instructions in traditional programming languages but at a higher abstraction (and platform-independent) level.

Example. We show an operation[1] of the e-commerce system defined using Alf language: "newProduct", which creates a new product in the system.

```
activity newProduct(in _code:String, in _price:Real, in _specialPrice:Real, in _description:String,
in _substitutedProducts:Product[0..*]){
  p = new Product();
  p.code = _code;
  p.price = _price;
  p.specialPrice = _specialPrice;
  p.description = _description;
  for (i in 1.._substitutedProducts→size()) {
   CanBeSubstitutedBy.createLink(p1=>self,p2=>_substitutedProducts[i]);
  }
}
```

4   Our Method

Our method aims to verify at design-time if an action-based operation is *Strongly Executable* (SE). We consider that an operation is SE if it is always successfully executed, i.e. if every time we execute the operation (whatever values are given as arguments for its parameters), the effect of the actions included in the operation evolves the initial state of the system to a new system state that satisfies all integrity constraints of the structural model.

Given an input structural and behavioural models, our method (see Figure 2) returns either a positive answer (meaning that the operation is SE) or a corrective feedback. This corrective feedback consists in a set of actions and conditions that should be added to the operation in order to make it SE. Extending the operation with this feedback is a necessary condition but not a sufficient one to immediately guarantee the SE of the operation since the added actions may in its turn induce other constraint violations. Therefore, the extended operation must be recursively reanalyzed with our method until we reach a SE status.

When analyzing the SE of the operation, we must take into account all possible *execution paths* (an operation is SE iff all its paths are SE). Therefore, the first step of the method is to compute such paths (Section 4.1). Once the paths have

---

[1] Operation methods are specified as UML activities in Alf.

been computed, the rest of the method is applied on each path. Step 2 (Section 4.2) analyzes individually each action in the path p to see if it may violate some integrity constraint of the structural model. Finally, Step 3 (Section 4.3) performs a contextual analysis of each potentially violating action to see if other actions or conditions in p compensate or complement its effect to ensure that we always reach a consistent state at the end of the operation. If all potential violation actions can be discarded we can conclude that p is SE.

Our method performs an over-approximation analysis. This implies that it may return *false positives*, that is, it may return as a non-SE an operation which is actually SE. The designer intervention is necessary to confirm non-SE in those cases. On the other hand, the method does not return *false negatives* (in our opinion, more critical than the above), that is, when it states that an operation is SE, this statement is always true. Over-approximation is due to the lack of exhaustiveness in the comparison of conditions in the operation to favour the efficiency of the process. We believe this is a reasonable trade-off for the method.

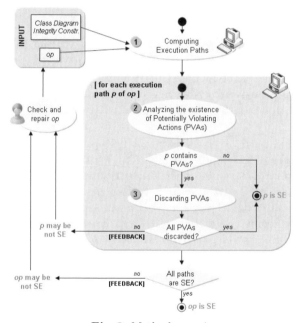

Fig. 2. Method overview

4.1   Step 1: Computing the Execution Paths of the Operation

An *execution path* of an operation op is a consecutive sequence of actions that may be followed during the execution of op in a given execution scenario. For trivial operations (e.g. with neither conditional or loop structures) there is a single execution path but, in general, several ones will exist.

We propose to represent each operation as a directed graph. Then, execution paths are all paths in the graph that start at the initial vertex, end at the final vertex and does not include repeated arcs.

Example. Figure 3 shows the directed graph of operation "newProduct". Two execution paths may be derived: the first one, executed when the new product has no substituted products (the loop is not executed); and the second one, executed otherwise.

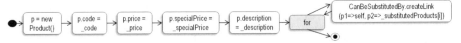

Fig. 3. Execution paths of "newProduct"

4.2   Step 2: Analyzing the Existence of Potentially Violating Actions

This step analyzes each action in the path to see if its effect can change the system state in a way that some integrity constraint becomes violated. If so, this action is declared as a *Potentially Violating Action* (PVA) and we refer to the constraints the PVA can violate as *Susceptible Violated Constraints* (SVC). If the path has no PVAs, is SE. Otherwise, we need to continue the analysis with the next step.

To detect PVAs we rely on the method published in [5] that receives as input a CD and a set of constraints and automatically determines the actions that may violate each constraint of the model. Thus, we may determine if a path contains PVAs by comparing the list of actions in the path with the list of actions returned by this method. All actions in the intersection of both sets are PVAs.

Example. Second path of "newProduct" (first path is not explicitly shown since it is a subset of this one) contains four PVAs: PVA_1, which may violate four mandatory constraints (when the attributes *code*, *price*, *specialPrice* and *description* are not initialized); PVA_2, which may violate the *productPrimaryKey* constraint (when the system contains another product with the same *code*); PVA_3, which may violate the *specialPrice* constraint (when _specialPrice $\geq self.price$); and PVA_4 which may violate the *symmetricAssociation* constraint (when the opposite link is not created).

Potentially Violating Actions of "newProduct" (second path):
- PVA_1: p = new Product()
    $SVC_{1.1}$: The attribute "code" of class "Product" must have at least one value
    $SVC_{1.2}$: The attribute "price" of class "Product" must have at least one value
    $SVC_{1.3}$: The attribute "specialPrice" of class "Product" must have at least one value
    $SVC_{1.4}$: The attribute "description" of class "Product" must have at least one value
- PVA_2: p.code = _code
    $SVC_{2.1}$: *productPrimaryKey* constraint
- PVA_3: p.specialPrice = _specialPrice;
    $SVC_{3.1}$: *specialPrice* constraint
- PVA_4: CanBeSubstitutedBy.createLink(p_1=>self,p_2=>_substitutedProducts[i])
    $SVC_{4.1}$: *symmetricAssociation* constraint

Since all paths of "newProduct" are susceptible to be non-SE (given that all of them contain some PVAs) we must proceed with the last step of our method.

4.3   Step 3: Discarding Potentially Violating Actions

It may happen that the context in which a PVA is executed within the path guarantees that the effect of the PVA is never going to actually violate any of its SVCs. Roughly, there are two ways to discard a PVA: (1) when the path contains a guard (i.e. a conditional structure) that ensures the PVA will only be executed in a safe context; and (2) when the path contains another action which counters or complements the effect of the PVA in order to maintain the integrity of the system. In this last step, we analyze the set of PVAs returned by the previous step and try to discard them by analyzing the two possibilities commented above. If all PVAs can be discarded, the path is classified as SE. If not, the path (and consequently the operation) is marked as non-SE and the corresponding corrective feedback is provided.

We have determined a set of *discarding conditions*, that is, the conditions that a path must satisfy in order to discard a specific PVA. Due to space limitations, we do not show here these conditions (the interested reader may found it in [17]), but we illustrate a subset of these conditions using our running operation.

Example. In the following we try to discard the PVAs of our running path according to our discarding conditions. For each PVA and SVC, we show the conditions that the path should satisfy to discard that PVA. Then, $\{sat\}$ states that the condition is satisfied by the path, while $\{not\ sat\}$ states the opposite.

Conditions to discard the PVAs of "newProduct" (second path):
- $PVA_1, SVC_{1.1}$: The attribute "code" of object "p" must be initialized $\{sat\}$
- $PVA_1, SVC_{1.2}$: The attribute "price" of object "p" must be initialized $\{sat\}$
- $PVA_1, SVC_{1.3}$: The attribute "specialPrice" of object "p" must be initialized $\{sat\}$
- $PVA_1, SVC_{1.4}$: The attribute "description" of object "p" must be initialized $\{sat\}$
- $PVA_2, SVC_{2.1}$:
  - option 1: Must exist a guard which ensures the PVA will only be executed when there is not another product with the same "code" $\{not\ sat\}$
  - option 2: Must exist a product with the same "code" and its value is modified $\{not\ sat\}$
  - option 3: Must exist a product with the same "code" and this product is destroyed $\{not\ sat\}$
- $PVA_3, SVC_{3.1}$: Must exist a guard which ensures the PVA will only be executed when "_specialPrice<_price" $\{not\ sat\}$
- $PVA_4, SVC_{4.1}$: Must exist a creation of the symmetric link of type "CanBeSubstitutedBy" between objects "_substitutedProducts[i]" and "self" $\{not\ sat\}$

Second path of "newProduct" does not satisfy all discarding conditions, hence, our method concludes it is not SE (and the same for the first path).

In the following we show the repaired operation *newProduct* once the feedback provided by our method has been integrated. The added sentences are preceded by a right arrow ($\rightarrow$). Each of them fixes one of the problems detected above. For the sake of simplicity, we only show one possible reparation.

```
activity newProduct(in _code:String, in _price:Real, in _specialPrice:Real, in _description:String,
in _substitutedProducts:Product[0..*] sequence){
→ if (not Product::allInstances()→exists(p|p.code=_code)) {
  → if (_specialPrice<_price) {
      p = new Product();
      p.code = _code;
      p.price = _price;
      p.specialPrice = _specialPrice;
      p.description = _description;
      for (i in 1.._substitutedProducts→size()) {
         CanBeSubstitutedBy.createLink(p1=>self,p2=>_substitutedProducts[i]);
         → CanBeSubstitutedBy.createLink(p1=>_substitutedProducts[i],p2=>self);
      }
  → }
→ }
}
```

5   Conclusions and Further Work

We have proposed a lightweight method for assisting the designer during the specification of executable behavioural models. In particular, our method verifies the Strong Executability (SE) of action-based UML operations (although our method could be used with models written in other languages) wrt the integrity constraints imposed by the structural model at design-time. The main characteristics of our method are its efficiency (since no simulation/animation of the behaviour is required) and feedback (for non-executable operations, it is able to identify the source of the inconsistency and suggest possible corrections). For these reasons, our method is easy to integrate in existing CASE tools.

As a further work, we plan to study the executability of operations when they are combined with other UML behavioural diagrams and explore the integration of our verification method in a more complete verification framework that could help designers choose the most appropriate verification technique for the model they have defined, depending on the target property and the verification trade-offs (completeness, efficiency,...) they are ready to accept.

Acknowledgements. This work has been partly supported by the Ministerio de Ciencia y Tecnología under TIN2008-00444 project, Grupo Consolidado.

References

1. Abdelhalim, I., Sharp, J., Schneider, S., Treharne, H.: Formal verification of tokeneer behaviours modelled in fUML using CSP. In: Dong, J.S., Zhu, H. (eds.) ICFEM 2010. LNCS, vol. 6447, pp. 371–387. Springer, Heidelberg (2010)
2. Alur, R.: Model Checking: From Tools to Theory. In: 25 Years of Model Checking, pp. 89–106 (2008)
3. Baker, P., Bristow, P., Jervis, C., King, D.J., Thomson, R., Mitchell, B., Burton, S.: Detecting and Resolving Semantic Pathologies in UML Sequence Diagrams. In: ESEC/SIGSOFT FSE, pp. 50–59 (2005)
4. Cabot, J., Clarisó, R., Riera, D.: Verifying UML/OCL Operation Contracts. In: Leuschel, M., Wehrheim, H. (eds.) IFM 2009. LNCS, vol. 5423, pp. 40–55. Springer, Heidelberg (2009)

5. Cabot, J., Teniente, E.: Determining the Structural Events That May Violate an Integrity Constraint. In: Baar, T., Strohmeier, A., Moreira, A., Mellor, S.J. (eds.) UML 2004. LNCS, vol. 3273, pp. 320–334. Springer, Heidelberg (2004)
6. Eshuis, R.: Symbolic Model Checking of UML Activity Diagrams. ACM Transactions on Software Engineering and Methodology 15(1), 1–38 (2006)
7. Farré, C., Teniente, E., Urpí, T.: Checking query containment with the CQC method. Data Knowledge Engineering 53(2), 163–223 (2005)
8. Graw, G., Herrmann, P.: Transformation and Verification of Executable UML Models. Electr. Notes Theor. Comput. Sci. 101, 3–24 (2004)
9. Grosu, R., Smolka, S.A.: Safety-Liveness Semantics for UML 2.0 Sequence Diagrams. In: ACSD, pp. 6–14. IEEE Press, Los Alamitos (2005)
10. Hanus, M.: Programming with Constraints: An Introduction by Kim Marriott and Peter J. Stuckey. MIT Press, Cambridge (1998); J. Funct. Program, 11(2):253–262, 2001.
11. Latella, D., Majzik, I., Massink, M.: Automatic Verification of a Behavioural Subset of UML Statechart Diagrams Using the SPIN Model-checker. Formal Asp. Comput. 11(6), 637–664 (1999)
12. Lilius, J., Paltor, I.: vUML: A Tool for Verifying UML Models. In: ASE, pp. 255–258 (1999)
13. OMG. UML 2.0 Superstructure Specification (ptc/07-11-02) (2007)
14. OMG. Concrete Syntax for UML Action Language (Action Language for Foundational UML), version Beta 1, (2010), www.omg.org/spec/ALF
15. OMG. Semantics Of A Foundational Subset For Executable UML Models (fUML), version 1.0 (2011), www.omg.org/spec/FUML
16. Planas, E., Cabot, J., Gómez, C.: Verifying Action Semantics Specifications in UML Behavioral Models. In: van Eck, P., Gordijn, J., Wieringa, R. (eds.) CAiSE 2009. LNCS, vol. 5565, pp. 125–140. Springer, Heidelberg (2009)
17. Planas, E., Cabot, J., Gómez, C.: Lightweight Verification of Executable Models (Extended Version) (2011), http://gres.uoc.edu/pubs/VerifyingExecModels.pdf
18. Queralt, A., Teniente, E.: Reasoning on UML conceptual schemas with operations. In: van Eck, P., Gordijn, J., Wieringa, R. (eds.) CAiSE 2009. LNCS, vol. 5565, pp. 47–62. Springer, Heidelberg (2009)

Towards a Model of Services Based on Co-creation, Abstraction and Restriction

Maria Bergholtz , Paul Johannesson, and Birger Andersson

Department of Computer and Systems Sciences, Stockholm University,
Isafjordsgatan 39. SE 164 40 Kista, Sweden
{maria,pajo,ba}@dsv.su.se

Abstract. The term service is today defined and used in a multitude of ways, and there is no usage characteristic that is common for all of these ways. As a consequence natural language terms used for describing services are ambiguous and often confusing. The lack of a common agreed upon definition of the term makes it difficult to understand and classify services as well as distinguish them from non-service concepts. In this paper, we do not propose a new definition of service but a model of services that helps in analysing the concept. The model is based on three perspectives: service as a means for co-creation of value, service as a means for abstraction, and service as a means for providing restricted access to resources.

Keywords: service, service model, service definition, service resource, service process, service delivery, Resource-Event-Agent ontology, Hohfeld's classification of Rights, conceptual modeling.

1 Introduction

The increasing interest in services has created a multitude of alternative views and definitions, often conflicting, of the service concept. The lack of a common view of the service concept makes it difficult to reason about, describe and classify services in a uniform way.

One attempt to defining services has focused on identifying properties (such as intangibility, inseparability, heterogeneity, and perishability [20]) that distinguish them from other kinds of recourses. However, [3, 4, 16, 5] and others have argued that the suggested properties are neither necessary nor sufficient for something to be a service. For example, not only services are intangible but also other kinds of resources, such as information and IPRs. Heterogeneity can be observed also in the production of certain goods and information, such as handicraft objects and newspaper articles.

An alternative way of identifying services is to view them as perspectives on the *use* and *offering* of resources [3]. This view is shared by the Unified Services Theory [16], which also bases its definition of services on the use and exchange of resources; here service processes are processes where customers always provide significant input resources, as opposed to non-service processes where customers only select what output resources to buy and pay for.

M. Jeusfeld, L. Delcambre, and T.W. Ling (Eds.): ER 2011, LNCS 6998, pp. 476–485, 2011.
© Springer-Verlag Berlin Heidelberg 2011

Services may also be understood as a means for abstraction. A common view found in [18, 13, 14, 10, 17] is services as an abstraction of activities that once started will achieve some user goal, usually defined as a change of state in (user) resources.

An often mentioned advantage of services is that the management (infrastructure, maintenance, technology, etc.) of resources are moved from customer to provider [12]. This is a consequence of the principle that service provision does not entail ownership transfer [12], [20]. The concept of service can be used as a means for providing restricted resource access without ownership transfer [2].

The diversity of service views and definitions, and the fact that these views are often conflicting, suggest that a multi perspective approach is required. We will introduce a number of service *perspectives* rather than propose a single service definition. We identify three main service perspectives from the literature introduced in the previous paragraphs: service as a means for co-creation of value [16, 10], service as a means for abstraction [18, 13, 14, 10, 17], and service as a means for providing resource access without ownership transfer [20, 2]. The purpose of the paper is to propose a conceptual model of services based on these three perspectives. The model has its theoretical foundation in the REA ontology [11] and Hohfeld's classification of rights, [8]. REA is used because it is a well established ontology of business collaboration with the basic view that resources are exchanged between agents according to agreements. Hohfeld's classification of rights is used as means for analysing what kinds of rights are transferred in exchanges of services and other kinds of resources. The work reported here builds on the work of [2], which is also based on a multi perspective view of analysing services. The main differences are (i): a new foundation for the model based on distinguishing between service as a resource and service as a process, (ii) the alignment of the model concepts with the core REA ontology.

The remainder of this paper is structured as follows. In Section 2, we briefly outline the REA ontology and Hohfeld's classification of rights. In Section 3, we introduce the three perspectives of services and elaborate them together with their corresponding conceptual models in Sections 4 - 6. Section 7 concludes the paper.

2   The REA Ontology and Hohfeld's Classification of Rights

The REA (Resource-Event-Agent) ontology was originally formulated in [11] and developed further in a series of papers, e.g. [7, 9]. The ontology is based on the core concepts of resources, events, and agents, which are described in the following subsections.

2.1   Resources

A resource is something that is of value for at least one agent, e.g., a car or Internet access. Based on the degree to which a resource is tied to an agent, resources can be classified into three categories: *internal resources* that are existent dependent on one agent, for example skills, knowledge and experiences, *shared resources* that are existence dependent on two or more agents, for example relationships and rights, and *independent resources* that can exist independently of any agent, for example land and information.

2.2 Conversion Processes

Resources are not unchanging but can be transformed, i.e. they can be produced, modified, used, or consumed. Resources are transformed in so called conversion processes consisting of conversion events. A *conversion event* represents a transformation of a single resource. A conversion event that creates a new resource or increases the value of an existing resource is called a *production event*. A conversion event that consumes a resource or decreases the value of a resource without consuming it, is called a *consumption event* or a *usage event*, respectively. Usage events are using resources that may be reused in several conversion events, (similar to the concept of 'assets' [6]), while consumption events use up resources (similar to the concept of 'consumables' [6]). Examples of conversion events are the production of bread, the repair of a car, and the consumption of a liter of fuel.

A *conversion process* is a set of conversion events including at least one production event and at least one consumption or usage event. The latter requirement expresses a duality relationship between production and consumption/usage events, stating that in order to produce or improve some resource, other resources have to be used or consumed in the process. For example, in order to produce a car, a number of other resources have to be used, such as steel, knowledge, and labour.

2.3 Exchange Processes

Resources can also be exchanged between agents, which occur in exchange processes consisting of exchange events. An *exchange event* is the transfer of rights on some resource to or from an agent. If the exchange event means that the agent receives rights on a resource, we call the event a *take event*. If the exchange event means that the agent gives up rights on a resource, we call the event a *give event*.

An *exchange process* is a set of exchange events including at least one give event and one take event. Similarly to conversion processes, this requirement expresses a duality relationship between take and give events - in order to receive a resource, an agent has to give up some other resource. For example, in a purchase (an exchange process) a buying agent has to provide money to receive some goods. Two exchange events take place in this process: one where the amount of money is decreased (a give event) and another where the amount of goods is increased (a take event).

2.4 Hohfeld's Classification of Rights

In the sections above, we have used the notion of rights in an informal way. As a more precise understanding of rights will be required for characterizing different kinds of resources and exchanges, we here introduce a rights classification based on the work of W. N. Hohfeld, [8], who identified four broad categories of rights: claims, privileges, powers, and immunities (not used in this paper).

- One agent has a *claim* on another agent if the second agent is required to act in a certain way for the benefit of the first agent, typically by carrying out some action. Conversely, the second agent is said to have a duty, or an obligation, to the first agent. An example is a person who has a claim on another person to pay an amount of money, implying that the other person has a duty to pay the amount.

- An agent has a *privilege* on an action if she is free to carry out that action without any interference from the environment in which the action is to be carried out. By environments is here meant social structures such as states, organizations or even families. Some examples of privileges are free speech and the fact that a person owning some property has privileges to use it in various ways.
- A *power* is the ability of an agent to create or modify a relationship. An example is that a person owning a piece of land has the power to sell it to someone else, thereby creating a new ownership relationship for that piece of land.

Most relationships are governed by a combination of several of these rights. For example, owning a car means to have privileges on using it and also the power to lend or sell it, i.e. creating new ownerships involving other agents.

2.5 Offerings, Commitments, and Contracts

Exchange processes can be governed by agreements that specify when and how resources are to be exchanged. The two most important types of agreements are offerings and contracts consisting of commitments. A *commitment* on a resource type is a duty for an agent to carry out a conversion or exchange event for an instance of that resource type. For example, an agent may have a duty towards another agent to transfer the ownership (an exchange event) of a car (instance of a car type) to that agent. A *contract* is a collection of commitments and possibly additional rules governing their interrelationships.

An *offering* for a resource type is a conditional obligation for one agent to some community of agents to enter into a commitment for that resource type. For example, an agent may provide a sales-offering for a certain car model, meaning that she is prepared to sell cars of that model, i.e. enter into commitments for the car model. An offering is similar to a commitment but differs from it by not being binding until another agent has accepted it. Thus, when an offering is accepted, it will result in a commitment. A set of offerings can be collected into a *bundled offering*, analogously to a contract.

Fig. 1 summarises the notions introduced so far in the form of a UML class diagram. In the following sections, we will suggest further analysis and specialisations of these notions in order to clarify the different perspectives on services. Almost all of the concepts in the conceptual model presented here may exist on both a knowledge level and an operational level. According to [6], the operational level models concrete, tangible individuals in a domain, while the knowledge level models information structures that characterize categories of individuals on the operational level. The diagrams of figure 1 through 5 hence distinguish between knowledge level concepts such as Resource Types (categories of Resources such as Car model, Agent type, Real Estate) and operational level concepts such as Resources (specific and often tangible concepts like a specific car or a concrete piece of land), Event Types and Events, and so forth for every concept in the model. Due to space limitations, we include both knowledge and operational level concepts in the diagrams only when both concepts are required to illustrate a focal point in the model.

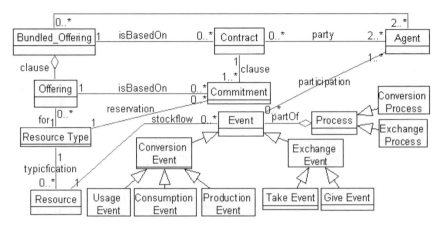

Fig. 1. REA ontology (adopted and extended from [15])

3   Service Perspectives

In the following sections, we will introduce a conceptual model for services. The model does not propose a single service definition but instead suggests a number of service perspectives based on the ways resources can be used and exchanged. This approach is reflected in the model, which does not include the term "service" but instead a family of related terms, including "service resource", "service offering", and "service process". We have identified three main perspectives on services: service as a means for co-creation of value [16, 10], service as means for abstraction [18, 13, 14, 10, 17], and service as a means for providing resource access without ownership transfer [20, 2]:

- Service as a means for *co-creation of value*. For most kinds of production of goods, customers are not involved. Instead, goods are produced internally at a supplier who later on sells the goods to a customer who uses them without the involvement of the supplier. In contrast, services are created and used in an interaction between supplier and customer.
- Service as a means for *abstraction*. Services can provide an abstraction mechanism, where resources are specified through their function and not their construction. In other words, a resource is defined in terms of the effects it has in a process, not in terms of its properties or constituents. For example, a hair dressing service can be defined in terms of the effects it has on someone's hair, not in terms of the resources being used in the execution of the service, such as scissors or electric machines.
- Service as a means for providing *restricted resource access*. An agent can provide access to some of her resources to another agent by transferring the ownership of them. However, such an ownership transfer may in some situations be undesirable or even legally impossible. Thus, there is a need for a way of offering access to resources without transferring ownership, and services provide a mechanism for this purpose. For example, instead of selling transportation vehicles, transportation services are provided.

The model, based on these three perspectives, will be presented in a series of UML-diagrams, all of which have the REA ontology as their point of departure. Fig. 2 and 3 show services as co-creation of value, while Fig. 4 and Fig. 5 show services as abstraction mechanisms and providers of resource access without ownership transfer.

4   Service as a Means for Co-creation

For a typical goods producing company, its interactions with customers can be quite limited. Without any involvement of the customers, the company procures raw materials and other assets from suppliers and uses these resources to produce goods to be sold. The only role of the customer is to select which goods to purchase and pay for them. Thus, the company carries out a conversion process in isolation transforming input resources to output resources, see Fig. 2a.

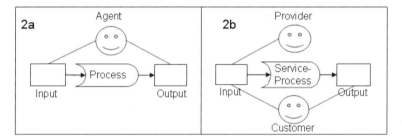

Fig. 2. Single agent process versus service-process

In contrast, a service can never be carried out by a provider in isolation, as it always requires a customer to take part in the process. In such a service process, the provider and the customer together co-create value, as both of them provide resources to be used or consumed in the process. For example, in a photo sharing service, the service provider will supply hardware and software, while the customer will provide photos and labour. Together, they engage in a process that results in value for the customer, shareable photo albums. Pictorially, a service process can be viewed as in Fig. 2b, which shows how both a service provider and a customer jointly contribute to the service process that produces an output for the benefit of the customer.

In order to make the concept of service as co-creation more precise, it is useful to distinguish between service as a process and service as a resource. The word "service" is sometimes used to denote a process, e.g., in the phrase "Today, our company carried out 25 car repair services". In other cases, "service" is used to denote a resource, e.g., "Our company offers car repair services for the fixed price of 200 euros".

A *service process*, see Fig. 3, is a conversion process that uses or consumes resources from two agents, called provider and customer, and produces resources that are under the control of the customer. The provider in the service process has to actively participate in the process, while the customer may be passive. For example, a customer driving a borrowed car is not a service process, while a customer being driven by (a representative of) the provider is. Thus, a service process differs from other processes in three ways: First, some of the input resources are under the control of one agent, the provider, while the output resources are under the control of another agent, the customer. This means that the provider uses or consumes her resources in the service process for the benefit of another agent. Secondly, not only the provider but also the customer provides resources as input to the service process. Thirdly, the provider actively takes part in the service process.

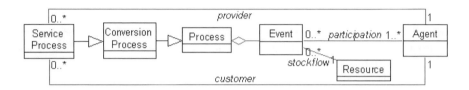

Fig. 3. REA-ontology from Fig. 1 expanded with Service Process to highlight co-creation of value between provider and customer

5   Service as a Means for Abstraction

To be able to specify resources in an abstract way provides several advantages. It becomes easier for a provider to describe the benefits of an offering when she can focus on the effects of the resource offered and abstract away from its accidental features. The provider can address the needs and wants of the customer and clarify how these are fulfilled by her offering without going into detail about its composition. Furthermore, the provider does not have to commit to any specific way of delivering her offering; instead, she can choose to allocate the resources needed in a flexible and dynamic way.

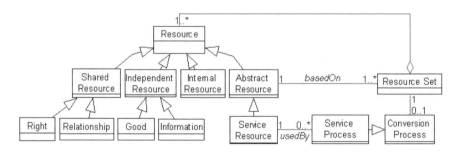

Fig. 4. Service as an abstraction mechanism

A *service resource* is an abstract resource that is defined only through its use and effects in a service process, i.e. what changes it can bring to other resources when consumed in such a process. For example, a hair cut service is defined through the effects it has on the hair style of a person. It is not defined by means of the concrete resources used when cutting the hair, such as labour and scissors. Rather, the concrete resources to be used are left unspecified and can change over time. On one day the hair dresser may use scissors and on another day an electric machine, but in both cases he provides a hair cut service. Thus, the same service resource can be based on different sets of other resources, as shown in Fig. 4, and when it is consumed exactly one of these resource sets will be used.

6 Service as a Means for Providing Restricted Resource Access

When satisfying a need, an agent can often choose between using a service or some other kind of resource, like goods or information. Using a service instead of another kind of resource provides several benefits, as the service consumer does not own the service. This means that she does not need to take on typical ownership responsibilities, like infrastructure management, integration, and maintenance. For example, a person can satisfy her transportation needs either by buying and driving a car or by using a taxi service. In the former case, she will own the car required for the transportation, i.e. she will be responsible for cleaning it, repairing it, getting the right insurances, and many other infrastructure and maintenance tasks. When using a taxi service, on the other hand, she does not have to care about any of these responsibilities but can focus solely on how to use the taxi to best satisfy her transportation needs. Thus, services provide a convenient way of offering and accessing resources by allowing agents to use them without owning them.

Fig. 5 depicts three different ways for an Agent to make its resources available to other agents through offerings:

- an agent may offer to sell a resource to another agent, i.e. to transfer the ownership of the resource to the other agent, as modelled by Ownership Offering. A transfer of ownership means that a number of rights are transferred from seller to buyer, in Fig. 5 modelled by class Right. The rights transferred include powers and privileges according to Hohfelds's classification of rights in section 2.4. For example, an agent offering to sell a book to a customer means that the agent is offering the customer privileges to use the book as well as the power to transfer the ownership of the book to yet another agent if she so wishes.

- an agent may offer to lend a resource or provide access to it in a Lending Offering. This means to offer an agent to get certain privileges on the resource for a period of time but without getting any ownership, i.e. the borrower is not granted the power to change the ownership of the resource. Optionally, the borrower may get some other powers, such as lending the resource to a third agent.

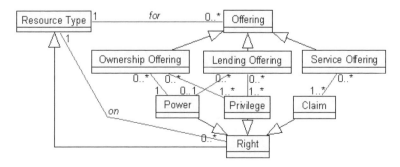

Fig. 5. Service as a means for restricted access provisioning

- an agent may make a Service Offering to a potential customer, which is the most abstract way of providing access to an agent's resources. A service offering means that the provider offers to use some of her service resources in a service process that will benefit the customer. Effectively, the provider restricts access to these resources. In particular, the customer is not offered any powers or privileges on any concrete resources. Instead, she is offered a claim on the provider to contribute to a certain service process.

7   Concluding Remarks

In this paper, we have proposed a conceptual model of the notion of service. A main characteristic of the model is that it describes services from three perspectives - service as a means for co-creation of value, for abstraction, and for access restriction.

The work presented here was partly motivated by a language problem identified by Wittgenstein [19]. He contends that a word is defined by its use, that it can be used in different ways, and that there is no usage characteristic that is common for all these ways. In the context of services, this is particularly problematic since no common agreed upon definition of the term exists and the natural language terms used are often confusing. Analysing services along the dimensions co-creation, abstraction and restriction mechanisms makes it possible to distinguish between similarly labeled but different concepts. For instance, a 'health care insurance service' is different from a 'burglar insurance service' (there is little to no customer participation in the latter and hence it is not a service process).

Our three perspectives can be compared to those introduced in [1]. There the chosen perspectives are called 'service value', 'service offering', and 'service process'. The service value perspective is analogous to our abstraction perspective, where a service is described by the effects it produces, but it also contains elements from our co-production perspective. The service offering perspective is related to our view of services as a means for restricted access to resources. The service process perspective describes how a service offering is put into operation, but in contrast to our proposal the authors do not investigate realization issues in detail.

In addition to their theoretical contributions, we believe that the results of the paper will find applications in structuring service descriptions and developing service classifications. Further research will investigate these issues as well as consolidate the proposed model.

References

1. Akkermans, et al.: Value Webs: Ontology-Based Bundling of Real-World Services. IEEE Intelligent Systems 19(4) (July/August 2004)
2. Bergholtz, M., Andersson, B., Johannesson, P.: Abstraction, restriction, and co-creation: Three perspectives on services. In: Trujillo, J., Dobbie, G., Kangassalo, H., Hartmann, S., Kirchberg, M., Rossi, M., Reinhartz-Berger, I., Zimányi, E., Frasincar, F. (eds.) ER 2010. LNCS, vol. 6413, pp. 107–116. Springer, Heidelberg (2010)
3. Edvardsson, B., Gustafsson, A., Roos, I.: Service portraits in service research: a critical review. Int. Jour. of Service Industry Management 16(1), 107–121 (2005)

4. Goldkuhl, G., Röstlinger, A.: Beyond goods and services - an elaborate product classification on pragmatic grounds. In: Proc. of Quality in Services (QUIS 7), Karlstad university (2000)
5. Ferrario, R., Guarino, N., Fernandez Barrera, M.: Towards an Ontological Foundations for Services Science: the Legal Perspective. In: Sartor, G., Casanovas, P., Biasiotti, M., Fernandez Barrera, M. (eds.) Approaches to Legal Ontologies. Springer, Heidelberg (2009)
6. Fowler, M.: Analysis Patterns. Reusable Object Models. Addison-Wesley, Reading (1997)
7. Geerts, G., McCarthy, W. E.: An Accounting Object Infrastructure For Knowledge-Based Enterprise Models. IEEE Int. Systems & Their Applications, pp. 89-94 (1999)
8. Hohfeld, W.N.: Fundamental Legal Conceptions. Greenwood Press, Westport (1978)
9. Hruby, P.: Model-Driven Design of Software Applications with Business Patterns. Springer, Heidelberg (2006); ISBN: 3540301542
10. Lusch, R.F., Vargo, S.L., Wessels, G.: Towards a conceptual foundation for service science: Contributions from service-dominant logic. IBM Systems Journal 47(1) (2008)
11. McCarthy, W. E.: The REA Accounting Model: A Generalized Framework for Accounting Systems in a Shared Data Environment. The Accounting Review (1982)
12. NESSI, http://www.nessi-europe.com
13. OASIS. Reference Model for Service Oriented Architecture 1.0, http://www.oasis-open.org/committees/download.php/19679/soa-rm-cs.pdf
14. Preist, C.: A Conceptual Architecture for Semantic Web Services. In: McIlraith, S.A., Plexousakis, D., van Harmelen, F. (eds.) ISWC 2004. LNCS, vol. 3298, pp. 395–409. Springer, Heidelberg (2004)
15. REA-ontology, http://reatechnology.com/what-is-rea.html
16. Scott, E., Sampson, C., Froehle, M.: Foundation and Implications of a Proposed Unified Services Theory. Production and Operations Management 15(2), 329–343 (2006)
17. United Nations, Dept. of Economic and Social Affairs. Common DataBase (CDB) Data Dictionary (February 19, 2008),
    http://unstats.un.org/unsd/cdbmeta/gesform.asp?getitem=398
18. Web Services Architecture W3C Working Group (2004),
    http://www.w3.org/TR/2004/NOTE-ws-arch-20040211/
19. Wittgenstein, L.: The Blue and Brown Book, pp.1-74. New York: Harper&Row (1980),
    http://www.geocities.jp/mickindex/wittgenstein/witt_blue_en.html
20. Zeithaml, V.A., Parasuraman, A., Berry, L.L.: Problems and Strategies in Services Marketing. Journal of Marketing 49, 33–46 (1985)

A Semantic Oriented Method for Conceptual Data Modeling in OntoUML Based on Linguistic Concepts[*]

Lucia Castro[1], Fernanda Baião[1], and Giancarlo Guizzardi[2]

[1] NP2Tec – Research and Practice Group in Information Technology,
Federal University of the State of Rio de Janeiro (UNIRIO), Rio de Janeiro, Brazil
[2] Ontology and Conceptual Modeling Research Group (NEMO), Computer Science
Department, Federal University of Espírito Santo (UFES), Espírito Santo, Brazil
{lucia.castro,fernanda.baiao}@uniriotec.br,
gguizzardi@inf.ufes.br

Abstract. Conceptual data models, as means of communication, must have semantic quality. Such quality relies on the model's completeness and validity in relation to the concepts it is supposed to represent. Since the modeler acquires such concepts mostly from texts created in a natural language, a semantic-oriented linguistic approach should be adopted for building unambiguous conceptualizations. Also, the chosen modeling language must offer enough constructs for the creation of a faithful representation, like OntoUML. Such languages, however, may require a learning period that modelers hardly can afford. This paper proposes a modeling method that consists of systematic steps to promote the understanding of the concepts inherent to the domain to be modeled. The method application is illustrated in an example. Additional evaluations of the proposed method included a case study, which results indicated that it makes modeling less complex by allowing for modeling choices to be dealt with within the realm of the natural language.

Keywords: Conceptual modeling, linguistics, OntoUML, semantics.

1 Introduction

Conceptual data modeling *"is by far the most critical phase of database design and further development of database technology is not likely to change this situation"* [1], and the model is a tool for intentional communication and reasoning, i.e., human activities. This paper addresses the conceptual data modeling process, which comprises two main activities: the acquisition of concepts used in the domain being modeled, and the representation of the acquired concepts in a modeling language (ML). The modeler obtains such concepts from texts produced in a natural language (NL); here, the term *text* is used in the same sense as in [2] and [3] and does not imply written material, but any product of the discourse of a community.

Discourse is described in [4] as the speech activity of an individual according to determined circumstances, and Bunge [5] defines universe of discourse as *"The*

---

[*] This research is funded by FAPES (45444080/09) and CNPq (481906/2009-6).

M. Jeusfeld, L. Delcambre, and T.W. Ling (Eds.): ER 2011, LNCS 6998, pp. 486–494, 2011.

collection of the possible referents of a discourse". In other words, the universe of discourse comprises the real-world things about which the discourse of an individual is generated through the texts he/she produces. Individual, in this case, is a community that deals with such universe in its professional activities, the members of which are said to be the domain specialists. The conceptual data model must express the domain interpretations of such specialists; the modeler must conceal personal experiences and interpretations from both the modeling process and the model itself.

The conceptual data modeling process is, then, similar to a translation activity, in terms that it consists of understanding concepts represented in a (natural) language and then representing those same concepts in a different (modeling) language. Thus, it was only natural that researchers resorted to linguistics for support in the development of methods and solutions for the modeling process, as presented in [6] and its references. However, such projects view modeling activities from the perspective of the (meta)model adopted, and linguistic concepts are used as means to support modeling decisions. Also, their work focuses on the syntactic analysis of texts, barely mentioning semantics at all; yet, translating, as well as modeling, is an activity based on "meaning", therefore handling semantics in its essence.

As with a NL to NL translation, the model is ideally expected to have the same meaning as the texts in the NL; this means to say that a conceptual model must have semantic quality. Lindlam *et al* [7] state that for a model to have semantic quality it has to be valid and complete in relation to the universe of discourse it represents. However, the modeler does not have access to such universe and his/her work has to be based on the interpretation of the domain specialists of that domain. This article presents a semantic-oriented method for conceptual data modeling that makes use of the theories of semantic types proposed by Dixon [8], as well as linguistic concepts, so as to systematically address this interpretation; this method is the result of the research presented in [9]. The ML adopted is OntoUML [10], [11], [12], [13], a well founded conceptual ML that comprises a semantically rich set of constructs. It is divided into six sections, as follows: section 2 discusses languages, both natural and modeling ones; section 3 describes the proposed conceptual data modeling method; section 4 presents a theoretical example for the application of the proposed method, section 5 discusses the method evaluation and section 6 concludes the article.

2   Languages

Bunge [5] describes language as basically a *"System of signs serving to communicate and think."* Natural language is the designation given to languages natively spoken by humans for communication. All facts and phenomena related to NLs are studied in Linguistics, which comprises semantics (study of the relations between the signs and their referents), syntax (study of the relations among signs) and pragmatics (the study of the relations between signs and the one who uses them); from these, semantics stands out since *"Understanding how we mean and how we think is a vital issue for our intuitive sense of ourselves as human beings."* [14].

The lexicon of a NL (its words) is divided into word *classes* or *parts of speech* [15] [16], that can be either *closed* (have fewer members and cannot normally be extended) or *open* (can be indefinitely extended). Open class items (nouns, adjectives, verbs and adverbs) are the ones that carry the semantic load. Dixon [5] states that the open class items of any (natural) language can be grouped into classes he names *semantic types*. All the words of a semantic type share a common meaning component and a typical set of grammatical properties, as, for instance, its association with a part of speech. The most important semantic types for conceptual modeling purposes, at least in English and other structurally similar languages, are the ones related to concrete-referenced nouns, since this is the class of words that name types of things. Dixon [5] groups such nouns as follows: Animate (in this case, animals), Human and its subclasses (Kin, Rank and Social Groups), Parts (body and others) and Inanimate and its subclasses (Artefacts, Celestial and Weather, Environment and Flora). Verbs are important for establishing relations between concepts. Semantic types associated with verbs are classified as Primary (*"refer to some activity or state; verbs that can make up sentences by themselves"*) and Secondary (*"those providing semantic modification of some other verb"*). Semantic Types associated with Adjectives, on the other hand, are divided in 11 subclasses: Dimension, Physical Property, Speed, Age, Colour, Value, Difficulty, Volition, Qualification, Human Propensity and Similarity.

Apart from using their NLs for communication, men have been creating abstractions (i.e., building models) of real-world things in a way to understand and cope with reality [17]. For models to be understandable and useful to a community, they must be created from a system of symbols and connecting rules (grammar) known to all members of that community. Such systems are MLs, which are artificial languages also used for communication and to help reasoning, through the creation of models instead of texts. This work adopts OntoUML as ML, that, due to its underlying foundational ontology (UFO) [10] [13], provides constructs enough to allow for the creation of semantically accurate models. However, using such a language can present a problem since it requires a deeper knowledge of the philosophical concepts that are the bases for its constructs meanings, and a training period that most modelers cannot afford.

Different from NLs, MLs do not provide a lexicon; consequently, the translation between a NL and a ML must be done through the comparison between NL constructs (here, semantic types) and the constructs of the ML (the NL sign representing the concept being modeled appears in the model as the label of a construct). Bunge [5] defines *construct* as *"a concept, proposition, or set of propositions, such as a classification, a theory, or a moral or legal code"*; both natural and modeling languages have meaningful constructs. For instance, each of Dixon's semantic types [8] can be considered a construct, as well as each category described in the ML. Constructs are defined in terms of meta-properties, which must be compared during the modeling process so that the meaning restrictions imposed by the NL constructs are present in the model, reflected in the ML construct used in each representation.

3   The Method

This paper proposes a method for the creation of conceptual data models in OntoUML. The main goals are: to provide means for modelers to understand the concepts presented in the texts produced by domain specialists; to prevent modelers' from representing their own interpretation of the domain, instead of the specialists'; to allow for modeling decisions to be made within the realm of the NL, so that even modelers with little experience in OntoUML are able to create accurate models; to help creating models that have semantic quality, by ascertaining that the representations are valid and complete; and to provide means for this semantic quality to be maintained through time. The proposed method consists of six steps:

Step 1 – Breaking the text into kernel sentences - The modeler decomposes the NL texts produced by domain specialists into kernel sentences. Kernel sentences are affirmative, active sentences that do not have co-ordinate or subordinate clauses [18] [19]. They form the deep structure (meaning) of a text, whereas the surface structure (form) of the text is the result of transformations applied to the deep structure (e.g., identical subject suppression and passivization [19]). To extract the kernel sentences from a text, one should reverse such transformations. A simple example could be the sentence *John went to the beach and was taken home afterwards*. The sentence includes two clauses co-ordinated by the conjunction *and*. *John* is suppressed in the second clause, since it is the subject in both. Also, we know that someone took *John* home after he left the beach. The technique, thus, for "breaking" complex sentences is looking for co-ordinate and subordinate conjunctions and understanding how they relate clauses, identifying suppressed subjects, and converting sentences from passive to active voice, whenever applicable. When a resulting active voice sentence does not have an explicit subject, the word "someone" should be used as substitute (this specifies points to be clarified with the user in Step 2). So, for the example above, we could have two kernel sentences: *John went to the beach* and *Someone took John home afterwards*. Kernel sentences must be arranged in a numbered list in the order they appear in the text, so that reading the list is like reading the text itself.

As the modeler decomposes the text into simple sentences, he/she may find that pieces of information are missing or find ambiguities that will have to be explained by the domain specialists. One way of spotting missing information is to identify the verb semantic types and their related semantic roles and make up questions according to those roles. For instance, the verb *give* imply that something (*gift*) that belonged to someone (*donor*) will now belong to someone else (*recipient*). Table 1 presents some

Table 1. Questions for spotting semantic roles

Semantic Type	Semantic Role	Questions
Affect	Agent	***Who*** *<verb> <Target>* **with** *<Manip>?*
	Target	*<Agent> <verb>* **whom/what** *<Manip>?*
	Manip	*<Agent> <verb> <Target>* **with what?**
Giving	Donor	***Who*** *<verb> <Gift>***to** *<Recipient>?*
	Gift	*<Donor> <verb>* **what to** *<Recipient>?*
	Recipient	*<Donor> <verb> <Gift>* **to whom/what?**
Corporeal	Human	***Who*** *<verb> <Substance>?*
	Substance	*<Human> <verb>* **what?**
Competition	Competitor	***Who*** *<verb>?*
	Activity	***Competitor*** *<verb> <Activity>?*
Social Contract	None	***Who*** *<verb>* **who?**
Using	None	***Who*** *<verb>* **what?**

of the semantic types for verbs [5], their related semantic roles and the questions that might be asked in order to discover missing information. The modeler should write a list with all questions and doubts, in the same order as they appear in the text; this list, as well as the list of simple sentences, is the output for Step 1.

Step 2 – Clearing doubts - The modeler must then meet with domain specialist(s) and clear all doubts. According to the answers provided by the domain specialists, the modeler updates the list of simple sentences, explicating previously unknown subjects, and eliminating synonyms and ambiguities.

Step 3 – Identifying signs - The modeler must identify the conceptually significant NL signs present in the sentence list. In English, as well as in other similarly structured languages, such symbols will be nouns, verbs and adjectives. Such signs must be organized in a table with columns for the subject, the verb and the objects of each simple sentence – each row of the table will represent a simple sentence.

Step 4 – Linking signs to Semantic Types - The modeler must associate each of the identified signs with one of the semantic types. As semantic types are not mutually exclusive, the modeler must be careful so as to make the association that is applicable in that specific context or domain. The output for this phase is the table of signs; each row presents the sign and the semantic type to which it was associated.

Step 5 – Mapping Semantic Types to OntoUML constructs – In this step, the modeler systematically identifies a preliminary set of OntoUML constructs that will be needed to model the concept each sign previously identified represents. This is conducted by applying the mappings defined in [9]; some mapping examples are illustrated in Table 2. This mapping tends to be fairly stable and, as such, it can be organized in a table that can be accurately used in most situations.

Step 6 – Creating the model - Once the semantic types have been mapped to the ML constructs, the model can be created and taken to the domain specialist for validation, before the final model is produced.

Table 2. Semantic Types to OntoUML constructs Mapping

Semantic Type	OntoUML Construct	Semantic Type	OntoUML Construct
Animate	*Kind*	Social Group	*Kind*
Human	*Kind*	Part	When the part is a component, *kind* When the part is an ingredient, *quantity* When the part is a member, *kind* When the part is a sub-collection, *collective*
Kin	*Role*	Inanimate	*Kind*
Rank	*Role*	Artefact	*Kind*

4 Example

In their seminal conceptual modeling book [1], Battini *et al* provide exercise case studies for students. We have selected a small excerpt of the text for one of such exercises (pp 268--269) for our example modeling.

"In the library of a computer science department, books can be purchased both by researchers and by students. Researchers must indicate the grant used to pay for the book; each student has a limited budget, which is fixed each year by the dean of the college."

The list of simple sentences produced in step 1 is:

0.   In the library of a computer science department
1.   Researchers can purchase books
2.   Students can purchase books
3.   Researchers pay for books with grants
4.   Researchers must indicate the grant used to pay for the book
5.   Each student has a limited budget
6.   Each student pays for books from their budget
7.   The Dean of the college fixes students' budgets every year

The question produced in Step 1 is answered in Step 2 as follows:

Q: When you say "grant", do you refer to the amount of money or to a document, like a grant report, or a grant certificate?
A: It refers to the amount of money (library budget).

Table 3 presents the signs identified in each sentence.

Table 3. List of signs

Sentence	Signs			
0	Library	Comp. Sci. Dept.		
1	Researcher	Purchase	Book	
2	Student	Purchase	Book	
3	Researcher	Pay	Book	Grant
4	Researcher	Indicate	Grant	Book
5	Student	Have	Limited Budget	
6	Student	Pay	Book	Budget
7	Dean	Fix	Student	[yearly] Budget

The next step is the association of identified signs with semantic types. Table 4 presents the list of signs and the rationale behind their associations.

The modeler then must map semantic types to OntoUML constructs, following table 2. For example, a Social Group is mapped to Kind, Rank to Role, Giving to Relator and Artefact to Kind (detailed rationale beyond this mapping is explained in [9] and [20]). Finally, the modeler creates an OntoUML model and validates it with domain specialists. Figure 1 presents the produced version of our example model.

Table 4. List of signs and their associations with semantic types

Sign	Semantic Type
Computer Science Dpt.	Noun phrase that refers to a division of an institution, i.e., it has a concrete reference, is related to humans and is a **Social Group**.
Library	Noun that also refers to a division of an institution; also has a concrete reference, is related to humans and is a **Social Group**.
Researcher	Sign refers to a human but qualifying the person according to a position and/or responsibility; the semantic type should be **Rank**.
Purchase	Purchase is a Primary A verb, of the type **Giving**, i.e., one that always involves 3 semantic roles: a donor, a donated thing and a recipient.
Book	An object (concrete and inanimate) produced by men, thus, an **Artefact**.
Student	Sign refers to a human but qualifying the person according to a position and/or responsibility; the semantic type should be **Rank**.
Grant	Sign refers to an amount of money given by an organization for a particular purpose; a nominalization of the verb *to grant*, it's meaning relates a Primary A verb of the type **Giving**.
Budget	Sign refers to an amount of money set aside for a particular purpose; a nominalization of the verb *to budget*, it's meaning relates to a Primary A verb of the type **Giving**, since the Dean fixes the amount of money a Student has at his/her discretion, and this procedure is repeated every year.
Dean	Sign refers to a human but qualifying the person according to a position and/or responsibility; the semantic type should be **Rank**.

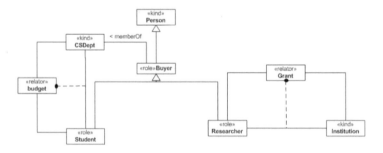

Fig. 1. OntoUML example model

5   Method Evaluation

The method presented in this paper was evaluated through a case study and an experiment. Due to space restrictions, details about this evaluation are presented in [20]. The results of the experiment showed that modelers found it easier to discuss concepts in terms of NL constructs, and that the model produced according to the proposed method was complete and valid, i.e., the model had semantic quality.

6   Conclusion

This work proposed a method for conceptual data modeling in OntoUML that is based on linguistic analysis and on the semantic types theory proposed by Dixon [5]. We developed the mapping of each of those semantic types to the constructs of a well-founded ontological ML, OntoUML. MLs differ from NLs in that the meaning of representations do not come from signs but from constructs; thus, the modeler must compare NL constructs (semantic types) to the ML ones, from the meta-properties inherent to each of them. One quality trait of the produced model relies on its semantic equivalence to the descriptions provided in the NL. The use of ontological languages to achieve semantic quality is not a novelty and the semantic gain of an OntoUML model over a correspondent ER one is evidenced in [12]. However, the semantics of such language constructs is much less intuitive for the modeler than the semantics of the constructs of his NL; thus, discussing concepts and understanding the metaproperties that apply to them is much easier if done in the NL. The method proposed in [20] uses linguistics to achieving semantic quality in conceptual models, not only by the application of semantic principles but also by providing a systematized list of activities to achieve this goal.

The outputs of each step of the method form a record of the modeler's rationale throughout the modeling process; this is important for keeping the semantic quality of the created method. NLs are essentially ambiguous, and provide several ways of saying the same thing; also, NLs are in constant evolution and semantics are affected by it, i.e., the meaning of signs may change with time. MLs, on the contrary, need to provide for unambiguous representations of concepts; and models are static representations that may provide erroneous information as time passes. Consequently, recording the reasons why constructs and signs were chosen to represent a concept is a way of maintaining the semantic quality: people who read the model in the future can use the documentation created during the modeling process to understand such choices and the semantics behind them.

References

1. Batini, C., Ceri, S., Navathe, S.: Conceptual Database Design. Benjamin/Cummings (1992)
2. Eco, U.: Semiotics and the Philosophy of Language. Indiana Univ. Press (1984)
3. Koch, I.: Introdução à Linguística Textual. WMF Martins Fontes (2009) (in Portuguese)
4. Bechara, E.: Moderna Gramática Portuguesa. Nova Fronteira (2009) (in Portuguese)
5. Bunge, M.: Philosophical Dictionary. Prometheus Books, Amherst (2003)
6. Castro, L., Baiao, F., Guizzardi, G.: A Survey on Conceptual Modeling from a Linguistic Point of View. Technical Report, Rela Te-DIA (2009)
7. Lindlam, O., Sindre, G., Sølvberg, A.: Understandig Quality in Conceptual Modeling. IEEE Software 11(2), 42–49 (1994)
8. Dixon, R.M.W.: A Semantic Approach to English Grammar. Oxford University Press, Oxford (2005)
9. Castro, L., Baião, F., Guizzardi, G.: A Linguistic Approach to Conceptual Modeling with Semantic Types and OntoUML. In: EDOC 2010, Intl. Workshop on Vocabularies, Ontologies and Rules for the Enterprise (VORTE 2010), Vitoria (2010)
10. Guizzardi, G.: Ontological Foundations for Structural Conceptual Models. CTIT (2005)
11. Benevides, A.B., Guizzardi, G.: A Model-Based Tool for Conceptual Modeling and Domain Ontology Engineering in OntoUML. In: Filipe, J., Cordeiro, J. (eds.) Enterprise Information Systems. Lecture Notes in Business Information Processing, vol. 24, pp. 528–538. Springer, Heidelberg (2009)

12. Guizzardi, G., Lopes, M., Baião, F., Falbo, R.: On the Importance of Truly Ontological Distinctions for Ontology Representation Languages: An Industrial Case Study in the Domain of Oil and Gas. In: Halpin, T., Krogstie, J., Nurcan, S., Proper, E., Schmidt, R., Soffer, P., Ukor, R. (eds.) Enterprise, Business-Process and Information Systems Modeling. Lecture Notes in Business Information Processing, vol. 29, pp. 224–236. Springer, Heidelberg (2009)
13. Benevides, A.B., Guizzardi, G., Braga, B.F.B., Almeida, J.P.A.: Assessing Modal Aspects of OntoUML Conceptual Models in Alloy. In: Heuser, C.A., Pernul, G. (eds.) ER 2009. LNCS, vol. 5833, pp. 55–64. Springer, Heidelberg (2009)
14. Jackendoff, R.: Foundations of Language. Oxford University Press, Oxford (2002)
15. Greenbaum, S.: The Oxford English Grammar. Oxford University Press, Oxford (1996)
16. Quirk, R., Greenbaum, S.: A University Grammar of English. Longman, London (1973)
17. Schichl, H.: Models and History of Modeling. In: Kallrath, J. (ed.) Modeling Language in Mathematical Optimization, pp. 25–36. Kluwer Academic Publishers, Norwell (2004)
18. Chomsky, N.: Aspects of the Theory of Syntax. MIT Press, Cambridge (1965)
19. Chomsky, N.: Syntactic Structures. Mouton de Gruyter, New York (2002)
20. Castro, L.: Abordagem Linguística para a Modelagem Conceitual de Dados com Foco Semântico, MSc Dissertation, Unirio, Rio de Janeiro (2010) (in Portuguese)

Content-Based Validation of Business Process Modifications

Maya Lincoln and Avigdor Gal

Abstract. Researchers become increasingly interested in developing tools for evaluating the correctness of business process models. We present a methodology for content-based validation of changes to business processes, relying on an automatic extraction of business logic from real-life business process repositories. Each process step in a repository is automatically transformed to a *descriptor* - containing objects, actions, and related qualifiers. From the collection of descriptors we induce taxonomies of action sequence, object lifecycle, and object and action hierarchies that form the logical foundation of the presented validation process. The method utilizes these taxonomies to identify process deficiencies that may occur due to process model modification, and suggests alternatives in order to correct and validate the models.

Keywords: Business process modeling, Content-based validation, Business process compliance.

1 Introduction

In recent years, researchers have become increasingly interested in developing tools for evaluating the correctness of business process models, using verification [21,14,13], validation [24,9,3,5], and compliance [1,4,19,2,15] methods. We observe that the validation process cannot be done globally but is rather specific to an organization or a specialized domain for which the processes are designed. To illustrate, consider Example 1.

Example 1. Fig. 1 illustrates two processes, one that deploys a *Make to Stock* (MtS) production policy and the other uses a *Make to Order* (MtO) production policy. The execution pattern of the MtS process includes six sub-processes (Fig. 1a). The MtO process, on the other hand, would start with a different flow of

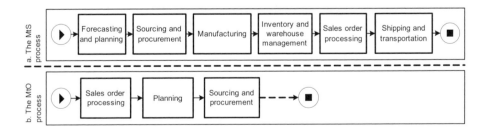

Fig. 1. An example of the MtS and MtO high-level processes

M. Jeusfeld, L. Delcambre, and T.W. Ling (Eds.): ER 2011, LNCS 6998, pp. 495–503, 2011.
© Springer-Verlag Berlin Heidelberg 2011

sub-process, although some of them are also included in the MtS flow, *e.g.*, the "Sales order processing" sub-process (Fig. 1b). From a validation perspective, any inclusion of forecasting related activities in the MtO process would be redundant if not erroneous. Furthermore, aiming to process sales orders in the context of MtS prior to completing a forecasting activity would be lacking if not impossible. Such validation cases, that we refer to as "content-based validation" propagate into lower level process models and will neither be identified by structural verification methods, nor by semantic/data based validation methods. Hence, the need for content-based validation becomes apparent.

Our work presents a content-based validation framework that uses organizational standards to evaluate the correctness of both newly designed and modified processes. A unique feature of the proposed framework, in the context of process validation, is the creation of a repository that captures organizational standards by using natural language processing analysis to capture simultaneously action and object patterns. Our contribution to the compliance domain is in the *dynamic* construction and adjustment of patterns - avoiding the need to design and maintain external, static rules.

We propose to *automatically* extract business logic from process repositories using the PDC model [7,8]. Each process step is encoded automatically as a *descriptor* that represents objects, actions, and qualifiers. The collection of all process descriptors formulates taxonomy models of action sequence, object life-cycle, and object and action hierarchies that support the validation process. The proposed method identifies content-based validation deficiencies, from which required corrections can be deduced.

The proposed method can support business analysts in validating new process models or in changing existing models, by marking contextually non-valid process segments and suggesting possible corrections. Our contribution includes: (1) proposing a *content-based* validation of business process models that require no additional semantics or pre-defined patterns. The validation process is agnostic to the process model type (*e.g.*, BPMN, Petri net, YAWL, *etc.*); (2) identifying conflicts that may occur in business process models by adding new knowledge; and (3) being able to examine new knowledge that has no prior reference or representation in the existing repository.

The paper is organized as follows: we provide a classification of the related work in Section 2, positioning our work with respect to previous research. In Section 3 we present the descriptor model. Then, we describe the content-based validation method in Section 4. We conclude in Section 5.

2   Related Work

To position our work within the vast research on business process validation, we group current related works into three major research fields: business process *verification, validation* and *compliance* (see illustration in Fig. 2). Business process *verification* (left-hand side of Fig. 2) addresses the question of "does this process model work?." This research stream largely focuses on avoiding errors

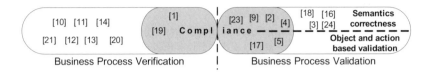

Business Process Verification   Business Process Validation

Fig. 2. Related work segmentation

at the structural level of the process model, *e.g.*, deadlocks or incorrect data links. Business process *validation* (right-hand side of Fig. 2) addresses the question "does this process model work well?." To answer this question it is required to examine the *content*, *data* and *context* layers of process models, aiming to validate the process logic. For example, a process model that contains the step "Pay for received goods" before the step "Receive goods" can be verified but may not be valid. Business process *compliance* addresses both verification and validation issues (see shaded area in Fig. 2), answering the question "does this process comply with a reference model/pattern?."

Business Process Verification. Works such as [21,13] focus on avoiding errors at the structural level. Special emphasis was put on correctness of change operations [12], mainly the insertion and moving of activities [14], as well as on defining the soundness criterion and related derivatives, *e.g.*, [10,11,20], aiming to check whether proper execution completion is possible or guaranteed.

Business Process Validation. Semantics correctness was defined using annotations, *e.g.*, [9], ontologies, *e.g.*, [18], and combinations of the two, *e.g.*, [23,24,3]. This domain also includes data flow analysis, *e.g.*, [16]. Within this stream, [5], for example, deals with compliance of business process models to a set of given reference object lifecycles, and the work in [17] defines a concept of action patterns, which are closely related to semantic content of a process model. We position our work in this area of process validation, but unlike other works in this field, our approach: (1) does not require any predefined pattern or rule to determine validation, and (2) deals simultaneously with action sequences and object lifecycles.

Business Process Compliance. Compliance works mainly focus on validating a combination of process data and structure [1,23,4,19,2]. The frameworks in [9,2], for example, provide general criteria for assessing the compliance of processes with semantic constraints. More specifically, certain compliance works were aimed at supporting specific tasks, *e.g.*, identifying violations of execution order compliance rules [1].

Our proposed framework does not rely on predefined patterns, but it rather suggests a content-aware validation method that dynamically extracts business logic from real-life business process repositories. The automatic extraction of organizational content from process model repositories distinguishes our work from previous contributions, and creates a platform for developing enabling applications for content-based validation.

3   The Descriptor Model

In this section we provide a formal descriptor space model. Section 3.1 describes the descriptor model and Section 3.2 describes descriptor-based taxonomies.

3.1   The Process Descriptor Repository

In this section we describe a descriptor model, based on [8,7]. Fig. 3 provides an illustrating example (using YAWL [22]) of a business process model of the process "Evaluate Supplier Performance," describing a flow of activities aimed at fulfilling the process goal.

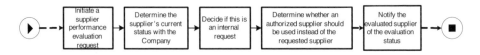

Fig. 3. The "Evaluate Supplier Performance" process model

In the Process Descriptor Catalog model ("PDC") [8,7] each activity is composed of one action, one object that the action acts upon, and possibly one or more action and object qualifiers. Qualifiers extend the description of actions and objects. In particular, a qualifier of an object is roughly related to an object state. State-of-the-art Natural Language Processing (NLP) systems, *e.g.,* the *Stanford Parser*,[1] also used in [6], can serve to automatically decompose process and activity names into *process/activity descriptors*. For example, in Fig. 3, the activity "Notify the evaluated supplier of the evaluation status" generates an activity descriptor containing the object "supplier," the object qualifier "evaluated," the action "notify," and the action qualifier "of the evaluation status."

In general, given an object, o, an object qualifier, q_o, an action, a, and an action qualifier, q_a, we denote a descriptor, d, as follows: $d = (o, q_o, a, q_a)$. A *complete action* is an action with its qualifier, and similarly, a *complete* object is an object with its qualifier. We denote by $o(d)$ the complete object part of the descriptor, *e.g.,* "evaluated supplier" in the example.

A *process repository* is a collection of interconnected process models, where the execution of an activity in one process model may invoke the execution of another activity in another process model.

3.2   Descriptor-Based Taxonomies

From the descriptor model's two atomic elements, *objects* and *actions*, we construct four taxonomies, namely an *action hierarchy model*, an *object hierarchy model*, an *action sequence model*, and an *object lifecycle model*. The action and object taxonomy models organize a set of activity descriptors according to the relationships among business actions and objects both hierarchically and in terms of execution order, as detailed next.

---

[1] http://nlp.stanford.edu:8080/parser/index.jsp

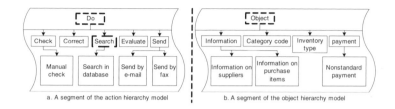

Fig. 4. Segments of action and object hierarchy models

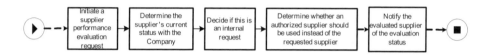

Fig. 5. Segments of the action sequence model and the object lifecycle model

The hierarchical dimension of actions and objects is determined by their qualifiers. We define an Action Hierarchy Model (AHM) to be a tree $T = (A, E)$, where A represents actions and an edge (a_i, a_j) in E exists if a_j is more specific than a_i. An Object Hierarchy Model (OHM) is defined similarly. To illustrate, segments of an action hierarchy model and an object hierarchy model are presented in Fig. 4. For example, the action "Manual check" is a subclass (a more specific form) of "Check" in the action hierarchy model, since the qualifier "Manual" limits the action of "Check" to a reduced action range.

The descriptor model induces two object-based models. The Action Sequence Model (ASM) is a graph of ordered complete actions (an "action sequence") that are applied to a complete object (see illustration in Fig. 5a). For example, the ASM of the object "New supplier details" contains the following action sequence: "Receive," followed by "Examine," "Approve," and "Document."

The Object Lifecycle Model (OLM), is a graph of ordered complete objects that expresses the possible ordering of the object's states (see illustration in Fig. 5b). This sequence is built by locating the same object with different qualifiers along the process diagram. For example, the object "New supplier" is part of the object lifecycle of "Supplier" in Fig. 5b.

Note that ASM and OLM are defined as sets of sequences and not as a single sequence, since different unconnected processes in the repository may involve the same object, and therefore contribute a different sequence to these models.

Based on the activity decomposition model, the operational range of a business process repository is compiled into a descriptor space (DS), in which each activity is represented by a coordinate of its four descriptor components. The generated descriptor space is a quad-dimensional space, in which the coordinates represent the object dimension, the action dimension, and their qualifiers.

4   The Content-Based Validation Method

We now present a method for validating changes in process repositories using the descriptor model. Business logic and business rules, as reflected in an existing process repository, are valuable assets of an enterprise. Therefore, the suggested validation method aims at seeking consistency of new knowledge, as reflected in model changes, with existing knowledge, and alert if inconsistencies are revealed. In doing so, the method is conservative with respect to existing knowledge and indifferent to new knowledge that has no representation in the existing repository. Note that some inconsistencies may reflect new valid knowledge in an enterprise modus-operandi (*e.g.*, changes in the execution order of activities). Nevertheless, the suggested method will also alert such inconsistencies, not because they are necessarily wrong, but in order to enable the designer to correct either the new knowledge or the existing repository if required.

The validation of changes in existing process repositories is based on the compliance of a change with the business logic and business rules as automatically extracted from these repositories (before changes were applied). We define two atomic change types, namely *Add* and *Delete*. We consider a modification of the position of an existing activity and a modification of an existing descriptor (*e.g.*, a change of its object or its action) as a combination of a *Delete* change followed by an *Add* change. Also, more complex changes, such as the change of a chain of activities, is broken into atomic changes and analyzed accordingly. Finally, we note that newly designed processes are validated by examining the addition of each new activity.

The method examines the validity of an atomic change based on the business logic as expressed in an underlying process repository (see Section 3). The suggested framework provides process designers with information regarding the validity of a change, which guides them regarding possible corrections that may be applied.

The validation method is initiated when a process designer makes an atomic change to an existing process model, denoted by v_{ch}. When the designer adds a new activity or deletes an existing one, the activity's name is decomposed automatically into a process descriptor format, d_{ch}, as detailed in Section 3.1. Then, the new ASM and OLM for $o(d_{ch})$, denoted ASM_{ch} and OLM_{ch} respectively, are created.

The validation method examines the atomic change based on the content rules that are explicitly given in a repository and exposed by the four object and action taxonomies (Section 3.2). As a result, it produces a list of validation deficiencies (detailed in Section 4).

Validation Deficiencies. Using the four taxonomies, it is possible to define three error types, as follows:

1. An Invalid Action Sequence error (*Err-IAS*) occurs whenever an atomic change in a process repository causes a violation of the action sequence model of an object in the existing process repository. For example, the actions "Create," "Submit," and "Review" are all applied sequentially to the object

"Requisition" in the same process model within a given process repository. When deleting the activity "Submit requisition" from this process model - a new action sequence is created containing the action "Create" followed by "Review." Since no such sequence of actions is applied to the object "Requisition" in the original process repository (see Fig. 5a), it is considered a violation of this object's action sequence. Similarly, this error type can also occur when adding a new activity "Approve requisition" before "Review requisition."

2. An Invalid Object Lifecycle error ($Err\text{-}IOL$) similarly occurs whenever an atomic change in a process model violates an object lifecycle as represented in the existing process repository.
3. An Unknown Descriptor Combination error ($Err\text{-}UDC$) occurs when a newly added descriptor is not represented in the original process repository.

The condition for the occurrence of an error of type $Err\text{-}IAS$ is as follows: $Err\text{-}IAS=true$ if $ASM_{ch}(o(d_{ch})) \nsubseteq ASM_{orig}(o(d_{ch}))$. Given a changed descriptor, d_{ch}, $ASM_{orig}(o(d_{ch}))$ is the original ASM of $o(d_{ch})$ *before* applying that change. Similarly, the condition for Err-IOL is:
$Err\text{-}IOL=true$ if $OLM_{ch}(o(d_{ch})) \nsubseteq OLM_{orig}(o(d_{ch}))$ and the condition for Err-UDC is: $Err\text{-}UDC=true$ if $d_{ch} \notin DS_{orig}$.

For example, let us examine a case of a new activity "Verify inventory type" that is added between the activities "Search for inventory type" and "Insert inventory type" in a given process repository. In this example: $o(d_{ch})=$"inventory type" and therefore $ASM_{orig}(o(d_{ch})) =\{$(Define, Verify, Correct), (Search, Insert, Define, Correct)$\}$ (see Fig. 5a). After adding the new activity, the following new action sequence model is created: $ASM_{ch}(o(d_{ch})) =\{$(Define, Verify, Correct), (Search, Verify, Insert)$\}$. Since the sequence (Search, Verify, Insert) is not a subset of any of the paths in ASM_{orig}, $Err\text{-}IAS$ is invoked.

5   Conclusions

We proposed a methodology for content-based validation of business process models that focuses on deficiency identification. The suggested methodology can save process modification time and support non-expert designers in validating business process models.

This work can be applied in real-life scenarios, yet we suggest to: (1) extend the empirical study, and (2) introduce a transactional concept that will allow analyzing several atomic changes together.

References

1. Awad, A., Smirnov, S., Weske, M.: Towards Resolving Compliance Violations in Business Process Models. In: GRCIS. CEUR-WS. org (2009)
2. El Kharbili, M., Stein, S., Markovic, I., Pulverm, E.: Towards a framework for semantic business process compliance management. In: Proc. of the Workshop on Governance, Risk and Compliance for Information Systems, pp. 1–15. Citeseer (2008)

3. Farahbod, R., Glässer, U., Vajihollahi, M.: Specification and validation of the business process execution language for web services. In: Zimmermann, W., Thalheim, B. (eds.) ASM 2004. LNCS, vol. 3052, pp. 78–94. Springer, Heidelberg (2004)
4. Governatori, G., Milosevic, Z., Sadiq, S.: Compliance checking between business processes and business contracts. In: 10th IEEE International Enterprise Distributed Object Computing Conference, EDOC 2006, pp. 221–232. IEEE, Los Alamitos (2006)
5. Kuster, J., Ryndina, K., Gall, H.: Generation of business process models for object life cycle compliance. In: Alonso, G., Dadam, P., Rosemann, M. (eds.) BPM 2007. LNCS, vol. 4714, pp. 165–181. Springer, Heidelberg (2007)
6. Leopold, H., Smirnov, S., Mendling, J.: Refactoring of process model activity labels. In: Hopfe, C.J., Rezgui, Y., Métais, E., Preece, A., Li, H. (eds.) NLDB 2010. LNCS, vol. 6177, pp. 268–276. Springer, Heidelberg (2010)
7. Lincoln, M., Golani, M., Gal, A.: Machine-assisted design of business process models using descriptor space analysis. In: Hull, R., Mendling, J., Tai, S. (eds.) BPM 2010. LNCS, vol. 6336, pp. 128–144. Springer, Heidelberg (2010)
8. Lincoln, M., Karni, R., Wasser, A.: A Framework for Ontological Standardization of Business Process Content. In: Int. Conf. on Enterprise Information Systems, pp. 257–263 (2007)
9. Ly, L.T., Rinderle-Ma, S., Goser, K., Dadam, P.: On enabling integrated process compliance with semantic constraints in process management systems. Information Systems Frontiers, 1–25 (2009)
10. Mendling, J., van der Aalst, W.M.P.: Formalization and verification of ePCs with OR-joins based on state and context. In: Krogstie, J., Opdahl, A.L., Sindre, G. (eds.) CAiSE 2007 and WES 2007. LNCS, vol. 4495, pp. 439–453. Springer, Heidelberg (2007)
11. Puhlmann, F., Weske, M.: Investigations on soundness regarding lazy activities. In: Dustdar, S., Fiadeiro, J.L., Sheth, A.P. (eds.) BPM 2006. LNCS, vol. 4102, pp. 145–160. Springer, Heidelberg (2006)
12. Reichert, M., Dadam, P.: ADEPT flex-supporting dynamic changes of workflows without losing control. J. of Intelligent Information Systems 10(2), 93–129 (1998)
13. Reichert, M., Dadam, P., Bauer, T.: Dealing with forward and backward jumps in workflow management systems. Software and Systems Modeling 2(1), 37–58 (2003)
14. Rinderle, S., Reichert, M., Dadam, P.: Correctness criteria for dynamic changes in workflow systems–a survey. Data & Knowledge Engineering 50(1), 9–34 (2004)
15. Russell, N., ter Hofstede, A.H.M., Edmond, D., van der Aalst, W.M.P.: Workflow data patterns: Identification, representation and tool support. In: Delcambre, L.M.L., Kop, C., Mayr, H.C., Mylopoulos, J., Pastor, Ó. (eds.) ER 2005. LNCS, vol. 3716, pp. 353–368. Springer, Heidelberg (2005)
16. Sadiq, S., Orlowska, M., Sadiq, W., Foulger, C.: Data flow and validation in workflow modelling. In: Proc. 15th Australasian database conference, vol. 27, pp. 207–214. Australian Computer Society, Inc. (2004)
17. Smirnov, S., Weidlich, M., Mendling, J., Weske, M.: Action patterns in business process models. Service-Oriented Computing, 115–129 (2009)
18. Soffer, P., Kaner, M., Wand, Y.: Assigning ontology-based semantics to process models: The case of petri nets. In: Bellahsène, Z., Léonard, M. (eds.) CAiSE 2008. LNCS, vol. 5074, pp. 16–31. Springer, Heidelberg (2008)
19. Thom, L.H., Reichert, M., Chiao, C.M., Iochpe, C., Hess, G.N.: Inventing Less, Reusing More, and Adding Intelligence to Business Process Modeling. In: Bhowmick, S.S., Küng, J., Wagner, R. (eds.) DEXA 2008. LNCS, vol. 5181, pp. 837–850. Springer, Heidelberg (2008)

20. van der Aalst, W.M.P.: Verification of workflow nets. In: Azéma, P., Balbo, G. (eds.) ICATPN 1997. LNCS, vol. 1248, pp. 407–426. Springer, Heidelberg (1997)
21. van der Aalst, W.M.P.: Workflow verification: Finding control-flow errors using petri-net-based techniques. In: van der Aalst, W.M.P., Desel, J., Oberweis, A. (eds.) Business Process Management. LNCS, vol. 1806, pp. 19–128. Springer, Heidelberg (2000)
22. van der Aalst, W.M.P., Ter Hofstede, A.: YAWL: yet another workflow language. Information Systems 30(4), 245–275 (2005)
23. Weber, I., Hoffmann, J., Mendling, J.: Semantic business process validation. In: Proc. of Int. Workshop on Semantic Business Process Management (2008)
24. Weber, I., Hoffmann, J., Mendling, J.: Beyond soundness: on the verification of semantic business process models. Distributed and Parallel Databases 27(3), 271–343 (2010)

Visual Change Tracking for Business Process Models

Sonja Kabicher, Simone Kriglstein, and Stefanie Rinderle-Ma

University of Vienna, Faculty of Computer Science
Rathausstrasse 19/9, 1010 Vienna, Austria
{sonja.kabicher,simone.kriglstein,stefanie.rinderle-ma}@univie.ac.at

Abstract. Basically there are two options to display process change: (a)
showing the corresponding process model before and after the change, or
(b) including change tracking options within the process model. In this
paper we want to find out how to support users best in grasping process changes. For this, first of all, a conceptualization of Change Tracking Graphs (CTG) is provided that is independent of any process meta
model. The CTGs are then visualized in different ways following aesthetic criteria on the one side and mental map aspects on the other side.
Further, different visual properties are applied. All different combinations of change representation for process models are evaluated based
on an empirical study with 117 participants. This study provides a first
stepstone towards a more user-centric application of process change.

Keywords: Business Process Modeling, Information Visualization,
Conceptual Model Evolution.

1 Introduction

In this work we present an visual framework for change tracking in business
process models. Following a human-centric view, we argue that the inclusion
of change information in a graph supports traceability and transparency of the
changes, and allows the user to achieve change awareness by providing a picture
of the whole process and its elements affected by the change. The following
challenges of considering change tracking in graphs are focused in this work: (a)
How to consider change as content in graphs?, (b) How to layout change tracking
graphs?, and (c) How to visualize change in the change tracking graph? To
tackle these questions, our approach includes: (1) the description of the change
tracking graph and the change tracking states of graph elements by means of a
general series-parallel digraph, (2) the description of change as it is considered
in tracking graphs, namely by means of change patterns and the assignment
of visual properties to changed elements in the change tracking graph, (3) the
description of two intuitive options of change tracking graph layouting (future
perspective, and past perspective), and (4) a survey to elicit users' preferences
concerning change tracking graph layouting and the visualization of changes in
the change tracking graph. Our hypotheses are the following:

M. Jeusfeld, L. Delcambre, and T.W. Ling (Eds.): ER 2011, LNCS 6998, pp. 504–513, 2011.
© Springer-Verlag Berlin Heidelberg 2011

Hypothesis 1: Change tracking in the business process model supports the process user in getting a holistic view of the changes implemented.

Hypothesis 2: There is a varying preference of the process users concerning the layout of the change tracking model that is either grounded in the layout of the initial model (focusing on the mental map) or in the layout of the adjusted model (considering particular aesthetic criteria).

Hypothesis 3: Particular visual properties (like *color(hue)* and *brightness*) help the process user to better understand the change performed on the business process model.

In this work we focused on the control flow of business process models, particularly considering activities, execution constraints, and their ordering. Other components of business process modeling, like information modeling (data representation) are not further considered in this work.

2   Main Issues of Visual Change Tracking

In this section we discuss the corestones of our visual framework for change tracking: aesthetic criteria, mental map, and visual properties.

2.1   Aesthetic Criteria

Aesthetic criteria are particularly important when layouts are produced for human consumption and should optimize the graph drawing to increase the readability [12] [14]. There are various aesthetic criteria discussed in the visualization research community, some of the commonly used ones are, for example, edge crossing minimization, bend minimization, layout size/area minimization, angle maximization, length minimization of edges, reflection of symmetries, clustering of nodes to reveal the structure of the graph, and layered drawings [14][8] [20][28][23]. Often the aesthetic criteria are only presented for drawing static graphs without changes. Therefore, it is recommended to preserve the mental map of a graph after each update [9][7][3]. However, the aesthetic criteria often compete against each other and depending on the priorities set for particular aesthetic criteria the graphs vary in their layout [20]. Already existing experimental results show that there is a trade-off between aesthetic criteria for 'drawing a graph nicely' and efforts to preserve the mental map [20]. Therefore, we analyze the mental map separately from the common aesthetic criteria to find out which approach is better suited for the visualization of changes in business processes.

2.2   Mental Map

Graphs which represent business processes are usually dynamic graphs, because business processes can change over time. The changes can spoil the layout of the graph (e.g., an added node may overlap an existing node) and therefore layout algorithms were developed which rearrange nodes and edges in consideration of aesthetic criteria [10]. However, layout algorithm which completely rearrange the nodes and edges are not helpful, because they destroy the abstract structural information which users form about a graph (or called users' *mental map* about a graph) [10][3]. Therefore, other aspects gained importance especially for dynamic graphs which concentrate on the preservation of user's mental map. In other words, these aspects take the initial model's layout into account when changes are implemented. It is argued that similarity of the graph's layout (or layout stability [22]) before and after change helps the user to keep their orientation in the graph [22]. This saves much time otherwise users have to relearn the structure of the graph after each update [6]. Keeping the mental map means that the layout of a graph is preserved as much as possible after a change. This can be supported, e.g., by the following requirements [10][22][21][7]: (a) move as few nodes as possible (only the part of the graph should be affected by the change where the change occurs), (b) move nodes as little as possible and (c) keep uniform scaling.

2.3   Visual Properties

Visualizations encode the components of data by means of visual properties [2]. According to [5], there exist planar (e.g. *spatial position*) and retinal variables (e.g. *color(hue)*, *size*, *brightness*, *shape*, *texture*, and *orientation*). In case of business process models, the spatial positions defines the flow of the process and retinal variables can be used to make changes in processes transparent. It is important that the visual properties support users to interpret the data quickly and therefore it has to be avoided that visual properties are used as decorative elements, or as unnecessary graphical effects. The choice of the visual properties depends strongly on their purpose and therefore not all visual properties work well for each visualization. For example, *orientation* of elements plays a role according to aesthetic criteria for graph drawing which can be a contradiction with the recommendation to maximize consistent flow direction for the visualization of business processes [4]. Or, the usage of the visual properties *shapes* and *textures* is restricted because *shapes* or *textures* often strongly depend on the used business process modeling notations. To make change information between processes transparent in our approach, we concentrate on the visual properties *color(hue)*, *brightness*, and *size* which allow us to be independent of the used business process modeling notations and aesthetic criteria.

3   Visual Framework for Change Tracking in Graphs

In this section we introduce our approach of including change tracking information in graphs. In the following, we use the term *graph* to refer to series-parallel digraphs. In a first step we describe our approach by means of a series-parallel digraph, as such a graph serves as an illustrative general graph for business process models. In a second step we show the application of our approach to particular workflow modeling notations.

For our approach we assume that change is to be conducted to an already existing graph by following a predefined set of change patterns [29] at a specific date. To perform change on a graph, some pre- and postconditions need to be met, as listed in the following. Precondition 2 and Postcondition 3 refer to quality metrics of graphs (e.g., correctness). As we use change patterns for performing the change on existing graphs, the quality metrics are assumed to be maintained when graphs are changed. Therefore, we do not further discuss quality metrics in this work.

Precondition 1: There already exists an initial graph A.
Precondition 2: The initial graph A corresponds to certain quality metrics.
Precondition 3: Change is predefined by means of change patterns.

Postcondition 1: Three graphs are available: initial graph A, change tracking graph A^*, and adjusted graph A'.
Postcondition 2: The graph A^* is designed according to two layouts. A^*_{MM} considers the layout of the initial graph A. A^*_{AC} considers the layout of the adjusted graph A'.
Postcondition 3: The graph A' correspond to certain quality metrics.

Change Tracking Graph. The change is conducted by transforming the initial graph A to the adjusted graph A'. Thus, A' is the resulting process schema from the application of the change to A. In our approach we introduce the *change tracking graph A** which contains the graph elements of the initial graph A that are not affected by the change, the graph elements of A that are deleted, and the graph elements that are added during change. Further, we introduce three possible change tracking states of graph elements. Graph elements that are inserted are signed as *activated* elements, deleted elements are denoted as *deactivated* elements, and graph elements that are not affected by the change are marked as *initial* elements.

Change Primitives. We could compute A, A', A^* based on the set-based definition as presented above. However, as change is typically applied in an incremental manner, and we do actually know the change, we opt for determining the change tracking graphs by exploiting the changes. The basis for this is that we can express all kinds of change patterns by means of the following change primitives [25]: 'delete node', 'delete edge', 'insert node', and 'insert edge'. Using the two change primitives *insert* and *delete* also allows us to easily mark the change conducted with particular visual properties without challenging the graph user with an exaggerated number of new visual appearances of the graph elements. All presented change patterns in [29] can be separated into these four change primitives. In Figure 1, the sequence of the change primitives is presented for the change patterns serialInsert, Delete, serialMove, Replace, Swap, and Parallelize process fragment(s). The selected change patterns serve as illustrative examples of change and provide an insight into our approach.

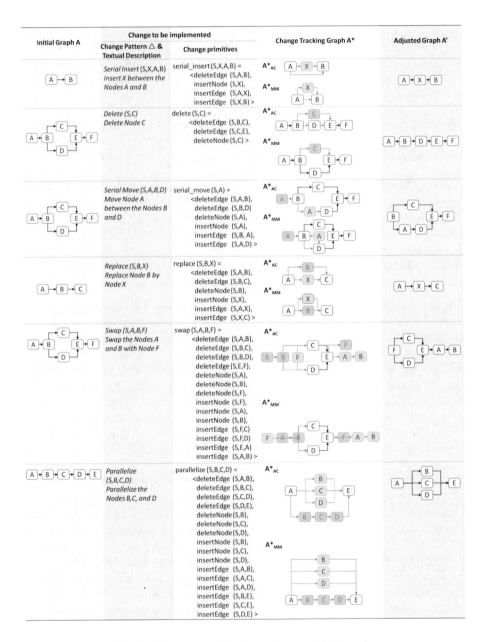

Fig. 1. Change tracking in series-parallel digraphs

Visual Properties. Based on the change tracking state the graph elements are marked by means of selected visual properties. As mentioned in Section 2 we propose to use the visual properties *color(hue)*, *brightness*, or *size* to visualize change in the change tracking graph A*, as they do not change the shape of the elements used in a particular process modeling notation (e.g., changing a square into a circle). We further propose that graph elements that are not effected by the change remain in their original notation.

Layout. There are two options of layouting the change tracking graph A*. One layout option is to consider the layout of the initial graph A in A^*, called A^*_{MM} that intends to maintain the current *mental map* of the process captured in the initial graph A, and thus reflects the *past* layout in A^*. Preserving the mental map of the initial graph A means to keep the graph as much as possible unchanged after change by moving as few nodes as possible and by moving the nodes as little as possible. Deleted elements remain on their initial positions in order to reflect the layout of A, and then the inserted elements are considered in the layout. The alternative option refers to the *future* layout in A^* by taking the layout of the adjusted graph A' into consideration that is characterized by prioritized *aesthetic criteria* applied to the remaining initial and inserted (activated) graph elements. The resulting change tracking graph is called A^*_{AC}. We suggest the following aesthetic criteria mentioned backward-sorted according to their priorities: focus on the control flow, minimization of edge crossing and number of overlapping elements, maximization of connecting node and edge orthogonality, and minimization of the number of bends. The inserted and initial graph elements are placed according to the aesthetic criteria first, and then the deleted elements are considered in the layout.

4   Survey

The goal of the survey was to evaluate, if visualization of changes can support users, and which visual properties they prefer for making changes in graphs visible. Further, we wanted to find out, if users prefer to see changes in the initial graph, or if they prefer to trace the changes in the layout of the adjusted graph. For this survey, we primarily concentrated on the extremes of both layout approaches, as according to Purchase and Samra [24] extremes of layout adjustment (low and high mental map preservation in dynamic graphs) produce better performance than a layout approach that makes a compromise.

4.1   Methodology

The user survey included questions and tasks to analyze our hypotheses and contained closed, open-ended and rank-ordered questions. In addition to an introduction, a description about the purpose of the survey, and demographic and introductory questions, the questionnaire was structured into two parts: visual properties and layout. The part *visual properties* included questions and tasks to analyze Hypothesis 1 and Hypothesis 3. We wanted to find out (a) if the participants perceive it is absolutely necessary to visualize changes in graphs and (b) if the different visualization properties help them to trace changes. To answer these questions the initial graph along with the adjusted graph was presented to the participants who were then asked to identify the changes that occurred. In a next step, three further graphs were shown and each graph visualized the change information with the help of another visual property. For the visual property *color(hue)* the color orange was used to visualize deleted elements, and the color green was used for added elements. In contrast to *color(hue)*, light gray (for deleted elements) and dark gray (for new elements) were used representing the visual property *brightness*. To evaluate the visual property *size*, deleted elements were shown smaller, and new elements were visualized larger than the already existing elements. After each graph version, participants were asked if they had the feeling to see all changes in comparison with the version which shows no change information. The part *layout* concentrated on Hypothesis 2, and to analyze, if the participants prefer to track changes in the initial graph (with focus on the mental map) or to see the changes already in the adjusted graph which considers the aesthetic criteria. To answer this question, the participants saw both layout versions in regard to their visual properties and they were asked which of these layout versions they prefer. We undertook a pre-test involving three persons to be sure that the questions and tasks were clear and consistent with the survey goals. Based on their feedback the questionnaire was modified.

4.2   Results

We primarily concentrated on persons who had at least basic knowledge about business processes and experiences with graph visualizations. The findings of our empirical study were based on 117 interviewees, mainly computer science students, but also business process specialists from industry and science. For the evaluation, we used generalized examples to be independent from a specific domain which allows us to get a large number of participants.

The gathered data was analyzed in a descriptive way. For the responses from the open-ended questions, we applied the qualitative content analysis to evaluate participants' reflections. The findings of our empirical study are listed according to our hypotheses.

Hypothesis 1: When no change information was visualized in the graph, the most of the participants (51.3%) were unsure or had not the feeling (27%) to identify all changes between the initial and adjusted graph. Only 1.7% of the particpants preferred the version without change visualization. The results about the rating how well the different versions supported the participants to detect changes underpinned our observation that change visualizations are helpful for users to trace changes in business processes.

Hypothesis 2: The results of the comparison showed that there exists no clear favorite. Half of the respondents stated that they preferred to see changes in the adjusted graph, and the other half of the participants found it more helpful to see the changes in the initial graph to have a better orientation.

Hypothesis 3: Most participants (70%) preferred the visual property *color (hue)* followed by the visual property *brightness* (40% of the the participants) and more than half of the respondents stated that they were completely sure to see all changes with the help of the visual property *color(hue)* or *brightness.* The participants noted that colors (52 nominations) and brightness (37 statements) helped them to get a good overview about the changes which occured in the graph. However, it was also mentioned that the colors were too dominant and grabbed the viewer's attention too much (stated by 3 participants). Furthermore, it was mentioned that the usage of color is often insufficient for users who were color blind (mentioned by 3 participants). To avoid this problem, it would be a good alternative to combine color with brightness. Only 5% of the particpants preferred the visual property *size.* The most named reasons were that the representation was unclear and the nodes and edges were difficult to read when the size was perceived too small (8 statements). The users' preferences in regard to the different visual properites were also recognizable in the rating results concerning how well the different versions support the participants to detect changes.

5   Related Work

In respect to graph layout, there exist many layout approaches (e.g., [27] [19] [11] [15]) and aesthetic criteria (e.g., [14] [28] [23]) for general graph classes. Furthermore, several layout approaches targeted specifically toward business process graphs were published (e.g., [12] [1] [26]). While most of the works on graph drawing concentrate on single static graphs, visual representation of graphs which can change over time (e.g, by adding or deleting nodes or edges) have received little attention [9] [3]. Especially in business process, changes can occur over time and therefore it is necessary that users are notified about the relevant changes. Several works exist which discuss approaches to support user to trace changes, for example, [18] present an traceability-based change notification approach. Furthermore, in the field of UML there exist several approaches to make changes transparent, e.g., for detecting differences between class diagrams [16]. Although there exist several approaches to make changes in software transparent (e.g., [17,13]), change visualization for business processes has received little attention in the last years. In our work, we present a conceptualization for change tracking in series-parallel digraphs in general which is independent of any process meta model.

6   Conclusion

In this work, we presented a visual framework for change tracking in series-parallel digraphs in general by introducing the change tracking graph. Two different layouts of the change tracking graphs were presented, in which the tracked change was embedded. We conduced an analysis of user preferences with 117 participants, mainly computer science students, which helped us to find out that change tracking was helpful for the users to identify the conducted changes on the process model, and most of the users preferred the visual property *color(hue)* to visualize change in the change tracking model. About half of the survey participants preferred to see the past layout designed according to mental map aspects whereas the others preferred to see the future layout designed according to aesthetic criteria. We derive from this result, that probably both layouts should be offered to the process users when change is performed on process models so that each process user can choose his or her preferred layout.

In future work, we will concentrate on large collections of business processes and process model sets that, e.g. contain a vast number of subprocesses, in order to analyze how change can be represented throughout various modeling levels, e.g. in the reference model, in subprocess and process families. Moreover, we will investigate how our approach can help to make changes transparent between similar processes or between different versions of a process. Further, we will work on an adequate implementation focusing on usability aspects and continue to refine the visualizations of change.

References

1. Albrecht, B., Effinger, P., Held, M., Kaufmann, M.: An automatic layout algorithm for bpel processes. In: Proc. of the 5th International Symposium on Software Visualization, pp. 173–182. ACM, New York (2010)
2. Andrienko, N., Andrienko, G.: Exploratory Analysis of Spatial and Temporal Data: A Systematic Approach. Springer, Heidelberg (2005)
3. Beck, F., Burch, M., Diehl, S.: Towards an aesthetic dimensions framework for dynamic graph visualisations. In: Proc. of the 2009 13th International Conference Information Visualisation, pp. 592–597. IEEE Computer Society, Los Alamitos (2009)
4. Bennett, C., Ryall, J., Spalteholz, L., Gooch, A.: The Aesthetics of Graph Visualization. In: Cunningham, D.W., Meyer, G.W., Neumann, L., Dunning, A., Paricio, R. (eds.) Computational Aesthetics 2007: Eurographics Workshop on Computational Aesthetics in Graphics, Visualization and Imaging, pp. 57–64 (2007)
5. Bertin, J.: Semiology of graphics: diagrams, networks, maps / Jacques Bertin; translated by William J. Berg. University of Wisconsin Press (1983)
6. Bridgeman, S., Tamassia, R.: A user study in similarity measures for graph drawing. In: Mutzel, P., Jünger, M., Leipert, S. (eds.) GD 2001. LNCS, vol. 2265, pp. 231–235. Springer, Heidelberg (2002)
7. Coleman, M.K., Parker, D.S.: Aesthetics-based graph layout for human consumption. Softw. Pract. Exper. 26, 1415–1438 (1996)
8. Davidson, R., Harel, D.: Drawing graphs nicely using simulated annealing. ACM Trans. Graph 15, 301–331 (1996)
9. Diehl, S., Goerg, C., Kerren, A.: Preserving the mental map using foresighted layout. In: Proc. of Joint Eurographics IEEE TCVG Symposium on Visualization, pp. 175–184. Springer, Heidelberg (2001)
10. Eades, P., Lai, W., Misue, K., Sugiyama, K.: Preserving the mental map of a diagram. In: Proc. of COMPUGRAPHICS, vol. 91, pp. 24–33 (1991)
11. Eades, P., Lin, T., Lin, X.: Two tree drawing conventions. Int. J. Comput. Geometry Appl. 3(2), 133–153 (1993)

12. Effinger, P., Siebenhaller, M., Kaufmann, M.: An interactive layout tool for bpmn. In: Proc. of IEEE International Conference on Commerce and Enterprise Computing, pp. 399–406. IEEE Computer Society, Los Alamitos (2009)
13. Eick, S.G., Graves, T.L., Karr, A.F., Mockus, A., Schuster, P.: Visualizing software changes. IEEE Trans. Softw. Eng. 28, 396–412 (2002)
14. Fleischer, R., Hirsh, C.: Graph drawing and its applications. In: GD 2001, pp. 1–22. Springer, Heidelberg (2001)
15. de Fraysseix, H., Pach, J., Pollack, R.: Small sets supporting fary embeddings of planar graphs. In: Proc. of the Twentieth Annual ACM Symposium on Theory of Computing, pp. 426–433. ACM, New York (1988)
16. Girschick, M.: Difference detection and visualization in uml class diagrams. Tech. rep. (2006)
17. Gracanin, D., Matkovic, K., Eltoweissy, M.: Software visualization. ISSE 1(2), 221–230 (2005)
18. Helming, J., Koegel, M., Naughton, H., David, J., Shterev, A.: Traceability-based change awareness. In: Schürr, A., Selic, B. (eds.) MODELS 2009. LNCS, vol. 5795, pp. 372–376. Springer, Heidelberg (2009)
19. Hong, S.-H., Eades, P., Quigley, A., Lee, S.-H.: Drawing algorithms for series-parallel digraphs in two and three dimensions. In: Whitesides, S.H. (ed.) GD 1998. LNCS, vol. 1547, pp. 198–209. Springer, Heidelberg (1999)
20. Lee, Y.-Y., Lin, C.-C., Yen, H.-C.: Mental map preserving graph drawing using simulated annealing. In: Proc. of the 2006 Asia-Pacific Symposium on Information Visualisation, vol. 60, pp. 179–188. Australian Computer Society, Inc. (2006)
21. Misue, K., Eades, P., Lai, W., Sugiyama, K.: Layout adjustment and the mental map. Journal of Visual Languages and Computing 6(2), 183–210 (1995)
22. Paulisch, F.N., Tichy, W.F.: Edge: An extendible graph editor. Software: Practice and Experience 20(S1), S63–S88 (1990)
23. Purchase, H.C.: Metrics for graph drawing aesthetics. Journal of Visual Languages & Computing 13(5), 501–516 (2002)
24. Purchase, H.C., Samra, A.: Extremes are better: Investigating mental map preservation in dynamic graphs. In: Stapleton, G., Howse, J., Lee, J. (eds.) Diagrams 2008. LNCS (LNAI), vol. 5223, pp. 60–73. Springer, Heidelberg (2008)
25. Rinderle, S., Reichert, M., Jurisch, M., Kreher, U.: On representing, purging, and utilizing change logs in process management systems. In: Dustdar, S., Fiadeiro, J.L., Sheth, A.P. (eds.) BPM 2006. LNCS, vol. 4102, pp. 241–256. Springer, Heidelberg (2006)
26. Six, J.M., Tollis, I.G.: Automated visualization of process diagrams. In: Goodrich, M.T., Kobourov, S.G. (eds.) GD 2002. LNCS, vol. 2528, pp. 45–59. Springer, Heidelberg (2002)
27. Sugiyama, K.: Graph drawing and applications for software and knowledge engineers. Series on software engineering and knowledge engineering, vol. 11. World Scientific, Singapore (2002)
28. Taylor, M., Rodgers, P.: Applying graphical design techniques to graph visualisation. In: Proc. of the Ninth International Conference on Information Visualisation, pp. 651–656. IEEE Computer Society, Los Alamitos (2005)
29. Weber, B., Reichert, M., Rinderle-Ma, S.: Change patterns and change support features - enhancing flexibility in process-aware information systems. Data Knowl. Eng. 66, 438–466 (2008)

An Empirical Analysis of Human Performance and Error in Process Model Development

Alexander Nielen[1], Denise Költer[2], Susanne Mütze-Niewöhner[1],
Jürgen Karla[2], and Christopher M. Schlick[1]

[1] Institute of Industrial Engineering and Ergonomics at RWTH Aachen University,
Bergdriesch 27, 52062 Aachen, Germany
`{a.nielen,s.muetze,c.schlick}@iaw.rwth-aachen.de`
[2] Institute of Business Information Systems at RWTH Aachen University,
Templergraben 64/V, 52062 Aachen, Germany
`{koelter,karla}@winfor.rwth-aachen.de`

Abstract. Process models capture important corporate know-how for an effective Business Process Management. Inconsistencies between process models and corporate reality are a common phenomenon in corporate practice. Human performance in process model development is a major source for these inconsistencies. In this contribution, a human performance analysis of process model development paying special attention to the concept of human error was conducted. It was found that the frequencies of the omissions and erroneous executions of notation elements are significantly higher for novices than for experienced modelers. Moreover, experienced modelers inherently adhere to a verb-object activity labeling style. The overall empirical results indicate that experienced modelers achieve higher process model quality with less expenditure of time than novices.

Keywords: Process Modeling, Model Quality, Human Error, Human Reliability Analysis.

1 Introduction

Process models are of utmost importance to Business Process Management [1]. They capture important corporate know-how, facilitate continuous improvement efforts, and provide a basis for the certification according to a commonly-accepted quality standard. Further benefits of process modeling refer to information systems specification [2], knowledge management implementation and maintenance [3], process reengineering [4], organizational transparency [5], and workflow design assistance [6].

Several frameworks and guidelines have been developed to ensure high process model quality, including the Guidelines of Modeling (GoM) [7] the SEQUAL framework [8], or the seven Process Modeling Guidelines (7PMG) [9]. These frameworks provide validated sets of rules and put an emphasis on essential quality parameters for process models.

The main information sources for process model development are interviews of speech, observation of actions, and documentary analyzes. Alongside with a chain of

M. Jeusfeld, L. Delcambre, and T.W. Ling (Eds.): ER 2011, LNCS 6998, pp. 514–523, 2011.

multiple personal interactions, various error-prone transformation processes take place. These cognitive processes are accompanied by communication interferences, misconceptions and information losses. Their occurrence has a negative impact on the information content and therefore on the quality of the process model [10]. Consequently, many process models do not match with corporate reality and a major effort has to be made in order to iteratively eliminate inconsistencies between the process model and the real workflow. Thus, there is the evident need to further increase the effectiveness and efficiency of process model development through a human performance and error analysis under laboratory conditions.

2 Background

Experienced process modelers and managers with an academic background are typically entrusted with process model development [11]. In corporate practice one often encounters employees that are not familiar with formal modeling languages [12] and often lack a methodological background [13]. A participatory approach [14] relying on an active involvement of non-academic employees in process development, maintenance, and improvement requires that this target group achieves a similar level of process model quality in order to be a true alternative to the traditional approach.

An empirical analysis with a focus on human performance and error can provide a scientific basis for quantifying differences, to identify procedural weaknesses and to reach conclusions about the reliability of process model development. To the best of the authors' knowledge there is no empirical research with regard to human performance and error in process model development so far.

2.1 Human Performance in Process Model Development

For the investigation of human performance and error in process model development, Rasmussen's differentiation of skill-based, rule-based and knowledge-based behavior can be taken as a basis [15]. Following these three levels of human performance, process model development can be reviewed as rule-based behavior from an experienced modeler´s point of view. In case predefined procedures and patterns cannot be applied, process model development relates to knowledge-based behavior. This behavior is typical for novices who have no prior experience in process model development. Compared to rule-based behavior, knowledge-based behavior usually requires a higher mental effort for problem solving, a greater duration of time and is more prone to erroneous actions.

2.2 Human Error in Process Model Development

The concept of human error cannot be separated from levels of human performance in process modeling. Following Reason's [16] definition for the concept of human error, two major aspects are essential for the remainder of the paper: the representation or non-representation of an action, i.e., an error of omission, and the erroneous execution of an action.

The in-depth analysis of human error is an important part of a Human Reliability Analysis (HRA). By using HRA in the context of process model development, cause-effect relationships of incorrectly performed actions are put into focus. In order to successfully apply HRA, it is important to identify all actions that will be subject to examination in the course of the HRA. To allow for a HRA to identify errors in process model development and to subsequently derive the most efficient countermeasures, the authors followed the VDI 4006 standard [17].

In preparation of the laboratory study, particular emphasis was put on the development of an error classification scheme. It is based on Reason's [16] generic error types of omission and erroneous execution (see Fig. 1). With regard to the element "activity", the error classification accounts for activity omissions and parameterization. An activity is declared as wrongly parameterized if it does not relate to the required information, tools or shortcomings. Erroneous execution is impaired when wrong assignment to an organizational unit or wrong mode occurs. Wrong activity mode is noticed when an inadequate choice of either a serial, parallel, conditional, synchronous or iterative activity was made.

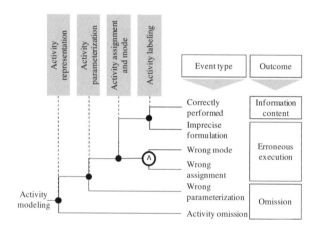

Fig. 1. Event tree for activity-level error classification

Activity labeling was also assigned to the category of erroneous execution as it is an important quality aspect of process models [18]. Following the division according to [18], verb-object is considered as the best-case labeling style. An action-noun labeling also provides adequate comprehension from the part of the model user. The adherence to neither of these styles is classified as an imprecise formulation.

3   Laboratory Study

With regard to the absence of empirical research on human performance and error in process modeling, this paper addresses the following research question: How do performance and error of novices differ from those of experienced modelers? And what practical implications can be drawn for the participatory approach?

3.1 Methods

Modeling Tasks. Three text-based modeling tasks were created, namely (1) coffee trade, (2) diamond commodity chain, and (3) simulation project. During task creation, particular attention was paid to a comparable task size, an easy to understand language and that no specialized knowledge is required. Sample solutions for each modeling task served as a reference baseline against which the elaborated tasks of the subjects were measured. As it is not possible to anticipate or identify all erroneous actions in process model development, we referred to the actions with the greatest potential for decreasing the information content of the process model.

Experimental Design. The task sequence of the above mentioned modeling tasks was varied in the laboratory study in order to exclude position effects. The allotted time for each modeling task was not limited and the entire experiment was videotaped from a vertical angle.

For task solving, the process modeling language C3—an acronym for coordination, cooperation, and communication—was chosen [19]. Its graphical elements primarily descended from the UML notation in 1999 and were complemented with graphical elements for cooperative process modeling. C3 is capable of representing manufacturing and development processes as well as inter-departmental relations and decision processes [14]. The C3 graphical elements are similar to UML and match other modeling languages such as the EPC and BPMN. The elements applied in the laboratory study comprise C3 objects and connectors (see Fig. 2).

Apparatus. The working area was a whiteboard mounted on a height-adjustable table. Thus, the subjects could take an ergonomic position to solve the tasks. This setup was preferred to a computer-based design because it allowed to exclude the influence of prior experience with modeling tools, e.g., Microsoft Visio or SemTalk.

The subjects used plastic shapes for representing the C3 objects. The C3 connectors had to be drawn on the whiteboard. Labeling the C3 shapes as well as writing on the whiteboard had to be carried out with a board marker.

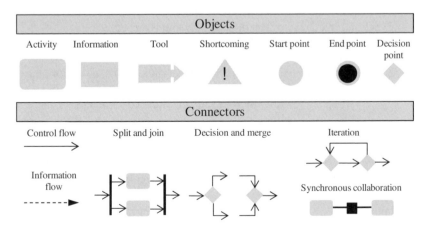

Fig. 2. Graphical elements of C3 applied in the laboratory study

Subjects. A total of 39 subjects—21 men and 18 women aged between 21 and 36 years (26.4 years, SD = 4.25)—participated in the laboratory study. The sample was divided into experienced modelers and novices. The group of experienced modelers consisted of 12 men and 7 women. They had prior work experience in process modeling. This sample consisted of research assistants from industrial engineering, business information systems, and operations research. Each subject of this group had at least one year professional experience.

The novices had no prior experience in process modeling. This sample consisted of 9 men and 11 women who were students from psychology, sociology, and medicine. All subjects were either employees or students of RWTH Aachen University in Germany. All subjects had the German A-Level, i.e., the German university entrance qualification. The research assistants held an academic degree in their scientific discipline, three held a doctorate degree.

Procedure. Prior to the main experiment, the personal data were collected, i.e., age, profession, and prior experience in process modeling. An introduction phase of approximately 10 minutes followed. Each subject was introduced into C3 by means of a design template. The template showed a sample process model with brief explanations of the C3 graphical elements. The subjects had to read up the explanations and could ask questions on C3 in order to resolve possible uncertainties.

The main experiment comprised the three modeling tasks in sequential order. Except the design template there were no auxiliary means allowed. A five minute break was granted after the completion of each modeling task. Communication with the investigator was not allowed during the development of each process model.

Dependent and Independent Variables. In accordance with the experimental design, the independent variable was the level of expertise of the subjects (experienced modeler versus novice). Prior experience in process modeling determined whether the subjects were assigned to the group of experienced modelers or the group of novices. The following three dependent variables were considered:

- Model development time
- Types and frequency of errors (see Fig. 1)
- Types and frequency of task labeling style in terms of
  - frequency with which the subject adhered to an verb-object style such as *sign contract* for task labeling,
  - frequency with which the subject adhered to an action-noun style such as *task assignment* for task labeling, and
  - frequency with which the subject adhered to neither of these styles for task labeling.

Hypotheses and Statistical Analysis. The following hypotheses were formulated:

- Model development time for novices is significantly higher than for experienced modelers (H_1).
- Frequency of errors is significantly higher for novices than for experienced modelers (H_2).

- The task labeling style of experienced modelers does significantly differ from those of novices (H_3). It is expected that experienced modelers inherently adhere to a verb-object activity labeling style.

The statistical analysis was conducted with the statistical software package SPSS Version 18.0. A two-way analysis of variance (ANOVA) with repeated measures was calculated to test hypothesis H_1. For multi-level comparison of means the Bonferroni post-hoc test was calculated. For significant results the effect size ω^2 was calculated according to [20]. Chi-square tests were calculated to test the hypotheses H_2 and H_3. The significance level for each analysis was set at $\alpha=0.05$.

3.2 Results

Model Development Time. The results of the ANOVA show a significant main effect of prior experience in process modeling on model development time ($F(1,38) = 5.787$, $p = 0.021$) with a small effect size of $\omega^2=0.1$. The first hypothesis can therefore be accepted. The mean model development time for each modeling task including the 95% confidence intervals is shown in Fig. 3.

With regard to the coffee task, the model development time for experienced modelers is 11.47% shorter than for novices. This difference is, however, not statistically significant ($F(1,38) = 1.992$, $p = 0.166$). Regarding the diamond task, the model development time for experienced modelers is 24.56% shorter than for novices. This difference is statistically significant ($F(1,38) = 5.135$, $p = 0.029$). Concerning the simulation task, model development time for experienced modelers is 10.44% shorter than for novices. This difference is not statistically significant ($F(1) = 1.376$, $p = 0.248$).

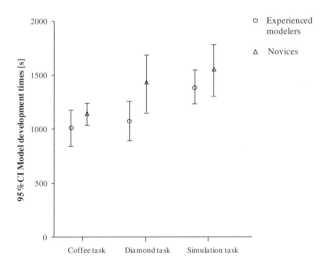

Fig. 3. Model development times [s] for the modeling tasks

Frequency of Errors. According to the defined event tree for activity-level error classification (see Fig. 1), activity omissions for experienced modelers and novices were captured. The associated statistic ($\chi^2(2) = 7.080$, $p=0.008$) proves that there are significant differences between experienced modelers and novices with regard to activity omissions.

The contingency table of error frequencies and the total number of actually identified activities is shown in Table 1. The associated statistic ($\chi^2(1) = 7.080$, $p = 0.008$) shows that there are significant differences between the two levels of expertise with regard to activity parameterization.

Table 1. Contingency table of activity-level error frequencies

	Activity parameterization		Activity assignment and activity mode		Total number of modeled activities
	Correct execution	Wrong execution	Correct execution	Wrong execution	
Experienced modelers	563 (88.1%)	76 (11.9%)	548 (85.8%)	91 (14.2%)	639
Novices	511 (82.8%)	106 (17.2%)	477 (77.3%)	140 (22.7%)	617

Regarding activity assignment and activity mode, the associated statistic ($\chi^2(1) = 14.931$, $p = 0.000$) shows a statistically significant difference. Hypothesis H_2 can be accepted as error frequencies for both errors of omission and commission differ significantly for experienced modelers and novices.

Activity Labeling Style. Three activity labeling styles were distinguished as shown in Table 2. The associated statistic ($\chi^2(2) = 195.285$, $p = 0.000$) shows a statistically significant difference between the two levels of expertise. H_3 can be accepted as the labeling style of experienced modelers does significantly differ from those of novices.

Table 2. Contingency table of labeling style frequencies

	Activity labeling style			Total number of modeled activities
	Verb-object	Action-noun	Neither	
Experienced modelers	376 (58.8%)	120 (18.8%)	143 (22.4%)	639
Novices	130 (21.1%)	281 (45.5%)	206 (33.4%)	617

3.3 Discussion

With regard to model development time, experienced modelers developed the process models on average faster than novices. A statistically significant difference was found for the diamond task. The observed time differences might have been influenced by individual differences in terms of text comprehension and motivational aspects. Some experienced modelers did not know the C3 notation and probably needed some extra time to get used to its syntax and semantics. More complex workflows and a larger sample size might lead to more pronounced results.

Concerning error frequencies, activity omissions were considerably higher for novices than for experienced modelers. With regard to activity parameterization as well as activity assignment and mode, the differences between experienced modelers and novices proved to be significant. Experienced modelers seemed to have a better understanding of what is relevant for the information content of a process model and incorporate this information more conscientious into the process model. Experienced process modelers achieved higher consistency with the predefined sample solutions whereas novices left out more information and developed process models with less information content. Higher omission rates can be expected for more complex real world scenarios.

Regarding activity labeling style, experienced modelers seemed to have an inherent preference for verb-object activity labeling (58.8%). Novices preferred the action-noun labeling in most of the cases (45.5%) and had generally more variety in their labeling style. In approximately one third of the cases (33.4%), the novices followed neither a verb-object nor an action-noun labeling style. The corresponding activities may be misinterpreted by a model user and might lead to inadequate working procedures. These results empirically support the findings from Mendling et al. [18] who supposed that experienced process modelers tend to use a verb-object activity labeling style.

The authors affirm that there are some limitations. First, sample size is considerably small and the sample only consists of research assistants and students from a technical university. Future research should collect data from practitioners who might face different cognitive bottlenecks in process model development. The factors that contribute to the occurrence of errors might also be highly context-dependent. Human aspects mainly include motivation and vigilance; system limitations include the limited working area. A major difference to process model development in corporate practice might be that the information for process model development could be recalled by a subject at any time during the main experiment by simply reading up the text. In a real world scenario, the transformation processes are more prone to interferences and, therefore, process models might have a greater variety and frequency of errors.

4   Conclusion and Outlook

Methods of industrial engineering bear the potential to improve the efficiency of process model development. A promising approach is to conduct an empirical analysis of human performance and error in process model development. The presented experimental study on process model development represents the preparatory work for a participatory approach in process model development and accounted for a defined scope of errors of omission and execution. The overall results indicate that experienced modelers achieve better model quality than novices through higher consistency with the corresponding reality segment.

With regard to future research activities, a detailed video analysis might provide new insights on successful strategies in process model development. To this purpose, the depth of the empirical analysis will be revised and updated. Expected results might have the potential to further enhance human performance in process model development and improve training concepts on process modeling for novices. In order to facilitate the computer-aided development of complex process models, it might be valuable to apply a second-generation HRA method such as CREAM [21] to process model development.

Acknowledgments. The research was supported by the Interdisciplinary Management Practice of RWTH Aachen University and funded by the Excellence Initiative of the German federal and state governments.

References

1. Becker, J., Kahn, D.: Der Prozess im Fokus. In: Becker, J., Kugeler, M., Rosemann, M. (eds.) Prozessmanagement. Springer, Berlin (2008)
2. Mendling, J., Recker, J.: Extending the Discussion of Model Quality: Why Clarity and Completeness may not be enough. In: Pernici, B., Gulla, J.A. (eds.): CAiSE 2007 Workshop Proceedings Vol. I - Eleventh International Workshop on Exploring Modeling Methods in Systems Analysis and Design (EMMSAD 2007), Trondheim, pp 109–121 (2007)
3. Wong, K.Y.: Critical success factors for implementing knowledge management in small and medium enterprises. Industrial Management & Data Systems 105(3), 261–279 (2005)
4. Schuh, G., Friedli, T., Kurr, M.A.: Prozessorientierte Reorganisation. Reengineering-Projekte professionell gestalten und umsetzen. Carl Hanser Verlag, München (2007)
5. Indulska, M., Green, P., Recker, J., Rosemann, M.: Business Process Modeling: Perceived Benefits. In: Laender, A.H.F., Castano, S., Dayal, U., Casati, F., de Oliveira, J.P.M. (eds.) ER 2009. LNCS, vol. 5829, pp. 458–471. Springer, Heidelberg (2009)
6. van der Aalst, W.M.P., ter Hofstede, A.H.M., Weske, M.: Business Process Management: A Survey. In: van der Aalst, W.M.P., ter Hofstede, A.H.M., Weske, M. (eds.) BPM 2003. LNCS, vol. 2678, pp. 1–12. Springer, Heidelberg (2003)
7. Schuette, R., Rotthowe, T.: The Guidelines of Modeling - An Approach to Enhance the Quality in Information Models. In: Ling, T.-W., Ram, S., Li Lee, M. (eds.) ER 1998. LNCS, vol. 1507, pp. 240–254. Springer, Heidelberg (1998)
8. Krogstie, J., Sindre, G., Jorgensen, H.: Process models representing knowledge for action: a revised quality framework. European Journal of Information Systems 15, 91–102 (2006)
9. Mendling, J., Reijers, H.A., van der Aalst, W.M.P.: Seven Process Modeling Guidelines (7PMG). In: Information and Software Technology (IST), vol. 52(2), pp. 127–136. Elsevier B.V, Amsterdam (2010)
10. Jakobs, E.M., Spanke, J.: Sprache als Erfolgsfaktor industrieller Prozessmodellierung. In: Steinmann, C. (eds.) Evolution der Informationsgesellschaft. Markenkommunikation im Spannungsfeld der neuen Medien. VS, Wiesbaden (2011)
11. Weske, M.: Business Process Management – Concepts, Languages, Architectures. Springer, Berlin (2007)
12. Luo, W., Tung, Y.A.: A Framework for Selecting Business Process Modeling Methods. Industrial Management & Data Systems 99(7), 312–319 (1999)

13. Kalpic, B., Bernus, P.: Business Process Modeling in Industry – The Powerful Tool in Enterprise Management. Computers in Industry 47, 299–318 (2002)
14. Nielen, A., Jeske, T., Schlick, C., Arning, K., Ziefle, M.: Interdisciplinary Assessment of Process Modeling Languages Applicable for Small to Medium-sized Enterprises. In: Callaos, N., Chu, H.-W., Krittaphol, W., Lesso, W., Savoie, M. (eds.) The 8th International Conference on Computing, Communications and Control Technologies: CCCT 2010, IMCIC, Copyright Manager, Winter Garden, Florida, vol. II, pp. 47–52 (2010)
15. Rasmussen, J.: Skills, Rules, and Knowledge; Signals, Signs, and Symbols, and Other Distinctions in Human Performance Models. IEEE Transactions on Systems, Man, and Cybernetics 15(2), 234–243 (1983)
16. Reason, J.: Human Error. Cambridge University Press, Cambridge (1990)
17. VDI 4006: Human Reliability Methods for Quantitative Assessment of Human Reliability. VDI-Gesellschaft (2003)
18. Mendling, J., Reijers, H.A., Recker, J.: Activity Labeling in Process Modeling: Empirical Insights and Recommendations. In: Information Systems (IS). Special Issue on Vocabularies, Ontologies and Rules for Enterprise and Business Process Modeling and Management, vol. 35(4), pp. 467–482. Elsevier B.V, Amsterdam (2010)
19. Killich, S., Luczak, H., Schlick, C., Weissenbach, M., Wiedenmaier, S., Ziegler, J.: Task Modelling for Cooperative Work. Behaviour & Information Technology 18(5), 325–338 (1999)
20. Field, A.: Discovering Statistics Using SPSS, 2nd edn. Sage Publications, London (2005)
21. Hollnagel, E.: Cognitive Reliability and Error Analysis Method: CREAM. Elsevier, Amsterdam (1998)

Panel: New Directions for Conceptual Modeling

Jeffrey Parsons[1], Antoni Olivé[2], Sudha Ram[3],
Gerd Wagner[4], Yair Wand[5], and Eric Yu[6]

[1] Memorial University of Newfoundland
St. John's, NL, Canada
`jeffreyp@mun.ca`
[2] Universitat Politècnica de Catalunya
Barcelona, Catalonia, Spain
`antoni.olive@upc.edu`
[3] University of Arizona
Tucson, AZ, USA
`ram@eller.arizona.edu`
[4] Brandenburg University of Technology
Cottbus, Germany
`wagnerg@tu-cottbus.de`
[5] University of British Columbia
Vancouver, BC, Canada
`yair.wand@sauder.ubc.ca`
[6] University of Toronto
Toronto, ON, Canada
`eric.yu@utoronto.edu`

Abstract. This panel examines potential opportunities for conceptual modeling research in new domains.

1 Panel Objective

This year marks the 30th ER conference. During this time, research in conceptual modeling has made significant progress. Advances in conceptual modeling have made important contributions to requirements analysis, database design, and information systems development. In view of the changing landscape in which information technology applications are developed and used, this is an appropriate time to consider where we are in conceptual modeling research and what the future might hold. In particular, this panel will focus on emerging and understudied domains for the application of conceptual modeling research. Panelists will consider what conceptual modeling research brings to understanding phenomena in new or non-traditional domains. Equally importantly, they will reflect on new conceptual modeling research issues arising from the demands and requirements of these domains. The objective of the panel is to spark increased interest in conceptual modeling and the ER conference by encouraging audience members to consider new opportunities for applying conceptual modeling.

M. Jeusfeld, L. Delcambre, and T.W. Ling (Eds.): ER 2011, LNCS 6998, pp. 524–525, 2011.
© Springer-Verlag Berlin Heidelberg 2011

2 Position Statements

2.1 Antoni Olivé

One of the most important changes in economic and social activities is that of globalization. This has an impact on the information systems used by organizations and people, in the conceptual schemas of those systems, and in the way those schemas are developed. Until now, the main focus in conceptual modeling has been on "local" worlds. Globalization demands conceptual modeling in a global world.

2.2 Sudha Ram

Conceptual modeling has a role in many new and emerging areas, such as biological data integration and web analytics. Techniques are needed to explicitly model the semantics of biological sequence data to allow easy processing of ad hoc queries. Conceptual modeling can also be extended to the area of web analytics to distinguish between classes of data and instances incorporating temporal and spatial information.

2.3 Gerd Wagner

Despite their long histories and their common focus on modeling, the Conceptual Modeling (CM) and Discrete Event Simulation (DES) communities have not paid much attention to each other. I will argue that DES can benefit a lot from adopting and adapting results of CM research, and that the recent trend in CM towards ontological foundations is also highly relevant for DES.

2.4 Yair Wand

Conceptual modeling emerged as a way to understand application requirements for information systems, but has extended beyond this original purpose. Theoretical and empirical findings are applied in other domains and conceptual models can be used for other than their original purposes. In particular, I will show how conceptual modeling research has generated results that can be applied also in the natural sciences.

2.5 Eric Yu

There are tremendous opportunities as well as challenges for extracting meaning and significance from the vast petabytes of data being generated every day from diverse sources. What conceptual modeling techniques are needed to make sense of these data? How do we abstract from diverse sources to create coherent understanding? How can we go from raw data to insightful interpretation to enable decision making?

Panel: Modeling for the Future Internet

Arne Berre[1] and Michele Missikoff[2] (Moderators)

[1] SINTEF, Oslo, Norway
[2] CNR-IASI, Rome, Italy

The Internet is a paradigmatic example of a successful system that has not been designed by using any of the available modelling methods. The components have been realised and deployed, then the Internet (seen as a socio-technical system) has evolved (and is still evolving) in a spontaneous, bottom-up fashion. What can we learn from this that we can apply to other complex socio-technical systems?

We need to explore if there are new design and engineering paradigms that will emerge for complex systems. From 'story telling' to user-generated mashups, to crowdsourcing: are there new paradigm that are challenging our 'traditional' way of addressing modeling and, in general, software engineering? At the same time, emerging technologies such as Internet of Things with smart objects, autonomic computing, self-configuring/healing systems indicate that there are large areas where the need of human intervention is simply superfluous. Are we at a turning point in the development of the Future Internet Application Systems? And therefore do we need to deeply rethinking our ideas, methods, tools, aimed at modelling for developing complex socio-technical systems? How we will use the Future Internet infrastructure, with Internet of People, Internet of Content and Knowledge, Internet of Services to invent, model, create, deploy, and manage the future interoperable 'cloudy' software applications?

Questions and issues that will be discussed include: What is being done today, what are the challenges – and where the conceptual modelling research community should direct its efforts. Is there a limit (in terms of complexity) to what an engineering discipline of modelling can do? Is it true that without a systematic application of the human intelligence complex ICT systems cannot exist? Or should we start to embrace new (complementary?) paradigms that accept a limitation in human planning/driving in the development of systems, beyond a certain complexity threshold? Autonomic systems are able to self evolve, self adjust, self healing without human intervention. Complexity theory teaches us that it is impossible to keep under control the behaviour of reality in all possible cases. On another plan, user-centred analysis shows that, for instance, storytelling (i.e., people reporting on their concrete experiences) is more reliable than the abstract modelling of a fragment of the reality.

The Panel intends to address these themes with an open innovation approach, with the help of distinguished panellists, and in particular: Robert Meersman, Klaus Fischer, Sergio Gusmeroli, Elio Salvadori, Bernhard Thalheim, and the moderators: Arne Berre and Michele Missikoff. Below, a few position statements of Klaus, Sergio, and Robert are reported.

Klaus Fischer – The term modelling is unfortunately used in many different areas. Geometrical 3D modelling in CAD system is a well-know example. Purely

M. Jeusfeld, L. Delcambre, and T.W. Ling (Eds.): ER 2011, LNCS 6998, pp. 526–527, 2011.

mathematical models are used in statistics and a set of linear equations can be understood as a model by linear programmers. With the advent of the Unified Modeling Language (UML) proposed by the Object Management Group (OMG) the term modeling got widely adapted for software design.

Recently OMG introduced the Model Driven Architecture (MDA) that distinguishes three different abstraction levels: the *metamodel*, the set of *model instances* that comply with the metamodel, and the *program code* that is generated from the model instance and give them its semantic interpretation, at least in an operational sense. However, it is desirable to express as much of this semantics as possible in the model instances or even at the level of the metamodel.

Important aspects for model instances are their consistency and the completeness. Theorem provers might be used to check for these properties on concrete model instances. Today such tools only exist in specialized areas.

Sergio Gusmeroli – Modelling the FI is a precondition for implementing the three main aspects of a FI-based architecture: virtualisation (or abstraction), self-management, and orchestration (or mashup).

While FI Network and Software modelling (aimed at IaaS, SaaS) have already started decisively in the FI Assembly movement and its associated projects, not enough has been done so far regarding the Platform level (i.e., PaaS). The notion of Development and Delivery platforms is pervading every FI aspect from the obvious IoS (GSDP: Global Service Delivery Platform with search, discovery, orchestration, execution functions, and service development platforms with facilities for user innovation, business-IT integration, application mashup, collective intelligence and crowdsourcing), to the IoT (event driven architectures and platforms, real-digital world interconnection, distributed decision making), to the IoC&K (3D and video delivery platforms and marketplaces, user generated videos and contents).

What is it common between IoS, IoT, IoC&K delivery platforms? Could we model common features and services? What's the difference between one GSDP and another? What synergy may exist between user-generated services and user-generated content?

Robert Meersman – The Ultimate Modeling Challenge is posed by the inherently hybrid nature of systems interoperating within the social fabric created by the Future Internet.

Ontology construction must become viewed as a complex, social, and distinctly methodological modeling activity. It must lead to formalized semantic agreement involving its stakeholder communities and the various social processes within those communities. Few of such social processes are as yet formally modeled; in fact requirements are often relatively poorly understood by system modelers, nor by and large mapped onto the desired enterprise workflows.

I shall claim that modeling of such systems will therefore likely explicitly involve hybrid aspects of information (i.e. the co-existence of formal reasoning and "informal" human interactions). Correspondingly, "hybrid ontologies" will need to be modeled and deployed within their supporting social implementation environments.

Author Index